ROBERT BURNS
THE MAN AND THE POET

Robert Burns, 1795/6, Reid.
Courtesy Scottish National Portrait Gallery.

ROBERT BURNS

THE MAN AND THE POET

A Round, Unvarnished Account

Robert T. Fitzhugh

*Illustrated with Photographs
and Maps*

HOUGHTON MIFFLIN COMPANY BOSTON

Second Printing   c

Copyright © 1970 by Robert T. Fitzhugh
All rights reserved. No part of this work may be
reproduced or transmitted in any form by any
means, electronic or mechanical, including
photocopying and recording, or by any
information storage or retrieval
system, without permission
in writing from the
publisher.

Library of Congress
Catalog Card Number: 76–96066

Printed in the United States of America

PREFACE

Deep in the general heart of men
His power survives.
WORDSWORTH

This book aims to deliver a round, unvarnished account of Robert Burns, one of the dozen major British poets, and a man of striking paradoxes. He has always fascinated both the parson and the profane, the Scot and the non-Scot, the bawdy and the sentimental, the patriot and the reformer, the Left and the Right, and those who relish song or satire. Of late he has attracted new-model analysts whose attentions would have probably pleased and certainly puzzled him. All of which is merely to say that Burns has always been an incandescent figure who moves readers according to their taste and interest. He flashed into popularity in 1786, and his fame endures around the world.

In his verse, Burns is ever a conscious and sophisticated craftsman, and in his famous vernacular poems he is a poet of superb gifts and grace, who adapted the popular forms and materials which he used as models, stamping his own work with brilliant originality. Given a marginal gloss, the vernacular poems are perfectly clear; in fact, much easier to read than Shakespeare. Burns is, moreover, one of the few literary figures who, like Dr. Johnson and Lord Byron, have a striking personality.

Burns is here presented mainly as he spoke for himself, and as those who knew him spoke of him. It is a sound principle to take him at his word unless there is specific reason to believe he may have been mistaken. At times, however, he was consciously vague, and occasionally he was given to syncopated statement. Within the limits of human fallibility, punctuation and spelling of quoted matter have been reproduced exactly.

Since there would be small reason for a life of Robert Burns had he not been a poet, the poetry is quoted extensively, both as prime biographical material and as a delight in itself. It should be noted, however, that Burns' poems and his songs are treated separately. Burns did not think of the songs as poems; they were always written for tunes, and were intended to be sung.

While avoiding dialogue with preceding biographers, this life attempts to deal straightforwardly with controversies, presenting the evidence, indicating probabilities, but not forcing conclusions. All readers who are familiar with the scholarship and criticism on Burns will recognize the many debts in this book, which are hereby acknowledged fully, freely, and happily. More detailed acknowledgment will appear in the Post Scripts to the various sections. A List of Major Sources, each with the abbreviation used for reference to it, will be found on page 445.

PERSONAL NOTE

This biographer's humility was quickened by his discovering that some cherished perceptions had been anticipated, and that even distinguished predecessors had erred. He can only hope that his own work will be a helpful addition and summary, and that any errors will be inconspicuous.

Writing a book is a lonely course with much comforting support along the way. Friends and colleagues are patiently curious about one's progress and often make helpful suggestions; strangers become wonderfully kind; and librarians graciously lighten one's burdens. To be particular: my colleague Bruce Park read and commented on an early and disorderly version of the manu-

script, and my fellow-Burnsian John Weston took time he could
ill afford to criticize the nearly completed text. Dr. Stanley Bardwell, my physician, interested himself in Burns' health record and
wrote a clinical analysis of the available data. Professors Raymond
Bentman, T. Crawford, David Daiches, Joel Egerer, James Kinsley, Ross Roy, and Robert Thornton answered questions and
argued points to my great advantage. Mr. H. J. R. Bankes made
available a photograph of Maria Riddell's portrait; Sir Thomas
Innes, Lord Lyon King of Arms, responded most courteously to
an inquiry; Mr. Charles P. Finlayson, Keeper of Manuscripts,
Edinburgh University Library, searched university records for the
date of Robert Riddell's honorary degree; Jinny and Wendy
Neefus and Bill Coons, of Hudson, New York, went far beyond
the call of duty in helping prepare illustrations; Mr. W. A.
Findlater of Dublin sent details of his ancestor, Alexander Findlater, Burns' Excise Supervisor, and the photostat of a letter from
Burns to him; Dr. Douglas Guthrie of Edinburgh supplied ex-
planations of Eighteenth Century medical terms; Mr. Edward
McKiernan, Librarian of the Free Public Library, Campbeltown,
searched newspaper files and found a long-sought-for confirmation; Mr. Desmond Donaldson, County Librarian, Dumfriesshire,
in response to a question about another matter, sent a copy of John
Syme's obituary; Dr. Dwight Burkhardt interrupted his own work
to make Xerox copies of articles in medical journals; and my
fellow Player John Mulholland, and the Players librarian, Mr.
Louis A. Rachow, took a warm interest in providing engaging
details of Learned Pigs. For encouragement and valuable criticism
I want to thank Mr. Craig Wylie and Mrs. Daphne Ehrlich of
Houghton Mifflin Company.

A collection of useful books built up over the years, and the
magic of Xerox, made it possible to write this book in the relaxed
quiet of a New York State farmhouse. For most helpful assistance,
my thanks go to the staffs of the Widener Library, the British
Museum, the library of Brooklyn College, the New York Public

Library, the Yale University Library, the Huntington Library, and the libraries of the University of Michigan, the University of Pennsylvania, and the University of Virginia. Likewise to the staffs of *English Language Notes, University of Colorado Studies, Queens Quarterly,* and the *Dalhousie Review,* and to the Saltire Society.

A special word of appreciation is due the National Library of Scotland and the Scottish National Portrait Gallery for many courtesies, and to Hodder and Stoughton, Ltd., and the Clarendon Press for generous permissions to quote.

Finally, Brooklyn College has facilitated my work by giving me a reduced teaching load for two semesters.

ROBERT T. FITZHUGH

No Ruz Farm
Craryville, New York
January 25, 1970

CONTENTS

Preface   vii

Chronological Table   xv

I. Profile   1

II. Growth   17

III. Poet   51
    1. Epistles and Satires   51
    2. Bard   83
    3. Love Affairs   91
    4. Kilmarnock Edition   107

IV. Lion   124
    1. Edinburgh   124
    2. Tours   147
    3. Clarinda   172

V. Married Man   191
    1. Aftermath   191
    2. Farmer and Exciseman   204
    3. Ellisland and the Riddells   231

VI. Song   288

VII. Last Years   350

Appendix A   391
Scots Vernacular Poems Which Influenced
Burns

Appendix B   415
Medical Opinion and Data Upon Which It
Is Based

Appendix C   430
Burns' Autobiographical Letter to Dr. John
Moore

Appendix D   440
The Child in Highland Mary's Grave

List of Major Sources   445

Post Scripts   449

Index   483

ILLUSTRATIONS

Endpaper — Nithdale above Ellisland, 1805
Frontispiece — Robert Burns, 1795/6, Reid

Following page 236

Likenesses of Burns

Robert Burns, 1787, Nasmyth
Robert Burns, 1787, Beugo, after Nasmyth
Robert Burns drawn 1796/7. Skirving after Nasmyth, and not from life
Robert Burns, 1787 (?), Nasmyth
Robert Burns, 1787, Miers
Robert Burns. Painted 1828 presumably from Nasmyth drawing

Members of the Burns Family

Gilbert Burns, brother of Robert Burns
Agnes Broun, mother of Robert Burns
Jean Armour Burns (1767–1834)
Robert Burns, eldest son of the poet
Elizabeth Hyslop Burns, daughter of Robert Burns by Anne Park
Colonel William Nicol Burns, son of Robert Burns
Lieutenant Colonel James Glencairn Burns, son of Robert Burns

Friends of Burns and Memorabilia

Mrs. Frances Anna Dunlop
Lord Glencairn

A Learned Pig
Margaret Chalmers
William Smellie
Agnes M'Lehose ("Clarinda")
Glasses given Clarinda by Burns in parting
Maria Riddell (Mrs. Walter Riddell)
Robert Riddell of Glenriddell
Hermitage at Friar's Carse, near Ellisland
Francis Grose
John Syme
Alexander Cunningham
Jessie Lewars
Dr. James Maxwell

Buildings and Places Associated with Burns

Alloway Kirk, 1805
Burns' Birthplace, Alloway, 1805
Burns' Cottage
Mt. Oliphant
Lochlea
Mossgiel
Ellisland
Burns' last residence

Maps

Places in Southern Scotland associated with Robert Burns   20–21
Places in Northern Scotland associated with Robert Burns   150–151

CHRONOLOGICAL TABLE

An independent compilation, with details from the chronology prepared by DeLancey Ferguson for *Pride and Passion*, this table is designed to supplement a text in which relationships or situations are often presented entire, although they may overlap others in time.

1757 December 15, William Burnes (1721–1784) marries Agnes Broun (1737–1820).

1759 January 25, Robert Burns is born at Alloway. (His brother Gilbert is also born there, September 28, 1760; and his sisters Agnes, September 30, 1762, and Annabella, November 14, 1764.)

1765 Robert and Gilbert begin their schooling under John Murdoch.

1766 William Burnes rents Mt. Oliphant farm, moving in at Whitsunday. (William Burns is born there, July 30, 1767; John, July 10, 1769; and Isabella, June 27, 1771.)

1768 Robert and the family distressed by *Titus Andronicus*.

1772 Robert and Gilbert go in alternate weeks to study at Dalrymple.

1773 Robert studies grammar and French with Murdoch in Ayr for several weeks; he writes *Handsome Nell*.

1775 Burns attends his first dancing school; during the summer he goes to Kirkoswald.

1777 The William Burnes family moves to Lochlea Farm.

1780 The Tarbolton Bachelor's Club is organized.

1781 Burns is jilted by Alison Begbie (?); in July, he becomes a Mason; and late in the summer, he goes to Irvine, where he meets Richard Brown and suffers a severe illness. William Burnes' dispute with his Lochlea landlord begins.

1783 In January, Burns wins a £3 prize for flaxseed; in April, he begins his Commonplace Book; and in the autumn, with Gilbert, he rents Mossgiel farm.

1784 January 27, William Burnes is successful at law against his landlord. February 13, William Burnes dies. The family soon moves to Mossgiel.

1785 May 22, Elizabeth Paton bears Burns a daughter, Elizabeth. He begins to write his major poetry, and he meets Jean Armour.

1786 Burns plans emigration to Jamaica. April 3, he issues proposals for his Kilmarnock edition; he is repudiated by the Armours; May 14 (?), he takes farewell of Mary Campbell. In late July, the Kilmarnock edition is published; September 3, Jean bears twins, Robert and Jean; in October, Mary Campbell dies; November 27, Burns leaves Mauchline for Edinburgh, arriving November 29; December 14, the Edinburgh edition of the *Poems* is announced.

1787 April 17, the Edinburgh *Poems* are published; April 21, Burns sells his copyright to Creech. May 5–June 1, Burns tours the Borders; June 2 (?), he receives Meg Cameron's appeal in Dumfries; June 8, he returns to Mauchline. In late June, he tours the West Highlands, and on July 25, he reports Jean to be "in for it again." During July, Burns writes his autobiographical letter to Dr. Moore, dated August 2. August 15, he settles with Meg Cameron in Edinburgh; and August 25–September 16, he tours the Highlands with William Nicol. In early October, he visits Stirling, Harvieston, and the two Ochtertyres; and in late November, Dalswinton. December 4, back in Edinburgh, he meets Agnes M'Lehose (Clarinda), and the night of December 7/8, he dislocates his knee.

1788 January 4, Burns visits Mrs. M'Lehose for the first time; the affair grows in fervency until he leaves Edinburgh, February 18. February 25, he returns to Mauchline, after visiting Glasgow, Paisley, Dunlop, and Kilmarnock; he establishes Jean in a room in Mauchline, and goes off to visit Ellisland with John Tennant, returning March 2. March 3, Jean bears twins, one dying March 10 and one March 23. March 18, in Edinburgh, Burns signs a lease of Ellisland (the terms having been agreed on with Patrick Miller, March 13). March 20, Burns leaves Edinburgh, after taking ardent farewells of Agnes M'Lehose. (While in the city he had negotiated his Excise commission, issued officially July 14.) During April and May, Burns receives Excise instructions in Tarbolton from his friend James Findlay, and qualifies for duty. June 12, he settles at Ellisland; and August 5, he and Jean acknowledge their previous irregular marriage. In November, Jenny Clow bears Burns a son; and in December, Jean joins him at the Isle.

1789 Mid-February–February 28, Burns goes to Edinburgh to close accounts with Creech and to settle with Jenny Clow. August 19, Francis Wallace Burns is born to Jean. September, Burns begins his Excise duties, and by November 8 is ill with a "most violent cold."

1790 In July, Burns is transferred to the Dumfries 3d Division, tobacco. July 24, William Burns dies in London. December 1, Burns sends MS of *Tam o' Shanter* to Francis Grose.

1791 January 27, Burns is placed on the list of those eligible for promotion to Examiner and Supervisor. March 31, Anne Park bears Burns a daughter, Elizabeth; April 9, Jean bears him a son, William Nicol. April 11, Grose's *Antiquities* is published, with *Tam o' Shanter*. (The poem had appeared in two magazines during March.) June 19–22, Burns visits Ayrshire to attend his brother Gilbert's wedding; August 25, the Ellisland crops are sold; September 10, the Ellisland lease is renounced; early November, the Ellisland "farming things" things are sold; November 11, Burns moves to Dumfries. December 1 (?)–December 11 (?), Burns goes to Edinburgh, where he takes further farewells of Agnes M'Lehose, now planning to rejoin her husband in Jamaica.

1792 February 29, the schooner *Rosamond* is captured; April 10, Burns is made an honorary member of the Royal Company of Archers, Edinburgh; April 19, the *Rosamond's* carronades are sold; by April 26, and perhaps as early as February, Burns is promoted to the Dumfries Port Division. September 16, he writes his first letter to George Thomson; November 21, Elizabeth Riddell Burns is born to Jean; late December, and early January, 1793, the Excise Board inquires into Burns' loyalty.

1793 February 1, France declares war against England. In February, the second Edinburgh edition of *Poems* is published, with additions. May 19, Burns moves to Mill Vennel; July 27–August 2, he takes his first Galloway tour with Syme; in August, the sedition trials are held in Edinburgh; c. August 30, Burns sends *Scots Wha Hae* to Thomson. At the end of December, the party occurs which results in the Riddell quarrel.

1794 January 12, Burns returns Maria Riddell's Commonplace Book; April 21, Robert Riddell dies. June, c. 24–c. 28, Burns again tours Galloway with Syme; August 12, James Glencairn Burns is born to Jean; in late December, Burns is appointed Acting Supervisor. The final edition during Burns' life of *Poems*, Edinburgh, is published this year.

1795 In January, Burns helps organize the Dumfries Volunteers; in January (?), Mrs. Riddell seeks a reconciliation; in April, Alexander Findlater resumes his duties as Supervisor; in September, Elizabeth Riddell Burns dies. From December on, Burns is severely ill.

1796 July 3–18, Burns is at the Brow; July 21, he dies, and is buried July 25, the day his son Maxwell is born.

ROBERT BURNS

THE MAN AND THE POET

I

PROFILE

What an antithetical mind! — tenderness, roughness —
delicacy, coarseness — sentiment, sensuality —
soaring and grovelling, dirt and deity —
all mixed up in that compound of inspired clay!

LORD BYRON

Robert Burns was a witty compound of satire, sentiment, and sex, a man of "general talents" and of great personal force. One of his shrewdest admirers felt that poetry was "actually not his *forte*." However that may have been, during a few brilliant years while he was obscure and free and sure of a sympathetic audience for Scots vernacular poetry, he created a body of work that made him one of the major poets who have written in the British Isles. Largely by following the cues of Robert Fergusson, and those of a few other minor models, Burns turned his poverty-stricken life, and the affairs of obscure Mauchline parish, into a splendid body of Poems Chiefly in the Scottish Dialect. "Where materials would have been wanting perhaps to almost every other mortal, he like an electrical kite soars aloft, & draws down etherial [fire] from heaven." Thus William Nicol, the gifted and irascible Latin master, a friend for whom Burns named a son, and from whom he once got an affectionate letter of reproof beginning "Dear Christless Bobie." *

* This facetious greeting is the only known occasion when Burns was called "Bobbie" by anyone who knew him. Affectionately, he was "Robbie," and familiarly, "Rob," "Rab," or "Robin."

When publication had brought fame, and marriage had brought a family and a government job to support it, and when the great excitement of his Mauchline years had cooled, Burns found that he had lost his freedom to speak as he wished, and had gained a more sophisticated audience with whom he felt no easy rapport. He had, moreover, said what he wanted to say, in the way he knew best how to say it, and he did not wish to repeat. With different poetic modes, both before and after his Kilmarnock and Edinburgh editions, he had only limited success. But when he turned again to the vernacular, in *Tam o' Shanter*, he wrote his finest poem. Those who advised Burns that he would not be read in Scots have been proved wrong the past hundred and seventy years.

It is said that burdensome and uncongenial work as an Exciseman during Burns' last decade interfered with his writing, but he said no, and his burden was certainly not so great then, particularly after he moved to Dumfries in 1791, as it had been when he produced his famous poems. Indeed, the *volume* of his poetic output did not decline much. He remained the vital, sociable man he had been since boyhood, alert to his times, provoked by the riddle of religion, full of irreverent delight at the human comedy, patriotic, quixotic, outraged by man's inhumanity to man, bedeviled by sex, the center of any company he was ever in. Three weeks before his death, his mind was "seldom greater." If not flush in his later years, he was not poverty-stricken, either; nor was he carefu'; and he lived simply on his income in the "hugry-mugry" fashion he was used to — at times a little in debt or behind in his rent, not frequenting his house too much latterly, but a kind and solicitous husband, and an affectionate father concerned for his children.

Burns was an honest man, a generous man, a "feeling" man (he called himself the "child of skinless sensibility"), and sometimes a pawky man, but he was never, nor did he ever want to be, a respectable bourgeois. He remained a peasant with a healthy disrespect for the "dirt o' gentry." "He knew, felt, and ardently loved what is good and great, and occasionally practiced these emotions — But too often 'his pulses maddening play' drove him headlong from these heights." So wrote his most intimate friend of the later years, John Syme. He himself had confided to his Commonplace Book, March, 1784 (age 25): "I have often coveted the acquaintance of that part of mankind commonly known by the ordinary phrase of Blackguards, . . . those who by thoughtless Prodigality, or headstrong Passions have been driven to ruin: . . . I have yet found among them, in not a few instances, some of the noblest Virtues, Magnanimity, Generosity, disinterested friendship and even modesty, in the highest perfection."

During his last six years, until his death in 1796, Burns remained essentially, and not surprisingly, much the man he had been in the previous decade. For this reason, observations of Burns in this period, like the following by Maria Riddell, his close friend, are interesting for their retrospective illumination of him throughout his mature life:

Many others, perhaps, may have ascended to prouder heights in the regions of Parnassus, but none certainly ever outshone Burns in the charms — the sorcery, I would almost call it, of fascinating conversation, the spontaneous eloquence of social argument, or the unstudied poignancy of brilliant repartee; nor was any man, I believe, ever gifted with a larger portion of the, "*vivida vis animi.*"

His personal endowments were perfectly correspondent to the qualifications of his mind: his form was manly; his action, energy itself; devoid in great measure perhaps of those graces, of that polish, acquired only in the refinement of societies where in early life he could have no opportunities of mixing; but where, such was the irresistible power of attraction that encircled him, though his appearance and manner were always peculiar, he never failed to delight and excel. His figure seemed to bear testimony to his earlier destination and employments. It seemed rather moulded by nature for the rough exercises of Agriculture, than the gentler cultivation of the Belles

Lettres. His features were stamped with the hardy character of independence, and the firmness of conscious, though not arrogant, pre-eminence; the animated expressions of countenance were almost peculiar to himself; the rapid lightnings of his eye were always the harbingers of some flash of genius, whether they darted the fiery glances of insulted and indignant superiority, or beamed with the impassioned sentiment of fervid and impetuous affections. His voice alone could improve upon the magic of his eye: sonorous, replete with the finest modulations, it alternately captivated the ear with the melody of poetic numbers, the perspicuity of nervous reasoning, or the ardent sallies of enthusiastic patriotism.

The keenness of satire was, I am almost at a loss whether to say, his forte or his foible; for though nature had endowed him with a portion of the most pointed excellence in that dangerous talent, he suffered it too often to be the vehicle of personal, and sometimes unfounded animosities. . . . The vivacity of his wishes and temper was indeed checked by almost habitual disappointments, which sat heavy on a heart, that acknowledged the ruling passion of independence, without having ever been placed beyond the grasp of penury. . . .

He was seldom, indeed never, implacable in his resentments, and sometimes it has been alleged, not inviolably faithful in his engagements of friendship. . . . His inconstancy and caprice, I am inclined to believe, originated less in levity of sentiment, than from an extreme impetuosity of feeling. . . . He was candid and manly in the avowal of his errors, and *his avowal* was a *reparation*. . . .

The penchant Burns had uniformly acknowledged for the festive pleasures of the table, and toward the fairer and softer objects of nature's creation, has been the rallying point from whence the attacks of his censors have been uniformly directed; and to these, it must be confessed, he shewed himself no stoic.

Thus runs Mrs. Riddell's famous testimony, "so discerning and impartial in understanding, that it remains the best thing written of him by a contemporary critic."

Robert Burns grew up under the influence and control of an affectionate, shrewd, and pious father, whom he revered, and whom he later described as a man of "stubborn, ungainly Integrity, and headlong ungovernable Irascibillity." William Burnes saw life as "a continual struggle between animal instinct and controlling reason," a struggle to attain inner peace and to "exalt the mind above irregular passions," and so to give animal life pleasure and joy and thus achieve the beauty of holiness. He did not subscribe to the orthodox Calvinist belief in predestination, but felt that heaven was open to all who lived a good life and sincerely repented of their sins. Burns was deeply impressed by this teaching, and speaks of his own "idiot piety" as a child.

He also speaks of "cheerless gloom" and galley slave labor. The Burns family leased and rented land which they farmed. They were not hired farm laborers, cotters. They lived as others of their class, a no less grinding life for being common. They ate poorly and worked hard, Robert doing his full share. But William saw to it that his boys learned to write well, and Robert certainly learned to read and to understand what he read. No one has yet made a full study of Burns' reading, but its extent and acuteness are at once apparent to anyone familiar with the Eighteenth Century and with Burns' letters. He was very much a man of his time.

Upon his father's death in February, 1784, Robert became head of the family and set out earnestly with his brother to make a success of farming on his own. But as one might imagine of a young man who had been restricted as he had been, Burns' irregular passions and animal instincts asserted themselves both before his father's death, and considerably more afterward. Putting his religious beliefs to one side, he became the buoyant leader of some high-spirited young men in the community; he challenged the "auld licht" Calvinism that prevailed in his parish, voicing his father's opinions; and he fathered a bastard on Elizabeth Paton. It was not so much his challenge to the auld lichts, or his reckless general self-assertion, or his fornication, that made him notorious in a conservative rural district, as the poems he wrote rejoicing in what he had done and calling down ridicule on worthies whom he had shocked and who wished to discipline him. The simple result was that by 1786 when Burns (age 27) had failed as a farmer, and had written the poems which made him famous; when the Kirk Session had denounced him, and he was dodging a warrant sworn out by James Armour for support of his daughter Jean's coming child; he decided to resolve his difficulties by emigrating to Jamaica. But before leaving Scotland he wished to try for fame as a poet by publishing, and thought that he might make enough money from his venture to pay his passage. He succeeded on both counts, but he did not go to Jamaica, and he paid some of the money to Elizabeth Paton to settle *her* paternity claim. The warrant of James Armour was allowed to lapse. Burns' edition brought out in nearby Kilmarnock is probably the most notable first volume of poems ever published. It contains much of his best poetry, it made his name, and it got him free of his Mauchline enemies. But it did not change him much. He continued, for example, to help support his mother, brother, and daughter at Mossgiel, even to sinking half his Edinburgh profits in the enterprise. Burns had warm family loyalties. He once spoke casually of his youthful correspondent, James Candlish, as "the earliest friend except my only brother that I have on earth," and when his poor Uncle Robert died, he took his uncle's children into his own home.

This is not the place to tell the story of Burns' loves, but it is the place to put straight the general pattern of his life and character, in which his relations with women are both prominent and revealing. Burns fascinated women of all classes and degrees. His address to them was "extremely deferential, and always with a turn either to the pathetic or humorous, which engaged their attention particularly." He was handsome and vital. His approach no doubt varied with the station and qualities of the woman, but essentially he regarded women as "the blood-royal of life," and lovemaking as life's greatest pleasure. He puts it all candidly to his correspondent George Thomson:

I am a very Poet in my enthusiasm of the Passion. — The welfare
& happiness of the beloved Object, is the *first* & *inviolate* sentiment
that pervades my soul; & whatever pleasures I might wish for, or
whatever might be the raptures they would give me, yet, if they
interfere & clash with that *first* principle, it is having these pleasures
at a dishonest price; & Justice forbids, & Generosity disdains the
purchase! — As to the herd of the Sex, who are good for little or
nothing else, I have made no such agreement with myself; but where
the Parties are capable of, & the Passion is, the true Divinity of love —
the man who can act otherwise than I have laid down, is a Villain!

A brief account of his life with Jean Armour will tell much
about him, and her, and Eighteenth Century Ayrshire.* Robert
and Jean met as village neighbors, and fell in love; and Jean
became pregnant. He offered to marry her, and indeed thought
he had done so, but her parents refused to recognize him, as too
poor, and probably too scandalous, for a son-in-law. Outraged,
he submitted to public rebuke in church for fornication in order
to receive a certificate as a bachelor from his minister. Jean bore
twins, one of whom died, Robert's mother taking the other,
Robert, Jr. After Burns' winter in Edinburgh, he returned rich
by Mauchline standards, and famous. Jean's parents made him
welcome and locked the two in a room. Burns eventually went
back to Edinburgh to settle accounts with his publisher, where
he had the famous affair with Clarinda, thinking little of Jean,
again pregnant, and when he returned to Mauchline in the spring
of 1788, he wrote to Robert Ainslie, in Edinburgh, of his meeting
with Jean, now nearly come to term.

Mauchline, 3d March, 1788

My dear Friend,
    . . . I have been through sore tribulation, and under much buffet-
ing of the Wicked One, since I came to this country. Jean I found
banished like a martyr — forlorn, destitute, and friendless; all for the

* The attitudes and mores of the Ayrshire peasantry of that time were not those
of the Victorian and later middle class.

good old cause: I have reconciled her to her fate: I have reconciled her to her mother: I have taken her a room: I have taken her to my arms: I have given her a mahogany bed: I have given her a guinea; and I have fucked her till she rejoiced with joy unspeakable and full of glory. But — as I always am on every occasion — I have been prudent and cautious to an astounding degree; I swore her, privately and solemnly, never to attempt any claim on me as a husband, even though anybody should persuade her she had such a claim, which she has not, neither during my life, nor after my death. She did all this like a good girl, and I took the opportunity of some dry horselitter, and gave her such a thundering scalade that electrified the very marrow of her bones. O, what a peacemaker is a guid weel-willy pintle! It is the mediator, the guarantee, the umpire, the bond of union, the solemn league and covenant, the plenipotentiary, the Aaron's rod, the Jacob's staff, the prophet Elisha's pot of oil, the Ahasuerus' sceptre, the sword of mercy, the philosopher's stone, the horn of plenty, the Tree of Life between Man and Woman. . . .

Your faithful Friend,
R. B.

Despite his resolves, within a few days he had married Jean. It was a contented marriage. She was devoted to him and cherished him, in Professor Ferguson's happy adaptation, "not weighing his merits, but pardoning his offenses." He reported the event to his friends in a formula:

Shortly after my last return to Ayrshire, I married "my Jean." This was not in consequence of the attachment of romance perhaps; but I had a long and much-loved fellow creature's happiness or misery in my determination, and I durst not trifle with so important a deposite. Nor have I any cause to repent it. If I have not got polite tattle, modish manners, and fashionable dress, I am not sickened and disgusted with the multiform curse of boarding-school affectation; and I have got the handsomest figure, the sweetest temper, the soundest constitution, and the kindest heart in the country.

Burns and Jean had five more children,* the last born the day

---

* When Burns was farming at Ellisland, he wrote his friend and Excise Supervisor, Alexander Findlater, when sending him some eggs, "Mrs. B——, like a

of his funeral. Jean also took into her household Burns' daughter by Anne Park, and Robert Chambers reports her having said with unique authority, "Oor Robin should hae had twa wives."

Of Burns' later years, John Syme noted, "Tho Burns did not resort much to his own house yet he ever spoke affectionately & endearingly of his wife & family."

Maria Riddell wrote to Dr. Currie, December 28, 1799:

Burns said little or nothing about his Wife to me latterly, but as I believe her conduct, subsequent to their union by marriage, was exemplary towards him, so it is just to add that he always spoke of her with a high tribute of respect and esteem. He did not love her, but he was far from insensible to the indulgence and patience, "the meekness with which she bore her faculties" on many occasions very trying to the tempers of most individuals of our sex.

The "occasions" of infidelity mentioned by Mrs. Riddell are given greater significance by a letter from Thomas Telford, the engineer, to Thomas Boyd, Dumfries contractor.

Shrewsbury, 7th Decr. 1794

DEAR SIR

. . . I hope you informed my friend Robin Burns that I was very desirous of paying my respects, but tell him that unless he leaves off his baudy songs, that "he'll get his Fairen. — 'In Hell they'll roast him like a Herring.'" — Tho if he goes on in his old way not even a *she Devil* will be able to meet with a Milt* in him.

But after you have abused him properly, do tell him, that the first time I meet Mr. Alison, we will drink his health, for in case we should be consigned to a *Neuk* in his neighbourhood, it would prove some consolation to be on decent terms with one another. — Farewell — I am yours very sincerely

THOS TELFORD

good true wife, looking on my taste as a Standard, & knowing that she cannot give me anything — *eatable* — more agreable than a new-laid egg, she begs your acceptance of a few."
* *milt* — the secretion of the male generative organs of fishes.

Of Burns and liquor, three considerations must hold: he was a sociable man in a hard-drinking world, he had organically poor health, and he enjoyed low social position. As C. K. Sharpe, "the Scottish Walpole," remarks, "His intemperance was venial — when one considers that the gentry with whom he associated generally caroused with brandy and water whenever they met in the morning — and never dined together without getting drunk." And Catherine Carswell comments, "We need go no further than two great contemporaries of Burns who were blessed with better constitutions and kinder nurtures than fell to his share. Between them they ruled the British Empire for many years during which they were seldom sober." Like William Pitt, and Henry Dundas, his lieutenant for Scotland, Burns did his work. Unlike them, he also wrote his songs. He said, "I love drinking now and then. It defecates the standing pool of thought." He also wrote, "Occasional hard drinking is the devil to me. — Against this I have again & again bent my resolution, & have greatly succeeded. — Taverns, I have totally abandoned: it is the private parties in the family way, among the hard drinking gentlemen of this country, that does me the mischief — but even this, I have more than half given over." (January 2, 1793, to Mrs. Dunlop.)

As a young man, writing poems about Scotch Drink, Burns had little money for dissipation, and his brother reports that he was of sober habit. In Edinburgh, he seems to have enjoyed much convivial company. As he grew older, his friend Syme reports, "He loved wine and would take it freely & in considerable quantities but I never saw him brutally drunk — I have seen many *gentlemen* more drunk than ever I saw Burns — I never saw Burns drink a *dram* but as any Gentleman might." This in the Eighteenth Century might cover a good deal. Alexander Findlater comments: "That when he sat down in an evening with a few friends whom he liked, he was apt to prolong the social hour beyond the bounds which prudence would dictate, is unquestionable." Finally, on March 11, 1828, Sir Walter Scott wrote to John Lockhart, then engaged on his life of Burns, "I heard from Mr. Miller Dalswinton's [Burns' landlord's] eldest son . . . when Burns came to stay at Dalswinton all night as he often did, he used to stipulate for a bottle of brandy in his sleeping-room and drink it well nigh out before morning."

The pattern of indulgence here, and elsewhere, is clear enough. Likewise, elsewhere, the pattern of continued responsible activity as Exciseman and poet and head of a family. Likewise a record of poor health and illness all his life, and a rapid decline during his last eighteen months. He died of rheumatic fever, with possible terminal bacterial endocarditis. But there is no indication of alcoholism, and Burns no more died a drunken wastrel than Walter Scott or William Pitt. He did, however, provide a ready example for ill-informed clerical and other moralists who would not have been so active had Burns been a laird, or a lord, or obscure, or rich. An excellent case in point is that celebrated rake, Burns' neighbor James Boswell. Burns' "failings" and "follies" also made handy targets for those who noted he was not a gentleman, and who felt it unbecoming in him to hold liberal opinions on social reform, and to think and speak with improper respect of his betters.

Much of his biography, also, has been written with care not to offend the living, and particularly the upper classes, even at Burns' expense. Indeed, the patronizing tone and the class angle have been persistent elements in Burns biography since his death, mixed with dogged persistence in editing his character and selecting from his writing to fit special tastes. The present biographer, for example, was refused access to a considerable body of material in the nineteen thirties because it would "ruin the romantic concept of Burns," and he has no reason to believe that the guardian's attitude has changed.

Burns as he lived is much better than any revision, and the more fully he comes to be known, the more surely is his pre-

diction to Jean on his deathbed being fulfilled: "Don't be afraid.
I'll be more respected a hundred years after I'm dead than I am
at present."

From the first, Burns wrote poetry because he wanted to say
something he felt strongly about. He rhymed "for fun." His interests were men and their ways, and his own position in the
world. He was bawdy, political, satiric, sentimental, impudent,
humorous. He wrote of people he knew, and he spoke with the
voice of men like his father, driven by landlords and oppressed
by a class system. With life for his ilk short and bleak, and its
only pleasures friendship and lovemaking, Burns accepted the
prospect of "crazy, weary, joyless Eild [old age]" at forty, with
beggary a likely prospect and death a kindly release, and he set
out to enjoy his pleasures while he had youth.

He celebrated in his poems the honest man of good heart, and
the sweet sonsy [jolly] lass, and the joys of friendship and love.
He dignified simple life and spoke with zest of those even lower
down than himself. He cried out for recognition of ability, wit,
and worth, and he denounced oppression, privilege, and the unevenness of fortune. He contrasted the spontaneous, impulsive,
"feeling" life with considered, dull attention to profit and advantage (what he called "Catch-the-plack"). He ridiculed pretension
in religion, in politics — and in general. He depicted local life and
customs. And he proclaimed that a poet should feel, should speak
the language of the heart, should have a spark o' Nature's Fire.

Once he had pretty well exhausted his favorite themes in
poetry, by 1787, Burns turned to an earlier enthusiasm, Scots
song, becoming for a time "absolutely crazed" about it, and
until his death serving as virtual editor of one famous collection
and a major contributor to another. There was an Eighteenth
Century vogue in both England and Scotland for Scotch folk
songs and for songs in the folk manner (Professor Kinsley speaks
of "more than thirty collections" between 1700 and 1782), so that
here again Burns found himself writing for a sympathetic audience, in a congenial tradition, in the Scots-English mixture of his

successful work, and with freedom to write as he pleased, particularly for his publisher and friend James Johnson. Moreover, instead of merely celebrating his native district as he had done in his poems, he was now celebrating all of Scotland, which pleased him. The range of human experience which he covered was much wider, also, than in his poems. And in the dramatic setting of songs he could say things which his position as a "Placeman" and head of a family would have made it ticklish to say outright. His songs were a major undertaking, requiring gifted craftsmanship and energetic devotion, and yielding rich satisfaction. Burns was busy with them until he died.

Some of his songs Burns merely collected and sent on to editors, others he ransacked from printed collections, many he modified, often building a song from a fragment or a chorus. Frequently he created songs for tunes without words. Always he composed with music in his head. He described his method to George Thomson:

Untill I am compleat master of a tune, in my own singing, (such as it is) I can never compose for it. — My way is: I consider the poetic Sentiment, correspondent to my idea of the musical expression; then I chuse my theme; begin one Stanza; when that is composed, which is generally the most difficult part of the business, I walk out, sit down now & then, look out for objects in Nature around me that are in unison or harmony with the cogitations of my fancy & workings of my bosom; humming every now & then the air with the verses I have framed: when I feel my Muse beginning to jade, I retire to the solitary fireside of my study, & there commit my effusions to paper; swinging, at intervals, on the hind-legs of my elbow-chair, by way of calling forth my own critical strictures, as my pen goes on. —

Seriously, this, at home, is almost invariably my way. — What damn'd Egotism!

Burns wrote again to Thomson on the same subject in 1794:

Whenever I want to be more than ordinary *in song;* to be in some degree equal to your diviner airs; do you imagine I fast & pray for the celestial emanation? — Tout au contraire! I have a glorious recipe, the very one that for his own use was invented by the Divinity of Healing & Poesy when erst he piped to the flocks of Admetus. — I put myself on a regimen of admiring a fine woman; & in proportion to the adorability of her charms, in proportion you are delighted with my verses.

A fuller discussion of Burns' achievement in song will be found in Section VI; many think it even greater than his achievement in poetry. Technically the songs are a virtuoso performance in marrying words to music, in fitting sentiment and illustration to melody. There is nothing comparable in our literature. Two dozen of the songs are among the finest lyrics we have, and these lyrics are true lyrics, for singing to music, not just for reading.

It should be added that since the Scots folk muse was often high-kilted, Burns created polite versions for publication, while making for himself and his friends a private collection of the choicer bawdry. "There is, there must be, some truth in original sin," he wrote to his friend Cleghorn. "My violent propensity to Bawdy convinces me of it. — Lack a day! if that species of Composition be the Sin against 'The Haly Ghaist,' 'I am the most offending soul alive.'" Here, too, he was mainly collector or improver, but sometimes also creator.

The key to any understanding of Burns is recognition of him as a complex, contradictory, and paradoxical man. In politics, for example, he recognized that the Union of Scotland and England in 1707 had brought security, economic opportunity, and relief from religious and political factionalism. But he lamented the loss of independence, he found Mary Queen of Scots more attractive than Queen Elizabeth I, and he responded better to the exiled Stuart kings than to those "obscure, beef-witted, insolent . . . foreigners" George I, II, and III. He supported the French Revolution in its early stages, and the American Revolution in retrospect. Yet he would have maintained himself to be a sturdy patriot, and so he was. His experiences with landlords and factors, a class system, and rotten borough government gave him great sympathy for the "Rights of Man" and for general social reform. Yet he joined a volunteer regiment when Great Britain was threatened by invasion from France.

Burns enjoyed attention from gentry and aristocracy, among whom he had friends and correspondents, and he was perfectly assured with them, if not always comfortable or gracious. But in general he envied those above him and spoke bitterly of patronizing superiors, privileged dullness, and class discrimination. He preferred honest worth to birth and breeding. "The rank is but the guinea's stamp, / The man's the gowd for a' that." And "gowd" Burns was more likely to find in humble circumstances. It is unfortunate that so little is on record of Burns among his own kind, and so much about his associations with his "superiors."

"He was prone to scarify, blister & reprobate timid, mean, crouching folks — but not to put himself forward as magnanimous & independent. — At times however he aimed at being the Superior — and to demolish competition." So, again, John Syme, echoing similar comments by others. But Burns could also be winning, kindly, generous, sympathetic.

Parish squabbles and windy preachers amused him, and petty parish tyranny infuriated him, especially when provoked by his own behavior. He retained a strong religious faith in a benevolent Creator, and he came to feel about Calvinist original sin that "the whole business is reversed, . . . We come in to this world with a heart & disposition to do good for it," but we soon find ourselves "under a kind of cursed necessity of turning selfish" in our own defense. "Experience of the weakness, not the strength, of human powers" made him "glad to grasp at revealed religion." Basically he felt that "The heart benevolent and kind / The most resembles God." His feelings about an afterlife varied, but he subscribed generally to this view: "All my fears & cares are of this world: if there is Another, an honest man has nothing to fear from it." And he added, "I hate a Man that wishes to be a Deist, but I fear, every fair, unprejudiced Enquirer must in some degree be a Sceptic." He continued a churchgoer and sermon critic, he led family worship at Mossgiel and Ellisland, and in his letters he was given to extended moral and theological reflections. Although he ridiculed preordained damnation, and salvation by faith alone, without good works, he wrote of the old Covenanters who had fought and died for that belief:

> The Solemn League and Covenant
>   Now brings a smile, now brings a tear.
> But sacred Freedom, too, was theirs:
>   If thou'rt a slave, indulge thy sneer.

Any effort to produce an orderly, consistent Burns must fail. He was not a man of doctrine or dogma. Like most of us, he had some loosely centered strong feelings which he expressed variously to different people in different circumstances. And like most of us he tended in his opinions to gratify his ego and relieve his distress.

One final, and summary, paradox. We can know Burns only when we see that the poetry was the man. If we rejoice in the poetry we must rejoice in the poet. Had he not been the man he was, he had not written the poetry he did. "His character," wrote his first editor and biographer, James Currie, "is displayed in almost every poem he wrote, to such as have the comprehension necessary to receive it. The very circumstance of Burns having pourtrayed himself in such vivid colours, is a decisive proof of his superior genius. . . . Inferior minds shrink from a full exposure of themselves."

II

GROWTH

And the Spring comes slowly up this way.
CHRISTABEL

Robert Burns was much like his father — intelligent, thoughtful, hard-working, kind, honest, independent, scrupulous in money matters, and fiercely proud ("the sport of strong passions"). These are disqualifying circumstances for commercial success, and as farmers, both father and son failed to prosper. A further reason for the family poverty was that during Burns' youth and young manhood, farmers without capital were hard pressed in Ayrshire. War brought inflation, depressed business, raised prices. In anticipation of more productive farming methods, landlords increased rents, taking their income out of the hides of tenants who knew only the older ways, or who had no money to improve with.

Burns' father, William Burnes (1721–1784),* was unable to rent good farms, he paid too much for those he did rent, and he tried to make a go of it by overworking himself and, later, his family. His motives were excellent and characteristic. He wished so far as possible to be his own man, and he wanted to keep his children about him so that they would grow up in a good atmosphere and not have to leave home and become farm

* "Burnes" was pronounced with two syllables in William's native Kincardineshire, but "Burrrns" in Ayrshire. After their father's death, Robert and his brother Gilbert adopted the spelling "Burns."

laborers or house servants, as they would have, had he continued working for wages.

William had come to Ayrshire, via Edinburgh, from Dunnotar, in the northeast, below Aberdeen, where his family of solid tenant farmers had fallen on hard times. After working for several employers as a gardener, he leased seven acres at Alloway, near Ayr, from a Dr. Campbell, and built on them with his own hands the "auld clay biggin," now one of the most famous tourist attractions in the world. On December 15, 1757, he married Agnes Broun (1732–1820), red-haired and fair and sensible, and set up housekeeping in his new cottage. There, on January 25, 1759, Robert their first child was born. William was thirty-eight.

His intention had been to set up as a nurseryman and market-gardener, but the enterprise did not prosper, and he continued employment, as gardener and overseer, for Provost William Fergusson, of Ayr, on his nearby estate of Doonholm. During the next six years, he and Agnes had another son, Gilbert, and two daughters, Agnes and Annabella, and the two-room cottage became a tight fit for the family. Needing more room, and wishing to better himself and his family, William rented from Dr. Fergusson an upland farm of seventy Scots acres named Mt. Oliphant,* about two miles away. Unable to dispose of his lease on the Alloway holding, he rented the cottage and seven acres, and borrowed £100 from his employer to stock the new farm, moving in at Whitsunday, 1766. There the family lived until Whitsunday, 1777, when they moved to Lochlea farm, ten miles away in Tarbolton parish. William and Agnes then had seven children.

The extra living space at Mt. Oliphant was probably an attic where the boys might sleep, a common feature of the "but and ben" (outer and inner room) farm cottage. Such a cottage "with its walls of stone or rammed clay, its earthen floor and thatched roof, and with the fire seldom built up except for cooking, had

---

* Gilbert Burns said later it was "almost the very poorest soil . . . in a state of cultivation." (Currie I, 69.)

a winter chill and dampness that bred tuberculosis in the young and rheumatism in the old. . . . The stable was usually under the same roof, and its reek mingled with the dampness and the smell of unwashed humanity. . . . Outside the door was the . . . glaur hole, manure heap of man and beast alike." Oatmeal porridge supported the human inhabitants, each resident dipping at meals with his spoon from a common bowl. Barley soup, cabbage, bread, cheese, and occasional potatoes filled out the menu. Animals that died were eaten if possible.

We lived very sparingly [reports Gilbert Burns]. For several years butcher's meat was a stranger in the house, while all the members of the family exerted themselves to the utmost of their strength and rather beyond it, in the labours of the farm. My brother, at the age of thirteen, assisted in threshing the crop of corn, and at fifteen was the principal labourer on the farm, for we had no hired servant, male or female. The anguish of mind we felt at our tender years, under these straits and difficulties, was very great. To think of our father growing old (for he was now above fifty) broken down with the long continued fatigues of his life, with a wife and five other children, and in a declining state of circumstances, these reflections produced in my brother's mind and mine sensations of the deepest distress. I doubt not but the hard labour and sorrow of this period of his life, was in great measure the cause of that depression of spirits with which Robert was so often afflicted through his whole life afterward. At this time he was almost constantly afflicted in the evenings with a dull headache, which, at a future period of his life, was exchanged for a palpitation of the heart, and a threatening of fainting and suffocation in his bed, in the night time. . .

Nothing could be more retired than our general manner of living at Mt. Oliphant; we rarely saw anybody but the members of our own family. There were no boys of our own age, or near it, in the neighbourhood. . . . My father was for some time almost the only companion we had. He conversed familiarly on all subjects with us, as if we had been men; and was at great pains, while we accompanied him in the labours of the farm, to lead the conversation to such subjects as might tend to increase our knowledge, or confirm us in virtuous habits.

Places in
Southern Scotland
Associated with
ROBERT BURNS

There are few details about Robert as a boy. He seems to have been a reserved, moody youngster, and he remarks that he was by no means a favorite with anybody, although "a good deal noted for a retentive memory and a stubborn, sturdy something" in his disposition. The midwife at his birth is reported to have said Burns was the smallest and poorest child she ever saw born — nothing but skin. And once when his teacher was called from the room and the other children broke into an uproar, Robert hid himself in a chest. Returning, the master signaled for order by striking the chest with his tawz (a strap fringed at one end, traditional symbol and instrument of authority). Poor Robbie, inside, was so upset that he screamed and had to be sent home sobbing. Another picturesque detail is that about ten days after Robert's birth, a storm blew in the gable of the cottage's clay wall above the fireplace, necessitating the removal of mother and baby to a neighbor's while repairs were made.

The one thing we do know a good deal about is Robert's schooling, and his early reading, which influenced him strongly. He learned to read and to understand what he read, and he learned to write clear, grammatical prose. The schooling began in his sixth year (1765) at Alloway Mill nearby, under a man named Campbell, who soon gave up teaching to manage the workhouse in Ayr. Subsequently, William Burnes arranged with an earnest and pedantic young man, John Murdoch, to take over the school. Murdoch's account for Currie after Burns' death of his two years at Alloway is valuable as the earliest report on Robert by an outsider, here a friendly and observant one.

In 1765, about the middle of March, Mr. W. Burnes came to Ayr, and sent to the school where I was improving in writing, . . . desiring that I would come and speak to him at a certain inn, and bring my writing-book with me. . . . In the month of May following, I was engaged by Mr. Burnes, and four of his neighbours, to teach, and accordingly began to teach the little school at Alloway. . . . My five employers undertook to board me by turns, and to make up a certain salary, at the end of the year, provided my quarterly payments from the different pupils did not amount to that sum.

My pupil Robert Burns was then between six and seven years of age; his preceptor about eighteen. Robert, and his younger brother Gilbert, had been grounded a little in English before they were put under my care. They both made a rapid progress in reading, and a tolerable progress in writing. In reading, dividing words into syllables by rule, spelling without book, parsing sentences, &c. Robert and Gilbert were generally at the upper end of the class, even when ranged with boys by far their seniors. The books most commonly used in the school were, the *Spelling Book*, the *New Testament*, the *Bible*, *Mason's [Masson's] Collection of Prose and Verse*, and Fisher's *English Grammar*. They committed to memory the hymns and other poems of that collection, with uncommon facility. This facility was partly owing to the method pursued by their father and me in instructing them, which was, to make them thoroughly acquainted with the meaning of every word in each sentence that was to be committed to memory. . . . As soon as they were capable of it, I taught them to turn verse into its natural prose order; sometimes to substitute synonymous expressions for poetical words, and to supply all the ellipses. . . .

Gilbert always appeared to me to possess a more lively imagination, and to be more of a wit, than Robert. I attempted to teach them a little church-music. Here they were left far behind by all the rest of the school. Robert's ear, in particular, was remarkably dull, and his voice untunable. . . . Robert's countenance was generally grave, and expressive of a serious, contemplative, and thoughtful mind.

After two years, Murdoch left the school and the neighborhood, and William Burnes undertook to teach the boys arithmetic at home by candlelight. Just before leaving, Murdoch came to say goodbye.

He brought us [says Gilbert] as a present and memorial of him, a small compendium of English Grammar, and the tragedy of *Titus Andronicus*, and by way of passing the evening, he began to read the play aloud. We were all attention for some time, till presently the whole party was dissolved in tears. A female of the play (I have but a confused remembrance of it) had her hands chopt off, and her tongue cut out, and then was insultingly desired to call for water to wash her hands.* At this, in an agony of distress, we with one voice desired he would read no more. My father observed, that if we would not hear it out, it would be needless to leave the play with us. Robert replied, that if it were left he would burn it.

Here is the second example of Robert's turbulent sensibility.

In case John Murdoch should seem unduly straitened, his exit from Ayr may be noted. Having returned to become one of the English teachers in the Ayr school, and feeling aggrieved with the Reverend Dr. Dalrymple (who had baptized Robert), Murdoch retired first to an inn and then to a private house, voicing his opinion that the doctor was as revengeful as hell and as false as the devil. He also said that the doctor was a hypocrite and a damned liar. For these slanders, he was summarily dismissed February 14, 1776, and left town. Robert remained on friendly terms with him, however, and Murdoch was chief mourner at Burns' younger brother's funeral in London some years later.

Besides arranging for the Alloway school, William sent Robert for a part of the summer of 1772, when he was thirteen years old, to a school three miles away at Dalrymple to improve his handwriting. The following summer, Murdoch having by then returned to Ayr, Robert lived with him for three weeks, studying English and French. Finally, during the summer of 1775, the boy spent some weeks with his mother's brother at Kirkoswald, near the seacoast about ten miles south, so that he might learn "Mensuration, Surveying, and Dialling, &c." at the local school. He speaks of geometry and trigonometry, and of sines and cosines.

At Kirkoswald, Burns learned more than mathematics. He made, as he says,

progress in the knowledge of mankind. — The contraband trade was at that time very successful; scenes of swaggering riot and roaring dissipation were as yet new to me; and I was no enemy to social life. —

---

* The stage direction reads, "Enter the Empress' sons with Lavinia, her hands cut off, and her tongue cut out, and ravished."

Here, though I learned to look unconcernedly on a large tavern-bill, and mix without fear in a drunken squabble, yet I went on with a high hand in my Geometry; till the sun entering Virgo, a month which is always carnival in my bosom, a charming Fillete who lived next door to the school overset my Trigonomertry, and set me off at a tangent from the sphere of my studies. . . . Stepping out to the garden one charming noon to take the sun's altitude, I met with my Angel. . . . It was vain to think of doing any more good at school.

At the age of eighteen, when his family moved from Mt. Oliphant to Lochlea farm, Robert had long been a "reader when he could get a book," and a reader of substantial books. "Robert read . . . with an avidity and industry scarcely to be equalled. . . . For no book was so voluminous as to slacken his industry, or so antiquated as to damp his researches." Murdoch's drill, especially his emphasis that words had precise meanings and should be used precisely, had made Robert "an excellent English scholar."

Burns' reading had given him some knowledge of Greek and Roman religion; of ancient history, and English and Scottish history;* and of the geography of the world. He knew his Bible intimately, and the popular science and astronomy used as evidence of religious truth. He was soaked in Calvinist theology, including a *Manual of Religious Belief*, the joint product of Murdoch and William Burnes, mildly liberal in its views. He had read a selection of polite letters by Eighteenth Century authors, which he used as models for his own letters. Perhaps most important, and maybe a little later, he had been enthralled by Henry Mackenzie's *Man of Feeling*, and by Laurence Sterne's *Tristram*

---

* He wrote to Dr. John Moore, author of travel books and, later, a novel: "The two first books I ever read in private, and which gave me more pleasure than any two books I ever read again, were, the life of Hannibal and the history of Sir William Wallace. — Hannibal gave my young ideas such a turn that I used to strut in raptures up and down after the recruiting drum and bagpipe, and wish myself tall enough to be a soldier; while the story of Wallace poured a Scotish prejudice in my veins which will boil along there till the flood-gates of life shut in eternal rest." (F I, #125, 106.)

Shandy, both of which greatly influenced his opinions and his prose style.

All of this reading, as well as most of the poetry he admired, was in English, which Burns learned to speak and write "with fluency, and precision, and originality . . . more particularly as he aimed at purity in his turn of expression, and avoided more successfully than most Scotchmen, the peculiarities of Scottish phraseology." It should be noted that Burns spoke English like an educated Scotsman, with Scots accent and flavor,* and wrote English, except when in his poetry he adopted a literary Scots-English largely of his own devising.

But neither Murdoch, nor William Burnes, nor Robert's reading, had much to do with his turning to poetry. He writes to Dr. Moore:

You know our country custom of coupling a man and a woman together as Partners in the labors of Harvest. — In my fifteenth autumn [1773], my Partner [Nelly Kirkpatrick] was a bewitching creature who just counted an autumn less. — My scarcity of English† denies me the power of doing her justice in that language; but you know the Scotch idiom, She was a bonie, sweet, sonsie lass. — In short, she altogether unwittingly to herself, initiated me in a certain delicious Passion, which in spite of acid Disappointment, gin-horse Prudence and bookworm Philosophy, I hold to be the first of human joys, our dearest pleasure here below. — How she caught the contagion I can't say; you medical folks talk much of infection by breathing the same air, the touch, &c. but I never expressly told her that I loved her. — Indeed I did not well know myself, why I liked so much to loiter behind with her, when returning in the evening from our labors; why the tones of her voice made my heartstrings thrill like an Eolian harp; and particularly, why my pulse beat such a furious ratann when I

---

* Burns was certainly familiar with broad Scots, and could doubtless speak it, but no evidence survives that he used it except a facetious letter to his friend William Nicol. (F I, #112, 94–95.)

† A rhetorical device and an echo from Sterne, no doubt, who frequently confesses similar inabilities, and once even supplies the reader blank pages to fill with a description to his liking. Burns had no more difficulty than Sterne in saying exactly what he wanted to in English prose.

looked and fingered over her hand, to pick out the nettle-stings and thistles. — Among her other love-inspiring qualifications, she sung sweetly; and 'twas her favorite reel to which I attempted giving an embodied vehicle in rhyme. — I was not so presumptive as to imagine that I could make verses like printed ones, composed by men who had Greek and Latin; but my girl sung a song which was said to be composed by a small country laird's son, on one of his father's maids, with whom he was in love; and I saw no reason why I might not rhyme as well as he, for excepting smearing sheep and casting peats, his father living in the moors, he had no more Scholarcraft than I had. — Thus with me began Love and Poesy; which at times have been my only, and till within this last twelvemonth have been my highest enjoyment.

In August, 1783, Burns copied the song he wrote for Nelly into his Commonplace Book.

Song

(Tune, *I am a man unmarried*)

O once I lov'd a bonny lass
    Ay and I love her still
And whilst that virtue warms my breast
    I'll love my handsome Nell.
        Fal lal de lal &c.

As bonny lasses I hae seen,
    And mony full as braw;   *fine*
But for a modest gracefu' mien,
    The like I never saw.

A bonny lass I will confess,
    Is pleasant to the e'e;
But without some better qualities
    She's no a lass for me.

But Nelly's looks are blythe and sweet,
    And what is best of a',
Her reputation is compleat
    And fair without a flaw.

> She dresses ay sae clean and neat,
>   Both decent and genteel;
> And then there's something in her gate
>   Gars ony dress look weel.   *makes*
>
> A gaudy dress and gentle air
>   May slightly touch the heart;
> But it's innocence and modesty
>   That polisses the dart.
>
> 'Tis this in Nelly pleases me;
>   'Tis this enchants my soul;
> For absolutely in my breast
>   She reigns without controul.

In the previous April, Burns had written, "If anything on earth deserves the name of rapture or transport it is the feelings of green eighteen in the company of the mistress of his heart when she repays him with an equal return of affection." And in August he continued, "For my own part I never had the least thought or inclination of turning Poet till I got once heartily in Love, and then Rhyme and Song were, in a manner, the spontaneous language of my heart."

Of a time several years after composing *Handsome Nell*, he writes,

Poesy was still a darling walk for my mind, but 'twas only the humour of the hour. — I had usually half a dozen or more pieces on hand; I took up one or other as it suited the momentary tone of the mind, and dismissed it as it bordered on fatigue. — My Passions when once they were lighted up, raged like so many devils, till they got vent in rhyme; and then conning over my verses, like a spell, soothed all into quiet.

The tumult through which most young men pass while coming to terms with themselves began late for Burns and lasted long. Its first recorded incident fell during the year of Kirkoswald, when Burns was seventeen. He defied his father and went to a village dancing school. (Being fond of dancing, he apparently went to another school three years later, and perhaps to others in between.) More serious strains followed. During the Lochlea years (1777–1784), he had a near nervous breakdown, he suffered a religious crisis, he had girl trouble ("My heart was compleatly tinder, and was eternally lighted up by some Goddess or other"), he wanted to marry but could see no way to afford a wife or family, he found his work grinding and his lot inescapable, he experienced legal oppression and class tyranny, he felt he had abilities and he knew the futile stirrings of ambition ("The great misfortune of my life was, never to have An Aim").

In these troubled years, he tells us, his "sole principles of action" were "vive l'amour et vive la bagatelle." He helped found a Bachelor's Club in Tarbolton village, he became an active and enthusiastic Mason, he continued his extensive reading, he kept at his work, and he became known as an amusing and keen-witted debater, particularly on religious subjects, in kirkyard, field, or smithy. He felt he had been "sent into the world to see, and observe," and his delight was to "study men, their manners, and their ways," a phrase he had picked up from Alexander Pope. Moreover, he had no intention of keeping his observations to himself; he started his Commonplace Book later to record some of them, with a stated hope that the record might be read some day by others.

So, despite many distresses and heavy work, Burns was a buoyant and vital young man. Gilbert says of him,

Though when young he was bashful and awkward in his intercourse with women, yet when he approached manhood, his attachment to their society became very strong, and he was constantly the victim of some fair enslaver. The symptoms of his passion were often such as nearly to equal those of the celebrated Sappho. I never indeed knew that he *fainted, sunk, and died away;* but the agitations of his mind and body, exceeded any thing of the kind I ever knew in real life. He had always a particular jealousy of people who were richer than himself, or who had more consequence in life. His love, therefore, rarely settled on persons of this description. When he selected any one out of the sovereignty of his good pleasure to whom he should pay his particular attention, she was instantly invested with a sufficient stock of charms, out of the plentiful stores of his own imagination; and there was often a great dissimilitude between his fair captivator, as she appeared to others, and as she seemed when invested with the attributes he gave her. One generally reigned paramount in his affections; . . . but . . . Robert was frequently encountering other attractions, which formed so many under-plots in the drama of his love. As these connexions were governed by the strictest rules of virtue and modesty, (from which he never deviated till he reached his 23d year,) he became anxious to be in a situation to marry.

Robert had earlier described this period of his life "[After a hard day's work] I spent the evening in the way after my own heart. — A country lad rarely carries on an amour without an assisting confident. — I possessed a curiosity, zeal and intrepid dexterity in these matters which recommended me a proper second in duels of that kind; and I dare say, I felt as much pleasure at being in the secret of half the amours in the parish, as ever did Premier at knowing the intrigues of half the courts of Europe."

The Tarbolton Bachelor's Club was founded in 1780 by young men from that village and surrounding farms, and its history, written by Burns, and its Rules, heavily influenced by him, tell much about the club and its chief instigator.

History of the Rise, Proceedings, and Regulations of the *Bachelor's Club*

> Of birth or blood we do not boast,
> Nor gentry does our club afford;
> But ploughmen and mechanics we,
> In Nature's simple dress record.

. . . By far the greater part of mankind are under the necessity *of earning the sustenance of human life by the labour of their bodies,* whereby, not only the faculties of the mind, but the nerves and sinews of the body, are so fatigued, that it is absolutely necessary to have recourse to some amusement or diversion, to relieve the wearied man, worn down by the necessary labours of life.

As the best of things, however, have been perverted to the worst of purposes, so, under the pretence of amusement and diversion, men have plunged into all the madness of riot and dissipation; and instead of attending to the grand design of human life, they have begun with extravagance and folly, and ended with guilt and wretchedness. Impressed with these considerations, we the following lads in the parish of Tarbolton, viz. Hugh Reid, Robert Burns, Gilbert Burns, Alexander Brown, Walter Mitchel, Thomas Wright, and William M'Gavin, resolved for our mutual entertainment to unite ourselves into a club or society, under such rules and regulations, that while we should forget our cares and labours in mirth and diversion, we might not transgress the bounds of innocence and decorum.

At their first meeting, with Burns presiding, they debated the topic, "Suppose a young man, bred a farmer, but without any fortune, has it in his power to marry either of two women, the one a girl of large fortune, but neither handsome in person, nor agreable in conversation, but who can manage the household affairs of a farm well enough; the other of them a girl every way agreable, in person, conversation, and behavior, but without any fortune: which of them shall he choose?"

Views on this matter are recorded in a letter from Burns to his friend John Tenant, Jr., September 13, 1784. After discussing a girl with a portion of £300, Burns continues, "We talk of air & manner, of beauty & wit, and lord knows what unmeaning nonsense; but — there — is solid charms for you — who would not be in raptures with a woman that will make him 300 £ richer? — And then to have a woman to lye with when one pleases, without running any risk of the cursed expense of bastards and all the other concomitants of that species of Smuggling — these are solid views of matrimony — "

The next year the club admitted new members. "The club being thus increased," the history continues, "we resolved to meet

at Tarbolton on the race-night, the July following, and have a
dance in honour of our society. Accordingly we did meet, each
one with a partner, and spent the evening in such innocence
and merriment, such cheerfulness and good humour, that every
brother will long remember it with pleasure and delight."

The Rules and Regulations provide for times of meeting and
procedure; for the selection of members, the choice of topics for
debate, and the maintenance of proper decorum. Fines for impropriety were to be applied to the reckoning at the inn where
the club met. Before dismissal, there was to be a "general toast
to the mistresses of the club." The 10th regulation deserves full
quotation:

Every man proper for a member of this society, must have a frank,
honest, open heart; above anything dirty or mean; and must be a
professed lover of one or more of the female sex. No haughty, self-
conceited person, who looks upon himself as superior to the rest of
the club, and especially no mean-spirited, worldly mortal, whose only
will is to heap up money, shall upon any pretense whatever be
admitted. In short, the proper person for this society is, a cheerful,
honest-hearted lad, who, if he has a friend that is true, and a mistress
that is kind, and as much wealth as genteelly to make both ends
meet — is just as happy as this world can make him.

The Bachelor's Club was short-lived, perhaps because Burns
lost interest in it when he became a Mason the next year, in
1781. A village Masonic lodge such as he joined was a sort of
convivial credit union and mutual benefit society, and Robert
seems to have been a leading spirit, becoming Depute Master in
time. Lodge St. David, Tarbolton, to which he was admitted
July 4, 1781, represented a "junchen" of Lodge St. David and
Lodge St. James which had taken place only nine days before.
In a subsequent separation, Burns chose Lodge St. James. His
Masonic activity declined after his leaving Ayrshire in 1786, but
a great moment in his life was the famous toast to him at St.
Andrew's Lodge, Edinburgh, by the Grand Master, "Caledonia,

& Caledonia's Bard, brother Burns," "which rung through the whole Assembly with multiplied honors and repeated acclamations."

His activities about Tarbolton gave Burns a seeming purpose, and relief from his problems, and entertainment; but no real settlement.

The only two doors by which I could enter the fields of fortune [he wrote] were, the most niggardly economy, or the little chicaning art of bargain-making: the first is so contracted an aperture, I never could squeeze myself into it; the last, I always hated the contamination of the threshold. — Thus, abandoned of aim or view in life; with a strong appetite for sociability, as well from native hilarity as from a pride of observation and remark; a constitutional hypochondriac taint which made me fly solitude; add to all these incentives to social life, my reputation for bookish knowledge, a certain wild, logical talent, and a strength of thought something like the rudiments of good sense, made me generally a welcome guest; so 'tis no great wonder that always "where two or three were met together, there was I in the midst of them."

In a memorandum, titled "Egotisms from my own Sensations," dated by R. H. Cromek "May," and placed between quotations from the Commonplace Book for 1784 and 1785, Robert writes, "I don't well know what is the reason of it, but somehow or other though I am, when I have a mind, pretty generally beloved; yet, I never could get the art of commanding respect. — I imagine it is owing to my being deficient in what Sterne calls 'that understrapping virtue of discretion.' — I am so apt to a *lapsus linguae*, that I sometimes think the character of a certain great man, I have read of somewhere, is very much *apropos* to myself — that he was a compound of great talents and great folly. N.B. To try if I can to discover the causes of this wretched infirmity, and, if possible, to mend it."

Burns refers to a particularly distressing incident of about this time in his letter to Dr. Moore. "A belle-fille whom I adored and who had pledged her soul to meet me in the field of matrimony, jilted me with peculiar circumstances of mortification," and helped to bring on a severe melancholia in the winter of 1781–82. It is tempting to assume that this girl was the Ellison or Alison Begbie whom Burns' youngest sister, Mrs. Begg, identified as the jilter. But his sister would have been a young girl at the time, and not necessarily too well informed about her grown brother's love affairs. Drafts of five letters seem to refer to this proposal and jilting. They are addressed merely to "A" or "E," and the first, to "A" (of which there is a manuscript), makes a proposal of marriage. The three following letters, to "my dearest E," discuss love and courtship, and the last ruefully acknowledges a rejection. They are dignified, self-conscious, and solemn. The proposal takes this form: "I hope you will forgive me when I tell you that I most sincerely & affectionately love you. — I am a stranger in these matters A——, as I assure you, that you are the first woman to whom I ever made such a declaration so I declare I am at a loss how to proceed. —

". . . I hope my inexperience of the world will plead for me — I can only say I sincerely love you & there is nothing on earth I so ardently wish for, or could possibly give me so much happiness, as one day to see you mine." Letters number two and three equate love and virtue. In letter two, he writes, "I verily believe, my dear E., that the pure genuine feelings of love are as rare in the world as the pure genuine principles of virtue and piety. . . . I have often thought that if a well-grounded affection be not really a part of virtue, 'tis something extremely akin to it. Whenever the thought of my E. warms my heart, every feeling of humanity, every principle of generosity kindles in my breast. It extinguishes every dirty spark of malice and envy which are but too apt to infest me. I grasp every creature in the arms of universal benevolence, and equally participate in the pleasures of the happy, and sympathise with the miseries of the unfortunate."

Letter number three continues the theme. "The love I have for you is founded on the sacred principles of virtue and honor. . . . Believe me, my dear, it is love like this alone which can render the marriage state happy." In letter four, he protests, "There is one rule which I have hitherto practiced, and which I shall invariably keep with you, and that is, honestly to tell you the plain truth." But, alas, in letter five, he is shocked to find that she can only wish him happiness and be his friend.

It is not even certain that Burns sent these letters to anyone, but they are similar in style and tone to one that he sent his father soon after they are presumed to have been written, and their chief biographical significance lies in their suggestion that Burns was a circumspect and proper young man so late as his twenty-second year.

A change in him, marking the arrival of his long-postponed maturity, began when he left home for seven or eight months in the summer of 1781. While marketing the flax which he and his brother raised on land taken from their father, Robert got the idea that he might improve his condition by turning flax-dresser and merchant, and so he went from Lochlea to the nearby town of Irvine to learn the trade. He also speaks of the venture as a "whim."

In Irvine he had one partner named Peacock, who may have been a relative of his mother, and one who, he says, was dishonest, but they may not have been the same. And one partner's wife set the shop afire during a New Year welcome to 1782, leaving Burns with the clothes he stood up in. But he stayed on after the misadventure for several months. Just who owned the shop which burned down is a matter of dispute, but the importance of Robert's six months in Irvine lies elsewhere than in his flax dressing and the fire. Most notably, he met a sailor, Richard Brown, and he may have read the Scotch poems of Robert Fergusson. A controversy, centering about the date of a copy of Fergusson's poems which Burns owned, has lately arisen over the occasion

of his first meeting with these poems. It is obvious that the volume in question may not have provided his first acquaintance
with Fergusson, and the fact that he did not begin to imitate
Fergusson's poems until 1784–85 is no evidence as to when he
first read them. The only significant fact in the case is Burns'
statement to Dr. Moore. After mentioning that Brown had encouraged him in looser ways with women, he continues, "Here
his friendship did me a mischief; and the consequence was, that
soon after I resumed the plough,* I wrote the Welcome inclosed.
— My reading was *only* [italics supplied] encreased by two stray
volumes of Pamela, and one of Ferdinand Count Fathom, which
gave me some idea of Novels. — Rhyme, except some religious
pieces which are in print, I had given up; but meeting with
Fergusson's Scotch Poems, I strung anew my wildly-sounding
rustic lyre with emulating vigor."

The *only* italicized above suggests that Burns did not read
Fergusson at Irvine, but the chronology of the passage is slurred.
It is not clear just when he gave over writing poetry for a time,
but it may have been before he came to Irvine. And the Welcome
[*To His Bastart Wean*] celebrates a child born May 22, 1785,
three years after he left Irvine, in the spring of 1782. Whatever
the date, Burns' discovery of Fergusson was the chief formative
influence in making him a great poet.

Richard Brown was a man of much wider experience than
Burns and of considerable ability; he soon became master of a
West Indiaman. He gave Burns his first thought of publication by
suggesting that he send some of his poems to a magazine. Just
what poems Robert showed Brown no one can say, but he may
have had available *The Death and Dying Words of Poor Mailie*,
and songs like *Winter, a Dirge*, or *Corn Rigs*. It may be he even
showed Brown some of the religious poems he mentions to
Dr. Moore. But *Corn Rigs* is a more likely choice, and an

---

* The time assigned by Gilbert for Robert's departure from "the strictest rules
of virtue and modesty." (F I, #125, 113.)

excellent song.* Robert had gone far since he wrote *Handsome Nell.*

Corn Rigs

It was upon a Lammas night,
  When corn rigs are bonie,   *ridges or rows*
Beneath the moon's unclouded light,
  I held awa to Annie;
The time flew by, wi' tentless heed;   *careless*
  Till, 'tween the late and early,
Wi' sma' persuasion she agreed
  To see me thro' the barley.
    Corn rigs, an' barley rigs,
      An' corn rigs are bonie:
    I'll ne'er forget that happy night,
      Amang the rigs wi' Annie.

The sky was blue, the wind was still,
  The moon was shining clearly;
I set her down, wi' right good will,
  Amang the rigs o' barley:
I ken't her heart was a' my ain;   *knew*
  I lov'd her most sincerely;
I kiss'd her owre and owre again,
  Amang the rigs o' barley.

I lock'd her in my fond embrace;
  Her heart was beating rarely:
My blessings on that happy place,
  Amang the rigs o' barley!
But by the moon and stars so bright,
  That shone that hour so clearly!
She ay shall bless that happy night
  Amang the rigs o' barley.

I hae been blythe wi' comrades dear;
  I hae been merry drinking;
I hae been joyfu' gath'rin gear;   *making money*
  I hae been happy thinking:

* In his letter to Dr. Moore, Burns places this song before his twenty-third year, although the present version may represent later emendations. (F I, #125, 112.)

But a' the pleasures e'er I saw,
Tho' three times doubled fairly —
That happy night was worth them a',
Amang the rigs o' barley.
Corn rigs, an' barley rigs,
An' corn rigs are bonie:
I'll ne'er forget that happy night,
Amang the rigs wi' Annie.

In Irvine, Burns also went through a religious ferment which must have been at least part cause of the desperate depression, already mentioned, which accompanied "alarming symptoms of a Pleurisy or some other dangerous disorder" that afflicted him there. The comparatively liberal theology of William Burnes was no longer satisfactory to Robert. There was a God, Burns felt sure, but what sort of a God was he, and in what relation did he stand to man? What was expected of man, with the passions God had given him? Burns never settled these matters to his satisfaction, but at Irvine he seems to have relieved himself finally of oppressive concern.

In a very early song, *Winter, a Dirge,* probably written before he went to Irvine, Burns accepts man's miserable estate and pleads to God, "Since to enjoy Thou dost deny, / Assist me to resign." But in *A Prayer in the Prospect of Death,* from the Irvine period, after admitting his human weakness and frailty, Burns finds comfort in the reflection, "But Thou art good, and goodness still / Delighteth to Forgive." And in *Stanzas Written in Prospect of Death,* on the same occasion, Burns wonders why he is loth to leave this earthly scene, which is not pleasant. He trembles before an angry God because he is guilty, and he promises never more to disobey, but he knows he is weak, and he asks for divine assistance. Neither of these poems expresses the Calvinist position.

Paraphrase of the First Psalm advances an ancient paradox. God grants peace and rest to the good, "But hath decreed that wicked men / Shall ne'er be truly blest." This decree seems harsh to Burns, and unworthy a benevolent God who created the wicked in the first place. *The Ninetieth Psalm Versified* recites the familiar theme that man is brought into the world and flourishes briefly, like the flower in beauty's pride, "But long ere night, cut down it lies / All wither'd and decay'd." He comes to no resolution, but in a later song, *Tho' Fickle Fortune*, he concludes, "Then come, Misfortune, I bid thee welcome — / I'll meet thee with undaunted mind!" And in a "wild rhapsody," *My Father Was a Farmer*, he resolves, "The past was bad, and the future hid; its good or ill untrièd, O, / But the present hour was in my pow'r, and so I would enjoy it, O."

A blank verse passage entitled *Remorse* (1783), an outgrowth of his reading Adam Smith's *Theory of Moral Sentiments*, adds complementary reflections:

> Of all the numerous ills that hurt our peace;
> That press the soul, or wring the mind with anguish;
> Beyond comparison the worst are those
> By our own folly, or our guilt brought on. . . .
> Lives there a man so firm, who, while his heart
> Feels all the bitter horrors of his crime,
> Can reason down its agonizing throbs,
> And, after proper purpose of amendment,
> Can firmly force his jarring thoughts to peace?
> O happy, happy, enviable man!
> O glorious magnanimity of soul!

It is feelings like this which led Burns to rejoice in Milton's Satan when he read *Paradise Lost*.

Some years later, a heart-wrung comment in a letter to Margaret Chalmers reveals continuing stress. "There are just two creatures I would envy, a horse in his native state traversing the forests of Asia, or an oyster on some of the desart shores of Europe. The one has not a wish without enjoyment, the other has neither wish nor fear."

A notable result of the stirrings of Burns' spirit during the confused years at Lochlea was his development of a flexible, easy, and often pungent English prose style. Most of Burns' prose is in letters, and too often his letters merely convey inflated commonplaces or protective politeness to social superiors, or waft sentiment and elephantine gallantry to women. But even as he discovered his way in poetry, so he learned, when he was on easy terms with a correspondent and had something to say, to write forceful English prose. The pity is that there were not more such correspondents, and that we do not have more of these letters, so suggestive of Burns' conversation which everyone found enchanting, and almost no one recorded.

His early letters are studied compositions based on models he found in his school reader, or in a volume of "letters by the most eminent writers, with a few sensible directions for attaining an easy epistolary style." An excellent example of this early manner at its best, and a most revealing document as well, is a letter from Burns to his father, written from Irvine, December 27, 1781.

HONORED SIR,

I have purposely delayed writing in the hope that I would have the pleasure of seeing you on Newyearday but work comes so hard upon us that I do not chuse to come, as well for that, as also for some other little reasons which I shall tell you at meeting. — My health is much about what it was when you were here only my sleep is rather sounder and on the whole I am rather better than otherwise tho it is but by very slow degrees. — The weakness of my nerves has so debilitated my mind that I dare not, either review past events, or look forward into futurity; for the least anxiety, or perturbation in my breast, produces most unhappy effects on my whole frame. — Sometimes, indeed, when for an hour or two, as is sometimes the case, my spirits are a little lightened, I glimmer a little into futurity; but my principal, and indeed my only pleasurable enjoyment is looking backwards & forwards in a moral & religious way — I am quite transported at the thought that ere long, perhaps very soon, I shall bid an eternal adiew to all the pains, & uneasiness & disquietudes of this weary life; for I assure you I am heartily tired of it, and, if I do not very much deceive myself I could contentedly & gladly resign it. —

The Soul uneasy & confin'd from home
Rests & expatiates in a life to come.

POPE

It is for this reason I am more than pleased with the 15th, 16th &
17th verses of the 7th Chapter of Rev:n* than any ten times as many
verses in the whole Bible, & would not exchange the noble enthusiasm
with which they inspire me, for all that this world has to offer — As
for this world I despair of ever making a figure in it — I am not formed
for the bustle of the busy nor the flutter of the Gay. I shall never again
be capable of it. — Indeed, I am altogether unconcern'd at the
thoughts of it. I foresee that very probably Poverty & Obscurity await
me & I am, in some measure prepared & daily preparing to meet
& welcome them. — I have but just time & paper to return you my
grateful thanks for the many Lessons of Virtue & Piety you have given
me — Lessons which were but too much neglected when they were
given but which, I hope have been remembered ere it is yet too
late — Present my dutiful respects to my Mother & my Compnts to
Mr & Mrs Muir and with wishing you all a merry Newyearday I shall
conclude

I am, Honored Sir, your dutiful son
Robt Burns

my meal is nearly out but I am going to borrow till I get more —

Four days later came the New Year party at the shop, and the
fire.

Although in the latter part of the letter he is imitating and
even quoting from Chapter LV of his favorite novel, *The Man
of Feeling*, Burns here is obviously distressed. In his Commonplace Book, as we have seen, he speaks of a "dangerous disorder" † from which he suffered at this time, and he specifies in the
letter itself his other causes for depression: religious concern,
poor diet, hard work, and frustration. Certainly, also, he was
lonely. It is probable that he lived by himself, and cooked his
own porridge, with meal sent from home.

* A depiction of the joys of heaven.
† Possibly smallpox, then prevalent in Irvine. See Health Record, Appendix B.

The following letter, written two and a half years later, reveals a much brighter spirit, and a much lighter style, in describing to his cousin the adventures of a local orgiastic cult, the Buchanites.

Mr. James Burness   Writer   in Montrose

Mossgiel, 3d August 1784

My dear Sir,

I ought in gratitude to have acknowledged the receipt of your last kind letter before this time; but without troubling you with any apology I shall proceed to inform you that our family are all in health at prest and we were very happy with the unexpected favor of John Caird's company for near two weeks; & I must say it of him he is one of the most agreable, facetious warm-hearted lads I was ever acquainted with. —

We have been surprised with one of the most extraordinary Phenomena in the moral world, which, I dare say, has happened in the course of this last Century. — We have had a party of the Presbytry Relief as they call themselves, for some time in this country. A pretty thriving society of them has been in the Burgh of Irvine for some years past, till about two years ago, a Mrs Buchan from Glasgow came among them, & began to spread some fanatical notions of religion among them, & in a short time, made many converts among them, & among others their Preacher, one Mr Whyte, who upon that account has been suspended & formally deposed by his brethren; he continued however, to preach in private to his party, & was supported, both he, & their spiritual Mother as they affect to call old Buchan, by the contributions of the rest, several of whom were in good circumstances; till in spring last the Populace rose & mobbed the old leader Buchan, & put her out of the town; on which, all her followers voluntarily quitted the place likewise, & with such precipitation, that many of them never shut their doors behind them; one left a washing on the green, another a cow bellowing at the crib without meat or anybody to mind her, & after several stages, they are fixed at present in the neighbourhood of Dumfries. — Their tenets are a strange jumble of enthusiastic jargon, among others, she pretends to give them the Holy Ghost by breathing on them, which she does with postures & practices that are scandalously indecent; they have likewise disposed of all their affects & hold a community of goods, & live nearly an idle life, carrying on a great farce of pretended devotion in barns, & woods, where they lodge & lye all together, & hold likewise a community of women, as it is another of their tenets that they can commit no moral sin. — I am personally acquainted with most of them, & I can assure you the above mentioned are facts. —

This My Dr Sir, is one of the many instances of the folly of leaving the guidance of sound reason, & common sense in matters of Religion. — Whenever we neglect or despise these sacred Monitors, the whimsical notions of a perturbated brain are taken for the immediate influences of the Deity, & the wildest fanaticism, & the most inconstant absurdities, will meet with abettors & converts. —Nay, I have often thought, that the more out-of-the-way & ridiculous their fancies are, if once they are sanctified under the sacred name of Religion, the unhappy, mistaken votaries are the more firmly glued to them. —

I expect to hear from you soon, & I beg you will remember me to all friends, & believe me to be,

my Dr Sir your affectionate Cousin,
ROBERT BURNESS*

There has been much speculation about Burns' relations with the Buchanites, and with one Buchanite lass, Jean Gardner, in particular, but reliable details are lacking.

During the harsh experience of his late adolescence and early manhood, Burns also developed his views on social injustice and the need for social reform. They were personal, not theoretical. The Mt. Oliphant years had been bleak, and had ended bitterly. During the landlord's life, William Burnes had been able to make compromises on rent day, but after Provost Fergusson died, the factor did his duty, pressed for the rent, wrote threatening letters, and made the family miserable. It seemed to Burns that if honesty and hard work were not enough to make a decent living for a man and his family, then there was something wrong with the system. The Lochlea experience showed to him even more clearly the cruel disadvantage of the land system to a tenant, and the opportunities open to landlords for oppression almost without recourse for a poor man. It seemed unjust that a landed

---

* Burns used this spelling when writing to his cousin, who himself used it.

aristocracy and gentry should enjoy their comforts at such great burden to people like himself. And he resented the privileges of well-born dullness, and the indifference of those favored by fortune to those beneath them. "He could not well conceive of a more mortifying picture of human life than a man seeking work." As he put it,

> See yonder poor, o'erlabor'd wight
> So abject, mean, and vile,
> Who begs a brother of the earth
> To give him leave to toil;
> And see his lordly fellow worm
> The poor petition spurn,
> Unmindful, tho' a weeping wife
> And helpless offspring mourn.

It was experience and feeling of this sort which lay behind Burns' warm response later to cries for Freedom and Liberty, for the Rights of Man, and for reform of a corrupt government managed by a privileged few for their special advantage.

The troubles which William Burnes had with his Lochlea landlord can be described simply, now that most of the legal documents have been discovered, and they are important to an understanding of both the father's integrity and the son's antipathy to moneyed gentry. When David McClure and William made their oral agreement about the Lochlea rent in 1777, McClure allowed a certain amount to William for improvements he was to make on the farm. By 1781 when McClure was desperate for money and denied the allowance which William Burnes claimed, Burnes suspended the payment of rent. On August 18, 1783, an arbitration decided in Burnes' favor, ordering him to pay McClure £231 7s 8d, which he had available, and disallowing claims against him for upward of £500. But on May 17, 1783, McClure had seized Burnes' crops and stock, to insure payment of his claims; and in the meantime, McClure's creditors had laid claims to Burnes' rent for themselves. To extricate himself from this dual demand, the harassed old man took an expensive step for one in his position: he raised an action of "multiple poinding" in the highest court in Scotland, the Court of Session, and was ordered to pay the creditors not the landlord — just two weeks before he died of tuberculosis. The expense of his defense, and the rent due, seem to have taken all his money, and the strain of the three years undoubtedly hastened his end. The family distress was acute. Their only substantial assets after William's death were claims for unpaid wages which he had allowed his children. These, rating as preferred claims, were paid before those of other creditors, and with this money the family moved promptly to Mossgiel farm, a few miles away in Mauchline parish. Robert and Gilbert, in the prospect of disaster, had sublet it even before William's death, from a friendly lawyer and fellow-Mason, Gavin Hamilton, of Mauchline.

An account of William Burnes will serve to complete the story of Robert Burns' youth and the environment from which he emerged to dazzle the world two years after his father died. The close-knit family at Lochlea felt the father's loss deeply, and Robert was particularly distressed by the old man's saying on his deathbed that he feared for his oldest son.

Testimony about William Burnes unanimously speaks of him as a superior man. Murdoch comments on his "solid reasoning, sensible remark, and a moderate seasoning of jocularity," and emphasizes the happy home life at Alloway and Mt. Oliphant, and the devotion between Agnes and her husband. Murdoch continues, "He was a tender and affectionate father; he took pleasure in leading his children in the path of virtue; not in driving them, as some parents do, to the performance of duties to which they themselves are averse. . . . He had the art of gaining the esteem and good-will of those that were labourers under him. I think I never saw him angry but twice: the one time it was with the foreman of the band, for not reaping the field as he was desired; and the other time it was with an old man, for using smutty

innuendos and *doubles entendres*. . . . As he was at no time
overbearing to inferiors, he was equally incapable of that passive,
pitiful, paltry spirit, that induces some people to *keep booing
and booing* in the presence of a great man. He always treated
superiors with a becoming respect, but he never gave the smallest encouragement to aristocratical arrogance."

Dr. Currie, citing "one who knew him toward the latter end of
his life," describes William as "above the common stature, thin,
and bent with labour, his countenance . . . serious and expressive . . . and the scanty locks on his head . . . gray." He then
quotes the famous passage describing family worship in *The Cotter's Saturday Night,* which Gilbert says was written as a picture
of his father.

> The cheerfu' supper done, wi' serious face,
>   They round the ingle, form a circle wide;   *fire*
> The sire turns o'er, wi' patriarchal grace,
>   The big ha'-Bible, ance his father's pride.
> His bonnet rev'rently is laid aside,
> His lyart haffets wearing thin and bare;   *gray temples*
>   Those strains that once did sweet in Zion glide,
> He wales a portion with judicious care,   *selects*
>   And "Let us worship God!" he says, with solemn air.

The final observation of William Burnes links him with his
sons, and is particularly interesting in its details about Robert.
Dr. John M'Kenzie, then of Mauchline, attended William Burnes
in his final illness.

When I first saw William Burns [he writes], he was in very ill health,
and his mind suffering from the embarrassed state of his affairs. His
appearance certainly made me think him inferior, both in manner and
intelligence, to the generality of those in his situation; but before
leaving him, I found that I had been led to form a very false conclusion of his mental powers. After giving a short, but distinct account, of
his indisposition, he entered upon a detail of the various causes that
had gradually led to the embarrassment of his affairs; and these he
detailed in such earnest language, and in so simple, candid, and

pathetic a manner, as to excite both my astonishment and sympathy. His wife spoke little, but struck me as being a very sagacious woman, without any appearance of forwardness, or any of that awkwardness in her manner which many of these people shew in the presence of a stranger. . . . Gilbert and Robert Burns were certainly very different in their appearance and manner, though they both possessed great abilities, and uncommon information. Gilbert partook more of the manner and appearance of the father, and Robert of the mother. Gilbert, in the first interview I had with him at Lochlea, was frank, modest, well informed, and communicative. The poet seemed distant, suspicious, and without any wish to interest or please. He kept himself very silent, in a dark corner of the room: And before he took any part in the conversation, I frequently detected him scrutinizing me during my conversation with his father and brother. . . . From the period of which I speak, I took a lively interest in Robert Burns; and, before I was acquainted with his poetical powers, I perceived that he possessed very great mental abilities, an uncommonly fertile and lively imagination, a thorough acquaintance with many of our Scottish poets, and an enthusiastic admiration of Ramsay and Fergusson. Even then, on subjects with which he was acquainted, his conversation was rich in well chosen figures, animated, and energetic. Indeed, I have always thought that no person could have a just idea of the extent of Burns's talents, who had not an opportunity to hear him converse. His discrimination of character was great beyond that of any person I ever knew; and I have often observed to him, that it seemed to be intuitive. I seldom ever knew him to make a false estimate of character, when he formed the opinion from his own observation.

Most of the poetry Burns wrote before he was twenty-five is lost. The little of his early verse we now have, and the dates are not certain, is mostly songs about Tarbolton and Mauchline girls, and mostly in English, with an occasional flavoring of Scots words. The surviving early poetry, probably from a little later, is largely religious: prayers, reflections, paraphrases of psalms. From the beginning, Burns was imitative. As he wrote to his friend Peter Hill, "It is an excellent method for improvement, and what I believe every Poet does; to place some favorite classic Author, in our own walks of study & composition, before us as a model."

The models for his songs were all around him. He heard them from friends and neighbors and sweethearts; he heard them from his mother. He also had two collections of songs, one of which he says he "pored over . . . song by song, verse by verse; carefully noting the true tender or sublime from affectation or fustian."

For his early poetry, he had the work of Allan Ramsay in vernacular Scots; Ramsay provided a model for *The Death and Dying Words of Poor Mailie*, and, later, for the verse epistles. But the poets Burns admired before 1782, and continued to admire later, were didactic, sententious, formal writers for polite readers in England, and in Scotland. A great favorite was James Thomson, a Scot, noted for his long poem, *The Seasons*, in which he drew edifying moral reflections from generalized descriptions of nature; and Alexander Pope, in whom Burns found a source of quotations second only to Thomson. He was also fond of William Shenstone, a writer of insipid elegies, *e.g., Elegy XVIII He Repeats the Song of Colin, a discerning Shepherd, Lamenting the State of the Woolen Manufactory.* Thomas Gray's *Elegy Written in a Country Churchyard* echoes throughout *The Cotter's Saturday Night*, and Oliver Goldsmith's *The Deserted Village* also provided many hints for that poem. Burns refers to both of these poets frequently. James Beattie, another Scot, was the famous author of a vapidly pleasant poem, *The Minstrel, or the Progress of Genius,* in which he condescended to native inspiration, and produced such reflections as

> And let us hope — to doubt is to rebel —
> Let us exult in hope, that all shall yet be well.

Edward Young (Hazlitt's "gloomy epigrammatist") is immortal for the line "How populous! how vital is the grave!" which comes from his *Night Thoughts on Life, Death, and Immortality.* And finally there is Robert Blair, still another Scot, who wrote *The Grave,* in which he announced

The task be mine
To paint the gloomy horrors of the tomb.

One finds frequent echoes of these men in Burns' poems, but not much work in their manner until after the vernacular flowering, when he was trying other modes because his success had "encouraged such a shoal of ill-spawned monsters to crawl into public notice under the name of Scots Poets, that the very term Scots Poetry borders on the burlesque." Workmanlike though his later imitations may be, Burns was unable to transmute his admired English models into poetry with his individual stamp and distinctive quality, as he had done with his vernacular models. Some of this later work has biographical interest, but as poetry, it is commonplace.

The spirit, the tone, the tune, the feel, the rhythm, the movement, the subjects, the verse forms, the conventions, and the diction of Burns' vernacular Scots poems all derived from a long tradition in Scotland, unfamiliar then and now to most readers of English literature. The suggestion that he write in this tradition was stimulated by his reading of Robert Fergusson. Burns greatly increased the dimensions of what he found. Where Fergusson wrote vividly of local occasions, scenes, and people, Burns at his best transcended the local characters and events which he described. His poems have a controlling theme, a view of life, not merely a central topic. Most important, and wholly undefinable, are the greater imagination and artistic power, the richness and flow of suggestive language, and the force of statement in Burns' work.

He developed a highly individualized style and idiom. He devised a mixture of general English and of Scots spoken in no particular area and by no particular group, to create the informal and conversational manner he wanted. He shifts back and forth from English to Scots as it suits his purpose, his rhythm, his rhyming need, his poetic mood. He tries to be simple, clear, and exciting. He speaks naturally, and to the heart.

Hearing his poetry read in proper Scots discovers grace and

rhythmic felicity and tonal sensitivity otherwise unsuspected, but he comes through well even if one cannot have that advantage. He has much to offer those who are willing to give a little for it, particularly if they have a taste for so full-blooded a poet, with so rich a zest for life. It is true that Burns' world has disappeared. But so has Chaucer's, and Shakespeare's, and Pope's, and Byron's. Great writers create their own worlds, in which those who come after find themselves.

The two years between his residence in Irvine and the death of William Burnes (1782–1784) were for Robert years of Masonic meetings, girls, reading, hard farm work, and worry, but little is known in particular of him during this time. When he became head of the family, and moved to Mossgiel farm, he and Gilbert made a vigorous effort to succeed as farmers, but bad seed and bad weather turned a meagre enterprise into a desperate one; and Robert brought other difficulties on himself, until his situation became intolerable. His personal problems as much as his meeting with Fergusson excited him to write vernacular poetry, and the poetry got him and the family out of their troubles.

III

POET

If Poetry comes not as naturally as Leaves to a tree it had better not come at all.

JOHN KEATS

The rough material of Fine Writing is certainly the gift of Genius; but I as firmly believe that the workmanship is the united effort of Pains, Attention, & repeated Trial.

BURNS TO HENRY ERSKINE

1. Epistles and Satires

On Robert Burns' twenty-fifth birthday (January 25, 1785), he was known about Tarbolton and Mauchline parishes as a raffish farmer whose family had had trouble with its landlord. By January, 1789, editions of his poems had been published in Kilmarnock, Edinburgh, Belfast, Dublin, London, Philadelphia, and New York. Although his first verse dates from 1773, when he was fourteen, and he continued to write poetry and songs thereafter, the poems that made his name were written between the summer of 1784 and the autumn of 1786. There survive twenty songs of previous date, some of them excellent in the versions we have; also a handful of solemn religious lyrics, and a few reflective poems of small merit. This work is mostly in English, but no doubt Burns' inner ear heard his lines pronounced with the Scots tone and quality. There is only one vernacular poem to give a hint of what was to follow, *The Death and Dying Words of Poor Mailie,* in which Burns records a favorite sheep's opinions on freedom and animal husbandry, and quotes her legacy of advice to her son and daughter. It is an engaging comic piece in a tradition initiated by William Hamilton of Gilbertfield with *The Last Dying Words of Bonnie Heck, a Famous Grey-Hound in the Shire of Fife* and continued by Allan Ramsay and others.

Burns' productive period began in the summer of 1784, according to his brother Gilbert's recollection, with the *Epistle to Davie,* although as revised and published at Kilmarnock, the poem is dated "January," and includes references to "Jean," presumably Jean Armour, whose relations with Burns began in the summer or fall of 1785. Here, as in his earlier work, Burns is soothing his passions by writing verse, but instead of celebrating girls, he is now formulating his ideas, and he begins to reveal a striking personality as he reflects on his reading and his experience of life. Not that his opinions are original or necessarily compelling. But Burns is that rarest of rarities, a sharply perceptive man of wit and sense and imagination, who speaks out candidly, and who can magnetize his readers. Most notable of all, his poetry seems conversational while actually written in complicated rhythms and with intricate rhyming. He was a gifted metrist, and was deeply concerned with his artisanship, but he wrote for people, in a manner they could enjoy directly and understand, and about matters they had experienced.

Burns has a wide range — humor, pathos, sarcasm, bawdry, impudence, sensitivity to nature, irony, tenderness, pawky sense, satire, moral sentiment. He is not polite or deferential; the reader must take him on his own terms. He responds fully to the forces of life, and he finds that respectability is a denial of humanity and a loss of vitality. He is willing to grant that a full life may be a short one, and may seem folly to those of worldly wisdom. Certainly what makes good poetry does not please the "unco guid." He remarks simply of his tempestuous life and of the poetry that sprang from it

---

* Davie was David Sillar, member of the Bachelor's Club, fiddler, and village rhymer.

The light that led astray
Was light from heaven.

And after he had listened to his conscience and married Jean Armour, and had assumed family responsibilities, he observed to Sillar, "I hear you have commenced, Married Man; so much the better, though your Muse may not fare the better for it. — I know not whether the Nine Gipseys are jealous of my Lucky, but they are a good deal shier since I could boast the important relation of Husband."

Burns wrote as an Ayrshire farmer about Ayrshire men and women, but Ayrshire men and women do not differ much from men and women in other places and times, even in China, it seems. Dr. Wen Yuan-Ning, on Burns' birthday in 1944, remarked on the BBC, "Burns . . . is everybody's poet. There are in all human beings, whether Scots or Chinese, feelings and thoughts that 'lie too deep for tears.' Burns in his poems and songs expresses these elemental thoughts and feelings in a way that would strike a responsive chord even in the breast of an unlettered peasant in China, could he but understand the tongue that Burns spoke." Burns' admirer and correspondent, Mrs. Dunlop, wrote him of a Portuguese who, to soothe his soul, would repeat Burns' verses instead of saying his prayers. And Burns' epistles, which were written to friends and neighbors on purely local and personal matters, touch the concerns of men everywhere.

A famous one, the *Epistle to Davie*, opens with a brief and characteristic description of the bitter weather outside, and of the poet snug inside. Burns shifts quickly to a comparison of the rich and the poor in such weather, and then broadens his comparison:

It's hardly in a body's pow'r,
To keep, at times, frae being sour,
    To see how things are shar'd;
How best o' chiels are whyles in want,   *chaps   sometimes*
While coofs on countless thousands rant   *dolts   roister*

And ken na how to ware't;   *spend*
But Davie, lad, ne'er fash your head,   *trouble*
    Tho' we hae little gear;   *wealth*
We're fit to win our daily bread,
    As lang's we're hale and fier: *whole   sound*
"Mair spier na, nor fear na,"   *ask not*
    Auld age ne'er mind a feg;   *fig*
        The last o't, the warst o't,
        Is only but to beg.

To lie in kilns and barnes at e'en,
When banes are craz'd, and bluid is thin,
    Is, doubtless, great distress!
Yet then content could make us blest;
Ev'n then, sometimes, we'd snatch a taste
    Of truest happiness.
The honest heart that's free frae a'
    Intended fraud or guile,
However Fortune kick the ba',
    Has ay some cause to smile;
        And mind still, you'll find still,
        A comfort this nae sma';
        Nae mair then, we'll care then,
        Nae farther can we fa'.

The beggar's lot here described was no romantic fantasy, but a likely enough prospect for poor folk like Burns, and a relief from their burdens as well. In stanza five, Burns brings his comparison to its conclusion, in a statement of one of his strongest beliefs:

It's no in titles nor in rank:
It's no in wealth like Lon'on Bank,
    To purchase peace and rest.
It's no in makin muckle, mair;   *much   more*
It's no in books, it's no in lear,   *learning*
    To make us truly blest:
If happiness hae not her seat
    An' center in the breast,
We may be wise, or rich, or great,
    But never can be blest!

Nae treasures nor pleasures
Can make us happy lang;
The heart ay's the part ay
That makes us right or wrang.

The remaining stanzas speak of the joys of love and friendship.

Burns found suggestions and models and themes for his verse epistles in similar graceful but rather empty epistles exchanged between Hamilton of Gilbertfield and Allan Ramsay. The complex fourteen-line stanza of the *Epistle to Davie* which Burns handles with such ease and felicity, dates back at least to 1597, to Alexander Montgomerie's *The Cherry and the Slae,* which Burns probably found in Ramsay's anthology, *The Ever Green.* There followed a score of similar epistles, jocular, witty, loosely constructed, some of them merely good-natured expressions of friendship and gratitude, but many loaded with careful statements of Burns' views on poetry, on the unevenness of fortune, on pretence and hypocrisy, on Ayrshire kirk affairs, and on his life and lot and love adventures. For most of them he chose the traditional six-line stanza which he uses in the *Epistle to J. Lapraik,** where, after extending cordial greetings, he comments on poets and poetry, particularly his own.

But, first an' foremost, I should tell,
Amaist as soon as I could spell,
I to the crambo-jingle fell;   *rhyming*
    Tho' rude an' rough —
Yet crooning to a body's sel,   *humming*
    Does weel eneugh

I am nae poet, in a sense;
But just a rhymer like by chance,
An' hae to learning nae pretence;
    Yet, what the matter?
Whene'er my Muse does on me glance,
    I jingle at her.

* Lapraik was a farmer, and a rhymer like Sillar.

Your critic-folk may cock their nose,
And say, "How can you e'er propose,
You wha ken hardly verse frae prose,
    To make a sang?"
But, by your leaves, my learned foes,
    Ye're maybe wrang.

What's a' your jargon o' your Schools,
Your Latin names for horns an' stools?
If honest Nature made you fools,
    What sairs your grammers?   *serves*
Ye'd better taen up spades and shools   *shovels*
    Or knappin-hammers.   *stone-breaking*

A set o' dull, conceited hashes   *dunderheads*
Confuse their brains in college-classes,
They gang in stirks, and come out asses,   *young bullocks*
    Plain truth to speak;
An' syne they think to climb Parnassus   *then*
    By dint o' Greek!

Gie me ae spark o' Nature's fire,
That's a' the learning I desire;
Then, tho' I drudge thro' dub an' mire   *puddle*
    At pleugh or cart,
My Muse, tho' hamely in attire,
    May touch the heart.

Clearly, Burns feels that poetry is not just a matter of forms, rules, and conventions — a series of gracefully turned clichés; it must express the poet's feelings, and spring from inner compulsions. It is for both the simple and the sophisticated. Burns continues in his epistle with some personal comments, expresses a desire for friendship with Lapraik, and adds a characteristic challenge:

Awa ye selfish, warly race,   *worldly*
Wha think that havins, sense, an' grace,   *manners*
Ev'n love an' friendship should give place
        To Catch-the-Plack!   *get the money*
I dinna like to see your face,
        Nor hear your crack.

But ye whom social pleasure charms,
Whose hearts the tide of kindness warms,
Who hold your being on the terms,
    "Each aid the others,"
Come to my bowl, come to my arms,
    My friends, my brothers!

The *Second Epistle to J. Lapraik* continues the theme of the
honest man which closed the *Epistle to Davie.*

My worthy friend, ne'er grudge an' carp,
Tho' Fortune use you hard an' sharp;
Come, kittle up your moorland harp   *tickle*
    Wi' gleesome touch!
Ne'er mind how Fortune waft an' warp;   *woof*
    She's but a bitch.

. . . .

Do ye envý the city gent,
Behint a kist to lie an' sklent;   *counter   cheat*
Or purse-proud, big wi' cent. per cent.
    An' muckle wame,   *big belly*
In some bit brugh to represent   *borough*
    A bailie's name?   *magistrate's*

Or is't the paughty feudal thane,   *haughty*
Wi' ruffl'd sark an' glancing cane,   *shirt   shining*
Wha thinks himsel nae sheep-shank bane,   *important*
    But lordly stalks;
While caps an' bonnets aff are taen,
    As by he walks?

. . . .

For thus the royal mandate ran,
When first the human race began:
"The social, friendly, honest man,
    Whate'er he be,
'Tis he fulfills great Nature's plan,
    And none but he."

In *To William Simpson* of Ochiltree,* Burns speaks at length
of his desire to celebrate Ayrshire in his poems, and includes a
famous comment on how poetry comes to a poet.

* A schoolmaster.

The Muse, nae poet ever fand her,   *found*
Till by himsel he learn'd to wander,
Adown some trottin burn's meander,   *brook's*
 An' no think lang:
O, sweet to stray, an' pensive ponder
 A heart-felt sang!

The warly race may drudge an' drive,   *worldly*
Hog-shouther, jundie, stretch, an' strive;   *ply the elbows*
Let me fair Nature's face descrive,
 And I, wi' pleasure,
Shall let the busy, grumbling hive
 Bum owre their treasure.   *Hum*

Burns is particularly brisk in a satiric epistle which comments on the pretence and hypocrisy of his adversaries, the clergy: *To the Rev. John M'Math,* Inclosing a Copy of "Holy Willie's Prayer" which he had requested, Sept. 17, 1785.* After commenting on his shots at some clerics and clerical practices, Burns continues,

I own 'twas rash, an' rather hardy,
That I, a simple, countra Bardie,
Should meddle wi' a pack sae sturdy,
 Wha, if they ken me,
Can easy wi' a single wordie
 Louse Hell upon me.

But I gae mad at their grimaces,
Their sighin, cantin, grace-proud faces,
Their three-mile prayers an' hauf-mile graces,
 Their raxin conscience,   *elastic*
Whase greed, revenge, an' pride disgraces
 Waur nor their nonsense.   *Worst than*

· · · · · · · · · · · · · ·
O Pope, had I thy satire's darts
To gie the rascals their deserts,
I'd rip their rotten, hollow hearts,
 An' tell aloud
Their jugglin hocus-pocus arts
 To cheat the crowd!

* A Tarbolton clergyman.

God knows, I'm no the thing I should be,
Nor am I even the thing I could be,
But twenty times I rather would be
    An atheist clean
Than under gospel colors hid be
    Just for a screen.

An honest man may like a glass,
An honest man may like a lass;
But mean revenge an' malice fause   *false*
    He'll still disdain
An' then cry zeal for gospel laws
    Like some we ken.

The six-line stanza of the preceding epistles and of many other of Burns' poems had by his time "become the common inheritance of all such Scotsmen as could rhyme." Henley and Henderson trace it back to the trouvères. It was the vehicle for *Bonnie Heck,* and for the *Piper of Kilbarchan.* Ramsay and Fergusson were skillful in it. One of Burns' distinctions is that he could use so hackneyed a form with such vigor and freshness.

By far the most wide-ranging of the epistles is the buoyant one to James Smith,* in which Burns talks about his poetry, his views on life's burdens and rewards, his feelings about "douce folk that live by rule."

Dear Smith, the sle'est, pawkie thief,   *crafty*
That e'er attempted stealth or rief!   *plunder*
Ye surely hae some warlock-breef   *wizard-spell*
    Owre human hearts;
For ne'er a bosom yet was prief   *proof*
    Against your arts.

For me, I swear by sun an' moon,
And ev'ry star that blinks aboon,   *above*
Ye've cost me twenty pair o' shoon,   *shoes*

* Smith, a boon companion and member of the Court of Equity, kept a small draper's shop in Mauchline. He, like Richmond, found it convenient to leave the village, and eventually (1788) he emigrated to Jamaica, where he died.

Just gaun to see you;   *going*
And ev'ry ither pair that's done,
    Mair taen I'm wi' you.   *taken*

That auld, capricious carlin, Nature,   *gossip*
To mak amends for scrimpit stature,   *stunted*
She's turn'd you off, a human-creature
    On her first plan;
And in her freaks, on ev'ry feature
    She's wrote the Man.

Just now I've taen the fit o' rhyme,
My barmie noddle's working prime,   *yeasty brain is*
My fancy yerkit up sublime,
    Wi' hasty summon:
Hae ye a leisure-moment's time
    To hear what's comin?

Some rhyme a neebor's name to lash;
Some rhyme (vain thought!) for needfu' cash;
Some rhyme to court the countra clash,   *country*
    An' raise a din;
For me, an aim I never fash;   *trouble about*
    I rhyme for fun.

The star that rules my luckless lot,
Has fated me the russet coat,
An' damn'd my fortune to the groat;
    But, in requit,
Has blest me with a random-shot
    O' countra wit.

This while my notion's taen a sklent,   *turn*
To try my fate in guid, black prent;
But still the mair I'm that way bent,
    Something cries, "Hoolie!   *softly*
I red you, honest man, take tent!   *advise   heed*
    Ye'll shaw your folly:

"There's ither poets, much your betters,
Far seen in Greek, deep men o' letters,
Hae thought they had ensur'd their debtors,
    A' future ages;
Now moths deform, in shapeless tatters
    Their unknown pages."

Then farewell hopes o' laurel-boughs
To garland my poetic brows!
Henceforth I'll rove where busy ploughs
    Are whistling thrang;   *at work*
An' teach the lanely heights an' howes   *hollows*
    My rustic sang.

I'll wander on, wi' tentless heed   *careless*
How never-halting moments speed,
Till Fate shall snap the brittle thread;
    Then, all unknown,
I'll lay me with th' unglorious dead,
    Forgot and gone!

But why o' death begin a tale?
Just now we're living sound an' hale;
Then top and maintop crowd the sail,
    Heave Care o'er-side!
And large, before Enjoyment's gale,
    Let's tak the tide.

This life, sae far's I understand,
Is a' enchanted fairy-land,
Where pleasure is the magic-wand,
    That, wielded right,
Maks hours like minutes, hand in hand,
    Dance by fu' light.

The magic-wand then let us wield;
For, ance that five-an'-forty's speel'd,   *climbed*
See, crazy, weary, joyless Eild,   *Old Age*
    Wi' wrinkl'd face,
Come hostin, hirplin owre the field,   *coughing* *limping*
    Wi' creepin pace.

When ance life's day draws near the gloamin,
Then fareweel vacant, careless roamin;
An' fareweel chearfu' tankards foamin,
    An' social noise:
An' fareweel dear, deluding Woman,
    The joy of joys!

. . . .

O ye douce folk that live by rule,   *sedate*
Grave, tideless-blooded, calm an' cool,
Compar'd wi' you — O fool! fool! fool!

How much unlike!
Your hearts are just a standing pool,
Your lives a dyke!   *wall*

Nae hair-brained, sentimental traces
In your unletter'd, nameless faces!
In *arioso* trills and graces
          Ye never stray;
But *gravissimo*, solemn basses
          Ye hum away.

Ye are sae grave, nae doubt ye're wise;
Nae ferly tho' ye do despise   *wonder*
The hairum-scairum, ram-stam boys,
          The rattling squad:
I see ye upward cast your eyes —
          Ye ken the road!

Whilst I — but I shall haud me there,   *hold*
Wi' you I'll scarce gang onie where —   *go*
Then, Jamie, I shall say nae mair,
          But quat my sang,   *quit*
Content wi' you to make a pair,
          Where'er I gang.

Before noticing other poems, many of which deal with the kirk and some of its ministers, and with Burns' love affairs, it may be helpful to examine some background briefly. In his autobiographical letter to Dr. Moore, Burns says that even before he had moved from Mt. Oliphant, he was fond of debating religious topics. "Polemical divinity about this time was putting the country half-mad; and I, ambitious of shining in conversation parties on Sundays between sermons, funerals, &c. used in a few years more to puzzle Calvinism with so much heat and indiscretion that I raised a hue and cry of heresy against me which has not ceased to this hour." Sillar speaks of his friend's similar activities in Tarbolton. "He had in his youth paid considerable attention to the arguments for and against the doctrine of original sin, then making considerable noise in your neighbourhood [Ayr], and having perused Dr Taylor's work on that subject, and 'Letters on

Religion essential to Man,' when he came to Tarbolton, his opinions were of consequence favourable to . . . the moderate side. The religion of the people of Tarbolton at that time was purely the religion of their fathers, . . . and taught by one generation to another, uncontaminated by reading, reflection, and conversation. . . . The slightest insinuation of Taylor's opinions made his neighbours suspect, and some even avoid [Burns], as an heretical and dangerous companion." Sillar also reports that Burns wore the only tied hair in the parish, and wore his plaid "wrapped in a particular manner round his shoulders."

Burns continues in the letter to Dr. Moore, speaking now of the period of his residence at Mossgiel (1784–1786). "I now began to be known in the neighbourhood as a maker of rhymes.*
— The first of my poetic offspring that saw the light was a burlesque lamentation on a quarrel between two revd Calvinists, both of them dramatis person in my Holy Fair. . . . Holy Willie's Prayer next made its appearance, and alarmed the kirk-Session so much that they held three several meetings to look over their holy artillery, if any of it was pointed against profane Rhymers. Unluckily for me, my idle wanderings led me, on another side, point-blank within the reach of their heaviest metal." In other words, his having made Jean Armour pregnant gave the elders a chance to get back at him for making sport of them.

In rural Ayrshire the Kirk held high ground in Burns' day. Liberal or Conservative, it feared the Devil, felt his presence, and made every effort to counter his seductions. The instrument for opposing vice and supporting virtue was the Kirk Session, a council of parish elders presided over by the minister. This body had the right and duty to inquire into private behavior, and to recommend censure, private or public. Contumacy could bring denial of church membership, and denial meant serious loss of social standing.

But the Kirk in Ayrshire was torn by inner stress. An Auld

---

* Village rhymers were a regular feature of Scots country life, another of the poetic traditions into which Burns fitted.

Licht party clung with passion to the orthodox Calvinist faith in foreordained salvation or damnation, while a New Licht party felt that good works might help a man into heaven, and that goodness of heart was important. The bitterness distinguishing the factions was intense, and there were further complications. In some parishes the ministers were elected, and tended to be Auld Licht like the congregations. In others, the patron of the parish presented the minister, and since the patrons were gentry and the gentry were more liberal than the peasantry, the presented ministers were probably New Licht even if their congregations were not. The right of patronage was hotly debated, and was widely resented by the people.

Burns viewed these all-too-human dissensions in the ranks of the Lord with genial relish, and when, as we have seen, two Auld Licht ministers quarreled over their parish boundaries and denounced each other publicly, he wrote a poem in ironic sympathy for the Auld Licht cause, whose champions had fallen from grace and weakened its position. *The Twa Herds* [Shepherds] "met with a roar of applause" from one side, and with furious resentment from the other. It is still a lively poem, but it requires too much explanation for ready enjoyment by a modern reader. Not so the three satires which followed, and which are among Burns' most famous and successful poems: *Holy Willie's Prayer, The Holy Fair,* and *Address to the Deil* [Devil].

Holy Willie's Prayer is one of the world's great and final satires. William Fisher, the speaker, was a member of the Mauchline Kirk Session which censured Burns for fornication.* Burns describes Fisher as "a rather oldish bachelor elder, in the parish of Mauchline, and much and justly famed for that polemical chattering which ends in tippling orthodoxy, and for that spiritualized

---

* Public rebuke in church by the minister of those guilty of fornication was a regular and popular feature of Sunday worship. Of this "sordid and general tyranny it is only necessary to say that the time-honoured Scottish tradition of fornication triumphantly survived all its terrors." (Edwin Muir, *John Knox,* 1930, 306–307, from Kinsley III, 1069.)

bawdry which refines to liquorish devotion." The unfortunate man was overcome in a snowstorm on his way home, February 13, 1809, and died in a roadside ditch. Burns seized happily on a discomfiture of Fisher and the Mauchline Kirk Session to ridicule them. In pursuit of its responsibilities, the Session had charged Burns' landlord, Gavin Hamilton, with neglect of public and family worship and contumacy. (His house adjoined the churchyard.) Hamilton promptly appealed to the Presbytry of Ayr, a superior court, which ordered the erasure of Mauchline session minutes against him, after which "the muse overheard Willie at his devotions." *

Originally, *Holy Willie's Prayer* was parochial, and even occasional. The "Calvinist intercession" and "language of the saints" which it parodies are now largely historic. But the pious hypocrite exists in all times, and Holy Willie is forever his name and symbol — in his confusion of virtue and self-interest, of piety and persecution, of godliness and complacent self-indulgence. Burns never printed this poem,† but it was widely circulated in manuscript. While it delighted lawyers like Robert Aiken in Ayr, who represented Hamilton in this matter, or clergymen like M'Math in Tarbolton, it as certainly roused the respectable community against its author.

> O Thou that in the Heavens does dwell,
> Wha, as it pleases best Thysel,
> Sends ane to Heaven an' ten to Hell
> A' for Thy glory,
> And no for onie guid or ill
> They've done before Thee!
>
> I bless and praise Thy matchless might,
> When thousands Thou hast left in night,
> That I am here before Thy sight,

* Hamilton was sustained again when the Session appealed to a higher body still, the Synod.
† It appeared, however, as an anonymous pamphlet in 1789. (Egerer, #16, 32.)

For gifts an' grace
A burning and a shining light
        To a' this place.

What was I, or my generation,
That I should get sic exaltation?   *such*
I, wha deserv'd most just damnation
        For broken laws,
Sax thousand years ere my creation,   *Six*
        Thro' Adam's cause!

When from my mither's womb I fell,
Thou might hae plung'd me deep in hell
To gnash my gooms, and weep, and wail
        In burning lakes,
Whare damnèd devils roar and yell,
        Chain'd to their stakes.

Yet I am here, a chosen sample,
To show Thy grace is great and ample:
I'm here a pillar o' Thy temple,
        Strong as a rock,
A guide, a buckler, and example
        To a' Thy flock!

But yet, O Lord! confess I must:
At times I'm fash'd wi' fleshly lust;   *troubled*
An' sometimes, too, in warldly trust,
        Vile self gets in;
But Thou remembers we are dust,
        Defiled wi' sin.

O Lord! yestreen, Thou kens, wi' Meg —   *last night*   *knowest*
Thy pardon I sincerely beg —
O, may't ne'er be a living plague
        To my dishonour!
An' I'll ne'er lift a lawless leg
        Again upon her.

Besides, I farther maun avow —   *must*
Wi' Leezie's lass, three times, I trow —
But, Lord, that Friday I was fou,
        When I cam near her,

Or else, Thou kens, Thy servant true
  Wad never steer her.   *rouse*

Maybe Thou lets this fleshly thorn
Buffet Thy servant e'en and morn,
Lest he owre proud and high should turn
  That he's sae gifted:
If sae, Thy han' maun e'en be borne
  Until Thou lift it.

Lord, bless Thy chosen in this place,
For here Thou has a chosen race!
But God confound their stubborn face
  An' blast their name,
Wha bring Thy elders to disgrace
  An' open shame!

Lord, mind Gau'n Hamilton's deserts:
He drinks, an' swears, an' plays at cartes,
Yet has sae monie takin arts
  Wi' great and sma',
Frae God's ain Priest the people's hearts
  He steals awa.

And when we chasten'd him therefore,
Thou kens how he bred sic a splore,   *row*
And set the world in a roar
  O' laughin at us:
Curse Thou his basket and his store,
  Kail an' potatoes!

Lord, hear my earnest cry and pray'r
Against that Presbyt'ry of Ayr!
Thy strong right hand, Lord, mak it bare
  Upo' their heads!
Lord, visit them, an' dinna spare,
  For their misdeeds!

O Lord, my God! that glib-tongu'd Aiken,
My vera heart and flesh are quakin
To think how we stood sweatin, shakin,
  An pish'd wi' dread,   *pissed*
While he, wi' hingin lip an' snakin,
  Held up his head.

Lord, in Thy day o' vengeance try him!
Lord, visit him wha did employ him!
And pass not in Thy mercy by them,
    Nor hear their pray'r,
But for Thy people's sake destroy them,
    An' dinna spare!

But, Lord, remember me and mine
Wi' mercies temporal and divine,
That I for grace an' gear may shine   *wealth*
    Excell'd by name;
And a' the glory shall be Thine —
    Amen, Amen!

Elizabeth Paton, the mother of Burns' first child, and the cause of his first Kirk Session rebuke, possibly in Tarbolton, had been a servant to Agnes Burnes at Lochlea, and had gone back to her home, Largieside, when the Burneses moved to Mossgiel. Betty, or Lizzie, is described as plain and of a masculine understanding. On May 22, 1785, she bore Burns a daughter, Elizabeth, whom he acknowledged, and who was eventually cared for by his mother at Mossgiel. The child grew up under the protection of her Uncle Gilbert. There is no recorded claim by Betty Paton that she had been deceived, and no claim for marriage, although there is a report that Robert's family disagreed over whether he should marry her or not. When he had raised a little money by the Kilmarnock edition of his poems, she did make a claim for "a certain sum," and on December 1, 1786, discharged "the said Robert Burns of all claims . . . against him for maintenance, cloathing and education of the said child, till it arrives at the fixed age of ten years compleat."

This affair was nothing unusual in Ayrshire peasant life. The minister's rebuke of Rab and Betty followed in due course, and the fine of a guinea, and that was that except for a delightful poem, *Welcome to a Bastart Wean*, a title more apt than the one favored by his Nineteenth Century editors, *A Poet's Welcome to His Love-Begotten Daughter*.

Thou's welcome, wean! Mishanter fa' me,   *child   Mishap befall*
If thoughts o' thee or yet thy mammie
Shall ever daunton me or awe me,
     My sweet, wee lady,
Or if I blush when thou shalt ca' me
     Tyta or daddie!

What tho' they ca' me fornicator,
An' tease my name in kintra clatter?   *country chatter*
The mair they talk, I'm kend the better;
     E'en let them clash!
An auld wife's tongue's a feckless matter   *feeble*
     To gie ane fash.   *trouble*

Welcome, my bonie, sweet, wee dochter!
Tho' ye come here a wee unsought for,
And tho' your comin I hae fought for
     Baith kirk and queir;
Yet, by my faith, ye're no unwrought for —
     That I shall swear!

Sweet fruit o' monie a merry dint,   *stroke*
My funny toil is no a' tint: *lost*
Tho' thou cam to the warl' asklent,
     Which fools may scoff at,
In my last plack thy part's be in't   *coin*
     The better half o't.

Tho' I should be the waur bestead,   *worse*
Thou's be as braw and bienly clad,   *fine   warmly*
And thy young years as nicely bred
     Wi' education,
As onie brat o' wedlock's bed
     In a' thy station.

Wee image o' my bonie Betty,
As fatherly I kiss and daut thee,
As dear and near my heart I set thee,
     Wi' as guid will,
As a' the priests had seen me get thee
     That's out o' Hell.

Gude grant that thou may ay inherit
Thy mither's looks an' gracefu' merit,

An' thy poor, worthless daddie's spirit
    Without his failins!
'Twill please me mair to see thee heir it
    Than stocket mailins.   *farms*

And if thou be what I wad hae thee,
An' tak the counsel I shall gie thee,
I'll never rue my trouble wi' thee —
    The cost nor shame o't —
But be a loving father to thee,
    And brag the name o't.

The second time Burns became a candidate for a Kirk Session's attention, the occasion was by no means routine. In addition to *Holy Willie's Prayer,* he had written and circulated *The Holy Fair* and *Address to the Deil;* he had led in organizing a mock Session, a Court of Equity or Fornicator's Court,* and he had boasted of his celebrity in a song, *The Fornicator.* Obviously the first rebuke had not taken.

The Fornicator

Ye jovial boys who love the joys,
    The blissful joys of Lovers,
Yet dare avow, with dauntless brow,
    When the bony lass discovers;
I pray draw near, and lend an ear,
    And welcome in a Frater,
For I've lately been on quarantine,
    A proven Fornicator.

* Designed ostensibly to discourage the desertion of girls "in trouble" by their quondam partners. The final stanza of a merry song, *Wha'll Mow* [Ride] *Me Now,* generally agreed to be by Burns (but whether his or not, no matter) will serve admirably as the motto of this sportive group.

    But Deevil damn the lousy loon
        Denies the bairn he got;
    Or lea's the merry arse he lo'ed   *leaves   loved*
        To wear a ragged coat.

A summons and decree of this "Court," in verse and by Burns, appears in Section VI.

Before the Congregation wide,
  I passed the muster fairly,
My handsome Betsy by my side,
  We gat our ditty rarely;
But my downcast eye by chance did spy
  What made my lips to water,
Those limbs so clean where I, between,
  Commenc'd a Fornicator.

With rueful face and signs of grace
  I pay'd the buttock-hire,
But the night was dark and thro' the park   *field*
  I could not but convoy her;
A parting kiss, I could not less,
  My vows began to scatter,
My Betsy fell — lal de dal lal lal,
  I am a Fornicator.

But for her sake this vow I make,
  And solemnly I swear it,
That while I own a single crown
  She's welcome for to share it;
And my roguish boy his Mother's joy
  And the darling of his Pater,
For him I boast my pains and cost,
  Although a Fornicator.

Ye wenching blades whose hireling jades
  Have tipt you off blue-boram,   *given you the clap*
I tell you plain, I do disdain
  To rank you in the Quorum;
But a bony lass upon the grass
  To teach her esse Mater,   *to be a mother*
And no reward but for regard,
  O that's a Fornicator.

Your warlike Kings and Heros bold,
  Great Captains and Commanders;
Your mighty Caesars fam'd of old,
  And conquering Alexanders;
In fields they fought and laurels bought,
  And bulwarks strong did batter,
But still they grac'd our noble list,
  And ranked Fornicator! ! !

On the second Sunday in August, Mauchline celebrated its annual communion service. Except for the disgraced and forbidden, everybody from the parish came, and many from other parishes. Since the church could not possibly hold them all at once, a tent was erected on the church grounds from which a relay of neighboring preachers competed for the favor of those outside, while successive groups of communicants received the sacrament in the church itself. In southwestern Scotland, "sacramental occasions" like this were called popularly and aptly, "Holy Fairs."

A prose account of them published in 1759, suggests that Burns may have had it in mind as he wrote his poem in 1785 about Mauchline Holy Fair. Its title was *A Letter from a Blacksmith to the Ministers and Elders of the Church of Scotland.* A few excerpts are instructive:

In Scotland they run from kirk to kirk, and flock to see a Sacrament, and make the same use of it that the papists do of their pilgrimages and processions — that is, indulge themselves in drunkenness, folly, and idleness. . . . At the time of the administration of the Lord's Supper, upon the Thursday, Saturday, and Monday, we have preaching in the fields near the church. Allow me, then, to describe it as it really is: at first you find a great number of men and women lying upon the grass; here they are sleeping and snoring, some with their faces toward heaven, others with their faces turned downwards, or covered with their bonnets; there you find a knot of young fellows and girls making assignations to go home together in the evening, or to meet in some alehouse; in another place you see a pious circle sitting around an ale-barrel, many of which stand ready upon carts for the refreshment of the saints. . . . In this sacred assembly there is an odd mixture of religion, sleep, drinking, courtship, and a confusion of sexes, ages and characters. When you get a little nearer the speaker, so as to be within reach of the sound, tho' not of the sense of his words, for that can only reach a small circle . . . you will find some weeping and others laughing, some pressing to get nearer the tent or tub in which the parson is sweating, bawling, jumping, and beating the desk; others fainting with the stifling heat, or wrestling to extricate themselves from the crowd; one seems very devout and serious, and the next moment is scolding or cursing his neighbours for squeezing or treading on him; in an instant after, his countenance is composed to the religious gloom, and he is groaning, sighing, and weeping for his sins: in a word, there is such an absurd mixture of the serious and comick, that were we convened for any other purpose than that of worshipping the God and Governor of Nature, the scene would exceed all power of farce.

Some details from *A General View of Agriculture in the County of Ayr*, Board of Agriculture Report, 1811, by William Aiton (b. 1760 — still alive 1847), suggest that there was little difference in many essentials between a holy fair and an ordinary one:

The manner in which the unmarried people, of both sexes, conduct themselves at fairs and races, is far from being decorous, and calls loudly for reformation. Great numbers of *lads* and *lasses* are collected at the fair, in the course of the afternoon, where they continue till about midnight. The country girls travel to the fair, (unless in time of frost) without shoes or stockings, with their coats tucked up, and retire to the corner of some park, near the fair, where they put on their shoes and perform the labours of the *toilette;* after which, they stalk into the fair, make *sham* calls at shops, or saunter among the crowd, till their rustic admirers, who are also on the *look-out,* invite them to the change-house. This is done by tapping the fair one on the shoulder, treading on her foot, or by some pantomimic gesture which she understands, and readily obeys, unless a swain, more to her mind, shall then make similar signals.

Nothing is so galling to the *lasses,* as to be allowed to stand long idle, in the market place, without being invited to the change-house by some young man. The place where groups of them stand, without being called upon, is termed, "the pitiful market."

A "sturdy fallow," having made his signals, struts off to the ale-house, his "clever hizzy," following at a short distance, proud of having gotten a "chance," and envied by such as have had none.

In the ale-house, the *lad* treats his *lass,* with ale, whisky, and sweet-meats, (called *fairings*), hugs her in his arms, tumbles her into a bed, if one can be found, though many persons be in the room, then, with one arm under her head, the other, and one of his legs over her, he enjoys a *tete a tete* conversation, longer or shorter, as the market happens to be brisk or slow. After a little time, they adjourn to some long-room, mason lodge, or barn, to dance reels. If the hall be much crowded at the time, they are obliged to maintain a struggle for the floor; which is done by the *lad* laying hold of his partner by the sides, and pushing her forward to the front of the crowd.

Towards night, when *John Barleycorn* has obtained possession of the *upper storey*, these struggles for the floor often lead to blows. During the affray, the weak part of the company, with the fiddler, get upon the benches, or run into a corner, while the more heroic, or those who are most intoxicated, take the post of honour. Few blows are struck in these uproars; they only pull and haul, and make a hideous noise. A few minutes exhaust their rage; — new company arrives; — the fiddler becomes arbiter; — the tattered nymphs collect their shoes, and adjust their deranged dress; — the fiddler strikes up a reel; — the dance proceeds, and the affray ends as it began, no one can tell how.

If the *lass* has already been called for, the *lad* holds by her to the utmost; but if she has not been asked for, he soon becomes indifferent and ultimately leaves her. If she has many lovers, they press into the room, and even into the bed, where she is reclining; lay hold of her by the arm, leg, or any part of her dress which they can come at; and by dint of importunity, little short of compulsion, they obtain an audience. While one is pouring out his requests, in whispers into her ear, another fixes his talons on any part of her body, which he can reach; — she listens to him, till others arrive; — they jostle each other; and all of them roar out her name, like so many auctioneers calling a roup. She continues, for a time, in a sort of passive uncertainty, yielding to the greatest force, sometimes getting upright, at other times, she is thrown upon the bed, till after enjoying several of these kind embraces, and hearing many supplications, one of the *sturdiest* of the *chiels* lays hold of her in his arms, whispers his prayer in her ear, and by main force, hurries her off holding her by the wrist, with one hand, and his other arm either round her neck or back, as a constable would keep hold of a thief, till he lodges her in a bedside, in another alehouse; at all which "she is nothing loath." — The disappointed lovers follow and renew their applications; — a similar farce is gone through, till one of them hurries her to another ale-house, and to another bed, if one can be found.

This is what they call "holding the fair," and it is continued till about midnight, when the *lads* and *lasses* begin to pair off, and return to the fair one's home, where they generally spend an hour or two by themselves, in the barn, byre, or cart shade, talking over the events of the day.

These accounts of village life, and the outraged piety which greeted Burns' poem *The Holy Fair* and other of his reflections on religious observance in his part of Ayrshire, suggest that he was but wittily clearsighted in revealing uncomfortable truth. And both Aiton and the Blacksmith give a vivid sense of what might be called the Breughel quality in Ayrshire peasant life, essential to an understanding of Burns and his poetry.

He opens his poem with a joyous salute to the summer morning, and then introduces his three allegorical maidens, Superstition, Hypocrisy, and Fun, appropriate companions with whom he sets off for the Sacramental Occasion. He gives a lively account of the country folk he meets — farmers, housewives, laborers, lasses, and then describes the churchyard scene with its mixture of piety, thirst, and lubricity, all of which find satisfaction. Then, after some shots at the local clergy, he shows the people on their way home. In *The Holy Fair*, Burns is genial, sympathetic, and deadly. He makes the most of his own dramatic situation, at once involved in the action and yet detached from it. He sets the scene and lets the actors destroy themselves. The structure of the poem manifests itself in the easy flow of events, detail strengthens tone, and style enriches theme. The poem grows to effortless perfection and dissolves with crushing simplicity.

> Upon a simmer Sunday morn,
> When Nature's face is fair,
> I walkèd forth to view the corn,
> An' snuff the caller air.   *fresh*

The rising sun, owre Galston Muirs,
  Wi' glorious light was glintin;
The hares were hirplin down the furs,   *hopping furrows*
  The lav'rocks they were chantin   *larks*
    Fu' sweet that day.

As lightsomely I glowr'd abroad   *gazed*
  To see a scene sae gay,
Three hizzies, early at the road,   *young women*
  Cam skelpin up the way.   *hastening*
Twa had manteeles o' dolefu' black,
  But ane wi' lyart lining;   *gray*
The third, that gaed a wee a-back *walked   behind a bit*
  Was in the fashion shining
    Fu' gay that day.

The twa appear'd like sisters twin,
  In feature, form, an' claes;   *clothes*
Their visage wither'd, lang an' thin,
  An' sour as onie slaes: *sloes*
The third cam up, hap-step-an'-lowp,
  As light as onie lambie,
An' wi' a curchie low did stoop,   *curtsey*
  As soon as e'er she saw me,
    Fu' kind that day.

Wi' bonnet aff, quoth I, "Sweet lass,
  I think ye seem to ken me;
I'm sure I've seen that bonie face,
  But yet I canna name ye."
Quo' she, an' laughin as she spak,
  An' taks me by the han's,
"Ye, for my sake, hae gi'en the feck   *most*
  O a' the Ten Comman's
    A screed some day.   *rip*

"My name is Fun — your cronie dear,
  The nearest friend ye hae;
An' this is Superstition here,
  An' that's Hypocrisy.
I'm gaun to Mauchline Holy Fair,   *going*
  To spend an hour in daffin: *frolic*
Gin ye'll go there, yon runkl'd pair, *If   wrinkled*

We will get famous laughin
    At them this day."

Quoth I, "Wi' a' my heart, I'll do't;
    I'll get my Sunday's sark on,   *shirt*
An' meet you on the holy spot;
    Faith, we'se hae fine remarkin!"   *we'll*
Then I gaed home at crowdie-time,   *went porridge-*
    An' soon I made me ready;
For roads were clad, frae side to side,
    Wi' monie a wearie body,
        In droves that day.

Here farmers gash, in ridin graith,   *respectable gear*
    Gaed hoddin by their cotters;   *jogging*
There swankies young, in braw braid-claith, *strapping lads*
    Are springin owre the gutters.
The lasses, skelpin barefit, thrang,   *hastening in a crowd*
    In silks an' scarlets glitter;
Wi' sweet-milk cheese, in monie a whang,   *thick slice*
    An' farls, bak'd wi' butter,   *cakes*
        Fu' crump that day.   *crisp*

When by the plate we set our nose,
    Weel heapèd up wi' ha'pence,
A greedy glowr black-bonnet throws,   *look the Elder*
    An' we maun draw our tippence.
Then in we go to see the show:
    On ev'ry side they're gath'rin;
Some carrying dails, some chairs an' stools,   *planks*
    An' some are busy bleth'rin   *gabbling*
        Right loud that day.

Here stands a shed to fend the show'rs,
    An' screen our countra gentry;
There Racer Jess, an' twa-three whores,
    Are blinkin at the entry.   *leering*
Here sits a raw o' tittlin jads,   *tattling jades*
    Wi' heaving breasts an' bare neck;
An' there a batch o' wabster lads   *weaver*
    Blackguardin frae Kilmarnock,
        For fun this day.

Here some are thinkin on their sins,
  An' some upo' their claes;   *clothes*
Ane curses feet that fyl'd his shins,   *soiled*
  Anither sighs an' prays:
On this hand sits a chosen swatch,   *sample*
  Wi' screw'd-up, grace-proud faces;
On that a set o' chaps, at watch,
  Thrang winkin on the lasses   **Busy**
    To chairs that day.

O happy is that man an' blest!
  Nae wonder that it pride him!
Whase ain dear lass, that he likes best,
  Comes clinkin down beside him!
Wi' arm repos'd on the chair back,
  He sweetly does compose him;
Which, by degrees, slips round her neck,
  An's loof upon her bosom,   *And his palm*
    Unkend that day.

[There follow six stanzas describing local preachers. Eventually the crowd seeks relief in taverns.]

Now butt an' ben the change-house fills, *kitchen and parlor* *tavern*
  Wi' yill-caup commentators;   *ale-cup*
Here's crying out for bakes an' gills,   *biscuits*
  An' there the pint-stowp clatters;
While thick an' thrang, an' loud an' lang,   *busy*
  Wi' logic an' wi' Scripture,
They raise a din, that in the end
  Is like to breed a rupture
    O' wrath that day.

Leeze me on drink! it gies us mair   *Blessings on*
  Than either school or college;
It kindles wit, it waukens lear   *learning*
  It pangs us fou o' knowledge: *crams*
Be't whiskey-gill or penny wheep,   *potent small beer*
  Or onie stronger potion,
It never fails, on drinkin deep,
  To kittle up our notion,
    By night or day.

The lads an' lasses, blythely bent
  To mind baith saul an' body,
Sit round the table, weel content,
  And steer about the toddy: *stir*
On this ane's dress, an' that ane's leuk,
  They're makin observations;
While some are cozie i' the neuk,   *corner*
  An' formin assignations
      To meet some day.

But now the Lord's ain trumpet touts,
  Till a' the hills are rairin,
And echoes back return the shouts;
  Black Russell is na sparin:
His piercin words, like Highlan' swords,
  Divide the joints an' marrow;
His talk o' Hell, whare devils dwell,
  Our verra "souls does harrow"
      Wi' fright that day!

A vast, unbottom'd, boundless pit,
  Fill'd fou o' lowin brunstane,   *full glowing brimstone*
Whase ragin flame, an' scorchin heat,
  Wad melt the hardest whun-stane!
The half-asleep start up wi' fear,
  An' think they hear it roarin;
When presently it does appear,
  'Twas but some neebor snorin
      Asleep that day.

'Twad be owre lang a tale to tell,
  How monie stories past;
An' how they crowded to the yill,
  When they were a' dismist;
How drink gaed round, in cogs an' caups,   *large and small wooden vessels*
  Amang the furms an' benches;
An' cheese an' bread, frae women's laps,
  Was dealt about in lunches,   *thick pieces*
      An' dawds that day.   *lumps*

In comes a gawsie, gash guidwife,   *jolly shrewd*
  An' sits down by the fire,
Syne draws her kebbuck an' her knife;   *Then cheese*
  The lasses they are shyer:

The auld guidmen, about the grace,
  Frae side to side they bother;
Till some ane by his bonnet lays,
  An' gies them't, like a tether,
    Fu' lang that day.

Waesucks! for him that gets nae lass,   *Alas!*
  Or lasses that hae naething!
Sma' need has he to say a grace,
  Or melvie his braw claething!   *soil with meal* *fine*
O wives, be mindfu', ance yoursel,
  How bonie lads ye wanted;
An' dinna for a kebbuck-heel
  Let lasses be affronted
    On sic a day.

Now Clinkumbell, wi' rattlin tow,   *Bellringer* *rope*
  Begins to jow an' croon;   *toll* *boom*
Some swagger hame as best they dow,   *can*
  Some wait the afternoon.   *[for the next round of preaching]*
At slaps the billies halt a blink, *gaps in fences* *fellows* *moment*
  Till lasses strip their shoon:
Wi' faith an' hope, an' love an' drink,
  They're a' in famous tune
    For crack that day.   *talk*

How monie hearts this day converts
  O' sinners and o' lasses!
Their hearts o' stane, gin night, are gane   *by nightfall* *gone*
  As saft as onie flesh is:
There's some are fou o' love divine:
  There's some are fou o' brandy;
An' monie jobs that day begin,
  May end in houghmagandie   *fornication*
    Some ither day.

In several variations, the eight-line stanza with a refrain of *The Holy Fair* had been traditional in poems of this kind for three hundred years, with its original in *Christis Kirk on the Green*. Both Ramsay and Fergusson had standardized the tag word "day" at the end of the refrain. Burns is skillful in giving this refrain an imaginative and structural variety.

Whatever may have been its relation to the Blacksmith's account of sacramental occasions quoted above, Burns' *The Holy Fair* is certainly modeled directly on Fergusson's *Leith Races* and *Hallow-Fair*. Where Ramsay was mainly quaint and humorous, Fergusson wrote vernacular poems with a spirited irreverence which Burns found congenial, and which he adopted and enriched in this poem and elsewhere. The relation of Burns' vernacular poetry to the Scots poems which suggested it is important to an understanding of what he accomplished and what he did not accomplish. A brief anthology as Appendix A will illustrate the tradition from which he worked. His originality can be appreciated only by those familiar with his sources.

Address to the Deil [Devil] is Burns' final poem of his irreverent trio, and his country neighbors must have found it little short of blasphemous. While it helped establish its author's reputation for irreligion, today it seems merely a lively recital of picturesque folklore, and its central character but a good-natured parody of Milton's Satan. Burns was no man to deny the pride and power of the Prince of Darkness, but he found only amusement in the Deil of peasant Ayrshire, and its Auld Licht clergy. The brimstone pit of pulpit oratory was for him no place even for a Devil, and he felt it was a sad comedown for Satan who had led the embattled seraphim to war, to be drowning unhappy travellers at fords and preventing cream from churning. Burns could only chuckle at such a Devil's police power over souls, especially his own. The poem was a lighthearted treatment of matters taken very seriously by some, and it incited retaliation by those offended.

> O Thou! whatever title suit thee —
> Auld Hornie, Satan, Nick, or Clootie —   *Hoofie*
> Wha in yon cavern grim an' sootie,
>   Clos'd under hatches,
> Spairges about the brunstane cootie,   *splashes   tub*
>   To scaud poor wretches!   *scald*

Hear me, Auld Hangie, for a wee,   *Hangman*
An' let poor damnèd bodies be;
I'm sure sma' pleasure it can gie,
    E'en to a deil,
To skelp an' scaud poor dogs like me   *strike   scald*
    An' hear us squeel.

Great is thy pow'r an' great thy fame;
Far kend an' noted is thy name;
An' tho' yon lowin heugh's thy hame,   *flaming pit's*
    Thou travels far;
An' faith! thou's neither lag, nor lame,   *backward*
    Nor blate, nor scaur.   *bashful   afraid*

Whyles, rangin like a roarin lion   *Sometimes*
For prey, a' holes an' corners tryin;
Whyles, on the strong-wing'd tempest flyin,
    Tirlin the kirks;   *Uncovering*
Whyles, in the human bosom pryin,
    Unseen thou lurks.

  . . . .
Let warlocks grim, an' wither'd hags,   *wizards*
Tell how wi' you, on ragweed nags,   *ragwort*
They skim the muirs an' dizzy crags,
    Wi' wicked speed;
And in kirk-yards renew their leagues,
    Owre howkit dead.   *exhumed*

Thence, countra wives, wi' toil an' pain,
May plunge an' plunge the kirn in vain;   *churn*
For O! the yellow treasure's taen
    By witching skill;
An' dawtit, twal-pint hawkie's gaen   *petted, twelve-pint cow's gone*
    As yell's the bill.   *dry as the bull*

Thence, mystic knots mak great abuse
On young guidmen, fond, keen an' croose;   *husbands   cocksure*
When the best wark-lume i' the house,   *tool*
    By cantraip wit,
Is instant made no worth a louse,
    Just at the bit.   *nick of time*

When thowes dissolve the snawy hoord *thaws snowy hoard*
An' float the jinglin icy board,
Then, water-kelpies haunt the foord,
    By your direction,
An' nighted trav'llers are allur'd
    To their destruction.

And aft your moss-traversing spunkies *bog jack-o'-lanterns*
Decoy the wight that late an' drunk is:
The bleezin, curst, mischievous monkies
    Delude his eyes,
Till in some miry slough he sunk is,
    Ne'er mair to rise.

. . . .

But a' your doings to rehearse,
Your wily snares an' fechtin fierce, *fighting*
Sin' that day Michael did you pierce
    Down to this time,
Wad ding a Lallan tongue, or Erse, *beat Lowland*
    In prose or rhyme.

An' now, Auld Cloots, I ken ye're thinkin, *Hoofs*
A certain Bardie's rantin, drinkin,
Some luckless hour will send him linkin, *hurrying*
    To your black Pit;
But, faith! he'll turn a corner jinkin, *dodging*
    An' cheat you yet.

But fare-you-weel, Auld Nickie-Ben!
O, wad ye tak a thought an' men'!
Ye aiblins might — I dinna ken — *perhaps*
    Still hae a stake:
I'm wae to think upo' yon den, *sad*
    Ev'n for your sake!

2. Bard

Burns' admirers have long trumpeted his broad humanity, his championship of Freedom and Equality, his challenge to the Establishment and to Kirk tyranny. They celebrate his patriotism and his success despite a lowly origin. They lament his failure to win patronage, and his early death. And they argue about whether he is a "national" voice. But his lasting fame arises from something else entirely — his distinction as a poet. And this distinction, like so much about Burns, is paradoxical. In his poems, he is essentially a wit, a moralist, a satirist — a son of the Eighteenth Century; but his forms and style differ greatly from those of his neo-classical predecessors and contemporaries. On the other hand, he wrote of simple subjects, in natural language and a concrete style, thereby foreshadowing much in Wordsworth.

Sensitive to rhythms, tonal effects, rhetorical emphasis — Burns used language with rare force and color to give the quality and texture of life, and to urge his own feelings.* There are reaches of human experience to which his Muse does not respond. One finds irony but no tragedy; warm feeling but not the depths of Wordsworth's sonnet on Westminster Bridge or of Keats' Odes. On the other hand, Wordsworth could not have written *Tam o' Shanter* or *The Jolly Beggars,* nor Keats *Holy Willie's Prayer* or *Corn Rigs.* To each poet his own, and Burns' own is very good indeed. "Bold, graphic, variable, expressive, packed with observations and ideas, the phrases go ringing and glittering on through verse after verse, through stave after stave, through poem after poem, in a way that makes the reading of this peasant a peculiar pleasure for the student of style." (Henley.)

Burns once described poetry as "Natural ideas expressed in melodious words," a phrase suggestive of the simplicity and conversational tone of his verse, which disguise its careful finish. Burns has little in common with poets who write in an elaborate or decorative style, like Spenser, or in the grand manner, like Milton. He is what he called himself, a Bard, recording experience in a traditional way for a popular audience — "a man speaking to men." With the metaphysical and symbolist traditions he has no connection at all, except as any poetry is what Robert

---

* Sir Walter Scott wrote, "Long life to thy fame and peace to thy soul, Rob Burns! When I want to express a sentiment which I feel strongly, I find the phrase in Shakespeare — or thee." (*The Journal of Sir Walter Scott,* New York, 1890. 383–84.)

Frost called a "constant symbol," saying something in terms of something else. But even here, Burns is not much given to indirection. He speaks straightforwardly, and is distinguished among our major poets by the small expansion of artifice between the impulse which strikes poetry from experience, and the poetic statement. Like the Eighteenth Century English poets whom he admired, Burns thought to "study men, their manners, and their ways," and he agreed that "True wit is Nature to advantage dressed." In his verse, with admirable economy, he sought the memorable phrase and the apt illustration for his observation — strengthening his statement and pointing his meaning with rhythm and rhyme. Although sensitive to external nature, he felt that "Exotic rural imagery is always comparatively flat," unless it serves to enrich remark.

As we have seen, the forms and style which Burns found congenial were Scots, as was the life he wrote about; and he felt that the eclectic and irregularly used Scots vernacular was essential in giving his verse the right movement, as well as desirable in coloring characters and incidents. He agreed with Ramsay, "The *Scotticisms,* which perhaps may offend some over-nice Ear, give new Life and Grace to the Poetry, and become their Place as well as the *Doric* dialect of *Theocritus,* so much admired by the best Judges." It should be noted that in poems like *Hallowe'en* and *The Auld Farmer's New-Year Morning Salutation to his Auld Mare, Maggie,* the Doric is appropriately much richer, while in many poems it is merely an occasional coloration. The use of dialect also increases the dramatic tension between Burns' innate peasant qualities and his acquired detachment from them. One must familiarize himself with Burns' special characteristics, as is true for all poets, particularly those of another day, but with him it is largely a matter of vocabulary. The prodigies of exegesis and digestion familiar in contemporary criticism are incongruous for one of his limpid simplicity. He fiddles no harmonics, and requires no guide to his feeling or purpose.

Burns belongs with noted predecessors: Chaucer (of the *Canterbury Tales*), Henryson (of the fables and *Robene and Makyne*), and Dunbar (in his less courtly moments). His parallels with Shakespeare are often noted: modest origins and scanty formal training; "native genius"; individuality in the use of established forms and subjects; a concrete style, a lyric gift, and metrical felicity; and zest for the human comedy. In Burns' own century, he shares top honors with Pope, his fellow wit and satirist. And of his successors, he has the strongest kinship with his neighbor and contemporary, Wordsworth, and with his fellow-Scot, Byron, in the deceptively casual *Beppo* and *Don Juan*.

One of the first qualities which a reader notices in Burns' poetry is the way his "countra wit" distills observation into proverbial statement. "O wad some Power the giftie gie us / To see oursels as ithers see us!" "It's aye the cheapest lawyer's fee / To taste the barrel." "Ne'er mind how Fortune waft an' warp; / She's but a bitch." "Nursing her wrath to keep it warm." "The best-laid schemes o' mice an' men / Gang aft agley." "Feel not a want but what yourselves create." "Nae man can tether time or tide." "But facts are chiels that winna ding, / And downa be disputed." "The heart ay's the part ay / That makes us right or wrang." "Man's inhumanity to man / Makes countless thousands mourn!" "Morality, thou deadly bane / Thy tens o' thousands thou hast slain!"

> Life is all a variorum,
>   We regard not how it goes;
> Let them prate about decorum,
>   Who have characters to lose.
>
> Ye high, exalted, virtuous dames,
>   Tied up in godly laces,
> Before ye gie poor Frailty names,
>   Suppose a change o' cases:
> A dear-lov'd lad, convenience snug,
>   A treach'rous inclination —
> But, let me whisper i' your lug,   *ear*
>   Ye've aiblins nae temptation.   *maybe*

But the informality which may give zest to a proverb is likely to blunt an epigram. Burns was fond of producing rhymed witticisms, many merely dull or strained, but a few pleasantly amusing, like his lines to Robert Ainslie's sister Rachel, in church:

> Fair maid, you need not take the hint,
>   Nor idle texts pursue;
> 'Twas guilty sinners that he meant,
>   Not angels such as you.

Many were virulent, however, and, as he told Maria Riddell, often written on people against whom he had no enmity. One of his best seems to have been of that kind:

On Lord Galloway

> Bright ran thy line, O Galloway,
>   Thro' many a far-famed sire!
> So ran the far-famed Roman way
>   So ended in a mire.

The subject of another has not been identified.

> Here cursing, swearing Burton lies,
>   A buck, a beau, or "Dem my eyes!"
> Who in his life did little good,
>   And his last words were — "Dem my blood!"

Perhaps his most famous epigram was provoked by a court duel between Burns' friend Henry Erskine, Dean of Faculty, and Islay Campbell, Lord Advocate — stanzas to the tune of *Killiecrankie.*

Lord Advocate

> He clench'd his pamphlets in his fist,
>   He quoted and he hinted,
> Till in a declamation-mist
>   His argument he tint it: *lost*

He gapèd for 't, he grapèd for 't,   *groped*
   He fand it was awa, man;   *found*
But what his common sense came short,
   He ekèd out wi' law, man.

Mr. Erskine

Collected, Harry stood awee,
   Then open'd out his arm, man;
His lordship sat wi' ruefu' e'e,
   And ey'd the gathering storm, man;
Like wind-driv'n hail it did assail,
   Or torrents owre a linn, man;   *cascade*
The bench sae wise, lift up their eyes,
   Hauf-wauken'd wi' the din, man.

But Burns' epigrams in general do not suggest "the ruffle's flutter and the flash of steel" so necessary to success in that difficult form. His style and language are, however, an ideal medium for his sophisticated account of mankind in the guise, largely, of Eighteenth Century Ayrshire countrymen.

It remains to suggest something of his grace at adjusting syntax and syllables to the demands of meter and rhyme, and his aptness at suiting tone, rhythm, and illustration to the matter at hand. His range and variety are happily illustrated in many of his opening stanzas.

The Holy Fair

Upon a simmer Sunday morn,
   When Nature's face is fair,
I walkèd forth to view the corn,
   An' snuff the caller air.   *fresh*
The rising sun, owre Galston Muirs,
   Wi' glorious light was glintin;
The hares were hirplin down the furs,   *furrows*
   The lav'rocks they were chantin   *larks*
      Fu' sweet that day.

To a Mouse

Wee, sleekit, cowrin, tim'rous beastie,
O, what a panic's in thy breastie!

Thou need na start awa sae hasty
  Wi' bickering brattle!   *hurrying scamper*
I wad be laith to rin an' chase thee,   *loth*
  Wi' murdering pattle!   *plough-staff*

Hallowe'en
  Upon that night, when fairies light
   On Cassilis Downans dance,   *[some small hills]*
  Or owre the lays, in splendid blaze,   *pastures*
   On sprightly coursers prance;
  Or for Colean the rout is taen,   *road taken*
   Beneath the moon's pale beams;
  There, up the Cove, to stray and rove,
   Amang the rocks and streams
    To sport that night:

  . . . .

  Some merry, friendly country-folks
   Together did convene,
  To burn their nits, an' pou their stocks, *nuts pull plants*
   An' haud their Hallowe'en
    Fu' blythe that night.

Death and Dr. Hornbook
  Some books are lies frae end to end,
  And some great lies were never penn'd:
  Ev'n ministers, they had been kend   *known*
   In holy rapture,
  A rousing whid at times to vend,   *lie*
   And nail't wi' Scripture.

Burns' metrical felicity is everywhere apparent, but perhaps it can be exemplified most happily by examples of the way he gives freshness and variety to the hackneyed *rime couée* which he favored.

Lines on Meeting with Lord Daer
  This wot ye all whom it concerns:
  I, Rhymer Rob, *alìas* Burns,
   October twenty-third,
  A ne'er-to-be-forgotten day,
  Sae far I sprachl'd up the brae
   I dinner'd wi' a Lord.

To a Mouse
> I'm truly sorry man's dominion
> Has broken Nature's social union,
> An' justifies that ill opinion
>   Which makes thee startle
> At me, thy poor, earth-born companion
>   An' fellow mortal!

On the Late Captain Grose's Peregrinations Thro' Scotland,
Collecting the Antiquities of that Kingdom
> Of Eve's first fire he has a cinder;
> Auld Tubalcain's fire-shool and fender;   *shovel*
> That which distinguishèd the gender
>   O' Balaam's ass;
> A broomstick o' the witch of Endor,
>   Weel shod wi' brass.

The Auld Farmer's New-Year Morning Salutation to his Auld Mare,
Maggie
> When thou and I were young and skiegh,   *skittish*
> An' stable-meals at fairs were driegh,   *tedious*
> How thou wad prance, an' snore, an' skriegh, *snort   whinny*
>   An' tak the road!
> Towns-bodies ran, an' stood abeigh,
>   An' ca't thee mad.

> When thou was corn't, an' I was mellow,
> We took the road ay like a swallow:
> At brooses thou had ne'er a fellow,   *wedding-races*
>   For pith an' speed;
> But ev'ry tail thou pay't them hollow,
>   Whare'er thou gaed.

The Cherry and the Slae stanza of the *Epistle to Davie* provides a more striking example of metrical virtuosity. See pp. 53–54. In his verse, Burns normally thought and wrote concretely.

Epistle to James Smith
> My barmie noddle's working prime.   *foaming*

The Vision
> There, lanely by the ingle-cheek,   *fire-side*
> I sat and ey'd the spewing reek,
> That fill'd, wi' hoast-provoking smeek, *cough-   smoke*

The auld clay biggin;   *building*
An' heard the restless rattons squeak
About the riggin.   *rooftree*

To a Mouse
That wee bit heap o' leaves an' stibble,
Has cost thee monie a weary nibble!
Now thou's turned out, for a' thy trouble,
But house or hald,   *Without   holding*
To thole the winter's sleety dribble,   *endure*
An' cranreuch cauld!   *hoar frost*

The Twa Dogs
That merry day the year begins,
They bar the door on frosty win's;
The nappy reeks wi' mantling ream,   *cream*
An' sheds a heart-inspiring steam;
The luntin pipe, an' sneeshin mill,   *smoking   snuff box*
Are handed round wi' right guid will;
The cantie auld folks crackin crouse,
The young anes ranting thro' the house —
My heart has been sae fain to see them,
That I for joy hae barkit wi' them.

Like many a distinguished fellow-poet, Burns left much that
interests few readers. As he himself said, "He must be an excellent
poet indeed whose every performance is excellent." But the two
hundred or so pages of his best work rank among the best we
have, and it is, as Carlyle affirmed, "of Nature's own and most
cunning workmanship."

3. *Love Affairs*

During the fifteen months after August, 1785, Burns continued
to write fine poetry at a spectacular rate; he carried on intense,
complex, and disturbing love affairs — with Jean Armour, and
Mary Campbell, and perhaps Bettsy Miller; he decided to leave
Scotland, but did not; he determined to publish his poems, and
did; he achieved a substantial fame and earned a little money;
and he was prevailed upon to try another edition in Edinburgh.
It was a time of fevered activity and intense excitement, a time

of depressing failure and notable success, a time of humiliation and of bold assertion, a time of joy and deep sorrow, and of hope and perplexity.

When Burns and Jean Armour became lovers, he was twenty-six, she twenty. She must have known his reputation and the reasons for it. He was handsome and electrifying and notorious. She was shapely and willing, and he delighted in her. By February, 1786, he referred to her pregnancy as news "not the most agreable," but he gave her a paper acknowledging her in some sort as his wife or wife-to-be. The paper is not known to exist, and speculation about its contents is futile, but it probably constituted legal marriage, and Burns certainly thought of Jean as his wife, although he could by no means afford to establish a household. It was about this time that he began to consider emigrating to Jamaica and working for wages there as a slave driver, a disagreable prospect, attractive only in contrast to his desperate situation at home.

Jean's father was a master mason. When he and his wife discovered Jean's pregnancy, they forced her to surrender the paper, and sought advice from their lawyer, and Burns' friend, Robert Aiken, who "mutilated" the paper, probably cutting out the names — a maneuver of dubious legal effect on a binding contract. But James Armour regarded an illegitimate grandchild as preferable to a penniless son-in-law, and he pursued his ends in this way. In late March the Armours packed Jean off to Paisley to stay with relatives, and Mrs. Armour denied knowing of her daughter's condition to an emissary from the Kirk Session, who came to inquire officially.

Burns was thunderstruck. He felt that Jean had betrayed him, and his spirit was deeply bruised. In April he wrote a famous letter to John Arnot, to which he added a note when copying it out for Robert Riddell some years later: "The story of the letter was this — I had got deeply in love with a young Fair-One, of which proofs were every day *arising* more & more to view. — I would gladly have covered my Inamorata from the darts of Calumny with the conjugal Shield, nay had actually made up some sort of Wedlock; but I was at that time deep in the guilt of being unfortunate, for which good & lawful objection, the Lady's friends broke all our measures, & drove me au desespoir."

In the letter itself, he writes in the manner of Lawrence Sterne:

I have lost, Sir, that dearest earthly treasure, that greatest blessing here below, that last, best gift which compleated Adam's happiness in the garden of bliss, I have lost — I have lost — my trembling hand refuses its office, the frighted ink recoils up the quill — Tell it not in Gath — I have lost — a — a — a Wife!

He describes the affair with an elaborate Shandean venereal metaphor.

I rarely hit where I aim: & if I want anything, I am almost sure never to find it where I seek it. — For instance, if my pen-knife is needed, I pulled out twenty things — a plough-wedge, a horse-nail, an old letter or a tattered rhyme, in short, everything but my pen-knife; & that at last, after a painful, fruitless search, will be found in the unsuspected corner of an unsuspected pocket, as if on purpose thrust out of the way. — Still, Sir, I had long had a wishing eye to that inestimable blessing, a wife. — My mouth watered deliciously, to see a young fellow, after a few idle, common-place stories from a gentleman in black, strip & go to bed with a young girl, & no one durst say, black was his eye; while I, for just doing the same thing, only wanting that ceremony, am made a Sunday's laughing-stock, & abused like a pick-pocket. — I was well aware though, that if my ill-starred fortune got the least hint of my connubial wish, my schemes would go to nothing. — To prevent this, I determined to take my measures with such thought & forethought, such a caution & precaution, that all the malignant planets in the Hemisphere should be unable to blight my designs. — Not content with, to use the words of the celebrated Westminster Divines, "the outward & ordinary means," I left no stone unturned; sounded every unfathomed depth; stopped up every hole & bore of an objection; but, how shall I tell it! notwithstanding all this turning of stones, stopping of bores, &c. — whilst I, with secret pleasure, marked my project swelling to the proper crisis, & was singing te Deum in my own fancy; or, to change the metaphor, whilst

I was vigorously pressing on the siege; had carried the counter-scarp, & made a practicable breach behind the curtin in the gorge of the very principal bastion; nay, having mastered the covered way, I had found means to slip a choice detachment into the very citadel; while I had nothing less in view than displaying my victorious banners on the top of the walls — Heaven & Earth must I "remember"! my damned Star wheeled about to the zenith, by whose baleful rays Fortune took the alarm, & pouring in her forces on all quarters, front, flank, & rear, I was utterly routed, my baggage lost, my military chest in the hands of the enemy; & your poor devil of a humble servant, commander in chief forsooth, was obliged to scamper away, without either arms or honors of war, except his bare bayonet & cartridge-pouch; nor in all probability had he escaped even with them, had he not made a shift to hide them under the lap of his military cloak. — . . . There is a pretty large portion of bedlam in the composition of a Poet at any time; but on this occasion I was nine parts & nine tenths, out of ten, stark staring mad.

Then, after a long passage of turgid rhetoric, he reports that he is looking for another wife. This letter to Arnot was written in April.

On June 12, he writes to David Brice:

I have no news to tell you that will give me any pleasure to mention, or you, to hear. — Poor, ill-advised, ungrateful Armour came home on friday last. — You have heard all the particulars of that affair; and a black affair it is. — What she thinks of her conduct now, I don't know; one thing I know, she has made me compleatly miserable. — Never man lov'd, or rather ador'd, a woman more than I did her: and, to confess a truth between you and me, I do still love her to distraction after all, tho' I won't tell her so, tho' I see her, which I don't want to do. — My poor, dear, unfortunate Jean! how happy I have been in her arms! — It is not the losing her that makes me so unhappy; but for *her* sake I feel most severely. — I foresee she is in the road to, I am afraid, *eternal* ruin; and those who made so much noise, and showed so much grief, at the thought of her being *my wife*, may, some day, see her connected in such a manner as may give them more real cause of vexation. — I am sure I do not wish it: may Almighty God forgive her ingratitude and perjury to me, as I from my very soul forgive her! and may His grace be with her and bless her in all future life! — I can have no nearer idea of the place of eternal punishment than what I have felt in my own breast on her account. — I have tryed often to forget her: I have run into all kinds of dissipation and riot, Mason-meetings, drinking matches, and other mischief, to drive her out of my head, but all in vain: and now for a grand cure: the Ship is on her way home that is to take me out to Jamaica; and then, farewell dear old Scotland, and farewell dear, ungrateful Jean, for never, never will I see you more.

The next day, June 13, Jean wrote to the Kirk Session admitting the pregnancy and naming Robert as the father.

Since Jean would not have him, Burns determined to establish himself unquestionably as a bachelor, and was promised a certificate to that effect by his minister, the Rev. William Auld of Mauchline, if he would stand in church for three Sundays, with Jean, and be rebuked publicly. He writes on July 9 to John Richmond, "I have waited on Armour since her return home, not by — from any the least view of reconciliation, but merely to ask for her health; and — to you I will confess it, from a foolish hankering fondness — very ill-plac'd indeed. — The Mother forbade me the house; nor did Jean shew that penitence that might have been expected. — However, the Priest, I am inform'd will give me a Certificate as a single man, if I comply with the rules of the Church, which for that very reason I intend to do." He reports he is to appear that morning for the first time, and that his book will be ready in a fortnight. A letter to Brice, July 17, adds a piquant detail: "Jean and her friends insisted much that she should stand along with me in the kirk, but the minister would not allow it, which bred a great trouble I assure you, and I am blamed as the cause of it, tho' I am sure I am innocent: but I am very well pleased, for all that, not to have had her company." He made his last appearance August 6, and considered himself freed from all obligations to Jean.

Meanwhile he was seeing his Kilmarnock volume through the

press. He had issued proposals for subscribers to it on April 14, 1786, and he sent his poems to the printer June 13. The volumes were ready in late July. He was also making plans for immediate departure to Jamaica once the book was out, these having been accelerated by James Armour's swearing out a warrant against him seeking support for the coming child. He had mentioned Jamaica to Arnot in April; on July 17 he tells Brice he expects to leave in October. But on July 30 he writes to Richmond from a hiding place where Armour cannot find him:

My hour is now come. — You and I will never meet in Britain more. — I have orders within three weeks at farthest to repair aboard the Nancy, Capn Smith, from Clyde, to Jamaica, and to call at Antigua. — This, except to our friend Smith, whom God long preserve, is a secret about Mauchlin. — Would you believe it? Armour has got a warrant to throw me in jail till I find security for an enormous sum. — This they keep an entire secret, but I got it by a channel they little dream of; and I am wandering from one friend's house to another, and like a true son of the Gospel "have nowhere to lay my head." — I know you will pour an execration on her head, but spare the poor, ill-advised girl for my sake; tho', may all the Furies that rend the injured, enraged Lover's bosom, await the old harridan, her Mother, untill her latest hour!

Two days later, the distracted man writes to Smith, "Against two things however, I am as fix'd as Fate: staying at home, and owning her conjugally. — The first, by Heaven I will not do! The last, by Hell I will never do! . . . If you see Jean tell her, I will meet her, So help me Heaven in my hour of need!"

On August 14 he postpones sailing, and on September 1, he writes that he won't sail until the end of the month. But by September 27 he is thinking of a second edition of his book, and says his departure is uncertain and will probably not take place until after harvest. By October 8 he has been discussing a new edition with his Kilmarnock printer, John Wilson, and he has considered becoming an Exciseman.

Through his poems he made helpful friends, and he writes
to Richmond on September 1, "The warrant is still in existence,
but some of the first Gentlemen in the county have offered to
befriend me; and besides, Jean will not take any step against me,
without letting me know, as nothing but the most violent men-
aces could have forced her to sign the petition. — I have called
on her once and again, of late; as she, at this moment, is threatened with the pangs of approaching travail; and I assure you, my
dear Friend, I cannot help being anxious, very anxious, for her
situation. — She would gladly now embrace that offer she once
rejected, but it shall never more be in her power." He then urges
Richmond to return and marry Jenny Surgeoner, of whom and
her child by Richmond he gives touching particulars.

On September 3 he rejoices to Richmond:

A Fragment - - - -

Chorus

Green grow the rashes O
Green grow the rashes O
The lasses they hae wimble bores,   *gimlet*
The widows they hae gashes O.

1.

In sober hours I am a priest;
    A hero when I'm tipsy, O;
But I'm a king and ev'ry thing,
    When wi' a wanton Gipsey, O.
    Green grow &c.

2.

'Twas late yestreen I met wi' ane
    An' wow, but she was gentle, O!
Ae han' she pat round my cravat,
    The tither to my p - - - - - O.
    Green grow &c.

3.

I dought na speak - - yet was na fley'd - -   *afraid*
My heart play'd duntie, duntie, O;
An' ceremony laid aside,
I fairly fun' her c-ntie, O. - - - -
Green grow &c.

■ - - - - - - - - - - - ■

- - - Multa desunt - - -

■ - - - - - - - - - - - ■

Sept: 3d Armour has just now brought me a boy and a girl at one
throw. - - God bless them poor little dears. - -

R. B.

His volume was a success. And with James Armour checked, and his certificate as a bachelor in his pocket, and Jean safely delivered, Burns thought less and less of emigration. He had also taken legal measures against Armour. On July 22, 1786, Burns assigned his interest in Mossgiel farm, and his profits from his poems and the copyright as well, to his brother Gilbert for support of his daughter by Betty Paton. Burns' later agreement with Betty, executed December 1, 1786, superseded this agreement.

But there was another reason for Burns to postpone his departure, and perhaps this was the "other mischief" he refers to in his letter to Brice. At the same time as the Armour affair, he had been involved deeply with Mary Campbell, the girl known to history as Highland Mary.* This relationship is so hedged around with controversy that it seems best to present details about it in their full complexity. First, there is a Mary Campbell who has nothing to connect her with Burns except that she was in the right places at the right times. In 1783, she was living in Dundonald Parish, which includes Irvine; by April, 1784, she had moved to Mauchline, from which she had gone to nearby Stair by February, 1786. On April 25, 1784, when the Mauchline

---

* There is a provocative note about still another heroine of this period. A letter to Richmond, dated September 27, concludes, "Bettsy Miller awaits me." (F I, #49, 44.) She appears in his *Belles of Mauchline*, and is a character in a jolly poem, *A Mauchline Wedding*. She is also probably the "quondam Eliza" of a letter to Smith of June 11, 1787. (F I, #113, 95.)

Kirk Session questioned her, she reported one John Hay to be the father of her child. Hay denied it at the time, but confessed later.* In 1781–1782, Burns was in Irvine; by March, 1784, he had moved to Mauchline; and in May, 1786, he said goodbye to his Mary Campbell on the banks of the Ayr in Stair.

Burns' Mary Campbell became a nurse in Gavin Hamilton's family in Mauchline in July, 1785. It has been argued that the mother of an illegitimate baby could not have been so received, and hence that the Dundonald Mary was not this girl, but the Armours did not feel that their daughter in the same village would be irredeemably disgraced by having such a child, and Betty Paton married after bearing one to Burns, and lived in good odor. Either could have secured a position from the Hamiltons. It has been argued also that Burns could not have become infatuated with a woman who had born a bastard, and could not have idealized her in his poetry. But one's experience of Burns and of life is limited, indeed, for such an argument to carry much weight. And while some of Burns' comments on Mary do idealize her, many do not. However, there is no evidence permitting a final decision whether the Dundonald girl was Burns' heroine or not.

The next item relating to Highland Mary is a negligible song, *My Highland Lassie, O,* which speaks of crossing the seas and pledges faithfulness forever. R. H. Cromek printed a note about it presumably by Burns. The manuscript has disappeared, but Cromek's once-questioned reliability has been supported by the late Davidson Cook and DeLancey Ferguson. The note reads:

This was a composition of mine in very early life, before I was known at all in the world. My Highland lassie was a warm-hearted, charming young creature as ever blessed a man with generous love.

* A minute of the Session, dated "1787. December 17," is revealing. "John Hay voluntarily confessed fornication with Janet Sillar and Mary Campbell and also with Euphan Bowie from the New Town of Ayr, and the father of a child brought forth by each of them, and also confessed fornication with Margaret Ceurdie and Agnes M'Cletchie, formerly confessed by him. The Sess. appointed him to confess publicly any day he pleased." (Ch-W I, 471.)

After a pretty long tract of the most ardent reciprocal attachment, we met by appointment, on the second Sunday of May, in a sequestered spot by the Banks of Ayr, where we spent the day in taking a farewel, before she should embark for the West-Highlands, to arrange matters among her friends for our projected change of life. At the close of Autumn following she crossed the sea to meet me at Greenock, where she had scarce landed when she was seized with a malignant fever, which hurried my dear girl to the grave in a few days, before I could even hear of her illness.

It should be noted that the lassie of this passage is not named.

Here one must decide what Burns meant by being blessed, over a pretty long tract of most ardent reciprocal attachment, with the generous love of a warm-hearted, charming young creature. A similar decision is required about a comment he made to George Thomson when sending him *Will Ye Go To The Indes, My Mary.* "You must know, that all my earlier love-songs were the breathings of ardent Passion." And finally, what is to be made of a stanza from *Thou Lingering Star* describing the famous parting of Burns and Mary, and particularly of the line, "The flowers sprang wanton to be pressed"?

> Ayr, gurgling, kiss'd his pebbled shore,
>   O'erhung with wild woods thickening green;
> The fragrant birch and hawthorn hoar
>   'Twin'd amorous round the raptur'd scene;   ·
> The flowers sprang wanton to be prest,
>   The birds sang love on every spray,
> Till too, too soon, the glowing west
>   Proclaim'd the speed of wingèd day.

The famous song *Highland Mary* is the only good one Burns wrote to his Mary. But does it suggest as has been maintained, that she was the one pure lily among his passion flowers?

> Ye banks and braes and streams around
>   The castle o' Montgomery,
> Green be your woods, and fair your flowers,
>   Your waters never drumlie!   *cloudy*

There Summer first unfald her robes,
  And there the langest tarry!
For there I took the last fareweel
  O' my sweet Highland Mary!

How sweetly bloom'd the gay, green birk,
  How rich the hawthorn's blossom,
As underneath their fragrant shade
  I clasp'd her to my bosom!
The golden hours on angel wings
  Flew o'er me and my dearie:
For dear to me as light and life
  Was my sweet Highland Mary.

Wi' monie a vow and lock'd embrace
  Our parting was fu' tender;
And, pledging aft to meet again,
  We tore oursels asunder.
But O, fell Death's untimely frost,
  That nipt my flower sae early!
Now green's the sod and cauld's the clay,
  That wraps my Highland Mary!

   . . . .

Three years after Mary's death, Burns was moved to write some highly charged rhetoric about her to Mrs. Dunlop. Surveying his uncertainties about a life after death, he says that if there were one, he should like to meet there his father, and his friend, Robert Muir. Then he continues, "There should I, with speechless agony of rapture, again recognize my lost, my ever dear Mary, whose bosom was fraught with Truth, Honor, Constancy, & Love." Obviously, her memory is still precious to him, but one wonders why he would meet her with "speechless agony of rapture."

It seems clear that he and his Mary had a passionate love affair at the same time he was involved with Jean Armour, and that they parted with vows, exchanged in May, not long after Jean had dishonored similar ones. Before Burns and Mary could meet again, she died of fever. It is difficult to see how, in a small village, Burns' Mary could have failed to know that her affair paralleled the well-publicized one with Jean Armour.

Soon after Burns had moved to Mauchline, he found a crony in John Richmond, clerk to Gavin Hamilton, his landlord. Richmond left Mauchline under a cloud in the late autumn of 1785. During Burns' 1786–1787 winter in Edinburgh, he shared Richmond's room and bed. As late as February 7, 1788, Burns is writing to him in the old terms of intimacy, although later their relations seem to have cooled. Richmond, therefore, is an excellent source of information about Burns during the period of their close friendship. The following story, attributed to him, is undated, but it obviously relates to a time before he had left Mauchline. These notes are taken from memoranda sent by Joseph Train* to John Lockhart while Lockhart was preparing his Life of Burns, published in 1828.

Highland Mary. — Truth deprives her history of much of its charm. — Her character was loose in the extreme. — She was *kept* for some time by a Brother of Lord Eglinton's,† and even while a servant with Gavin Hamilton, and during the period of Burns' attachment it was well known that her meetings with Montgomery were open and frequent. — The friends of Burns represented to him the impropriety of his devotedness to her, but without producing any change in his sentiments. — Richmond told Mr Grierson that Montgomery & Highland Mary frequently met in a small alehouse called the Elbow — and upon one occasion he & some of Burns's friends knowing they were actually together in the Elbow — and having often in vain tried to convince Robert of her infidelity, upon this occasion they promised to give ocular proof of their assertions. — The party retired to the Elbow — Richmond (Mr Grierson's informant) was one and they took their seats in the kitchin from which two rooms branched off to the right and left — being all the accommoda-

* Collector of Excise at Castle Douglas.
† At this time the master of St. James Lodge, Tarbolton, was Captain James Montgomerie, younger brother of Colonel Hugh Montgomerie afterward Earl of Eglinton. (H & H I, 389; Kinsley III, 1080.)

tion the house contained.* They had taken their position in the kitchin, to be sure that no one could leave the other rooms without being observed. — After waiting long, and when Burns was beginning to ridicule their suspicions, at last Mary Campbell appeared from one of the rooms — was jeered by the party, in a general way — blushed and retired. — Another long interval elapsed and Burns began to rally his spirits, which were very much sunk — and Montgomery (Colonel or Capt) walked out of the same room. — Burns coloured deeply — compressed his lip — and muttered, "*damn* it." After enduring considerable bantering from his friends he soon gave way to the general hilarity of the evening, and his friends thought he had seen enough of Highland Mary but in a few days after, he returned "like the dog to its vomit."

Train adds another note:

Highland Mary. — I should have added formerly that Grierson has a facsimile of the leaf of the Bible *exchanged* by Burns with Mary containing the inscription. — in addition to what has already appeared in print the Signature of Burns is followed by his Mason's Mark which if you are a *free* mason you will understand — it is thus: >—x—→ In place of any of the commonplace facsimiles generally given of Burns' handwriting, it is likely we will give a representation of the two leaves containing these inscriptions. Mr Grierson was permitted by the surviving relations to copy these inscriptions. — One curious circumstance is worth recording. — From what motive it is now difficult to say, but one of Mary Campbell's brothers pasted a slip of paper over the *signatures* of Burns — and to read these it is necessary to hold the leaf between the eye and the light. — I saw a letter from another of her brother's to Mr Grierson stating this circumstance — and containing a lock of Mary's hair. — (It is of the true Celtic hue, and *feel*) This contains some other interesting information. — I am promised copies of it — and of several other unpublished letters of Burns, by Mr G. — These were read to me — but after some weeks exertion I have hitherto been unable to procure them. — Grierson is a curious old fellow. — He has been an enthusiastic collector of such

---

* Chambers-Wallace reports (I, 474n) that Mauchline "contained a back lane called the 'Elbow' in which was a public-house kept by a sailor, nicknamed 'The Old Tar.'"

matters connected with Burns for upwards of 20 years — during which time he has repeatedly visited the various places of the Poet's residences.

These reports raise a large probability that Burns and his Mary Campbell had begun their affair in the autumn of 1785, before Richmond left for Edinburgh, or even earlier. The "Mr. Grierson" mentioned by Train is now known to have been James Grierson of Dalgoner, a diligent collector of reliable information about Burns, and a close friend of Anthony Dunlop, son of Burns' correspondent, Mrs. Frances Dunlop.* On October 24, 1817, Grierson himself noted,

Met with   Campbell spouse to James Anderson mason in Ardrossan 1817 and sister to Highland Mary Burns friend. She says Mary was tall, fair haird with blue eyes — they were daughters of Arch. Campbell mariner who resided at Dunoon Parish & Agnes Campbell his spouse, he died in Greenock 1815 & is buried in a lair of the new burying ground he bought from widow McPherson & his widow lives there in Scots land long vennal. Their sons are Robert & Archd Carpenters there — Mrs Andersons sons possess the Bible† Burns gave her in exchange — it is printed by Alexander Kincaids assignies at Edin 1782. The booksellers mark 5/6 2 vol small 12° on each volume is his mason mark. this son a mason works presently in Paisley. Mrs. A says her sister was buried in the old kirk ground Greenock, the new burying ground was not then begun & that widow McPherson & others know the place — during the fever she was insensible, except the last day of her life when her father asked if she knew where she was. Yes, she said, I am on my bridal bed. She died in the house of her uncle Alex Campbell, Greenock Her grandfather was tenant to Duke of Argyl but lost his farm rather than let his sons go into the army. Mrs. A showed the Bible to J. G. which she sent to Paisley to her son for, on purpose — on the first vol is in Burns hand writing "And ye shall not swear by my name falsely" — "I am the LORD" "Levit 19 Chap 12 verse" his name had been there but carefully rubed out except some letters   On the second vol

---

* Chambers-Wallace reports, also, that he knew Burns. (III, 13.)
† Further particulars of this Bible may be found in Ch-W I, 475–78. It is preserved in the Burns monument, Alloway.

there is also wrote in his hand "Thou shalt not for swear thyself but shalt perform unto the Lord thine Oath" "Matth: 35 Ch 33 verse On this vol had also been the mason mark & his name with date 1786. but papers had been pasted on & torn off so the writing is much defaced.

Leaves are folded in at or near various places as Isaiah 30 & 21. 34 & 10. 43 & 17. 55 & 16 [or 17 or 19] Jerem: x 27 [or x & 7, or Jerem 7; or Jerem 1 & 7]. 31 & 5. Ezek 18. 36 & 33. Hosea 4th 11 & 8. Zach. 13 Luke 17 & 14 John 13 & 14. 20 & 7. Rev 4 & 10* It seems evident that those two texts wrote at length in his hand, each *only* part of a verse & inscribed one in each vol. given to mary were intended strongly to alude to some secret known to them alone & it is more than probable this was some promise or Oaths he has not Oaths as in the original but *Oath* & he was not one of these men who had no meaning for what they did. — probably it was her who erased the name, conscious too of the meaning and not chusing to have the books in her possession on which were the texts connected with the name.

These memoranda of Grierson serve to identify and describe Mary Campbell, but even with them, specific proof of the nature of Burns' relations with her is lacking. One can only weigh all the available evidence and decide for himself. A further tantalizing bit is a passage from a letter to Robert Aiken, written in early October, 1786, about the time of Mary Campbell's death. "I have been feeling all the various rotations and movements within, respecting the Excise. There are many things plead strongly against it; the uncertainty of getting soon into business; the consequences of my follies, which may perhaps make it im-

---

* While too much should not be made of the passages marked in Mary's Bible, "Isaiah 30 & 21. 34 & 10." repeats the theme of the quotations from Leviticus and Matthew inscribed on the flyleaves of the Bible, "Jerem: 31 & 5" possibly refers to Burns' plan for taking Mary with him to the West Indes, and "Ezek 18" suggests repentance and forgiveness. "Hosea 4th 11 & 8.," "Zach. 13," "Luke 17 & 14," and "Rev 4 & 10" have a marked flavor of the Armour episode and its aftermath. In "John 13 and 14" there may be a reference to the famous ceremony of parting between Burns and Mary. But the great questions remain: Why did Mary's family preserve these references? And why did they try to obliterate Burns' name from the Bible?

practicable for me to stay at home; and besides I have for some time been pining under secret wretchedness, from causes which you pretty well know — the pang of disappointment, the sting of pride, with some wandering stabs of remorse, which never fail to settle on my vitals like vultures, when attention is not called away by the calls of society, or the vagaries of the Muse. Even in the hour of social mirth, my gaiety is the madness of an intoxicated criminal under the hands of the executioner." What, one wonders, did Aiken "pretty well know"? At this time, there would be little about Burns' edition, or his livelihood, or the Armour affair, to prompt such remarks.

He seems to have regarded Mary Campbell as a fiancée of sorts. Perhaps she was the "other wife" he was looking for when he wrote to John Arnot in April. But it is significant that, while Burns' letters are full of Jean, they say nothing of Mary either before or after she left Ayrshire. The affair with her came at the time when he was writing poems glorying in his prowess. And there is no hint throughout his life of any other "pure" romance. The evidence for one with Mary Campbell seems flimsy, indeed, while the relationship detailed and suggested in the documents above is all-too-human, and credible, and characteristic of Burns.

There has been much controversy about a child's coffin found in Mary Campbell's grave when her remains were exhumed and re-interred in 1920. It was not that of a baby born to Mary Campbell, but that of Agnes Hendry, who was born January 4, 1827 and who died February 27, 1827. These dates are taken from the Hendry family register of her brother Daniel S. Hendry, and were certified in a document in the present biographer's possession by Duncan M. Hendry on October 23, 1933.*

In mid-August, 1786, Burns had still some Kilmarnock volumes to get to their purchasers, he had an account to settle with his printer, he had a decision to make about Jamaica, he had an

* See Appendix D; also *Chronicle* 1918, 1920, 1921, 1922.

agreement to make with Betty Paton and Gilbert about little Betty's maintenance, he felt a concern for Jean, and a concern for Mary Campbell. He no longer had any concern about the Armour warrant. By late October, he had pretty well decided to print a new edition of his poems and to give up going to Jamaica; he had settled with his printer, and was negotiating a settlement with Betty Paton; Jean had born twins, and Mary was dead. Whatever the tensions and sorrows of the previous months had been, Burns was now free of compelling restraints. Friends were urging an edition in Edinburgh. Perhaps a comfortable arrangement for making a living might come to him if he went to the capital and met influential people. A new edition would probably make a good deal of money, which the family needed desperately. And the prospect of wider fame was delightful. So, on November 27, on a borrowed pony, he set out for a two day ride to Edinburgh. He had a royal reception at Covington Mains farm, near Biggar in Lanarkshire, en route, and arrived November 29 with a hangover. He had completed his career as a major poet, except for his most famous poem, *Tam o' Shanter*.

4. Kilmarnock Edition

Poems Chiefly in the Scottish Dialect, by Robert Burns, Kilmarnock, 1786, was a well-printed paper-bound volume of 240 pages, priced at three shillings. Burns and his friends had gathered over 300 subscriptions, enough to defray expenses, before printing began. In his original proposal to his subscribers, Burns had offered only Scotch poems, but he finally included half a dozen melancholy and moralizing English pieces apparently to increase the volume's appeal. And, it should be noted, although the subscribers and the presumed audience were to be almost entirely local, or at least Scottish, Burns added a liberal glossary of his Scots vocabulary. The 612 copies brought in £90, of which the printer's bill took £34/3/–; but Burns says that he cleared only £20. Perhaps the difference is accounted for partly by the

£9 passage money for Jamaica which he paid down, and may have lost. His settlement with Betty Paton took a substantial amount, and he must have given some to the family at Mossgiel. Burns cannot have had much in his pocket when he set out for Edinburgh.

The Kilmarnock volume made Burns famous at once. Review notices appeared promptly in Edinburgh and London. But Burns withheld from his book, or wrote within three months of its appearance, enough poems and songs to make another volume of the same size and quality. Some of this poetry, and a few songs, he added to his Edinburgh edition of April, 1787, but most of the poetry he never published at all. Later he sent the bulk of the songs to James Johnson and George Thomson for their collections. Of the unpublished poetry, some was too personal to appear publicly (A Poet's Welcome), or too likely to provoke recrimination (the epistle to John M'Math), or too broad (The Court of Equity), or even downright bawdy (The Fornicator).

Of the poems written by November, 1786, and not yet mentioned, there are five of limited interest — three moralizing and melancholy pieces (Despondency, Lament, and To Ruin), and two parochial poems that require heavy annotation (Hallowe'en and The Ordination). The opening stanzas of Hallowe'en are promising, but the poem progresses to a detailed account of Ayrshire folk customs, and fails to transcend its particularities. The Ordination concerns a Kilmarnock parish quarrel over patronage.

A song, and two minor poems, of serious social comment, are readable enough, and contain memorable passages. The song, Man Was Made to Mourn, is a vigorous recital of human suffering and injustice, and the inequality of human reward, with the famous lines,

> Man's inhumanity to man
> Makes countless thousands mourn.

This song concludes, in the words of the aged protagonist,

> The poor, oppressèd, honest man
> Had never, sure, been born,
> Had there not been some recompense
> To comfort those that mourn!
>
> O Death! the poor man's dearest friend,
> The kindest and the best!
> Welcome the hour my agèd limbs
> Are laid with thee, at rest!
> The great, the wealthy fear thy blow,
> From pomp and pleasure torn;
> But, oh! a blest relief to those
> That weary-laden mourn!

Of the two minor poems, one is bitterly ironic, with a cumbersome explanatory heading:

Address of Beelzebub: To the Right Honorable the Earl of Breadalbane, President of the Right Honorable the Highland Society, which met on the 23rd of May last, at the *Shakespeare*, Covent Garden, to concert ways and means to frustrate the desires of five hundred Highlanders who, as the Society were informed by Mr. M'Kenzie of Applecross, were so audacious as to attempt an escape from their lawful lords and masters whose property they were, by emigrating from the lands of Mr. Macdonald of Glengary to the wilds of Canada, in search of that fantastic thing — Liberty.

In this Address, the Devil, writing from Hell, urges the lords and masters to "lay aside a' tender mercies," and not merely to distrain and rob such ungrateful and troublesome tenants,

> But smash them! crush them a' to spails *chips*
> An' rot the dyvors i' the jails! *bankrupts*
> The young dogs, swinge them to the labour: *whip*
> Let wark an' hunger make them sober!
> The hizzies, if they're aughtlins fawsont *girls at all good looking*
> Let them in Drury Lane be lesson'd! *[as prostitutes]*

An' if the wives an' dirty brats
Come thiggin at your doors an' yetts,   *begging gates*
Flaffin wi' duds an' grey wi' beas',   *flapping with vermin fleas*
Frightin awa your deuks an' geese,
Get out a horsewhip or a jowler,   *bulldog*
The langest thong, the fiercest growler,
An' gar the tattered gypsies pack   *make beat it*
Wi' a' their bastards on their back!

The other poem, *A Dedication to Gavin Hamilton, Esq.* like
the Author's Preface to *Tristram Shandy*, appears in the middle
of the volume. It opens with some banter, and then proceeds to
ironic sympathy. Hamilton, although he is "the poor man's friend
in need, / The gentleman in word and deed," does not satisfy his
orthodox neighbors because he is generous and kind merely from
"carnal inclination" and not because he subscribes to proper Calvinist doctrine. Burns continues,

Morality, thou deadly bane,
Thy tens o' thousands thou hast slain!
Vain is his hope, whase stay an' trust is
In moral mercy, truth, and justice!

No — stretch a point to catch a plack;   *make money*
Abuse a brother to his back;
Steal thro' the winnock frae a whore,   *window*
But point the rake that taks the door;
Be to the poor like onie whunstane,
And haud their noses to the grunstane;
Ply ev'ry art o' legal thieving;
No matter — stick to sound believing.

He adds a good deal more in the same mordant vein.

There are also ten light-hearted and felicitous poems, laced and
graced with pungent observations, but all essentially *jeux d'esprit.*
These poems give an idea of the vivacity and salty readiness
which so delighted those who heard Burns speak. *Scotch Drink*

celebrates whiskey and Scotland, and parodies Fergusson's *Caller* [*Fresh*] *Water*, *To a Haggis* was written to amuse a gathering of Ayrshire friends, *Adam Armour's Prayer* is good-natured ridicule of his brother-in-law to be, *Poor Mailie's Elegy* pays further tribute to that immortal sheep, *The Inventory* presents a versified report to a tax gatherer, *Epistle to a Young Friend* gives "good advice" to Robert Aiken's (the tax gatherer's) son, *Tam Samson's Elegy* is rough joking on a good friend, *The Brigs of Ayr* has fun with municipal improvements pushed by Burns' friend John Ballantine, *Lines on Meeting with Lord Daer* is a bread and butter note celebrating a dinner, and *Nature's Law* bursts into joy on the birth of Jean's twins.

To this list may be added three more or less bawdy poems, one of which, *The Fornicator*, has already been quoted. The other two, *The Court of Equity* and *The Patriarch*, are given in Section VI.

Burns' songs have given him a quite different fame from that of the poems, although too often the distinction between his poetry and his songs is confused. A later section will consider the whole matter of Burns and Scottish Song, including *The Jolly Beggars — Love and Liberty*, essentially a collection of songs.

It remains to comment on a few major poems so far unnoticed but written by November 1786. First, *The Twa Dogs*, which Burns used to open the Kilmarnock volume. Here, after a famous description of the two *dogs*, not merely speakers in the guise of dogs, Burns has them discuss their masters, and the rich and the poor, and the gentles and the cotters, all with admirable good sense and humor, and then lets them part without coming to conclusions, although simple life obviously comes off the better, and the gentles are shown up for the hollow-hearted wastrels they too often are. In the central speech, dog Luath, the ploughman's collie, answers dog Caesar, the aristocratic democrat who would just as soon make love to a mongrel, and who has remarked that "surely poor-folk maun [must] be wretches!"

LUATH

They're nae sae wretched's ane wad think;
Tho' constantly on poortith's brink,   *poverty's*
They're sae accustom'd wi' the sight,
The view o't gies them little fright.

Then chance an' fortune are sae guided,
They're ay in less or mair provided;
An' tho' fatigu'd wi' close employment,
A blink o' rest's a sweet enjoyment.   *snatch*

The dearest comfort o' their lives,
Their grushie weans an' faithfu' wives;   *thriving*
The prattling things are just their pride,
That sweetens a' their fire-side.

An' whyles twalpennie worth o' nappy   *ale*
Can make the bodies unco happy:
They lay aside their private cares,
To mind the Kirk and State affairs;
They'll talk o' patronage an' priests,
Wi' kindling fury i' their breasts,
Or tell what new taxation's comin,
An' ferlie at the folk in Lon'on.   *wonder*

As bleak-fac'd Hallowmass returns,   *Halloween*
They get the jovial, ranting kirns,   *harvest-homes*
When rural life, of ev'ry station,
Unite in common recreation:
Love blinks, Wit slaps, an' social Mirth   *strikes*
Forgets there's Care upo' the earth.

That merry day the year begins,
They bar the door on frosty win's;
The nappy reeks wi' mantling ream,   *cream*
An' sheds a heart-inspiring steam;
The luntin pipe, an' sneeshin mill,   *smoking   snuff-box*
Are handed round wi' right guid will;
The cantie auld folks crackin crouse,   *chatting cheerfully*
The young anes ranting thro' the house —   *romping*
My heart has been sae fain to see them,
That I for joy hae barkit wi' them.

Still it's owre true that ye hae said
Sic game is now owre aften play'd;
There's monie a creditable stock
O' decent, honest, fawsont folk,   *respectable*
Are riven out baith root an' branch,
Some rascal's pridefu' greed to quench,
Wha thinks to knit himself the faster
In favor wi' some gentle master,
Wha, aiblins thrang a parliamentin',   *perhaps busy*
For Britain's guid his saul indentin' —

The Auld Farmer's New-Year Morning Salutation to his Auld Mare, Maggie, shows Burns being kindly and warm without the sentimentality to which he was prone. He catches the old man's feeling for his work partner of many years, and he creates sure and clean the quality and tone of a farmer's life. Much of the old man's affection for Maggie, for example, comes from her having done good work on the farm, and from her having given him healthy colts to sell. Here, as in *The Twa Dogs,* the language, the feeling, the purpose, the illustrations are finely at one.

This is not true of *The Cotter's Saturday Night,* in which the style and the statement are often at odds, and the commentary seems intrusive and self-conscious rather than a natural outgrowth of the narrative. What Burns says in *The Cotter* he says in Epistles and elsewhere — the simple and natural life is better than the artificial, love and friendship are life's richest rewards, the lower classes are the strength of the country, and Scotland for Aye. The poem, a projection of Burns' father and his household, idealizes the life of poverty, family affection, and honest work, and poor is he who denies the virtues it celebrates. The father's homecoming and the family gathering, the supper, and the Bible reading, are generally touching and right, but such lines as these jar the effect of stanza five:

The parents partial eye their hopeful years;
Anticipation forward points the view.

Stanzas nine and ten begin the self-conscious intrusions. And after stanza twelve, only the satiric seventeen is more than competent; and not a few stanzas seem contrived. Burns no doubt hoped to elevate the poem by introducing the manner of his admired English models, but the result is unfortunate.

And yet the poem is still widely admired, and properly so, for a reason neatly stated by Henley and Henderson. "Burns's verse falls naturally into two main divisions. One, and that the larger, appeals with persistency and force, on the strength of some broadly human qualities, to the world in general: for the reason that the world in general is rich in sentiment but lacks the literary sense. The other, being a notable and lasting contribution to literature, is the concern of comparatively few." Yet for the few, also, *The Cotter* certainly leaves its mark and makes its point, even while they are conscious of its defects.

Three of Burns' most famous poems help further to illustrate the remark quoted above, and all follow a similar pattern — a series of narrative-descriptive stanzas which lead up to a sententious conclusion. *To a Louse* is artistically by far the best, and by far the least popular. *To a Mountain Daisy* is generally agreed to be the weakest. But *To a Mouse* has always enjoyed high popularity, and critical esteem as well. The distress of the "wee, sleekit, cowrin, tim'rous beastie" is vivid and touching; and "the best laid schemes o' mice an' men gang aft agley," surely; but what of a mouse as a symbol for brotherhood? The general experience of man is otherwise. Who feels "social union" with a mouse? In this central symbolism the poem is artificial and contrived, and sentimental. And the self-pity of its conclusion is not appealing. But for the great majority who are "rich in sentiment but lack the literary sense," these remarks are beside the point. The poem moves them, and Burns was not writing for academic critics.

Professor Sir Walter Raleigh makes a shrewd comment to this same effect. "The Scottish people feel a hearty, instinctive, and just dislike for biographers of Burns. The life of Burns, full as it was of joy and generous impulse, full also of error, disappointment, and failure, makes a perfectly devised trap for the superior person. Almost everyone is superior to Robert Burns in some one point or other — in conjugal fidelity, in worldly prudence, or in social standing. Let him be careful to forget his advantages before he approaches this graveside, or his name will be added to the roll of the failures." True, and fair enough. But it could be wished that Sir Walter had added: The story of Burns is the more moving the more fully told, and the wonder of the man and his work the more deeply felt, the more completely it is understood. Romanticizing admirers no less than "superior persons" have too often made a monstrous caricature of Burns.

To a Louse seems a perfect poem. It opens briskly, it sets a memorable scene, it tells a lively story, it maintains its tone of genial irony with a rich association of incident and image, and it moves quickly and surely to its conclusion, probably the most famous stanza Burns ever wrote. It may be remarked that one's feeling about a louse, and about the occasion, are entirely appropriate to the satiric purpose of the poem, in which not one figure or image is inept, not one line weak. And the theme is quintessential Burns — the absurdity of pretence, especially religious pretence.

To a Louse

On seeing one on a lady's bonnet at church

Ha! whare ye gaun, ye crowlin ferlie?   *crawling wonder*
Your impudence protects you sairly,
I canna say but ye strunt rarely   *strut*
        Owre gauze and lace,
Tho' faith! I fear ye dine but sparely
        On sic a place.

Ye ugly, creepin, blastit wonner,   *marvel*
Detested, shunn'd by saunt an' sinner,
How daur ye set your fit upon her —
        Sae fine a lady!
Gae somewhere else and seek your dinner
        On some poor body.

Swith! in some beggar's hauffet squattle: *temples squat*
There ye may creep, and sprawl, and sprattle   *scramble*
Wi' ither kindred, jumping cattle,
   In shoals and nations;
Whare horn nor bane ne'er daur unsettle   *combs*
   Your thick plantations.

Now haud you there! ye're out o' sight   *hold*
Below the fatt'rils, snug an' tight;   *ribbon ends*
Na, faith ye yet! ye'll no be right,
   Till ye've got on it —
The vera tapmost, tow'ring height
   O' Miss's bonnet.

My sooth! right bauld ye set your nose out,
As plump an' grey as onie grozet: *gooseberry*
O for some rank, mercurial rozet,   *rosin*
   Or fell, red smeddum,   *insecticide*
I'd gie ye sic a hearty dose o't,
   Wad dress your droddum!   *backside*

I wad na been surpris'd to spy   *would not have*
You on an auld wife's flainen toy: *flannel cap*
Or aiblins some bit duddie boy,   *maybe   small ragged*
   On's wyliecoat;   *undervest*
But Miss's fine Lunardi! fye!   *balloon bonnet*
   How daur ye do't?   *dare*

O Jenny, dinna toss your head,
An' set your beauties a' abread!   *abroad*
Ye little ken what cursèd speed
   The blastie's makin!
Thae winks an' finger ends, I dread,   *Those*
   Are notice takin!

O wad some Power the giftie gie us
To see oursels as ithers see us!
It wad frae monie a blunder free us,
   An' foolish notion:
What airs in dress an' gait wad lea'e us,
   An' ev'n devotion!

A stanza from the epistle to William Simpson makes an apt comment on *The Vision*.

> The Muse, nae poet ever fand her,   *found*
> Till by himsel he learn'd to wander,
> Adown some trottin' burn's meander   *brook's*
>   An' no think lang;
> O, sweet to stray, an' pensive ponder
>   A heart-felt sang!

In *The Vision*, written over a period of time, and revised, Burns "thinks lang," for forty-six stanzas, and the poem is mainly a versified record of his thoughts about Scotland, and poetry, and his place as a "rustic bard." (He makes it clear that he feels he is one of the "humbler ranks.") Here is Burns' *apologia*, his *Defence of Poesie*, his view of his calling as an honorable one and significant to his country and his people. The poem opens with stanzas describing the poet weary after a day of threshing. Stanza four continues:

> All in this mottie, misty clime,   *dusty*
> I backward mus'd on wasted time:
> How I had spent my youthfu' prime,
>   An' done naething,
> But stringing blethers up in rhyme,
>   For fools to sing.

> Had I to guid advice but harkit,
> I might, by this, hae led a market,
> Or strutted in a bank and clarkit
>   My cash-account:
> While here, half-mad, half-fed, half-sarkit,   *-shirted*
>   Is a' th' amount.

Suddenly there appears the figure of Coila, in the trim shape of Jean Armour.

> A "hair-brain'd, sentimental trace,"
> Was strongly markèd in her face;

> A wildly-witty, rustic grace
> Shone full upon her;
> Her eye, ev'n turn'd on empty space,
> Beam'd keen with honor.

The lassie wears a mantle bearing a map of Ayrshire, with pictures on it of distinguished figures, historical and contemporary. She is the spirit of the district (Kyle), and a member of a "light aerial band" which Burns invents* to inspire Scotland and Kyle. Coila speaks of patriots, soldiers, poets, improving landlords, judges, professors, rustic bards, artisans, wooers — all important in the general society; she says she has had Burns in her care since his birth, and points to what he has done under her influence:

> "When youthful Love, warm-blushing, strong,
> Keen-shivering, shot thy nerves along,
> Those accents grateful to thy tongue,
>   Th' adorèd *Name,*
> I taught thee how to pour in song
>   To soothe thy flame.

> "I saw thy pulse's maddening play,
> Wild-send thee Pleasure's devious way,
> Misled by Fancy's meteor-ray,
>   By passion driven;
> But yet the light that led astray
>   Was light from Heaven.

> "I taught thy manners-painting strains
> The loves, the ways of simple swains,
> Till now, o'er all my wide domains
>   Thy fame extends;
> And some, the pride of Coila's plains,
>   Become thy friends."

Finally she encourages him,

> "Then never murmur nor repine;
> Strive in thy humble sphere to shine;
> And trust me, not Potosi's mine,   [*of gold, silver, and copper*]

---

* Professor J. C. Weston feels that Burns was influenced in the creation of his troop by Pope's sylphs in *The Rape of the Lock.*

Nor king's regard,
Can give a bliss o'ermatching thine,
A rustic Bard.

"To give my counsels all in one:
Thy tuneful flame still careful fan;
Preserve the dignity of Man,
With soul erect;
And trust the Universal Plan
Will all protect."

Then she places a holly wreath on his head, and "like a passing
thought" fades away. It should be noted that Coila encourages
her Scots poet in purest English, as a serious-minded and thoughtful Scot should. This elaborate poem is smoothly versified, and
of biographical interest, but after the opening stanzas it does not
have the full force and grace of Burns at his best.

As we have seen, Burns took his position as poet seriously, and
he enjoyed his success, but he recognized that it helped him little
in what he called "the sober science of life." In June, 1786, he had
written David Brice that his Kilmarnock edition was to be his
"last foolish action," after which he intended to "turn a wise man
as fast as possible." All during the exciting months which followed
in Edinburgh, he was worried about his problem of a livelihood,
made even greater by his more prominent position. He felt he
could not live on his poetry, and fame paid no bills. His essential
position was much the same after both his publications as before.

The greatest change for him was a broadening of his acquaintance. Burns responded warmly to those who offered him friendship, and he found much pleasure in three persons who were
attracted to him by the Kilmarnock volume in the autumn of
1786: the Rev. George Lawrie, of Newmilns, in nearby Loudon
parish; Dr. Thomas Blacklock, of Edinburgh; and Mrs. Frances
Anna Wallace Dunlop, of Dunlop, a few miles north of Kilmarnock.

Before Burns left for Edinburgh, he was entertained happily
by the Lawrie family at the Manse, where he left behind an

appropriate poem, the prayer *O Thou Dread Power.* In the capital, he frequently saw Mr. Lawrie's son, Archibald, who was pursuing his ministerial studies, and his daughter, Christina.

Dr. Blacklock was a man of some note. Blind since infancy, he had completed his studies, nonetheless, and had become a minister, but his parishioners objecting, after a few years he retired and accepted an annuity. In Edinburgh he boarded and tutored college students, and as a musician, minor poet, and man of learning, was well enough known to be visited by Dr. Johnson on his famous visit to Scotland. Mr. Lawrie had sent him a copy of Burns' poems, and in his letter of thanks, Dr. Blacklock spoke of them with enthusiasm, and urged a second edition. This letter encouraged Burns to consider an Edinburgh edition when it was forwarded to him. In the city, he came to know Blacklock, enjoyed his company, and met interesting people through him. He wrote Mr. Lawrie, "In Dr. Blacklock, whom I see very often, I have found what I would have expected in our friend, a clear head and an excellent heart."

With Mrs. Dunlop, Burns developed a strong and lasting friendship, and one of the more notable relations in literary history. When she first read his poems, she was ill and depressed. Her husband had recently died, and her estranged oldest son had been forced to sell her beloved family estate of Craigie to pay debts incurred by fashionable living. She found such consolation in the poems, and particularly in *The Cotter's Saturday Night,* that on November 14, she wrote Burns requesting a dozen copies, and expressing pleasure that he had celebrated her ancestor, the great Sir William Wallace, in *The Vision.* Burns replied at once, citing his early enthusiasm for Wallace, and sending five copies, all he could muster.

Frances Anna Wallace (1730–1815) was proud of her family — she actually descended from an uncle of the great hero. At eighteen she had made a runaway match with John Dunlop of Dunlop (1707–1785), of a family nearly as ancient as her own.

Frances and John Dunlop had seven sons and six daughters. (Mrs. Dunlop's father added piquancy to the family by choosing as his second wife his son-in-law's sister.) After John Dunlop's death, his widow lived in semi-retirement, mainly with her son Andrew at Dunlop House, but often with her son John at his farm, More-ham Mains, near Haddington, east of Edinburgh, and occasionally at Loudon Castle, which had been rented by a son-in-law. She was a tower of strength in domestic crises, and a friendly, sensible woman not without humor, given to writing long, involved sentences and bad poetry. In any estimate of Burns, it is notable that he won and kept the friendship of Frances Dunlop.

As with most good friends, they sometimes irritated one another, but they felt at ease and maintained a remarkable candor, discussing his love affairs, the intimate family concerns of them both, politics and other topics of the day, and literature, about which Mrs. Dunlop had some knowledge and strong if often distressing opinions. Although broad-minded and occasionally broad-spoken, she objected vigorously to "improprieties" in Burns' poems. She was tedious, prolix, and repetitious in her letters, complaining that he wrote less often than she and then did not answer her because he did not read what she had written. She often spoke of the comfort his poems had given her when she first read them, and of her continuing admiration for her "dr Burns." As Professor Ferguson remarks, he seems to have felt about her as many a man does toward his mother: she often bored him, but he loved her. She in turn gave him motherly advice, loved him much like a son, and treasured his letters, which she seems to have kept private and not shared with her children. She and Burns each turned instinctively to the other in times of distress such as family deaths, or of especial happiness such as a birth of children or grandchildren. She interested herself in his family, getting to know Gilbert, calling on Jean in Mauchline, and making friends with his cousin Fanny, his uncle Robert's daughter.

She also tried to help him in a practical way. Through her he learned that Adam Smith had suggested he secure a steady income by becoming a Salt Officer, a job with less opprobrium than the Excise carried, and with light duties, paying £35 a year. She made him acquainted with Dr. John Moore, a Scot, and an M.D., Glasgow, now a fashionable author living in London. She and Dr. Moore worked hard to have Burns appointed to a newly established chair of Agriculture at the University of Edinburgh. He called it an "idle project," and felt himself unsuited for the appointment, but he did consider seriously her suggestion that he buy a commission in the army. Mrs. Dunlop thought that Burns and his family would have been better off living in the country, but when he became an Exciseman and gave up farming, she helped him through her friendships with Commissioner Robert Graham and with Collector William Corbet's wife.

After a letter from Burns of January 12, 1795, Mrs. Dunlop withheld her correspondence until eighteen months later when she heard that he was dying. Apparently his offense was writing about the execution of the king and queen in France: "What is there in the delivering over a perjured Blockhead & an unprincipled Prostitute to the hands of the hangman, that it should arrest for a moment, attention?" Although liberal, Mrs. Dunlop was no democrat. She had an early sympathy with the French Revolution, but was outraged by the later violence. She also had two daughters married to royalist refugees, and four army sons and a grandson. Burns' expression of republican sympathies, particularly in this "indelicate" way, seems to have been too much for her. A year later, he wrote in vain to ask his offense, since he had heard nothing from her, but the following letter, written a week before his death, brought an immediate response, which, unhappily has not survived.

MADAM

I have written you so often without rec.g any answer, that I would not trouble you again but for the circumstances in which I am. — An illness which has long hung about me in all probability will speedily send me beyond that bourn whence no traveller returns. — Your friendship with which for many years you honored me was a friendship dearest to my soul. — Your conversation & especially your correspondence were at once highly entertaining & instructive. — With what pleasure did I use to break up the seal! The remembrance yet adds one pulse more to my poor palpitating heart!

Farewell!!!

ROBERT BURNS

July
10th

IV

LION

I am just a poor wayfaring Pilgrim on the road to Parnassus.
BURNS TO ROBERT MUIR

I am a Bard, of no regard
Wi' gentle folks an' a' that.
Love and Liberty

1. Edinburgh

Burns was lionized in Edinburgh, and he enjoyed it, but he had
to endure being patronized also, and he resented that. Canny
pursuit of his purpose — a new edition — netted him about £450,
a sum "for his relief" which Sir Walter Scott felt to be "extremely
trifling." And Burns suffered tedious delays in collecting even that
amount. He greatly increased his fame, a dear concern for him,
but his very success hampered further poetic development. Burns
finally left Edinburgh, as he had entered it, with but two practical
ways of supporting himself — tenant farming and tax collecting
(The Excise), both unattractive. He looked back on his venture
as a "hare-brained ramble," and on Edinburgh Society as a
"Greenland bay of Indifference." From the beginning he had
recognized that for this small group of "Patricians" who saw too
much of each other, he was merely a welcome novelty.

On his arrival in Edinburgh, Burns knew there only his old
crony John Richmond, still a lawyer's clerk, with whom he was to
share a room and a bed. But Burns had connections, whom he approached promptly and with dramatic results. The first was Sir

John Whitefoord, erstwhile Master of St. James Lodge, Tarbolton (Burns was Depute Master). Formerly of Ballochmyle, near Mauchline, Sir John had retired to Edinburgh upon selling his estate to cover losses incurred through a bank failure. Another Ayrshire Freemason, James Dalrymple of Orangefield, was a friend of Burns' patron John Ballantine, the Ayr banker, and a nephew of the Rev. Dr. William Dalrymple who had baptized Burns. More important, Mr. Dalrymple was cousin to James Cunningham, Lord Glencairn, a prominent member of that select club, the Caledonian Hunt, and a friend of the leading bookseller-publisher William Creech. Moreover, Lord Glencairn's brother had married Miss Isabella Erskine, sister to Lord Buchan and to Henry Erskine, Dean of the Faculty of Advocates. Within a week of his arrival, through Dalrymple and Sir John, Burns was welcomed by the best society of the city — landed aristocracy and gentry, and a select group of able but by no means distinguished professional people: judges, lawyers, doctors, ministers, and university professors. Burns' Masonic affiliation certainly quickened his progress, also. On December 7, ten days after his arrival, he attended a meeting of the most popular Edinburgh lodge, Canongate Kilwinning, and on February 1, 1787, he was made an "assumed member" of the lodge.

The Duchess of Gordon carried him to balls and assemblies so enthusiastically that it created a scandal heard in London. Lord Glencairn invited Burns to his house, persuaded the Caledonian Hunt to subscribe for 100 copies of a new edition, bestirred himself to get subscriptions from London, and seemingly introduced Burns to Creech. Professor Dugald Stewart, who had entertained Burns at his country home near Mauchline, continued his friendship, and brought the Kilmarnock volume to the attention of Henry Mackenzie. On December 7, Mackenzie published a review of it in *The Lounger*, a weekly periodical he was editing, thus supplementing reviews in the October, November, and December issues of the *Edinburgh Magazine*. Mackenzie was cordial, and Burns looked to him for advice, with at least one unfortunate result in negotiations with Creech over copyright. Lord Monboddo, Judge of the Court of Session, often had Burns to his house, and Burns celebrated his beautiful daughter Elizabeth in the *Address to Edinburgh*. Mr. Patrick Miller, brother of the Lord Justice-Clerk (mentioned in *The Vision*) and later President of the Court of Session, left a present of ten guineas, and soon suggested that he would be pleased to have the Ploughman Poet as a tenant on his newly bought estate of Dalswinton. The Earl of Eglinton, at the urging of his Countess, had an agent leave ten guineas subscription money. The young Walter Scott saw Burns at the home of Professor Adam Fergusson. Principal William Robertson, historian and friend of Adam Smith, said that while Burns' poems surprised him, his prose compositions were even more wonderful, and his conversation surpassed both.

Of greater significance than his being taken up by prominent people was an announcement on December 14 by Creech that an edition of Burns' poems was in the press, "to be published by subscription for the sole benefit of the author." In other words, the poems were to be published at Burns' risk, with Creech as his agent. The records of Burns' dealings with Creech are not known to have survived, but the bookseller managed the details of publication, perhaps for a commission. He also subscribed for 500 copies which he could sell at one shilling above the subscription price of five shillings.* Burns paid the printer and binder. His relations with Creech did not remain cordial for long, but Creech got the job done, and had the best experience and connections in Edinburgh for it. A second Commonplace Book, from the Edinburgh period, contains Burns' impressions of Creech.

> A little upright, pert, tart, tripping wight,
> And still his precious self his dear delight;
> Who loves his own smart shadow in the streets
> Better than e'er the fairest She he meets.

* James Grierson reports that Creech paid Burns only the "bookseller's price," not the subscription price for these copies. (Fitzhugh, 40.)

Much specious lore, but little understood
(Veneering oft outshines the solid wood),
His solid sense by inches you must tell,
But meet his subtle cunning by the ell!
A man of fashion, too, he made his tour,
Learn'd "vive la bagatelle et vive l'amour";
So travell'd monkies their grimace improve,
Polish their grin — nay, sigh for ladies' love!
His meddling vanity, a busy fiend,
Still making work his selfish craft must mend.

An important result of Burns' social success was that many people recorded their impressions of him, and four artists left well-authenticated likenesses of him. The Nasmyth sketch and full length painting give an accurate representation of what Burns looked like as he walked about Edinburgh. And the Nasmyth head, and particularly the Beugo engraving from it for which Burns gave additional sittings, are careful representations of his features. The Taylor portrait and the Miers silhouette supply interesting confirmation and added detail. Burns stood about five feet ten, and was strong and well knit, although not of a heavy frame, but his carriage and something about his shoulders disguised his height and his natural grace of movement. Swarthy, coarse-featured, with black hair falling over his high forehead, he tended to be moody and withdrawn in a large company, but grew animated in conversation, when his eyes would glow "like coals of living fire." Several comments of a time later than his winters in Edinburgh mention a tendency toward slovenly dress, and two speak of a pockmarked face although none of the portraits show it.

There is general agreement that Burns received adulation with dignity, and exerted himself in company because he saw it was expected of him, but was neither forward nor constrained. He was fully conscious of his abilities and depended on them and not on his situation as a ploughman poet to maintain his position. He exhibited ready wit and strong common sense, and spoke his mind independently and sometimes more forcefully than his well-bred hosts enjoyed. His conversation was frequently tinged with sarcasm, and "his deportment was plain and showed him ready to repel any insult with decision." One hostess who had not met him sent an invitation which he accepted if she would also invite a "learned pig" * then performing in a Grassmarket booth. Two observers speak of an affected rusticity, one of them the son of his printer, who describes Burns carrying a whip and cracking it in the printing shop. Two other observers felt that he had got a swelled head, but since until Burns' death he continued to speak cordially of one, David Ramsay, publisher of the *Edinburgh Courant*, it would appear that a friendship developed and continued between them nevertheless.

The general and enduring impression which Burns made on upper class Edinburgh was recorded by John Lockhart, writing thirty years later, in a biography praised by Sir Walter Scott.

There were many points in Burns's conversational habits which men, accustomed to the delicate observances of refined society, might be more willing to tolerate under the first excitement of personal curiosity, than from any very deliberate estimate of the claims of such a genius, . . . He by no means restricted his sarcastic observations on those whom he encountered in the world to the confidence of his notebook; but startled polite ears with the utterance of audacious epigrams, far too witty not to obtain general circulation in so small a society as that of the Northern capital, far too bitter not to produce a deep resentment, far too numerous not to spread fear almost as widely as admiration. . . . It needs no effort of imagination to conceive what the sensations of an isolated set of scholars (almost all either clergymen or professors) must have been in the presence of this big-boned, black-browed, brawny stranger, with his great flash-

---

* Learned pigs were a popular attraction in Burns' day. A learned pig was one trained to walk round with his proprietor inside a ring of cards and to pick up designated cards apparently by vocal direction but actually on a signal not perceived by the spectators. A common signal was the "snuffing" of the proprietor's nose. (William Frederick Pinchbeck, *The EXPOSITOR, or Many Mysteries Unraveled*, Boston, 1805.) The picture of a Learned Pig among the illustrations following page 236 is the frontispiece to Pinchbeck's book.

ing eyes, who, having forced his way among them from the plough-tail at a single stride, manifested in the whole strain of his bearing and conversation, a most thorough conviction that, in a society of the most eminent men of his nation, he was exactly where he was entitled to be; hardly deigned to flatter them by exhibiting even an occasional symptom of being flattered by their notice; by turns calmly measured himself against the most cultivated understandings of the time in discussion; overpowered the *bon mots* of the most celebrated convivialists by broad floods of merriment, impregnated with all the burning life of genius; astounded bosoms habitually enveloped in the thrice-piled folds of social reserve, by compelling them to tremble — nay, to tremble visibly — beneath the fearless touch of natural pathos; and all this without indicating the smallest willingness to be ranked among those professional ministers of excitement, who are content to be paid in money and smiles for doing what the spectators and auditors would be ashamed of doing in their own persons, even if they had the power of doing it; and, — last and probably worst of all, — who was known to be in the habit of enlivening societies which they would have scorned to approach, still more frequently than their own, with eloquence no less magnificent; with wit in all like-lihood still more daring; often enough, as the superiors whom he fronted without alarm might have guessed from the beginning, and had, ere long, no occasion to guess, with wit pointed at themselves.

An illustrative footnote to Lockhart is Henry Mackenzie's comment that Burns' admiration for Robert Fergusson was evidence of his "propensity for coarse dissipation." But then Fergusson had mocked Mackenzie's famous novel in a poem, *The Sow of Feeling*. Mackenzie noted, as though it were a degrading incon-sistency, that Burns enjoyed the attentions of important people, but resented class distinctions. However, he does give a rare bit of Burns' conversation. "He indulged his sarcastic humour* in talking of men, particularly if he thought them proud, or dis-dainful of Persons of inferior rank; his Observations were always

* Compare Mackenzie's observation, with Burns' comment to Mrs. Dunlop: "I hate an ungenerous sarcasm a great deal more than I do the devil — at least as Milton describes him; and though I may be rascally enough to be sometimes guilty of it myself, I cannot endure it in others." (F I, #219, 205.)

acute and forcibly expressed. I was walking with him one day
when we met a common Acquaintance not remarkable for Ability
or intellectual Endowments. I observed how extremely fat he had
lately grown. 'Yes,' said Burns, 'and when you have told that you
have exhausted the subject of Mr —— Fatness is the only quality
you can ascribe to him.' "

An extensive memorandum prepared for Dr. Currie by another
literary man, Dr. Robert Anderson, both supports and qualifies
the statements of Lockhart and Mackenzie. "I was struck with
[Burns'] appearance, so different from what I had expected in
an uneducated rustic. His person, though neither robust nor
elegant, was manly and pleasing; and his countenance, though
dark and coarse, uncommonly expressive and interesting. With
an air of keen penetration and calm thoughtfulness approaching
to melancholy, the usual attendant on genius, there was a kind
of stern pride and supercilious elevation about him not incompatible with openness and affability, which might perhaps be
properly termed a strong consciousness of intellectual excellence.
His dress was plain, but genteel,* like that of a farmer of the
better sort; a dark-coloured coat, light-figured waistcoat, shirt
with ruffles at the breast, and boots, in which he constantly visited
and walked about the Town. He wore his hair, which was black
and thin, in a queue, without powder."

Anderson continues that Burns was "decent, dignified, and
simple" in the large gathering where he first met him, and "perfectly easy, unembarrassed, and unassuming." As with everyone
who ever met Burns, Anderson found his conversation "captivat-
ing," and "even more fascinating than his poetry." He adds the
following details. "Though [Burns'] knowledge in many instances

---

* "After a brief residence in town, his plain rustic dress was exchanged for a
suit of blue and buff, the livery of Fox, with buckskins and top boots." (Ch-W
II, 34.) The jacket was buff, the waistcoat blue. These colors were perhaps a
tribute to his Whig (Foxite) patrons. But Edinburgh was overwhelmingly Tory
(Pittite). In a comment below on the ambivalence of Burns' politics, Anderson
remarks that Burns supported Pitt and descried Fox. Perhaps it may be said
that Burns was the prototype of the "independent liberal."

was superficial, yet he conversed on every subject in a manner
that evinced the strongest marks of genius, sagacity, and acuteness, combined with the most powerful sallies of wit, sarcasm,
and satire. With acuteness of intellect, which might sometimes
be termed shrewdness, he possessed a still more useful talent,
Good Sense, which enabled him instantly to discern what was
right or wrong in literature, morality, and the general affairs of
the world. He affected to despise those branches of knowledge
which he had not cultivated, particularly the abstract sciences.
'I know nothing of logic, or mathematics,' I have heard him say,
with great emphasis. 'I profess only poetry.' He was eager to
assert the dignity and importance of poetry, which he termed the
gift of heaven, though he frequently debased and degraded it
by the misapplication of his own great powers to mean and unworthy purposes.* He spoke of his own productions with great
complacency, and justified the faults imputed to them by loud
and vehement appeals from criticism to commonsense. He recited
his own beautiful Songs very readily, and with peculiar animation and feeling, though he affected † to be ignorant of the
principles of music."

Anderson then proceeds to list what the polite found offensive
in Burns' manner. While independent, he was the slave of "powerful, ardent, and irritable" passions. His pride sometimes showed
as insolence, sometimes as resentment. "He would not condescend
to practice the graces and respectful attentions of polite persons."
He had strong personal, political, and religious prejudices which
"misguided the rectitude of his judgment."

Burns' "morality with regard to women was lax; he transgressed
the rules of sobriety openly; he was accused of ingratitude —
perhaps justly, for he could not bear to conceive himself under
an obligation; but his integrity in business was never questioned.

* One wishes that Anderson had listed more particularly Burns' offenses against
elegant good taste. Perhaps he was one of those who advised omission of *The
Jolly Beggars — Love and Liberty* from the Edinburgh volume.
† No affectation; Burns had almost no formal knowledge of music.

Though proud and revengeful, he was naturally generous and compassionate; zealous in serving those he loved, and always ready to perform offices of kindness and humanity. Though he was accustomed to admit impure and profane thoughts into his mind, yet I never heard him utter a word offensive to decency in the company of ladies; and though addicted to convivial excesses, yet I never heard that he violated the rules of sobriety in private families."

Anderson reports that he and Burns met frequently, and were on good terms, although they did not agree on many topics. "Political disputes then ran high," he remarks. "I was a Whig, attached to the principles upon which the Revolution was effected, He was a tory, an idolater of monarchy, and a Jacobite as much as he could be. I was on the side of Fox and the parliament; He adhered to Pitt and the King." Burns "was not so much elated by the distinction he obtained in Edinburgh as might be expected. He knew that it would be transient, and he neglected not the means of turning it to his advantage," even urging that some poor verses to him be published because he "thought the printing them might do him service." "It was, . . . a part of the machinery . . . of his poetical character to pass for an illiterate ploughman who wrote from pure inspiration." When Anderson "pointed out some of the evident traces of poetical imitation in his verses, privately, [Burns] readily acknowledged his obligations, and even admitted the advantages he enjoyed in poetical composition from the *copia verborum*, . . . which the knowledge and use of the English and Scottish dialects afforded him; but in company he did not suffer his pretentions to pure inspiration to be challenged, and it was seldom done where it might be supposed to affect the success of the subscription for his *Poems*."

Anderson supplies a provocative anecdote.

The vanity which led many women of rank and character to seek his acquaintance and correspondence is remarkable. One instance, not generally known, I shall mention on account of its singular

romanticity, from the information of Mr. Dalzell. A Miss Carmichael,* a young poetess, who adored Burns and studied his manner,
had been invited to dine with him at Mr. Ramsay's. Sometime after
she took the romantic resolution of commencing a sentimental correspondence with him, and sent him a card requesting a meeting
in the glen between Arthur's Seat and Salisbury Craigs. Though she
was not handsome, he had little confidence in his own virtue, and
in the delicate embarrassment of the moment he called upon Mr.
Dalzell, who happened to be in Town, shewed him the card, and
begged he would accompany him to the place of meeting. Dalzell
readily agreed to go, and kept his appointment; but in the interval
Burns changed his mind and thought proper to go alone. The end
of this adventure is not known.

Burns' encounter with an eccentric clergyman will serve to
close this account of his life in polite Edinburgh circles. A discussion of Gray's *Elegy* having arisen during a breakfast party
at the house of a High School teacher, Alexander Christinson, the
minister attacked the poem generally, and Burns asked him to be
more particular. Unable to quote pointedly or to make effective
criticism, the minister fumbled until Burns lost patience and remarked, "Sir, I now perceive a man may be an excellent judge
of poetry by square and rule, and after all be a damned blockhead!" Upon which he turned to a child sitting in Mrs. Christinson's lap and said, "I beg your pardon, my little dear."

Burns recorded his own impressions of Edinburgh in his letters
and in a Commonplace Book which he started there. At first he
was amused and pleased, but troubled. "I am in a fair way of
becoming as eminent as Thomas a Kempis or John Bunyan," he
wrote to Gavin Hamilton. After two weeks in the city, he names
his new patrons to John Ballantine, and adds, "I tremble lest I
should be ruined by being dragged too suddenly into the glare
of polite & learned observation." At the same time he comments

---

* Rebekah Carmichael, to whom Burns presented a copy of Fergusson's poems.
(Ch-W II, 60–61.) Mr. Dalzell seems to have been Andrew Dalzell, Professor of
Greek in Edinburgh University.

to Robert Aiken, "Various concurring circumstances have raised my fame as a Poet to a height which I am absolutely certain I have not merit to support; and I look down on the future as I would into the bottomless pit."

An engaging interlude is a report to Ballantine on his and Richmond's landlady, a Mrs. Carfrae.

I have just now had a visit from my Landlady who is a staid, sober, piously-disposed, sculduddry-abhoring Widow, coming on her grand climacterick. — She is at present in sore tribulation respecting some "Daughters of Belial" who are on the floor immediately above. — My Landlady who as I said is a flesh-disciplining, godly Matron, firmly believes that her husband is in Heaven; and having been happy with him on earth, she vigorously and perseveringly practices some of the most distinguishing Christian virtues, such as, attending Church, railing against vice, &c. that she may be qualified to meet her dear quondam Bedfellow in that happy place where the Unclean & the ungodly shall never enter. — This, no doubt, requires some strong exertions of Self-denial, in a hale, well-kept Widow of forty five; and as our floors are low and ill-plaistered, we can easily distinguish our laughter-loving, night-rejoicing neighbors — when they are eating, when they are drinking, when they are singing, when they are &c., my worthy Landlady tosses sleepless & unquiet, "looking for rest but finding none," the whole night. — Just now she told me, though by the by she is sometimes dubious that I am, in her own phrase, "but a rough an' roun' Christian" that "We should not be uneasy and envious because the Wicked enjoy the good things of this life; for these base jades who, in her own words, lie up gandygoin with their filthy fellows, drinking the best of wines, and singing abominable songs, they shall one day lie in hell, weeping and wailing and gnashing their teeth over a cup of God's wrath!"

An oblique expression of Burns' sentiments about the "E'nbrugh gentry" was his application to erect a headstone over Robert Fergusson's unmarked grave. All who could come by a copy of the Kilmarnock edition, or who should soon read the volume being prepared by Creech, would find the following stanza in the epistle to William Simpson:

O Fergusson! thy glorious parts
Ill suited law's dry, musty arts!
My curse upon your whunstane hearts,   *whinstone*
    Ye E'nbrugh gentry!
The tythe o' what ye waste at cartes
    Wad stow'd his pantry!   *Would have stored*

By the end of his first winter, Burns tells Dr. Moore, "I have formed many intimacies and friendships here, but I am afraid they are all of them of too tender a construction to bear carriage a hundred and fifty miles." And to Mrs. Dunlop he writes at the same time, "I know what I may expect from the world, by and by; illiberal abuse and perhaps contemptuous neglect." A more explicit statement of distaste comes in a letter of January 27, 1788, after he had been in Edinburgh a year. "Why will Great people not only deafen us with the din of their equipage, and dazzle us with their fastidious pomp, but they must also be so very dictatorially wise? I have been questioned like a child."

A little later he tells William Nicol, "My mind has been vitiated by idleness"; and to William Dunbar he writes, "My late scenes of idleness and dissipation have enervated my mind to an alarming degree." Just as he was leaving Edinburgh finally, he writes to his farmer friend, Robert Cleghorn, "My Muse has degenerated into the veriest prose-wench that ever picked cinders or followed a Tinker."

In his frustration he adopted the same attitude which he had taken when at Irvine six years before:

Then come, Misfortune, I bid thee welcome —
I'll meet thee with undaunted mind!

But now he had a mighty protagonist to emulate. He writes to Mrs. Dunlop, April 30, 1787, "I am resolved to study the sentiments of a very respectable Personage, Milton's Satan — 'Hail horrors! hail infernal world!'" To James Smith in June, he cries, "Give me a spirit like my favorite hero, Milton's Satan." And to

Clarinda the following January he again champions Satan's "manly fortitude in supporting what cannot be remedied."

The Reverend Hugh Blair was a famous preacher, author of a rhetoric, and a great critical eminence. He was pleased to be gracious to Burns, who wrote in his Edinburgh Commonplace Book, "I never respect him with humble veneration; but when he kindly interests himself in my welfare, or, still more, when he descends from his pinnacle, and meets me on equal ground, my heart overflows with what is called *liking*. When he neglects me for the mere carcase of greatness, or when his eye measures the difference of our points of elevation, I say to myself with scarcely any emotion — What do I care for him or his pomp either?

"It is not easy forming an exact-judging judgment of any one: but, in my opinion, Dr Blair is merely an astonishing proof of what industry and application can do. Natural parts like his are frequently to be met with — his vanity is proverbially known among his acquaintances — but he is justly at the head of what is called fine writing; and a critic of the first — the very first rank in prose; even in poesy, a good bard of Nature's making can only take the *pas* of him. He has a heart, not of the finest water, but far from being an ordinary one. In short, he is a truly worthy and most respectable character." It should be noted that a famous *gaffe* by Burns was his admitting in Blair's presence a preference for the great man's assistant, Dr. Greenfield, as a preacher. A slip in conversation, it caused Burns acute distress, and Blair was gentleman enough not to notice it.

In Edinburgh, as in Mauchline and Tarbolton, Burns preferred men who were open and free-spoken, who enjoyed a convivial evening, and preferably, men who had something to them. The city abounded in such, even if they did not grace the politer drawing rooms. But the various social strata in Edinburgh rubbed shoulders in a curiously intimate way; there was a considerable

overlap between the convivial clubs and the more elegant as-
semblages, and many patricians rejoiced in deep potations. In
1787, Edinburgh was a vestigial remnant of medieval times, a
noisome warren of high buildings, narrow wynds (alleys), and
packed closes, where water was delivered by cart and slops were
thrown out the window. The main street, from which the wynds
sloped down to north and south, ran along a rocky ridge, with
Edinburgh Castle at the high, west, end, and Holyrood Palace
at the bottom to the east. The city had grown upward because
there was no room to expand. In the tall tenement buildings,
porters, chimney sweeps, and their ilk inhabited the cellars; upper
class people the lower floors; merchants and clerks the middle
levels; and workmen the attics. All were served by the same
narrow staircase, adorned with accumulations of refuse. Quarters
were crowded and hygiene unthought of. Perforce much of the
city's life was carried on in the street, or in taverns, the usual
place for lawyer and client to meet, or for merchants to seal a
bargain. During the previous decades there had been some expansion of the city to the south, and by 1787 the Georgian squares
north of Princes Street were also beginning to develop. But life
still centered in the old city.

Edinburgh could boast an intellectual and social sophistication
above that common to a provincial city, which it had become on
Scotland's union with England in 1707, when the Scottish parliament was absorbed into the English. However, Scotland still had
its own system of law, centering in Edinburgh; and its presbyterian national church, whose General Assembly resembled a
national legislature. The University of Edinburgh was noted, particularly its medical school. And the self-contained and self-
satisfied Society of the old capital thought of itself as distinguished by a special canon of refinement and cultivation. In
Burns' day, it included no famous men like Hume, earlier, or
Scott, later. Burns never met his equal there, and to quote a late
Nineteenth Century Scottish biographer, "It strikes us of this day

as almost ludicrous that he should have been patronised by men
of the undoubted though second-rate capacity of Dugald Stewart,
Hugh Blair, and Henry Mackenzie." Indeed, it never occurred
to these men and their friends that their chief if only claim to
fame would be their association with Burns.

A greater irony still was their professed distaste for the vernacular which they found so delightful in Burns' poems. They
wanted to speak and write English, as Burns himself did. For
them, Scots had become merely a dialect of the lower classes,
suitable perhaps for humorous or homely verse, but no longer a
literary language. Like Burns, they admired the English poets of
the Eighteenth Century, and Scots poets like Thomson and
Beattie, who wrote in the English manner.

A distinguishing mark of life in the old city was the convivial
clubs, for business and professional men, which met in taverns.
And it was among men who enjoyed amusements of this kind
that Burns found his lasting friends in Edinburgh. These clubs
were usually organized around some conceit, and a sanitized
account of one appears in Chapter XXXVI of *Guy Mannering*.
The Crochallan Fencibles, to which Burns was introduced by
his printer and Creech's partner, William Smellie, was pseudo-
military, each member having rank. The "Colonel" was William
Dunbar, a lawyer and Writer to the Signet. "Old sinful Smellie,"
as Burns called him, "that veteran of genius, wit, and Baudy,"
was "Adjutant." Smellie had edited the first *Encyclopaedia Bri-
tannica*, and had written many articles for it. He was author, also,
of a *Philosophy of Natural History*. Burns sketched him in lines
intended to be part of a long poem never completed:

> Crochallan came:
> The old cock'd hat, the brown surtout the same;
> His grisly beard just bristling in its might
> ('Twas four long nights and days to shaving night);
> His uncomb'd, hoary locks, wild-staring, thach'd
> A head for thought profound and clear unmatch'd;

Yet, tho' his caustic wit was biting rude,
His heart was warm, benevolent, and good.

Burns elsewhere speaks of Smellie as "a man positively of the first abilities & greatest strength of mind, as well as one of the best hearts & keenest wits that I have ever met with." The name of Smellie's club came from the favorite song, *Cro Chalein* (Gaelic for "Colin's Cattle"), of the innkeeper whose tavern they frequented — Donald (Dawney) Douglas, of Anchor Close, near Smellie's shop. "Fencibles" parodied the name of the home guard fencible regiments which had been raised when the regular army was overseas during the American war. Other members of the club were Charles Hay, later, as judge, Lord Newton, the "Major" (Hay is reported to have said, "Drinking is my occupation — law my amusement"); William Craig, cousin and protector of Burns' famous heroine "Clarinda," and later, as judge, Lord Craig, the "Provost"; Hon. Henry Erskine, Dean of the Faculty of Advocates; Lord Gillies, judge of the Court of Session; Hon. Alexander Gordon, advocate; Alexander Wight; John Dundas, Edmund Bruce, and William Dallas, Writers to the Signet; Captain Matthew Henderson, subject of an elegy by Burns; John Tennant of Glenconner, farmer, one-time factor for the Dowager Countess of Glencairn, and friend of William Burnes; William Nicol, Latin master of the High School; Allan Masterton, writing master at the High School; James Johnson, an engraver; Alexander Cunningham, lawyer, and, later, jeweler; Robert Cleghorn, a farmer from just outside Edinburgh; and one Williamson of Cardrona.

Anecdotes of Williamson, and of a Dr. Gilbert Stuart, who had died the August before Burns came to Edinburgh, will serve to illustrate the quality of fellowship distinguishing these men. Stuart had been associated with Smellie in getting out the *Edinburgh Magazine and Review*, which his intemperate expressions of "indignation against vice and meanness," and his personal vendettas against prominent people, helped bring to an untimely end, de-

spite Smellie's efforts to moderate Stuart's utterance. In the words
of Robert Kerr, Smellie's biographer, Dr. Stuart

occasionally indulged in fits of extreme dissipation, which ultimately
undermined his constitution, and hurried him to a premature grave.

In the course of one of his rambles, during the publication of the
Edinburgh Magazine and Review, Dr Stuart came one evening to the
house of Mr Smellie in a state of complete intoxication, and was
immediately put to bed. Awakening in the course of the night, he
conceived himself in a brothel, and alarmed the family by repeatedly
vociferating *house! house!* Mr Smellie came as soon as possible to
the bedside of his friend, to learn what he wanted, and endeavoured
to persuade him to go quietly again to sleep. On seeing Mr Smellie
almost naked, and still impressed with the idea of being in a house
of bad fame, he addressed Mr Smellie with great emphasis in nearly
the following words: "Smellie! I never expected to find you in such
a house. Get on your clothes, and return immediately to your wife
and family; and be assured I shall never mention this affair to any
one."

Robert Chambers, in his *Traditions of Edinburgh,* quotes from
a privately printed memoir that Williamson of Cardrona

got rather tipsy one evening after a severe *field-day*. When he came
to the head of Anchor Close, it occurred to him that it was necessary
that he should take possession of the castle [some half mile up the
hill]. He accordingly set off for this purpose. When he got to the
outer gate, he demanded immediate possession of the garrison, to
which he said he was entitled. The sentinel, for a considerable time,
laughed at him; he, however, became so extremely clamorous, that
the man found it necessary to apprise the commanding-officer, who
immediately came down to inquire into the meaning of such impertinent conduct. He at once recognized his friend Cardrona, whom
he had left at the festive board of the Crochallan-Corps only a few
hours before. Accordingly, humouring him in the conceit, he said:
"Certainly you have every right to the command of this garrison; if
you please, I will conduct you to your proper apartment." He accordingly conveyed him to a bedroom in his house. Cardrona took formal possession of the place, and immediately afterward went to bed.
His feelings were indescribable when he looked out of his bedroom

window next morning, and found himself surrounded with soldiers and great guns. Some time afterwards, this story came to the ears of the Crochallans; and Cardrona said he never afterward had the life of a dog, so much did they tease and harass him about his strange adventure.

Burns formed many lasting friendships among this group. Nicol became his travelling companion and spirited correspondent; Masterton and he collaborated on *Willie Brew'd a Peck o' Maut;* Cleghorn remained a most affectionate friend until Burns' death; Cunningham's devotion to Burns led him to attempt raising funds for the widow and children, an effort which drew little sympathy or response from the Patricians. With Johnson, a fellow folk-song enthusiast, Burns got out what is still the best collection of Scots traditional songs, *The Scots Musical Museum.*

By late February, 1787, when approximately the first three hundred pages of Burns' new edition had been printed,* it became evident that the number of subscriptions would require a larger edition than had been planned. As a result, these first pages were reset and additional sheets printed. The later sheets were all printed at once, together with the introductory matter. For bibliographical purists, the Edinburgh edition was then actually two editions, although the content of both is the same. Burns says that the total number of copies printed was three thousand. The book appeared April 17. Thereafter, Burns took an active interest in its distribution, at least partly to save commissions to booksellers. By early May, having done in Edinburgh what he came to do, Burns left, with no better idea of how to make a living than he had had when he arrived. Tenant farming for him had been a bitter experience, but none of his prominent new friends had offered anything at all, except Mr. Miller, who wanted him as a tenant farmer.

Burns seems to have felt that now his large edition had appeared, there would be little further demand for his poems, one

---

* With the famous misprint of "stinking" for "skinking" [watery] in stanza eight of the *Address to a Haggis.*

of the greatest mistakes in the history of publishing. Since Henry Mackenzie apparently agreed with him, the two of them drew up an agreement with Creech accepting Creech's offer to buy Burns' copyright for an added one hundred guineas. The agreement was made the day the poems appeared, April 17. Creech signed a note for the amount on October 23, and finally, at Burns' insistence, paid off the note without interest on May 30, 1788. But it was not until February, 1789, that Burns could report a final settlement of his account with the bookseller, and only then after frequent complaint, although Creech must have made substantial payments to Burns before that time. The delay kept Burns hanging around Edinburgh, cost him money, and hampered his reluctant plans for settling on a farm.

His feelings about Creech are revealed in the "frosty, keen" letter which he wrote him on January 24, 1788.

SIR,
    When a business, which could at any time be done in a few hours, has kept me four months without even a shadow of anything else to do but wait on it, 'tis no very favourable symptom that it will be soon done, when I am a hundred miles absent. — At any rate, I have no mind to make the experiment, but am determined to have it done before I leave Edinr — But why should I go into the country? till I clear with you, I don't know what to do, or what I have in my power to do. — You have declared yourself to the Publick at large, my friend, my Patron; at all times I gratefully own it: I beg you will continue to be so; and rather make a little exertion amid your hurried time, than trifle with a poor man in his very existence; I shall expect to hear from you tomorrow, or next day; and have the honor to be,

                                        Sir,
                                        your very humble ser

On March 25, 1789, Burns wrote of the final settlement to Mrs. Dunlop: "I clear about 440 or 450 £.* — To keep my brother

* Burns seems to have deducted from these sums his living expenses, including his tours, over about two years.

from ruin, and scattering my aged parent & three sisters comfort-
less in the world, I advanced him about 200£ of that money; this
you know was an indispensible affair, as their wellbeing is certainly to me as my own. — What money rests for myself, you will
guess is too little for my own stock; but my Master allows me
some money to build & enclose, & with that, I could have done —
if the farm would have done." In a word, by the time he got all
his much-needed money from Creech, he had found that the farm
would not do for him. What the result would have been had he
had sufficient capital is uncertain, but this is to anticipate. The
significant fact is that Creech had acted characteristically, and
for his own benefit. The *Biographical Dictionary of Eminent
Scotsmen,* originally edited by Creech's fellow townsman, Robert
Chambers, concludes its entry on Creech with the following
paragraph:

In private life Mr. Creech shone conspicuously as a pleasant companion and conversationalist, being possessed of an inexhaustible
fund of droll anecdote, which he could narrate in a characteristic
manner, and with unfailing effect. He thus secured general esteem,
in despite, it appeared, of extraordinary fondness for money, and
penuriousness of habits, which acted to the preclusion not only of
all benevolence and disposition, but even of the common honesty of
discharging his obligations when they were due.

Burns wrote nothing specifically for his new edition except the
wooden *Address to Edinburgh,* and a witty and ironic prose
*Dedication to the Noblemen and Gentlemen of the Caledonian
Hunt,* in which he assumes the role of the Ploughman Poet singing in his country's service, and addressing those who protect
her honor with conscientiousness, courage, knowledge, and public spirit.

MY LORDS, AND GENTLEMEN,
A Scottish Bard, proud of the name, and whose highest ambition is
to sing in his Country's service, where shall he so properly look for

patronage as to the illustrious Names of his native Land; those who bear the honours and inherit the virtues of their Ancestors? — The Poetic Genius of my Country found me as the prophetic bard Elijah did Elisha — at the *plough*; and threw her inspiring *mantle* over me. She bade me sing the loves, the joys, the rural scenes and rural pleasures of my natal Soil, in my native tongue: I tuned my wild, artless notes, as she inspired. — She whispered me to come to this ancient metropolis of Caledonia, and lay my Songs under your honoured protection: I now obey her dictates.

Though much indebted to your goodness, I do not approach you, my Lords and Gentlemen, in the usual stile of dedication, to thank you for past favours; that path is so hackneyed by prostituted Learning, that honest Rusticity is ashamed of it. — Nor do I present this Address with the venal soul of a servile Author, looking for a continuation of those favours: I was bred to the Plough, and am independent. I come to claim the common Scottish name with you, my illustrious Countrymen; and to tell the world that I glory in the title. — I come to congratulate my Country, that the blood of her ancient heroes still runs uncontaminated; and that from your courage, knowledge, and public spirit, she may expect protection, wealth, and liberty. — In last place, I come to proffer my warmest wishes to the Great Fountain of Honour, the Monarch of the Universe, for your welfare and happiness.

When you go forth to waken the Echoes, in the ancient and favourite amusement of your Forefathers, may Pleasure ever be of your party; and may Social-joy await your return! When harassed in courts or camps with the justlings of bad men and bad measures, may the honest consciousness of injured Worth attend your return to your native Seats; and may Domestic Happiness, with a smiling welcome, meet you at your gates! May Corruption shrink at your kindling, indignant glance; and may tyranny in the Ruler and licentiousness in the People equally find you an inexorable foe!

I have the honour to be,

With the sincerest gratitude and highest respect,

My Lords and Gentlemen,

Your most devoted humble servant,

ROBERT BURNS

Edinburgh,
April 4. 1787.

It is to be wondered how many members of the ruling class group thus addressed paid much attention to the Dedication which ridiculed their aristocratic pretensions, or, paying attention, felt its sting, which was a part of Burns' response to his experience of the Patricians. Another response was resentment at being told it was customary and would be expected that he print at his own expense a thirty-six page list of subscribers' names.

To his Edinburgh edition, Burns added five of his religious poems, seven songs, and six poems of importance: *Death and Dr. Hornbook, The Brigs of Ayr, The Ordination,* the *Address to the Unco Guid, Tam Samson's Elegy,* and the *Address to a Haggis.* This last poem, a famous *tour de force,* which has become a *pièce de resistance* on Burns Nights, had been written originally to surprise a party in Ayrshire when Burns recited it as a seemingly impromptu "grace." He used it similarly, probably without the element of surprise, at the home of Andrew Bruce, merchant, in Edinburgh. By the time the Edinburgh volume appeared, the poem had already been printed in the *Caledonian Mercury* and the *Scots' Magazine.*

In the business of getting out his book, Burns was attentive and shrewd. He promoted the edition by publicizing himself as the "heaven-taught Ploughman," a role Mackenzie had assigned in his *Lounger* review. He flattered the "literati" by seeming to consult them, but he wisely paid little attention to their advice. He was prompt with copy and diligent as a proof-reader. The Edinburgh edition added little to his stature as a poet, but it spread his fame throughout the English-speaking world, largely by prompting pirated editions he probably never heard of and certainly got no return from.

But Burns' newly established position hampered his poetic development. He no longer enjoyed the freedom of relative obscurity, or that buoyancy which gives the Kilmarnock poems so much of their enduring appeal. And his very success as a vernacular poet, he wrote to the Rev. Patrick Carfrae, had "brought an inundation of nonsense over the Land. — Subscription bills for Scots Poems have so dunned and daily do so dun the Public that the very term, Scots Poetry, totters on the brink of contempt." With this in mind, he wrote a little later to Lady Elizabeth Cunningham, sister of his friend and patron, Lord Glencairn, "I am aware that though I were to give the world Performances superiour to my former works, if they were productions of the same kind, the comparative reception they would meet with would mortify me. — For this reason I wish still to secure my old friend, Novelty, on my side, by the *kind* of my performances." A year before, he had commented on his novelty to Dr. Moore: "I know that a great deal of my late eclat was owing to the singularity of my situation, and the honest prejudice of Scotsmen."

This search for novelty led Burns to try odes, Popean satires, laments, monodies, political pieces, and much else, with small success, but he never attempted what he mentioned to Lady Elizabeth — drama, and it is likely that he would have failed there, also. For he regarded drama as chiefly a vehicle for sentiments and declamations, and he shows small gift for the complex structure or the character development desirable in good plays. But certainly he secured his old friend Novelty on his side when he turned to the vernacular again in his verse tale *Tam o' Shanter*, and this may well have been a strong motive for his writing that poem.

But Burns' problems as a man were more pressing than those as a poet. The refined women of Edinburgh fascinated him. To one, Margaret Chalmers, he proposed marriage without success; another, Agnes M'Lehose, he might have married, but she was married already. And he had his living to make. Patrick Miller continued to urge that Burns rent a farm on his Dalswinton estate. While well-disposed, Mr. Miller was no Maecenas. He was looking for intelligent farmers who could restore to productivity the neglected lands he had bought, and Burns' first thought of his proposal had been, "Mr. Miller is no Judge of land; and though I dare say he means to favour me, yet he may give me, in his opinion, an advantageous bargain that may ruin me." However, on his way home from Edinburgh, and without committing himself, he stopped to see Mr. Miller's farm. Afterward, he wrote to James Smith, "I cannot settle to my mind. Farming, the only thing of which I know anything, and heaven above knows but little do I understand of that, I cannot, dare not risk on farms as they are. If I do not fix, I will go for Jamaica. Should I stay in an unsettled state at home, I would only dissipate my little fortune, and ruin what I intend shall compensate my little ones for the stigma I have brought on their names."

As a famous man, with money, Burns' position in Mauchline was far different from what it had been when he left seven months before. He wrote to William Nicol, "I never, my friend, thought Mankind very capable of anything generous; but the stateliness of the Patricians in Edinr, and the servility of my plebeian brethren, who perhaps formerly eyed me askance, since I returned home, have nearly put me out of conceit altogether with my species." He repeats his admiration for the independence and defiance of hardship of Milton's Satan. The "mean, servile compliance" of the Armour family disgusted him particularly. He wrote later to Mrs. Dunlop, "I was made very welcome to visit my girl. — The usual consequences began to betray her: and as I was at that time laid up a cripple in Edinr she was turned, literally turned out of doors, and I wrote to a friend to shelter her, till my return."

2. Tours

Before settling himself, and while awaiting a settlement from Creech, Burns took four trips which carried him over much of Scotland. The first, en route from Edinburgh back to Mauchline, was partly with a young lawyer's apprentice, Robert Ainslie, whose high spirits delighted Burns. He wrote Ainslie afterward, "There is one thing for which I set great store by you as a friend, and it is this — that I have not a friend upon earth, besides your-self, to whom I can talk nonsense without forfeiting some degree of his esteem." But, as we shall see, the friendship wore itself out in a few years.

On Saturday, May 5, Burns and Ainslie rode out of Edinburgh, and came to Ainslie's home at Dunse that night. For the next month, Burns was busily entertained by a succession of local worthies as he rode about the beautiful Border country, visiting places of interest.* In his journal (one of two which he kept dur-ing his life), he notes "fine" ruins like those of Roxburgh, Jed-burgh, Dryburgh, and Melrose; he jots down information about farm practices, and prices, and rents; he speaks with enthusiasm of particularly lovely scenery. The many entries about places associated with Scots songs suggest that they were a major in-terest, for by this time Burns had agreed with James Johnson in Edinburgh to provide him with all the songs he could find for the *Scots Musical Museum.*

But, as always, Burns' chief interest was the people he met. The journal opens with a charming account of the Ainslie family, noting that the daughter, Rachel, was an "angel." Burns describes the minister at Dunse as a "revd., rattling, drunken old fellow," and sketches the celebrated traveler, Patrick Brydone, as "a man of quite ordinary natural abilities, ingenious but not deep, chear-ful but not witty, a most excellent heart, kind, joyous, & benev-olent but a good deal of the French indiscriminate complaisance — from his situation past & present an admirer of every thing that has a splendid title or possesses a large estate."

* Besides Dunse, he mentions Kelso, Coldstream, Roxburgh, Jedburgh (where he was made a Burgess), Melrose, Selkirk, Dryburgh, Inverleithing, Earlston, Berwick, Eyemouth (where he went sailing), St. Abb's (where he was "made a royal arch Mason of St. Ebbe's Lodge"), Dunbar; and after Ainslie returned to Edinburgh, a journey across northern England to Carlisle, from which place he returned to Scotland via Gretna, and came to Dumfries (where, also, he was made a Burgess). North of Dumfries he visited Dalswinton, and went on to Mauchline arriving there about June 10. On one occasion, his fame did not excuse him from municipal censure. John Sinton reports that in Carlisle, Burns paid a fine for release of his horse, which had been impounded for straying off limits onto corporation grass. (Sinton, *Burns Excise Officer and Poet,* 4th edition, Glasgow and Edinburgh, 1897. 20–21.)

After visiting a Captain Rutherford, Burns notes, "The Captn.
a specious polite fellow, very fond of money in his farming way,
but showed a particular respect to My Bardship . . . Miss Rutherford a beautiful girl, but too far gone woman to expose so much
of so fine a swelling bosom — her face tho' very fine rather in-
animately heavy." The Rev. Thomas Somerville of Jedburgh
Burns found to be "a man & a gentleman, but sadly addicted to
punning." (When this note was published in 1800, the good man
is said "to have absolutely abandoned punning.")

Burns' adventures with Miss Isabella Lindsay, whom he met
on a walking party, provide some particularly happy passages. A
Mrs. Fair and a Miss Lookup, sisters, "ugly & stupid," attempted
to monopolize him, but he had an eye on "Miss Lindsay, a good-
humor'd amiable girl; rather short et embonpoint, but handsome
and extremely graceful — beautiful hazle eyes full of spirit &
sparkling with delicious moisture — an engaging face & manner,
un tout ensemble that speaks her of the first order of female
minds." Shaking himself free from Mrs. Fair and Miss Lookup,
he "somehow or other got hold of Miss Lindsay's arm," and, he
continues, "Miss seems very well pleased with my Bardship's distinguishing her, and after some slight qualms which I could easily
mark, she sets the titter round at defiance, and kindly allows me
to keep my hold; and when parted by the ceremony of my introduction to Mr Somerville she met me half to resume my situation
— Nota Bene — the Poet within a point and a half of being
damnably in love — I am afraid my bosom still nearly as much
tinder as ever —

"The old, cross-grained, whiggish, ugly, slanderous hag, Miss
Lookup with all the poisonous spleen of a disappointed, ancient
maid, stops me very unseasonably to ease her hell-rankling bursting breast by falling abusively foul on the Miss Lindsays, particularly my Dulcinea; I hardly refrain from cursing her to her
face — May she, for her pains, be curst with eternal desire and
damn'd with endless disappointment." Two days later, Miss Lindsay is of a party which visited Esther Easton, "a very remarkable

Places in Northern Scotland Associated with ROBERT BURNS

(Including those mentioned in his journal of his Highland tour, 1787) woman for reciting Poetry of all kinds, and sometimes making Scotch doggerel herself — She can repeat by heart almost every thing she has ever read, particularly Pope's Homer from end to end — has studyed Euclid by herself, and in short is a woman of very extraordinary abilities — on conversing with her I find her fully to come up to the character given of her — She is very much flattered that I send for her, and that she sees a Poet who has put out a book as she says — She is, among other things, a great Florist — and is rather past the meridian of once celebrated beauty but alas! tho very well married, before that period she was violently suspected for some of the tricks of the Cytherean Déesse."

Burns then presented Miss Lindsay with his picture, "which she accepted with something more tender than gratitude." The end of this summer idyl is tender indeed. "Took farewell of Jedburgh with some melancholy, disagreable sensations — Jed, pure be thy chrystal streams, and hallowed thy sylvan banks! Sweet Isabella Lindsay, may Peace dwell in thy bosom, uninterrupted, except by the tumultuous throbbings of rapturous Love! That love-kindling eye must beam on another, not me; that graceful form must bless another's arms, not mine!" Ten days later he met Miss Betsy Grieve and her sister at Eyemouth, and wrote, "My Bardship's heart got a brush from Miss Betsy."

The heavyweight hosts in various places led him to imagine four of them as a sturdy team of ploughhorses. He also called on a Miss Clark, "a maiden, in the Scotch phrase, 'Guid enough but no brent new,' a clever woman, with tolerable pretensions to remark and wit; while Time had blown the blushing bud of bashful modesty into the full-bosomed flower of easy confidence — She wanted to see what sort of raree show an Author was; and to let him know that though Dunbar was but a little town, yet it was not destitute of people of parts."

On one return to Berrywell, the Ainslie house at Dunse, Burns "found Miss Ainslie all alone," and reflected, "Heavenly Powers

who know the weaknesses of human hearts support mine! what
happiness must I see only to remind me that I cannot enjoy it!"
He imagines the joys of lovemaking with Rachel, and adds later,
"Charming Rachel! may thy bosom never be wrung by the evils
of this life of sorrows, or by the villainy of the world's sons!"
Rachel died unmarried.

Just below his apostrophe to Rachel there are two revealing
comments: "I am taken extremely ill with strong feverish symptoms, & take a servant of Mr Hood's to watch me all night — embittering Remorse scares my fancy at the gloomy forebodings of
death — I am determined to live for the future in such a manner
as not to be scared at the approach of Death — I am sure that I
could meet him with indifference, but for 'The Something beyond
the grave.'

"I go with Mr Hood to see the roup [auction] of an unfortunate
Farmer's stock — rigid Economy & decent Industry, do you preserve me from being the principal Dramatis Persona in such a
scene of horrors!"

In Dumfries, besides the freedom of the burgh, Burns received
a letter from Mrs. James Hog, Buchanan's Land, Canongate, Edinburgh, written for one Meg Cameron, who was "in trouble."
Although his "sincere well-wisher," and apologetic, Meg described
herself as "out of quarters, without friends," her "situation . . .
really deplorable." She begged, "For God's sake, . . . write and let
me know how I am to do." She did not say that Burns was the
father. Burns at once wrote Ainslie a letter which reveals much
of the nature of their friendship. "My first welcome to this place
was the inclosed letter. — I am very sorry for it, but what is done
is done. — I pay you no compliment when I say that except for my
old friend Smith there is not any person in the world I would trust
so far. — Please call at the Jas Hog mentioned, and send for the
wench and give her ten or twelve shillings, but don't for Heaven's
sake meddle with her as a *Piece*. — I insist on this, on your honor;
and advise her out to some country friends. You may perhaps not

like the business, but I just tax your friendship thus far. — Call immediately, or at least as soon as it is dark, for God sake, lest the poor soul be starving. — Ask her for a letter I wrote her just now, by way of token. — it is unsigned. — Write me after the meeting."

The surviving fragment of another letter to Ainslie of June 25 seems to question Burns' responsibility: "The Devil's Day-book only April 14 or fifteen so cannot yet have increased her growth much. I begin, from that, and some other circumstances, to suspect foul play." But when Meg swore out a writ against him for support of her child, he answered and paid. In view of his letter below to Ainslie of July 29, 1787, Meg is probably the "Highland wench in the Cowgate" who surprised Burns by bearing him three bastards at a birth instead of merely the "gallant half Highlander" he speaks of below to Ainslie. There is no further record of Meg Cameron or her child or children.

The occasion of the July 29 letter was the birth of Ainslie's bastard son.

Give you joy, give you joy, My dear brother! may your child be as strong a man as Samson, as wise a man as Solomon, & as honest a man as his father. I have double health & spirits at the news. Welcome, Sir, to the society, the venerable Society, of Fathers!!!

> Lo, Children are God's heritage,
>   The womb's fruit his reward,
> The sons of youth as arrows are,
>   In strong men's hands prepar'd.
>
> Oh, happy is the man that hath
>   His quiver fill'd with those!
> He unashamed in the gate
>   Shall speak unto his foes!

But truce, with the Psalmist! I shall certainly give you a congratulatory Poem on the birthday myself. My ailing child is got better, and the Mother* is certainly in for it again, and Peggy† will bring a

---

* Jean Armour. The ailing child is one of her twins, probably Jean, who died the following autumn.
† Meg Cameron.

gallant half Highlander, and I shall get a farm, and keep them all about my hand, and breed them in the fear of the Lord and an oakstick, and I shall be the happiest man upon earth.

> "Sing, Up wi't, Aily, Aily;
> Sing down wi' kimmerland jock;
> Deil ram their lugs, quo' Willie,
> But I hae scour'd her dock!"   Encore!

Take the following random verses to the tune of Black joke.

> "My Girl she's airy, she's buxom and gay
> Her breath is as sweet as the blossoms in May;
>   A touch of her lips it ravishes quite;
> She's always good natur'd, good humor'd and free;
> She dances, she glances, she smiles with a glee;
>   Her eyes are the lightenings of joy and delight;
> Her slender neck, her handsome waist,
> Her hair well buckl'd, her stays well lac'd,
> Her taper white leg, with an et and a, c,
> For her a,b,e,d, and her c,u,n,t,
>   And Oh for the joys of a long winter night!!!"

A letter I just got from Creech's oblidges me to be in Edinr. against this day, or tomorrow se'nnight, and then what a shaking of hands, and what coveys of *good things*, between you & I! I will call for you at Mitchelson's* the moment I arrive.

> Then, hey, for a merry good fellow;
>   And hey for a glass of good strunt;   *spirits*
> May never we sons of Apollo
>   E'er want a good friend and a ——†

Writing sense is so damn'd dry, hide-bound a business, I am determined never more to have anything to do with it. I have such an aversion to right line and method, that when I can't get over the hedges which bound the highway, I zig-zag across the road just to keep my hand in. I am going to church, and will remember you in my prayers. Farewell.

ROBT. BURNS

* Samuel Mitchelson, lawyer, whom Ainslie served as apprentice-clerk.
† These lines were Burns' concluding stanza to the ballad *I'll tell you a tale of a wife. My Girl she's airy* above, he wrote in 1784 or earlier, and copied into his Commonplace Book.

In mid-June, shortly after he had returned to Mauchline from his Border Tour, Burns set off for the West Highlands, Mary Campbell's country. His route is uncertain and his purpose unrecorded. The previously mentioned letter to Ainslie of June 25 was written from Arrochar, on Loch Long, and it mentions an earlier stop at Inverary, which produced a famous squib:

> Whoe'er he be that sojourns here,
> I pity much his case,
> Unless he come to wait upon
> The Lord their God, 'His Grace.'
>
> There's naething here but Highland pride
> And Highland scab and hunger:
> If Providence has sent me here,
> 'Twas surely in an anger.

Two later records of the journey are happier. One is a ticket bearing that Mr. Burns, of Ayrshire, was "admitted and received a Burgess and Guild Brother" of Dumbarton, on June 29, 1787. The other, a letter to James Smith, reminiscent of Sterne, gives a lively account of Burns' progress down Loch Lomondside.

On our return, at a Highland gentleman's hospitable mansion, we fell in with a merry party, and danced till the ladies left us, at three in the morning. Our dancing was none of the French or English insipid formal movements; the ladies sung Scotch songs like angels, at intervals; then we flew at Bab the Bowster,* Tullochgorum, Loch Erroch Side, &c. like midges sporting in the mottie sun, or craws prognosticating a storm in a hairst day. When the dear lasses left us, we ranged round the bowl till the good-fellow hour of six; except a

---

* "Bab the bowster is an old favorite dance, and never omitted at penny weddings and other rustic balls. As practiced in the West of Scotland, it was rather a lengthy function. A row of men and a row of women faced each other, with one in the middle carrying a bolster. The company sang the refrain: —

> 'Wha learnt you to dance, you to dance, you to dance,
> Wha learnt you to dance, Bab at the bowster, brawly.'

At the close of the stanza, the holder of the bolster, laid it at the feet of one of the opposite sex, and then both knelt and kissed. The process was repeated, until all had participated, or until the company tired of the game." (*The Songs of Robert Burns*, ed. J. C. Dick, London, Edinburgh, and New York, 1903. 429.)

few minutes that we went out to pay our devotions to the glorious lamp of day peering over the towering top of Benlomond. We all kneeled; our worthy landlord's son held the bowl; each man a full glass in his hand; and I, as priest, repeated some rhyming nonsense, like Thomas-a-Rhymer's prophecies I suppose. After a small refreshment of the gifts of Somnus, we proceeded to spend the day on Lochlomond, and reached Dumbarton in the evening. We dined at another good fellow's house, and consequently, pushed the bottle; when we went out to mount our horses, we found ourselves "No vera fou but gaylie yet." My two friends and I rode soberly down the Loch side, till by came a Highlandman at the gallop, on a tolerably good horse, but which had never known the ornaments of iron or leather. We scorned to be out-galloped by a Highlandman, so off we started, whip and spur. My companions, though seemingly gaily mounted, fell sadly astern; but my old mare, Jenny Geddes, one of the Rosinante family, strained past the Highlandman in spite of all his efforts with the hair halter; just as I was passing him, Donald wheeled his horse, as if to cross before me to mar my progress, when down came his horse, and threw his rider's breekless a–e in a clipt hedge; and down came Jenny Geddes over all, and my Bardship between her and the Highlandman's horse. Jenny Geddes trode over me with such cautious reverence, that matters were not so bad as might well have been expected; so I came off with a few cuts and bruises, and a thorough resolution to be a pattern of sobriety for the future.

I have yet fixed on nothing with respect to the serious business of life. I am, just as usual, a rhyming, mason-making, raking, aimless, idle fellow. However, I shall somewhere have a farm soon. I was going to say, a wife too; but that must never be my blessed lot. I am but a younger son of the house of Parnassus, and, like other younger sons of great families, I may intrigue, if I choose to run all risks, but must not marry. . . .

As for the rest of my acts, and my wars, and all my wise sayings, and why my mare was called Jenny Geddes, they shall be recorded in a few weeks hence at Linlithgow,* in the chronicles of your memory, by Robt. Burns.

* Smith had by this time moved from Mauchline to Linlithgow, where Burns planned to visit him on his contemplated Highland Tour, which he began in August. Jenny Geddes was a resolute Presbyterian vegetable seller who objected to the introduction of the new Episcopal service-book on July 23, 1637, and threw a stool at the dean who dared read from it. She aimed so well that the cleric had to duck in the pulpit to avoid being hit. (Chambers, Traditions of Edinburgh, 119–120.)

By July 2, Burns is again at Mauchline, having passed through Paisley on his way from Dumbarton. During July he continued the love affair with Jean Armour which had been renewed in June, and wrote his famous autobiographical letter to Dr. Moore. The recipient of this letter, Dr. John Moore (1729–1802), had published a *View of Society and Manners in France, Switzerland, and Germany* (1779), and *in Italy* (1781). He also published *Medical Sketches* (1786), and a novel, *Zeluco* (1789). Dr. Moore, it may be recalled, was a friend of Mrs. Dunlop, who sent him a copy of Burns' Kilmarnock edition, which he in turn sent to Dr. James Currie, a friend of his son Graham. Another son was the famous Sir John Moore, hero of the battle of Coruña. Dr. Moore admired Burns, and although the two men never met, they exchanged many letters. As an established author, the doctor drew from Burns more respectful address than his position and his friendly but fatuous advice warranted.

By August 7, Burns was back in Edinburgh attempting to pry more money out of Creech, settling the claim of Meg Cameron (August 15), and arranging for a trip through the Highlands with William Nicol (1744–1797), which he had hinted at in his letter of June 30 to Smith. Nicol was a man of ability, given to drink and violent explosions of temper. He caused Burns some moments of embarrassment, but they remained friends until Burns' death, and Burns named a son after him. Nicol, a witty man, irreverent to respectability like Burns, gave the Bard recognition and response and a sympathy with his social and political views, which he found in no one else. The choice of Nicol as a travelling companion was another indirect, and perhaps imprudent,* comment on the Edinburgh gentry. Henry Cockburn, who had been his student, says that Nicol, "though a good man, an intense student, and filled, but rather in the memory than the head, with knowledge, was as bad a schoolmaster as it is possible to fancy. Un-

---

* Mrs. Dunlop wrote Burns in November, 1790, of Nicol, "who, the world says, has already damned you as an author." (RB & Mrs. D, 287.)

acquainted with the nature of youth, ignorant even of the characters of his own boys, and with not a conception of the art of the duty of alluring them, he had nothing for it but to drive them; and this he did by constant and indiscriminate harshness."

There are two other contemporary accounts of Nicol, and Burns, which throw revealing light on their relationship and on the feelings of upper class Edinburgh about each of them. The first, by Alexander Young, of Harburn, W.S., is self-explanatory.

I was just entering into business when Burns came first to Edinburgh; and one of my first clients was his friend Wm. Nicol, one of the masters of the High School, who was the son of a Tailor in the village of Ecclefechan in Annandale, employed and patronized by my Grandfather and his family; which services were zealously returned to me by Mr. Nicol in the line of my profession. I considered him, and, I believe justly, as one of the greatest Latin Scholars of the Age; and when I found him & Burns over their Whiskey-punch, (which I had sometimes the honor of partaking with them) bandying *extempore* translations and imitations of English, Scotch, & Latin Epigrams, I could not help considering them as good exemplifications of the Italian *Improvisatori*.

One remarkable instance still occurs to me. When Burns gave Nicol the following strange epitaph to translate into Latin —

> "Here lies old John Hildebrode
> Have mercy on him, Gude God,
> As he would hae on thee, if he were God
> And thou wert old John Hildebrode."

After a little consideration, Nicol gave furth a Latin edition of this nonsense; which I thought greatly superior to the original. I wrote it down, and long preserved it with some similar dogrel verses; but I now recollect the beginning only: —

> "Hic situs Hilbrodus,
> Quo non miserabilis alter" &c.

At this time, I looked upon Nicol as a far greater Poet and genius than Burns. He had considerable, indeed constant, employment in translating the Medical & Law Theses of the graduates at the University, for which he made liberal charges, but was very ill paid. I was employed by him to recover many of these claims from English students, concerning which I corresponded with the late Mr. Roscoe, (then an Attorney in Liverpool); and on communicating to Nicol some of Mr. Roscoe's letters signifying that several of his claims were considered to be doubtful, if not desperate, he fell into an extravagant rage, swore, the most unseemly oaths & uttered the grossest blasphemies, that "if our Saviour were again on Earth and had employed him to translate a Thesis without paying him for it, he would crucify him over again!" In consequence of these and similar exhibitions, I thought it prudent to detach myself from such companions; but I never had any quarrel with them.

After reading Young's memoranda, his friend the Rt. Hon. Charles Hope, later Lord Granton, added comments of his own.

I met Burns several times at dinner in different Houses, when he first came to Edinr but I was not at all intimate with Him That visit of his to Edinr was a great misfortune to him, & led to all his after follies & misconduct, & ultimately to his ruin & premature death — to all of which his intimacy with Nicol mainly contributed — Nicoll, as you say, was a good Scholar; but I did not consider him as a *better* Scholar than Adam or Fraser — His passions were quite ungovenable, & he was altogether a most unprincipled Savage — He persecuted poor Adam* by every means in his power; & at last was guilty of a brutal Assault on him, for which the Magistrates did not expell him, as they ought to have done — As a specimen of Nicols unprincipled disposition, & at the same time of his Selfish cunning, take the following Anecdote — You Know it was at that time the Custom for the Rector once a Week to go & examine the Class of one of the other Masters, who, at the same time, came to the Rectors Class & examined it — On one of those ocasions, when I was Dux of the Rectors Class, Nicol came to examine us —. He seemed to be in particular good humour, anticipating, I have no doubt, the triumph he expected over the Rector — He went on for some time in the usual way, hearing us translate & construe — He then began to put some difficult questions, which Several of the Boys could not answer, but on putting them to me & other boys at the Head of the Class, they were all answered — At

* Rector of the High School.

last He put a question which neither I nor any other Boy could answer — On which He turned to me & said, You are a pretty fellow, Sir to be at the Head of this School — not to be able to answer this question — I'll show you that your Cousin John Hope (the late Lord Hopetoun) in my Class can answer it, & make you ashamed of yourself — He then called the Janitor & desired Him to call John Hope to come to Him — John came & the Question was put to him, but John could not answer it — Nicol was evidently very angry, but He had the Selfish Cunning not to outrage the Son of Such a Man as Old Lord Hopetoun — So He merely desired Hope to go away & send Elliott, the Herriotter, to Him — Accordingly Elliott came, & the question was repeated to him, but He did not answer it either, on which the Savage lost all command of himself, flew at poor Elliott, seized & shook by both Ears, till He almost tore them off, & quite forgetting himself, exclaimed You Scoundrel, Have I not been dunning this into you for a week past — showing that He had been leading his Boys out of their depth, & attempting to make them get by rote things that they did not understand, in hopes of having it to say, that His Boys only in the third Class were farther advanced than the Rectors — This explosion operated like Electricity on the Class — There was a universal shout & Hiss, & we all ran out of the school, leaving Nicoll frantic but stupefied with rage — So much for Nicol.*

On August 23, Burns wrote from Edinburgh, asking Ainslie to add "Burns" to any name he gave his newly born son ("Zimri Burns Ainslie or Achitophel &c, &c,") and reporting that he and Nicol intended to travel in a chaise. "Nicol thinks it more comfortable than horse-back, to which I say, Amen," he adds. The two planned to take at least three weeks for their tour, and actually spent twenty-two days, covering 600 miles. The pace was hurried at times by Nicol's impatience. Burns' correspondence shows that he would have enjoyed less haste. He had invitations to present, he wanted to collect songs for Johnson, and he particularly wanted to visit his aunts and uncles about Stonehaven and Montrose. His journal reflects his hurry, being often hardly more than staccato jottings, or an itinerary. With digressions, he

* For a more temperate view of Nicol, by Dr. J. M. Adair, see p. 170.

and Nicol went from Edinburgh to Stirling, on up the north road to Inverness, and then east along the Moray Firth, cutting down to Peterhead, and continuing along the coast to Aberdeen, Stonehaven, Montrose, Dundee, Perth, and Queensferry, and so back to Edinburgh on September 16.

Lord Glencairn had given Burns a diamond stylus, and in Stirling he used it to write on a window pane his resentment that the old royal palace had been allowed to fall into disrepair.

> Here Stewarts once in glory reign'd,
> And laws for Scotland's weal ordain'd;
> But now unroof'd their palace stands,
> Their sceptre swayed by other hands:
> Fallen indeed, and to the earth,
> Whence grovelling reptiles take their birth
> The injured Stewart line is gone,
> A race outlandish fills their throne:
> An idiot race, to honour lost —
> Who know them best despise them most.

These sentiments about the reigning house of Hanover were hardly designed to gain Burns political favors from those who had favors to grant.

He and his fellow Jacobite visited Bannockburn and Killiecrankie, where the Scots had slaughtered the English, and Culloden, where the English had slaughtered Prince Charles' remaining supporters. They visited Ossian's grave near Crieff, and at Cawdor were shown the bed on which King Duncan had been murdered. Later they heard "that the muir where Shakespeare lays Macbeth's witch meeting is still haunted." At Scone they viewed a "picture of the Chevalier and his sister — Queen Mary's bed, the hangings wrought with her own hands." They met the famous fiddler Neil Gow and heard him play — "A short, stout-built, honest highland figure, with his grayish hair shed on his honest social brow — an interesting face, marking strong sense, kind openheartedness mixed with unmistrusting simplicity."

As on his Border Tour, Burns notes lovely scenery, ruins, and details about farming, and he is interested in the people he met. At the peak of his fame, he was received in the best houses. A typical entry is that recording his visit to Blair Athole, seat of the Duke of Athole, to whom he had an introduction.

[Friday, August 31] Blair — sup with the Duchess — easy and happy from the manners of the family — confirmed in my good opinion of my friend Walker.

[Saturday, September 1] — visit the scenes round Blair — fine, but spoilt with bad taste — Tilt and Garry rivers — falls on the Tilt — heather seat — ride in company with Sir William Murray and Mr. Walker to Loch Tummel — meanderings of the [Tummel], which runs through quondam Struan-Robertson's estate from Loch Rannoch to Loch Tummel — Dine at Blair — Company — General Murray, *rien* — Captain Murray, an honest Tar — Sir W. Murray, an honest, worthy man, but tormented with the hypochondria — Mrs. Graham, *belle et amiable* — Miss Cathcart — Mrs. Murray, a painter — Mrs. King — Duchess and fine family, the Marquis, Lords James, Edward and Robert — Ladies Charlotte, Amelia and [Elizabeth] — children dance — sup — Duke — Mr. Graham of Fintray — Mr. McLaggan, Mr. and Mrs. Stewart.

Mr. Robert Graham of Fintry was to prove a firm friend to Burns the Exciseman. The poet later visited Sir William Murray at his estate of Ochtertyre. "Walker" was Josiah Walker, whom Burns had met in Edinburgh through Dr. Blacklock; he was now a tutor in the Duke's family. He speaks as do so many others of Burns' "unembarrassed, plain, firm" manner, and reports that he was delighted with the Duke's children, and in turn delighted the company with his toast to them, "honest men and bonie lasses." Of another guest, "a man of a robust but clumsy person," Burns expressed the value he entertained for him "on account of his vigorous talents, although they were clouded at times by coarseness of manners; 'in short,' he added, 'his mind is like his body, he has a confounded strong in-kneed sort of a soul.'"

The Duke was expecting an important guest, Henry Dundas,

Pitt's political lieutenant for Scotland, and wished to keep Burns as "the best dainty with which he could entertain an honored guest." But, though "easy and happy," Burns acceded to Nicol's wishes and left on Sunday, sending back a few days later *The Humble Petition of Bruar Water* to pay his "debts of honour and gratitude."

Henry Mackenzie had given Burns introductions to Sir James Grant of Grant, and to his cousin, Mrs. Elizabeth Rose, of Kilravock. He and Nicol spent half a day with Sir James, dining, and going on "through mist and darkness to Dulsie, to lie." On their way to Fort George and Inverness, they called on Mrs. Rose, and on their way back east, they had breakfast with her, when Burns was delighted to have Miss Rose sing two Gaelic songs for him. Mrs. Rose and a Mr. Grant accompanied the travellers on their way some distance, and the following winter Burns sent her a letter and a volume of the *Scots Musical Museum*. He and Nicol spent that night with a celebrated naturalist, James Brodie of Brodie, who was, as Burns notes, "truly polite, but not just the highlander's cordiality."

At Fochabers, Burns presumed on his former friendship with the Duchess of Gordon to call at Castle Gordon. The journal entry is happy, but it omits some details. "Fine palace, worthy of the noble, the polite, the generous Proprietor — Dine — Company, Duke and Duchess, Ladies Charlotte and Madelina, Colonel Abercrombie and lady, Mr. Gordon and Mr. [*blank*], a clergyman, a venerable aged figure, and Mr. Hoy, a clergyman, I suppose, a pleasant open manner — The Duke makes me happier than ever great man did — noble, princely, yet mild, condescending and affable, gay and kind — The Duchess charming, witty, kind and sensible — God bless them! Come to Cullen to lie." In a letter to James Hoy, the Duke's librarian, Burns laments having been hurried away, and continues, "May that obstinate son of Latin Prose be curst to Scotch-mile periods, and damn'd to seven league paragraphs; while Declension & Conjugation, Gender, Number, and Time, under the ragged banners of Dissonance and Disarrange-

ment eternally rank against him in hostile array!!!!!!" He goes on
to recite his connection with Johnson's *Museum,* and to request
the Duke's words to *Cauld Kail in Aberdeen,* for which he thanks
Hoy in a later letter.

His reference to the "obstinate son of Latin Prose" was, of
course, to Nicol. On arrival at Fochabers, Burns had left his companion at the inn and walked up to the castle, where he was
warmly received and pressed to join the company, just sitting
down to dinner. Burns did, but rose soon and said he must rejoin
Nicol, whereupon the Duke sent a guest with Burns to insist that
Nicol return with them and become one of the party. But Nicol,
infuriated by the seeming neglect, had ordered the chaise to be
hooked up, and stormed that if Burns did not join him, he would
set off alone. Burns joined him and they drove away. At Banff
they breakfasted with a schoolmaster friend of Nicol's, who invited a boy to be present and to serve later as messenger and
guide on a proposed visit to Duff House nearby, mansion of the
Earl of Fife. This lad later remembered that "during breakfast,
Burns played off some sportive jests at his touchy *compagnon de
voyage,* about some misunderstanding which took place between
them at Fochabers, in consequence of Burns having visited the
castle without him."

The next day, Burns notes that they passed "Lord Aberdeen's
seat — entrance denied to every body, owing to the jealousy of
three-score over a kept country-wench." In Aberdeen, which Burns
calls a "lazy town," he met "Bishop Skinner, a non-juror, son of
the author of 'Tullochgorum,' a man whose mild, venerable manner is the most marked of any in so young a man." Bishop Skinner
wrote his father a lively account of this meeting, and his father
sent Burns a rhymed epistle which opened a brief and cordial
correspondence between them. The bishop's letter follows:

Calling at the printing office the other day, whom should I meet on
the stair but the famous Burns, the Ayrshire Bard! And on Mr.
Chalmers telling him that I was the son of *Tullochgorum,* there was
no help but I must step into the inn hard by and drink a glass with

him and the printer. Our time was short, as he was just setting off for the south and his companion hurrying him; but we had fifty "auld sangs" through hand, and spent an hour or so most agreably. — "Did not your father write the *Ewie wi' the crooked horn?*" — "Yes." — "O, an I had the lown that did it!" said he, in a rapture of praise; "but tell him how I love, and esteem, and venerate his truly Scottish muse." On my mentioning *his Ewie*, and how you were delighted with it, he said it was all owing to yours, which had started the thought. He had been at Gordon Castle, and come by Peterhead. "Then," said I, "you were within four Scottish miles of *Tullochgorum's* dwelling." Had you seen the look he gave, and how expressive of vexation; — had he been your own son you could not have wished a better proof of affection. "Well," said he at parting, and shaking me by the hand as if he had been really my brother, "I am happy in having seen you, and thereby conveying my long-harboured sentiments of regard for your worthy sire; assure him of it in the heartiest manner, and that never did a devotee of the Virgin Mary go to Loretto with more fervour than I would have approached his dwelling and worshipped at his shrine." He was collecting on his tour all the "auld Scots sangs" he had not before heard of, and likewise the tunes, that he might get them set to music. "Perhaps," said he, "your father might assist me in making this collection; or, if not, I should be happy in any way to rank him among my correspondents." "Then give me your direction, and it is probable you may hear from him sometime or other." On this he wrote his direction on a slip of paper, which I have enclosed that you may see it under his own hand. As to his personal appearance, it is very much in his favour. He is a genteel looking young man of good address, and talks with as much propriety as if he had received an academical education. He has indeed a flow of language, and seems never at a loss to express himself in the strongest and most nervous manner. On my quoting with surprise some sentiments of the Ayrshire *Plowman,* "Well," said he, "and a plowman I was from youth, and till within these two years had my shoes studded with a hundred *tackets.* But even then I was a reader, and had very early made all the English poets familiar to me, not forgetting the old bards of the best of all poetical books — the Old Testament."

Burns' journal records a visit to Stonehaven, where he met his relations, noting particularly "Robert Burnes, writer . . . , one of those who love fun, a gill, a punning joke, and have not a bad heart — his wife a sweet hospitable body, without any affectation of what is called town-breeding." Burns merely mentions Montrose, where his cousin James Burness lived, a "finely-situated handsome town," but in a letter to his brother Gilbert on his return to Edinburgh, he gives many details of their uncles, aunts, and cousins. "I spent two days among our relations, and found our aunts, Jean & Isbal [his father's sisters] still alive and hale old women, John Caird [husband of Williams Burnes' sister Elspeth], though born the same year with our father, walks as vigorously as I can; they have had several letters from his son in New York. — William Brand [husband of Isbal] is likewise a stout old fellow."

This pleasant visiting was interrupted by Nicol. In a letter to James Burness, Robert laments, "Mr Nicol and Mr Carnegie have taken some freak in their head, and have wakened me just now with the rattling of the chaise to carry me to meet them at Craigie to go on our journey some other road and breakfast by the way. — I must go, which makes me very sorry." On his return to Edinburgh he sent James Burness nine copies of his book to distribute for him.

Below Montrose, Burns went sailing along the coast from Auchmithie to Arbroath, and near Perth he noted "the scene of 'Bessy Bell and Mary Gray,'" and recorded having had "Reflections in a fit of the Colic." After a night at Kinross, the journal closes bleakly, "Come through a cold barren Country to Queensferry — dine — cross the Ferry, and come to Edinburgh."

Once back in the city, Burns turned again to the business of making a living. He had, of course, to choose from the opportunities open to him. So long ago as the previous autumn he had considered the Excise as an escape from farming. The service carried a certain social opprobrium, but the duties were not heavy, the income was respectable and regular, and there was opportunity for promotion to very comfortable positions indeed. But in Burns' day, all government jobs went by political favor, and he could find no one to help him to an Excise appointment. His

Edinburgh patrons felt that the Excise was an unworthy occupation for Scotia's Bard, and that a ploughman poet should naturally return to the romantic and honorable life of a farmer. About
that life, Burns was, as usual, sensible and clear-headed. He wrote
Mrs. Dunlop, "As to a Laird farming his own property; sowing
corn in hope, & reaping it, in spite of brittle weather, in gladness;
. . . 'tis a heavenly life! — but devil take the life, of reaping the
fruits that another must eat."

Since at the moment, however, he had no other practical choice,
he got in touch with Patrick Miller about the farm they had discussed, expressing fear that Mr. Miller might have left Dalswinton
before he could get there. "I am determined," he adds, "not to
leave Edinr till I wind up my matters with Mr Creech, which I
am afraid will be a tedious business."

After two weeks of waiting, he set out on another round of
visits, leaving Edinburgh about October 1 with a friend of Archibald Lawrie, Dr. James McKittrick Adair. Adair seems to have
been a headstrong, roving man, always off to a new start and never
winning through. He wrote for Dr. Currie a pleasant narrative
of his expedition with Burns, notable for the more genial picture
it gives of William Nicol than that projected by Alexander Young
and Lord Granton.

Burns' and Adair's destination was Harvieston, in the Devon
valley, near Stirling, where Burns had gone for a day while on his
tour with Nicol. The attractions there were Margaret Chalmers
and her cousin Charlotte Hamilton, relatives of Gavin Hamilton.
Burns' relations with Margaret were most happy, and his letters to
her are among his best. She told Thomas Campbell, the poet, that
Burns had proposed marriage to her, and the thought of what his
life might have been with her and a comfortable income is provocative. She was not a great deal above him in station, and she
was a woman of charm, intelligence, and literary taste. She and
Burns remained friends after her engagement and marriage to
Lewis Hay, a banker. The family connections here are complex.

Of three Murdoch sisters, Barbara had married Hamilton's father and so had become his step-mother; Euphemia had married a Mr. Chalmers and was now the widowed mother of two daughters, Cochran (Lady Mackenzie) and Margaret; and Charlotte had married John Tait of Harvieston. After her death, leaving a son and a daughter, Mr. Tait invited her sister, Mrs. Hamilton, now widowed also, to live at Harvieston with her son and her daughters Grace and Charlotte (Gavin Hamilton's half-brother and half-sisters), and manage his household until his own daughter grew up. Sometimes, Mrs. Chalmers visited there in the summer also with her daughters. In the latter years of her husband's life, the Chalmers family had lived on a farm near Mauchline, and it is probable that Burns had met Margaret Chalmers before he came to Edinburgh, where he saw her often, sometimes at Dr. Blacklock's.

Of his earlier visit to Harvieston, when Margaret had not been there, Burns had written to Gavin Hamilton, describing one of the pleasantest days of his life, "They are a family, Sir: though I had not any prior tie, though they had not been the brother & sisters of a certain generous friend of mine, I would never forget them. — I am told you have not seen them these several years, so you can have very little idea of what such young folks as they now are." He continues with a happy description of the children, reporting that he cannot speak of Charlotte "in common terms of admiration; she is not only beautiful but lovely." He reproaches Hamilton for not having seen more of such delightful relatives, and adds family gossip.

On the October visit, when Margaret was present, Burns intended to stay at Harvieston only briefly before going on to two other country houses, and then returning. But Adair stayed the fortnight, and paid successful court to Charlotte Hamilton. He reports to Dr. Currie that Burns smashed the window pane at Stirling on which he had written the couplets during his previous visit, and then goes on,

At Stirling we met with a company of travellers from Edinburgh, among whom was a character in many respects congenial with that of Burns. This was Nicol, one of the teachers of the High Grammar-School at Edinburgh — the same wit and power of conversation; the same fondness for convivial society, and thoughtlessness of to-morrow, characterized both; Jacobitical principles in politics were common to both of them; and these have been suspected, since the revolution in France, to have given place in each, to opinions apparently opposite. I regret that I have preserved no *memorabilia* of their conversation, either on this or other occasions, when I happened to meet them together. Many songs were sung; which I mention for the sake of observing, that then when Burns was called on in his turn, he was accustomed, instead of singing, to recite one or other of his own shorter poems, with a tone and emphasis, which though not correct or harmonious, were impressive and pathetic. This he did on the present occasion.

From Stirling we went next morning through the romantic and fertile vale of Devon to Harvieston, in Clackmannanshire, then inhabited by Mrs. Hamilton, with the younger part of whose family Burns had been previously acquainted. He introduced me to the family, and there was formed my first acquaintance with Mrs. Hamilton's eldest daughter, to whom I have been married for nine years. Thus was I indebted to Burns for a connexion from which I have derived, and expect further to derive, much happiness.*

Burns apparently disappointed the Harvieston party by insufficiently fervid appreciation of local scenery. But he relished two incidents which Adair describes. "A visit to Mrs. Bruce of Clackmannan a lady above ninety, the lineal descendant of that race which gave the Scottish throne its brightest ornament, interested his feelings more powerfully. This venerable dame, with characteristical dignity, informed me, on my observing that I believed

---

* Miss Hamilton and Dr. Adair were married November 16, 1789. Dr. Adair's aunt, a Mrs. Burke, writes after his death, to her niece, his sister Anne, Archibald Lawrie's wife [July 24, 1802]: "I am truly sorry to hear that my beloved James was denied the Blessing of domestic happiness . . . he never gave me the least hint of his unhappy situation." In a later letter, of February 18, 1804, she refers to "that oddaty Mrs Adair." (Volume II, *The Lawrie Family*, 60, a MS history by David Balfour Graham Langwell. Most courteously lent the present biographer by the author.)

she was descended from the family of Robert Bruce, that Robert Bruce was sprung from her family. Though almost deprived of speech by a paralytic affection, she preserved her hospitality and urbanity. She was in possession of the hero's helmet and two-handed sword, with which she conferred on Burns and myself the honour of Knighthood, remarking, that she had a better right to confer the title than *some people.*"

On their way back to Edinburgh, the two men visited Dunfermline Abbey. "Here," Adair reports, "I mounted the *cutty stool,* or stool of repentence, assuming the character of a penitent for fornication; while Burns from the pulpit addressed to me a ludicrous reproof and exhortation, parodied from that which had been delivered to himself in Ayrshire, where he had, as he assured me, once been one of seven who had mounted the *seat of shame* together.

"In the court-yard, two broad flag-stones mark the grave of Robert Bruce, for whose memory Burns had more than common veneration. He knelt and kissed the stone with sacred fervour, and heartily . . . execrated the worse than Gothic neglect of the first of Scottish heroes."

While Adair was courting Charlotte Hamilton, Burns went on his intended visits to John Ramsay of Ochtertyre, near Stirling, and to Sir William Murray, at another Ochtertyre, near Crief. Ramsay he had met through Dr. Blacklock, and Sir William had been a guest at Blair Athole during Burns' stay there. By October 8, he was "exceedingly comfortably situated" at Sir William's, after a few days with Mr. Ramsay, whom he hoped to visit again on the tenth on his way back to Harvieston.

"I have been in the company of many men of genius," Mr. Ramsay wrote to Dr. Currie, "some of them poets, but never witnessed such flashes of intellectual brightness as from him, the impulse of the moment, sparks of celestial fire! I never was more delighted, therefore, than with his company for two days, tête-a-tête. In a mixed company I should have made little of him; for, in the gamester's phrase he did not always know when to play off and when to play on. . . . When I asked him whether the Edinburgh Literati had mended his poems by their criticisms, 'Sir,' said he, 'these gentlemen remind me of some spinsters in my country, who spin their thread so fine, that it is neither fit for weft or woof.'" Mr. Ramsay suggested that Burns write poetry descriptive of "beautiful landscapes of rural life and manners," or a play like the *Gentle Shepherd* "which everyone who knows our swains in the unadulterated state, instantly recognizes as true to nature."

On his return to Edinburgh, Burns had expected to go at once to Dumfries, but on October 20 he wrote to Mr. Miller that he had caught such a cold his doctors had ordered him into close confinement. He continues:

From something in your last, I would wish to explain my idea of being your Tenant. — I want to be a farmer in a small farm, about a plough-gang, in a pleasant country, under the auspices of a good landlord. — I have no foolish notion of being a Tenant on easier terms than another. — To find a farm where one can live at all, is not easy — I only mean living soberly, like an old-style farmer, and joining personal industry. — The banks of the Nith are as sweet, poetic ground as any I ever saw; and besides, Sir, 'tis but justice to the feelings of my own heart, and the opinion of my best friends, to say that I would wish to call you landlord sooner than any landed gentleman I know. — These are my views & wishes; and in whatever way you think best to lay out your farms, I shall be happy to rent one of them. — I shall certainly be able to ride to Dalswinton about the middle of next week, if I hear you are not gone.

But he did not visit Dalswinton until late November. Those familiar with Burns' sentiments about landlords may hear overtones of irony in his compliments to Mr. Miller.

3. Clarinda

By early December Burns was back in Edinburgh from his visit to Dumfries, and he expected to leave the city within a few days when two accidents coincided to keep him there until February and to precipitate one of the most famous episodes of his life. He met Agnes Craig M'Lehose, and he wrenched his knee so badly that he could not leave his room for a month, or travel for two months and a half. The accident, caused by a drunken coachman, also led to Burns' finally securing an appointment in the Excise, which he had hoped for on coming to Edinburgh the previous December. One of his doctors, Alexander ("Lang Sandy") Wood, learning that Burns really desired the appointment, set wheels in motion to get it for him. The person chiefly responsible for securing it seems to have been Robert Graham of Fintry, now a member of the Scottish Board of Excise.

In writing to Margaret Chalmers about his appointment, Burns said, "I have chosen this, my dear friend, after mature deliberation. The question is not at what door of fortune's palace shall we enter in; but what doors does she open to us? . . . I got this without any hanging on, or mortifying solicitation; it is immediate bread, and though poor in comparison of the last eighteen months of my existence, 'tis luxury in comparison of all my preceding life: besides, the commissioners are some of them my acquaintances, and all of them my firm friends."

When Burns and Mrs. M'Lehose met, on Tuesday, December 4, they were greatly attracted to each other, and she invited him to tea on December 6, but he found it necessary to postpone the engagement with regret until December 8, Saturday. However, on Saturday morning he suffered his accident, and they were forced to carry on their affair entirely by correspondence until January 4. Even when they began to see one another, they continued to exchange letters frequently. The affair grew fervid, and he who would savor it fully must brace himself to read the full correspondence of Sylvander (Burns) and Clarinda (Mrs. M'Lehose); the Arcadian names were her suggestion. Most of the letters are tiresome, as love letters tend to be, but they reveal a skillful and often comic game of pretence which ended in pathetic frustration. Clarinda had arranged with a friend, Miss Erskine Nimmo (a friend, in turn, of Margaret Chalmers), for an introduction to Burns, and she promptly threw herself at his head. But her orthodox Calvinism, her cautious respectability, and her vulnerable position kept her from satisfying passions she was only too willing to arouse.* She was supporting herself and two small children on two tiny annuities which she would lose in the event of scandal. Burns began the affair with obvious thoughts of another conquest, but soon found himself checked and unable either to break off or to triumph.

Mrs. M'Lehose (1759–1841) was a flirtatious sentimentalist, small, plumpish, and pretty. Having lost her mother and sister in childhood, and being a lively girl, she married at seventeen, against advice, a young law-agent of pleasing manners, James M'Lehose. In a memoir, her grandson, W. C. M'Lehose, describes the consequences of this match.

Married at so early an age, before the vivacity of youth was passed, and, indeed, before it was fully developed, possessed of considerable personal attractions, a ready flow of wit, a keen relish for society, in which her conversational powers fitted her to excel, and a strong love of admiration; she appears to have displeased her husband, because she could not at once forego those enjoyments so natural to her time of life and situation. And he, without any cause, seems to have conceived the most unworthy jealousy, which led him to treat her with a severity most injudicious, and, to one of her disposition, productive of the worst consequences.

After four and a half years of marriage, and three children, one dying in infancy, Mrs. M'Lehose found her husband's treatment unendurable, and returned to her father, Andrew Craig, a Glas-

* Mrs. M'Lehose seems to be the only known woman of Burns' acquaintance to meet the specifications outlined in a letter to Alexander Cunningham of September, 1792: "I remember, in my Plough-boy days, I could not conceive it possible that a noble Lord could be a Fool, or that a Godly Man could be a Knave. — How ignorant are Plough-boys! — Nay, I have since discovered that a *godly woman* may be a ——— !" (F II, #506, 120.)

gow surgeon. A fourth child was born soon thereafter. M'Lehose exercised his rights, and as soon as it was practicable, took her children from her to force her return, but she held out. Before long he exhausted his resources, suffered a period of imprisonment for debt, returned the children, and finally left the country in November, 1784. He never thereafter contributed to the support of his wife and children, except for one remittance of £50, accompanied by grandiloquent directions for his son's education. For a time, the surgeons and the writers of Glasgow each made a small annuity to the neglected wife, but withdrew them when it was found that M'Lehose had a large income in Jamaica. A judgment against him produced no results until his death in 1812, when it enabled his widow to recover funds from an account he had long maintained in London.

Upon her father's death in 1782, Mrs. M'Lehose moved to Edinburgh, where she lived under the protection of her cousin, a lawyer and Burns' fellow-Crochallan, William Craig, later Lord Craig as Judge of the Court of Session. He supplemented her annuities, and supported her after the annuities were withdrawn. Agnes Craig's education had been sketchy and frivolous, but after separation from her husband, she industriously read the best authors, and practiced a polite style. She even wrote passable verses. A woman of quick mind and lively spirit, she led an active social life, and was much concerned with religion.

Like Mrs. Dunlop, she felt distress at outspokenness in Burns' poems, *The Holy Fair* being particularly offensive to her. The temper of her meetings with Burns is suggested by a method of censorship which she says she would have exercised over certain poems had she known him when he was preparing the Kilmarnock edition. "Had Clarinda known you, she would have held you in her arms till she had your promise to suppress them." A comment on their discussions of religion and morals is similar. "If you'd caress the 'mental intelligence' as you do the corporeal frame, indeed, Sylvander, you'd make me a philosopher."

Burns obviously discussed Clarinda with his friend Ainslie, a significant detail in itself, and eventually he took Ainslie to call, thereby initiating a long and cozy relationship between the two, of which there will be more information later. As one solid mark of friendship, Ainslie later took Mrs. M'Lehose's son into his law office.

Clarinda's letters speak of bad conscience on mornings after meetings with Burns, and even report conferences with her spiritual adviser, the Rev. John Kemp, whose imagination was "rich — his feelings delicate — his discernment acute." He talked to her "in the style of a tender parent" anxious for her happiness. Sylvander fumed at the reports of Mr. Kemp. Clarinda and Sylvander exchanged verses, discussed friendship and true love, and religion. She told him of her unhappy marriage, and he told her about Jean and gave her a copy of his autobiographical letter to Dr. Moore to read.

Clarinda had been converted to orthodox Calvinism, but she could not convert Sylvander, who did, however, give her a careful, thoughtful, and sophisticated statement of his theological position, one which combined various departures from orthodoxy.

He who is our Author and Preserver, and will one day be our Judge, must be — not for His sake in the way of duty, but from the native impulse of our hearts — the object of our reverential awe and grateful adoration. He is almighty and all-bounteous, we are weak and dependent; hence prayer and every other sort of devotion. — "He is not willing that any should perish, but that all should come to everlasting life;" consequently it must be in every one's power to embrace His offer of "everlasting life;" otherwise He could not, in justice, condemn those who did not. A mind pervaded, actuated, and governed by purity, truth, and charity, though it does not *merit* heaven, yet is an absolutely necessary prerequisite, without which heaven can neither be obtained nor enjoyed; and, by Divine promise, such a mind shall never fail of attaining "everlasting life:" hence the impure, the deceiving, and the uncharitable exclude themselves from eternal bliss, by their unfitness for enjoying it. The Supreme Being has put the immediate administration of all this, for wise and good ends known to Himself, into the hands of Jesus Christ — a great Personage, whose relation to Him we cannot comprehend, but whose relation to us is that of a Guide and Saviour; and who, except for our own obstinacy and misconduct, will bring us all, through various ways, and by various means, to bliss at last.

Burns here expands his father's belief, and combines the Arminian rejection of absolute predestination with the Arian position that Christ the Son was not consubstantial with the Father, and the Socinian doctrine that denied Christ's divinity but held his birth to be a miracle.

Burns is more explicit about his feelings toward Jesus in a later letter, to Mrs. Dunlop, in which he addresses Jesus Christ as "thou amiablest of characters," and adds, "I trust thou art no Imposter, & that thy revelation of blissful scenes of existence beyond death and the grave is not one of the many impositions which time after time have been palmed off on credulous mankind." He summarizes his position to Clarinda, "My creed is pretty nearly expressed in the last clause of Jamie Deans's grace, an honest weaver in Ayrshire: 'Lord, grant that we may lead a gude life! for a gude life maks a gude end; at least it helps weel!'"

On occasion, Clarinda had to remind Sylvander that she was a married woman, and that she could stand no scandal, and he protested that she misunderstood him. By mid-February, he had promised to be hers for life, which she understood as a promise to "wait" until her husband died. But as soon as Burns got back to Ayrshire and saw Jean's desperate situation, he cleared these sentimental fantasies out of his mind and acted decisively. When she learned of his marriage to Jean, Clarinda was understandably furious, but after some tempestuous interruptions, she resumed her relations with him, and wrote in her diary, December 6, 1831, "This day I can never forget. Parted with Burns in the year 1791, never more to meet in this world. Oh, may we meet in Heaven!" The occasion of their parting was a meeting in Edinburgh before she left for Jamaica in the hope of reconciliation with her husband. But on discovery that he had a native mistress and at least one mulatto child, she returned by the same boat.

If a lyric may be taken as evidence, this final parting from Burns was warm and tender.

> O May, thy morn was ne'er sae sweet
> As the mirk night o' December!
> For sparkling was the rosy wine,
> And private was the chamber,
> And dear was she I dare na name,
> But I will ay remember.

Even in good plain prose, however, Burns wrote his Nancy, no longer Clarinda, some letters after their parting which can only mean that they had returned to their old intimacy. On December 11, 1791, she is "my dearest Nancy," and a little later, "a creature very extraordinary," a lock of whose hair he is having put in a ring. On December 27, she is his "ever dearest Nancy," and he sends her the only good lines she ever inspired,

> Had we never lov'd sae kindly,
> Had we never lov'd sae blindly,
> Never met — or never parted —
> We had ne'er been broken hearted.

When Burns was finally able to leave Edinburgh on February 18, 1788, at the very height of his affair with Clarinda, he went to Glasgow "crazed with thought and anxiety," and had a happy meeting with his old Irvine friend Richard Brown, now a sea captain, and then on to Mauchline via Paisley and Kilmarnock, with a two day visit at Dunlop House. He complained of having to fight his "way severely through the savage hospitality of this country," where the object of all hosts was "to send every guest drunk to bed if they can." His letters to Clarinda became less frequent. One of February 23 from Mossgiel which reveals his impressions of Jean, and pays compliments to Clarinda, she showed

James Grierson in 1830! "I, this morning as I came home, called for a certain woman. — I am disgusted with her; I cannot endure her! I, while my heart smote me for the prophanity, tried to compare her with my Clarinda: 'twas setting the expiring glimmer of a farthing taper beside the cloudless glory of the meridian sun. — Here was tasteless insipidity, vulgarity of soul, and mercenary fawning; there, polished good sense, heaven-born genius, and the most generous, the most delicate, the most tender Passion. — I have done with her, and she with me." His report of the meeting to Ainslie, written in late February or early March reveals other and more compelling sentiments about Jean,* of whom Burns wrote to Brown March 7, "I found Jean — with her cargo very well laid in; but unfortunately moor'd, almost at the mercy of wind and tide: I have towed her into convenient harbour where she may lie snug till she unload;† and have taken command myself — not ostensibly, but for a time in secret. — I am gratified by your kind enquiries after her; as after all, I may say with Othello —

'Excellent wretch!
'Perdition catch my soul but I do love thee!' "

That neither of his heroines bore too heavily on Burns' mind is suggested by a letter he wrote to Clarinda (addressing her as "My dear Madam") five days after leaving Edinburgh, and before he had seen Jean. Of his visit to Paisley, he says,

My worthy, wise friend, Mr. Pattison, did not allow me a moment's respite. — I was there ten hours; during which time I was introduced to nine men worth six thousands; five men worth ten thousand; his brother, richly worth twenty thousands; and a young Weaver who will have thirty thousands good when his father, who has no more children

* Quoted in Profile, pp. 7–8.
† Four days before the date of this letter to Brown, on March 3, Jean had already born a second set of twins; one of them died March 10, and the other March 22.

than the said Weaver and a Whig-kirk,* dies. — Mr P—— was bred a zealous Anti-burgher; but, during his widowerhood, he has found their strictness incompatible with certain compromises he is often obliged to make with those Powers of darkness, the devil, the world and the flesh; so he, good, merciful man! talked privately to me, of the absurdity of eternal torments, the liberality of sentiment in indulging the honest instincts of Nature, the mysteries of Concubinage, &c. He has a son, however, that at sixteen has repeatedly minted at certain priviledges, — only proper for sober, staid men, who can use the *good things* of this life without *abusing* them; but the father's parental vigilance has hitherto hedged him in, amid a corrupt and evil world. His only daughter, who, "if the beast be to the fore, and the branks [bridle] bide hale," will have seven thousand pound, when her old father steps into the dark Factory-Office of Eternity with his well-thrumm'd web of life; has put him again and again in a commendable fit of indignation by requesting a harpsichord — "O, these damn'd boarding-schools!" exclaims my prudent friend; "she was a good spinner and sower, till I was advised by her foes and mine to give her a year of Edinr!"

After two bottles more, my much-respected friend opened up to me a project, a legitimate child of Wisdom and Goodsense: 'twas no less than a long-thought-on and deeply-matur'd design to marry a girl, fully as elegant in her form as the famous Priestess whom Saul consulted in his last hours; and who had been 2d maid of honor to his deceased wife. — This, you may be sure, I highly applauded; so I hope for a pair of gloves by and by.

During the month after he left Edinburgh, Burns was much torn. There was Jean, whom he decided to marry; there was Clarinda, still delicious, with whom he must break off; there was Mr. Miller's farm to be decided about; there was his Excise commission to be negotiated; and there was William Creech. Having installed Jean in a room provided by Dr. M'kenzie, with her mother to care for her, he hurried off once more to survey the farm with his friend John Tennant of Glenconner. " 'Tis merely out of Compliment to Mr Miller," he writes Clarinda, "for I know the

* A reference to expectations from his estate of the Whig (Cameronian) Kirk.

Excise must be my lot." Before leaving Edinburgh he had written
Margaret Chalmers, "I have altered all my plans of future life. A
farm that I could live in, I could not find; and, indeed, after the
necessary support my brother and the rest of the family required,
I could not venture on farming in that style suitable to my feelings. You will condemn me for the next step I have taken: I have
entered into the Excise. I stay in the West about three weeks, and
then return to Edinburgh for six weeks' instructions; afterwards,
for I get employ instantly, I go où il plait à Dieu — et mon Roi."
   But Tennant "staggered" Burns with a favorable judgment of
Ellisland farm, and he decided to rent it, keeping his Excise commission in case the farm proved a bad bargain, as he still feared
it might. Tennant's judgment of the land and the lease was probably sound enough, but Burns had no stomach for the long period
of development which Ellisland needed, nor the capital for it,
particularly in the style suitable to his feelings. By October, 1791,
he was writing to Peter Hill, Creech's old clerk, now in business
for himself, that prospects for an Excise supervisorship (what he
had had his eye on all the time) were good, but that he had not
been so fortunate in his farming. "Mr. Miller's kindness has been
just such another as Creech's was but this for your private ear."
   On Monday, March 10, Burns left for Edinburgh, via Glasgow,
collecting some money owed him en route; on March 13 he agreed
on terms of a lease with Mr. Miller (the lease being signed March
18), and by March 17 he wrote Clarinda, "My Excise affair is just
concluded." By the twentieth, after another session of "racking
shop accounts with Mr Creech," he is back in Glasgow on his way
to Ayrshire. During the week he had spent in Edinburgh, he told
Clarinda nothing of Jean, continued fervent meetings with her
(calling her his "dearest angel," and saying he loves her, has
loved her, and will love her to death, through death, and forever),
and gave her a pair of drinking glasses as a parting gift. It is small
wonder that he writes to Richard Brown apologizing for having
neglected a commission because "watching, fatigue, and a load

of Care almost too heavy for [his] shoulders, have in some degree
actually fever'd" him; by some of his experiences, probably those
with Creech, he "was convulsed with rage."

When Clarinda heard he was married — how is not known,
probably through Ainslie — she eventually wrote Sylvander ac-
cusing him of "perfidious treachery" and calling him a "villain."
He replied March 9, 1789,* that he had saved her from herself.

The letter you wrote me to Heron's carried its own answer in its
bosom: you forbade me to write you, unless I was willing to plead
guilty to a certain Indictment that you were pleased to bring against
me. — As I am convinced of my own innocence, and though conscious
of high imprudence & egregious folly, can lay my hand on my breast
and attest the rectitude of my heart; you will pardon me, Madam, if
I do not carry my complaisance so far as humbly to acquiesce in the
name of, Villain, merely out of compliment even to YOUR opinion;
much as I esteem your judgment, and warmly as I regard your worth.
— I have already told you, and I again aver it, that at the Period of
time alluded to, I was not under the smallest moral tie to Mrs B——;
nor did I, nor could I then know, all the powerful circumstances that
omnipotent Necessity was busy laying in wait for me. — When you
call over the scenes that have passed between us, you will survey the
conduct of an honest man, struggling successfully with temptations the
most powerful that ever beset humanity, and preserving untainted

---

* A letter written in August, 1788, has not survived, but Burns describes the
occasion of it to Ainslie, August 23. "I don't know if ever I told you some
very bad reports that Mrs Mc[Leho]se once told me of Mr Nicol. I had mentioned the affair to Mr Cruickshank, in the course of conversation about our
common friend, that a lady had said so & so, which I suspected had originated
from some malevolence of Dr Adams. — He had mentioned this story to Mr
Nicol cursorily, & there it rested; till now, a prosecution has commenced between
Dr A—— & Mr N——, & Mr N—— has press'd me over & over to give up the
lady's name. — I have refused this; & last post Mr N—— acquaints me, but in
very good natured terms, that if I persist in my refusal, I am to be served with
a summonds to compear & declare the fact. —
"Heaven knows how I should proceed! I have this moment wrote Mrs
Mc——se, telling her that I have informed you of the affair; & I shall write
Mr Nicol by Tuesday's post that I will not give up my female friend till
further consideration; but that I have acquainted you with the business & the
name; & that I have desired you to wait on him, which I intreat, my dear Sir,
you will do; & give up the name or not, as You & Mrs Mc——se's prudence shall
suggest." (F I, #266, 250.)

honor in situations where the austerest Virtue would have forgiven a fall — Situations that I will dare to say, not a single individual of all his kind, even with half his sensibility and passion, could have encountered without ruin; and I leave you to guess, Madam, how such a man is likely to digest an accusation of perfidious treachery!

Was I to blame, Madam, in being the distracted victim of Charms which, I affirm it, no man ever approached with impunity? — Had I seen the least glimmering of hope that these Charms could ever have been mine — or even had not iron Necessity — but these are unavailing words. —

I would have called on you when I was in town,* indeed I could not have resisted it, but that Mr Ainslie told me that you were determined to avoid your windows while I was in town, lest even a glance of me should occur in the street. —

When I have regained your good opinion, perhaps I may venture to solicit your friendship, but be that as it may, the first of her Sex I ever knew shall always be the object of my warmest good wishes.

In February, 1790, there was an acidulous exchange of letters, in one of which Burns sent Mrs. M'Lehose a song, *My Lovely Nancy*. And in October, 1790, Robert Ainslie visited Burns at Ellisland and sent a report of him to the still angry lady, with whom Ainslie is obviously on excellent terms.

Dumfries 18th Octr. 1790

I promised to write my Dear Friend and for that End now Seat myself at Dumfries — I have been with Burns since Friday — and as his duty as Exciseman engaged him this day, I have taken the Opportunity of coming here to Visit this Town — You desired that I should let you hear every thing regarding him & his family and how I was pleased — This is a difficult question as my short room here will not permitt me to be so full as I might — and part of the question admitts of Double Answers — I was pleased with Burns' hearty welcome of me — and it was an addition to his pleasure, that my Arrival was upon his *Kirn* night [harvest supper], when he Expected some of

---

* In February, 1789, he had visited Edinburgh to settle with Creech, and for another reason which will appear below.

his friends to help make merry, but much displeased with the Company when they arrived — They consisted of a Vulgar looking Tavern keeper from Dumfries; and his Wife more Vulgar — Mr. Miller of Dalswinton's Gardener and his Wife — and said Wife's Sister — and a little fellow from Dumfries, who had been a Clerk — These were the strangers, and the rest of the Company who are inmates of the house were Burns' Sister, and Mrs. Burns' Sister, who are Two common looking Girls who act as their Servants — and 3 Male and female cousins who had been Shearing for him — We spent the evening in the common way on Such occasions of Dancing, and Kissing the Lasses at the end of every dance — With regard to the helpmate She seems Vulgar & Common-place in a considerable degree — and pretty round & fat — She is however a kind Body in her Own way, and the husband Tolerably Attentive to her — As to the house, it is ill-contrived — and pretty Dirty, and *Hugry Mugry* — Tho last, not least Our Friend himself is as ingenious as ever, and Seem'd very happy with the Situation I have described — His Mind however now appears to me to be a great Mixture of the poet and the Excise Man — One day he Sitts down and Writes a Beautiful poem — and the Next he Seizes a cargo of Tobacco from some unfortunate Smuggler — or Roups out some poor Wretch for Selling liquors without a License From his conversation he Seems to be frequently among the Great — but No Attention is paid by people of any rank to his wife — Having found that his farm does not answer he is about to Give it up, and depend wholly on the Excise —

Now, having given you such a description of those you wished to hear of, As to myself, that Cursed melancholy, which I was complaining of, has been daily increasing — and All Burns' Jokes cannot dispell it — I sit silent & frail even amidst Mirth — and instead of that joyous Laugh which I used to have I frequently discover the Tear start into my Eyes, and Sigh most piteously — I know of no Sufficient reason for Such Misery, but the Effect of constitution, and am Sorry now to be Obliged to go among absolute Strangers — Nothing under the Sun would be so agreable as Seing you, and a letter from you would be the next Best — If you write to me, address to me to be left till called for at the post office of *Ayr*, where I shall be in a few days — and for fear of Accidents in that country, you may use the letter A or any such if you speak of Burns.

Burns & I drunk your health on Saturday at an inn & to Settle the

matter Got both Exceedingly drunk — you need say nothing of this
letter to any Body

yours most affectionately

R. AINSLIE

Mrs. M'Lehose
Lamont's Land
Canongate
Edinr.

Despite its underhandedness and patronizing tone, this letter
is certainly the best service Ainslie ever did Burns' memory. It
gives a unique and happy picture of peasant farmer Burns enjoying a party at home. The appreciative critic should never forget
that Burns was, in Henley's phrase, "essentially and unalterably
a peasant," and it is as a reminder of this cardinal fact that Ainslie's letter is of notable importance.

There are two recorded letters from Burns to Ainslie after this
date, both friendly, and a final comment on him in the last letter
from Burns to Clarinda in 1794.

My old Friend, Ainslie, has indeed been kind to you. — Tell him, that
I envy him the power of serving you. — I had a letter from him a
while ago, but it was so dry, so distant, so like a card to one of his
clients, that I could scarce bear to read it, & have not yet answered
it. — He is a good, honest fellow; and *can* write a friendly letter,
which would do equal honor to his head & his heart, as a whole sheaf
of his letters I have by me will witness; & though Fame does not blow
her trumpet at my approach *now* as she did *then,* when he first
honored me with his friendship, yet I am as proud as ever; & when I
am laid in my grave, I wish to be stretched at my full length, that I
may occupy every inch of ground I have a right to.

Mrs. M'Lehose continued to write, with some bitterness, but
she sent Burns one of her poems early in 1791. He replied wist-
fully, sending her *Sweet Sensibility how charming.* Then in November, 1791, she made a discovery which must have wrenched
her. During the delirious winter of 1788, upon leaving her, Burns

had often sought out a serving girl, one Jenny Clow, who had born him a son the following November, and whose suit for support he had answered during his visit to Edinburgh of February, 1789, when Clarinda said she would not even go near her windows for fear of seeing him. Now ill, destitute, and probably dying, this girl had found out Mrs. M'Lehose, and through her, sent an appeal to Burns for assistance. After describing Jenny's plight, Mrs. M'Lehose adds nastily, "You have now an opportunity to evince you indeed possess those fine feelings you have delineated, so as to claim the just admiration of your country. I am convinced I need add nothing farther to persuade you to act as every consideration of humanity as well as gratitude must dictate. I am, sir, your sincere well-wisher."

Burns replied November 23, with some clumsy irony, in the third person. The significant paragraph reads,

Mrs. M—— tells me a tale of the poor girl's distress that makes my very heart weep blood. I will trust that your goodness will apologize to your delicacy for me, when I beg of you, for heaven's sake, to send a porter to the poor woman — Mrs. M., it seems, knows where she is to be found — with five shillings in my name; and, as I shall be in Edinburgh on Tuesday first, for certain, make the poor wench leave a line for me, before Tuesday, at Mr. Mackay's White Hart Inn, Grassmarket, where I shall put up; and before I am two hours in town, I shall see the poor girl, and try what is to be done for her relief. I would have taken my boy from her long ago, but she would never consent.

I shall do myself the very great pleasure to call for you when I come to town, and repay you the sum your goodness shall have advanced.

There is no further information about Jenny Clow and her son.

During this visit to Edinburgh, there was a reconciliation between Burns and his "dearest Nancy," and their final meeting, when he must have learned of her intention to rejoin her husband. She sailed in February, 1792, arrived in Jamaica in April, and was back in Edinburgh by August, her health temporarily impaired. He wrote her the next spring inquiring about her health, and sending her a book;* and again in 1794 reporting that when he was asked to propose a toast, he always offered "Mrs. Mac." He is writing with a bottle by him on the table, and he has recently quarreled with Maria Riddell. Mrs. M'Lehose is still "ever dearest," and his "lovely Clarinda." The letter includes his unhappy Monody and Epigram provoked by the quarrel with Mrs. Riddell, and asks Clarinda's opinion of them.

The record does not close even here. After Burns' death, Agnes M'Lehose wanted her letters back, and on September 19, 1796, Alexander Cunningham (1763?–1812) in Edinburgh wrote John Syme in Dumfries, "I have today had another call from a Mr Ainslie W.S. *whom I suspect does* Mrs McLehose's business demanding her Letters — he wished very much to introduce me to her which I declined for two reasons — I never accept of an invitation from any Man without intending to make the retort courteous & his manners and behavior† seem quite opposite to what I would wish to meet with even in a common acquaintance besides involving me in an introduction to a Woman who for aught I know may be as chaste as Diana but who bears a quisquis‡ character in the World & which might lead to many perplexities."

Cunningham wanted permission to publish the Clarinda correspondence in the edition he and Syme were promoting to raise money for Burns' family, but Mrs. M'Lehose refused. In a further effort to secure permission, Syme asked Maria Riddell to see what she could do, and the two ladies exchanged enthusiastic letters about their "archangel," as Mrs. Riddell called him. Later,

---

* Burns' note to his transcript of this letter in the Glenriddell MS calls it "fustian rant of enthusiastic youth," a fair enough description but purposefully deceptive dating.

† Ainslie became for many years an elder of the Old Kirk, St. Giles, and wrote *A Father's Gift to his Children* and *Reasons for the Hope that is in us*. (*The Land of Burns*, I, 89.)

‡ In *James Currie The Entire Stranger and Robert Burns*, p. 334, Professor Robert D. Thornton prints the following footnote: "In the N.L.S., MS. 587 (1181), an undated letter from Ainslie to Mrs. M'Lehose, Ainslie speaks of the 'end of the week which you have appointed as the Termination of my Banishment.'"

she regretted her exuberance, and did not wish it known that she had corresponded with Clarinda. She writes to Dr. Currie, May 6, 1800, "I hope you have kept my correspondence with Clarinda *entre nous*. I have had the ingenuity to get back my letters, alleging their utility for furnishing information to Burns's biographer, and I have heard some circumstances of our Bard's heroine that have rather diminished my Sentimental ardour! And I was a little afraid for the future sake of those rare epistles of mine, which might, all things considered, have placed me in an awkward predicament."

Mrs. M'Lehose continued as a bright and active member of her social circle for forty years, and was described at seventy as "a well looked little woman" by James Grierson. She survived her children, all of her grandchildren except one, and most of her friends. Her grandson, W. C. M'Lehose, writes of her, "When later years thinned the ranks of her friends, and diminished the number of her invitations, it was with great difficulty she became reconciled to a more retired mode of life." In her last years her mind remained clear and alert, but she lost her memory. She died October 22, 1841, aged 82.

Although Burns had acknowledged Jean as his wife* by living with her publicly, she and he went through a ceremony of marriage in Gavin Hamilton's office, a few doors from their room, before a Justice of the Peace. And on August 5, "they both acknowledged their irregular marriage" before the Kirk Session, expressed sorrow, were rebuked, and absolved of any scandal, Burns giving a guinea for the poor on the occasion.

In June 1788 he wrote Ainslie, "Were it not for the terrors of my ticklish situation respecting provision for a family of children, I am decidedly of opinion that the step I have taken is vastly for my happiness. As it is, I look to the Excise scheme as certainty of

---

* James Grierson, in 1829, reports Clarinda as follows: "Burns in marrying Jean Armour behaved better than Jean could have expected — but B said in the situation she was and hurried out of doors by her father what could he do." (Fitzhugh, 41.) Compare Burns' letter to Clarinda of March 9, 1789, pp. 182–83.

maintenance; a maintenance, luxury, to what either Mrs. Burns or I was born to." And on September 9, he opens his mind to his old friend and fellow-student of French, the engraver John Beugo, "You do not tell me if you are going to be married. — Depend upon it, if you do not make some damned foolish choice, it will be a very great improvement on the Dish of Life. — I can speak from Experience, tho' God knows, my choice was as random as Blind-man's-buff. I like the idea of an honest country Rake of my acquaintance, who, like myself, married lately. — Speaking to me of his late step, 'L——d, man,' says he, 'a body's baith cheaper and better sair't [served]!' "

He comments in a different tone to Mrs. Dunlop. "The most placid good-nature — & sweetness of disposition; a warm heart, gratefully devoted with all its powers to love [me deleted] one; vigorous health & sprightly chearfulness, set off to the best advantage by a more than common handsome figure; these, I think, in a woman, may make a tolerable good wife, though she should never have read a page but the Scriptures of the Old & New Testament, nor have danced in a brighter Assembly than a Penny-pay Wedding."

After getting his appointment to the Excise and leasing his farm* and marrying Jean, Burns set vigorously and sensibly about doing what was to be done. Mr. Miller had made him an allowance for improvements, and he contracted with a Dumfries builder for a farmhouse at Ellisland. To qualify for duty as an Exciseman, he took instructions† from James Findlay, Excise officer at Tarbolton, in April and May. He busied himself securing furniture and stocking his farm. Memory of the Edinburgh excitement brought nostalgia at times, but he had foreseen that his vogue would be brief. He wrote to the "Colonel" of the Crochallans, William Dunbar, "I have dropt all conversation and all read-

---

* For 76 years, the first three at £50, the rest at £70.
† Burns' commission was dated July 14, 1788, but he did not go on duty then. (Snyder, 314–315.)

ing (prose reading) but what tends in some way or other to my serious aim," but he expresses pleasure at Dunbar's offer of correspondence.

The great days were over, and if things were now not just as he would have liked them to be, he recognized that his poetry and his fame were owing to the same causes as his discouragement and frustration — that is, to his temperament and his lot in life. In his work, as in his life, Burns is a vivid symbol of the desperation most men feel. If for him the desperation was not so quiet at times, and if he sought relief, be it noted that he lived his life forthrightly. After his death, William Nicol made a wry and pointed comment about Burns' "firmness." "The Fanatics have now got it into their heads, that dreadful bursts of penetential sorrow issued from the heart of our friend, before he expired. But if I am not much mistaken in relation to his firmness, he would disdain to have his dying moments disturbed with the sacerdotal gloom & the sacerdotal howl. He knew that he would negotiate wt. God alone, concerning his immortal interests." And Burns' friend, James Gray, echoes Maria Riddell. "Though he was often well nigh broken-hearted by the severity of his fate yet he was never heard to complain."

V

MARRIED MAN

To make a happy fireside clime
To weans and wife,
That's the true pathos and sublime
Of human life.

BURNS, *Epistle to Dr. Blacklock*
Ellisland, 21st Oct., 1789

The dramatic climax of Burns' life was the 1786–1788 period of his Kilmarnock volume and his Edinburgh residence. But the subsequent eight years offer rich biographical materials for an understanding of the private man — of his daily life, his friendships, his social and political views, his livelihood, his household, the wide range of his interests, the quality of his mind and spirit. And they reveal the irony that he lived these years under the burden of an unrecognized but debilitating and fatal illness.

Summary judgments and dramatic foreshortenings can only distort seriously, as they have done in the past, the complex truth of Robert Burns during these years. Hence the Boswellian narrative which follows.

Burns' major interest during this period was Scots song. Section VI offers a full and detailed account of his achievement, in both music and lyrics, as a song collector and song writer.

1. Aftermath

In January, 1788, while recovering from his knee injury and thinking of his prospects, Burns wrote Mrs. Dunlop, "Lately I was a sixpenny private, and, God knows, a miserable soldier enough; now I march to the campaign, a starving cadet: a little more conspicuously wretched.

"I am ashamed of all this; for though I do want bravery for the warfare of life, I could wish, like some other soldiers, to have as much fortitude or cunning as to dissemble or conceal my cowardice."

He never achieved the relatively comfortable refuge from life's "warfare" which he yearned for, and, being the man he was, he probably could not have, but during the next few years, Burns made a successful marriage, he secured a steady income, and he improved materially on his previous standard of living. With canny vigilance he continued to pursue advancement in the Excise service by recommending himself to his superiors and by soliciting favor from influential friends. His prospects for promotion to a well-paid position were good when he died. Ever mindful of his responsibilities to Jean and his children, Burns lived his last seven years as a low-grade civil servant who looked forward to an upper-grade sinecure in time. His occupation in these years was not congenial to him, but better than tenant farming, and no other choices presented themselves except an offer of work on the London *Morning Chronicle* in 1794, a position which he felt was too insecure to risk.

Burns continued to write poetry after 1786, but produced only a handful of important poems, including his most important one of all, *Tam o' Shanter*. His great interest and satisfaction lay in providing songs for two editors, James Johnson and George Thomson. Johnson, barely literate, simply and gratefully took what Burns sent him for the *Scots Musical Museum,* and between them they produced a collection which Burns correctly predicted would "defy the teeth of time."

Thomson and his book, a *Select Collection of Original Scotish Airs*, were different. He had no taste for folk song, and planned an elegant work for a polite audience, preferring English words and insisting on drawing room decorum. He was forever suggesting improvements to Burns, one of which resulted in an egregious and now forgotten version of *Scots Wha Hae*. Burns complied with Thomson's requests amiably when he could, but often refused just as amiably. "I have long ago made up my mind as to my own reputation in the Business of Authorship," he wrote Thomson, "& have nothing to be pleased, or offended at, in your adoption or rejection of my verses." By refusing all payment, Burns retained complete independence, saying that his songs might be considered "either *above*, or *below* price," and that "to talk of money, wages, fee, hire &c. would be downright Sodomy of Soul!"

The most generous term for Thomson's treatment of Burns is paltry. Once his contributor was dead, Thomson felt free to alter texts at will, as, indeed, he did harmonies which he commissioned from Beethoven. He ignored Burns' wishes and instructions, he made an unsubstantiated claim to exclusive copyright in the songs Burns had sent him, and he inked out passages in Burns' letters to him which he found unpleasant and which posterity finds revealing about his chicanery. Different rates of fading helped DeLancey Ferguson to discover this device in 1928, after Thomson had enjoyed a century and a quarter's reputation for generosity in making the correspondence available.

But Thomson left one surprising docket. When, a week before his death, Burns was being severely dunned by a tailor for the cost of his Volunteer's uniform, he turned to Thomson, among others, for help. "After all my boasted independence," he wrote, "curst necessity compels me to implore you for five pounds. — A cruel scoundrel of a Haberdasher to whom I owe an account, taking it into his head that I am dying, has commenced a process, & will infallibly put me into jail. — Do, for God's sake, send me that sum, & that by return of post. — Forgive me this earnestness, but the horrors of a jail have made me half distracted. — I do not ask all this gratuitously; for upon returning health, I hereby promise & engage to furnish you with five pounds' worth of the neatest song-genius you have seen. O I tryed my hand on Rothiemurche this morning. — The measure is so difficult, that it is impossible to infuse much genius into the lines — They are on the other side. Forgive me!"

Thomson sent the five pounds, but noted on Burns' letter, "This idea is exaggerated — he could not have been in any such danger at Dumfries nor could he be in such necessity to implore aid from *Edinr.*"

"On the other side" was

> Fairest maid on Devon banks,
>   Crystal Devon, winding Devon,
> Wilt thou lay that frown aside,
>   And smile as thou wert wont to do?
>
> Full well thou know'st I love thee dear —
> Couldst thou to malice lend an ear!
> O, did not Love exclaim: — "Forbear,
>   Nor use a faithful lover so!"
>
> Then come, thou fairest of the fair,
> Those wonted smiles, O, let me share,
> And by thy beauteous self I swear
>   No love but thine my heart shall know!

This song, reminiscent of Peggy Chalmers and days at Harvieston in the Devon valley, was his last.

Thomson capped his relations with the man who had been so generous to him by writing an ill-informed and patronizing obituary which did Burns' memory severe and lasting and gratuitous injury. But happily Burns knew nothing of that. James Johnson, a very poor man, subscribed four pounds for the relief of Burns' widow. George Thomson, two guineas.

That he should write fifty-six letters in four years to a man like Thomson illustrates one important reason why Maria Riddell should speak of Burns' habitual disappointment, and why James Gray should describe him as "broken-hearted by the severity of his fate." Where could he find, not companions, but companionship? Who shared his interest in a country where "they have as much idea of a Rhinoceros as of a Poet"? Thomson did not share Burns' tastes, and he may have been a nuisance at times, but at least he was someone Burns could write to about his central interest (the two men never met, although Thomson may have seen Burns in Edinburgh), and in whom he could find some relief from his loneliness.

This loneliness was exasperated by a temperament which made it impossible for Burns to seek and to slip into a complacent and comfortable acceptance by his superiors in station, with whom his prominence thrust him into frequent association. As he wrote to David McCulloch in 1794, "I am indeed ill at ease whenever I approach your Honorables & Right Honorables." And the more prominent he became, and the more his family depended on him, the less he could relieve his mind. As he said of himself, "Mine is the madness of an enraged Scorpion shut up in a thumb-phial." To understand Burns in his later years, one must recognize the pressure of these tensions, and the fact that his Edinburgh experience had heightened them. The letters provide ample illustration.

In one to Deborah Duff Davies, he wrote, "I remember, & 'tis almost the earliest thing I do remember, when I was quite a boy, one day at church, being enraged at seeing a young creature, one of the maids of his house, rise from the mouth of the pew to give way to a bloated son of Wealth and Dullness, who waddled surlily past her. — Indeed the girl was very pretty; and he was an ugly, stupid, purse-proud, money-loving, old monster, as you can imagine." This early resentment of snobs and snobbery, and of class distinction and social arrogance, especially that deriving from money, sharpened as Burns grew older, when his "extreme impetuosity" and his "skinless sensibility" produced notable explosions, usually private, but sometimes public. A relatively mild outburst is his ironic paragraph to Mrs. Dunlop, May 27, 1788, at the end of his Edinburgh experiences.

There are few circumstances relating to the unequal distribution of the good things of this life that give me more vexation (I mean in what I see around me) than the Importance that the Great bestow on their trifles and small matters in family affairs, compared with the same, the very same things on the contracted Scale of a Cottage. — Last afternoon I had the honor to spend an hour or two at a good woman's fireside, where the homely planks that composed the floor were decorated with a splendid Carpet, and the gay table sparkled with Silver & China. — 'Tis now about term-day, and there has been a revolution among those creatures who, tho' in appearance, Partakers & equally noble Partakers, of the same Nature with Madame; yet are from time to time, their nerves, their sinews, their health, strength, wisdom, experience, genius, time, nay a good part of their very thoughts, sold for months & years, anxious Drudges, sweating, weary slaves, not only to the necessities, the conveniences, but the Caprices of the Important Few. — We talked of the insignificant Creatures; nay, notwithstanding their general stupidity & Rascality, did some of the poor devils the honor to commend them — But, light be the turf upon his breast who taught — "Reverence Thyself!" we looked down on the unpolished Wretches, their impertinent wives and clouterly brats, as the lordly Bull does on the little, dirty Ant-hill, whose puny inhabitants he crushes in the carelessness of his ramble, or tosses in the air in the wantonness of his pride.

A variation on the theme comes in a letter to Peter Hill, January 17, 1791. Speaking of Poverty, Burns says,

Owing to thee, the Man of unfortunate dispositions & neglected education, is condemned as a fool for his dissipation; despised & shunned as a needy wretch, when his follies as usual have brought him to want; & when his unprincipled necessities drive him to dishonest practices, he is abhorred as a miscreant, & perishes by the justice of his country. — But far otherwise is the lot of the Man of Family & Fortune. — His early extravagance & folly, are fire & spirit; his consequent wants, are the embarrasments of an Honest Fellow; & when, to remedy the matter, he sets out with a legal commission to plunder distant provinces & massacre peaceful nations, he returns laden with the spoils of rapine & murder, lives wicked & respected, & dies a Villain &

a Lord. — Nay, worst of all — Alas for hapless Woman! the needy creature who was shivering at the corner of the street, waiting to earn the wages of casual prostitution, is ridden down by the chariot wheels of the Coroneted Rep, hurrying on to the adulterous assignation; she, who without the same necessities to plead, riots nightly in the same guilty trade!!!

Biographers who lament that Burns left Athole House when on his Highland Tour, a day or so before the great Henry Dundas was to arrive (and presumably be so delighted with Burns that he would "do something for him") ignore the attitude of the Dundas family to Burns which he reveals in a letter to Alexander Cunningham of March 11, 1791.

I have two or three times in my life composed from the wish, rather than from the impulse, but I never succeeded to any purpose. — One of these times I shall ever remember with gnashing of teeth. — 'Twas on the death of the late Lord President Dundas [of the Court of Session]. — My very worthy & most respected friend, Mr Alexr Wood, Surgeon, urged me to pay a compliment in the way of my trade to his Lordship's memory. — Well, to work I went, & produced a copy of Elegiac verses some of them I own rather commonplace, & others rather hidebound, but on the whole though they were far from being in my best manner, they were tolerable; & had they been the production of a Lord or a Baronet, they would have been thought very clever. — I wrote a letter, which however was in my very best manner, & inclosing my Poem, Mr Wood carried altogether to Mr Solicitor Dundas [the Lord President's son, Robert, Jr.] that then was, & not finding him at home, left the parcel for him. — His Solicitorship never took the smallest notice of the Letter, the Poem, or the Poet. — From that time, highly as I respect the talents of the Family, I never see the name, Dundas, in the column of a newspaper, but my heart seems straitened for room in my bosom; & if I am obliged to read aloud a paragraph relating to one of them, I feel my forehead flush, & my nether lip quivers. — Had I been an obscure Scribbler, as I was then in the hey-day of my fame; or had I been a dependant Hanger-on for favor or pay; or had the bearer of the letter been any other than a gentleman who has done honor to the city in which he lives, to the

Country that produced him, & to the God that created him, Mr Solicitor might have had some apology.*

A much more violent, and public, eruption resulted when the funeral procession of a Mrs. Oswald (d. December 6, 1788) displaced Burns from a comfortable inn on a wintry night. Unhappily, such exhibitions of spleen became increasingly characteristic. In a letter to Dr. Moore, to whom he sent his *Ode Sacred to the Memory of Mrs. Oswald of Auchencruive,* he describes the event, and his outrage that even the corpse of one who was rich could affront the lowly.

The inclosed Ode is a compliment to the memory of the late Mrs Oswald of Auchencruive. — You, probably, knew her personally, an honor of which I cannot boast; but I spent my early years in her neighbourhood, and among her servants and tenants I know that she was detested with the most heartfelt cordiality. — However, in the particular part of her conduct, which roused my Poetic wrath, she was much less blameable. — In January last, on my road to Ayrshire, I had put up at Bailie Whigham's in Sanquhar, the only tolerable inn in the place. — The frost was keen, and the grim evening and howling wind were ushering in a night of snow and drift. — My horse & I were both much fatigued with the labors of the day, and just as my friend the Bailie and I, were bidding defiance to the storm over a smoking bowl, in wheels the funeral pageantry of the late, great Mrs Oswald, and poor I am forced to brave all the horrors of the tempestuous night, and jade my horse, my young favorite horse whom I had just christened Pegasus, twelve miles farther on, through the wildest moors & hills of Ayrshire, to New Cumnock, the next Inn. — The powers of Poesy & Prose sink under me, when I would describe what I felt. — Suffice it to say, that when a good fire at New Cumnock had so far recovered my frozen sinews, I sat down and wrote the inclosed Ode.

The opening lines of the Ode, and the strophe are sufficient to give a sense of its bitter tone and poverty of style.

* Burns' fellow-Crochallan, and Mr. Solicitor Dundas' fellow-lawyer, Charles Hay, also urged Burns to write the poem. Lord President Dundas died December 13, 1787. (F I, #164, 147.)

Dweller in yon dungeon dark,
Hangman of creation, mark!
Who in widow-weeds appears,
Laden with unhonoured years,
Noosing with care a bursting purse,
Baited with many a deadly curse?

STROPHE

View the wither'd beldam's face:
Can thy keen inspection trace
Aught of Humanity's sweet, melting grace?
Note that eye, 'tis rheum o'erflows —
Pity's flood there never rose.
See those hands ne'er stretch'd to save,
Hands that took, but never gave.
Keeper of Mammon's iron chest,
Lo, there she goes, unpitied and unblest,
She goes, but not to realms of everlasting rest!

Burns liked this poem. He sent a copy of it to Mrs. Dunlop soon after he wrote it, and it appeared in Stuart's *Star*, London, on May 7, 1789, over an easily penetrated pseudonym. Burns also included it in his 1793 edition.

In a practical burst of resentment against privilege, Burns vigorously defended one of the "children of Dependence" against aristocratic persecution when James Clarke, schoolmaster at Moffat, was accused of undue severity by school officials with support from the Earl of Hopeton. Burns rallied his friends to Clarke's cause, wrote petitions for him to present, lent him money, and eventually won the day. Triumphantly he wrote in the Glenriddell letterbook, after a copy of one of the petitions, "Bravo! Clarke. — In spite of Hopeton & his myrmidons thou camest off victorious!"

It is often wondered at that Burns was both a Jacobite and a Jacobin, a supporter of the divine-right-of-kings Stuarts and of the French Revolution democrats, but the reason is simple enough. He wrote in Glenriddell's interleaved *Scots Musical Museum*, "Except when my passions were heated by some accidental cause, my Jacobitism was merely by way of, *Vive la bagatelle.*" When his passions were heated, he could write to Mrs. Dunlop, "Nothing can reconcile me to the common terms 'English ambassador, English court,' &c. And I am out of all patience to see that equivocal character, Hastings, impeached by 'the Commons of England.'" Essentially, the Stuart cause touched his Scots patriotism; moreover, Queen Mary was an attractive woman, and the "Scotish Muses were all Jacobites." "And, surely," he continued, "the gallant though unfortunate house of Stewart, the kings of our fathers for so many heroic ages, is a theme much more interesting than an obscure beef-witted insolent race of foreigners whom a conjuncture of circumstances kickt up into power and consequence." This comment on the Hanoverians was, at least, written in the privacy of Robert Riddell's library, unlike the indiscreet lines on the window at Stirling.

That Burns was not merely bilious in such pointed and apt comments on the Hanoverians is suggested by the historical sense revealed in a thoughtful and well-informed letter to the Editor of the *Edinburgh Evening Courant,* inspired by an anti-Stuart sermon:

I went last Wednesday to my parish church, most cordially to join in grateful acknowledgments to the Author of all Good, for the consequent blessings of the Glorious Revolution. To that auspicious event we owe no less than our liberties religious and civil — to it we are likewise indebted for the present Royal Family, the ruling features of whose administration have ever been, mildness to the subject, and tenderness of his rights. Bred and educated in revolution principles, the principles of reason and common sense, it could not be any silly political prejudice that made my heart revolt at the harsh abusive manner in which the Reverend Gentleman mentioned the House of Stuart, and which, I am afraid, was too much the language of that day. We may rejoice sufficiently in our deliverance from past evils, without cruelly raking up the ashes of those whose misfortune it was, perhaps, as much as their crimes, to be the authors of those evils; and may bless God for all his goodness to us as a nation, without, at the same time, cursing a few ruined powerless exiles, who only harboured ideas, and made attempts, that most of us would have done, had we been in their situation.

"The bloody and tyrannical house of Stuart" may be said with propriety and justice, when compared with the present Royal Family, and the liberal sentiments of our days. But is there no allowance to be made for the manners of the times? Were the royal contemporaries of the Stuarts more mildly attentive to the rights of man? Might not the epithets of "bloody and tyrannical" be with at least equal justice, applied to the house of Tudor, of York, or any other of their predecessors?

The simple state of the case, Mr. Printer, seems to me to be this — At that period the science of government — the true relation between King and subject, like other sciences, was but just in its infancy, emerging from the dark ages of ignorance and barbarism. The Stuarts only contended for prerogatives which they knew their predecessors enjoyed, and which they saw their contemporaries enjoying; but these prerogatives were inimical to the happiness of a nation and the rights of subjects. In this contest between Prince and People, the consequence of that light of science which had lately dawned over Europe, the Monarch of France, for example, was victorious over the struggling liberties of the subject: With us, luckily, the Monarch failed, and his unwarrantable pretensions fell a sacrifice to our rights and happiness. Whether it was owing to the wisdom of leading individuals, or to the justlings of party, I cannot pretend to determine; but likewise happily for us, the kingly power was shifted into another branch of the family, who, as they owed the throne solely to the call of a free people, could claim nothing inconsistent with the covenanted terms which placed them there.

The Stuarts have been condemned and laughed at for the folly and impracticability of their attempts, in 1715 and 1745. That they failed, I bless my God most fervently; but cannot join in the ridicule against them. — Who does not know that the abilities or defects of leaders and commanders are often hidden until put to the touchstone of exigence; and that there is a caprice of fortune, an omnipotence in particular accidents, and conjunctures of circumstance, which exalt us as heroes, or brand us as madmen, just as they are for or against us?

Burns then makes a telling connection between the English opposition to Stuart tyranny which ended in the Glorious Revolu-

tion of 1688, and a more recent revolution against English ministerial and parliamentary tyranny, that of the American colonies.

Man, Mr. Printer, is a strange, weak, inconsistent being — Who would
believe, Sir, that in this our Augustan age of liberality and refinement,
while we seem so justly sensible and jealous of our rights and
liberties, and animated with such indignation against the very memory
of those who would have subverted them, who would suppose that a
certain people, under our national protection, should complain, not
against a Monarch and a few favourite advisers, but against our
whole legislative body, of the very same imposition and oppression,
the Romish religion not excepted, and almost in the very same terms
as our forefathers did against the family of Stuart! I will not, I cannot,
enter into the merits of the cause; but I dare say, the American
Congress, in 1776, will be allowed to have been as able and as en-
lightened, and, a whole empire will say, as honest, as the English
Convention of 1688; and that the fourth of July will be as sacred to
their posterity as the fifth of November is to us.

To conclude, Sir, let every man, who has a tear for the many
miseries incident to humanity, feel for a family, illustrious as any
in Europe, and unfortunate beyond historic precedent; and let every
Briton, and particularly every Scotsman, who ever looked with reverential pity on the dotage of a parent, cast a veil over the fatal mistakes
of the Kings of his forefathers.

Put in this way, Burns' sympathy for the old Scots royal house
which had won independence from England, his national pride,
his hatred of tyranny, and his enthusiasm for the Rights of Man
and for the Promise of Liberty, Equality, and Fraternity offered
by the French Revolution then developing — all form a persuasive
sequence. *Scots Wha Hae* is its ringing statement, particularly
stanzas Five and Six, and a noble prelude to the Jacobin cry, "A
man's a man for a' that."

> For a' that, an' a' that,
> It's comin yet for a' that,
> That man to man the world o'er
> Shall brithers be for a' that.

Burns' enthusiasm for the promise held out by France was widely shared in the early 1790's in Great Britain. The English constitutional settlement of 1688 had been degraded and corrupted by a self-perpetuating oligarchy until in Burns' day there was a general eagerness and pressure for Parliamentary and other reform, and the reformers were greatly encouraged by events in France. All this bred fear of "revolution" among the ruling class, and after France declared war on England in February, 1793, the British government, to preserve "sound institutions" and aristocratic power, embarked on a savage program of repression in a series of infamous trials. In Scotland, the prosecution was even more severe, and the court procedure more scandalous, than in England. A famous orator, Thomas Muir, given a sentence in August 1793 of fourteen years transportation to Botany Bay in a notoriously rigged trial, was sent out in 1794, and rescued by an American vessel in 1796, which took him to France. In reading of certain remarks and behavior of Burns during these years, one should bear in mind the public tension and official policy illustrated by the fate of Muir and many others like him.

Burns was no doctrinaire reformer; he had no plan for improving the world. But he had suffered from poverty and oppression, and he resented the casual acceptance of inequality by the privileged. Had his income been more comfortable, he might have found his disabilities more tolerable. "The most cordial believers in a Future State," he wrote Mrs. Dunlop, "have ever been the Unfortunate." And as he remarked to Mrs. Robert Graham, "I was born a poor dog; and however I may occasionally pick a better bone than I used to do, I know that a poor dog I must live & die." The practical basis of his discouragement he voiced to Mrs. Dunlop, "I hope, if I am spared with them, to show a set of boys that will do honor to my cares & name; but I am not equal to the task of rearing girls. — Besides, I am too poor: a girl should always have a fortune." In the same spirit, he reflected to his old Crochallan Colonel, William Dunbar, "To a father who himself knows the world, the thought that he shall have Sons to usher into it, must fill him with dread; but if he have Daughters, the prospect in a thoughtful moment is apt to shock him."

When he made these comments, Burns did not know, nor could it have been known in his day, that he suffered from an infection which was soon to kill him. During his later years, Burns' normal tendency to melancholia was intensified by the pains and debility of the disease, and his mention of "blue devils" became increasingly frequent. Just when he contracted his recurring illness, rheumatic fever, is difficult to determine, but his first mention of revealing symptoms came during his residence at Irvine, 1781–1782. The earlier dull headache after days of heavy labor at Mt. Oliphant farm, of which Gilbert Burns speaks, was most likely due to the physical exhaustion of an overworked adolescent boy.

Clinical details are lacking for an assured diagnosis of Burns' final illness, but his letters, and a few other sources, provide a fairly full record, which has been examined by four physicians* in the last forty years. They all speak of rheumatic fever and endocarditis, and they all agree that Burns showed no signs of alcoholism. Upon examining the record, the last of these four physicians, Dr. Stanley Bardwell, of Hudson, New York, gives for the first time a full clinical analysis of available data in support of his opinion that Burns' terminal illness resulted from an original infection which produced rheumatic fever, which, in turn, may have produced bacterial endocarditis, an infection of the valves of the heart.

2. Farmer and Exciseman

The summer of 1788 was busy and often bleak for Burns. While Jean remained in Mauchline, in part receiving instruction about the duties of a farm wife under Robert's mother and sisters, he

---

* Sir James Crichton-Browne (*Burns From a New Point of View*, London, 1926), Harry B. Anderson (*Annals of Medical History*, X March, 1928, 47ff.), S. Watson Smith (*British Medical Journal*, December 30, 1944, 864), and Stanley Bardwell (see Appendix B).

organized his farm and superintended the building of a house and outbuildings at Ellisland. As he wrote to Peter Hill from Mauchline, "From Ellisland in Nithsdale* to Mauchline in Kyle† is forty and five miles; there a house a-building, & farm enclosures and improvements to tend; here a new — not so much indeed a *new* as a *young* wife." Burns rode back and forth, spending a week or ten days in each place, leaving unsupervised his farm workers and the contractor for his buildings while he was in Ayrshire. When at his farm, he was "a solitary Inmate of an old, smoky 'Spence' [best room]" in the far from weathertight hut of the outgoing tenant, David Cullie, and his wife — decent and pious folk who were suspicious of Burns' orthodoxy and astonished at his knowledge of the Bible. In a verse epistle to Hugh Parker, an Ayrshire friend, he describes his plight.

> In this strange land, this uncouth clime,
> A land unknown to prose or rhyme;
> Where words ne'er cross't the Muse's heckles,   *hackles*
> Nor limpit in poetic shackles:
> A land that Prose did never view it,
> Except when drunk he stacher't thro' it: *staggered*
> Here, ambush'd by the chimla cheek,   *chimney corner*
> Hid in an atmosphere of reek,
> I hear a wheel thrum i' the neuk   *spin   corner*
> I hear it — for in vain I leuk: *look*
> The red peat gleams, a fiery kernel
> Enhuskèd by a fog infernal.
> Here, for my wonted rhyming raptures,
> I sit and count my sins by chapters;
> For life and spunk like ither Christians,
> I'm dwindled down to mere existence;
> Wi' nae converse but Gallowa' bodies,
> Wi' nae kend face but Jenny Geddes.   *known*

Burns' first day at Ellisland was June 12 (he called it "the elbow of existence"), and during the following lonely summer and

* Dumfriesshire
† Central Ayrshire

autumn, he wrote many letters from there and from Mauchline to old cronies in Edinburgh, letters often tinged with nostalgia. His most frequent correspondent, however, was Mrs. Dunlop, to whom he unburdened his mind, sure of her affectionate interest. That he should take time for so much letter-writing indicates something of his attitude toward his farm, and of the attention he gave it.

Professor Ferguson printed forty-six letters from the period June–December, 1788, many of them long, and they reveal an active, vigorous man who discusses books, songs, his poems, his marriage, his farm, and his general concerns. By September he was beginning to doubt the wisdom of having taken the farm at all. He wrote to Robert Graham at harvest time, on September 10, "My farm, now that I have tried it a little, tho' I think it will in time be a saving bargain, yet does by no means promise to be such a Pennyworth as I was taught to expect. — It is in the last stage of worn-out poverty, & will take some time before it pay the rent. — I might have had the Cash to supply the defficiencies of these hungry years, but I have a younger brother and three sisters, on a farm in Ayr-shire; and it took all my surplus, over what I thought necessary for my farming capital, to save not only the comfort but the very existence of that fireside family-circle from impending destruction. — This was done before I took the farm; and rather than abstract my money from my brother, a circumstance which would ruin him, I will resign the farm and enter immediately into the service of your Honours [the Excise Board]. — But I am embarked now in the farm; I have commenced married man; and I am determined to stand by my Lease, till resistless Necessity compel me to quit my ground." Ellisland became increasingly burdensome to him until he escaped from it completely into the Excise three years later.

He goes on to report that, since the Excise officer in the district surrounding Ellisland, one Leonard Smith, has recently become "quite opulent" by inheritance, perhaps the Board would consider replacing Smith with himself. Graham replied promptly on September 14, and Burns, suffering from influenza, thanked him for his "generous favor" on the twenty-third. By the following September (1789), Burns had been given the district, and reports to Mrs. Dunlop, "Five days in the week, or four at least, I must be on horseback, and very frequently ride thirty or forty miles ere I return; besides four different kinds of book-keeping to post every day." His pay was £50 a year, which compared very favorably with the incomes of ministers and school teachers. The reduced farming activity was left largely to servants, with Jean in charge of the dairying. "Burns kept twelve cows, and made butter and cheese," she reported.

The intervening year strengthened Burns' doubts about the suitability of farming for him. In March, 1789, he wrote Mrs. Dunlop,

You remember, Madam, I had two plans of life before me; The Excise & farming. — I thought, by the glimmering of my own prudence, the Excise was my most eligible scheme; but all my Great friends and particularly you, were decidedly, & therefore decided me, for farming. — My master, Mr Miller, out of real tho' mistaken benevolence, sought me industriously out, to set me on this farm, as he said to give me a lease that would make me comfortable & easy. — I was a stranger to the country, the farm and the soil, and so ventured on a bargain, that instead of being comfortable, is & will be a very, very hard bargain, if at all practicable. . . . My brother's lease is near expiring; he may be able to live by my lease as he can with propriety do things that I *now* can not do; I will plant him in this farm & throw myself on the Excise at large, where I am sure of immediate & constant bread.

Construction of the new house dragged on, but Burns wrote happily to Jean on October 14, 1788:

MY DEAREST LOVE,
You need not come on Sunday to meet me on the road, for I am

engaged that day to dine with Mr Logan at Laycht, so it will be in the evening before I arrive at Mauchline. —

You must get ready for Nithsdale as fast as possible, for I have an offer of a house in the very neighbourhood with some furniture in it, all which I shall have the use of for nothing till my own house be got ready; I am determined to remove you from Ayrshire immediately, as I am a sufferer by not being on my farm myself. — We will want a Maid servant, of consequence: if you can hear of any to hire, ask after them. — The apples are all sold & gone. — I am extremely happy at the idea of your coming to Nithsdale, as it will save us from these cruel separations. — The house is one in which a Mr Newal lived during the summer, who is gone to Dumfries in Winter. — It is a large house, but we will only occupy a room or two of it. —

I am ever, my dearest Madam,
Your faithful husband & humble servt
ROBT BURNS

But Jean did not join him at this house, The Isle, until early December, and they were still there the following April 15, sometime after which they moved into the still unfinished Ellisland farmhouse. Young Robert, their only surviving child, did not follow Jean to Nithsdale for about six months, but Burns did take in his uncle Robert's children William and Fanny on their father's death in January; and his brother William spent a long time with them during the winter. William was an amiable but ineffective youth seeking employment as a saddler. Robert helped him with clothes and money, and tried without much success to get him a job. William drifted to the neighborhood of Carlisle, then across to Newcastle, and finally to London, where, in a short time, he died of a fever. Robert's letters to him are affectionate, and full of good advice, which William asked for in his own well-expressed missives to his big brother. When the family moved to Ellisland, Burns' sister Agnes joined them.

Burns' letters are full of references to his work on the farm, and to the farm's demands and worries. "Every minute," he tells

Mrs. Dunlop on April 21, 1789, "has five minutes worth of business to do, and every crown has a twenty shilling errand to run." This latter theme he expanded in December. "My poor distracted mind is so torn, so jaded, so racked & bedevil'd with the task of the superlatively Damn'd — MAKING ONE GUINEA DO THE BUSINESS OF THREE — that I detest, abhor, and swoon at the very word, Business, though no less than four letters of my very short Sirname are in it." Obviously pressed for funds, Burns was looking to active duty in the Excise for relief.

By May 13, 1789, less than a year after he had come to Ellisland, Burns is writing Robert Graham of a conversation with Collector Mitchell, and by July 31, he and Mitchell have had a long and friendly talk about removing Leonard Smith and installing Robert Burns in his place, which should "be productive of at least no disadvantage to the Revenue." If the Board agrees to the change, Burns' salary will enable him to carry on and enjoy the improvement of his farm. He has considered giving up the farm entirely, but, he adds, "The worst of it is, I know there are some respectable Characters who do me the honor to interest themselves in my welfare & behaviour, and as leaving the farm so soon may have an unsteady giddy-headed appearance, I had perhaps better lose a little money than hazard such people's esteem." By August 19 he can write Mrs. Dunlop of his appointment, and say that he expects to begin duty the first of September. He seems to have been appointed September 7, but he was not sworn in until October 27. However, his name appeared on the official list of officers October 10, and he was assigned to full duty at once without serving the customary period as an "expectant." (See addendum, p. 482.)

Illness and injury were prompt results of Burns' new activities. Two months after he went on duty, he caught a "most violent cold," and suffered severely from it (and later from a "diseased nervous system") until mid-January, 1790, having to give up his Excise-books for a time. "My nerves are in a damnable State," he wrote Gilbert on January 11. "I feel that horrid hypochondria pervading every atom of both body & soul." The following September (1790), he "was seized with a slow, illformed Fever," and also had "a most malignant Squinancy" * which nearly carried him off.

In January, 1791, he fell — "not from my horse but with my horse" † — and injured his arm and hand, but he could write with them in February. And in March his horse came down with him and broke his right arm. Waiting for him on his return home from the accident was Janet Little, a poetical milkmaid and a protégée of Mrs. Dunlop, who had come to seek encouragement. Jenny reported that he chatted "at seeming ease and good humor," but could not lie down in bed, and was obliged to sit in a chair all night, in very violent pain.

Finally, in October, 1791, he is "a poor devil nailed to an elbow chair, writhing in anguish with a bruised leg, laid on a stool before him." It was high time when, in early November, he gave up riding about and moved to Dumfries. No doubt these experiences contributed to the despondency which Mrs. Burns thought induced him to give up Ellisland.

Burns' feelings about his position as Exciseman were mixed. The extra income was welcome. To Richard Brown he wrote, "I have indeed been extremely lucky in getting an additional income of £50 a year, while, at the same time, the appointment will not cost me above £10 or £12 per annum of expenses." To Lady Elizabeth Cunningham, sister of Lord Glencairn, he remarked, "People may talk as they please of the ignominy of the Excise, but what will support my family and keep me independent of the world is to me a very important matter; I had much rather that my Profession borrowed credit from me, than that I borrowed credit from my Profession." To Robert Ainslie

---

* "Phlegonous tonsillitis." See Appendix B.
† Perhaps Jenny Geddes, although in March, 1789, he wrote to Dr. Moore of a "young favorite horse" which he had just christened Pegasus — no doubt the one celebrated in his lines *Pegasus at Wanlockhead*. (F I, #322, 315.)

he was more colorful. "For the ignominy of the Profession," he wrote, "I have the encouragement which I once heard a recruiting Sergeant give to a numerous if not a respectable audience in the Streets of Kilmarnock — 'Gentlemen, for your further & better encouragement, I can assure you that our regiment is the most blackguard corps under the crown, and consequently with us an honest fellow has the surest chance for preferment.' " After two years, he wrote to his friend Cleghorn, "The Excise, after all has been said against it, is the business for me. — I find no difficulty in being an honest man in it; the work of itself, is easy." He adds that he has been put on the Supervisor list and hopes for early promotion, which will place him in a "respectable situation."

An Exciseman's duties were complex and exacting in Burns' day, even if Burns found them easy to perform. When, the year after his death, there was published *An Abridgement of all the Statutes now in Force Relative to the Revenue of the Excise in Great Britain,* the *abridgement* ran to nine hundred octavo pages. Burns did not enjoy this convenience, but had to pore through Acts of Parliament, general orders, and memoranda to learn his job.

The following were subject to Excise duties: — Auctions, bricks and tiles, beer, candles, coaches, cocoa-nuts, coffee, cyder, perry, verjuice, glass, hops, hides and skins, malt, mead or Metheglin, paper, pepper, printed calico and silk goods, soap, British spirits, foreign spirits, starch, salt, stone bottles, sweets, tea, tobacco and snuff, wine, and wire. The duty upon these articles was, in nearly every case, charged during the manufacture, and the surveillance of the processes entailed upon the officer frequent visits by day and night, on Sunday and Saturday. For example, soap-boilers were surveyed every four hours, candlemakers every six hours, and even brick-makers had sometimes to be surveyed twice a day. Each article had several rates of duty. Tanners had to pay fourteen different rates, per lb., per skin, and per dozen skins, according to the kind of hide; and even hare and rabbit skins were not allowed to escape. There were seventy-eight rates of paper duty according to size, kind, and quality, and other similar instances could be given. Of course, no single Excise officer had all these manufactures in his station; but he generally had a number of them, and he was never allowed to forget his responsibility with regard to them all. He was expected to detect within the bounds of the district allotted to him every article upon which the king's dues had not been paid. . . . In those days a tax was levied on almost every article in daily use in the household.

A zealous officer was supposed to supplement his pay with his half-share of the fines, and of the proceeds from sales of seized goods, for which he was responsible. After he had been on active duty for a year, Burns indicates in a letter to Robert Graham that his "Decreet" will be more than his annual salary. "As my Division consists of ten large parishes, & I am sorry to say, hitherto very carelessly surveyed, I had a good deal of business for the Justices; & I believe my Decreet will amount to between fifty & sixty pounds. — I took, I fancy, rather a new way with my Frauds. — I recorded every Defaulter; but at the Court, I myself begged off every poor body that was unable to pay, which seeming candour gave me so much implicit credit with the Hon. Bench, that with high Complnts they gave me such ample vengeance on the rest, that my Decreet is double the amount of any Division in the District."

In a letter to Collector Mitchell of the same time, Burns reflects on the immutable difficulties of enforcing the law against offenders with influential friends:

I wish & pray that the goddess of Justice herself would appear tomorrow among our Honble Gentlemen, merely to give them a word in their ear, that, "Mercy to the Thief, is Injustice to the Honest Man." For my part, I have galloped over my ten parishes these four days, untill this moment that I am just alighted, or rather, that my poor jackass skeleton of a horse has let me down; for the miserable devil has been on his knees half a score of times within the last twenty miles, telling me in his own way "Behold, am not I thy faithful jade of a horse, on which thou hast ridden these many years!!!" In short, Sir, I have broke my horse's wind, & almost broke my own neck, besides some injuries in a part that shall be nameless, owing to a hard-hearted stone of a saddle; & I find that every Offender has so many Great Men to espouse his cause, that I shall not be surprised if I am committed to the strong Hold of the Law tomorrow for insolence to the dear friends of the Gentlemen of the Country.

In the letter to Graham quoted above (September 4, 1790), he expands his discontent with farming. "I am going either to give up, or subset my farm directly. — I have not liberty to subset, but if my Master will grant it me, I propose giving it just as I have it to myself, to an industrious fellow of a near relation of mine [his brother Gilbert]. — Farming this place in which I live, would just be a livelihood to a man who would be the greatest drudge in his own family, so is no object; & living here hinders me from that knowledge of the business of Excise which it is absolutely necessary for me to attain." He goes on to hope he can get a Port Division with its easier duties and higher pay, and that he can eventually become an Examiner or Supervisor, all with the support of well-placed people, including Mr. Graham. And by January 27, 1791, he had been placed on the list of those recommended for Examiner and Supervisor. But so early as September 11, 1790, John Syme had written Alexander Cunningham of Burns, "He says he is immediately to be promoted in the Excise line," and Nicol had written to Ainslie on August 13 that Burns was already an Examiner. It would seem that he had had prematurely high hopes of advancement.

Mrs. Dunlop, ever his friend, seems to have had a hand in getting Burns' name put on the list of Supervisors, through her friendship with Robert Graham, and with the wife of General Supervisor William Corbet.* Burns wrote her in March, 1790,

---

* Corbet inquired of Burns' Supervisor, Alexander Findlater, about him, and received the following reply, dated December 20, 1790, an important testament to his abilities and performance as an Exciseman: "Dear Sir, Mr. Burns informs me that, in consequence of a communication between you & some of his friends, he

that the farm was a "ruinous bargain," which he must give up by Martinmas, 1791, when his rent is to rise £20, and he will consider himself "well quit" if he be no more than a hundred pounds out of pocket. He continues,

I can have in the Excise-line what they call a foot-walk whenever I chuse; that is an appointment to a Division where I am under no necessity of keeping a horse.* — There is in every Sea-port town, one or two Officers, called Port-Officers, whose income is at least seventy pounds per ann. — I will petition Mr Graham & stretch all my interest, to get one of these; and if possible on Clyde. — Greenock & Port-Glasgow are both lucrative places in that way, & to them my views are bent. — You formerly wrote me, if a Mr Corbet in the Excise could be of use to me. — If it is a Corbet who is what we call one of our General Supervisors, of which we have just two in Scotland, he can do everything for me. — Were he to interest himself properly for me, he could easily by Martinmas 1791 transport me to Port Glasgow port Division, which would be the ultimatum of my present Excise hopes. — He is a Willm Corbet, & has his home, I believe, somewhere about Stirling. — One word more, and then to have done with this most ungracious subject: all this business of my farm &c. is for your most private ear: it would be of considerable prejudice to me to have it known at present."

---

has stated his case to you by letter, & exprest his wishes on account of his family, of being translated to a more beneficial appointment: — And as at our last interview at Stirling you hinted a desire of being certified of the propriety of his Character as an officer of the Revenue; I shall, abstracted from every Consideration of his other talents, which are so universally admired, in a few words give you my Opinion of him. — He is an active, faithful, & zealous officer, gives the most unremitting attention to his office (which, by the bye is more than I at first looked for from so eccentric a Genius) and tho' his experience must as yet be small, he is capable, as you may well suppose, of achieving a much more arduous task than any difficulty that the theory or practice of our business can exhibit. — In short, — being such as I have described — and believe me, I have not 'o'erstep'd the modesty of' *truth* — he is truly worthy of your friendship; and if your recommendation can help him forward to a more eligible situation, you will have the merit of conferring an Obligation on a man who may be considered a credit to the profession." (Author's transcript of original in Burns College Museum, Alloway, published *Chronicle*, 1931.)

* He received an appointment the following July (1790) to the Dumfries third division, tobacco, but what difference this appointment may have made in his life is not clear. (Sinton, 59.)

Burns' Ellisland lease bound him to enclose the property and build "a dwelling house, Barn, byre and stable," for which improvements Mr. Miller was to advance £300. There was no provision for a sublease or for an escape. But in 1791, Mr. Miller received an offer of £1900 for the farm from a neighbor, John Morin of Laggan, which he was glad to accept because Ellisland was separated from the rest of his estate by the River Nith.* On September 10, 1791, Burns signed a release of his "Tack," and he told Robert Cleghorn that he had got "some little consideration" for his lease, but he does not say what.

He had previously sold off the crops on August 25, an occasion he described to Thomas Sloan. "I sold my crop on this day se'ennight past, & sold it very well: a guinea an acre, on an average, above value. — But such a scene of drunkenness was hardly ever seen in this country. — After the roup was over, about thirty people engaged in a battle, every man his own hand, & fought it out for three hours. — Nor was the scene much better in the house. — No fighting, indeed, but folks lying drunk on the floor, & decanting, untill both my dogs got so drunk by attending them, that they could not stand. — You will easily guess how I enjoyed the scene; as I was no further over than you used to see me. — Mrs B——& family have been in Ayr-shire these many weeks." The customary refreshment on such occasions had produced the customary results, even if somewhat more dramatic than usual.

In early November Burns sold off his "horses, cows, farming things, &c." on such terms that he could report to Mrs. Dunlop, "I have got rid of my farm with little, if any loss . . . by that peculiar Good Luck that for some years past" had attended all his motions. On November 11, 1791, he moved Jean, Robert Jr., Francis Wallace, and William Nicol into three small rooms above the Stamp Office in the Wee or Stinking or Carwart's Vennel (now Bank Street), Dumfries, within sound of the river. The

* Fourteen years later, Morin sold Ellisland for £4430.

landlord was Captain John Hamilton, of Allershaw, who proved Burns' practical friend by his considerate restraint when rent was overdue. On May 19, 1793, Burns moved to another and more comfortable of Captain Hamilton's properties, the stone house in the Mill Vennel (now Burns Street), where he died three years later, and where Jean continued to live.

With proceeds from the two sales at Ellisland, Burns paid off some obligations, including his five pound, ten shilling debt to "Mr Robert Burn, Architect, for erecting the stone over poor Ferguson." Burns wrote to Peter Hill, "He was two years in erecting it, after I commissioned him for it; & I have been two years paying him, after he sent me his account; so he & I are quits. — He had the hardiesse to ask me interest on the sum; but considering that the money was due by one Poet, for putting a tomb-stone over another, he may, with grateful surprise, thank Heaven that he ever saw a farthing of it."

Burns used other proceeds to visit Edinburgh in late November and early December, when he relieved Jenny Clow and renewed his affair with Clarinda.

Transcripts of official Excise records show that Burns succeeded to the Dumfries first, or Port, Division on April 26, 1792. He reports this promotion to Maria Riddell in a letter dated by Professor Ferguson "February, 1792." The manuscript has not been traced, and the date seems early, although here, as when Burns began his Excise duties, the official entry may have been delayed. "I am happy," he wrote Mrs. Riddell, "to inform you I have just got an appointment to the first or Port Division as it is called, which adds twenty pounds to my Salary. My Excise Income is now Cash paid Seventy pounds a year: and this I hold untill I am appointed Supervisor. . . . My Perquisites I hope to make worth 15 or 20£ more." This was Burns' last promotion, although he was made Acting Supervisor, December, 1794–April, 1795, during the illness of Supervisor Findlater.

The Board's records and Burns' own correspondence reveal

him to have been guilty of occasional small errors, inadvertence, or carelessness. That is all. He did his work conscientiously, and the Board treated him favorably. It was the emphatic opinion of Supervisor Findlater that he "would, if he had lived, have been promoted in due course; and that, at a shorter period of service than any of his predecessors." After Burns' death in July, 1796, the man below him on the list was made Examiner January 12, 1797, and Supervisor the following August 10. Burns would have received these promotions had he lived, with a salary of £120–£200.

In March, 1795, while he was Acting Supervisor, Burns replied to an offer of assistance from Patrick Heron, M.P., that the Supervisor's "business is an incessant drudgery, and would be nearly a compleat bar to every species of literary pursuit." However, he continues, the moment he is appointed Supervisor, he may be nominated on the Collector's list, "and this is always a business purely of political patronage. A Collectorship varies much, from better than two hundred a year to near a thousand. They also come forward by precedency on the list; and have, besides a handsome income, a life of complete leisure. A life of literary leisure, with a decent competence, is the summit of my wishes." Upon his promotion to Supervisor, he concludes, he would be most grateful for assistance from a politically powerful friend in securing a Collectorship.

Burns would almost certainly have been a Supervisor by the time of his letter to Heron, had his well-placed and well-intentioned friends got him into the Excise during the 1786–1787 winter, as he had wished. Had they done so, he would have avoided the exasperation of his farm, and he might well have been more comfortable financially, also.

Burns' most celebrated exploit as an Excise officer was his leading a party to board a grounded smuggling schooner, the *Rosamond*, in the Solway estuary below Dumfries. He later purchased four carronades at the sale of the seized vessel and sent them to the revolutionary government in France. The seizure is best followed in the picturesque narrative of Riding Officer Walter Crawford's journal, with a few minor emendations. The journal begins January 12, 1792. On February 26, Crawford heard of the smuggler.

26 E[vening] 4 [o'clock] Gone to Dumfries to acquent the Supervisor and Officers that a landing [of smugglers] was expected that week, In the mean time having left a person in whom I could thorowghly confide to ride Express to me on the first appearance of a landing for which he was delligently to watch.

27 E 11 My Express arrived informing me that a landing was making or about to be made, on which I set off with Mr Lewars directly, leaving Messrs. Burns, Penn & Ranking to follow as fast as possible.

By the 28 m[orning] 5 arrived at Annan and immediately sett out with the Party of Dragoons, Searched Mr M'Dowall's [a notorious smuggler] and most of the Smuglers house[s] between that and the Shore, and about Noon Rode down to the shore where I was informed that the Vessal could not gett off for want of Watter. I made an attempt to Board her with the Millitary But when wee offered to app[r]och they hailed ws that they would fire on us if wee app[r]oched any farther.

As my Party had only Pistols and were but few in number and a great number of men appearing to be on Deck I stoped the Soldiery and riding up to the Vessal allone asked liberty to Come on board which after some altercation they granted. I Boarded her and found Twenty four men under arms with fifteen round of shott each.

I returned to shore and consulting with the Officers and Millitary we agread that greater force would be absolutly necessary, In consequence of which Mr Lewars sett off for Dumfries to Bring twenty four more Dragoons while I went to Ecclefechan for the Party there with which I patroled the roads till the arrivall of Mr. Lewars with the additionall force from Dumfries.

On the 29 m 9 wee approached the Vessall with the following force, Dragoons from Dumfries Twenty Three, Annan Thirteen, Ecclefechan Eight, in all Forty four fully accoutered and on horse-back. The vessal having fallen down the Sollway Firth abouth a mill from where she was yesterday and being about a mile within sea mark, most of which space being covered with watter, and a very heavy Currant running between us and the Vessel we deemed it imposible to get at her either on foott or on horseback, so we aggread to search the coast for Boats in which to board her. But the Country People guessing our design got the start of us and staved every Boat on the Coast before we Could reach them, the vessel in the mean time keeping up a fire of grape shott and musquetry, we resolved as last resource to attempt the passage on foott as the quick sands made the riding on horseback dangerous or rather impossible.

We drew up the Millitary in three divisions determined to approach her & attact her if the s[t]ream was foardable, one party fore and aft and the Third on her Broadside, the first party being Commanded by Quarter Master Manly, the Second by my self and the Third led by Mr Burns.

Our orders to the Millitary were to reserve there fire till within eight yards of the vessel, then to pour a volley and board her with sword & Pistol. The vessel keept on firing thou without any damage to us, as from the situation of the ship they could not bring their great guns to bear on us, we in the mean time wading breast high, and in Justice to the party under my Command I must say with great alacrity; by the time we were within one hundred yards of the vessel the Crew gave up the cause, gott over side towards England which shore was for a long way dry sand. As I still supposed that there were only Country people they were putting ashore and that the Crew were keeping under Cover to make a more vigourous immediate resistance, we marched up as first concerted, but found the vessel compleatly evacuuated both of the Crew and every movable on board except as per inventory, the smugglers as their last instance of vengen[c]e having poured a six-pounder Carronade through her Broadside. She proved to be the Roseomond of Plymouth, Alexander Patty Master, and about one hundred tons burthen schooner r[igged].

This document rests in the National Library of Scotland, with two others relating to Burns and the *Rosamond*. The first, in Burns' hand, is a record of the guarding, repair, and refloating of the vessel, and her preparation for sale. The second, in the hand of Burns' fellow officer, John Lewars, is an inventory of the ship and her "furniture." Proceeds of the sale (April 19, 1792) were £166/16/6, and the expenses of preparation £45/15/4, leaving prize money of £121/1/2. The Excisemen's share of this latter sum is not recorded.

These documents were collected and supplied to Sir Walter Scott by Joseph Train, Supervisor of Excise for Castle Douglas. Train also speaks of Lewars' journal which recorded Burns' purchase of the four carronades, and of a sale catalogue with a note in Burns' hand that he had purchased them for £3. The whereabouts of Lewars' journal and of the sale catalogue are not now known; however, Sir Walter interested himself in the story, and learned that the carronades had been intercepted by the Customs at Dover. No record of this interception has come to light. For Burns to purchase the guns and despatch them to France was perfectly legal. England and France were not at war until the following February. But for an Exciseman, this expression of his feelings was dramatically reckless.

That these feelings were much excited at this time is suggested by Burns' having subscribed, November 13, 1792, to the *Gazetteer*, an Edinburgh paper just established by William Johnston, a reputable reforming politician soon to be imprisoned in the "sedition" drive. Further evidence appears in Burns' letter to Mrs. Dunlop of December 6.

We, in this country, here have many alarms of the Reform, or rather the Republican spirit, of your part of the kingdom. — Indeed, we are a good deal in commotion ourselves, & in our Theatre here, "God save the king" has met with some groans and hisses, while, Ça ira has been repeatedly called for. — For me, I am a *Placeman*, you know, a very humble one indeed, Heaven knows, but still so much so as to gag me from joining in the cry. — What my private sentiments are, you will find out without an Interpreter. — In the meantime, I have taken up the subject in another view, and the other day, for a pretty Actress's benefit-night, I wrote an address which I will give on the other page, called "The Rights of Woman."

The Rights of Woman

An Occasional Address

Spoken by Miss Fontenelle on her Benefit Night
November 26, 1792

While Europe's eye is fix'd on mighty things,
The fate of empires and the fall of kings;
While quacks of State must each produce his plan,
And even children lisp the Rights of Man;
Amid this mighty fuss just let me mention
The Rights of Woman merit some attention.

First, in the sexes' intermix'd connexion
One sacred Right of Woman is Protection:
The tender flower, that lifts its head elate,
Helpless must fall before the blasts of fate,
Sunk on the earth, defac'd its lovely form,
Unless your shelter ward th' impending storm.

Our second Right — but needless here is caution —
To keep that right inviolate's the fashion:
Each man of sense has it so full before him,
He'd die before he'd wrong it — 'tis Decorum!
There was, indeed, in far less polish'd days,
A time, when rough rude Man had naughty ways:
Would swagger, swear, get drunk, kick up a riot,
Nay, even thus invade a lady's quiet!
Now, thank our stars! these Gothic times are fled;
Now, well-bred men — and you are all well-bred —
Most justly think (and we are much the gainers)
Such conduct neither spirit, wit, nor manners. *

* John Syme's account (November 21, 1794) to Alexander Cunningham of the Caledonian Hunt's visit two years later to Dumfries, suggests the quality of genteel behavior ironically glanced at here. "Our Caledonian Hunt went off with dissipation without fashionable gaiety — There was not one of Noble blood at the Races if we except Maule — The exhibitions of the Bucks were splendid if we give that title to rioting. Drinking three bottles each day, disturbing the players, staggering in at the Assembly — some even dancing in boots — displayed the spirit and genius of modern manners — Baker, one of the knowing english Squires on the Turf made an elegant appearance by insulting in the

For Right the third, our last, our best, our dearest:
That right to fluttering female hearts the nearest,
Which even the Rights of Kings, in low prostration,
Most humbly own — 'tis dear, dear Admiration!
In that blest sphere alone we live and move;
There taste that life of life — Immortal Love.
Smiles, glances, sighs, tears, fits, flirtations, airs —
'Gainst such an host what flinty savage dares?
When awful Beauty joins with all her charms,
Who is so rash as rise in rebel arms?

But truce with kings, and truce with constitutions,
With bloody armaments and revolutions;
Let Majesty your first attention summon:
Ah! ça ira! the Majesty of Woman!

At unspecified times, probably during the fall of 1792, Burns is reported to have made such provocative toasts as one to the

---

grossest manner Squire Walter Riddel of this place who pursued him to Durham and made him ask pardon which is published in our papers of last week. Maule and others you would hear, pickled our friend Harry Welsh — by daubing his hair with mustard etc & sticking toothpic quills in it by way of hedgehogging the man — This lad, Cunningham, must be distracted — his behavior here has been horrible and I dare say will make a desert about him if ever he appears again in this quarter — But say nothing of this as from me — Maule, I suppose you have heard, fell in love with Patricia Gordon of Halleaths — a very beautiful & valuable young girl — and he is to marry her in the first week of Decemr — This is certainly to take place if we judge from every indication — clothes making settlement *do* etc. etc." (Author's transcript, see P.S. for p. 365.)

It will be recalled that the Caledonian Hunt had subscribed to one hundred copies of Burns' Edinburgh edition, and had received its Dedication, whose ironic sting will be more fully appreciated if it is re-read with the above account in mind. (*Cp.* pp. 143–44; see also p. 277n and pp. 10–11.) Burns left a poor if bitter epigram on Maule — "*To the Hon. Wm. R. Maule of Panmure* Extempore: On seeing the Hon. Wm. R. Maule of Panmure driving away in his fine and elegant phaeton on the race ground at Tinwald Downs, October, 1794."

> Thou Fool, in thy phaeton towering,
>   Art proud when that phaeton's praised?
> 'Tis the pride of a Thief's exhibition
>   When higher his pillory's rais'd.

It should also be noted that the subject of this epigram, in 1817, twenty-one years after Burns' death, settled £50 a year on Burns' widow. Within a year and a half, however, James Glencairn Burns' improved circumstances allowed him to relieve Maule of this voluntarily assumed obligation. (Ch-W IV, 295.)

last verse of the last chapter of the last book of kings. Whatever he may have done, he had written to Mrs. Dunlop, April 3, 1789, "Politics is dangerous ground for me to tread on, and yet I cannot for the soul of me resist an impulse of anything like Wit." The impulse got him into trouble, for about this time he was reported to the Excise Board as disaffected, and Collector Mitchell was instructed to look into the matter. Burns wrote frantically to Robert Graham, and since there has been so much statement and counterstatement about this affair, it seems best to present the relevant documents entire, and let Burns speak for himself. Here is his letter to Graham, December 31, 1792.

Sir,

I have been surprised, confounded & distracted by Mr Mitchel, the Collector, telling me just now, that he has received an order from your Honble Board to enquire into my political conduct, & blaming me as a person disaffected to Government. Sir, you are a Husband — & a father — you know what you would feel, to see the much-loved wife of your bosom, & your helpless, prattling little ones, turned adrift into the world, degraded & disgraced from a situation in which they had been respectable & respected, & left almost without the necessary support of a miserable existence. — Alas, Sir! must I think that such, soon, will be my lot! And from the damned, dark insinuations of hellish, groundless Envy too! — I believe, Sir, I may aver it, & in the sight of omnipotence, that I would not tell a deliberate Falsehood, no, not though even worse horrors, if worse can be, than those I have mentioned, hung over my head; & I say, that the allegation, whatever villain has made it, is a Lie! To the British Constitution, on Revolution principles, next after my God, I am most devoutly attached! —

You, Sir, have been much & generously my Friend — Heaven knows how warmly I have felt the obligation, & how gratefully I have thanked you. — Fortune, Sir, has made you powerful, & me impotent; has given you patronage, & me dependance. — I would not for my *single Self* call on your Humanity; were such my insular, unconnected situation, I would despise the tear that now swells in my eye — I could brave Misfortune, I could face Ruin: for at the worst, "Death's thousand doors stand open;" but, good God! the tender concerns that I have mentioned, the claims & ties that I, at this moment, see & feel around

me, how they ennerve Courage, & wither Resolution! To your patronage, as a man of some genius, you have allowed me a claim; & your
esteem, as An Honest Man, I know is my due: to these, Sir, permit
me to appeal; & by these may I adjure you to save me from that
misery which threatens to overwhelm me, & which, with my latest
breath I will say it, I have not deserved.

On the same day that he wrote to Graham, he wrote to Mrs.
Dunlop that "some envious, malicious devil" had raised a little
demur about his political principles. "I have set, henceforth," he
continued, "a seal on my lips as to these unlucky politics, but to
you I must breathe my sentiments." * Unfortunately that portion
of the manuscript containing his sentiments has been torn away.
Within five days, Burns had been reassured by Robert Graham,
and had replied in a letter which stated the truth and nothing
but the truth, but perhaps not quite the whole truth.

Sir,
    I am this moment honored with your letter: with what feelings I
received this other instance of your goodness, I shall not pretend
to describe. —
    Now, to the charges which Malice & Misrepresentation have brought
against me. —
    It has been said, it seems, that I not only belong to, but head a
disaffected party in this place. — I know of no party in this place,
Republican or Reform, except an old party of Borough-Reform; with
which I never had anything to do. — Individuals, both Republican &
Reform, we have, though not many of either; but if they have associated, it is more than I have the least knowledge of: & if there exists
such an association, it must consist of such obscure, nameless beings,
as precluded any possibility of my being known to them, or they to
me. —

---

* In September, 1793, Burns presented a copy of John De Lolme's *The British
Constitution* to the Dumfries public library, with the following inscription: "Mr
Burns presents this book to the Library & begs they will take it as a Creed of
British Liberty — untill they find a better. R. B." But the day after the pres-
entation he retrieved the volume and pasted the sheet with the inscription and
the one next to it together, to hide his indiscretion. The copy of De Lolme may
be seen in the Burns House, Dumfries. (F II, #589, 211; Ch-W IV, 55.)

I was in the playhouse one night, when Ça Ira was called for. — I was in the middle of the Pit, & from the Pit the clamour arose. — One or two individuals with whom I occasionally associate were of the party, but I neither knew of the Plot, nor joined in the Plot; nor ever opened my lips to hiss, or huzza, that or any other Political tune whatever. — I looked on myself as far too obscure a man to have any weight in quelling a Riot; at the same time as a character of higher respectability, than to yell in the howlings of a rabble. — This was the conduct of all the first Characters in this place; & these Characters know, & will avow, that such was my conduct. —

I never uttered any invectives against the king. — His private worth, it is altogether impossible that such a man as I, can appreciate; and in his Public capacity, I always revered, & ever will, with soundest loyalty, revere, the Monarch of Great Britain, as, to speak in Masonic, the sacred Keystone of our Royal Arch Constitution. —

As to Reform Principles, I look upon the British Constitution, as settled at the Revolution, to be the most glorious Constitution on earth, or that perhaps the wit of man can frame; at the same time, I think, & you know what High and distinguished Characters have for some time thought so, that we have a good deal deviated from the original principles of that Constitution; particularly, that an alarming System of Corruption has pervaded the connection between the Executive Power and the House of Commons. — This is the Truth, the Whole truth, of my Reform opinions; opinions which, before I was aware of the complection of these innovating times, I too unguardedly (now I see it) sported with: but henceforth, I seal up my lips. — However, I never dictated to, corresponded with, or had the least connection with, any political association whatever — except, that when the Magistrates & principal inhabitants of this town, met to declare their attachment to the Constitution, & their abhorrence of Riot, which declaration you would see in the Papers, I, as I thought my duty as a Subject at large, & a Citizen in particular, called upon me, subscribed the same declaratory Creed. —

Of Johnston, the publisher of the Edinr Gazetteer, I know nothing. — One evening in company with four or five friends, we met with his prospectus which we thought manly & independent; & I wrote to him, ordering his paper for us. — If you think that I act improperly in allowing his Paper to come addressed to me, I shall immediately countermand it. — I never, so judge me, God! wrote a line of prose

for the Gazetteer in my life. — An occasional address, spoken by Miss
Fontenelle on her benefit-night here, which I called, the Rights of
Woman, I sent to the Gazetteer; as also some extempore stanzas on
the Commemoration of Thomson: both of these I will subjoin for your
perusal. — You will see that they have nothing whatever to do with
Politics. — At the time when I sent Johnston one of these poems, but
which one, I do not remember, I inclosed at the request of my warm
& worthy friend, Robt Riddel Esq: of Glenriddel a prose Essay signed
Cato, written by him, & addressed to the delegates for the County
Reform, of which he was one for this County. — With the merits, or
demerits, of that Essay, I have nothing to do, farther than transmitting
it in the same Frank, which Frank he had procured me. —

As to France, I was her enthusiastic votary in the beginning of
the business. — When she came to shew her old avidity for conquest,
in annexing Savoy, &c. to her dominions, & invading the rights of
Holland, I altered my sentiments. — A tippling Ballad which I made
on the Prince of Brunswick's breaking up his camp, & sung one convivial evening, I shall likewise send you, sealed up, as it is not every
body's reading. — This last is not worth your perusal; but lest Mrs
Fame should, as she has already done, use, & even abuse, her old
priviledge of lying, you shall be the master of everything, le pour et
le contre, of my political writings & conduct.

He concludes by reporting that the Supervisor of the Galloway
district has been paralyzed, and suggesting that perhaps the
Board might be disposed to fill this Supervisor's place. Two days
later he wrote Graham again on the subject, but he did not get
the job.

On this occasion, General Supervisor Corbet came to Dumfries to inquire, an indication that the Board took the matter
seriously. John Syme, in a note to Alexander Peterkin, describes
the results. "Mr Corbet admonished Burns — but found no
grounds, save some witty sayings — Mr Corbet, Mr Findlater
Burns & I dined together once or twice on the occasion." Findlater confirms Syme in a letter to the *Glasgow Courier*, March,
1834. Burns himself reviews the event in a letter to John Francis
Erskine, of Mar, who had offered him assistance on hearing that

he had been dismissed. He prefixed the following explanatory note to a copy of the letter which he made in the Glenriddell letter book.

In the year 1792-3, when Royalist & Jacobin had set all Britain by the ears, because I unguardedly, rather under the temptation of being witty than disaffected, had declared my sentiments in favor of Parliamentary Reform, in the manner of that time, I was accused to the Board of Excise of being a Republican; & was very near being turned adrift in the wide world on that account. — Mr Erskine of Mar, a *gentleman indeed,* wrote to my friend Glenriddell to know if I was really out of place on account of my Political principles; & if so, he proposed a Subscription among the friends of Liberty for me, which he offered to head, that I might be no pecuniary loser by my political Integrity. —This was the more generous, as I had not the honor of being known to Mr Erskine. I wrote him as follows. —

[Dumfries, 13th April, 1793]

Sir,

Degenerate as Human Nature is said to be, &, in many instances, worthless & unprincipled it certainly is; still there are bright examples to the contrary; examples, that even in the eyes of Superiour Beings must shed a lustre on the name of Man. — Such an example have I now before me, when you, Sir, came forward to patronise & befriend a distant, obscure stranger; merely because Poverty had made him helpless, & his British hardihood of mind had provoked the arbitrary wantonness of Power. — My much-esteemed friend, Mr Riddell of Glenriddell, has just read me a paragraph of a letter he had from you. — Accept, Sir, of the silent throb of gratitude; for words would but mock the emotions of my soul. —*

You have been misinformed, as to my final dismission from the Excise: I still am in the service. — Indeed, but for the exertions of a gentleman who must be known to you, Mr Graham of Fintry, a gentleman who has ever been my warm & generous friend, I had, without so much as a hearing, or the smallest previous intimation,

---

* A few days after Burns' death, Alexander Cunningham approached Mr. Erskine for a subscription to the fund being raised in behalf of Jean and the children. He wrote Syme, "When I waited on Mr Erskine of Marr you will be surprised to hear he seem'd luck warm." (Author's transcript, see P.S. for p. 365.)

been turned adrift, with my helpless family, to all the horrors of Want. — Had I had any other resource, probably I might have saved them the trouble of a dismissal; but the little money I gained by my Publication, is almost every guinea embarked, to save from ruin an only brother; who, though one of the worthiest, is by no means one of the most fortunate of men. —

In my defence to their accusations, I said, that whatever might be my sentiments of Republics, ancient or modern, as to Britain, I abjured the idea. — That a Constitution which, in its original principles, experience had proved to be every way fitted for our happiness in society, it would be insanity to sacrifice to an untried visionary theory. — That, in consideration of my being situated in a department, however humble, immediately in the hands of the people in power, I had forborne taking any active part, either personally, or as an author, in the present business of Reform. — But that, where I must declare my sentiments, I would say that there existed a system of corruption between the Executive Power & the Representative part of the Legislature, which boded no good to our glorious Constitution; & which every patriotic Briton must wish to see amended. — Some such Sentiments as these I stated in a letter to my generous Patron, Mr Graham, which he laid before the Board at large, where it seems my last remark gave great offence; & one of our Supervisors general, a Mr Corbet, was instructed to enquire, on the spot, into my conduct, & to document me — "that *my* business was to *act*, not to think; & that whatever might be Men or Measures, it was for me to be silent & obedient." — Mr Corbet was likewise my steady friend; so between Mr Graham & him, I have been partly forgiven: only, I understand that all hopes of my getting officially forward are blasted.

But they were not blasted as we shall see. Burns' letters and songs reveal that although he did not change his sentiments, he was more careful after the inquiry. The incident closes on a lighter note. When William Nicol heard that Burns had got into trouble for speaking out of turn, he wrote in friendly reproof. Burns copied Nicol's letter into the Glenriddell letter book, with a prefatory note: "From my worthy friend Mr. Nicol of the High School, Edinr: alluding to some temeraire conduct of mine in the political opinions of that day. — "

DEAR CHRISTLESS BOBIE,

What is become of thee? Has the Devil flown off with thee, as the glade [hawk] does with a bird? — If he should do so, there is little matter, if the reports concerning thy *imprudence* are true. — What concerns it thee whether the lousy Dumfriesian fiddlers play Cà Ira, or God save the king? Suppose you had an aversion to him, you could not, as a gentleman, wish God to use him worse than he has done. — The infliction of Ideocy is no sign of Friendship or Love;* & I am sure, damnation is a matter far beyond your wishes or ideas: — But of this kind are only the insidious suggestions of ill-minded persons; for your good sense will ever point out to you, as well as to me, a bright model of political conduct, who flourished in the victorious reign of Queen Anne viz. the vicar of Bray, who during the convulsions of Great Britain, which were without any former example, saw eight reigns, in perfect security; because he remembered that precept of the *sensible, shrewd, temporizing* Apostle — "we ought not to resist the Higher Powers — "

You will think I have gotten a pension from Government; but I assure you, no such thing has been offered me. — In this respect, my vanity prompts me to say, they have not been so *wise* as I would have wished them; for I think their Honors have employed as impotent Scribblers. —

Enough of Politics. — What is become of Mrs. Burns & the dear bairns? How is my Willie? Tell her, though I do not write often, my best wishes shall ever attend her & the family. — My wife, who is in a high devotional fit this evening, wishes that she & her children may be reckoned favorites of the Lord — and numbered with the Elect. — She indeed leaves your Honor & Me to shift for ourselves; as, as far as she can judge from the criteria laid down in Guthrie's trial of a saving interest, that both you & I are stamped with marks of Reprobation.

May all the curses from the beginning of Genesis to the end of Revelation, light, materially & effectually, on thy enemies; & may all the blessings of the Covenant be eminently exemplified in thy person, to the glory of a forgiving Deity!

Here, or elsewhere, I am always thine sincerely

Edinr 10th Febry — 93 WILLM NICOL

* A reference to George III's temporary insanity.

Before copying his reply to Nicol in the letter book, Burns comments, "As my friend Nicol, though one of the worthiest, & positively the cleverest fellow I ever knew, yet no man, in his humours, having gone greater lengths in imprudence, unholiness, &c. than he; I wrote him as follows. [February 20, 1793]"

O thou, wisest among the Wise, meridian blaze of Prudence, full-moon of Discretion, & Chief of many Counsellors! — How infinitely is thy puddle-headed, rattle-headed, wrong-headed, round-headed slave indebted to thy supereminent goodness, that from the luminous path of thy own right-lined rectitude, thou lookest benignly down on an erring Wretch, of whom the zig-zag wanderings defy all the powers of Calculation, from the simple copulation of Units up to the hidden mystery of Fluxions! May one feeble ray of that light of wisdom which darts from thy sensorium, straight as the arrow of Heaven against the head of the Unrighteous, & bright as the meteor of inspiration descending on the holy & undefiled Priesthood — may it be my portion; so that I may be less unworthy of the face and favour of that father of Proverbs & master of Maxims, that antipode of Folly & magnet among the Sages, the wise & witty Willie Nicol! Amen! Amen! Yea, so be it! ! ! [And so on for another paragraph, finally concluding] May thy pity & thy prayer be exercised for, O thou lamp of Wisdom & mirror of Morality!

Thy devoted slave
RB

To Alexander Cunningham on the same day he sent the following dialogue:

Quere, What is Politics?
Answer, Politics is a science wherewith, by means of nefarious cunning, & hypocritical pretence, we govern civil Polities for the emolument of ourselves & our adherents. —
Quere, What is a Minister?
Answer, A Minister is an unprincipled fellow, who by the influence of hereditary, or acquired wealth; by superiour abilities; or by a lucky conjuncture of circumstances, obtains a principal place in the administration of the affairs of government. —

Q. What is a Patriot?
A. An individual exactly of the same description as a Minister, only out of Place.

Two years later, in December, 1794, Burns was made Acting Supervisor in Dumfries, and wrote to Mrs. Dunlop, "My Political sins seem to be forgiven me." But in that same letter, his calling the king and queen of France "a perjured Blockhead & an un-principled Prostitute" so offended Mrs. Dunlop, apparently, that she broke off the correspondence.

3. Ellisland and the Riddells

Ellisland farm lay along the west bank of the river Nith, sur-rounded by hills, the farmhouse on a high bank overlooking the river. Six miles north of Dumfries and a half mile east of the road to Kilmarnock, it was a beautiful spot, but remote, and after his excitement of the past few years, lonely for Burns. In time he collected and enjoyed a circle of acquaintance, but he had no one to know him for what he was. Indeed, he had enjoyed little enough of that recognition in Edinburgh. At Ellisland, as before and later, galling ambiguities plagued him. He was fond of Jean and she devoted to him. But she played only a limited part in his life. As he wrote to Mrs. Dunlop shortly after his marriage, "I can easily *fancy* a more agreable companion for my journey of Life, but upon my honor, I have never *seen* the individual Instance!" (He had looked for a more cultivated wife without success.) "You are right," he continued, "that a Bachelor state would have ensured me more friends; but, from a cause you will easily guess, conscious Peace in the enjoyment of my own mind, and unmistrusting Confidence in approaching my God, would seldom have been of the number." He loved his children dearly, but his family was an oppressive responsibility which limited his utterance and burdened him, body and spirit. The struggle to get ahead was distasteful to him, not the less because he recognized that he was accepting burdens which he himself had created. He wrote his best vernacular poem at Ellisland, and many fine songs, but at the same time he was searching, unsuccessfully, for other modes. He achieved there a measure of stability and security, yet it was a time of anticlimax, restraint, and frustration.

He was both a farmer and Exciseman, yet neither the one nor the other, nor a comfortable combination of the two. He was famous for a brilliant success, which had brought him little satisfaction. He had no heart for life's "warfare," and he was often melancholy and ill, yet the immediate impression of anyone who reads his letters and notes his activities is one of buoyancy and vigor. Burns may have been at ease with his conscience at Ellisland, but his life was not in a style "suitable to his feelings," and he was no more at ease with himself than he had been at Lochlea or Mossgiel, even if for somewhat different reasons. His was not an uncommon human condition, but recognition of it is a help to understanding what he said and did.

The greatest irony of all was his position. Success had opened the way for him to enter homes of the gentry and aristocracy, but always as a tame lion. He often enjoyed it, and yet resented his reception, for the class line never disappeared between him and such people, although a few of them made him comfortable. He was usually on display, and it is too bad that so much is recorded of Burns in such circumstances, and so little when he was among cronies, or at home, or going about his business. He seldom figured among his social superiors as more than a celebrity who, although fascinating, was uncouth and awkward, and these relationships often ended in disdain or distress. With his own ilk, and among tradespeople and certain professional people, he found much good company with whom he felt comfortable; and, just as he always had, he continued to enjoy companions of "low ranks, but men of talent & humour." Never in his life, however, at Ellisland or elsewhere, except for Nicol and Smellie, perhaps, did he meet anyone of near his own calibre.

In his first year at Ellisland, Burns speaks of working with his laborers and of being tired, but his life there was certainly not the grind he had known at Lochlea or Mossgiel. After October, 1789, he devoted his efforts largely to the Excise, which was not heavy work, however tedious and time-consuming and often wearisome it may have been. One result of this change was a reduction in Burns' letter writing. Prolonged ill-health at the end of 1789, and during 1790, must have contributed to the reduction, also. But an examination of the 239 surviving and published letters of the period June, 1788–November, 1791, reveals great vigor of mind and wide interests, and the list of his correspondents is extensive and varied. He wrote most often, and with great freedom, to Mrs. Dunlop — about public events, religion, his family, his farm, his poetry, his opinions, and his general experience. She replied with many more letters than he sent her, full of affectionate concern and interest.

Correspondence with Crochallans* and similar cronies in Edinburgh was heavy, but that with "stately patricians" was light, although there is a sprinkling of letters to aristocracy and gentry. A few letters went to old Ayrshire friends like Sillar and Richard Brown, many to his brothers Gilbert and William, and one to his cousin James Burness. Dr. Moore continued to write and receive letters, and a series passed between Burns and the Grahams of Fintry. In August, 1789, by request, Burns also supplied Dr. Moore's protégée and amanuensis, Helen Maria Williams, with an elaborate critique of her poem, *The Slave Trade*, in which he found both sense and grammar wanting on occasion. Of one passage he remarks, "Either my apprehension is dull, or there is something a little confused in the apostrophe to Mr Pit. — . . . Try it in prose." Later he comments, "If you insert the word, Like, where I have placed As, you must alter Darts, to,

---

* "Many letters of Burns to Mr Smellie which remained, being totally unfit for publication, and several of them containing severe reflections on many respectable people still in life, have been burnt." (Robert Kerr, *Memoirs of the Life Writings and Correspondence of William Smellie*, 1811. II, 350.)

Darting, and Heeds, to Heeding, in order to make it grammar."
Touching homage to John Murdoch! One engaging note went to
Bruce Campbell, of Milrig, with a ballad for James Boswell,
Burns' old Mauchline neighbor, in hopes that proved vain of an
introduction; Boswell docketed the letter, "13 Novr 1788 Mr.
Robert Burns the Poet expressing very high sentiments of me."
Eight of his letters are either public or addressed to editors, and
his correspondence reveals an alert and informed interest in
public affairs.

A selection from the correspondence of these relatively quiet
years furnishes a lively record of Burns' interests, his tastes, his
good sense, his warm family feeling, his wit, the rich personality
which fascinated those who knew him, and his mode of expression. Although there are few records of Burns' electric conversation, these letters to his intimates provide a happy indication
of what it must have been like.

1. From a letter to Robert Ainslie, June 30, 1788:

I have just now been interrupted by one of my new Neighbours,
who has made himself absolutely contemptible in my eyes by his silly,
garrulous pruriency. — I know it has been a fault of my own too; but
from this moment I abjure it as I would the service of Hell!

2. From a letter to William Stewart, factor on the Closeburn
Estates north of Ellisland, with a bawdy song, July 9, 1788:

I enclose you the Plenipo. — You will see another, The Bower of bliss;
'tis the work of a Revd Doctor of the Church of Scotland — Would
to Heaven a few more of them would turn their fiery Zeal *that way!*
There, they might *spend* their Holy fury, and shew the *tree* by its
fruits! ! !

3. From a letter to Mrs. Dunlop, describing a dinner with his
landlord, Patrick Miller, August 16, 1788:

I was yesterday at Mr Miller's to dinner; the first time since I have been his Tenant. — My reception was quite to my mind: from the lady of the house, quite flattering. — I believe in my conscience that she respects me more on account of my marrying a woman in circumstances somewhat similar to her own, when she commenced Mrs Millar. — See what it is to be rich! I was going to add, & to be great; but to be rich is to be great. — She sometimes hits on a couplet or two impromptu. — She repeated one or two to the admiration of all present. — My suffrage as a professional man, was expected: I for once went, agonizing, over the belly of my conscience — Pardon me, ye, my adored Household gods, Independence of Spirit & Integrity of Soul! In the course of conversation, Johnson's musical Museum, A Collection of Scots Songs with the music, was talked of. — We got a song on the Harpsichord, beginning —

"Raving winds around her blowing" —

The Air was much admired: the Lady of the house ask'd me whose were the words — "Mine, Madam — they are my very best verses!" sacré Dieu! she took not the smallest notice of them! — The old Scots Proverb says well — "King's caff [chaff] is better than ither folks corn." — I was going to make a New Testament quotation about "casting Pearls," but that would be too virulent. — The Lady is actually a woman of sense & taste: a proof, if the subject needed, that these two said qualities, so useful & ornamental to Human Nature, are by no means inseparably of the family of Gules, Purpure, Argent, Or, &c. —

4. A letter to Jean, September 12, 1788:

MY DEAR LOVE,

I received your kind letter with a pleasure which no letter but one from you could have given me. — I dreamed of you the whole night last; but alas! I fear it will be three weeks yet, ere I can hope for the happiness of seeing you. — My harvest is going on. — I have some to cut down still, but I put in two stacks today, so I am as tired as a dog. —

You might get one of Gilbert's sweet milk cheeses [words missing] & send it to [MS torn]

On second thoughts, I believe you had best get the half of Gilbert's web of Table-linen, and make it up; tho' I think it damnable dear, but it is no out-laid money to us you know. — I have just now consulted my old Landlady about table-linen, & she thinks I may have the best for two shillings per yard; so after all, let it alone untill I return; and some day soon I will be in Dumfries, and will ask the prices there. — I expect your new gowns will be very forward, or ready to make, against I be home to get the Baiveridge [salute]. — I have written my long-thought-on letter to Mr Graham, the Commissioner of Excise; & have sent him a sheetful of Poetry besides. — Now I talk of Poetry, I had a fine Strathspey among my hands to make verses to, for Johnson's Collection which I [remainder of MS wanting]

5. From a letter to Mrs. Dunlop at Moreham Mains (her son's farm), November 13, 1788, speaking of a recent visit to Dunlop House:

I had the very great pleasure of dining at Dunlop yesterday. — Men are said to flatter women because they are weak; if it is so, Poets must be weaker still; for Misses Rachel & Keith [Mrs. Dunlop's daughters], and Miss Georgina Mckay, with their flattering attentions & artful compliments, absolutely turned my head. — I own they did not lard me over as a Poet does his Patron or still more his Patroness, nor did they sugar me up as a Cameronian Preacher does J-s-s C-st; but they so intoxicated me with their sly insinuations & delicate innuendos of Compliment that if it had not been for a lucky recollection how much additional weight & lustre your good opinion & friendship must give me in that circle, I had certainly looked on myself as a person of no small consequence.

6. From a letter to Dr. Blacklock, November 15, 1788:

A wife's head is immaterial, compared with her heart — & — Virtue's (as for Wisdom, what Poet pretends to it) — "ways are ways of pleasantness, & all her paths are peace."

7. From a letter to Mrs. Dunlop, December 7, 1788, commenting on George III, recently declared insane:

As for G. R. whom you commiserate so much in your Moreham mains epistle (you see I have read both sheets, notwithstanding your wicked

LIKENESSES OF BURNS

Robert Burns, 1787, Nasmyth. Painted for Burns' Edinburgh Edition. *Courtesy Scottish National Portrait Gallery.*

Robert Burns, 1787, Beugo, after Nasmyth, and from sittings by Burns. Probably the best likeness. Frontispiece to Edinburgh Edition.

Robert Burns drawn 1796/7. Skirving, after Nasmyth, and not from life, but said by Sir Walter Scott to be "the only good portrait of Burns." *Courtesy Scottish National Portrait Gallery.*

Robert Burns, 1787 (?), Nasmyth.
Courtesy Scottish National Portrait Gallery.

Robert Burns, 1787, Miers.

Robert Burns. Painted 1828, presumably from Nasmyth drawing.
Courtesy Scottish National Portrait Gallery.

MEMBERS OF THE BURNS FAMILY

Gilbert Burns,
brother of Robert Burns.

Agnes Broun,
mother of Robert Burns.

Jean Armour Burns, 1821.
Courtesy Scottish National Portrait Gallery.

Robert Burns,
eldest son of the poet.

Elizabeth Hyslop Burns,
daughter of Robert Burns
by Anne Park.

Colonel William Nicol Burns,
son of Robert Burns.

Lieutenant Colonel
James Glencairn Burns,
son of Robert Burns.

FRIENDS OF BURNS
AND MEMORABILIA

Mrs. Frances Anna Dunlop.

Lord Glencairn.

A Learned Pig. From the John
Mulholland Magic Collection, The
Walter Hampden Memorial Library
at the Players, New York. *Courtesy
Mr. Mulholland and the Library.*

Margaret Chalmers.

William Smellie.

Agnes M'Lehose ("Clarinda").

Glasses given Clarinda by Burns in parting.

Maria Riddell (Mrs. Walter Riddell), Sir Thomas Lawrence.
Courtesy the present owner, H. J. R. Bankes, Esq.

Robert Riddell
of Glenriddell.

Hermitage at Friars' Carse,
near Ellisland.

Francis Grose.

John Syme.

Alexander Cunningham.

Jessie Lewars.

Dr. James Maxwell.

BUILDINGS AND PLACES
ASSOCIATED WITH BURNS

Alloway Kirk, 1805.

Burns' Birthplace, Alloway, 1805.

Drawings from James M'Bain, *Burns' Cottage*, 1904. The ground plan and scale show the size and William Burnes' arrangement of the but (outer room or kitchen), ben (inner room or parlor), byre (cowshed), and barn traditional in the Ayrshire farmstead.

Three farmsteads, with different arrangements
of the but, ben, barn, and byre.

Mt. Oliphant

Lochlea.

Mossgiel.

Ellisland.

Burns' last residence (house at left).

surmise) I am not sure whether he is not a gainer, by how much a Madman is a more respectable character than a Fool.

8. From a letter to Mrs. Dunlop, "New-year-day Morning, 1789":

This Day; the first Sunday of May; a breezy, blue-skied noon some time about the beginning, & a hoary morning & calm sunny day about the end, of Autumn; these, time out of mind, have been with me a kind of Holidays. — Not like the Sacramental, Executioner-face of a Kilmarnock Communion; but to laugh or cry, be chearful or pensive, moral or devout, according to the mood & tense of the Season & Myself.

9. From a letter to Robert Ainslie, January 6, 1789, congratulating him on his having become a Writer to the Signet:

I grant you enter the lists of life, to struggle for bread, business, notice, and distinction, in common with hundreds. — But who are they? Men like yourself, and of that aggregate body, your compeers, seven-tenths of them come short of your advantages natural and accidental; while two of those that remain, either neglect their parts, as flowers in a desert, or misspend their strength, like a bull goring a bramble bush.

10. A letter to his cousin, James Burness, in Montrose, February 9, 1789:

My dear Sir,

Why I did not write to you long ago is what, even on the rack I could not answer. — If you can in your mind form an idea of indolence, dissipation, hurry, cares, change of country, entering on untried scenes of life — all combined; you will save me the trouble of a blushing apology. — It could not be want of regard for a man for whom I had a high esteem before I knew him — an esteem which has much increased since I did know him; and this caveat entered, I shall plead guilty to any other indictment with which you shall please to charge me. —

After I parted from you, for many months, my life was one continued scene of dissipation. — Here, at last, I am become stationary, and

have taken a farm and — a wife. The farm lies beautifully situated on
the Nith, a large river that runs by Dumfries, & falls into the Solway
Firth. — I have gotten a lease on my farm as long as I pleased; but
how it may turn out is just a guess, and it is yet to improve and inclose, &c.; however I have good hopes of my bargain on the whole. —

My Wife is, my Jean, with whose story you are partly acquainted. —
I found I had a much-loved fellow-creature's happiness or misery
among my hands, and I durst not trifle with so sacred a deposite. —
Indeed I have not any reason to repent the step I have taken, as I
have attached myself to a very good wife, & have shaken myself loose
of a very bad failing. —

I have found my book, a very profitable business; and with the
profits of it have begun life pretty decently. — Should Fortune not
favour me in farming, as I have no great faith in her fickle Ladyship,
I have provided myself in another resource, which, however some
folks may affect to despise it, is still a comfortable shift in the day of
misfortune. — In the heyday of my fame, a gentleman whose name at
least I dare say you know, as his estate lies somewhere near Dundee,
Mr Graham of Fintry, one of the Commissioners of Excise, offered me
the commission of an Excise-Officer. — I thought it prudent to accept
of the offer, and accordingly I took my Instructions, and have my
Commission by me. — Whether I may ever do duty, or be a penny the
better for it, is what I do not know; but I have this comfortable
assurance that, come whatever ill fate will, I can on my simple petition
to the Excise board, get into employ. —

We have lost poor uncle Robert this winter. — He had long been
weak, and with very little alteration in him, he expired Janry 3d. —
His Son William, has been with me this winter, & goes in May to bind
himself to be a Mason with my fatherinlaw who is a pretty considerable Architect in Ayrshire. — His other Son, the eldest, John, comes
to me, I expect in Summer. — They are both remarkable stout young
fellows, & promise to do well. — His only daughter, Fanny, has been
with me ever since her father's death and I purpose keeping her in my
family till she be quite woman grown, & be fit for better service. —
She is one of the cleverest girls, and has one of the most amiable dispositions, that I have ever seen. —

All friends in this country and Ayrshire are well. — Remember me
to all friends in the North. — My wife joins in Compliments to your
bedfellow & family. — I would write your brother-in-law, but have

lost his Address. — For goodness sake don't take example by me, but write me soon. — I am ever, My dear Cousin,

yours most sincerely —
ROBT BURNS

11. From a letter to Mrs. Dunlop, April 21, 1789:

Two mornings ago as I was, at a very early hour, sowing in the fields, I heard a shot, & presently a poor little hare limped by me, apparently very much hurt. — You will easily guess, this set my humanity in tears and my indignation in arms. — The following was the result, which please read to the young ladies — I believe you may include the Major [her son], too; as whatever I have said of shooting hares, I have not spoken one irreverend word against coursing them.

He adds the first copy of *On seeing a fellow wound a hare with a shot.*

12. From a letter to the Rev. Patrick Carfrae, April 27, 1789, giving advice about a proposed edition of poems by a farmer-poet known to Mrs. Dunlop, one James Mylne:

I have, Sir, some experience of publishing; and the way in which I would proceed with Mr Mylne's Poems is this. — I would publish in two or three English & Scots Public Papers any one of his English Poems which should, by private judges, be thought the most excellent, and mention it, at the same time, as one of the many poetical productions which a Lothian Farmer of respectable character left behind him at his death. — That his friends had it in idea to publish soon, by subscription, a Collection of his Poems, for the sake of his numerous family (I think Mrs Dunlop informed me that he had a numerous family) — not in pity to that Family, but in justice to what his friends think the Poetic Merits of the deceased; and to secure in the most effectual manner, to those tender connections whose right it is, the pecuniary reward of those merits. — After thus advertising the Public of the design, I would proceed to disperse Subscription bills. — Suppose the book to be 200, a few odd pages, and that there are printed, 600 copies. — This, on elegant paper, & stitched, or in boards, will be done for less than forty pounds. — Though not above 300 Subscribers are got, that at 4sh. or even at 3sh. per Copy price to Subscribers, will more than pay costs; and thus, without risking anything, and with a probability of considerable profits as the work should succeed in the world, I would bring Mr Mylne's poetic Merits to that Bar which is alone competent to decide on them, the Voice of the public. —

From what I have seen of his works, & from what an abler Judge, my honored friend Mrs Dunlop, has often mentioned to me of those works of his which I have not seen, I have the Most sanguine hopes that Mr Mylne's Poems will be a very respectable & much esteemed addition to that species of Polite Literature.

13. From a letter to his younger brother William, then in New-castle-on-Tyne, May 5, 1789:

Your falling in love is indeed a phenomenon. To a fellow of your turn it cannot be hurtful. I am, you know, a veteran in these campaigns, so let me advise you always to pay your particular assiduities and try for intimacy as soon as you feel the first symptoms of the passion; this is not only best, as making the most of the little entertainment which the sportabilities of distant addresses always gives, but is the best preservative for one's peace. I need not caution you against guilty amours — they are bad everywhere, but in England they are the very devil.

14. A letter to James Johnson, of the *Scots Musical Museum*, June 19, 1789:

MY DEAR FRIEND,

What are you doing, and what is the reason that you have sent me no proof sheet to correct? Though I have been rather remiss in writing you, as I have been hurried, puzzled, plagued & confounded with some disagreable matters, yet believe me, it is not owing to the smallest neglect or forget of you, my good Sir, or your patriotic work. — Mr Clarke & I have frequent meetings & consultations on your work. — I have given him three or four songs which he is preparing for you. — One is, the Caledonian Hunt, as it seems the verses I sent you don't suit it; another is, The Braes o' Ballochmyle, to which I have likewise given him new words, & a third is, The poor Thresher. — Let me hear from you first post, and forgive this seeming neglect in a care-

less fellow of an indolent Poet, who is as lazy as the Packman that
laid down his pack until he would f——t.
  My best complnts to your father & Mr Barclay.

I am ever, dear Sir, yours sincerely,
ROBT BURNS

15. From a letter to Mrs. Dunlop, June 22, 1789:

I have just heard Mr Kirkpatrick preach a sermon. He is a man
famous for his benevolence, and I revere him; but from such ideas of
my Creator, good Lord, deliver me! Religion, my honored friend, is
surely a simple business, as it equally concerns the ignorant and the
learned, the poor and the rich. That there is an incomprehensible
Great Being, to whom I owe my existence; and that He must be intimately acquainted with the operations and progress of the internal
machinery, and consequent outward deportment, of this creature
which He has made; these are, I think, self-evident propositions.
That there is a real and eternal distinction between virtue and vice,
and, consequently, that I am an accountable creature; that from the
seeming nature of the human mind, as well as from the evident im-
perfection, nay, positive injustice, in the administration of affairs
both in the natural and moral worlds, there must be a retributive
scene of existence beyond the grave; must, I think, be allowed by
every one who will give himself a moment's reflection. I will go further, and affirm, that from the sublimity, excellence, and purity of
His doctrine and precepts, unparalleled by all the aggregated wisdom
and learning of many preceding ages, though, *to appearance* He
Himself was the obscurest and most illiterate of our species — therefore
Jesus Christ was from God. . . .
  Whatever mitigates the woes, or increases the happiness, of others,
this is my criterion of goodness; and whatever injures society at
large, or any individual in it, this is my measure of iniquity.

**16. From a letter to Mrs. Dunlop, describing Captain Francis
Grose, July 17, 1789:**

Captn Grose, the well-known Author of the Antiquities of England
& Wales, has been through Annandale, Nithsdale & Galloway, in the
view of commencing another Publication, The Antiquities of Scot-

land. — As he has made his head-quarters with Captn Riddel, my nearest neighbour, for these two months, I am intimately acquainted with him; & I have never seen a man of more original observation, anecdote & remark. — Thrown into the army from the Nursery, & now that he is the father of a numerous family who are all settled in respectable situations in life, he has mingled in all societies, & known every body. — His delight is to steal thro' the country almost unknown, both as most favorable to his humour & his business. — I have to the best of my recollection of the old buildings, &c. in the County, given him an Itinerary thro' Ayr-shire. — I have directed him among other places to Dunlop house, as an old building worthy of a place in his collection. — It would have been presumption in such a man as I, to offer an introductory letter between such folks as Captn Grose & Major Dunlop, tho' for the honour of my native county I could have wished that Captn Grose had been introduced to the Dunlop family, & the Major would have been of much use to him in directing him thro' the farther corner of Cunningham, a place I little know, however if you discover a chearful-looking grig of an old, fat fellow, the precise figure of Dr Slop, wheeling about your avenue in his own carriage with a pencil & paper in his hand, you may conclude, "Thou art the man!"

Perhaps after all I may pluck up as much impudent importance as write to the Major by him. — He will go for Ayr-shire in four or five days, but I have directed him thro' Carrick & Kyle first.

17. From a letter to Peter Hill, February 2, 1790, about an Edinburgh whore:

What are you doing, and how are you doing? Have you lately seen any of my few friends? What is become of the Borough Reform, or how is the fate of my poor Namesake Mademoiselle Burns, decided? Which of their grave Lordships can lay his hand on his heart and say that he has not taken advantage of such frailty; nay, if we may judge by near six thousand years experience, can the World do without such frailty? O man! but for thee, & thy selfish appetites & dishonest artifices, that beauteous form, & that once innocent & still ingenuous mind, might have shone conspicuous and lovely in the faithful wife and the affectionate mother; and shall the unfortunate sacrifice to thy pleasures have no claim on thy humanity? As for those flinty-bosomed, puritannic Prosecutors of Female Frailty, & Persecutors of Female Charms — I am quite sober — I am dispassionate — to shew you that I am so I shall mend my Pen ere I proceed — It is written, "Thou shalt not take the name of the Lord thy God in vain," so I shall neither say, G—— curse them! nor G—— blast them! nor G—— damn them! but may Woman curse them! May Woman blast them! May Woman damn them! May her lovely hand inexorably shut the Portal of Rapture to their most earnest Prayers & fondest essays for entrance! And when many years and much port and great business have delivered them over to Vulture Gouts and Aspen Palsies, *then* may the dear bewitching Charmer in derision throw open the blissful Gate to tantalize their impotent desires which like ghosts haunt their bosoms when all their powers to give or receive enjoyment, are for ever asleep in the sepulchre of their fathers!!!

The lady mentioned in this letter was a Miss Margaret Matthews who took "Burns" * as a *nom de guerre* because of its celebrity on her arrival in Edinburgh. When she was proceeded against for disorders in her "house," William Creech heard the case as magistrate and gave her a stiff sentence. On appeal, Bailie Creech's decision was overturned, to his intense annoyance, and the newspapers made sport of him. One London paper announced, "Bailie Creech, of literary celebrity in Edinburgh, is about to lead the beautiful and accomplished Miss Burns to the hymeneal altar." When Creech threatened suit, the paper agreed to a retraction, and printed the following: "In a former number we noticed the intended marriage between Bailie Creech of Edinburgh, and the beautiful Miss Burns of the same place. We have now the authority of that gentleman to say that the proposed marriage is not to take place, matters having been otherwise arranged to the mutual satisfaction of both parties and their respective friends."

* Throughout his life Burns enjoyed producing epigrams, epitaphs, and miscellaneous versified witticisms. One of the few to combine grace, wit, and enduring point, was intended to be placed under the portrait of "Miss Burns."

> Cease, ye prudes, your envious railing!
> Lovely Burns had charms: confess!
> True it is she had ae failing:
> Had ae woman ever less?

18. A letter to William Nicol, February 9, 1790, in part about Nicol's mare, named "Peg Nicholson" after a mad washerwoman who had attempted to assassinate George III:

MY DEAR SIR,

That d—mned mare of yours is dead. I would freely have given her price to have saved her; she has vexed me beyond description. Indebted as I was to your goodness beyond what I can ever repay, I eagerly grasped at your offer to have the mare with me. That I might at least shew my readiness in wishing to be grateful, I took every care of her in my power. She was never crossed for riding above half a score of times by me or in my keeping. I drew her in the plough, one of three, for one poor week. I refused fifty-five shillings for her, which was the highest bode I could squeeze for her. I fed her up and had her in fine order for Dumfries fair; when four or five days before the fair, she was seized with an unaccountable disorder in the sinews, or somewhere in the bones of the neck; with a weakness or total want of power in her fillets; and, in short, the whole vertebrae of her spine seemed to be diseased and unhinged; and in eight and forty hours, in spite of the two best farriers in the country, she died and be d—mned to her! The farriers said that she had been quite strained in the fillets beyond cure before you had bought her; and that the poor devil, though she might keep a little flesh, had been jaded and quite worn out with fatigue and oppression. While she was with me, she was under my own eye, and I assure you, my much valued friend, everything was done for her that could be done; and the accident has vexed me to the heart. In fact, I could not pluck up spirits to write you on account of the unfortunate business.

There is little new in this country. Our theatrical company, of which you must have heard, leave us in a week. Their merit and character are indeed very great, both on the stage and in private life; not a worthless creature among them; and their encouragement has been accordingly. Their usual run is from eighteen to twenty-five pounds a night: seldom less than the one, and the house will hold no more than the other. There have been repeated instances of sending away six, and eight, and ten pounds a night for want of room. A new theatre is to be built by subscription; the first stone is to be laid on Friday first to come. Three hundred guineas have been raised by thirty subscribers, and thirty more might have been got if wanted.

The manager, Mr. Sutherland, was introduced to me by a friend from Ayr; and a worthier or cleverer fellow I have rarely met with. Some of our clergy have slipt in by stealth now and then; but they have got up a farce of their own. You must have heard how the Rev. Mr. Lawson of Kirkmahoe, seconded by the Rev. Mr. Kirkpatrick of Dunscore, and the rest of that faction, have accused in formal process, the unfortunate and Rev. Mr. Heron of Kirkgunzeon, that in ordaining Mr. Nelson to the cure of souls in Kirkbean he, the said Heron, feloniously and treasonably bound the said Nelson to the confession of faith, *so far as it was agreable to reason and the Word of God!*

Mrs. B. begs to be remembered most gratefully to you. Little Bobby and Frank are charmingly well and healthy. I am jaded to death with fatigue. For these two or three months, on an average, I have not ridden less than two hundred miles per week. I have done little in the poetic way. I have given Mr. Sutherland two Prologues; one of which was delivered last week. I have likewise strung four or five barbarous stanzas, to the tune of Chevy Chase, by way of Elegy on your poor unfortunate mare, beginning (the name she got here was Peg Nicholson):

> Peg Nicholson was a good bay mare
>   As ever trod on airn: *iron*
> But now she's floating down the Nith,
>   And past the mouth o' Cairn.
>
> Peg Nicholson was a good bay mare,
>   An' rode thro' thick an' thin;
> But now she's floating down the Nith
>   And wanting even the skin.
>
> Peg Nicholson was a good bay mare,
>   An' ance she bore a priest;
> But now she's floating down the Nith,
>   For Solway fish a feast.
>
> Peg Nicholson was a good bay mare,
>   An' the priest he rode her sair;
> An' much oppress'd an' bruis'd she was,
>   As priest-rid cattle are.

My best compliments to Mrs. Nicol, and little Neddy, and all the family. I hope Ned is a good scholar, and will come out to gather nuts and apples with me next harvest.

I am ever, my dearest Friend, yours,
ROBT BURNS

19. A letter to William Burns, February 10, 1790:

MY DEAR WILLIAM

I would have written you sooner but I have mislaid Mr Murdoch's letter, and cannot for my life lay my hand on it; so I cannot write him for want of a direction. — If I find it afterwards, I will write him & inclose it to you in London. — Now that you are setting out for that place, put on manly resolve, & determine to persevere; & in that case you will less or more be sure of success. — One or two things allow me to particularize to you. — London swarms with worthless wretches who prey on their fellow-creatures' thoughtlessness or inexperience. — Be cautious in forming connections with comrades and companions. — You can be pretty good company to yourself, & you cannot be too shy of letting anybody know you farther than to know you as a Sadler. — Another caution; I give you great credit for your sobriety with respect to that universal vice, Bad Women. — It is an impulse the hardest to be restrained, but if once a man accustoms himself to gratifications of that impulse, it is then nearly, or altogether impossible to restrain it. — Whoring is a most ruinous expensive species of dissipation; is spending a poor fellow's money with which he ought to clothe & support himself nothing? Whoring has ninety nine chances in a hundred to bring on a man the most nauseous & excrutiating diseases to which Human nature is liable; are disease & an impaired constitution trifling considerations? All this independant of the criminality of it. —

I have gotten the Excise Division in the middle of which I live. — Poor little Frank is this morning at the height in the Smallpox. — I got him inoculated, & I hope he is in a good way. —

Write me before you leave Newcastle & as soon as you reach London. — In a word, if ever you be, as perhaps you may be, in a strait for a little ready cash, you know my direction. — I shall not see you beat, while you fight like a Man.

Farewell! God bless you!
ROBT BURNS

20. From a letter to Mrs. Dunlop, April 10, 1790, in which Burns mentions his favorite novel, *The Man of Feeling*:

Still, with all my admiration of M'kenzie's writings, I do not know if they are the fittest reading for a young man who is about to set out, as the phrase is, to make his way into life. Do you not think, Madam, that among the few favored of Heaven in the structure of their minds (for such there certainly are) there may be a purity, a tenderness, a dignity, an elegance of soul, which are of no use, nay, in some degree, absolutely disqualifying, for the truly important business of making a man's way into life? If I am not much mistaken, my gallant young friend Anthony [Mrs. Dunlop's son] is very much under these disqualifications.

21. From a letter to Mrs. Dunlop, July 9, 1790, giving particulars of electioneering in Burns' neighborhood:

I have just got a summons to attend with my men-servants armed as well as we can, on Monday at one o'clock in the *morning* to escort Captn Miller from Dalswinton in to Dumfries to be a Candidate for our Boroughs which chuse their Member that day. — The Duke of Queensberry & the Nithsdale Gentlemen who are almost all friends to the Duke's Candidate, the said Captn [Patrick Miller's son], are to raise all Nithsdale on the same errand. — The Duke of Buccleugh's, Earl of Hopeton's people, in short, the Johnstons, Jardines, and all the Clans of Annandale, are to attend Sir James Johnston who is the other Candidate, on the same account. — This is no exaggeration. — On Thursday last, as chusing the Delegate for the boro' of Lochmaben, the Duke & Captn Miller's friends led a strong party, among others, upwards of two hundred Colliers from Sanquhar Coal-works & Miners from Wanlock-head; but when they appeared over a hill-top within half a mile of Lochmaben, they found such a superiour host of Annandale warriors drawn out to dispute the Day, that without striking a stroke, they turned their backs & fled with all the precipitation the horrors of blood & murther could inspire. — What will be the event, I know not. — I shall go to please my Landlord, & to see the Combustion; but instead of trusting to the strength of Man, I shall trust to the heels of my horse, which are among the best in Nithsdale.

In this election Burns, who disliked the Duke of Queensberry, supported Sir James Johnston, and wrote a series of election ballads in his behalf. *The Five Carlins,* ironically impartial, alone retains any interest.

22. A letter to Burns' old Tarbolton friend, schoolmaster John Wilson [Dr. Hornbook], September 11, 1790, in reply to a request for advice whether Wilson should try to improve his income by turning lawyer's clerk in Edinburgh:

I am truly sorry, my dear Sir, that you find yourself so uncomfortably situated in Tarbolton; the more so, as I fear you will find on trial that the remedy you propose, is worse than the disease. — The life of an Edinr Quill-driver at twopence a page, is a life I know so well — that I should be very sorry any friend of mine should ever try it. — To young lads, bred to the law, & meaning to push their way in that department & line of life, practicing as a copying Clerk is to them a necessary step; but to a gentleman who is unacquainted with the science of law, & who proposes to live merely by the drudgery of his quill, he has before him a life of many sorrows. — Pardon me, my dr Sir, this freedom: I wish only to keep you, as far as my knowledge of life can, from being misled by that seducing Slut, Fancy, under the mask of Hope. — The Excise is impracticable to you. — No man above thirty, or who has more than two children, is admissible. — However, you are the best judge of your present situation & future hopes; & as I wish to be of all the service to you that is in my scanty power, I inclose you a card to a friend of mine, the only one I have in Edinr, to whom I could with any hope of success make such a request. —

Allow me to mention one suggestion to you. — Your present appointment may be held by deputy, at least untill you go to Edinr & see what you have to expect there: let me beg of you for Mrs Wilson's sake, and your sweet little flock, not to quit the Present, poor as it is, untill you be pretty sure of your hold on the Future. —

I am afraid, too, that at this season, in vacation, you will find few of the Gentlemen of the law in town. — Had you not better defer your journey untill the Court sit down?

Mrs Burns joins me in best Complnts to Mrs Wilson. —
Farewell! & believe me to be, my dear Sir,
Yours sincerely
ROBT BURNS

Wilson took Burns' advice and gave up his Edinburgh scheme.

23. From a letter to the Rev. George Husband Baird, offering assistance to an edition of the poems of Michael Bruce, February 28, 1791:

Why did you, my dear Sir, write to me in such a hesitating style on the business of poor Bruce? Don't I know, & have I not felt, the many ills, the peculiar ills, that Poetic Flesh is heir to? — You shall have your choice of all the unpublished poems I have; & had your letter had my address, so as to have reached me in course of post (it but came to hand this morning) I should have directly put you out of suspense about it. — I suppose I need not premise, that I still reserve these my works so much in my power, as to publish them on my own account, if so the spirit move me, at any *after* period. — I only ask that some prefatory advertisement in the Book, as well as the Subscripn bills, may bear, that the Publication is solely for the behoof of Bruce's Mother: I would not leave Ignorance the least room to surmise, or Malice to insinuate, that I clubbed a share in the work from mercenary motives. . . .

I have taxed your friendship with the trouble of transmitting the enclosed letter to Dr Moore, . . . I leave it open for your perusal, I mean the printed sheet. — It is one of my latest productions [*Tam o' Shanter*]; & I dare say you may have it, if you will, to accompany Bruce's works.

The generous offer of *Tam o' Shanter* was not accepted, "in consequence of the opposition of Dr [Hugh] Blair and Dr Moore, who argued that from the moral tendency of Bruce's poetry, the insertion of Burns's . . . would be as gross a violation of propriety as the exhibition of a farce after a tragedy."

24. From the letter to Dr. John Moore enclosed in the above, also dated February 28, 1791:

What a rocky-hearted, perfidious Succubus was that Queen Elizabeth! — Judas Iscariot was a sad dog to be sure, but still his demerits shrink to insignificance, compared with the doings of the infernal Bess Tudor. — Judas did not know, at least was by no means sure, what or who that Master was; his turpitude was simply, betraying a worthy man who had ever been a good Master to him: a degree of turpitude which has even been outdone by many of his kind since. — Iscariot, poor wretch, was a man of nothing at all per Annum, & by consequence thirty pieces of silver was a very serious temptation to *him*, but to give but one instance, the Duke of Queensberry, the other day, just played the same trick on *his* kind Master, tho' His Grace is a man of thirty thousand a year, & come to that imbecille period of life when no temptation but Avarice can be supposed to affect him.

25. A letter to Alexander Findlater, Burns' Excise Supervisor, "Sunday even: [June, 1791]," about a lapse in the performance of Excise duties. The "Lorimer" of the letter was Burns' neighbor and friend, and the father of a girl he wrote songs about.

DEAR SIR,

I am both much surprised & vexed at that accident of Lorimer's Stock. — The last survey I made prior to Mr Lorimer's going to Edinr I was very particular in my inspection & the quantity was certainly in his possession as I stated it. — The surveys I have made during his absence might as well have been marked "key absent" as I never found any body but the lady, who I know is not mistress of the keys, &c. to know anything of it, and one of the times, it would have rejoiced all Hell to have seen her so drunk. I have not surveyed there since his return. — I know the gentleman's ways are, like the grace of G——, past all comprehension; but I shall give the house a severe scrutiny tomorrow morning, & send you in the naked facts. —

I know, Sir, & regret deeply that this business glances with a malign aspect on my character as an Officer; but as I am really innocent in the affair, & as the gentleman is known to be an illicit Dealer, & particularly as this is the *single* instance of the least shadow of carelessness or impropriety in my conduct as an Officer, I shall be peculiarly unfortunate if my character shall fall a sacrifice to the dark maneouvres of a Smuggler. —

I am, Sir, your oblidged & obedient humble servt
ROBT BURNS

26. A letter to David Newall, proprietor of the Isle, undated but probably in the spring of 1790:

DR SIR,

Inclosed is a state of the account between you and me and James Halliday respecting the drain. I have stated it at 20d. per rood, as in fact, even at that, they have not the wages they ought to have had, and I cannot for the soul of me see a poor devil a loser at my hand.

Humanity, I hope, as well as Charity, will cover a multitude of sins, a mantle, of which — between you and me — I have some little need.

I am, Sir, yours,
ROBT BURNS

During his last months at Ellisland, 1791, Burns' life was "chequered, joy & sorrow," by the following events:

1. He was deeply distressed by Lord Glencairn's death on January 30, which moved him to write his *Lament for James Earl of Glencairn.*

2. He had to pay a £20 bill, which he had endorsed for a friend, evidence that his credit was good if his judgment was not, and that he had funds. But the payment drained them. He wrote to David Sillar, who had asked for a loan, "It is not in my power to give you any assistance. — I am just five shillings rich at present; tho' I was considerably richer three days ago, when I was obliged to pay twenty pounds for a man who took me in, to save a rotten credit. — I heedlessly gave him my name on the back of a bill where-in I had no concern, & he — gave me the bill to pay." Burns seems not to have suffered unduly, for on June 16 he wrote Thomas Boyd, builder of his Ellisland house,

Dear Sir,

As it is high time that the account between you & me were settled, if you will take a bill of Mr Alexr Crombie's to me for twenty pounds in part, I will settle with you immediately; at least, against Wedensday se'nnight, as I am to be out of the country for a week. — Mr Crombie cannot take it amiss that I endeavour to get myself clear of his bill in this manner, as you owe him and I owe you.

3. The absence spoken of to Boyd was a visit to Kilmarnock, June 19–22, for his brother Gilbert's wedding to Jean Breckenridge.

4. Burns put aside a suggestion by Alexander Cunningham that he address a poem to the Royal Company of Archers in Edinburgh, the King's bodyguard for Scotland, who apparently were considering their fellow member Cunningham's suggestion of admitting Burns. He could not, he said, compose merely from the wish. But the select and aristocratic group admitted Burns to membership just the same, on April 10, 1792.

5. He was invited to be present at the Earl of Buchan's estate when the Earl planned to crown a bust of James Thomson, poet of *The Seasons,* with a wreath. Burns declined the invitation in a letter which began with polite irony, "Language sinks under the ardor of my feelings, when I would thank your Lordship for the honour, the very great honour, you have done me," but he sent an innocuous *Address to the Shade of Thomson.* When he learned later that the bust had been broken in a drunken frolic before the coronation, forcing the Earl to crown, instead, a volume of Thomson's poems, Burns wrote *On Some Commemorations of Thomson,* not one of his distinguished poems, but not innocuous, either.

> Dost thou not rise, indignant Shade,
>   And smile wi' spurning scorn,
> When they wha wad hae starved thy life
>   Thy senseless turf adorn?

They wha about thee mak sic fuss
Now thou art but a name,
Wad seen thee damn'd ere they had spar'd
Ae plack to fill thy wame.   *farthing belly*

Helpless, alane, thou clamb the brae
Wi' meikle honest toil,
And claucht th'unfading garland there,   *clutched*
Thy sair-won, rightful spoil.

And wear it there! and call aloud
This axiom undoubted: —
Would thou hae Nobles' patronage?
First learn to live without it!

"To whom hae much, more shall be given"
Is every great man's faith;
But he, the helpless, needful wretch,
Shall lose the mite he hath.

This was the poem Burns sent to Captain Johnston of the *Gazetteer*, cited later as evidence of his disaffection to government.

6. Finally, Burns ignored Creech's suggestion that he bring out a new edition.

At Ellisland farm, Burns' neighbor to the north was Captain Robert Riddell of Glenriddell (1755–1794), a good and amiable man recently retired at twenty-eight from the Prince of Wales Light Dragoons, and married (1784) to a Miss Elizabeth Kennedy. He enjoyed "an easy fortune," and William Smellie reported himself "sometimes *threatened* and *frightened*" with the "gigantic" Riddell's "immense *fist* and stentorian *voice*." The Captain lived as a country gentleman on his estate of Friars' Carse, pursuing an interest in folksong and local antiquities, corresponding with leading antiquaries, entertaining antiquaries and artists, and greatly enjoying convivial society. He was also an amateur musician, a church elder, and a political liberal. Although by his own account "no Draughtsman," he accompanied friends on trips to visit and sketch antiquities, and in May, 1794, after his death, there was published his *Collection of Scotch, Galwegian, and Border Tunes,* 37 pages, 7 shillings.* The University of Edinburgh in January, 1794, gave him an LL.D. in recognition of his "uncommon knowledge."

Although Riddell was widely esteemed as a man, contemporaries did not value his achievements highly. The Stenhouse edition of Johnson's *Scots Musical Museum* carries this note on Riddell's collection of tunes: "Robert Riddell of Glenriddell, Esq., was much respected, and attained some celebrity as an antiquarian, although his researches were not very profound, and some of his theories fanciful. [Mr. Charles Kirkpatrick Sharpe says,] 'Mr Riddell was an excellent man, but no musician; as I have been assured by a competent judge, whose partiality to the author would have made him very sensible of any merit his compositions might possess. . . .' Mr Riddell was member of several learned societies, and communicated various papers which were inserted in their Transactions." These latter Sir Walter Scott describes as "truly the most extravagant compositions that ever a poor Man abandoned by providence to the imaginations of his own heart had the misfortune to devise."

In commenting on Allan Cunningham's description of Robert Riddell as a "distinguished antiquarian," and much other praise, Riddell's schoolfellow, Alexander Young, of Harburn, W. S., remarks,

Robert Riddell of Glenriddell, so often mentioned in this Work with much applause, was my Schoolfellow, and in the same class with me at Dr. Chapman's in Dumfries.

In that Class also were Dr. William Charles Wills of London, Dr. James Currie of Liverpool, Dr. George Bell of Manchester, Wm. Cunningham of Enterkin &c.; and I am sure it would have astonished

---

* The volume was published by James Johnson, of the *Museum,* who told Burns, "I have not sold 10 copies." (Ch-W IV, 89.)

all these as much as it does me, to read such praises of the most heavy, dull youth, the least of a Scholar, and the most incorrigible dolt ["blockhead" deleted] in our class. He did not come much forward into the World; after we quitted school, ["and I know no ill of him" deleted] I used to meet him at the Assizes and Dumfries Elections, when we always shook hands cordially, in remembrance of old Class fellowship; but that he should have been commemorated, as is done in these volumes, seems to me most extraordinary. I think the secret must have lain in his marrying an excellent and amiable lady of the name of Kennedy, whom all his old School fellows admired, as much as they under-valued him.

Burns responded warmly to offers of friendship, and when Riddell offered his, the two men grew quickly to be on excellent terms. Burns, for example, felt free to ask if he might borrow a laborer from Riddell to help in his first harvest. Riddell gave his new neighbor a key to a "Hermitage" which he had had built on his grounds, as a suitable adornment of former abbey lands. He apparently had a romantic hope that the Bard would meditate in quiet there and produce poetry. Burns dutifully responded in the first month, inscribing some oracular couplets on a Hermitage window pane, but there is no record of his frequenting the place.

Verses in Friars Carse Hermitage

June 1788

Thou whom chance may hither lead,
Be thou clad in russet weed,
Be thou deckt in silken stole,
Grave these maxims on thy soul: —

Life is but a day at most,
Sprung from night in darkness lost;
Hope not sunshine every hour,
Fear not clouds will always lour.

Happiness is but a name,
Make content and ease thy aim.
Ambition is a meteor-gleam;
Fame a restless airy dream;
Pleasures, insects on the wing
Round Peace, th' tend'rest flow'r of spring;
Those that sip the dew alone —
Make the butterflies thy own;
Those that would the bloom devour —
Crush the locusts, save the flower.
For the future be prepar'd:
Guard wherever thou can'st guard;
But, thy utmost duly done,
Welcome what thou can'st not shun.
Follies past give thou to air —
Make their consequence thy care.
Keep the name of Man in mind,
And dishonour not thy kind.
Reverence with lowly heart
Him, whose wondrous work thou art;
Keep His Goodness still in view —
Thy trust, and thy example too.

Stranger, go! Heaven be thy guide!
Quod the Beadsman on Nidside.

Of a 1792 quarto issue of this poem, apparently anonymous, with a vignette by Robert Riddell's friend Francis Grose, Stenhouse remarks, "Mr [Charles Kirkpatrick] Sharpe . . . says . . . , 'Sir Walter Scott told me that this production puzzled him — it was much too good for the one [Riddell?] and much to bad for the other [Grose?].'"

Burns rejoiced to find that Riddell was a folk-song enthusiast, and their shared interest seems to have stimulated both men, one evidence of it being an interleaved set of the first four volumes of the *Museum* with notes by Burns and Riddell — 152 by Burns (to which Riddell added ten more comments); nineteen by Riddell alone; with seventeen more by an unknown hand. (Seventeen leaves presumably with additional comments, have been excised and are now missing.) Burns ordered another interleaved *Museum* for himself, now in the Ewart Public Library, Dumfries.

Out of compliment to his friendly neighbor, Burns prepared for him a manuscript volume of some of his poems, and another of some of his letters — the letters in his own hand, but some of the poems in that of an amanuensis. The poetry volume includes also a copy in another hand of the autobiographical letter to Dr. Moore, and both volumes contain comments by Burns. In the poetry volume he wrote the following compliment to the Riddells:

As this Collection almost wholly consists of pieces local or unfinished, fragments the effusion of a poetical moment & bagatelles strung in rhyme simply pour passer le temps, the Author trusts that nobody in to whose hands it may come will without his permission give or allow to be taken, copies of anything here contained; much less to give, to the world at large, what he never meant should see the light. — At the Gentleman's requests, whose from this time it shall be, the Collection was made; and to him, & I will add, to his amiable Lady, it is presented, as a sincere though small tribute of gratitude for the many many happy hours the Author has spent under their roof. — *There,* what Poverty even though accompanied with Genius must seldom expect to meet with at the tables & in the circles of Fashionable Life, his welcome has ever been, The cordiality of Kindness, & the warmth of Friendship. — As, from the situation in which it is now placed, this M.S.S. may be preserved, & this Preface read, when the hand that now writes & the heart that now dictates it may be mouldering in the dust; let these be regarded as the genuine sentiments of a man who seldom flattered any, & never those he loved. —

27th April 1791   ROBT BURNS

Burns also wrote a song to celebrate the Riddells' wedding anniversary in 1788. R. H. Cromek prints a note by Burns on this song, but the leaf in the interleaved *Museum* opposite the printed song, which presumably carried the note, is one of those which has been removed. The sentiments, however, are substantially repeated in a letter to Riddell. The note as printed by Cromek reads, "I composed this song out of compliment to one of the happiest and worthiest married couples in the world, Robert Riddel, Esq. of Glenriddel, and his lady. At their fireside — I have enjoyed more pleasant evenings than at all the houses of fashionable people in this country put together; and to their kindness and hospitality I am indebted for many of the happiest hours of my life." There is no reason to doubt the candor of this statement, or of the note in the manuscript book of poems, or of the letter, but it should be remembered that they were all written for the Riddells to see. And subsequent events lend them irony.

Burns was much at Friars' Carse, and Riddell was pleased to have guests meet him. On such occasions, Burns felt free, when the guests had franking privileges, to ask for franks for his letters. He had access to Riddell's library, and the two of them set up the Monkland Friendly Society, a local book club, for which Burns was the managing agent, ordering books from his friend Peter Hill, acting as librarian, and in August or September of 1791, writing the account below of the enterprise for Sinclair's *The Statistical Account of Scotland*, 1792.

To store the minds of the lower classes with useful knowledge, is certainly of very great consequence, both to them as individuals, and to society at large. Giving them a turn for reading and reflection, is giving them a source of innocent and laudable amusement; and besides, raises them to a more dignified degree in the scale of rationality. Impressed with this idea, a gentleman in this parish, Robert Riddell, Esq: of Glenriddel, set on foot a species of circulating library, on a plan so simple, as to be practicable in any corner of the country; and so useful, as to deserve the notice of every country gentleman, who thinks the improvement of that part of his own species, whom chance has thrown into the humble walks of the peasant and the artisan, a matter worthy of his attention.

Mr. Riddell got a number of his own tenants, and farming neighbours, to form themselves into a society, for the purpose of having a library among themselves. They entered into a legal engagment, to abide by it for 3 years; with a saving clause or two, in cases of removal to a distance, or of death. Each member, at his entry, paid 5s.; and at each of their meetings, which were held every fourth Saturday, 6d. more. With their entry money, and the credit which they took on the faith of their future funds, they laid in a tolerable stock of books at the commencement. What authors they were to purchase, was always to be decided by the majority. At every meeting, all the books, under certain fines and forfeitures, by way of penalty, were to be produced; and the members had their choice of the volumes in rotation. He whose name stood, for that night, first on the list, had his choice of what volume he pleased in the whole collection; the second had his choice after the first; the third after the second, and so on to the last. At next meeting, he who had been first on the list at the preceding meeting, was last at this; he who had been second, was first; and so on, through the whole 3 years. At the expiration of the engagment, the books were sold by auction, but only among the members themselves; and each man had his share of the common stock, in money or in books, as he chose to be a purchaser or not.

At the breaking up of this little society,* which was formed under Mr. Riddell's patronage, what with benefactions of books from him, and what with their own purchases, they had collected together upwards of 150 volumes. It will easily be guessed, that a good deal of trash would be bought. Among the books, however, of this little library, were, Blair's Sermons, Robertson's History of Scotland, Hume's History of the Stewarts, The Spectator, Idler, Adventurer, Mirror, Lounger, Observer, Man of Feeling, Man of the World, Chrysal, Don Quixotte, Joseph Andrews, &c. A peasant who can read, and enjoy such books, is certainly a much superior being to his neighbour, who, perhaps, stalks beside his team, very little removed, except in shape, from the brutes he drives.

Another happy note in the relations of Burns and Robert Riddell is the substantial assistance Riddell gave in the campaign to

---

* "The society, though reorganized after three years, maintained its existence and supported the library until February 2, 1931, when by formal vote it was disbanded, and the books distributed to appropriate places." (Snyder, 325.)

defend the Moffat schoolmaster, James Clarke, from charges of undue severity to his pupils.

While Burns enjoyed himself frequently at Friars' Carse, there is no record of his having spent the night there, as he did at the Millers', or of Robert Riddell's having been a guest at Ellisland farmhouse. And it is certain that Friars' Carse was one of the houses Burns had in mind when he wrote Mrs. Dunlop in December of 1792, after he had moved to Dumfries, "It is the private parties in the family way, among the hard drinking gentlemen of this county, that does me the mischief." Robert Riddell's convivial tastes are given classic illustration by the "Whistle" contest.

Riddell had a family relic — a whistle, which tradition held should become the property of that competitor who could blow it when all others were under the table. Riddell agreed to contest possession of the whistle with his cousins, Alexander Fergusson of Craigdarroch, lawyer and Justice of the Peace, and Sir Robert Laurie, M. P. for Dumfriesshire. The contest, refereed by John McMurdo, Chamberlain to the Duke of Queensberry at Drumlanrig, was held October 16, 1789, and was won by Craigdarroch. "He drank upds of 5 bottles of Claret." There has been argument about whether Burns was present during the contest as a witness, and he may have been, but he certainly was amused by it, and celebrated it with a ballad, *The Whistle*, in the course of which he complimented Mrs. Riddell. Mrs. Burns thought that her husband had been present, but only as a toping spectator.

Burns' enjoyment of Robert Riddell's convivial friends had one far more happy result than *The Whistle;* it led to his writing *Tam o' Shanter.* That "dainty chield," Captain Francis Grose, the "fine fat, fodgel wight [dumpy fellow], / O' stature short but genius bright," began his extended visits to Friars' Carse in April, 1789, as he went about sketching and collecting information for his two-volume work, *The Antiquities of Scotland.* Grose was jolly and full of stories, and Burns found him a congenial companion. The poem, *On The Late Captain Grose's Peregrinations*

Thro' Scotland, a happy memorial to their friendship, jocularly notes the captain's indefatigable researches.

By some auld, houlet-haunted biggin,	*owl-haunted building*
Or kirk deserted by its riggin,	*roof*
It's ten to ane ye'll find him snug in	
Some eldritch part,	*fearful*
Wi' deils, they say, Lord saf's! colleaguin	*save us*
At some black art.	

. . . .

Of Eve's first fire he has a cinder;	
Anld Tubalcain's fire-shool and fender;	*-shovel*
That which distinguishèd the gender	
O' Balaam's ass;	
A broomstick o' the witch of Endor,	
Weel shod wi' brass.	

Forbye, he'll shape you aff fu' gleg	*Besides smartly*
The cut of Adam's philibeg;	*kilt*
The knife that nicket Abel's craig	
He'll prove you fully,	
It was a faulding jocteleg,	*clasp knife*
Or lang-kail gullie.	*cabbage knife*

But wad ye see him in his glee —
For meikle glee and fun has he —
Then set him down, and two or three
    Guid fellows wi' him:
And port, O port! shine thou a wee,
    And then ye'll see him!

During the association between Burns and Grose it came to be agreed that Grose would include in his book a sketch of ruined Alloway Kirk, where Burns' father was buried, and that Burns would write a poem to go with it. Before writing the poem, he sent Grose a letter recounting legends of the Kirk, some of which he later used in *Tam o' Shanter.*

Sir,
    Among the many Witch Stories I have heard relating to Aloway Kirk, I distinctly remember only two or three.

Upon a stormy night, amid whirling squalls of wind and bitter blasts of hail, in short, on such a night as the devil would chuse to take the air in, a farmer or a farmer's servant was plodding and plashing homeward with his plough-irons on his shoulder, having been getting some repairs on them at a neighbouring smithy. His way lay by the Kirk of Aloway, and being rather on the anxious look-out in approaching a place so well known to be a favorite haunt of the devil and the devil's friends and emissaries, he was struck aghast by discovering, through the horrors of the storm and stormy night, a light, which, on his nearer approach, plainly shewed itself to proceed from the haunted edifice. Whether he had been fortified from above on his devout supplication, as is customary with people when they suspect the immediate presence of Satan; or whether, according to another custom, he had got courageously drunk at the smithy, I will not pretend to determine; but so it was that he ventured to go up to, nay into the very Kirk. — As good luck would have it, his temerity came off unpunished. The members of the infernal junto were all out on some midnight business or other, and he saw nothing but a kind of kettle or caldron, depending from the roof, over the fire, simmering some heads of unchristened children, limbs of executed malefactors, &c. for the business of the night. It was, in for a penny, in for a pound, with the honest ploughman; so without ceremony he unhooked the caldron from off the fire, and pouring out the damnable ingredients, inverted it on his head, and carried it fairly home, where it remained long in the family a living evidence of the truth of the story.

Another story, which I can prove to be equally authentic, was as follows.

On a market day in the town of Ayr, a farmer from Carrick, and consequently whose way lay by the very gate of Aloway kirk-yard, in order to cross the river Doon at the old bridge, which is about two or three hundred yards farther on than the said gate, had been detained by his business till by the time he reached Aloway, it was the wizard hour, between night and morning.

Though he was terrified with a blaze streaming from the kirk, yet as it is a well known fact, that to turn back on these occasions is running by far the greatest risk of mischief, he prudently advanced on his road. When he had reached the gate of the kirk-yard, he was surprised and entertained, through the ribs and arches of an old gothic window which still faces the highway, to see a dance of witches merrily footing it round their old sooty blackguard master, who was keeping them all alive with the power of his bagpipe. The farmer stopping his horse to observe them a little, could plainly descry the faces of many old women of his acquaintance and neighbourhood. How the gentleman was dressed, tradition does not say; but the ladies were all in their smocks; and one of them happening unluckily to have a smock which was considerably too short to answer all the purpose of that piece of dress, our farmer was so tickled that he involuntarily burst out, with a loud laugh, "Weel luppen, Maggy wi' the short sark!" and recollecting himself, instantly spurred his horse to the top of his speed. I need not mention the universally known fact that no diabolical power can pursue you beyond the middle of a running stream. Lucky it was for the poor farmer that the river Doon was so near, for notwithstanding the speed of his horse, which was a good one, against he reached the middle of the arch of the bridge, and consequently the middle of the stream, the pursuing, vengeful hags were so close at his heels, that one of them actually sprung to seize him: but it was too late; nothing was on her side of the stream but the horse's tail, which immediately gave way to her infernal grip, as if blasted by a stroke of lightning; but the farmer was beyond her reach. — However, the unsightly, tailless condition of the vigorous steed was to the last hours of the noble creature's life, an awful warning to the Carrick farmers, not to stay too late in Ayr markets. —

The last relation I shall give, though equally true, is not so well identified as the two former, with regard to the scene: but as the best authorities give it for Aloway, I shall relate it. —

On a summer's evening, about the time that Nature puts on her sables to mourn the expiry of the chearful day, a shepherd boy belonging to a farmer in the immediate neighbourhood of Aloway Kirk, had just folded his charge, and was returning home. As he passed the Kirk, in the adjoining field, he fell in with a crew of men and women, who were busy pulling stems of the plant ragwort. He observed that as each person pulled a ragwort, he or she got astride of it, and called out, "Up horsie!" on which the ragwort flew off, like Pegasus, through the air with its rider. The foolish boy likewise pulled his ragwort, and cried with the rest, "Up horsie!" and, strange to tell, away he flew with the company. The first stage at which the cavalcade stopt, was a merchant's wine cellar in Bourdeaux, where, without saying, by your leave, they quaffed away at the best the cellar could afford, untill the morning, foe to the imps and works of darkness, threatened to throw light on the matter, and frightened them from their carousals. —

The poor shepherd lad, being equally a stranger to the scene and the liquor, heedlessly got himself drunk; and when the rest took horse, he fell asleep and was found so next day by some of the people belonging to the merchant. Somebody that understood Scotch, asking him what he was, he said he was such-a-one's herd in Aloway, and by some means or other getting home again, he lived long to tell the world the wondrous tale.

> I am, Dr Sir,
> ROBT BURNS

In addition to drawing on lore of the kind which Burns had heard from his mother and from Betty Davidson while he was a boy, the poem obviously owes a good deal to Burns' memories of his summer at Kirkoswald and the smugglers on the Carrick shore, and its hero is presumably modeled on a farmer from that district, Douglas Graham of Shanter farm, who had a boat called the *Tam o' Shanter*. Jean Burns is reported to have said that Robert composed this poem in one day while walking along the banks of the Nith, and it may well be that he composed some of it in this way. He was accustomed to composing in his head, and while walking or riding. But the poem as we know it was certainly the result of more than some hours' strolling. As Burns said, "All my poetry is the effect of easy composition, but of laborious correction." And he wrote to Lady Henrietta Don, "Though the rough material of fine writing is undoubtedly the gift of genius, the workmanship is as certainly the united effort of labor, attention and pains." (January, 22, 1789, the same day as a letter to Henry Erskine with almost the same statement. See epigraph at beginning of Section III. He had made a similar statement to Dr. Moore on January 4.) There is an even more pointed remark in a letter to Mrs. Dunlop. When she objected at New Year, 1791, to the improprieties of *Tam,* and pronounced it a bad poem, Burns said nothing to her about her unhappiness until he wrote on April 11, announcing the birth on April 9 of William Nicol Burns, who was "rather stouter but not so handsome" as Mrs. Dunlop's god-son, Francis Wallace Burns (b. August 18, 1789). "Indeed," said Burns disarmingly, "I look on your little Namesake to be my chef d'oeuvre in that species of manufacture, as I look on 'Tam o' Shanter' to be my standard performance in the Poetical line. 'Tis true, both the one & the other discover a spice of roguish waggery that might perhaps be as well spared; but then they also shew in my opinion a force of genius & *a finishing polish* [italics supplied] that I despair of ever excelling." *

So fine a critic as Hazlitt, when lecturing on Burns, said of *Tam o' Shanter,* "I shall give the beginning of it, but I am afraid I shall hardly know when to leave off." And he proceeded to read it all. How could he have done otherwise? What need he have said *about* it?

Like all great art, *Tam o' Shanter* delights, and defies criticism.

* This is a convenient place to record that on March 31, ten days before little William's appearance, Anne Park, the niece of Mrs. Hyslop, hostess at the Globe Inn, Dumfries, bore Burns a daughter, Elizabeth. This child was first taken to Mossgiel, and then, later, was admitted to Burns' own family and raised with his other children, by Jean. There is no further word of Anne Park, who is presumed to have died in childbirth or soon after. Burns remained on excellent terms with Mr. and Mrs. Hyslop, and wrote about Anne a song of which he said, "I think it is the best love-song I ever composed in my life."

> Yestreen I had a pint o' wine,
> A place where body saw na;
> Yestreen lay on this breast o' mine
> The raven locks of Anna.
>
> . . . . .
>
> Ye Monarchs take the East and West,
> Frae Indus to Savannah!
> Gie me within my straining grasp
> The melting form of Anna. —
>
> Then I'll despise Imperial charms,
> An Empress or Sultana,
> While dying raptures in her arms,
> I give and take wi' Anna.

One can notice its ambiguities and irony and ambivalence, its realism and grotesque fancy, its humor and horror, its diablerie and satire; the irresistible flow of its narrative; the force of its statement and the brilliant compulsion of its language; the wonderfully interwoven sophistication and folklore; the subtle and assured metrics; the rhetorical power, the variety of scene, the richness of texture, the vividness of detail; and the background both of form and of literary tradition — such as the wild ride; but when one has finished, as Hazlitt knew, one has done little to explain the poem's power or to increase its delight. It stands alone in our literature.*

Tam o' Shanter
A Tale

Of Brownyis and of Bogillis full is this Buke.
Gawin Douglas

When chapman billies leave the street,	*pedlar fellows*
And drouthy neebors neebors meet;	*thirsty*
As market-days are wearing late,	
An' folk begin to tak the gate;	*road*
While we sit bousing at the nappy,	*ale*
An' getting fou and unco happy,	*full very*
We think na on the lang Scots miles,	
The mosses, waters, slaps, and styles,	*swamps gaps in walls*
That lie between us and our hame,	
Whare sits our sulky, sullen dame,	
Gathering her brows like gathering storm,	
Nursing her wrath to keep it warm.	

* Note on chronology: Burns and Grose were absorbed in lore of Alloway Kirk by the summer of 1790, and Burns recited a part of *Tam o' Shanter* to Ainslie in late October. By November, Mrs. Dunlop had seen a version which apparently lacked the witch dance. Burns sent the poem to Grose December 1, and by February, Grose had returned him some proof sheets, of which he sent one to Dr. Moore on February 28 (1791). The poem appeared March 18, 1791, in the *Edinburgh Herald,* and in the *Edinburgh Magazine* for March. Grose printed it as a footnote, pp. 199–201, in his second volume, which was published April 11. (F II, #401, #437; H & H I, 439; RB & Mrs. D, 286, 289; *Chronicle,* 1935, 9; Egerer, 36; Kinsley, 1347–1364.)

This truth fand honest Tam o' Shanter   *found*
As he frae Ayr ae night did canter:
(Auld Ayr, wham ne'er a town surpasses,
For honest men and bonie lasses).

O Tam, had'st thou but been sae wise,
As taen thy ain wife Kate's advice!   *As to have taken*
She tauld thee weel thou was a skellum,   *no-count*
A blethering, blustering, drunken blellum   *chattering   babbler*
That frae November till October,
Ae market-day thou was nae sober;
That ilka melder wi' the miller,   *meal-grinding*
Thou sat as lang as thou had siller;   *silver*
That ev'ry naig was ca'd a shoe on,   *every   called*
The smith and thee gat roaring fou on;
That at the Lord's house, even on Sunday,   [*a Kirkoswald tavern*]
Thou drank wi' Kirkton Jean till Monday.   [*the hostess*]
She prophesied, that, late or soon,
Thou would be found deep drown'd in Doon,
Or catch'd wi' warlocks in the mirk   *wizards   dark*
By Alloway's auld, haunted kirk.

Ah! gentle dames, it gars me greet,   *makes me weep*
To think how monie counsels sweet,
How monie lengthen'd, sage advices
The husband frae the wife despises!

But to our tale: — Ae market-night,
Tam had got planted unco right,
Fast by an ingle, bleezing finely,   *fire*
Wi' reaming swats, that drank divinely;   *foaming new ale*
And at his elbow, Souter Johnie,   *Cobbler*
His ancient, trusty, drouthy cronie: *thirsty*
Tam lo'ed him like a very brither;
They had been fou for weeks thegither.
The night drave on wi' sangs and clatter;
And ay the ale was growing better:
The landlady and Tam grew gracious
Wi' secret favours, sweet and precious:
The Souter tauld his queerest stories;
The landlord's laugh was ready chorus:
The storm without might rair and rustle,
Tam did na mind the storm a whistle.

Care, mad to see a man sae happy,
E'en drown'd himsel amang the nappy.
As bees flee hame wi' lades o' treasure,
The minutes wing'd their way wi' pleasure:
Kings may be blest but Tam was glorious,
O'er a' the ills o' life victorious!

But pleasures are like poppies spread:
You seize the flow'r, its bloom is shed;
Or like the snow falls in the river,
A moment white — then melts forever;
Or like the borealis race,
That flit ere you can point their place;
Or like the rainbow's lovely form
Evanishing amid the storm.
Nae man can tether time or tide;
The hour approaches Tam maun ride: *must*
That hour, o' night's black arch the key-stane,
That dreary hour Tam mounts his beast in;
And sic a night he taks the road in,
As ne'er poor sinner was abroad in.

The wind blew as 'twad blawn its last;
The rattling showers rose on the blast;
The speedy gleams the darkness swallow'd;
Loud, deep, and lang the thunder bellow'd:
That night, a child might understand,
The Deil had business on his hand.

Weel mounted on his gray mare Meg,
A better never lifted leg,
Tam skelpit on thro' dub and mire,   *hurried   puddle*
Despising wind, and rain, and fire;
Whiles holding fast his guid blue bonnet,   *Now*
Whiles crooning o'er some auld Scots sonnet   *song*
Whiles glow'ring round wi' prudent cares,
Lest bogles catch him unawares: *goblins*
Kirk-Alloway was drawing nigh,
Whare ghaists and houlets nightly cry.   *owls*

By this time he was cross the ford,
Whare in the snaw the chapman smoor'd;   *smothered*

And past the birks and meikle stane, *birches   great*
Whare drunken Charlie brak's neck-bane;
And thro' the whins, and by the cairn, *furze   pile of stones*
Whare hunters fand the murder'd bairn;
And near the thorn, aboon the well, *above*
Whare Mungo's mither hang'd hersel.
Before him Doon pours all his floods;
The doubling storm roars thro' the woods;
The lightnings flash from pole to pole;
Near and more near the thunders roll:
When, glimmering thro' the groaning trees,
Kirk-Alloway seem'd in a bleeze;
Thro' ilka bore the beams were glancing, *every chink*
And loud resounded mirth and dancing.

   Inspiring bold John Barleycorn,
What dangers thou canst make us scorn!
Wi' tippeny, we fear nae evil; *ale*
Wi' usquabae, we'll face the Devil! *whisky*
The swats sae ream'd in Tammie's noddle,
Fair play, he car'd na deils a boddle. *not   farthing*
But Maggie stood, right sair astonish'd,
Till, by the heel and hand admonish'd,
She ventur'd forward on the light;
And, vow! Tam saw an unco sight!

   Warlocks and witches in a dance:
Nae cotillion, brent new frae France, *brand*
But hornpipes, jigs, strathspeys, and reels,
Put life and mettle in their heels.
A winnock-bunker in the east, *window-seat*
There sat Auld Nick, in shape o' beast;
A tousie tyke, black, grim, and large, *shaggy dog*
To gie them music was his charge:
He screw'd the pipes and gart them skirl, *made them squeal*
Till roof and rafters a' did dirl. *ring*
Coffins stood round, like open presses, *cupboards*
That shaw'd the dead in their last dresses;
And, by some devilish cantraip sleight, *witching*
Each in his cauld hand held a light:
By which heroic Tam was able
To note upon the haly table,

A murderer's banes, in gibbet-airns;   *-irons*
Twa span-lang, wee, unchristen'd bairns;
A thief new-cutted frae a rape —
Wi' his last gasp his gab did gape;   **mouth**
Five tomahawks wi' bluid red-rusted;
Five scymitars wi' murder crusted;
A garter which a babe had strangled;
A knife a father's throat had mangled —
Whom his ain son o' life bereft —
The gray-hairs yet stack to the heft;
Wi' mair o' horrible and awefu',
Which even to name was be unlawfu'.
[Three Lawyers' tongues, turn'd inside out,
Wi' lies seam'd like a beggar's clout;
And Priests' hearts, rotten black as muck,
Lay stinking, vile, in every neuk.]*

As Tammie glowr'd, amaz'd, and curious,   *stared*
The mirth and fun grew fast and furious;
The piper loud and louder blew,
The dancers quick and quicker flew,
They reel'd, they set, they cross'd, they cleekit, †
Til ilka carlin swat and reekit   *every beldam sweated and steamed*
And coost her duddies to the wark,
And linket at it in her sark!   *skipped*

Now Tam, O Tam! had thae been queans,
A' plump and strapping in their teens!
Their sarks, instead of creeshie flannen,   *greasy flannel*
Been snaw-white seventeen hunder linen! —   *fine linen*
Thir breeks o' mine, my only pair,   **These breeches**
That ance were plush, o' guid blue hair,
I wad hae gi'en them off my hurdies   **buttocks**
For ae blink o' the bonie burdies!

---

* These vivid and characteristic lines appeared in the first printings of *Tam o'
Shanter*, but Burns deleted them in his 1793 Edinburgh edition at the suggestion
of his friend A. F. Tytler, the elegant and celebrated minor author, critic, historian, professor, lawyer, and finally judge. Tytler, in March, 1791, wrote Burns
that he was delighted with *Tam*, but remarked that these lines "though good in
themselves, . . . derive all their merit from the satire they contain," and "are
rather misplaced among circumstances of pure horror." (Ch-W III, 256–57; F II,
#445, 70.) In December, 1792, Burns thanked Tytler for "taking the trouble
of correcting the Presswork" of the 1793 edition. (F II, #526, 138.)
† "They whirled around in the reel, faced their partners, passed across the
circle of the dance, and linked arms and turned." (Kinsley III, 1362.)

But wither'd beldams, auld and droll,
Rigwoodie hags wad spean a foal   *withered   drive a foal from the*
Louping and flinging on a crummock,   *cudgel   /teat with fright*
I wonder did na turn thy stomach!

But Tam kend what was what fu' brawlie: *well*
There was ae winsome wench and wawlie,   *handsome*
That night enlisted in the core,
Lang after kend on Carrick shore
(For monie a beast to dead she shot,
An' perish'd monie a bonie boat,   *destroyed*
And shook baith meikle corn and bear,   *stole   much   barley*
And kept the country-side in fear).
Her cutty sark, o' Paisley harn,   *short smock   coarse cloth*
That while a lassie she had worn,
In longitude tho' sorely scanty,
It was her best, and she was vauntie. —   *proud*
Ah! little kend thy reverend grannie,
That sark she coft for her wee Nannie,   *bought*
Wi' twa pund Scots ('twas a' her riches),
Wad ever grac'd a dance of witches!

But here my Muse her wing maun cour,   *fold*
Sic flights are far beyond her power:
To sing how Nannie lap and flang
(A souple jad she was and strang),
And how Tam stood like ane bewitch'd,
And thought his very e'en enrich'd;
Even Satan glowr'd, and fidg'd fu' fain,   *twitched*
And hotch'd and blew wi' might and main   *hitched*
Till first ae caper, syne anither,   *then*
Tam tint his reason a' thegither,   *lost*
And roars out: "Weel done, Cutty-sark!"
And in an instant all was dark;
And scarcely had he Maggie rallied,
When out the hellish legion sallied.

As bees bizz out wi' angry fyke,   *fuss*
When plundering herds assail their byke;   *herdboys   hive*
As open pussie's mortal foes,   *the hare's*
When, pop! she starts before their nose;
As eager runs the market-crowd,
When "Catch the thief!" resounds aloud;

So Maggie runs, the witches follow,
Wi' monie an eldritch skriech and hollo.   *unearthly*

Ah, Tam! Ah, Tam! thou'll get thy fairin!
In hell they'll roast thee like a herrin!
In vain thy Kate awaits thy comin!
Kate soon will be a woefu' woman!
Now, do thy speedy utmost, Meg,
And win the key-stane of the brig;
There, at them thou thy tail may toss,
A running stream they dare na cross!
But ere the key-stane she could make,
The fient a tail she had to shake;   *devil*
For Nannie, far before the rest,
Hard upon noble Maggie prest,
And flew at Tam wi' furious ettle;   *purpose*
But little wist she Maggie's mettle!
Ae spring brought off her master hale,
But left behind her ain grey tail:
The carlin claught her by the rump,   *seized*
And left poor Maggie scarce a stump.

Now, wha this tale o' truth shall read,
Ilk man, and mother's son, take heed:
Whene'er to drink you are inclin'd,
Or cutty sarks run in your mind,
Think! ye may buy the joys o'er dear:
Remember Tam o' Shanter's mare.

Maria Riddell, wife of Robert's younger brother Walter, was literary, charming, witty, and accomplished. Daughter of William Woodley, Governor of the Leeward Isles, she had married at eighteen (September 16, 1790), at St. Kitts, the recently widowed Walter Riddell (1764–1802), who had inherited an Antiguan estate from his first and childless wife of a year. On August 31, 1791, after their return to England, Maria and Walter had a daughter, and on November 22, 1792, another, their last child. In the autumn of 1791, they came from London to the neighborhood of Dumfries, where Walter soon began to look for a country estate, and during the spring of 1792 he agreed to buy Goldilea for £16,000, paying £1000 down. He renamed it Wood-ley Park in honor of his wife, spent £2000 on improvements, and set up in considerable style. Burns apparently met Maria and her husband at Friars' Carse before he left Ellisland for Dum-fries in early November 1791, and he became a frequent visitor to Woodley Park.

By January 22, 1792, Maria had got from Burns a letter of introduction to his Crochallan friend, the printer Smellie, author of a *Philosophy of Natural History*. Maria wanted Smellie's opin-ion on a book she had written, eventually published as *Voyages to the Madeira and Leeward Islands; with Sketches of the Nat-ural History of these Islands*. Burns told Smellie that although Maria was a young lady of the first rank of fashion, and a "lively West-Indian girl of eighteen" (she was twenty), she was also a poet and a great admirer of Smellie's book. He urged that she would be a character that even in his own way "as a Naturalist & a Philosopher," would be an acquisition to his acquaintance. Smellie took to Maria, advised publication of her manuscript, and became her correspondent — solid testimony to her qualities of mind as well as to her charms.

Smellie wrote her, "When I considered your youth, and still more, your sex, the perusal of your ingenious and judicious work, if I had not previously had the pleasure of your conversation, the devil himself could not have frightened me into the belief that a female human creature could, in the bloom of youth, beauty, and consequently of giddiness, have produced a per-formance so much out of the line of your ladies works. Smart little poems, flippant romances, are not uncommon. But science, minute observation, accurate description, and excellent compo-sition, are qualities seldom to be met with in the female world." Smellie then continues gallantly, "Why did you grapple with a soldier? Mr Riddell I ever will revere, though not so much as yourself must do; but if I could have had the happiness of having the company of a lady so well qualified to assist me in my favourite study, we *two* should have made a COUPLE of figures in the literary world!" In the early autumn Smellie visited the Walter Riddells at Woodley Park, and Maria took him to the Dumfries Assembly. It is perhaps anticlimax to add that Smellie printed the *Voyages,* which were dedicated to him, the book being announced in November, 1792, as for sale by Cadell in London, and by Burns' friend Peter Hill, in Edinburgh. Burns received a copy from the author, which he promised to keep "sacred."

Relations between the Walter Riddells and the Robert Riddells were soon strained. By early autumn, 1792, Burns was promising Maria that if he saw Robert Riddell he would "say nothing at all, & listen to nothing at all" about her. As he wrote her later, "Your interest with the WOMEN is, I believe, a sorry business. — So much the better! 'tis God's judgment upon you for making such despotic use of your sway over the MEN." Maria was flirtatious, even flighty, as Burns himself had ample reason to note on another occasion. "I have often told you, my Dear Friend," he once wrote her, "that you had a spice of Caprice in your composition, & you have as often disavowed it; even perhaps while your opinions were, at the moment, irrefragably proving it."

Walter Riddell, like his brother Robert, was a convivial squire, and Woodley Park was another of the country houses complained of by Burns to Mrs. Dunlop, where he was urged to drink more than he wanted. But Walter seems not to have shared his brother's interest in books, antiquities, and songs. Burns thought poorly of him, and almost never mentions him in his letters to Maria. Professor Thornton gives evidence that Walter's relatives had limited confidence in him, and he seems to have been rather a wastrel. By June, 1793, after a year at Woodley Park, Walter found it necessary to return to the West Indies, presumably to raise money, and he remained out of Great Britain for almost a year. Once he returned, unsuccessful, he forfeited his deposit and expenditures on Woodley Park, and moved Maria to "a crazy, rambling, worm-eaten, cobweb-hunting chateau of the Duke of Queensberry," Tinwald House, where their style was much reduced. From this time on, Walter was a good deal from home. He and Maria moved to Halleaths in 1795, and left Scotland in 1797. She does not mention his death, 1802, in Antigua, in her diary.

Maria Riddell came into Burns' life just when he thought Clarinda was irrevocably leaving it, but while this new friendship provoked scandal, the twenty-four surviving letters from Burns to Maria give no indication of fervid evenings such as those with Mrs. M'Lehose. It should be noted that Mrs. Riddell carefully preserved Burns' letters to her, but was active in getting back her own letters to him after his death; none of them is known to biographers. Letters to others, however, such as those to Smellie, and to James Currie, reveal a bright, perceptive mind, and a crisp prose style.

Like Clarinda, Maria sought out Burns; like Clarinda, she was unhappily married and could write passable verse. But unlike Clarinda, she was no Calvinist, and no sentimentalist. Burns found Maria exciting. She was a sophisticated woman who could share his mind, and sympathise with his interests. He fascinated her, as he had so many women, and she played coquette with him. There are two periods in their relationship.

In the earliest surviving letter from Burns to Mrs. Riddell, she is "My Dearest Friend," whose report of better health was the welcomest letter he had ever received. He concludes, "God grant that you may live at least while I live, for were I to lose you it would leave a Vacuum in my enjoyments that nothing could fill up." Six months later he promises not to gossip about her, and "So, vive l'amour & vive la bagatelle!" A little later she is an "enviable creature," to be going to a bright party, but he begs her, "pity your melancholy friend." By January, 1793, he feels free to request her presence at the benefit night of an actor friend. In

April he is sending her a new song. "It is a trifling present, but —
'Give all thou canst' —

"Were my esteem for a certain Lady to be measured by a musical offering, that would not be less than the music of the Spheres
in score, or the Haleluias of the Hierarchies with all their accom-
paniments."

A little later, Burns sends Maria some smuggled French gloves
which his special knowledge as an Exciseman had enabled him to
procure for her. He wants to know if she will honor Thomson's
publication with a song, forwards one written to her, and adds,
"I am afraid that my song will turn out a very cold performance,
as I never can do any good with a love theme, except when I am
really & devoutly in love." The song is not particularly good, but
Burns' flimsy pretext that he was not in love can hardly have deceived Maria. Stanza III runs,

> The music of thy voice I heard,
>   Nor wist while it enslav'd me!
> I saw thine eyes, yet nothing fear'd,
>   Till fears no more had sav'd me!
> Th' unwary sailor thus, aghast
>   The wheeling torrent viewing,
> 'Mid circling horrors sinks at last
>   In overwhelming ruin.

Shortly after this letter, Mrs. Riddell accompanied her husband to
London, whence he departed abruptly for the West Indies.

In October, when Mrs. Riddell had returned alone from England, after a period of ill-health and distress, including the death
of her father, Burns sent her an epigram, and a song originally
written for Clarinda; he closed his letter, "Le bon Dieu vous
benisse!" Then in November come four letters close together, the
first jealous that she had been so surrounded by officers ("lobster-
coated Puppies") in her theatre box, that he could not get near
her; the second agreeing to visit her box "on Tuesday; when we
may arrange the business of the visit," asking advice of the "first

& fairest of Critics" about his revision of a song, calling her "Thou most amiable & most accomplished of Thy Sex," and closing with "fervent regard." The third letter complains that he is fretful and melancholy, like the Hebrew sage who foretold, "And behold, on whatsoever this man doth set his heart, it shall not prosper!" This letter concludes, "If my resentment is awakened, it is sure to be where it dare not squeak; & if in LOVE, as, God forgive me! I sometimes am; Impossibility presents an impervious barrier to the proudest daring of Presumption, & poor I, dare much sooner peep into the focus of Hell, than meet the eye of the goddess of my soul!

"Pray that Wisdom & Bliss be more frequent visitors of

RB"

By this time Maria Riddell must have known that she was playing with fire, and she had probably known it all along. The fourth November letter sends her a version of another poem, originally intended for Clarinda, which Maria had asked for. It concludes,

> By all on High, adoring mortals know!
> By all the conscious villain fears below,
> By what, Alas, much more my soul alarms,
> My doubtful hopes once more to fill thy arms!
> E'en shouldst thou, false, forswear each guilty tie,
> Thine, & thine only, I must live & die! ! !

When the inevitable explosion came, Maria chose to be insulted. Robert Riddell concluded that he must henceforth turn his back on Burns, and Burns felt himself ill-used. Just what happened, and just where, are both uncertain. But the morning after a customarily drunken evening in some country house* in late

---

* To the remarks of C. K. Sharpe (p. 10) and John Syme (p. 221–22) about genteel conviviality in and around Dumfries, may be added reminiscences of Mrs. Basil Montagu, formerly Anna Dorothea Benson, a friend of the Craiks of Arbigland, where she met Burns. Mrs. Montagu wrote to Jane Welsh Carlyle, protesting remarks which Allan Cunningham had attributed to her about Burns. "This he has put my name to, who have ever represented Burns as incapable of rudeness or vulgarity — on the contrary as gentle, modest in his manner to women, well bred and gentlemanly in all the courtesies of life, with a natural

December, 1793, Burns wrote the following letter to his hostess
of the night before. The text is Dr. Currie's, who gives the addressee as "Mrs. R * * * * *." Currie may have tinkered with the
text, but even if he did, what he printed is the closest to the incident that one can get.

MADAM,

I daresay that this is the first epistle you ever received from this
nether world. I write you from the regions of Hell, amid the horrors
of the damned. The time and manner of my leaving your earth I do
not exactly know, as I took my departure in a fever of intoxication,
contracted at your too hospitable mansion; but, on my arrival here,
I was fairly tried, and sentenced to endure the purgatorial tortures
of this infernal confine for the space of ninety-nine years, eleven
months, and twenty-nine days, and all on account of the impropriety
of my conduct yesternight under your roof. Here am I, laid on a bed
of pityless furze, with my aching head reclined on a pillow of ever-
piercing thorn, while an infernal tormentor, wrinkled, and old, and
cruel, his name I think is *Recollection,* with a whip of scorpions, forbids
peace or rest to approach me, and keeps anguish eternally awake. Still,
Madam, if I could in any measure be reinstated in the good opinion
of the fair circle whom my conduct last night so much injured, I
think it would be an alleviation to my torments. For this reason I
trouble you with this letter. To the men of the company I will make

---

politeness, poorly imitated by the artificial polish of society, since his manner
arose out of the chivalric respect and devotion he bore to the sex — a respect
that modulated his voice and veiled the flashing of his eyes, and gave a winning grace to the most trifling of his attentions; this and a thousand other
things all in commendation have I, from time to time, endeavoured to infuse
into the dense faculty of honest Allan; and, above all that, during the Carnival
of the Caledonian Hunt, 'when Universal Scotland all was drunk,' I never saw
Burns once intoxicated, though the worthy Member for Dumfries, and the good
Laird of Arbigland, and twenty more that might be named, were much more
tipsy than Tam o' Shanter, for he could see witches and warlocks, but they
could neither see or stand, and were brought home in a state of inglorious in-
sensibility. I have told him twenty times that Burns always left a dinner party,
if there were women, for the drawing room long before any other man joined
it; and this in his thick skull has produced the following brilliant remark from
Mrs. Montagu: 'He drank as other men drank.' . . . Poor Burns! Misfortune
pursues thee even to the grave! — So it is with almost all great men; reverence
keeps silent all who loved them, and Traders take up the theme." (*Chronicle*
1927, 187.)

no apology. — Your husband, who insisted on my drinking more than I chose, has no right to blame me; and the other gentlemen were partakers of my guilt. But to you, Madam, I have much to apologize. Your good opinion, I valued as one of the greatest acquisitions I had made on earth, and I was truly a beast to forfeit it. There was a Miss I—— too, a woman of fine sense, gentle and unassuming manners — do make, on my part, a miserable d—mned wretch's best apology to her. A Mrs G——, a charming woman, did me the honor to be prejudiced in my favor; this makes me hope that I have not outraged her beyond all forgiveness. — To all the other ladies please present my humblest contrition for my conduct, and my petition for their gracious pardon. O all ye powers of decency and decorum! whisper to them that my errors, though great, were involuntary — that an intoxicated man is the vilest of beasts — that it was not in my nature to be brutal to anyone — that to be rude to a woman, when in my senses, was impossible with me — but —

❊ ❊ ❊ ❊ ❊ ❊

Regret! Remorse! Shame! ye three hellhounds that ever dog my steps and bay at my heels, spare me! spare me!

Forgive the offenses, and pity the perdition of, Madam,

Your humble slave,

Since Maria Riddell's husband was out of the country, this letter could not have been addressed to her. If the addressee was, indeed, a Mrs. R * * * * *, it seems likely that she was Elizabeth Riddell (Mrs. Robert), and the terms of the letter support that attribution. Moreover, Burns' next letter to Maria seems hardly in the tone of one to a woman who had just received an abject apology from him. And he is certainly puzzled that she has cut him. He writes,

I have this very moment got the song from Sim [John Syme], & I am sorry to see that he has spoilt it a good deal. — It shall be a lesson to me how I lend him any thing again.

I have sent you Werter: truly happy to have any, the smallest, opportunity of obliging you. —

Tis true, Madam, I saw you once since I was at Woodley park; &

that once froze the very life-blood of my heart. — Your reception of me was such, that a wretch, meeting the eye of his Judge, about to pronounce sentence of death on him, could only have envied my feelings & situation. —

But I hate the theme; & never more shall write or speak of it.

One thing I shall proudly say; that I can pay Mrs R—— a higher tribute of esteem, & appreciate her amiable worth more truly, than any man whom I have seen approach her — nor will I yield the pas to any man living, in subscribing myself with sincerest truth

Her devoted humble servt

RB

It might seem from this letter that the incident, whoever the addressee of the letter from Hell may have been, took place at Woodley Park. But wherever it took place, within a fortnight, Burns is returning Maria Riddell's Common Place Book since he has forfeited her esteem. As for his unknown offense against her, he says, "To admire, esteem, prize and adore you, as the most accomplished of Women, & the first of Friends — if these are crimes, I am the most offending thing alive."

The traditional story of what happened at the dinner to produce Burns' apology is that the gentlemen over their wine began to discuss the Rape of the Sabines and decided to enact something similar when they rejoined the ladies. Mrs. Carswell, a descendant of Patrick Miller, reports a strong tradition that army officer guests planned the affair as a "rag" to humiliate Burns the Jacobin. "Such fun might have cropped up as easily at an Ellisland Hallowe'en, a Tarbolton penny bridal or an Irvine Hogmanay [New Year]. . . . But . . . this was a frolic of the gentry. . . . So when Robert had carried out his part with hearty despatch and all the latitude the occasion called for, he was stupefied to find himself alone." Possibly. The only direct account is his own, and it is not at variance. And if something of the sort took place, whom had he laid his hands on? Maria is certainly the most likely candidate.

Neighborhood gossip, as reported by Charles Kirkpatrick

Sharpe, had Maria causing a quarrel between Burns and her brother-in-law, and it held her conduct with Burns to be scandalous. But there is better information. Robert Riddell's sister-in-law, Rachel Kennedy, wrote to Burns' biographer Currie, "In the post-humous Volumes of poor Burns which y[ou edit] [MS damaged] allude to ought *not* to appear, as it refers to some circumstances of improper conduct of Burns to Mrs. Walter Riddell which she represented to Mr. Riddell, and which he thought (in his brother's absence) [he ou]ght to resent, and therefore declin'd taking a[ny f]urther notice of Burns. . . . She uniformly expressed herself *my* friend and was highly flattering in her attentions to me, but I found it quite necessary to break off all intercourse with her long before she left this Country."

Although Miss Kennedy does not refer specifically to such an incident as that described in the letter from Hell, it is unlikely that Burns would have been permitted *two* occasions for serious offense. And it is plain that Maria Riddell's conduct with him had caused family distress, wholly aside from whatever causes had led to the break with her husband's brother's wife's sister.

Some question arises whether even Robert Riddell was the husband of the letter from Hell, for in that letter, the husband is included with those who were "partakers" of his guilt. But after the incident, he continued to speak warmly of Robert Riddell. To be sure, Burns did not nourish grudges, and most of his remarks came after Riddell's death, which followed the incident by only four months. But even so, he would hardly speak so of a man who had offended him and broken their friendship. Whatever his feelings for Robert Riddell, Burns continued his low opinion of Walter, and his break with Elizabeth (Mrs. Robert) was complete. He spoke bitterly of both so late as February, 1796. If Robert Riddell was not the husband of the letter from Hell, then the letter was not addressed to his wife. And who then was the Mrs. R * * * * *? It is even possible, of course, that the party took place neither at Friars' Carse, with Elizabeth as hostess, nor at Woodley Park, and that the Mrs. R * * * * * was neither Elizabeth nor Maria. There is simply not evidence enough to make out a straightforward story. But one thing is abundantly clear. Burns' friendship with gentry had again ended in humiliation and bitterness, and he was the victim of class loyalty. Had a social equal of the Riddells so offended, there would have been an apology, perhaps, and maybe a lingering coolness, but not the ostracism which was visited on Burns. This was the sort of class-conscious treatment which infuriated him, and to which he was most sensitive, as "the sport, the miserable victim of rebellious pride, hypochondriac imagination, agonizing sensibility, and bedlam passions," of which he had written long ago to Margaret Chalmers. He responded as he had when Mrs. Oswald's funeral cortege had driven him from a comfortable fire out into the cold because he was a peasant and she had been rich gentry.

To Maria Riddell when he returned her Common Place Book, he wrote, "In a face where I used to meet the kind complacency of friendly confidence, *now* to find cold neglect & contemptuous scorn — is a wrench that my heart can ill bear. — It is however some kind of miserable good luck; that while De-haut-en-bas rigour may depress an unoffending wretch to the ground, it has a tendency to rouse a stubborn something in his bosom, which, though it cannot heal the wounds of his soul, is at least an opiate to blunt their poignancy."

During the next few months, perhaps after Robert Riddell's death on April 21, Burns wrote a *Monody on a Lady famed for her Caprice,* which he sent to Clarinda and to Mrs. Dunlop, and which Currie published in 1800, with the name Eliza substituted for Maria. The opening stanza and the Epitaph are a sufficient sample.

> How cold is that bosom which Folly once fired!
>   How pale is that cheek where the rouge lately glisten'd!
> How silent that tongue which the echoes oft tired!
> How dull is that ear which to flatt'ry so listen'd!
>   .   .   .   .

The Epitaph

Here lies, now a prey to insulting neglect,
What once was a butterfly, gay in life's beam:
Want only of wisdom denied her respect,
Want only of goodness denied her esteem.

To Mrs. Dunlop he described the subject of the Monody as "a fantastical fine-fashioned Dame of my acquaintance," and to Clarinda he wrote, "The subject of the foregoing is a woman of fashion in this country, with whom, at one period, I was well acquainted. — By some scandalous conduct to me, & two or three other gentlemen here as well as me, she steered so far to the north of my good opinion, that I have made her the theme of several illnatured things. — The following epigram struck me the other day as I passed her carriage. —

If you rattle along like your Mistress's tongue,
Your speed will out-rival the dart:
But, a fly for your load, you'll break down on the road,
If your stuff be as rotten's her heart."

Burns sent this epigram to Patrick Miller, Jr., in London, with the title, *Extempore Pinned to a Lady's Coach,* and signed "Nith." He asked, "How do you like the following clinch? . . . If your friends [the editors of the *Morning Post*] think this worth insertion, they are welcome." The editors did not think it worth insertion.

Sometime later, perhaps in early 1795, Burns wrote for Syme and some other cronies a parody of Pope's *Eloisa to Abelard,* called *From Esopus to Maria,* distinguished by ill-temper and general ineptitude, but containing several good lines. One line asks whether Lord Lonsdale "Must make a vast monopoly of Hell," with his villainy, and a couplet says of Maria,

"Who calls thee, pert, affected, vain coquette,
A wit in folly, and a fool in wit!"

She probably never saw this poem, and after about a year of estrangement sought a reconciliation. In early 1795, during the late winter or spring, Burns wrote the capricious lady a third-person letter, in obvious response to an advance, requesting a book from her and asking for a sight of any poem which she might have written. Some time later, he thanks her cordially and in the first person, for the book, and tells her he is having a miniature painted of himself which she may see by calling on the painter, Reid, and mentioning that he had spoken to her of the picture. "Both the Miniature's existence & its destiny," he adds, "are an inviolable secret, & therefore very properly trusted in part *to you*." In his next letter he says that he is sending the miniature to her, and reports he is "so ill as to be scarce able to hold this miserable pen to this miserable paper."

From the spring of 1795, Burns was a dying man, and he seems to have known it, for he writes to Mrs. Riddell in June or July, "The health you wished me in your Morning's Card is I think, flown from me forever." During the summer he advised her how to get a job in the Customs for a protégé, adding some pleasant badinage. A little later he criticizes a poem of hers in a brief note, and about the same time sends her a song of his own. That autumn, in deep distress at the death of little Elizabeth Riddell Burns (b. Nov. 21, 1792), he wishes that Maria may never experience such a loss, and he sends her a book of music. There are no more letters until June, 1796, when he excuses himself from attending her at a loyalty celebration.

I am in such miserable health as to be utterly incapable of shewing my loyalty in any way. — Rackt as I am with rheumatisms, I meet every face with a greeting like that of Balak to Balaam — "Come, curse me Jacob; & come, defy me Israel!" — So, say I, come, curse me that East-wind; & come, defy me the North!!! Would you have me in such circumstances copy you out a Love-song? No! If I must write, let it be Sedition, or Blasphemy, or something else that begins with a B, so that I may grin with the grin of iniquity, & rejoice with the rejoicing of an apostate Angel. —

— "All good to me is lost;
Evil, be thou my good!" —

I may perhaps see you on Saturday, but I will not be at the Ball. — Why should I? — "Man delights not me, nor woman either!" Can you supply me with the Song, "Let us all be unhappy together" — Do, if you can, & oblige

le pauvre miserable,

RB

Burns saw Maria Riddell for the last time about two weeks before his death.

Between December, 1793, and June or July, 1794, Burns twice wrote letters similar to the one from Hell, each resulting from an unfortunate mixture of alcohol and politics. Both of these letters are to men, as are two others, one earlier and one later, mere notes of the morning after. One of these latter (from early 1792, to John McMurdo, referee of the Whistle contest) apologizes for undue turbulence the evening before and sends a song just composed which is convincing evidence that the turbulence has subsided; the other (written, probably in February, 1794, to Samuel Clarke, Jr.) regrets inability to keep a breakfast appointment made convivially some hours earlier.

A letter written to Major William Robertson of Lude, December 3, 1793, before the Riddell quarrel, is self-explanatory. It begins: "Heated as I was with wine yesternight, I was perhaps rather seemingly impertinent in my anxious wish to be honored with your acquaintance. — You will forgive it: 'twas the impulse of heart-felt respect." Burns had heard Glenriddell say that Robertson was the father of Scotch County Reform, and wished "to take him by the hand," for, as he continues, "in times such as these, Sir, when our Commoners are barely able, by the glimmer of their own twilight understandings, to scrawl a frank; and when Lords are — what gentlemen would be ashamed to be; to whom shall a sinking Country call for help? To the *independent country gentleman!*" Several months later, he sent Robertson another

copy of *Wilt Thou be my Dearie?*, the Major having given the first
one to a lady to further his cause with her. Burns thanks him for
giving the song "first celebrity" by singing it.

A letter to Samual Clarke, Jr., of June or July, 1794, and dated
"Sunday morning," is both more serious and more amusing.

DR SIR,

I was, I know, drunk last night, but I am sober this morning. —
From the expressions Captn Dods made use of to me, had I nobody's
welfare to care for but my own, we should certainly have come, according to the manners of the world, to the necessity of murdering
one another about the business. — The words were such as generally, I believe, end in a brace of pistols; but I am still pleased to think
that I did not ruin the peace & welfare of a wife & a family of children in a drunken squabble. — Farther, you know that the report of
certain Political opinions being mine, has already once before brought
me to the brink of destruction. — I dread lest last night's business
may be misrepresented in the same way. — You, I beg, will take
care to prevent it. — I tax your wish for Mr Burns's welfare with the
task of waiting as soon as possible, on every gentleman who was
present, & state this to him, & as you please, shew him this letter. —
What after all was the obnoxious toast? — "May our success in the
present war [against France] be equal to the justice of our cause."
— a toast that the most outrageous frenzy of loyalty cannot object to.
— I request & beg that this morning you will wait on the parties
present at the foolish dispute. — The least delay may be of unlucky
consequence to me. — I shall only add, that I am truly sorry that a
man who stood so high in my estimation as Mr Dods, should use me
in the manner in which I conceive he has done.

Presumably Clarke had no difficulty in getting a sobered Captain Dods to see the absurdity of his resentment, for nothing more
is heard of the matter.

Burns took occasion of the first letter to Samuel Clarke to protect his Excise flank. He writes,

You very oblidgingly mentioned something of your intimacy with
Mr Corbet, our Supervisor General. Some of our folks about the

Excise Office, Edinr had, & perhaps still have conceived a prejudice against me as being a drunken dissipated character. — I might be all this, you know, & yet be an honest fellow; but you know that I am an honest fellow and am nothing of this. — You may in your own way let him know that I am not unworthy of subscribing myself

My dear Clarke, YOUR FRIEND

R. BURNS

VI

SONG

He coude songes make and well endite.

CHAUCER

Song — verse married to music — was Burns' earliest, his latest, his strongest, and his most enduring poetic interest. His early verse, "a darling walk" of his mind, was much of it love-songs, "the breathings of ardent Passion." "The earliest thing of Composition" to delight him was Addison's hymn, *How Are Thy Servants Blest, O Lord!* His own first composition was a song to a girl, and he notes two later songs he had composed at seventeen. As a boy and young man, Burns stored his mind with songs, some of them favorites of his mother's, some popular in the country side, some published in chapbooks, or in Ramsay's *Tea-Table Miscellany,* or in another, unidentified, collection of which he wrote, "The Collection of Songs was my vade mecum. — I pored over them, driving my cart or walking to labor, song by song, verse by verse; carefully noting the true tender or sublime from affectation and fustian. — I am convinced I owe much to this for my critic-craft such as it is." That his early interest in songs was well known is evident from a comment he made, after he had begun to assist with the *Scots Musical Museum,* to his boyhood friend James Candlish. "This, you will easily guess, is an undertaking exactly to my taste."

The relative amounts of space given to songs and to other matters in Burns' Commonplace Book of 1783–1785 emphasizes his enthusiasm. Aside from scattered references in his letters, the

Commonplace Book is the only solid evidence available of Burns'
early poetic interest and production. Of its forty-two pages with
entries, twenty-three contain songs, fragments of songs, or comments on songs. There are, in addition, four pages of rhymed
prayers, one of epitaphs, and nine pages with three poems — *The
Death and Dying Words of Poor Mailie* and two epistles to John
Lapraik. The other five pages are given to varied reflections.

Great interest attaches to passages in the Commonplace Book
of carefully considered comment on Scots song. It has been held
hitherto that Burns reached his views independently, as a result
of native good taste and perception, and it may well be so, but
Professor Kinsley has recently shown that some of Burns' opinions
find parallels in the published criticism of his day.

During September, 1785, he wrote,

There is a certain irregularity in the old Scotch Songs, a redun-
dancy of syllables with respect to that exactness of accent & measure
that the English Poetry requires, but which glides in, most melo-
diously with the respective tunes to which they are set. For instance,
the fine old Song of The Mill Mill O, to give it a plain prosaic reading
it halts prodigiously out of measure; on the other hand, the Song set
to the same tune in Bremner's Collection* of Scotch Songs which begins "To Fanny fair I could impart &c." it is most exact measure, and
yet let them both be sung before a real Critic, one above the biasses of
prejudice, but a thorough Judge of Nature, — how flat & spiritless will
the last appear, how trite, and tamely methodical, compared with the
wild-warbling cadence, the heart-moving melody of the first. — This
particularly is the case with all those airs which end in a hypermetrical
syllable. — There is a degree of wild irregularity in many of the compositions & Fragments which are daily sung to them by my compeers,
the common people — a certain happy arrangement of old Scotch syllables, & yet, very frequently, nothing, not even *like* rhyme, or sameness
of jingle at the ends of the lines. — This has made me sometimes imagine that perhaps, it might be possible for a Scotch Poet, with a nice
judicious ear, to set compositions to many of our most favorite airs, particularly that class of them mentioned above, independent of rhyme altogether.

* Robert Bremner was editor of several collections of Scots airs.

Later he comments on a song he had written,

I have even tryed to imitate, in this extempore thing, that irregularity in the rhyme which, when judiciously done, has such a fine effect on the ear. —

Fragment — Tune — Galla Water

Altho' my bed were in yon muir,
　Among the heather, in my plaidie,
Yet happy happy would I be
　Had I my dear Montgomerie's Peggy. —

When o'er the hill beat surly storms,
　And winter nights were dark and rainy;
I'd seek some dell, and in my arms
　I'd shelter dear Montgomerie's Peggy. —

Were I a Baron proud and high,
　And horse and servants waiting ready,
Then a' 'twad gie o' joy to me,
　The sharin't with Montgomerie's Peggy. —

Finally he suggests the best way to compose a song to one of the traditional tunes. "These old Scottish airs are so nobly sentimental that when one would compose to them; to south the tune, as our Scotch phrase is, over & over, is the readiest way to catch the inspiration and raise the Bard into that glorious enthusiasm so strongly characteristic of our old Scotch Poetry."

It should be noted that here Burns is expressing delight in values which he continued to cherish, and stating principles which influenced him not only in his later extensive work with songs, but in his poetry, also. He urges the primacy of melody in song, the grace of a "wild irregularity," the happy effects of escaping from the "sameness of jingle at the end of the line," the sublimity that grows from simplicity or natural expression, and the need for "Scotch syllables" to bring out the full flavor of Scotch tunes. It is important to remember that while many of Burns' songs make charming short poems, and are often thought of as poems, Burns wrote them as songs and considered them to be songs. The music for a song always came first with him; almost all the songs were written for specific tunes, and they should be heard with tunes, preferably the tunes for which Burns wrote them.

Further evidence of his early interest in popular songs and his wide knowledge of them, is his famous cantata, *The Jolly Beggars*, or *Love and Liberty*. Many think it his finest production. Said to have been inspired by a brief visit with John Richmond and James Smith to a beggars' revel at Poosie Nansie Gibson's dive in Mauchline, this work, like most of Burns', is derivative. The cast, the structure, the verse forms, and the songs are all traditional. Burns seems to have experimented with *Love and Liberty*, and to have pruned it, as he was accustomed to do. Richmond speaks of songs by a sweep, a sailor, and Nansie's daughter Racer Jess, all now lost; and the Merry Andrew section survives only on a separate sheet. The cantata is structurally much better without it. Burns wished to include *Love and Liberty* in his Edinburgh edition, but his wish was opposed by the elegant and Reverend Dr. Hugh Blair, and the cantata was omitted. Perhaps it should be noted that Burns had omitted the cantata from his Kilmarnock volume, also. In September, 1793, Burns wrote to George Thomson, "I have forgot the Cantata you allude to, as I kept no copy, & indeed did not know that it was in existence; however, I remember that none of the songs pleased myself, except the last — something about,

'Courts for cowards were erected,
'Churches built to please the priest' — "

This "puissant and splendid production," as Matthew Arnold called it, was first published in a chapbook in Glasgow (1799), as *The Jolly Beggars*, the title on the manuscript used by the publisher. But *Love and Liberty*, the title on another manuscript, describes the sentiments and theme of the piece far better.

The descriptive passages of *Love and Liberty* (which Burns called "recitativos," an odd term for him to use in describing Scots vernacular verse) are some of the most vivid and memorable poetry he ever wrote, and they give the songs a great lift. The songs themselves are lively, and appropriate for their singers, but one can easily understand Burns' dissatisfaction with them. The soldier, his doxy, the female thief, the bullying tinker, and the ballad singer in his second song all use a moderately polite English which is out of character and out of key with the introduction and the setting. If in successful art every element must combine to strengthen the central effect, then, despite the vigor of these songs, Burns was right that they are in some degree unsatisfactory. The fiddler's song, only, is tinged with the Doric and quite in character, with its refrain "Whistle owre the Lave o't" (a traditional cant phrase of bawdy ambiguity — roughly equivalent to "Let's not worry about that").

The Anglified songs are picturesque, but they lack the realistic vulgarity appropriate to the occasion and the singers. Moreover, the cantata is not well-suited to performance, although it is performed from time to time, and the songs give a good effect as detached pieces, particularly *John Highlandman*. The recitativos are something else again — pungent, humorous, dramatic — done with an assured brevity that gives vitality to a stale convention. They bring the group in Poosie Nansie's grimy hostel sharply alive. And here again, as in all of Burns' great poems, there is the rich, fresh language, the memorable phrasing, the swift finality of style.

Despite its unevenness, *Love and Liberty* moves irresistibly from the initial tableau of the ragged veteran and his doxy through the increasingly dramatic conflicts involving the fiddler, the trull, and the tinker, to the thunderously received first song of the Bard, and then to his fiery second, when, literally, all Hell breaks loose.

There are other verse tales than *Tam o' Shanter* in our literature, if few so good, and none in the Eighteenth Century. Where at all, however, is there anything to approach *Love and Liberty*?

Love and Liberty

A Cantata

1

Recitativo

When lyart leaves bestrow the yird,	*gray*
Or wavering like the Bauckie-bird,	*bat*
Bedim cauld Boreas' blast;	
When hailstanes drive wi' bitter skyte	*slanting stroke*
And infant Frosts begin to bite,	
In hoary cranreuch drest;	*hoarfrost*
Ae night at e'en a merry core	
O' randie, gangrel bodies,	
In poosie-Nansie's held the splore,	*riotous frolic*
To drink their orra dudies:	*extra rags*
Wi' quaffing, and laughing,	
They ranted an' they sang;	
Wi' jumping, and thumping,	
The vera girdle rang.	*griddle*

First, niest the fire, in auld, red rags,	*next*
Ane sat; weel brac'd wi' mealy bags,	
And knapsack a' in order;	
His doxy lay within his arm;	
Wi' usquebae an' blankets warm,	*whisky*
She blinket on her Sodger;	
An' ay he gies the tozie drab	*tipsy*
The tither skelpan kiss,	*another smacking*
While she held up her greedy gab	*mouth*
Just like an aumous dish:	*beggar's bowl for alms*
Ilk smack still, did crack still,	
Just like a cadger's whip;	*horse driver's*
Then staggering, an' swaggering,	
He roar'd this ditty up —	

1

Song
Tune: *Soldier's Joy*

I am a Son of Mars who have been in many wars,
　　And show my cuts and scars wherever I come;
This here was for a Wench, and that other in a trench,
　　When welcoming the French at the sound of the drum.
　　　　Lal de daudle &c.

My Prenticeship I past where my Leader breath'd his last,
　　When the bloody die was cast on the heights of Abram;
And I served out my TRADE when the gallant GAME was play'd,
　　And the MORO low was laid at the sound of the drum.

I lastly was with Curtis among the FLOATING BATT'RIES,
　　And there I left for witness, an arm and a limb;
Yet let my Country need me, with Elliot to head me,
　　I'd clatter on my stumps at the sound of a drum.

And now tho' I must beg, with a wooden arm and leg,
　　And many a tatter'd rag hanging over my bum,
I'm as happy with my wallet my bottle and my Callet,　　*woman*
　　As when I us'd in scarlet to follow a drum.

What tho', with hoary locks, I must stand the winter shocks,
　　Beneath the woods and rocks, oftentimes for a home,
When the tother bag I sell and the tother bottle tell,
　　I could meet a troop of Hell at the sound of the drum.

2

Recitativo

He ended; and the kebars sheuk,	*rafters shook*
Aboon the chorus roar;	*above*
While frighted rattons backward leuk,	*rats*
An' seek the benmost bore;	*inmost hole*
A fairy FIDDLER frae the neuk	*from the corner,*
He skirl'd out, ENCORE,	*shrilled out*
But up arose the martial CHUCK,	*wench*
An' laid the loud uproar —	

2

SONG
Tune: *Sodger Laddie*

I once was a Maid tho' I cannot tell when,
And still my delight is in proper young men:
Some one of a troop of DRAGOONS was my dadie,
No wonder I'm fond of a SODGER LADDIE.
    Sing lal de dal &c.

The first of my LOVES was a swaggering blade,
To rattle the thundering drum was his trade;
His leg was so tight and his cheek was so ruddy,
Transported I was with my SODGER LADDIE.

But the godly old Chaplain left him in the lurch;
The sword I forsook for the sake of the church;
He ventur'd the SOUL, and I risked the BODY,
'Twas then I prov'd false to my SODGER LADDIE.

Full soon I grew sick of my sanctified Sot,
The Regiment at large for a husband I got;
From the gilded SPONTOON to the FIFE I was ready,   *pike*
I asked no more but a SODGER LADDIE.

But the PEACE it reduc'd me to beg in despair,
Till I met my old boy in a CUNNINGHAM fair;
His RAGS REGIMENTAL they flutter'd so gaudy,
My heart it rejoic'd at a SODGER LADDIE.

And now I have lived — I know not how long,
And still I can join in a cup and a song;
But whilst with both hands I can hold the glass steady,
Here's to thee, MY HERO MY SODGER LADDIE.

3

RECITATIVO

Then niest outspak a raucle Carlin   *next*   *coarse old woman*
Who ken't fu' weel to cleek the Sterlin;   *knew how*   *snatch*
For mony a pursie she had hooked,
An' had in mony a well been douked: *ducked*

Her LOVE had been a HIGHLAND LADDIE,
But weary fa' the waefu' woodie!   *ill betide noose*
Wi' sighs an' sobs she thus began
To wail her braw JOHN HIGHLANDMAN.   *fine*

3

SONG

Tune: *O, an' ye were dead, Gudeman*

A highland lad my Love was born,
The lalland laws he held in scorn: *lowland*
But he still was faithfu' to his clan,
My gallant, braw John Highlandman.

Chorus

Sing hey my braw John Highlandman!
Sing ho my braw John Highlandman!
There's not a lad in a' the lan'
Was match for my John Highlandman.

With his philibeg, an' tartan plaid,   *kilt*
An' guid Claymore down by his side, *Highland sword*
The ladies' hearts he did trepan   *beguile*
My gallant, braw John Highlandman.
    Sing hey &c.

We ranged a' from Tweed to Spey,
An' liv'd like lords an' ladies gay:
For a lalland face he feared none,
My gallant, braw John Highlandman.
    Sing hey &c.

They banish'd him beyond the sea,
But ere the bud was on the tree,
Adown my cheeks the pearls ran,
Embracing my John Highlandman.
    Sing hey &c.

But Och! they catch'd him at the last,
And bound him in a dungeon fast,
My curse upon them every one,
They've hang'd my braw John Highlandman.
    Sing hey &c.

And now a widow I must mourn
The pleasures that will ne'er return;
No comfort but a hearty can,
When I think on John Highlandman.
　　　Sing hey &c.

4

RECITATIVO

A pigmy Scraper wi' his Fiddle,
Wha us'd to trystes an' fairs to driddle,　　*cattle markets　totter*
Her strappan limb an' gausy middle,　　　　　　　　*buxom*
　　　(He reach'd nae higher)
Had hol'd his heartie like a riddle　　　　　　　　　*sieve*
　　　An' blawn't on fire.

Wi' hand on hainch, and upward e'e,　　　　　　　*haunch*
He croon'd his gamut, ONE, TWO, THREE,
Then in an ARIOSO key,
　　　The wee Apollo
Set off wi' ALLEGRETTO glee
　　　His GIGA SOLO —　　　　　　　　　　　*jig-song*

4

SONG
　　Tune: *Whistle owre the lave o't*

Let me ryke up to dight that tear,　　　　　*reach　wipe*
An' go with me an' be my DEAR;
An' then your every CARE an' FEAR
　　　May whistle owre the lave o't.　　　*rest of it*

Chorus

I am a Fiddler to my trade,
An' a' the tunes that e'er I play'd,
The sweetest still to WIFE or MAID,
　　　Was whistle owre the lave o't.

At KIRNS an' WEDDINS we'se be there,　　*harvest homes　we'll*
An' O sae nicely's we will fare!
We'll bowse about till Dadie CARE　　　　　　*boose*
　　　Sing whistle owre the lave o't.
　　　　　I am &c.

Sae merrily's the banes we'll pyke,   *bones pick*
An' sun oursells about the dyke;
An' at our leisure when ye like
   We'll whistle owre the lave o't.
     I am &c.

But bless me wi' your heav'n o' charms,
An' while I kittle hair on thairms   *tickle gut strings*
HUNGER, CAULD, an' a' sic harms
   May whistle owre the lave o't.
     I am &c.

5

RECITATIVO

Her charms had struck a sturdy CAIRD,   *tinker*
 As weel as poor GUTSCRAPER;
He taks the Fiddler by the beard,
 An' draws a roosty rapier —   *rusty*
He swoor by a' was swearing worth
 To speet him like a Pliver,   *spit Plover*
Unless he would from that time forth
 Relinquish her forever:
Wi' ghastly e'e poor Tweedledee
 Upon his hunkers bended,   *haunches*
An' pray'd for grace wi' ruefu' face,
 An' so the quarrel ended;
But tho' his little heart did grieve,
 When round the TINKLER prest her,
He feign'd to snirtle in his sleeve   *snigger*
 When thus the CAIRD address'd her —

5

SONG
Tune: *Clout the Caudron* *Mend Cauldron*

My bonie lass I work in brass,
 A TINKLER is my station;   *tinker*
I've travell'd round all Christian ground
 In this my occupation;

I've ta'en the gold an' been enroll'd
    In many a noble squadron;
But vain they search'd when off I march'd
    To go an' clout the CAUDRON.
        I've ta'en the gold &c.

Despite that SHRIMP, that withered IMP,
    With a' his noise an' cap'rin;
An' take a share with those that bare
    The BUDGET and the APRON!   *leather bag*
And *by* that STOWP! my faith and houpe,   *pot   hope*
    And *by* that dear KEILBAIGIE,   *whiskey*
If e'er ye want, or meet with scant,
    May I ne'er WEET MY CRAIGIE!   *wet my throat*
        And by that Stowp, &c.

6

RECITATIVO

The Caird prevail'd — th'unblushing fair
    In his embraces sunk;
Partly wi' LOVE o'ercome saw sair,   *sore*
    An' partly she was drunk:
SIR VIOLINO with an air
    That show'd a man o' spunk,
Wish'd UNISON between the pair,
    An' made the bottle clunk
        To their health that night.

But hurchin Cupid shot a shaft,   *urchin*
    That play'd a DAME a shavie —   *trick*
The Fiddler RAK'D her fore and aft,
    Behint the Chicken cavie: *coop*
Her lord, a Wight of Homer's craft,
    Tho' limpan wi' the Spavie,   *Spavin*
He hirpl'd up an' lap like daft,   *hobbled   leapt*
    An' shor'd them DAINTY DAVIE   *offered them a night of it*
        O' boot that night.

He was a care-defying blade,
    As ever Bacchus listed!   *enlisted*
Tho' Fortune sair upon him laid,
    His heart she ever miss'd it.

He had no WISH but — to be glad,
  Nor WANT but — when he thristed: *thirsted*
He hated nought but — to be sad,
  And thus the Muse suggested
    His sang that night.

6

SONG
Tune: *For a' that an' a' that*

I am a BARD of no regard,
  Wi' gentle folks an' a' that;
But HOMER LIKE the glowran byke,   *staring crowd*
  Frae town to town I draw that.

Chorus

For a' that an' a' that,
  An' twice as muckle's a' that
I've lost but ANE, I've TWA behin',
  I've WIFE ENEUGH for a' that.

I never drank the Muses' STANK,   *pond*
  Castalia's burn an' a' that,   *stream*
But there it streams an' richly reams,   *froths*
  My HELICON I ca' that.
    For a' that &c.

Great love I bear to all the FAIR,
  Their humble slave and a' that;
But lordly WILL, I hold it still   *sexual appetite*
  A mortal sin to thraw that.   *thwart*
    For a' that &c.

In raptures sweet this hour we meet,
  Wi' mutual love an' a' that;
But for how lang the FLIE MAY STANG   *desire   sting*
  Let INCLINATION law that.   *determine*
    For a' that &c.

Their tricks an' craft hae put me daft,
  They've ta'en me in, an' a' that,

But clear your decks an' here's the SEX
  I like the jads for a' that.   *jades*
      For a' that an' a' that,
        An' twice as muckle's a' that,
     My DEAREST BLUID to do them guid
       They're welcome till't for a' that.   *to it*

7

RECITATIVO

So sung the BARD — and Nansie's waws   *walls*
Shook with a thunder of applause
  Re'echo'd from each mouth!
They toom'd their pocks, they pawn'd their duds,   *emptied their bags*
They scarcely left to coor their fuds,   *cover their buttocks*
  To quench their lowan drouth: *burning*
Then owre again the jovial thrang   *throng*
  The Poet did request,
To lowse his PACK an' wale a sang,   *loose   choose a song*
  A BALLAD o' the best.
      He, rising, rejoicing,
        Between his twa DEBORAHS,
     Looks round him an' found them
     Impatient for the Chorus.

7

SONG
Tune: *Jolly Mortals, fill your glasses*

See the smoking bowl before us,
  Mark our jovial, ragged ring!
Round and round take up the Chorus,
  And in raptures let us sing —

Chorus

A fig for those by law protected!
  LIBERTY's a glorious feast!
Courts for Cowards were erected,
  Churches built to please the PRIEST.

What is TITLE, what is TREASURE,
What is REPUTATION's care?
If we lead a life of pleasure,
'Tis no matter HOW or WHERE.
A fig for &c.

With the ready trick and fable
Round we wander all the day;
And at night, in barn or stable,
Hug our doxies on the hay.
A fig for &c.

Does the train-attended CARRIAGE
Thro' the country lighter rove?
Does the sober bed of MARRIAGE
Witness brighter scenes of love?
A fig for &c.

Life is all a VARIORUM,
We regard not how it goes;
Let them cant about DECORUM,
Who have character to lose.
A fig for &c.

Here's to BUDGETS, BAGS and WALLETS!
Here's to all the wandering train!
Here's our ragged BRATS and CALLETS!
One and all cry out, AMEN!

A fig for those by law protected,
LIBERTY's a glorious FEAST!
COURTS for Cowards were erected,
CHURCHES built to please the priest.

Just how much Burns knew about music is puzzling. In September, 1785, he wrote, "I set about composing an air in the old Scotch style. I am not Musical Scholar enough to prick down my tune properly, so that it can never see the light, and perhaps 'tis no great matter." However, Burns learned to read music after a fashion, and became intimately familiar with many books of Scotch airs. In 1791, he told Johnson that he had "all the music of

the country," except one collection, which he wished to have. It
should be mentioned also that church instruction in music was
customary in Burns' day, and we have seen that John Murdoch
attempted some elementary musical training at the Alloway
school.* As a young man, Burns bought a fiddle, on which he
learned to play slow tunes.

He often mentioned having had songs played or sung for him,
particularly after his association with James Johnson had begun.
The journals of his tours record his being sung to with pleasure,
and during his winter with William Cruikshank while he was
nursing his injured knee, he enjoyed hours of listening to young
Janet Cruikshank play on her harpsichord. He mentions his wife's
singing many times, and when he lived at Ellisland he had as
neighbor one Kirsty Flint, whose lusty voice was at his service.
At Ellisland also, he speaks of having had "an able Fiddler" with
him, and in Dumfries he thanks Johnson for making him acquainted with Nathaniel Gow, another fiddler. Later during the
Dumfries years he mentions "Fraser, the Hautboy player," a
"musical Highlander," and a "Singing Master." And there is frequent mention in his letters of Stephen Clarke, the Edinburgh
organist and musical editor of the Museum, who was often about
Dumfries professionally. From these and other sources Burns
learned with precision, and carried in his head, the body of
Scotch folk tunes, and many others as well.

Although he won his first fame with poems on his life, and
opinions, and conflict with the Kirk, his Edinburgh experience
did not divert him from a main interest in vernacular poetry.
Rather, his discovery that in Edinburgh the patricians, the gentry, the literati, the Crochallans — all were enthusiasts about
folk songs, served to encourage him in returning to his earlier
and still strong interest. We have seen, also, that after his great

---

* He found Robert's voice untunable. In later life Burns responded to calls for
his songs by reciting them. His mature singing voice was harsh. (See Anderson, 147; Adair, 189; and Syme, 413.)

success, he felt "Scots poetry" had become "contemptible" through the rush of petty and often imitative Scots versifiers into print, and that he feared mortification if he continued to write even superior poetry of that sort since it no longer offered novelty. Songs, however, were another matter.

The task he set himself was to provide words for all the tunes which he liked and felt were worth preserving. When, as often was true with dance tunes, there were no words, he wrote them, frequently taking hints from titles or other songs; when there were fragments, he expanded or combined them; when there were good verses, he adopted them; and when existing songs seemed faulty, he mended them. He took no money for his work, and he did not acknowledge authorship. He rhymed for fun, and for Scotland, and his great enthusiasm extended far beyond merely composing words for tunes. In January 1793, for example, he wrote to Thomson, "Lochaber and the braes of Ballenden, excepted, so far as the locality either from the title of the air, or the tenor of the Song, could be ascertained, I have paid my devotions at the particular shrine of every Scots Muse." In simple language, he had visited the site associated with every Scots song that he knew except two. And, more important, after he began his association with Johnson in 1787, Burns was alert and active in collecting unpublished songs *and tunes*. He was as much concerned with the music of the *Scots Musical Museum* as with the song texts.

Burns did not live to publish his projected volume of the songs he wished to acknowledge, or his notes on Scots song, although many of the notes do survive in the interleaved *Museum* which he prepared for Robert Riddell, and on sheets in the Laing collection of the University of Edinburgh. The extent of Burns' knowledge and the scope of his activity, and often even the fact or proportion of his authorship of individual songs, must be determined largely from these notes, or from letters. But anyone who examines this material recognizes at once that Burns had, as he said, "paid more attention to every description of Scots songs than perhaps any body living has done." Fortunately, Thomson preserved Burns' letters to him (they are now in the Morgan library); and the Johnson letters and memoranda for volumes I–IV of the *Museum* are in the British Museum, with others known and in private hands. In addition, Burns' general correspondence is full of songs and comments on songs.

James Johnson was content to take what Burns sent him, but George Thomson chose to suggest melodies for which Burns should write lyrics, and then to suggest changes in the lyrics. Thomson can be indexed quickly as a man who objected to *Comin' Thro' the Rye* because young ladies might not like to sing about kissing. A typical proposal from him was that Burns substitute "Ne'er made sic anither" in the lines, "For Nature made her what she is / And never made anither." Burns refused the suggestion. For "mammie's wark" [work], Thomson preferred "mother's wark," and Burns remarked cryptically, "If you think this last is better, you may adopt it." Thomson demurred at the tune for which Burns wrote *Scots Wha Hae,* and at the third line of the first stanza:

> Scots wha hae wi' Wallace bled,
> Scots, wham Bruce has often led,
> Welcome to your gory bed, —
> Or to victorie.

Burns replied, "Your idea, 'honour's bed,' is, though a beautiful, a hacknied idea; so, if you please, we will let the line stand as it is. I have altered the song as follows." He repeats the stanza, modifying the last line to read "Or to glorious victorie" so that it might accommodate Thomson's tune. The two additional syllables in each fourth line produced such results as "Traitor! Coward! turn & flie!" "Caledonian! on wi' me!" and "But they shall be — shall be free!" Public disapproval forced Thomson to restore Burns' original lines when Currie printed them in his biography in 1800.

Without extensive background, the mass of detailed comment about lines, phrases, titles, and tunes in the Burns-Thomson correspondence is tiresome, but there are frequent passages in Burns' letters which reveal his knowledge, his taste, and his concern about the relation of words to music. Salty comments also enliven his letters. For example, "I have begun anew, Let me in this ae night. — Do you think that we ought to retain the old Chorus? I think we must retain both the old chorus & the first Stanza of the old Song. — I do not altogether like the third line of the first Stanza, but cannot alter it to please myself. — I am just three stanzas deep in it.

[Here he quotes the stanzas.]

How do you like this? and would you have the denouement to be successful or otherwise? Should she 'let him in,' or not?" In the song as printed she does not.

Burns and Thomson disagreed about what Burns called "simplicity," and about the related desirability of a Scots vocabulary. Thomson was for English elegance, English words, and propriety. But Burns wrote to him, "Let me tell you, that you are too fastidious in your ideas of Songs & ballads." And later, "Give me leave to criticize your taste in the only thing in which it is in my opinion reprehensible: (you know I ought to know something of my own trade) of Pathos, Sentiment, & Point, you are a compleat judge; but there is a quality more necessary than either, in a Song, & which is the very essence of a Ballad, I mean Simplicity — now, if I mistake not, this last feature you are a little apt to sacrifice to the foregoing." Elsewhere he writes, "There is a pastoral simplicity, a something that one may call, the Doric style & dialect of vocal music, to which a dash of our native tongue & manners is particularly, nay peculiarly apposite."

He later gives an example. "There is a naïveté, a pastoral simplicity, in a slight intermixture of Scots words & phraseology, which is more in unison (at least to my taste, & I will add, to every genuine Caledonian taste,) with the simple pathos, or rustic sprightliness, of our native music, than any English verses whatever. — For instance, in my *Auld Rob Morris*, you propose instead of the word, 'descriving,' to substitute the phrase 'all telling', which would spoil the rusticity, the pastoral, of the stanza." In the interleaved *Museum*, Burns cites lines from *There's Nae Luck about the House* as "unequalled almost by anything I ever heard or read." In the stanza he admired, the sailor's wife, on hearing of her husband's return, sings,

> His very foot has music in't
> As he comes up the stair.
> And will I see his face again?
> And will I hear him speak?
> I'm downright dizzy wi' the thought —
> In truth I'm like to greet!   *weep*

Burns continues to emphasize this critical principle in letters to Thomson. "I still have several M. S. S. Scots airs by me, which I have pickt up, mostly from the singing of country lasses. — They please me vastly; but your learned lugs [ears] would perhaps be displeased with the very features for which I like them. — I call them Simple; you would pronounce them Silly." And elsewhere, "Now let me declare off from your taste. — Toddlin hame is a song that to my taste is an exquisite production of genius. — That very Stanza you dislike

> 'My kimmer & I lay down to sleep   *gossip (girl)*
> [And twa pint stoups at our bed feet   *tankards*
> And ay when we waken'd we drank them dry;
> What think you of my wee kimmer and I?']

is to me a piece of charming native humour. — What pleases me, as simple & naive, disgusts you as ludicrous & low."

Apparently Thomson was not alone in his feelings. "The legion of Scotish Poetasters of the day," Burns wrote, "whom your brother Editor, Mr Ritson, ranks with me as my coevals, have always mistaken vulgarity for simplicity; whereas Simplicity is as much eloignée from vulgarity, on the one hand, as from affected point & puerile conceit, on the other." Thomson proved obdurate, however, and his niggling moved Burns to his famous outburst, "These English Songs gravel me to death." However, he continued to supply a good many of them at Thomson's insistence, acceding to Thomson's requests when he could, and noting once, "The rhythm of the song is abused as you desired."

In the matter of revision, Burns made a distinction between traditional songs and the work of individual poets. He wrote of some tampering by his acquaintance, Josiah Walker, "Let a Poet, if he chuses, take up the idea of another, & work it into a piece of his own; but to mangle the works of the poor Bard whose tuneful tongue is now mute forever in the dark & narrow house, by Heaven 'twould be Sacriledge! I grant that Mr Walker's version is an improvement; but, I know Mr Walker well, & esteem him much; let him mend the Song as the Highlander mended his gun: he gave it a new stock, a new lock, & a new barrel."

Burns also had strong objections to elegant modification of Scots folk music. Of Thomson's musical editor, Joseph Pleyel, he exclaims, "Whatever Mr Pleyel does, let him not alter one iota of the original Scots Air [of the tune for *Highland Mary*]; . . . Let our National Music preserve its native features. They are, I own, frequently wild, & unreducable to the modern rules; but on that very eccentricity, perhaps, depends a great part of their effect."

Of sophisticated formal music, Burns had little or no understanding, but the "nobly sentimental" Scotch airs delighted him as much as the songs for them. Here he found no response from the improving Thomson, to whom he wrote, "I am sensible that my taste in Music must be inelegant & vulgar, because people of undisputed & cultivated taste can find no merit in many of my favorite tunes. — Still, because I am cheaply pleased, is that any reason why I should deny myself that pleasure? — Many of our Strathspeys, ancient & modern, give me most exquisite enjoyment, where you & other judges would probably be shewing signs of disgust. — For instance, I am just now making verses for Rothemurche's Rant, an air which puts me in raptures: & in fact, unless I be pleased with the tune, I never can make verses to it." This final statement should be noted most particularly, since Burns speaks often of trying with small success to write for tunes suggested by Thomson which he had no liking for.

Elsewhere he comments, "You know that my pretensions to musical taste, are merely a few of Nature's instincts, untaught & untutored by Art. — For this reason, many musical compositions, particularly where much of the merit lies in Counterpoint, however they may transport & ravish the ears of you, Connoisseurs, affect my simple lug no otherwise than merely as melodious Din."

Burns felt that no tune was complete without words to sing it by. "I think that it is better," he wrote, "to have mediocre verses to a favorite air than none at all." Indeed, the very quality of the music made it difficult, often, to provide words at all. "If you mean, my dear Sir," he wrote Thomson in his third letter to him, "that all the Songs in your Collection shall be Poetry of the first merit, I am afraid you will find difficulty in the undertaking more than you are aware of. — There is a peculiar rhythmus in many of our airs, and a necessity of adapting syllables to the emphasis, or what I would call, the *feature notes,* of the tune, that cramps the Poet, & lays him under almost insuperable difficulties." But Burns did not reconcile himself to a merely utilitarian mediocrity. He "had rather be the author of five well-written songs than of ten otherwise," and he suppressed songs which he did not feel were tolerable, or told Thomson to do so.

It is with these difficulties in mind that Burns wrote to the Rev. John Skinner, "The world may think slightingly of the craft of song-making, if they please, but as Job says — 'O that mine adversary had written a book!' — let them try. There is a certain something in the old Scotch songs, a wild happiness of thought and expression, which peculiarly marks them, not only from English songs, but also from the modern efforts of song-wrights, in our native manner and language."

It was Burns' ability to surmount the difficulties he mentions, and to capture the "certain something in the old Scotch songs" . which is his distinguishing achievement. He knew that many of his songs were "trifling enough perhaps, but they served as a vehicle to the music." As he said elsewhere, of the *Museum*, "Once for all, let me apologize for many silly compositions of mine in this work. Many beautiful airs wanted words; in the hurry of other avocations, if I could string a parcel of rhymes together any thing near tolerable, I was fain to let them pass." It is, however, an illuminating experience to compare Burns' songs with those he worked from, or with the common fare of the song books. His standards were high, and his achievement unsurpassed in technical skill, and in working within the spirit and manner of the folk songs he loved.

On another difficulty, that of keeping fresh and original, Burns makes a brilliant and bawdy comment to Thomson.

Originality is a coy feature, in composition, & in a multiplicity of efforts in the same style disappears entirely. . . . Some years ago, when I was young, & by no means the saint I am now, I was looking over, in company with a belle lettre friend, a Magazine Ode to Spring, when my friend fell foul of the recurrence of the same thoughts, & offered me a bet that it was impossible to produce an Ode to Spring on an original plan. — I accepted it, & pledged myself to bring in the verdant fields, — the budding flowers, — the chrystal streams, — the melody of the groves, — & a love-story into the bargain, & yet be original. Here follows the piece, & wrote for music too!

Ode to Spring — Tune — The tither morn. —

When maukin bucks, at early fucks,	*hare*
In dewy grass are seen, Sir,	
And birds, on boughs, take off their mows	*coits*
Among the leaves sae green, Sir;	

Latona's sun looks liquorish on
  Dame Nature's grand impètus
Till his prick go rise, then westward flies
  To roger Madame Thetis.

Yon wandering rill that marks the hill,
  And glances o'er the brae, Sir,
Slides by a bower where many a flower
  Sheds fragrance on the day, Sir;
There Damon lay, with Sylvia gay,
  To love they thought no crime, Sir;
The wild-birds sang, the echoes rang,
  While Damon's arse beat time, Sir. —

First, wi' the thrush, his thrust & push
  Had compass large & long, Sir;
The blackbird next, his tuneful text,
  Was bolder, clear & strong, Sir:
The linnet's lay then came in play,
  And the lark that soar'd aboon, Sir;   *above*
Till Damon fierce, mistimed his arse,
  And fucked quite out of tune, Sir.

Now for decency. — A great critic, Aikin on songs, says that love
& wine are the exclusive themes for song-writing. — The following
is on neither subject, & consequently is no Song; but will be allowed,
I think, to be two or three pretty good *prose* thoughts inverted into
rhyme.

Is There for Honest Poverty follows. The rapid shift in tone and
spirit is highly characteristic of Burns' letters.

Those to Johnson and Thomson also teem with detailed and
precise directions for fitting words to melodies. In these instructions there is much to indicate that he had come to understand
musical notation. Of *O Saw Ye Bonie Lesley*, he writes to Thomson in November, 1792,

Every seventh line ends with three syllables, in place of the two in
the other lines, but you will see in the sixth bar of the second part,
the place where these three syllables will always recur, that the four

semiquavers usually sung as one syllable will with the greatest propriety divide into two — thus

For Na – ture made her   what she is,   And &c., &c., &c.,

Characteristic later comments show both Burns' concern over musical settings, and the extent and kind of his musical knowledge. For example, "The bonie brucket [soot-marked] lassie — I enclose you a song to it, as I think it should be set; & with a better effect than the modulation in the Museum." To Johnson he wrote of *Turn Again, Thou Fair Eliza,* "The song will not sing to your tune; but there is a Perthshire tune in McDonald's collection of *Highland Airs* which is much admired in this country; I intended the verses to sing to that air. . . . There is another air in the same collection, an Argyleshire air, which with a trifling alteration will do charmingly. . . . The alterations are: in the fourth bar of the first and third strains, which are to be the tune, instead of the crotchet C, and the quavers G and E, at the beginning of the bar make an entire minim in E, I mean E, the lowest line."

Again, to Thomson, he comments on an air for the Jacobite verses, *There'll Never Be Peace Till Jamie Comes Hame.* "It is a little irregular in the flow of the lines; but where two short syllables, that is to say, one syllable more than regular feet, if those two syllables fall to the space of one, crotchet-time, composed of two different quavers under a slur, it has, I think, no bad effect, to divide them." And of another song, he says, "If you honor my verses by setting the air to it, I will vamp up the old Song, & make it English enough to be understood. — I have sent you my song noted down to the air, in the way I think that it should go; I believe you will find my set of the air to be one of the best."

These comments on music may be concluded with a touching analogy. "Conjugal love is a Passion which I deeply feel, & highly

venerate; but somehow it does not make such a figure in Poesy
as that other species of the Passion —

'Where Love is Liberty & Nature law. — '

Musically speaking, the first is an instrument of which the gamut
is scanty & confined, but the tones inexpressibly sweet; while
the last has powers equal to all the intellectual Modulation of
the Human Soul."

For one with Burns' rhythmic sense, it is not surprising to find
that with him composition was often accompanied by physical
action. During his years at Ellisland he speaks of having composed while on horseback, and in Dumfries there are frequent
references to songs which were the result of walks. He no doubt
also welcomed a respite on these walks from the healthy confusion of his household. Once he writes of having tried out a
song *viva voce* ("I sat, & raved, under the shade of an old thorn,
till I wrote one to suit the measure"). We have already seen
that he could not make verses for a tune unless he liked it and
could feel it. Moreover, he was a pragmatist, noting, "Making a
poem is like begetting a son: you cannot know whether you have
a wise man or a fool, untill you produce him to the world & try
him."

For convenience, Burns' two famous statements about his
methods of composition are herewith repeated. In connection
with the second, it may be noted that though his early songs
were "breathings of ardent passion," he had to adopt a formula
to raise his spirits at age thirty-five. Both comments are addressed to George Thomson, the first in 1793, the second in 1794.

1. "Untill I am compleat master of a tune, in my own singing,
(such as it is) I never can compose for it. — My way is: I consider the poetic Sentiment, correspondent to my idea of the
musical expression; then chuse my theme; begin one Stanza;
when that is composed, which is generally the most difficult part

of the business, I walk out, sit down now & then, look out for objects in Nature around me that are in unison or harmony with the cogitations of my fancy & workings of my bosom; humming every now & then the air with the verses I have framed: when I feel my Muse beginning to jade, I retire to the solitary fireside of my study, & there commit my effusions to paper; swinging, at intervals, on the hindlegs of my elbow-chair, by way of calling forth my own critical strictures, as my pen goes on."

2. "Do you think that the sober, gin-horse routine of existence could inspire a man with life, & love, & joy — could fire him with enthusiasm, or melt him with pathos, equal to the genius of your Book? — No! No!!! — Whenever I want to be more than ordinary *in song;* to be in some degree equal to your diviner airs; do you imagine I fast & pray for the celestial emanation? — Tout au contraire! I have a glorious recipe, the very one that for his own use was invented by the Divinity of Healing & Poesy when erst he piped to the flocks of Admetus. — I put myself on a regimen of admiring a fine woman; & in proportion to the adorability of her charms, in proportion you are delighted with my verses."

J. C. Dick notes than Burns recorded "about forty" tunes not published before, and provided songs for them; and that he edited many airs in instrumental collections for singing. "Very few of the tunes of Burns' songs had been printed with words until they were set to his verses." Dick estimates that only about 200 Scots tunes were available in publications when Burns began his work, and reports that Johnson had appropriated most of the best ones for the first of his volumes. In all, Burns sent some 350 songs to Johnson and Thomson, and for them he "embodied the whole cycle of Scottish Song, both as a writer of original songs, and as, for want of a better definition, a reconstructor of the songs of the past." Burns was no mere collector like David Herd, and certainly no scholar-antiquarian like Joseph Ritson; more than anything else he was a greatly gifted folk-artist, working among traditional materials and making them his own, often turning commonplace work into "living, emotional song."

As Sir Walter Scott has put it, few songs, "whether serious or humourous, passed through his hands without receiving some of those magic touches which, without greatly altering the song, restored its original spirit, or gave it more than it had ever possessed. So dexterously are these touches combined with the ancient structure that the *rifacciamento,* in many instances, could scarcely have been detected without the avowal of the bard himself."

Among the songs which Burns sent to Johnson, two of the happiest combinations of "poetic sentiment," "musical expression," "theme," and illustrations in harmony, are *Sweet Tibbie Dunbar* and *Ay Waukin, O.* Like many other excellent songs in the canon, they have great charm when sung, but only limited appeal when read. *Ay Waukin, O* is especially fine.

Sweet Tibbie Dunbar

O, wilt thou go wi' me, sweet Tibbie Dunbar?
O, wilt thou go wi' me, sweet Tibbie Dunbar?
Wilt thou ride on a horse, or be drawn in a car,
Or walk by my side, O sweet Tibbie Dunbar?

I care na thy daddie, his lands and his money;
I care na thy kin, sae high and sae lordly;
But say that thou'lt hae me for better or waur,   *worse*
And come in thy coatie, sweet Tibbie Dunbar.   *short petticoat*

Ay Waukin, O

Chorus

Ay waukin, O,   *wakeful*
   Waukin still and weary:
Sleep I can get nane
   For thinking on my dearie.

Simmer's a pleasant time:
  Flowers of every colour,
The water rins owre the heugh,   *crag*
  And I long for my true lover.

When I sleep I dream,
  When I wauk I'm eerie,   *apprehensive*
Sleep I can get nane
  For thinkin on my dearie.

Lanely night comes on,
  A' the lave are sleepin,   *rest*
I think on my bonie lad,
  And I bleer my een wi' greetin.   *eyes   weeping*

Ay waukin, O,
  Waukin still and weary:
Sleep I can get nane
  For thinking on my dearie.

Although Burns was widely familiar with ballads, he had little interest in them. But in his letters it was his common practice to use the words "ballad" and "song" almost interchangeably, a practice which reveals that he thought of songs as situation pieces, little stories, like ballads only shorter. Burns in his songs did not weave gossamer threads into mood pieces. Rather, he used concrete language and a compact style to develop human relationships. Most of his early songs, and some of the later ones, grew out of personal experience — often passionate, but they are not private or particular or confessional. While they may reflect Burns' experience, and feelings, and sense of life, the songs depict experience transmuted into art that is representative and general. And many of them, it should be noted, are for women to sing. As Burns wrote to Jean McMurdo of a song he had written about her, "Every composition of this kind must have a series of Dramatic incident in it, so I have had recourse to my invention." Many of these songs make charming little poems, but when they

are read, if they have choruses* or refrains, these pleasant adornments of a song grow monotonous. There follows a brief selection
of these "dramatic lyrics."

Last May a Braw Wooer

Last May a braw wooer cam down the lang glen,
  And sair wi' his love he did deave me.   *deafen*
I said there was naething I hated like men:
  The deuce gae wi'm to believe me, believe me —
  The deuce gae wi'm to believe me!

He spak o' the darts in my bonie black een,
  And vow'd for my love he was diein.
I said, he might die whcn he liket for Jean:
  The Lord forgie me for liein, for liein —
  The Lord forgie me for liein!

A weel-stocket mailen, himsel for the laird,   *farm*
  And marriage aff-hand were his proffers:
I never loot on that I kenn'd it, or car'd,   *let*
  But I thought I might hae waur offers, waur offers —   *worse*
  But I thought I might hae waur offers.

But what wad ye think? In a fortnight or less
  (The Deil tak his taste to gae near her!)
He up the Gate-Slack to my black cousin, Bess!
  Guess ye how, the jad! I could bear her, could bear her —
  Guess ye how, the jad! I could bear her.

But a' the niest week, as I petted wi' care,   *next*
  I gaed to the tryste o' Dalgarnock,   *cattle-fair*
And wha but my fine fickle lover was there?
  I glowr'd as I'd seen a warlock, a warlock —   *stared*
  I glowr'd as I'd seen a warlock.

But owre my left shouther I gae him a blink,
  Lest neebours might say I was saucy.

* Burns told George Thomson, "I am not fond of choruses to songs." (F II,
#580, 193.)

My wooer he caper'd as he'd been in drink,
And vow'd I was his dear lassie, dear lassie —
And vow'd I was his dear lassie!

I spier'd for my cousin fu' couthy and sweet;   *asked   loving*
Gin she had recover'd her hearin?
And how her new shoon fit her auld, shachl'd feet?   *shoes   shapeless*
But heavens! how he fell a swearin, a swearin —
But heavens! how he fell a swearin!

He beggèd, for gudesake, I wad be his wife,
Or else I wad kill him wi' sorrow;
So e'en to preserve the poor body in life,
I think I maun wed him to-morrow, to-morrow —   *must*
I think I maun wed him to-morrow!

Duncan Gray

Weary fa' you, Duncan Gray!   *woe befall*
(Ha, ha, the girdin o't!)   *girthing*
Wae gae by you, Duncan Gray   *Woe go with*
(Ha, ha, the girdin o't!)
When a' the lave gae to their play,   *rest*
Then I maun sit the lee-lang day,   *must   live-long*
And jeeg the cradle wi' my tae,   *jog   toe*
And a' for the girdin o't!

Bonie was the Lammas moon
(Ha, ha, the girdin o't!),
Glowrin a' the hills aboon   *above*
(Ha, ha, the girdin o't!).
The girdin brak, the beast cam down,
I tint my curch and baith my shoon,   *lost   kerchief   shoes*
And, Duncan, ye're an unco loon   *rogue*
Wae on the bad girdin o't!

But Duncan, gin ye'll keep your aith   *if   oath*
(Ha, ha, the girdin o't!),
I'se bless you wi' my hindmost breath   *I'll*
(Ha, ha, the girdin o't!).
Duncan, gin ye'll keep your aith,

The beast again can bear us baith,
And auld Mess John will mend the skaith   *damage*
And clout the bad girdin o't.   *patch*

Willie Wastle

Willie Wastle dwalt on Tweed,
The spot they ca'd it Linkumdoddie.
Willie was a wabster guid   .   *weaver*
Could stown a clue wi' onie bodie.   *have stolen skein*
He had a wife was dour and din,   *sullen   dark*
O, Tinkler Madgie was her mither!   *Tinker*
Sic a wife as Willie had,   *Such*
I wad na gie a button for her.

She has an e'e (she has but ane),
The cat has twa the very colour,
Five rusty teeth, forbye a stump,   *besides*
A clapper-tongue wad deave a miller;   *deafen*
A whiskin beard about her mou,
Her nose and chin they threaten ither: *each other*
Sic a wife as Willie had,
I wad na gie a button for her.

She's bow-hough'd, she's hem-shin'd   *bandy-legged haim-shinned*
Ae limpin leg a hand-breed shorter;   *one hand-breadth*
She's twisted right, she's twisted left,
To balance fair in ilka quarter;   *either*
She has a hump upon her breast,
The twin o' that upon her shouther: *shoulder*
Sic a wife as Willie had,
I wad na gie a button for her.

Auld baudrans by the ingle sits,   *Auld pussie*
An' wi' her loof her face a-washin;   *paw*
But Willie's wife is nae sae trig,
She dights her grunzie wi' a hushion;   *wipes snout footless stocking*
Her walie nieves like midden-creels,   *ample fists manure-baskets*
Her face wad fyle the Logan Water: *foul*
Sic a wife as Willie had,
I wad na gie a button for her.

Wha Is That at My Bower Door

"Wha is that at my bower door?"
  "O, wha is it but Findlay!"
"Then gae your gate, ye'se nae be here." *go your way you'll*
  "Indeed maun I!" quo' Findlay.   *must*
"What mak ye, sae like a thief?"
  "O, come and see!" quo' Findlay.
"Before the morn ye'll work mischiéf?"
  "Indeed will I!" quo' Findlay.

"Gif I rise and let you in" —   *If*
  "Let me in!" quo' Findlay —
"Ye'll keep me wauken wi' your din?"
  "Indeed will I!" quo' Findlay.
"In my bower if ye should stay" —
  "Let me stay!" quo' Findlay —
"I fear ye'll bide till break o' day?"
  "Indeed will I!" quo' Findlay.

"Here this night if ye remain" —
  "I'll remain!" quo' Findlay —
"I dread ye'll learn the gate again?"   *way*
  "Indeed will I!" quo' Findlay.
"What may pass within this bower"
  ("Let it pass!" quo' Findlay!)
"Ye maun conceal till your last hour" —
  "Indeed will I!" quo' Findlay.

Tam Glen

My heart is a-breaking, dear tittie,   *sister,*
 Some counsel unto me come len':
To anger them a' is a pity,
 But what will I do wi' Tam Glen?

I'm thinking, wi' sic a braw fellow *such fine*
 In poortith I might mak a fen'. *poverty shift*
What care I in riches to wallow,
 If I mauna marry Tam Glen?   *must not*

There's Lowrie the laird o' Dumeller:
  "Guid day to you, brute!" he comes ben.   *in*
He brags and he blaws o' his siller,   *money*
  But when will he dance like Tam Glen?

My minnie does constantly deave me, *mother* *deafen*
  And bids me beware o' young men.
They flatter, she says, to deceive me —
  But wha can think sae o' Tam Glen?

My daddie says, gin I'll forsake him,   *if*
  He'd gie me guid hunder marks ten.
But if it's ordain'd I maun take him,
  O, wha will I get but Tam Glen?

Yestreen at the valentine's dealing,   *Last night*
  My heart to my mou gied a sten,   *mouth* *leap*
For thrice I drew ane without failing,
  And thrice it was written "Tam Glen"!

The last Halloween I was waukin   *wakefully watching*
  My droukit sark-sleeve, as ye ken — *wetted shift-*
His likeness came up the house staukin, *stalking*
  And the very grey breeks o' Tam Glen! *breeches*

Come, counsel, dear tittie, don't tarry!
  I'll gie ye my bonie black hen,
Gif ye will advise me to marry   *If*
  The lad I lo'e dearly, Tam Glen.

I'm O'er Young to Marry Yet

Chorus

I'm o'er young, I'm o'er young,
  I'm o'er young to marry yet!
I'm o'er young, 'twad be a sin
  To tak me frae my mammie yet.

I am my mammie's ae bairn,   *only child*
  Wi' unco folk I weary, Sir,   *strange*
And lying in a man's bed,
  I'm fley'd it make me eerie, Sir. *afraid apprehensive*

Hallowmass is come and gane,
  The nights are lang in winter, Sir,
And you an' I in ae bed —
  In trowth, I dare na venture, Sir!

Fu' loud and shrill the frosty wind
  Blaws thro' the leafless timmer, Sir,   *timber*
But if ye come this gate again,   *way*
  I'll aulder be gin simmer, Sir.   *older be by summer*

Chorus

I'm o'er young, I'm o'er young,
  I'm o'er young to marry yet!
I'm o'er young, 'twad be a sin
  To tak me frae my mammie yet.

What Can a Young Lassie

What can a young lassie,
What shall a young lassie,
What can a young lassie
  Do wi' an auld man?
Bad luck on the penny
That tempted my minnie   *mother*
To sell her puir Jenny
  For siller an' lan'!   *money*

He's always compleenin
Frae mornin to eenin;
He hoasts and he hirples   *coughs   hobbles*
  The weary day lang;
He's doylt and he's dozin;   *muddled   impotent*
His blude it is frozen —
O, dreary's the night
  Wi' a crazy auld man!

He hums and he hankers,
He frets and he cankers,
I never can please him
  Do a' that I can.

He's peevish an' jealous
Of a' the young fellows —
O, dool on the day   *woe*
    I met wi' an auld man!

My auld auntie Katie
Upon me taks pity,
I'll do my endeavour
    To follow her plan:
I'll cross him an' wrack him
Until I heartbreak him,
And then his auld brass
    Will buy me a new pan.

O, Steer Her Up, an' Haud Her Gaun

O, steer her up, an' haud her gaun —   *rouse* *keep her going*
  Her mither's at the mill, jo,
An' gin she winna tak a man,   *if* *will not*
  E'en let her tak her will, jo.
First shore her wi' a gentle kiss,   *threaten*
  Then ca' another gill, jo,   *call for*
An' gin she tak the thing amiss,   *if she should take*
  E'en let her flyte her fill, jo.   *scold*

O, steer her up, an' be na blate,   *bashful*
  An' gin she take it ill, jo,
Then leave the lassie till her fate,
  And time nae langer spill, jo!   *waste*
Ne'er break your heart for ae rebute, *one rebuff*
  But think upon it still, jo,
That gin the lassie winna do't,
  Ye'll fin' anither will, jo.

It goes without saying that one's delight in productions like
these is greatly increased when they are sung.

Of course, songs inseparably linked to melodies in the public
mind are among Burns' most famous.

Ye Banks and Braes

Ye banks and braes o' bonie Doon,
  How can ye bloom sae fresh and fair;
How can ye chant, ye little birds,
  And I sae weary, fu' o' care!
Thou'll break my heart, thou warbling bird,
  That wantons thro' the flowering thorn:
Thou minds me o' departed joys,
  Departed, never to return. —

Oft hae I rov'd by bonie Doon,
  To see the rose and woodbine twine;
And lika bird sang o' its Luve,
  And fondly sae did I o' mine. —
Wi' lightsome heart I pu'd a rose,
  Fu' sweet upon its thorny tree;
And my fause Luver staw my rose,   *stole*
  But, ah! he left the thorn wi' me. —

A comparison of this song with an earlier version, *Ye Flowery Banks o' Bonie Doon,* generally agreed to be poetically superior, illustrates simply the special requirement of song. When the song quoted above "is sung to the melody forever associated with it," says Professor T. Crawford, "the extra syllables cease to be redundant, and the song emerges as quite different in mood from the other. . . . When considered as a *song,* and not merely as a verbal pattern, it becomes a beautifully poignant expression of love's melancholy, . . . When associated with the music, the repetition of 'departed' and the stock expression 'never to return' add immeasurably to the pathos."

Green Grow the Rashes, O

Chorus

Green grow the rashes, O;
Green grow the rashes, O;
The sweetest hours that e'er I spend,
Are spent among the lasses, O.

There's nought but care on ev'ry han',
   In every hour that passes, O:
What signifies the life o' man,
   An' 'twere na for the lasses, O.

The war'ly race may riches chase,   *worldly*
   An' riches still may fly them, O;
An' tho' at last they catch them fast,
   Their hearts can ne'er enjoy them, O.

But gie me a cannie hour at e'en,
   My arms about my dearie, O;
An' war'ly cares an' war'ly men,
   May a' gae tapsalteerie, O!   *topsy-turvy*

For you sae douce, ye sneer at this;   *grave*
   Ye're nought but senseless asses, O:
The wisest man the warl' e'er saw,   *world*
   He dearly lov'd the lasses, O.

Auld nature swears, the lovely dears
   Her noblest work she classes, O:
Her prentice han' she try'd on man,
   An' then she made the lasses, O.

Chorus

   Green grow the rashes, O;
   Green grow the rashes, O;
The sweetest hours that e'er I spend,
   Are spent among the lasses, O.

Comin Thro' the Rye

Chorus

O, Jenny's a' weet, poor body,   *wet*
   Jenny's seldom dry:
She draigl't a' her petticoatie,   *draggled*
   Comin thro' the rye!

Comin thro' the rye, poor body,
   Comin thro' the rye,

She draigl't a' her petticoatie,
Comin thro' the rye!

Gin a body meet a body
Comin thro' the rye,
Gin a body kiss a body,
Need a body cry?

Gin a body meet a body
Comin thro' the glen,
Gin a body kiss a body,
Need the warld ken?

Chorus
O, Jenny's a' weet, poor body,
Jenny's seldom dry:
She draigl't a' her petticoatie,
Comin thro' the rye!

The popular lines below derive from a second set (#418) in the *Museum,* which Professor Kinsley feels Burns had nothing to do with.

Ilka lassie hae her laddie,
Nane they say hae I;
But a' the lads they smile at me
When comin' thro' the rye.

The bawdy possibilities in this theme, Burns explored elsewhere.

Sweet Afton

Flow gently, sweet Afton, among thy green braes!
Flow gently, I'll sing thee a song in thy praise!
My Mary's asleep by thy murmuring stream —
Flow gently, sweet Afton, disturb not her dream!

Thou stock dove whose echo resounds thro' the glen,
Ye wild whistling blackbirds in yon thorny den,

Thou green-crested lapwing, thy screaming forbear —
I charge you, disturb not my slumbering fair!

How lofty, sweet Afton, thy neighbouring hills,
Far mark'd with the courses of clear, winding rills!
There daily I wander, as noon rises high,
My flocks and my Mary's sweet cot in my eye.

How pleasant thy banks and green vallies below,
Where wild in the woodlands the primroses blow;
There oft, as mild Ev'ning weeps over the lea,
The sweet-scented birk shades my Mary and me.

Thy crystal stream, Afton, how lovely it glides,
And winds by the cot where my Mary resides!
How wanton thy waters her snowy feet lave,
As, gathering sweet flowerets, she stems thy clear wave!

Flow gently, sweet Afton, among thy green braes!
Flow gently, sweet river, the theme of my lays!
My Mary's asleep by thy murmuring stream —
Flow gently, sweet Afton, disturb not her dream!

Auld Lang Syne

Chorus

For auld lang syne, my dear,
For auld lang syne,
We'll tak a cup o' kindness yet
For auld lang syne!

Should auld acquaintance be forgot,
And never brought to mind?
Should auld acquaintance be forgot,
And auld lang syne!

And surely ye'll be your pint-stowp,   *pay for*
And surely I'll be mine,
And we'll tak a cup o' kindness yet
For auld lang syne!

We twa hae run about the braes,
　And pou'd the gowans fine,　　　　*pulled　daisies*
But we've wander'd monie a weary fit　　　*foot*
　Sin' auld lang syne.

We twa hae paidl'd in the burn　　　*paddled　brook*
　Frae morning sun till dine,　　　　　　*noon*
But seas between us braid hae roar'd　　*broad*
　Sin' auld lang syne.

And there's a hand, my trusty fiere,　　　*comrade*
　And gie's a hand o' thine,
And we'll tak a right guid-willie waught　　*draught*
　For auld lang syne!

Chorus
For auld lang syne, my dear,
　For auld lang syne,
We'll tak a cup o' kindness yet
　For auld lang syne!

There were many "auld lang syne" songs before Burns', and he said he took down this one "from an old man's singing." Professor Kinsley discusses possible revisions, but comes to the conclusion that, "There remains no good evidence on which to question Burns's story that he got *Auld Lang Syne* from oral tradition." The air to which it is now sung was selected by George Thomson, possibly after consultation with Burns.

Burns once complained to Thomson that it was difficult "to ascertain the truth respecting our Poesy & Music." "I myself," he continued, "have lately seen a couple of Ballads sung through the streets of Dumfries, with my name at the head of them as the Author, though it was the first time ever I had seen them." But he tried to collect all the information he could about Scots song, recording much of it in Riddell's interleaved *Museum,* and more in the Laing collection notes. He gives the authorship of songs, assigns their native regions or the occasion of their composition, quotes fragments or versions of traditional songs, makes critical comments, and records engaging anecdotes. The ensuing legend about *The Kirk Wad Let Me Be* is in the Laing notes.

Tradition in the Western parts of Scotland tells this old song . . . once saved a Covenanting Clergyman out of a scrape. It was a little prior to the Revolution, a period when being a Scots Covenanter was being a Felon, one of their clergy who was at that very time hunted by the merciless soldiery, fell in, by accident, with a party of the military. The soldiers were not exactly acquainted with the person of the Rev. gentleman of whom they were in search; but from some suspicious circumstances they fancied that they had got one of that cloth and opprobious persuasion among them in the person of this stranger. "Mass John," to extricate himself, assumed such a freedom of manners (very unlike the gloomy strictness of his sect), and among other convivial exhibitions, sung (and, some traditions say, composed on the spur of the occasion) "Kirk wad let me be," with such effect, that the soldiers swore he was a d——d honest fellow, and that it was impossible *he* could belong to these hellish conventicles, and so gave him his liberty.

In the interleaved *Museum,* Burns records the source of *O'er the Moor Amang the Heather.* "This song is the composition of a Jean Glover, a girl who was not only a whore, but also a thief; and in one or other character has visited most of the Correction Houses in the West. She was born, I believe, in Kilmarnock. I took down the song from her singing as she was strolling through the country, with a slight-of-hand blackguard." Of *The Bush Aboon Traquair,* he notes, "This, another beautiful song of Mr. Crawford's composition. In the neighbourhood of Traquair, tradition still shows the old 'bush'; which, when I saw it in the year '87, was composed of eight or nine ragged birches. The Earl of Traquair has planted a clump of trees near by, which he calls *The new bush.*"

Burns attaches one of his regional notes to *Dumbarton's Drums Beat Bonny, O!* "This is the last of the West Highland airs; and from it, over the whole tract of country to the confines of Tweed-side, there is hardly a tune or song that one can say has taken its origin from any place or transaction in that part of Scotland. The oldest Ayr Shire reel is *Stewarton lasses,* which was made by the father of the present Sir Walter Montgomery Cunning-ham, alias Lord Lyle; since which period there has indeed been local music in that country in great plenty. *Johnnie Faa* is the only old song which I could ever trace as belonging to the ex-tensive county of Ayr."

Burns was evidently delighted with the following anecdote, which will serve to conclude this brief selection from his memo-randa. "*Kate of Aberdeen,* is, I believe, the work of poor Cunning-ham the player; of whom the following anecdote, though told before, deserves a recital. A fat dignitary of the Church coming past Cunningham one Sunday as the poor poet was busy plying a fishing-rod in some stream near Durham, his native country, his reverence reprimanded Cunningham very severely for such an occupation on such a day. The poor poet, with that inoffensive gentleness of manners which was his peculiar characteristic, re-plied, that he hoped God and his reverence would forgive his seeming profanity of that sacred day, 'as he had no dinner to eat, but what lay in the bottom of that pool.' This, Mr. Woods, the player who knew Cunningham well and esteemed him much, assured me was true."

It is ironic that Burns' heroic efforts to "embody" Scots folk song should have helped to inhibit its continued "localizing," and hence should have straitened its vitality. The whole Eighteenth Century movement toward collection and publication of folk songs hastened their translation from songs for singing into songs for performance and listening. And when a poet like Burns, or one of his lesser contemporaries like Lady Nairne, the Rev. John Skinner, Lady Anne Barnard, or Jane Eliot took a hand in the process, the result of these publications was art song as well. This is not to say that all of Burns' songs were of high quality, or even always better than the materials he worked from. Some were not, and he knew it. But his towering achievement served to stabilize his own localizings as the common forms, although independent development did continue, particularly with the bawdy songs of which he produced polite versions.

On the whole, it seems fair to say that the *Scottish Musical Museum* soon became what it has remained, the standard repository of traditional songs and airs in its day as formulated by Burns, and that, to quote Gavin Greig, "The songs of Robert Burns have never been sung by our peasantry in general; or, putting it more widely, we may say that Scottish book-songs have never been the songs of the mass of the Scottish people. This statement, so far as we know, is made for the first time in good black print. It is to me quite astounding that the Scottish people themselves should put forward the songs of Burns, Lady Nairne, Tannahill, Hogg, and Scott, as their own authentic native minstrelsy — as the songs that are and have been all along sung by swain and maid in the field and by the fireside; and that speakers and writers should work themselves into a fine frenzy over what is largely a delusion."

For Scots, of course, Burns' songs have special interest as expressions of national character and feeling, and country dwellers nowadays are said to find them more appealing than city folk. But even in Scotland, changing tastes, and particularly the "pop" hit tune as promoted by recordings and broadcasts, have reduced the popularity of Burns' songs. From the sophisticated, on the other hand, there is complaint that Burns stands in the way of a contemporary flowering of Scots poetry.

For the larger audience, as for Scotsmen, the two-score famous songs of Burns whether they are sung, or read as poems, provide a lively gallery of characters and strong appeal to a wide range of human feeling. Gaiety, bawdry, tenderness, humor, patriotism, passion, despair, bacchanalianism, and much else, in a variety of moods and voices, are common to all times and countries, no matter what their local dress.

And for those interested in the technique of suiting poetry to sentiment, and sentiment to melody, and of felicitously developing theme and situation with economy, Burns offers never ending excitement.

It remains to discuss *The Merry Muses* and related matters, and the first of these matters to understand plainly is that Scotland possesses "a wonderful quantity of indecorous traditionary verse, not of an inflammatory character, but simply expressive of a profound sense of the ludicrous in connection with the sexual affections. Such things, usually kept from public view, oozed out in merry companies such as Burns loved to frequent." So wrote Robert Chambers in 1851, in his life of Burns. And the contemporary expert on pornography, Mr. G. Legman, reports a "truly remarkable" body of such verse still to be circulating in Scotland, credit for stimulating which is customarily given to the repressions of the Calvinist Kirk. Sydney Goodsir Smith and Hugh MacDiarmid both vouch for the comparative superiority of Scots to other bawdry.

As we have seen, Burns wrote down a bawdy song in the 1783–85 Commonplace Book (*My Girl She's Airy*), and his correspondence is full of "uninflammatory" bawdry thereafter, particularly references to and quotations from songs. Alexander Cunningham summarized the matter nicely: "His poetry & letters were often so blended with Religion Politics Love & Bawdry that the greatest care must be taken" to edit them carefully. Some blander bawdry has long been regularly printed in editions of Burns — *Here's His Health in Water, The Rantin Dog, Wha Is That at My Bower Door*, songs from *The Jolly Beggars — Love and Liberty*. And a large number of Burns' contributions to Johnson and Thomson had their origins in popular bawdy songs. Publication in the *Museum* and the *Select Collection* of polite songs to the familiar bawdy tunes must have created widespread tension, probably agreeable. Some of the more notable derivations from bawdy originals are *Green Grow the Rashes, O, Duncan Gray, Duncan Davison, John Anderson,* and *Tho' Women's Minds.*

The Crochallans and similar groups specialized in bawdy songs, and rejoiced in Burns with his wide knowledge of them. He mentions in several of his letters a private collection of what he called "cloaciniad verse," and he promised to send Andrew Erskine a copy of some clandestine poems, on Erskine's request. Just what form Burns' collection took is not clear; perhaps a notebook, but more likely single sheets. In 1815 Allan Cunningham copied some songs from a MS belonging to a Mr. I. Gracie of Dumfries, who had received it from his father, the Dumfries banker James Gracie, who in turn had received it from Burns himself. The whereabouts of any MSS sent to Erskine, or of the Gracie MS, are not known.

Textual, bibliographical, editorial, and historical problems relating to Burns and bawdy songs are "riddling, perplexed, and labyrinthical" in the extreme. Just what Burns' collection contained is not known; what Allan Cunningham saw is not certain; and what, if anything, Burns sent to Erskine is also unknown. But that Burns was familiar with such materials and delighted in them is plain enough; and with bawdy songs he followed the same courses as with more polite ones. He worked as a folk artist with familiar materials, "localizing" what he found. It remains conjectural much of the time whether a particular version of a bawdy song is "by" Burns, or "mended by" him, or merely "old." From the Mauchline days on, he had many friends who shared the national taste for bawdry with him, and to them he sent bawdy songs or poems when he came upon them or composed them.

After Burns' death there appeared a pamphlet of 128 pages (122 pages of text), with a date of 1799, and with some pages watermarked 1799, and some 1800. It bore the title: *"The MERRY MUSES of Caledonia*; a Collection of FAVOURITE SCOTS SONGS, ANCIENT and MODERN: selected for the use of the CROCHALLAN FENCIBLES.

> Say Puritan, can it be wrong,
> To dress plain truth in witty song?
> What honest Nature says, we should do,
> What every lady does, — or would do."

It is not known who edited this pamphlet, or who printed it, or from what sources the contents were derived, but it does contain some songs by Burns, and others probably by him, together with many traditional songs; all of the kind described by Robert Chambers. During the Nineteenth Century, many clandestine volumes appeared with the *Merry Muses* title, but not until 1843 was Burns' name connected with one.* These later volumes present a great variety of English and Scots bawdry — most of it wholly unconnected with Burns, or with the original collection. A popular issue, much "copied," bore the date 1827 (the date of it was probably 1872), and the phrase on the title page, "Not for maids, ministers, or striplings." The Burns Federation sponsored a *Merry Muses* in 1909, edited by its Secretary, Duncan McNaught ("Vindex"), with the ostensible purpose of showing that Burns was chiefly interested in providing purified versions of the national minstrelsy. Only since 1959 in Great Britain, and 1964 in the United States, have reliable texts, and detailed, plain discussions of the whole area, been available. Those who would inform themselves more fully are cordially referred to the Postscript to this section.

Some of Burns' bawdry has already been introduced into this volume where it was appropriate. A selection follows, both of

---

* A gathering published as *The Giblet Pie* in 1806 claimed that some of its songs were "taken from the Original Manuscripts of R. Burns." (Legman, *Merry Muses*, 269.)

items by Burns, and of items which he refers to or knew and liked.

1. By all tests of style and sentiments, *Wha'll Mow Me Now?* is Burns' song, although there is no direct evidence of authorship.

O, I hae tint my rosy cheek,	*lost*
Likewise my waste sae sma';	
O wae gae by the sodger lown	*woe,*
The sodger did it a'.	

Chorus

O wha'll mow me now, my jo,	*ride sweetheart*
And wha'll mow me now:	
A soldier wi' his bandileers	
Has bang'd my belly fu'.	

Now I maun thole the scornfu' sneer	*must endure*
O' mony a saucy quine;	*wench*
When, curse upon her godly face!	
Her cunt's as merry's mine.	

Our dame hauds up her wanton tail,	
As due as she gaes lie;	
An' yet misca's a young thing,	*abuses*
The trade if she but try.	

Our dame can lae her ain gudeman,	
An' mow for glutton greed;	
An' yet misca' a poor thing,	*abuse*
That's mowin' for its bread.	

Alake! sae sweet a tree as love,	
Sic bitter fruit should bear!	
Alake, that e'er a merry arse,	
Should draw a sa'tty tear.	*salty*

But deevil damn the lousy loon,	
Denies the bairn he got!	
Or lea's the merry arse he lo'ed,	
To wear a ragged coat!	

2. *The Case of Conscience,* a parody of Calvinist morality, was sent by Burns to his friend, Provost Robert Maxwell of Lochmaben, December 20, 1789.

I'll tell you a tale of a Wife,
    And she was a Whig and a Saunt;   *Hypocrite   Saint*
She liv'd a most sanctify'd life,
    But whyles she was fash'd wi her cunt. *at times   troubled*

Poor woman! she gaed to the Priest   *went*
    And till him she made her complaint;   *to*
"There's naething that troubles my breast
    Sae sair as the sins o' my cunt.

"Sin that I was herdin at hame,   *Since*
    Till now I'm three score and ayont,
I own it wi' sin and wi' shame,
    I've led a sad life wi' my cunt."

He bade her to clear up her brow,
    And no be discourag'd upon 't;
For holy gude women enow   *enough*
    Were mony times waur't wi' their cunt.   *worsted*

It's naught but Beelzebub's art,
    But that's the mair sign of a saunt,   *more*
He kens that ye're pure at the heart,
    Sae levels his darts at your cunt.

What signifies Morals and Works,
    Our works are no wordy a runt!   *worth   cabbage stalk*
It's Faith that is sound, orthodox,
    That covers the fauts o' your cunt.   *faults*

Were ye o' the Reprobate race
    Created to sin and be brunt,   *burned*
O then it would alter the case
    If ye should gae wrang wi' your cunt.

But you that is Called and Free
    Elekit and chosen a saunt,
Will't break the Eternal Decree
    Whatever ye do wi' your cunt?

And now with a sancify'd kiss
Let's kneel and renew covenant:
It's this — and it's this — and it's this —
That settles the pride o' your cunt.

Devotion blew up to a flame;
No words can do justice upon't;
The honest auld woman gaed hame
Rejoicing and clawin her cunt.

Then high to her memory charge;
And may he who takes it affront,
Still ride in Love's channel at large,
And never make port in a cunt! ! !

3. After reviewing grounds for ascribing *The Patriarch* to Burns, Professor Kinsley says, "I am inclined . . . to accept this attribution."

As honest Jacob on a night,
Wi' his beloved beauty,
Was duly laid on wedlock's bed,
And noddin' at his duty:
Tal de dal, &c.

"How lang," she says, "ye fumblin' wretch,
Will ye be fucking at it?
My eldest wean might die of age,   *child*
Before that ye could get it.

"Ye pegh, and grane, and groazle there, *puff grunt*
And make an unco splutter,
And I maun ly and thole you here, *must endure*
And fient a hair the better." *devil a*

Then he, in wrath, put up his graith, *tool*
"The deevil's in the hizzie! *wench*
I mow you as I mow the lave, *rest*
And night and day I'm bisy.

"I've bairn'd the servant gypsies baith, *got with child*
Forbye your titty, Leah; *Also sister*

Ye barren jad, ye put me mad,
   What mair can I do wi' you.

"There's ne'er a mow I've gi'en the lave,
   But ye ha'e got a dizzen;
And damned a ane ye'se get again,   *one you'll*
   Altho' your cunt should gizzen."   *wither*

Then Rachel calm, as ony lamb,
   She claps him on the waulies,   *genitals*
Quo' she, "Ne'er fash a woman's clash, *pay heed to* *chatter*
   In trowth, ye mow me braulies.   *admirably*

"My dear 'tis true, for mony a mow,
   I'm your ungratefu' debtor;
But ance again, I dinna ken,
   We'll aiblens happen better."   *perhaps*

Then honest man! wi' little wark,   *work*
   He soon forgat his ire;
The patriarch, he coost the sark,   *cast* *shirt*
   And up and till't like fire! ! !   *to it*

4. Both Professor Ferguson and Professor Kinsley accept *Nine Inch Will Please a Lady* as Burns' song.

"Come rede me, dame, come tell me, dame,   *advise*
   My dame come tell me truly,
What length o' graith, when weel ca'd hame, *gear* *driven*
   Will sair a woman duly?"   *serve*
The carlin clew her wanton tail,   *scratched*
   Her wanton tail sae ready —
"I learn'd a sang in Annandale,
   Nine inch will please a lady. —

"But for a koontrie cunt like mine,   *country*
   In sooth, we're nae sae gentle;
We'll tak tway thumb-bred to the nine, *two* *thumb-breadths*
   And that's a sonsy pintle: *comely penis*
O leeze me on my Charlie lad,   *I take delight in*
   I'll ne'er forget my Charlie!
Tway roarin' handful's and a daud   *lump*
   He nidge't it in fu' rarely. —   *thrust*

"But weary fa' the laithron doup,   *lazy rump*
  And may it ne'er be thrivin!
It's no the length that maks me loup,   *jump*
  But it's the double drivin. —
Come nidge me, Tam, come nudge me, Tam,
  Come nidge me o'er the nyvel!   *navel*
Come lowse & lug your battering ram,   *loose draw out*
  And thrash him at my gyvel!"   *gabel*

5. The parody ballad, *Grim Grizzel*, is authentic Burns, and according to Professor Kinsley, authentic Scots rustic humor.

Grim Grizzel was a mighty Dame
  Weel kend on Cluden-side:
Grim Grizzel was a mighty Dame
  O' meikle fame and pride.   *great*

When gentles met in gentle bowers
  And nobles in the ha',
Grim Grizzel was a mighty Dame,
  The loudest o' them a'.

When lawless Riot rag'd the night
  And Beauty durst na gang,   *go about*
Grim Grizzel was a mighty Dame
  Wham nae man e'er wad wrang.

Nor had Grim Grizzel skill alane
  What bower and ha' require;
But she had skill, and meikle skill,
  In barn and eke in byre.   *also cowshed*

Ae day Grim Grizzel walkèd forth,
  As she was wont to do,
Alang the banks o' Cluden fair,
  Her cattle for to view.

The cattle shit o'er hill and dale
  As cattle will incline,
And sair it grieved Grim Grizzel's heart
  Sae muckle muck tae tine.   *much lose*

And she has ca'd on John o' Clods,
  Of her herdsmen the chief,

And she has ca'd on John o' Clods,
And tell'd him a' her grief: —

"Now wae betide thee, John o' Clods!
  I gie thee meal and fee,   *give*
And yet sae meickle muck ye tine
  Might a' be gear to me!   *wealth*

"Ye claut my byre, ye sweep my byre,   *clean out*
  The like was never seen;
The very chamber I lie in
  Was never half sae clean.

"Ye ca' my kye adown the loan   *call my cattle   lane*
  And there they a' discharge:
My Tammie's hat, wig, head and a'
  Was never half sae large!

"But mind my words now, John o' Clods,
  And tent me what I say: *heed*
My kye shall shit ere they gae out,
  That shall they ilka day.   *every*

"And mind my words now, John o' Clods,
  And tent now wha ye serve;
Or back ye'se to the Colonel gang,   *you'll*
  Either to steal or starve."

Then John o' Clods he lookèd up
  And syne he lookèd down;   *then*
He lookèd east, he lookèd west,
  He lookèd roun' and roun'.

His bonnet and his rowantree club   *mountain ash*
  Frae either hand did fa';
Wi' lifted een and open mouth
  He naething said at a'.

At length he found his trembling tongue,
  Within his mouth was fauld: *enfolded*
"Ae silly word frae me, madám,
  Gin I daur be sae bauld.   *If   dare   bold*

"Your kye will at nae bidding shit,
    Let me do what I can;
Your kye will at nae bidding shit,
    Of onie earthly man.

"Tho' ye are great Lady Glaur-hole,   *mud-hole*
    For a' your power and art
Tho' ye are great Lady Glaur-hole,
    They winna let a fart."

"Now wae betide thee, John o' Clods!
    An ill death may ye die!
My kye shall at my bidding shit,
    And that ye soon shall see."

Then she's ta'en Hawkie by the tail,   *Bossy*
    And wrung wi' might and main,
Till Hawkie rowted through the woods   *bellowed*
    Wi' agonizing pain.

"Shit, shit, ye bitch," Grim Grizzel roar'd,
    Till hill and valley rang;
"And shit, ye bitch," the echoes roar'd
    Lincluden wa's amang.   *walls [of ruined Lincluden abbey]*

6. Burns wrote to his fellow-Crochallan, Robert Cleghorn, on October 25, 1793, sending him the song below: "From my late hours last night, & the dripping fogs & damn'd east-wind of this stupid day, I have left me as little soul as an oyster. — 'Sir John, you are so fretful, you cannot live long.' — 'Why, there is it! Come, sing me a Baudy-song to make me merry!!!' "

Act Sederunt of the Session —
A Scots Ballad —

In Edinburgh town they've made a law,
    In Edinburgh at the Court o' Session,
That standing pricks are fauteors a',   *offenders*
    And guilty of a high transgression. —

Chorus

Act Sederunt o' the Session,   *official act*
Decreet o' the Court o' Session,
That standing pricks are fauteors a',
And guilty of a high transgression.

And they've provided dungeons deep.
Ilk lass has ane in her possession;   *each*
Until the wretches wail and weep,
They there shall lie for their transgression. —

Chorus

Act Sederunt o' the Session,
Decreet o' the Court o' Session,
The rogues in pouring tears shall weep,
By act Sederunt o' the Session. —

7. Burns' experience with kirk session discipline obviously lay behind his burlesque called variously *Libel Summons* or *The Court
of Equity.*

In Truth and Honour's name — Amen —
Know all men by these Presents plain: —

This fourth o' June, at Mauchline given,
The year 'tween eighty five and seven,
We, Fornicators by profession,
As per extractum from each Session,   *by authentic document*
In way and manner here narrated,
Pro bono Amor congregated;
And by our brethren constituted,
A Court of Equity deputed. —
With special authoris'd direction
To take beneath our strict protection,
The stays-out-bursting, quondam maiden,
With Growing Life and anguish laden;
Who by the rascal is deny'd,
That led her thoughtless steps aside. —
He who disowns the ruin'd Fair-one,
And for her wants and woes does care none;

The wretch that can refuse subsistence
To those whom he has given existence;
He who when at a lass's by-job,   *side-line (fornication)*
Defrauds her with a frig or dry-bob;   *cheats her of orgasm*
The coof that stands on clishmaclavers   *dolt   palavering*
When women haflins offer favors: —   *halfway*
All who in any way or manner
Distain the Fornicator's honor,
We take cognisance thereanent,
The proper Judges competent. —

First, Poet Burns he takes the chair;
Allow'd by a', his title's fair;
And pass'd nem. con. without dissension,
He has a Duplicate pretension. —   [*Betty Paton & Jean Armour*]
Next Merchant Smith, our worthy Fiscal,
To cow each pertinaceous rascal;
In this, as every other state,
His merit is conspicuous great:
Richmond the third, our trusty Clerk,*
The minutes regular to mark,
And sit dispenser of the law,
In absence of the former twa;
The fourth our Messenger at Arms,
When failing all the milder terms,
Hunter, a hearty, willing brother,
Weel skill'd in dead and living leather. —   *shoeleather   pudenda*
Without Preamble less or more said,
We, body politic aforesaid,
With legal, due Whereas, and Wherefore,
We are appointed here to care for
The interests of our constituents,
And punish contraveening truants,
Keeping a proper regulation
Within the lists of Fornication. —

Whereas, our Fiscal, by petition,
Informs us there is strong suspicion,
You Coachman Dow and Clockie Brown,   *Clockmaker*
Baith residenters of this town;   *Both*

* Richmond had left Mauchline for Edinburgh before this poem was written.
His inclusion on the Court was part of the fun.

In other words, you, Jock, and, Sandy,
Hae been at wark at Houghmagandie;   *Fornication*
And now when facts are come to light,
The matter ye deny outright. —

First, You, John Brown, there's witness borne,
And affidavit made and sworn,
That ye hae bred a hurly-burly
'Bout Jeany Mitchel's tirlie-whirlie,
And blooster'd at her regulator,   *blustered*
Till a' her wheels gang clitter-clatter. —   *go*
And farther still, ye cruel Vandal,
A tale might even in hell be scandal!
That ye hae made repeated trials
Wi' drugs and draps in doctor's phials,
Mixt, as ye thought, wi' fell infusion,
Your ain begotten wean to poosion. —
And yet ye are sae scant o' grace,
Ye daur to lift your brazen face,   *dare*
And offer for to take your aith,   *oath*
Ye never lifted Jeany's claith. —   *dress*
But tho' ye should yoursel manswear,
Laird Wilson's sclates can witness bear,   · *slates*
Ae e'ening of a Mauchline fair,
That Jeany's masts they saw them bare;
For ye had furl'd up her sails,
And was at play — at heads and tails. —   *maidenhead   penis*

Next, Sandy Dow, you're here indicted
To have, as publickly you're wyted,   *charged*
Been clandestinely upward whirlin
The petticoats o' Maggy Borelan,
And giein her canister a rattle,
That months to come it winna settle. —
And yet, ye offer your protest,
Ye never herried Maggy's nest;
Tho', it's weel ken'd that at her gyvel   *gabel*
Ye hae gien mony a kytch and kyvel. —   *jerk and thump*

Then Brown and Dow, before design'd,
For clags and clauses there subjoin'd,   *incumbrances*
We, Court aforesaid, cite and summon,
That on the fifth o' July comin,

The hour o' cause, in our Court-ha',
At Whitefoord's arms, ye answer Law!*

This, mark'd before the date and place is,
Sigillum est, per,
                    Burns the Preses.

This Summons and the signet mark,
Extractum est, per,
                    Richmond, Clerk.

At Mauchline, idem date of June,
'Tween six and seven, the afternoon,
You twa, in propria personae,
Within design'd, Sandy and Johny,
This Summons legally have got,
As vide witness underwrote:
Within the house of John Dow, vintner,
Nunc facio hoc
                    Gullelmus Hunter.

There follow certain traditional bawdy songs in which Burns
rejoiced.

8. *Andrew an' his Cuttie Gun* Burns called "the work of a
Master."

Blythe, blythe, blythe was she,	
Blythe was she but and ben;	*out and in*
An' weel she lo'ed it in her nieve,	*fist*
But better when it slippit in.	
When a' the lave gaed to their bed,	*rest went*
And I sat up to clean the shoon,	
O wha think ye cam jumpin' ben,	
But Andrew an' his cuttie gun?	*little*
Or e'er I wist he laid me back,	
And up my gamon to my chin;	*petticoat*

* At this point in several MSS, there are 59 lines of adjuration from the court
to the culprits, omitted by Burns in revision.

And ne'er a word to me he spak,
  But liltit out his cuttie gun.

The bawsent bitch she left the whalps,   *with white stripe on face*
  And hunted round us at the fun,
As Andrew fodgel'd wi his arse,   *fidgeted*
  And fir'd at me the cuttie gun.

O some delights in cuttie stoup,   *little tankards*
  And some delights in cuttie-mun,   *old song*
But my delight's an areselins coup,   *tumble*
  Wi' Andrew an' his cuttie gun.

Blythe, blythe, blythe was she,
Blythe was she but and ben;
An' weel she lo'ed it in her nieve,
But better when it slippit in.

9. Burns called *The Grey Goose and the Gled,* "a droll Scots song, more famous for its humor than delicacy."

As I look'd o'er yon castle wa',
  I spied a grey goose an' a gled;   *hawk*
They had a feight between them twa,   *fight*
  An' o' as their twa hurdies gaed.   *buttocks went*

Wi' a hey ding it in, an' a how ding it in,
  An' a hey ding it in, it's lang today.
Fal lary tele, tale, lary tale,
  Fal lary tal, lal lary tay.

She heav'd up, and he strack down,
  Between them twa they made a mow;
That ilka fart that the carlin gae,   *every woman gave*
  It's four o' them wad fill'd a bowe.   *six bushels*
    With a hey, &c.

Temper your tail, the carlin cried,
  Temper your tail by Venus' law;
Gird hame your gear, gudeman, she cried,   *Push tool*
  Wha the deil can hinder the wind to blaw?   *blow*
    With a hey, &c.

For were ye on my saddle set,
   An' were ye weel girt in my gear,   *equipment*
Gin the wind o' my arse blew ye out o' my cunt,
   Ye'll never be reckon'd a man o' wier.   *valor*
     With a hey, &c.

He plac'd his Jacob whare she did piss,
   And his bollocks whare the wind did blaw,
An' he grippet her fast by the gushet o' her arse,   *crack*
   And he gave her cunt the common law.
     With a hey, &c.

10. *As I Cam o'er the Cairney Mount,* "an excellent but somewhat licentious song," appeared with asterisks, and purified, in the *Museum* (#577 in Professor Kinsley's edition of Burns). Herewith an older version.

As I cam o'er the Cairney mount,
   And down amang the blooming heather,
The Highland laddie drew his durk
   And sheath'd it in my wanton leather.

   O my bonnie, bonnie Highland lad,
     My handsome, charming Highland laddie;
   When I am sick and like to die,
     He'll row me in his Highland plaidie.   *roll*

With me he play'd his warlike pranks,
   And on me boldly did adventure,
He did attack me on both flanks,
   And push'd me fiercely in the centre.

A furious battle then began,
   Wi' equal courage and desire,
Altho' he struck me three to one,
   I stood my ground and receiv'd his fire.

But our ammunition being spent,
   And we quite out o' breath an' sweating,
We did agree with ae consent,
   To fight it out at the next meeting.

11. Versions of *John Anderson, My Jo* go back at least until 1630. Burns seems to have adapted his famous song from the set below which was printed in the *Merry Muses.*

John Anderson, my jo, John,   *sweetheart*
 I wonder what ye mean,
To lie sae lang i' the mornin'
 And sit sae late at e'en?
Ye'll bleer a' your een, John,   *eyes*
 And why do ye so?
Come sooner to your bed at e'en,
 John Anderson, my jo.

John Anderson, my jo, John,
 When first that ye began,
Ye had as good a tail-tree
 As ony ither man;
But now its waxen wan, John,
 And wrinkles to and fro;
I've twa gae-ups for ae gae-down,
 John Anderson, my jo.

I'm backit like a salmon,
 I'm breastit like a swan;
My wame it is a down-cod,   *belly down pillow*
 My middle ye may span:
Frae my tap-knot to my tae, John,
 I'm like the new-fa'n snow;
And it's a' for your convenience,
 John Anderson, my jo.

O it is a fine thing
 To keep out o'er the dyke;   *wall*
But its a meikle finer thing,
 To see your hurdies fyke;   *buttocks fidget*
To see your hurdies fyke, John,
 And hit the rising blow;
It's then I like your chanter-pipe, *fingering stem of bagpipe*
 John Anderson, my jo.

When you come on before, John,
 See that ye do your best;

When ye begin to haud me,
　　See that ye grip me fast;
See that ye grip me fast, John,
　　Until that I cry "Oh!"
Your back shall crack or I do that,
　　John Anderson, my jo.

John Anderson, my jo, John,
　　Ye're welcome when ye please;
It's either in the warm bed
　　Or else aboon the claes: *above   clothes*
Or ye shall hae the horns, John,
　　Upon your head to grow;
An' that's the cuckold's mallison   *curse*
　　John Anderson, my jo.

With the matter now plainly before them, readers may well ponder why *The Merry Muses* remained clandestine for so long, and, indeed, whether Burns' taste for bawdry merits the celebrity which suppression has given it.

VII

LAST YEARS

Alas! Alas! a devilish change indeed.

BURNS TO JOHN RANKINE

During Burns' last four years, his political and social opinions offended many, his sarcasms continued to wound people, and his reputation for irreligion endured. His temperament grew more explosive as his health worsened, and as he grew less hopeful of recognition, reward, and security. He continued to enjoy bawdry and convivial parties, and to relish low caste company when it was amusing, and he was held to have loose ways with women. Burns in Dumfries was simply Rab Mossgiel grown older and more experienced in the world.

He did his work as before, he loved his family and supported it in modest comfort,* he was ready with assistance to the less fortunate, and he lived within his income. But John Syme said,

---

* In December, 1793, he writes Mrs. Dunlop of his daughter Elizabeth by Jean, "these four months a sweet little girl, my youngest child, has been so ill, that every day, a week or less threatened to terminate her existence." Then he continues, "There had much need be many pleasures annexed to the states of husband & father, for God knows, they have many peculiar cares. — I cannot describe to you, the anxious, sleepless hours these ties frequently give me. I see a train of helpless little folks: me, & my exertions, all their stay; & on what a brittle thread does the life of man hang! If I am nipt off at the command of Fate; even in all the vigour of manhood as I am, such things happen every day — gracious God! what would become of my little flock! — 'Tis here that I envy your people of fortune. A Father on his deathbed, taking an everlasting leave of his children, is indeed woe enough; but the man of competent fortune leaves his sons and daughters independency & friends; while I — but my God, I shall run distracted if I think any longer on the subject!" (F II, #605, 223.)

"Robin's heart and temper are not cold and frugal." He did not hain up [save] the bawbees [ha'pence]. There was obviously little spare cash.

Burns enjoyed respect and status in Dumfries. Both his correspondence and other evidence show him on good terms with many solid and prominent people. He remained creative, and a fascinating companion, until the end. The only noteworthy change in him during this period was that his illness grew more severe and his depression plagued him more frequently.

Despite increasing illness and distress, Burns retained his pungency and zest until his health finally broke completely. The February after he moved to Dumfries (1792), he sent Mrs. Dunlop a jar of brandy, with a letter in which he remarked that he knew better how to find smugglers than she did. By late summer of that year, he is busy "correcting the Press-work of two Publications," presumably a volume of the *Museum,* and the 1793 edition of his poems. The latter burden he soon turned over to Alexander Fraser Tytler,* but Professor Ross Roy has discovered that Burns himself superintended the edition which Creech brought out in 1794.

On September 10, 1792, he wrote an extensive letter to Alexander Cunningham, containing the following reflections on religion and marriage:

But of all Nonsense, Religious Nonsense is the most nonsensical; so enough, & more than enough of it. — Only, by the bye, will you, or can you tell me, my dear Cunningham, why a religioso turn of mind has always a tendency to narrow & illiberalize the heart? They are orderly; they may be just; nay, I have known them merciful: but still your children of Sanctity move among their fellow-creatures with a nostril snuffing putrescence, & a foot spurning filth, in short, with that conceited dignity which your titled Douglases, Hamiltons,

---

* Burns had supplied Creech with added material for this volume, including *Tam o' Shanter,* asking in return only some copies to give his friends. Even to get these, he had to dun Creech. (F II, #538, 151.)

Gordons, or any other of your Scots lordlings of seven centuries standing, display when they accidentally mix among the many-aproned Sons of Mechanical Life. . . .

Apropos, how do you like, I mean *really* like, the Married Life? — Ah, my Friend! Matrimony is quite a different thing from what your love-sick youths & sighing girls take it to be! — But Marriage, we are told, is appointed by G — & I shall never quarrel with any of HIS Institutions. — I am a husband of older standing than you, & I shall give you *my* ideas of the Conjugal State — (En passant, you know I am no Latin, is not "Conjugal" derived from "Jugum" a yoke?). — Well then, the scale of Good-wifeship I divide into ten parts — Good-Nature, four; Good-Sense two; Wit, one; Personal Charms, viz. a sweet face, eloquent eyes, fine limbs, graceful carriage (I would add a fine waist too, but that is so soon spoiled you know), all these one: as for the other qualities belonging to, or attending on, a Wife, such as fortune, connections, education, (I mean, education extraordinary), family-blood, &c. divide the two remaining degrees among them as you please; only, remember that all these minor properties must be expressed by *fractions;* for there is not any one of them in the aforesaid scale entitled to the dignity of an Integer.

A letter (dated January, 1793, by Professor Ferguson) to Provost David Staig of Dumfries, made detailed suggestions for improving the Burgh's revenue from ale. Shortly thereafter Burns requested a Burgess's privilege of free schooling for his children in the Dumfries academy. After pointing out that a good deal of ale comes into Dumfries untaxed, Burns continues, "I know that our Collector has a percentage on the Collection; but as it is no great object to him he gives himself no concern about what is *brought in* to the town. — The Supervisor would suit you better. — He is an abler & a keener man; &, what is all-important in the business, such is his official influence over, & power among, his Offrs that were he to signify that such was his wish, not a 'pennie' would be left uncollected. — It is by no means the case with the Collector. — The Offrs are not so immediately among his hands, & they would not pay the same attention to his mandates."

Not only would the reforms he suggests benefit the Burgh

revenue, they would also protect respectable Dumfries brewers from unfair competition. The reforms, Burns estimates, would increase revenue from this source by one third. Burns concludes, "These crude hints, Sir, are entirely for your private use. — I have by no means any wish to take a sixpence from Mr Mitchel's income: nor do I wish to serve Mr Findlater: I wish to shew any attempt I can, to do anything that might declare with what sincerity I have the honor to be,

Sir, your obliged humble servt

ROBT BURNS"

Sometime, apparently, before his break with Mrs. Riddell, she and Burns had found amusement in creating "armorial bearings" for him.* He first speaks of this project in a letter of March 3, 1794, to Cunningham. Burns was particularly concerned that the "pipe" in his design should be the true "stock & horn" of a Scottish shepherd.

There is one commission that I must trouble you with. — I lately lost a valuable Seal, a present from a departed friend, which vexes me much. — I have gotten one of your Highland pebbles,† which I fancy would make a very decent one; & I want to cut my armorial bearings on it: will you be so obliging as enquire what will be the expence of such a business? — I do not know that my name is matriculated, as the Heralds call it, at all; but I have invented one for myself; so, you know, I will be chief of the Name; & by courtesy of Scotland, will likewise be entitled to Supporters. — These, however, I do not intend having on my Seal. — I am a bit of a Herald; & shall give you, Secundum artem, my Arms. — On a field, azure, a holly-bush, seeded, proper, in base; a Shepherd's pipe & crook, Saltier-wise, also proper, in chief. — On a wreath of the colors, a woodlark perching on a sprig of bay-tree, proper, for Crest. — Two Mottoes: Round the top of the

* While in Edinburgh Burns had visited the Herald's Office to see if the name "Burns" was included in "that granary of Honors." It was not. (F I, #125, 105.)

† From Mrs. Riddell, though he does not mention it, the quarrel being at its height.

Crest — "Wood-notes wild" — At the bottom of the Shield, in the usual place —

"Better a wee bush than nae bield." —   shelter

By the Shepherd's pipe & crook, I do not mean the nonsense of Painters of Arcadia, but a Stock-&-horn, & a Club; such as you see at the head of Allan Ramsay, in [David] Allan's quarto Edition of the Gentle Shepherd. — By the bye, do you know Allan? — He must be a man of very great genius. — Why is he not more known? Has he no Patrons; or do "Poverty's cold wind & crushing rain beat keen & heavy" on him? — I once, & but once, got a glance of that noble editn of the noblest Pastoral in the world, & dear as it was; I mean, dear as to my pocket, I would have bought it; but I was told that it was printed & engraved for Subscribers only. — He is the *only* Artist who has hit *genuine* Pastoral costume. — What my dear Cunningham, is there in riches, that they narrow & encallous the heart so? — I think, that were I as rich as the sun, I would be as generous as day; but as I have no reason to imagine my soul a nobler one than every other man's, I must conclude that wealth imparts a bird-lime quality to the Possessor, at which the man, in native poverty, would have revolted.

By May, he is writing to Thomson in delight about illustrations for *The Cotter's Saturday Night* which David Allan is doing, and he also comments on the seal. Of the illustrations he says, "I would humbly propose that in No 1st instead of the Younker knitting stockings, I would, in preference to your 'Trump', to put a stock & horn among his hands, as if he were screwing & adjusting it." At the end of his letter, commenting on the seal, he says, "My 'seal' is all well, except that my 'Holly' must be a *bush*, not a *tree*, as in the present shield. — I also enclose it, & will send the pebble by the first opportunity."

In November he writes to Thomson again with concern that Allan get the "stock & horn" right, giving explicit details.

Tell my friend, Allen (for I am sure that we only want the trifling circumstance of being known to one another, to be the best friends on earth) that I much suspect he has, in his plates, mistaken the figure of the stock & horn. — I have, *at last,* gotten one; but it is a very rude instrument. — It is composed of three parts; the stock, which is the hinder thigh-bone of a sheep, such as you see in a mutton-ham: the horn, which is a common Highland cow's horn, cut off at the smaller end, untill the aperture be large enough to admit the "stock" to be pushed up through the horn, untill it be held by the thicker or hip-end of the thigh-bone; & lastly, an oaten reed exactly cut & notched like that which you see every shepherd-boy have when the corn-stems are green & full-grown. — The reed is not made fast in the bone, but is held by the lips, & plays loose in the smaller end of the "stock;" while the "stock," & the horn hanging on its larger end, is held by the hands in playing. — The "stock" has six, or seven, ventiges on the upper side, & one back-ventige, like the common flute. — This of mine was made by a man from the braes of Athole, & is exactly what the shepherds wont to use in that country. — However, either it is not quite properly bored in the holes, or else we have not the art of blowing it rightly; for we can make little of it. — If Mr Allen chuses, I will send him a sight of mine; as I look on myself to be a kind of brother-brush with him. — "Pride in Poets is nae sin," & I will say it, that I look on Mr Allen & Mr Burns to be the only genuine & real Painters of Scottish Costume in the world. —

Farewell!

R. BURNS

Something of Burns' position in Dumfries is suggested by the recognition he was granted. On November 30, 1792, he was elected senior warden of the Dumfries Lodge of Masons. On March 5, 1793, the committee in charge of the public library in Dumfries, "by a great majority resolved to offer to Mr Robert Burns a share in the library, free of any admission-money and the quarterly contributions to this date, out of respect and esteem for his abilities as a literary man; and they directed the secretary to make this known to Mr Burns as soon as possible, that the application which they understood he was about to make in the ordinary way might be anticipated." A few months later, Burns was, by vote, appointed a member of the committee.

In March of 1793, Burns reminded "the Lord Provost, Bailies, & Town Council of Dumfries" that they had made him an Honorary Burgess in 1787, and requested that they grant him the Burgess's privilege of free schooling in the town academy. The request was granted. In January, 1795, he was one of the organizers of the Royal Dumfries Volunteers, and for some months he served as a member of the directing committee. The Corps included many of Dumfries' most respected people, and membership was a social distinction.

A fellow Volunteer was James Gray, Latin Master and Rector at the Dumfries Academy 1794–1801, and then Latin Master at the Edinburgh High School 1801–1822. His second wife was Clarinda's friend and Burns' correspondent, Mary Peacock. In 1822, accompanied by his wife, Gray went to India as chaplain for the East India Company. He and Burns were friends in Dumfries, and in 1814 Gray wrote a defense of Burns for Alexander Peterkin, which he recast for Gilbert Burns in 1820. These statements have a good deal of special pleading in them, and the passages below are the more convincing, therefore, in their admissions.

In his letter to Peterkin, Gray writes of Burns,

It is not, however, denied that he sometimes mingled with society unworthy of him. He was of a social and convivial nature. He was courted by all classes of men for the fascinating powers of his conversation, but over his social scene uncontrolled passion never presided. Over the social bowl, his wit flashed for hours together, penetrating whatever it struck, like the fire from heaven; but even in the hour of thoughtless gaiety and merriment, I never knew it tainted by indecency. It was playful or caustic by turns, following an allusion through all its windings; astonishing by its rapidity, or amusing by its wild originality, and grotesque yet natural combinations, but never, within my observation, disgusting by its grossness.

Gray's redaction for Gilbert is more detailed.

It was my good fortune to be introduced to [Burns] soon after I went to Dumfries. This was early in 1794, and I saw him often and intimately during the remainder of his life. I sometimes met him in the scene of conviviality, and there, if any where, I must have received conviction of that intellectual and moral degredation of which we have heard so much; but no such impression was made on my mind. He seemed to me to frequent convivial parties from the same feelings with which he wrote poetry, because nature had eminently qualified him to shine there, and he never on any occasion indulged in solitary drinking. He was always the living spirit of the company, and by the communications of his genius, seemed to animate every one present with a portion of his own fire. He indulged in the sally of wit or humour, of striking originality, and sometimes of bitter sarcasm, but always free from the least taint of grossness. I was, from the commencement of my acquaintance with him, struck with his aversion to all kinds of indelicacy, and have seen him dazzle and delight a party for hours together by the brilliancy and rapidity of his flashes, without even an allusion that could give offense to vestal purity. I never saw him intoxicated; and, indeed, I am convinced, that though his company was courted by men of all ranks, and he was much in society of a convivial nature, that he was very seldom in a state of inebriation.

I often met him at breakfast parties, which were then customary in Dumfries, and sometimes enjoyed a morning walk with him; and on these occasions, if he had been suffering from midnight excesses, it must have been apparent. On the contrary, his whole air was that of one who had enjoyed refreshing slumbers, and who arose happy in himself, and to diffuse happiness on all around him; his complexion was fresh and clear, his eye brilliant, his whole frame vigorous and elastic, and his imagination ever on the wing. His morning conversations were marked by an impassioned eloquence, that seemed to flow from immediate inspiration, and shed an atmosphere of light and beauty around every thing it touched, alternately melting and elevating the soul of all who heard him. He had read much, and possessed a most powerful memory, which never exhibited any symptoms of that decay, which must have been the consequence of habitual intoxication; so far from it, he gleaned all that was valuable from every book he perused, which he could either quote in the words of the original, or make the ideas his own, and embody them in a more beautiful form.

Charles Kirkpatrick Sharpe (1780?–1851) was the third son of Burns' correspondent Charles Sharpe of Hoddam, in Annandale, east of Dumfries. During his boyhood, C. K. Sharpe became familiar with Burns' appearance, and he knew those who knew Burns well. Later, as "The Scottish Walpole," he met almost everyone of importance in Scotland. The following memorandum of his, dated January 8, 1808, appears on the back of a receipt from his father's agents, Walker and Gordon.

I do not choose to remember — or rather to record — Burns's frailties, however such things might amuse the public — he was exactly like other people as to his faults — these, however, bore no proportion to his genius.

He was very unlucky in his position — tho those called his superiors pretended at first to relish his compositions and conversation, they were not fitted, for the greater part, to do so — he must quickly have discovered this — hence his rudeness in conversation, which was much complained of.

Mr Riddell was a man of very limited understanding — Mr Mac-Murdo, and perhaps one gentleman more, were the only people in Dumfriesshire who really could understand his merit.

Some of his gentle friends were foolish, crack brained Whigs, democrats who, I have no doubt, egged him on, nay inspired, his extravagant notions, which did him so much harm — this was suggested to me by a person, who though he entertained very different political notions from Burns, loved, admired, and befriended him to the last.

Archibald Lawrie (1768–1837), son of the Rev. George Lawrie of Loudon, at whose home Burns had been a welcome guest, saw something of Burns in Edinburgh. In 1794, Archibald married Anne M'Kittrick Adair, sister of Burns' friend and fellow-traveller, Dr. Adair, who married Charlotte Hamilton. He met Miss Adair at Dunlop House, and Mrs. Dunlop actively promoted the match. Archibald was appointed assistant to his father at Loudon, became an officer, not a chaplain, of a militia regiment, and won a reputation as a sporting parson. In 1793, while on his way a-courting — unsuccessfully — in England, Lawrie passed through Dumfries, and sought out his old friend Burns. He recorded their meeting in his journal:

Before supper I sent for Mr Burns the poet, who came soon after I sent for him, but could not sup with me. He came into the room where I was supping with a number of strangers, and there he sat from 11 at night till 3 next morning. I left them about 12, and had a most confounded and extravagant Bill to pay next morning, which I grudged exceedingly, as I had very little of Burns's company; he was half drunk when he came, and completely drunk before he went away in the morning. . . . Thursday, 20th. After breakfast called on Mr B., found him at home, took a plateful of broth with him, and afterwards he took a walk with me thro the town of Dumfries, and along the banks of the Nith, which was extremely pleasant. After having walked some time with Mr B., I returned again with him to his house, where I stayed and dined and spent the day; after dinner we had some charming music from a Mr Fraser, master of a band of soldiers raised by and belonging to Lord Breadalbane; having drunk tea, we went to a wood upon the banks of the river Nith, where Mr Fraser took out his [haut boy] and played a few tunes most delightfully, which had a very pleasing effect in the wood. We then left this rural retirement, walked back to the town where I parted with Mr B., and continued my walk with a Mr Lewis [Lewars], a friend of Burns, who dined in company with me. The night coming on, I went with Mr Lewis and supped with him on cold mutton and eggs, at 12 o'clock left his house; went to the Inn, King's Arms, and ordered the chambermaid to show me to bed; having rested my mare one day more, which she had not the slightest occasion for, but the temptation of Burns company I could not withstand.

When Burns' acquaintance, Josiah Walker, wrote a biographical preface to Morison's *Burns* in 1811, he included an account of a visit to Burns in Dumfries.

Dr Currie is under a mistake when he says that Burns was confined in the house from October 1795 to the January following; for, in the month of November, I passed two days with him, when I observed no unfavorable change in his looks, his spirits, or his appetite.

Circumstances having, at that time, led me to Scotland, after an absence of eight years, during which my intercourse with Burns had been almost suspended, I felt myself strongly prompted to visit him. For this purpose, I went to Dumfries, and called upon him early in the forenoon. I found him in a small house of one story. He was sitting on a window-seat reading, with the doors open, and the family arrangements going on in his presence, and altogether without that appearance of snugness and seclusion which a student requires. After conversing with him for some time, he proposed a walk, and promised to conduct me through some of his favourite haunts. We accordingly quitted the town, and wandered a considerable way up the beautiful banks of the Nith. Here he gave me an account of his latest productions, and repeated some satirical ballads which he had composed, to favour one of the candidates at the last borough election. These I thought inferior to his other pieces, though they had some lines in which vigour compensated for coarseness. He repeated also his fragment of an *Ode to Liberty*, with marked and peculiar energy, and shewed a disposition which, however, was easily repressed, to throw out political remarks, of the same nature with those for which he had been reprehended. On finishing our walk, he passed some time with me at the inn, and I left him early in the evening to make another visit at some distance from Dumfries.

On the second morning after, I returned with a friend, who was acquainted with the poet, and we found him ready to pass a part of the day with us at the inn. On this occasion I did not think him quite so interesting as he had appeared at his outset. His conversation was too elaborate; and his expression weakened by a frequent endeavour to give it artificial strength. He had been accustomed to speak for applause, in the circles which he frequented, and seemed to think it necessary, in making the most common remark, to depart a little from the ordinary simplicity of language, and to couch it in something of epigrammatic point. In his praise and censure he was so decisive, as to render a dissent from his judgment, difficult to be reconciled with the laws of good breeding. His wit was not more licentious than is unhappily too venial in higher circles, though I thought him rather unnecessarily free in the avowal of his excesses. Such were the clouds by which the pleasures of the evening were partially shaded, but frequent corruscations of genius were visible between them. When it began to grow late, he shewed no disposition to retire, but called for fresh supplies of liquor, with a freedom which might be excusable, as we were in an inn, and no condition had been distinctly made, though it might easily have been inferred, had the inference been welcome, that he was to consider himself as our guest; nor was it till he saw us worn out, that he departed, about three in the morning, with a reluctance which probably proceeded less from being deprived of our company, than from being confined to his own. Upon the whole, I found this last interview not quite so gratifying as I had expected; although I discovered in his conduct no errors which I had not seen in men who stand high in the favour of society, or sufficient to account for the mysterious insinuations which I heard against his character. He, on this occasion, drank freely without being intoxicated, a circumstance from which I concluded, not only that his constitution was still unbroken, but that he was not addicted to solitary cordials; for if he had tasted liquor in the morning, he must have easily yielded to the excess of the evening.

Burns had a warm friend in young David McCulloch of Ardwell, near Gatehouse, and when he was ready to set out on a trip to that country in the summer of 1794, he wrote McCulloch on June 21: *

My dear Sir,

My long projected journey through your country is at last fixed; & on Wednesday next, if you have nothing of more importance than take a saunter down to Gatehouse, about two or three o'clock, I shall be happy to take a draught of Mckune's best with you. — Collector Syme will be at Glens about that time, & will meet us about dish-of-tea-hour. — Syme goes also to Kiroughtree; & let me remind you of your kind promise to accompany me there. — I will need all the friends I can muster, for I am indeed ill at ease whenever I approach your Honorables & Right Honorables. —

Yours sincerely
Robt Burns

At an undetermined date, but probably on the king's birthday, May 24, 1794, McCulloch encountered Burns in Dumfries; he

* McCulloch had been admitted a member of the Dumfries St. Andrews Lodge of Masons the previous May 6. (Ch-W IV, 121.)

later reported the meeting to John Lockhart when Lockhart was writing his *Life of Burns.** According to Lockhart,

> McCulloch was seldom more grieved, than when, riding into Dumfries one fine summer's evening to attend a country ball, he saw Burns walking alone, on the shady side of the principal street of the town, while the opposite part was gay with successive groups of gentlemen and ladies, all drawn together for the festivities of the night, not one of whom appeared willing to recognize him. The horseman dismounted and joined Burns, who, on his proposing to him to cross the street, said: "Nay, nay, my young friend — that's all over now;" and quoted after a pause some verses of Lady Grizel Baillie's pathetic ballad:

<table>
<tr><td>His bonnet stood ance fu' fair on his brow,</td><td></td><td></td></tr>
<tr><td>His auld ane look'd better than mony ane's new;</td><td></td><td></td></tr>
<tr><td>But now he lets't wear ony gate it will hing,</td><td>any way</td><td>hang</td></tr>
<tr><td>And casts himsel' dowie upon the corn-bing.</td><td>sad</td><td>-heap</td></tr>
</table>

<table>
<tr><td>Oh, were we young, as we ance hae been,</td><td></td></tr>
<tr><td>We sud hae been galloping down on yon green,</td><td>should</td></tr>
<tr><td>And linking it ower the lily-white lea, —</td><td>tripping</td></tr>
<tr><td>And werena my heart light, I wad die.</td><td></td></tr>
</table>

It was little in Burns's character to let his feelings on certain subjects escape in this fashion. He, immediately after citing these verses, assumed the sprightliness of his most pleasing manner; and taking his young friend home with him, entertained him very agreably until the hour of the ball arrived, with a bowl of his usual potation, and bonie Jean's singing some verses which he had recently composed.

In the spring of 1796, when Burns' illness was much advanced, Grace Aiken, a daughter of Burns' early friend, Robert Aiken, of Ayr, had occasion to pass through Dumfries, on her way to pay a visit in Liverpool.

Walking along the street towards the residence of her friend, Mrs Copland, she passed a tall, slovenly-looking man, of sickly aspect, who

---

* McCulloch's sister Elizabeth was the wife of Sir Walter Scott's brother Thomas. Lockhart was, of course, married to Sir Walter Scott's daughter Sophia. (Lockhart, Scott Douglas edition, 103.)

presently uttered an exclamation which made her turn round. It was Burns, but so changed from his former self that she could hardly have recognized him, except by his voice. When she asked him playfully if he had been going to pass her by without notice, he spoke as if he felt that it was proper for him, nowadays, to let his old friends be the first to hold forth the hand of friendship. At her pressing request he accompanied her to Mrs Copland's house; he even consented, after much entreaty, to go home and dress, so that he might return at four to dinner. He spent the evening cheerfully, and retired about midnight. The circumstance is worthy of notice, because neither Mrs Copland nor any of her friends — all members of the best society in Dumfries — had any objection to entertaining or meeting Burns. The hostess had not seen him for a considerable time, but from no cause affecting his reputation.

Burns' Dumfries neighbor Jesse Lewars, sister of his fellow-Exciseman John Lewars, helped nurse the poet during his final illness. She has left some pleasant reminiscences of Burns' and Jean's household.

As far as Burns was left to be guided by his own inclinations, his personal domestic habits were generally simple and temperate. As he was often detained by company from the dinner provided for him by his wife, she sometimes, if she thought he was likely to be absent, would not prepare that meal for him. When he chanced to come home and find no dinner ready, he was never in the least irritated, but would address himself with the greatest cheerfulness to any makeshift set before him. They generally had abundance of good Dunlop cheese, sent to them by their Ayrshire friends. The poet would sit down to bread and cheese, with his book by his side, and seem to the casual visitor as happy as a courtier at the feast of kings. He was always anxious that his wife should be well and neatly dressed, and did his utmost to counteract any tendency to carelessness — which she sometimes excused by alleging the duties of a nurse and mother — not only by gentle remonstrance, but by buying for her the best clothes he could afford. He rarely omitted to get for her any little novelty in female dress. She was, for instance, one of the first persons in Dumfries to wear a dress of gingham — a stuff which was at its first introduction rather costly, and used almost exclusively by the well-to-do.

John Syme (1755–1831), Distributor of Stamps in Dumfries, has been mentioned often in this book. In 1826, Dr. Robert Chambers found Syme to be "essentially a Scottish gentleman of 'the old school' — a well-bred *bon-vivant*," and he reports Syme's delight that when a host hesitated to draw the cork from another bottle, "Burns transfixed him by a comparison of his present position with that of Abraham lingering over the filial sacrifice." Syme's obituary in the *Dumfries Weekly Journal* spoke of him as "this talented, vivacious, peculiar, and most remarkable gentleman, whose memory deserves more than a passing notice," and went on to report that he "applied diligently to business, acted as factor for various gentlemen, and dispensed the rights of hospitality on a scale, certainly within his means, but still beyond the health and strength of almost any other human being. No man in the South of Scotland had half so extensive a circle of friends, and no man, it may be added, ever gave so many social parties. Mr. Syme hated to dine alone; and to him social converse, over a modicum of port, books, and a rubber, were the *summum bonum* of human happiness."

After Burns' death, Syme and Gilbert Burns went to Liverpool to stay with Dr. James Currie, in order to help him with the biography he was to write. "In those days there were no steam boats, and while returning to the Nith in an ordinary packet, a very terrible storm arose which appears to have alarmed even the boldest mariners. The excellent Gilbert, sick and frightened, hid himself below and spent his hours in prayer; but Mr. Syme, who was made of sterner stuff, who possessed nerves of iron and sinews of steel, remained on deck and assisted the crew as far as he could, until the vessel rounded St. Bees Head, and found temporary shelter in Whitehaven or Maryport."

In 1797, Maria Riddell wrote to James Currie, Syme's friend and employer (as factor on his estate), "I know Syme to be a careless & a very unsuspicious character. . . . He has a good head, united to an excellent heart, but I know that in matters of business he wants method; he is always in a labyrinth of papers and accounts, and, somewhat like the cuttlefish, he obscures himself altogether in a mist of his own creating." Syme himself provides a footnote to this comment. In a letter to Alexander Cunningham, he reports with shamefaced amusement that at the end of a long journey to go hunting, he discovered that he had not brought his dogs.

It will be remembered that Robert Chambers described Syme as a *bon-vivant*. In 1804, Mrs. Riddell wrote to Dr. Currie of Syme's marriage, "I think Syme did right, and has mended His *peccada* in the best possible way. I fancy the Lady never had beauty to allure, but merely, as Falstaff said, 'Rebellion came in his way, and he found it.' "

Syme's record of his intimacy with Burns has a candor rare in the documents available to Burns' biographers. Most of it survives in letters to his and Burns' friend Alexander Cunningham, in Edinburgh, but a valuable addition consists of comments on passages from early critics and biographers of Burns which Syme supplied to Alexander Peterkin when Peterkin was preparing his counterblast to them in 1815. Syme's account of a tour with Burns through Galloway in 1793* is particularly revealing.

From my Cabin at Troqueer near Dumfries
3d August 1793 — evening —

DEAR CUNNINGHAM

I had the distinguished favor and high gratification of receiving a large packet of choice pamphlets with your very acceptable letter of 24th July — They reached me on the 26th the evening before I set out with Burns on a tour thro the wilds and cultivated plains of Galloway some account of which tour I am so disposed to give you, and perhaps you are so disposed to receive that I trust you will graciously undertake to read to the end of this (to be) very long extended epistle —

I got Burns a grey Highland shelty to ride on — we dined the first

---

* As we have seen from Burns' letter to David McCulloch, he and Syme also toured southwestern Scotland again in 1794.

day of our Tour at Glendonwynnes of Parton — a beautiful situation on the banks of the Dee — in the evening we walked up a *bonny know* and had as grand a view of alpine scenery as can well be found — a delightful soft evening gave it all its great graces. Immediately opposite & within a mile of us we saw *Airds* a charming romantic place where dwelt Low the author of Mary weep no more for me — This was classical ground for Burns — He viewed the "highest hill which rises o'er the source of Dee" — He would have staid till "the passing spirit" had appeared had we not resolved to reach Kenmure that night — We arrived as Mr. & Mrs. Gordon were sitting down to Supper — *

Here is a genuine Baron's seat — the Castle, an old building stands on a large natural moat — In front the river Ken winds for miles thro the most fertile and beautiful Holm until it expands into a Loch 12 miles long, the banks of which on the South present a fine and soft landskape of green knolls, natural wood, and here and there a gray rock — In short I cannot conceive a scene more terribly romantic than the Castle of Kenmore, Burns thinks so much of it that he has long meditated on putting his thoughts in poetry descriptive of it — Indeed I take it he has begun the work — I should be very curious to see how his mind views it — We spent 3 days with Mr. Gordon whose polished hospitality is of an original and endearing kind. It is not only ask and it shall be given, seek & ye shall find but here is what you may wish to have, take it as you incline — Mrs. Gordon's lap dog Echo was dead — she would have an Epitaph — Several had been made — Burns was asked for one — He did not like the subject but to please the Lady he made the following —

> In wood & wild ye warbling throng
> Your heavy loss deplore
> Now half extinct your powers of Song
> Sweet Echo is no more
>
> Ye jarring screeching things around
> Scream your discordant joys,
> Now half your din of tuneless sound
> With Echo silent lies —

* During his late teens, while serving as an ensign in the 72nd regiment, Syme had formed a friendship which lasted until his death with a fellow officer, John Gordon, later Viscount Kenmure.

I don't give you this as a great thing — He does not like it — But I may give you one or two better things before I am done writing —

We left Kenmore and went to Gatehouse — I took him the moor road where savage & desolate regions extended wide around — The sky turned sympathetic with the wretchedness of the soil and treated the poor travellers to the full with a flood of misery — For 3 hours did the wild Elements "rumble their bellyful upon our defenseless heads — O, ho, twas foul" — we were utterly wet and we got vengeance at Gatehouse by getting utterly drunk — there is not such a scene of delightful beauty in Scotland as Gatehouse — As it is a stage on the road to Ireland I will not describe it — Tis well known to travellers and you likely have, or will see it —

From Gatehouse we went to Kirkcudb[righ]t thro a fine country but before I bring you there I must tell you Burns had got a pair of *jimmy* boots, which the wetness had rendered it an impossible task to get on — the brawny poet tried force & tore them in shreds — a whiffling vexation like this is more trying to the temper than a serious calamity — we were going to the *Isle* — Lord Selkirks and the forlorn Burns was quite discomfited — a sick stomach, headache &c lent their forces & the man of verse was quite *accablé*. Mercy on me how he did fume & rage — nothing would restore him in temper — I tried all I could think of, at length I got a lucky hit — across the bay of Wigton I showed him Ld. Galloway's house — he expectorated his spleen against the aristocratic elf, and regained a most agreeable temper — I have about half a dozen of capital extempores which I dare not write — But I may *repeat* and you shall hear them some time — I declare they possess as much point and classical *terseness* if I may so express myself, as anything I can imagine. O, he was in an epigrammatic humour indeed — I told him it was rash to crucify Ld. G—— in the way he was doing for tho he might not receive any favours at his hands yet he might suffer an injury — He struck up immediately

> Spare me thy vengeance G——— ay
> In quiet let me live;
> I ask no kindness at thy hand
> For thou hast none to give.

A Laird not very respectable is safer game — He does not love one Morrin* — He therefore gives a blow to him

* Purchaser of Ellisland.

When Morrin, deceased to the devil went down
Twas nothing would serve him but Satan's own crown;
Thy Fool-head, quoth Satan, that crown shall wear never:
I grant thou'rt as wicked, — but not quite so clever —

14th Augt.

The Interval from the first date to this has passed without my having time or word to finish what I have still to say in continuation of our Tour. I am to bring you to Kirkcudbt along with our Poet without boots. I carried the torn ruins across my saddle in despight of his fulminations and in contempt of apperances — and whats more Lord Selkirk carried them in his coach to Dumfries — & insisted they were worth the mending —

We reached Kirkcudbt about one, oclock — I had engaged us to dine with one of the first men in our Country L. Dalzell — But Burns' obstreperous independence would not dine but where he should as he said, eat like a Turk, drink like a fish & swear like the Devil — Since he would not dine with Dalzell in his own house he had nothing for it but (Dalzell) to dine with us in the Inn — we had a very agreeable party. In the evening we went to the *Isle* — Robert had not absolutely regained the milkiness of good temper, and it occurred once or twice to him that the Isle was the seat of a *Lord,* yet that Lord was not an *Aristocrate* He knew the family a little* — At length we got there about 8, as they were at tea & coffee — It is one of the most delightful places formed by the assemblage of every soft, but not tame object which constitutes natural and cultivated beauty But not to speak of its external graces let me tell you that we found all the female family (all beautiful) and some strangers at the Isle — and who else but Urbani — It is impossible to pay due respect to the family by putting them forward as principal figures on this paper when I have to tell you that *Urbani* sung us many Scotch Songs accompanied with music — The two young Ladies of Selkirk sung also — We had the song Lord Gregory which I asked for to have occasion to call upon Burns to *speak* his words to that tune — He *did speak* them — and such was the effect, that a dead silence ensued — Twas such a silence as a mind of feeling must necessarily preserve when it is touched, as I think sometimes & will happen, with that sacred en-

---

* Lord Daer with whom he had dined at Dugald Stewart's in 1786 was second son of the fourth Earl of Selkirk.

thusiasm which banishes every other thought than the contemplation and indulgence of the sympathy produced. . . .

We enjoyed a very happy evening — we had really a treat of mental and sensual delights — the latter consisting in abundance & variety of delicious fruits &c — the former you may conceive from our society — a company of 15 or 16 very agreeable young people.

We got to Dumfries next day — so Ends our Tour — I shall not dwell longer upon it, yet I could give you many other circumstances — but recollecting how Boswell treats of his Tour with Johnson & how he tells you of his, etc, etc, etc, I fear I might incur similar contempt. I have not seen Robert since.

I anxiously hope & pray that you Mrs. Cunningham and the dear little one will meet with all the happy things of this world — I remain Dear Cunningham —

Your old & affectionate companion & friend

JOHN SYME

At this point in the manuscript, Cunningham has inserted the following note: "Either on this ride to Dumfries or next day Burns I believe composed Scots wha hae with Wallace bled — the sublime address of Bruce to his troops. — Burns sent it soon after to J. Dalzell. He shewed it next day to J.S. in the stamp office." Burns, however, in a letter to George Thomson, dated by Professor Ferguson "About 30 August 1793," gives other particulars of *Scots Wha Hae*.

I am delighted with many little melodies which the learned Musician despises as silly & insipid. — I do not know whether the old air, "Hey tutti taitie," may rank among this number; but well I know that, with Fraser's Hautboy, it has often filled my eyes with tears. — There is a tradition, which I have met with in many places of Scotland, that it was Robert Bruce's March at the battle of Bannock-burn. — This thought, in my yesternight's evening walk, warmed me to a pitch of enthusiasm on the theme of Liberty & Independence, which I threw into a kind of Scots Ode, fitted to the Air, that one might suppose to be the gallant Royal Scot's address to his heroic followers on that eventful morning. —

Robert Bruce's march to BANNOCKBURN —
To its ain tune —

Scots, wha hae wi' WALLACE bled,
Scots, wham BRUCE has aften led,
Welcome to your gory bed, —
Or to victorie.—

Now's the day & now's the hour;
See the front o' battle lower;
See approach proud EDWARD's power,
Chains & Slaverie. —

Wha will be a traitor-knave?
Wha can fill a coward's grave?
Wha sae base as be a Slave?
— Let him turn & flie: —

Wha for SCOTLAND's king & law,
Freedom's sword will strongly draw,
FREE-MAN stand or FREE-MAN fa',
Let him follow me. —

By Oppression's woes & pains!
By your Sons in servile chains!
We will drain our dearest veins,
But they *shall* be free!

Lay the proud Usurpers low!
Tyrants fall in every foe!
LIBERTY's in every blow!
Let us DO — or DIE!!!

So may God ever defend the cause of Truth and Liberty, as he did that day! — Amen.!

RB

P.S. I shewed the air to Urbani, who was highly pleased with it, & begged me to make soft verses for it; but I had no idea of giving myself any trouble on the subject till the accidental recollection of that glorious struggle for Freedom, associated with the glowing ideas of some other struggles of the same nature, *not quite so ancient,* roused my rhyming mania.

Burns had seen Urbani at Lord Selkirk's on July 31 or August 1, and the gestation of *Scots Wha Hae* may well have been the result of that meeting, as Cunningham suggests, with the song taking final form as Burns reports to Thomson. The song is flaming evidence that Burns did not lighten his sympathies with the French Revolution in the summer of 1793, even though he may have become more discreet.

Robert Chambers quotes a Mr. Carson as source of the following anecdote, which forms an engaging supplement to Syme's account of the 1793 Galloway tour.

The only friends of the host and hostess invited to meet the travellers, Burns and Syme, at Kenmure, were the Rev John Gillespie, the highly esteemed minister of the parish, and myself.

On the evening preceding their departure, the bard having expressed his intention of climbing to the top of "the highest hill that rises o'er the source of Dee," there to see the arbour of Lowe, the author of the celebrated song "Mary's Dream," Mr Gordon proposed that they should all sail down the loch in his barge *Glenkens,* to the Airds Hill below Lowe's seat. Seeing that this proposal was intended in compliment by the worthy host both to the bard and to Mr Gillespie, who had been the patron of Lowe, the gentlemen all concurred; and the weather proving propitious next morning, the vessel soon dropt down to the foot of Loch Ken with all the party on board. Meanwhile, Mr Gordon's groom led the travellers' horses round to the Boat-o'-Rhone, saddled and bridled, that each rider might mount on descending from the poet's seat; but the barge unfortunately grounded before reaching the proposed landing-place — an obstruction not anticipated by any of the party. Mr Gordon, with the assistance of an oar, vaulted from the prow of the little vessel to the beach, and was soon followed in like manner by Mr Syme and myself; thus leaving only the venerable pastor of Kells and the bard on board. The former, being too feeble to jump, as we had done, to land, expressed a desire to remain in the vessel till Mr Gordon and I returned; upon hearing which, the generous bard instantly slipt into the water, which was, however, so deep as to wet him to the knees. After a short entreaty, he succeeded in getting the clergyman on his shoulders; on observing which, Mr Syme raised his hands, laughed immoderately and exclaimed: "Well, Burns, of all men on earth, you are the last I would have expected to see *priest-ridden!*" We laughed also, but Burns did not seem to enjoy the joke. He made no reply, but carried his load silently through the reeds to land.

When Mr Syme's account of this excursion with the bard into Galloway appeared in Dr Currie's first edition of the *Life and Works of Robert Burns,** the Glenkens people, who were actors in this part of the drama, were very much surprised to find the above incident not even alluded to. . . . We were all fully satisfied that it was by the bard's wading into the loch that his *new boots* were so thoroughly wet, and that the choler or independence next day manifested by him to Syme was only the result of his wounded feelings at having been made such a laughing-stock by his friend for merely rendering assistance due by common humanity to old age or infirmity, which Mr Gordon and myself charged ourselves afterward for having overlooked in that instance.

In giving excerpts from the following letter of Syme's, the *Burns Chronicle* (1934) omits the colorful account of Eighteenth Century "toasting."

DEAR CUNNINGHAM

. . . [Burns] says he cannot possibly be in Edinr where he should enjoy much happiness — particularly with you — He is confined here by his business and I dare say in part by his finances, for Robin's heart and temper are not cold and frugal — My Irish friend (Mr Large) filled him and me etc very *fu* last friday — A downright Irish Native & Robt. Burns in co — I defy apathy itself to escape a doze — Bi Jasus says the first & is that the way you fill in Scotland — arrah now we drink every good toast a bumper with us, & bad luck to him who shews daylight at the brim to a toast I give for *bi* the holy they are all of the vary best at all at all — now here's his majesty etc etc etc and many fine fellows in succession, to each of whom a bumper was necessary — other ways a pistol shot.

* Considerably embroidered by Currie.

It then became Robin to make a bumper — & hang the fellow for his toast made 13 — He gave — not a man — but a nation — Ireland — on which bi the holy says my friend we must have a round dozen to her before another toast be given — So that you see Cunningham how impossible it was to get free — . . .

I still am resolved upon paying you a visit before August — . . . I need not write the particulars I wish to communicate relative to Burns's production etc for I will regale you in conversation with some of these.

But the wild Bard has just now popped in while I was writing this and no less than a very elegant female figure of good rank reading a book aside me (She is the wife of an intimate acquaintance of mine — a writer in Kirkuidbr a very clever respectable woman whom I much esteem & so does Robin) Her husband was out — & Robin's confounding wit began to play — He remained all day — and was according to use & wont charming company. The wicked fellow had read a vehemently loyal advertisement by a Club of bucks here who call themselves the loyal *Native* Club — The individuals who compose it are neither Robins favorites nor mine, but we are far from differing from them on sentiments of loyalty — we differ on *sentiment* abstractedly considered — They know scarcely the meaning of the word sentiment & their Society consists mainly in roaring & drinking. Robin spouts the following — on the advertisement of the *Loyal Natives*

> Pray who are these *Natives* the rabble so ven'rate?
> They're our true ancient natives, and the breed unregen'rate:
> The ignorant savage that weather'd the storm,
> When the Man and the Brute differed but in the form.

Dont let any Dumfries person see this for one of the Savages if he heard it, might cut Robins pipe —

The following two passages from letters give pleasant details of Burns and Syme together. The first is from about May 1, 1795. "Burns and I are one and indivisible — but what with his occupation and mine we meet only by starts — or at least occasionally — & we drink as many *cups* of tea as *bottles* of wine together. We are two of the best *privates* in the Dumfries Royal Volunteers — But not to flatter myself or him, I would say that hang me if I should know how to be happy were he not in the way of making me so at times — " The second is dated February 24, 1796.

Burns tells me he had (if I did not misunderstand him) a long letter very lately from you — About a month ago he mentioned a scheme he was to follow which, if he accomplishes, will prove a very agreeable treat to you — He is to sit down as the spirit moves him and write you prose & poetry on every subject which strikes him — to form a sort of Journal business of it — and when it grows thro' two or three sheets to send the foliage — This will surely be a very valuable and entertaining farrago or Burnsana (is this a right term?)   I have prompted him to execute the design & shall not miss giving him the spur — He and I dined tete a tete last Sunday in my Cabin — quite sober — only one bottle of port betwixt us — I like this better than a debauch even in an Inn — Yet when two or three are gathered together in the name of friendship & *nostri-generis* — why, I would as soon have a bottle or a bottle & a half as a share of that quantity — We have a very superior fellow here — Dr Maxwell — who to an uncommon if not wonderful science in Physic adds the perfect manners and mind of a gentle man — you would be much attached him — without him & Burns I should find this place very blank & dreary —

The story draws very near its close in the next letter, of July 17, 1796. That of July 19 will be found later in the account of Burns' death.

My dear Cunningham

I had your favour covering letter to the Bard which I delivered personally. He poor fellow is in a very bad state of health — I really am extremely alarmed, not only by the cadaverous aspect and shaken frame of Burns, but from the accounts which I have heard from the first faculty here — But I entertain strong hopes that the vigour of his former stamina will conquer his present illness, and that by care & the attention & advice he receives from Dr Maxwell he will recover — I do not mean to alarm you but really poor Burns is very ill — However do not say whence you heard so — You are doing him a great kindness & benefit, and I am sure it is well bestowed — I cannot allow myself to imagine the business will fail, for God forbid there should be any rule of office that could not be dispensed with on such an occasion as the present.

Cunningham had urged the Excise Board to continue Burns at full pay even though he could not perform his duties. The Board felt that it must hold to its rule of granting only half pay in such circumstances, but Currie reports that Burns' "full emoluments were continued to him by the kindness of Mr [Adam] Stobbie, a young expectant in the Excise, who performed the duties of the office without fee or reward." Commissioner Graham sent a private contribution of £5.

Burns left an estate of approximately £300, and debts not above £20. But there were no liquid assets except the sums sent him in his last two weeks by James Burness and George Thomson, £15 in all, and the £5 from Robert Graham. James Burness sent another £5 for immediate necessities.

After Burns' death Cunningham undertook to raise a subscription in Edinburgh for the benefit of Jean and the children, but the response was discouraging. He wrote Syme August 9, 1796, "The truth is my dear Syme the poor Bards frailties excuse this vile word were not only so well known here but often I believe exaggerated that even the admirers of genius cannot be prevailed on to do what we all ought 'to forget and forgive' — "

On September 19, in discussing a proposed edition of Burns' poems and letters, Cunningham again writes to Syme, "To select & arrange what ought to be published of Burns's will be no easy task when you consider the variety of taste & opinions which obtain among men — and the necessity there is for the strictest delicacy being ever kept in View — His poetry & letters were often so blended with Religion Politics Love & Bawdry that the greatest care must be taken to render his thoughts & opinions consistent — "

In preparing for the extensive correctional comment in his

Preface to an 1815 edition of Currie (the copyright having expired), Alexander Peterkin had passages from several biographers and critics of Burns set in type, from which he pulled proofsheets. Three sheets survive which he sent to John Syme for comment. 2 1/3 sheets in 1935 were in possession of the Editor of the *Burns Chronicle,* with whose permission transcripts were prepared which are the basis of quotations here. 2/3 of the third sheet was then in the Watson Collection (1190) in the National Library of Scotland. Excerpts from these documents have appeared *ante.* Remaining items of interest follow.

Currie. "His temper now became more irritable and gloomy: he fled from himself into society, often of the lowest kind."

Syme deletes "the lowest kind" and substitutes "a low rank."

Syme: "Burns was fastidious on the point of going to meet strangers in a Tavern to shew himself as a Toy or wonder — when I had occasion to exhibit the Poet to a man of distinction who courted the favor, I wrote him a proper card of solicitation."

David Irvine: "His habits gradually became more pernicious."

Syme deletes "pernicious" and substitutes "inexcusable." *

Irvine: "Often did he acknowledge his numerous breaches of the duties of a husband and a father."

* An illustration of Syme's comment is the rhymed apology below from Burns to Mr. S. M'kenzie of Dumfries, which carries the following docket: "Mr. Robt Burns with a pretended excuse for having used my character ill — 1796 — Delivered to me by Mr. Syme, opposite the Inn possessed by Mrs. Riddick, in Bank Street." (Kinsley II, #520, 814.)

> The friend who wild from Wisdom's way
> The fumes of wine infuriate send,
> (Not moony madness more astray)
> Who but deplores that hapless friend?
>
> Mine was th'insensate, frenzied part,
> (Ah! why did I those scenes outlive,
> Scenes so abhorrent to my heart!)
> 'Tis thine to pity and forgive. —
> RB

Peterkin: "Ask Mrs Burns what were the breaches of Duty of which he was guilty."

The reply, in the margin, is neatly torn away. The proofsheet containing this material belonged to the late editor of the *Burns Chronicle*.

Syme: "Burns had much collision with world — could penetrate & appreciate character well & could acquit himself as well as any Lord of high & courtly race & experience."

Syme: "I conceived Burns to have been highly chivalrous & polite — quite devoid of vulgarity or meanness."

Sir Walter Scott: "To lay before him his errors, or to point out their consequences, was to touch a string that jarred every feeling with him. . . . It is a dreadful truth, that when racked and tortured by the well-meant and warm expostulations of an intimate friend, he at length started up in a paroxysm of frenzy, and, drawing a sword cane, which he usually wore, made an attempt to plunge it into the body of his adviser: in the next instant, he was with difficulty witheld from suicide."

Syme: "This happened to me — In my parlour at Rydale one afternoon Burns & I were very gracious & confidential — I did advise him to be temperate in all things — I might have spoken Daggers but I did not mean them — He shook to the inmost fibre of his frame, drew the sword cane, when I exclaimed, What! wilt thou thus, & in my own house? The poor fellow was so stung with remorse &c, that he dashed himself down on the floor — (which is a flagged floor) and beat his face against it — He shunned me during some weeks after from remorse and self-reproach — But we became better friends ever after."

As already mentioned by John Syme, Burns' chief physician in his terminal illness was his friend Dr. James Maxwell, whose father, Kirkonnel Maxwell, had followed Prince Charles in 1745.

Maxwell had studied medicine in France, had joined the Republican Army, and had helped guard the scaffold on which Louis XVI had been executed, dipping his handkerchief in the royal blood. Maxwell and Burns shared a combined Jacobitism and Jacobinism, and they and Syme and perhaps a few others were used to converse behind closed doors in violently loyalist Dumfries. Dr. Maxwell enjoyed high professional reputation, and he was most devoted in his attendance on Burns, but means were lacking at that time to diagnose Burns' illness, and Dr. Maxwell's advice to seek rest in pleasant surroundings, and gentle exercise, and sea bathing, was worthless at best. Nonetheless Burns tried to follow it, and went to Brow, on the Solway, near Dumfries, in early July, 1796. Brow is well described by Sir James Crichton-Browne:

Ten miles south-east of Dumfries, on the Solway shore, stands the meanest, shabbiest little spa in all the world. It consists of three white-washed cottages; a tank the size of a dining-table and lined with red-stone, into which, through an iron pipe, the mineral water trickles; an esplanade a score of yards long, of coarse tufted grass; and the pump-room, a dilapidated wooden shed, the walls and benches of which are graven over and over again with the initials of those who have sought healing at the Well. The country immediately around is flat and uninteresting. Inland there are a few stunted plantations of gnarled oaks and shaggy Scotch firs, which by their bent backs bear witness to the rough usage of the western winds, while in front there is a broad, flat, hillocky expanse, studded with bent grass and furze, and ending in the sea-beach, consisting of a mixture of sand and clay known locally as *sleetch*. This uninviting substance extends for several miles into the Solway Firth, with so slight a declination that the tide at low water recedes entirely out of sight and leaves to the eye a barren and cheerless waste.

On a dull day, with the skies draped in cloud and at low water, a more forlorn and desolate place than the Brow-Well — for that is how this spa is named, no one knows how or why — it would be difficult to imagine; but when the sun shines and the skies clear and the tide is in, it becomes a fascinating spot, for a magnificent panorama is disclosed to view. On the horizon on the east stretches the long range of the Cumberland and Westmoreland mountains, Skiddaw, Saddleback, Helvellyn, and the rest of them in an outline of fantastic beauty, and ending in the "sapphire promontory which men name St. Bees"; to the south "huge Criffel's hoary top ascends"; to the west, tier on tier, run the rugged Galloway hills, and then the ample woodlands that surround Comlongan Castle, while in the foreground sparkle the last ripples of the Atlantic flow.

But whatever its physical features may be, the Brow-Well must be regarded as a sacred precinct by all Scotsmen, for it was the scene of the last act of a memorable and deeply moving Scottish tragedy. It was the Gethsemane of Robert Burns.

Once at the Brow, removed from his friends and family, almost entirely alone, Burns sat under a hawthorne tree and saw his strength gradually slip away. Each day he waded out until the cold water came up to his armpits, and then waded back to sit under the hawthorne again and think of his daily more apparent end. Finally, on July 18, after he had become entirely certain the end was not far off, he climbed wearily into a carriage and was driven back to Dumfries.

At this time Maria Riddell was staying near Brow, and, hearing that Burns was there, she invited him to dinner and sent her carriage for him.

I was struck [she writes] with his appearance on entering the room. The stamp of death was impressed on his features. He seemed already touching the brink of eternity. His first salutation was "Well, Madam, have you any commands for the other world?" I replied, that it seemed a doubtful case which of us should be there soonest, and that I hoped he would yet live to write my epitaph. (I was then in a poor state of health.) He looked in my face with an air of great kindness, and expressed his concern at seeing me look so ill, with his accustomed sensibility. At table he ate little or nothing, and he complained of having entirely lost the tone of his stomach. We had a long and serious conversation about his present situation, and the approaching termination of all his earthly prospects. He spoke of his death without any of the ostentation of philosophy, but with firmness as well as feeling — as an event likely to happen very soon, and which gave him concern chiefly from leaving his four children so young and un-protected, and his wife in so interesting a situation — in hourly ex-pectation of lying-in of a fifth. He mentioned, with seeming pride and satisfaction, the promising genius of his eldest son, and the flattering marks of approbation he had received from his teachers, and dwelt particularly on his hopes of that boy's future conduct and merit. His anxiety for his family seemed to hang heavy upon him, and the more perhaps from the reflection that he had not done them all the justice he was so well qualified to do. Passing from this subject, he shewed great concern about the care of his literary fame, and particularly the publication of his posthumous works. He said he was well aware that his death would occasion some noise, and that every scrap of his writing would be revived against him to the injury of his future repu-tation: that letters and verses written with unguarded and improper freedom, and which he earnestly wished to have buried in oblivion, would be handed about by idle vanity or malevolence, when no dread of his resentment would restrain them, or prevent the censures of shrill-tongued malice, or the insidious sarcasms of envy, from pouring forth all their venom to blast his fame.

He lamented that he had written many epigrams on persons against whom he entertained no enmity, and whose characters he should be sorry to wound; and many indifferent poetical pieces, which he feared would now, with all their imperfections on their head, be thrust upon the world. On this account he deeply regretted having deferred to put his papers into a state of arrangement, as he was now quite incapable of the exertion. . . . The conversation was kept up with great evenness and animation on his side. I had seldom seen his mind greater or more collected. There was frequently a considerable degree of vivacity in his sallies, and they would probably have had a greater share, had not the concern and dejection I could not disguise, damped the spirit of pleasantry he seemed not unwilling to indulge.

We parted about sun-set on the evening of that day (the 5th of July, 1796); the next day I saw him again, and we parted to meet no more!

Burns left a moving record of his last days in letters which he wrote to friends and members of his family and to Jean. After his return to Dumfries, two days before his death, John Syme visited him and described the visit to Alexander Cunningham. Burns' first letter from Brow, written soon after his arrival, was to George Thomson.

Brow 4th July

My dear Sir,

I recd your songs: but my health being so precarious nay dangerously situated, that as a last effort I am here at a sea-bathing quarters. — Besides my inveterate rheumatism, my appetite is quite gone, & I am so emaciated as to be scarce able to support myself on my own legs. — Alas! is this a time for me to woo the Muses? However, I am still anxiously willing to serve your work; & if possible shall try: — I would not like to see another employed, unless you could lay your hand upon a poet whose productions would be equal to the rest. — You will see my alterations & remarks on the margin of each song. — You may think it hard as to "Cauld kail in Aberdeen," but I cannot help it. — My address is still Dumfries.

Farewell! & God bless you!

RBurns

There follow letters to Alexander Cunningham, to his father-in-law James Armour, to his brother Gilbert, to his cousin James Burness, to Jean, and to a friend begging the use of a gig to take him back to Dumfries. A letter to Mrs. Dunlop has already been quoted at the close of Section III, and one to George Thomson at the opening of Section V.

Brow-Sea-bathing quarters
July 7th

My dear Cunningham

I received yours here this moment and am indeed highly flattered with the approbation of the literary circle you mention; a literary circle inferiour to none in the two kingdoms. — Alas! my friend, I fear the voice of the Bard will soon be heard among you no more! For these eight or ten months I have been ailing, sometimes bedfast & sometimes not; but these last three months I have been tortured with an excruciating rheumatism, which has reduced me to nearly the last stage. — You actually would not know me if you saw me. — Pale, emaciated, & so feeble as occasionally to need help from my chair — my spirits are fled! fled! — but I can no more on the subject — only the Medical folks tell me that my last & only chance is bathing & country quarters & riding. — The deuce of the matter is this; when an Excise-man is off duty, his salary is reduced to 35£ instead of 50£. — What way, in the name of thrift, shall I maintain myself & keep a horse in Country-quarters — with a wife & five children at home, on 35£? I mention this, because I had intended to beg your utmost interest & all friends you can muster, to move our Commissrs of Excise to grant me the full salary. — I dare say you know them all personally. — If they do not grant it me, I must lay my account with an exit truly en poëte, if I die not of disease I must perish with hunger. —

I have sent you one of the songs: the other, my memory does not serve me with, & I have no copy here; but I shall be at home soon, when I will send it you. — Apropos to being at home, Mrs Burns threatens in a week or two to add one more to my Paternal charge, which if of the right gender, I intend shall be introduced to the world by the respectable designation of Alexr Cunningham Burns. My last was James Glencairn, so you can have no objection to the company of Nobility. —

Farewell —
RB

Mr Jas Armour   *Mason   Mauchline*

For Heaven's sake & as you value the welfare of your daughter, & my wife, do, my dearest Sir, write to Fife to Mrs Armour to come if possible. — My wife thinks she can yet reckon upon a fortnight. — The Medical people order me *as I value my existence*, to fly to sea-bathing & country quarters, so it is ten thousand chances to one that I shall not be within a dozen miles of her when her hour comes. — What a situation for her, poor girl, without a single friend by her on such a serious moment. —

I have now been a week at salt water, & though I think I have got some good by it, yet I have some secret fears that this business will be dangerous if not fatal. —

Your affectionate son —

July 10th   RBurns

DEAR BROTHER

It will be no very pleasing news to you to be told that I am dangerously ill, & not likely to get better. — An inveterate rheumatism has reduced me to such a state of debility, and my appetite is tottaly gone, so that I can scarcely stand on my legs. — I have been a week at sea-bathing, & I will continue there or in a friend's house in the country all the summer. — God help my wife & children if I am taken from their head! — They will be poor indeed. — I have contracted one or two serious debts, partly from my illness these many months & partly from too much thoughtlessness as to expense when I came to town that will cut in too much on the little I leave them in your hands. — Remember me to my Mother. —

Yours

July 10th RBURNS

Mr James Burness *Writer Montrose*
MY DEAREST COUSIN,

When you offered me money-assistance little did I think I should want it so soon. — A rascal of a Haberdasher to whom I owe a considerable bill taking it into his head that I am dying, has commenced a process against me, & will infallibly put my emaciated body into jail. — Will you be so good as to accomodate me, & that by return of post, with ten pound. — O, James, did you know the pride of my heart, you would feel doubly for me! Alas! I am not used to beg! The worst of it is, my health was coming about finely; you know & my Physician assures me that melancholy & low spirits are half my disease, guess then my horrors since this business began. — If I had it settled, I would be I think quite well in a manner. — How shall I use the language to you, O do not disappoint me! but strong Necessity's curst command. —

I have been thinking over & over my brother's affairs, & I fear I must cut him up; but on this I will correspond at another time, particularly as I shall need your advice. —

Forgive me once more for mentioning by return of Post. — Save me from the horrors of a jail!

My Compliments to my friend James, & to all the rest. — I do not know what I have written. The subject is so horrible, I dare not look it over again. —

Farewel

July 12th RBURNS

The threat of jail, though real enough for delinquent debtors in Burns' day, was probably not serious for him, but his melancholy was understandably deep, and it was sharpened by this prospect which he felt to be ominous. In his last letter to Jean, he makes an effort to be hopeful.

Brow, Thursday [14th]

MY DEAREST LOVE,

I delayed writing until I could tell you what effect sea-bathing was likely to produce. It would be injustice to deny that it has eased my pains, and I think has strengthened me; but my appetite is still extremely bad. No flesh nor fish can I swallow: porridge and milk are the only things I can taste. I am very happy to hear by Miss Jessy Lewars that you are all well. My very best and kindest compliments to her, and to all the children. I will see you on Sunday.

Your affectionate Husband,
R. BURNS

The next letter arranged for his return to Dumfries.

John Clark Esquire *Locherwoods*

Saturd: n^n[16th]

MY DEAR SIR,

my hours of bathing have interfered so unluckily as to have put it out of my power to wait on you. — In the meantime, as the tides are over I anxiously wish to return to town, as I have not heard any news of Mrs Burns these two days. — Dare I be so bold as to borrow your Gig? I have a horse at command, but it threatens to rain, & getting wet is perdition. Any time about three in the afternoon, will suit me exactly. —

Your most gratefully & sincerely
RBURNS

Burns' last letter was to his father-in-law.

Mr James Armour *Mauchline*

Dumfries, 18th July 1796

MY DEAR SIR,

Do for Heaven's sake, send Mrs Armour here immediately. My wife is hourly expecting to be put to bed. Good God! what a situation for her to be in, poor girl, without a friend! I returned from sea-bathing quarters today, and my medical friends would almost persuade me I am better; but I think and feel that my strength is so gone that the disorder will prove fatal to me.

Your Son-in-law,
R. Burns

The day after Burns returned from Brow, John Syme went to see him, and wrote at once to Cunningham.

Dumfries 19th July — 1796 — noon —

My dear Cunningham

I wrote you last Sunday and mentioned that our friend Burns was very ill — I conceive it to be a task (you would not forgive me did I omit it) to mention now, that I believe it is all over with him. I am this minute come from the mournful chambers in which I have seen the expiring genius of Scotland departing with Burns. Dr. Maxwell told me yesterday he had no hopes — today the hand of Death is visibly fixed upon him. I cannot dwell on the scene — It overpowers me — yet Gracious God were it thy will to recover him! He had life enough to acknowledge me — and Mrs. Burns said he had been calling on you and me continually — He made a wonderful exertion when I took him by the hand — with a strong voice he said, "I am much better today, — "I shall soon be well again for I command my spirits & my mind. But yesterday I resigned myself to death" — Alas it will not do. . . .

I will write you whenever any alteration of the case takes place — Meantime I feel from my soul I can give you no hopes.

Excuse the irregularity of this if necessary

Yours truly
J Syme

The illness is — the whole system debilitated & gone, beyond the power (perhaps) of man to restore —

Burns died Thursday, July 21, 1796, at five o'clock in the morning.

Of many ironies in Burns' career, his funeral was certainly not the least. Too late, it did him impressive honor, and of a sort he would not have relished. It was arranged by his devoted friend, John Syme, and during it a son was born to Jean, who, unaware of the promise her husband had made to Cunningham, named him Maxwell Burns. It would certainly have astonished many at the funeral to know that Burns would become a towering world figure, part of whose history would be the failure of such as they to recognize his worth.

The funeral was held on Monday, July 25, at the Dumfries Town Hall, from which the procession moved more than half a mile to the cemetery through streets lined by troops from the Angusshire Fencibles and the Cinque Ports Cavalry, both commands being then stationed in Dumfries. At the head marched a firing party of Burns' fellow-volunteers, and, behind them, the Cinque Ports Cavalry band playing the Dead March from *Saul*. Then came the bier supported by Volunteers, who changed at intervals. There followed Burns' relatives and "a number of the respectable inhabitants of the town and country." The remaining Volunteers came next, and a guard of Fencibles closed the procession. "A vast concourse of persons assembled, some of them from a considerable distance," and "the great bells of the churches tolled at intervals during the time of the procession. When arrived at the churchyard gate, the funeral party formed two lines and leaned their heads on their firelocks pointed to the ground. Through this space the corpse was carried and borne to the grave. The party then drew up alongside of it, and fired three volleys over the coffin when deposited in the earth."

Two stanzas from the poem with which Burns closed the Kilmarnock volume are his best epitaph.

> Is there a whim-inspirèd fool,
> Owre fast for thought, owre hot for rule,
> Owre blate to seek, owre proud to snool? —   *modest   cringe*

Let him draw near;
And owre this grassy heap sing dool,   *woe*
And drap a tear.

. . . .

The poor inhabitant below
Was quick to learn and wise to know,
And keenly felt the friendly glow
And softer flame;
But thoughtless follies laid him low
And stain'd his name.

Efforts of Cunningham in Edinburgh and Syme in Dumfries to collect funds for the benefit of Jean and the children met with limited success. In Liverpool, Dr. James Currie, a Dumfriesshire native and an early admirer of Burns, raised £70, and a London subscription produced £700. In all, £1200 was raised, invested, and turned over to the Bailies and Provost of Ayr; and Dr. Currie's four volumes in 1800, which he edited without compensation, raised £1400. On the income from these funds, Jean continued to live as a widow, quietly and sensibly, in the house where her husband had died. In later years, when her sons could assist her, she was most comfortable. She survived until March 26, 1834.

She refused offers to have her children educated away from her when they were young; eventually the three boys who grew to maturity received a good schooling. Robert (1786–1857), known in his family as "The Laird," got an appointment in the Stamp Office, London. He left an illegitimate son, who in turn left a son, who is reported to have died without issue. Burns has no known descendants by the male line. Maxwell Burns died in 1799, and Francis Wallace in 1803. William Nicol (1791–1872) and James Glencairn (1794–1865) became cadets in the East India Company's service, retiring as Colonel and Lieutenant Colonel. Burns' only direct descendants by Jean Armour are issue of James Glencairn's daughter Sarah.

Burns' daughter by Betty Paton, and his daughter by Anne

Park, each received £200 on marriage, from the subscription funds. Mrs. Carswell reports (1931) of Betty Paton, "Later she married happily and was respected by all. Today the wealthiest of all the blood of Burns, and the only one to reach the peerage of the United Kingdom, is descended from the child she bore the poet."

The caricature of Burns as a Heaven-Taught Ploughman who rose to meteoric fame and declined into dissipated poverty and neglect has faded, happily. But unfortunate ironies remain. His appeal to Scotsmen has served to foster the notion that he is but a local or national poet, and persistent fascination with his personality and his dramatic career, and with his all too human frailties, continues to shift interest from his having been a poet at all. Moreover this very interest in the man tends to ignore the complexity of his character; his good sense and candor and self-knowledge; and his share of that loneliness which is the lot of all great men, and particularly of great artists. The understanding which Burns foresaw would come to him eventually is possible only for those who have lived with him. To make this as nearly possible as can be today, this book has been written.

APPENDICES

APPENDIX A

SCOTS VERNACULAR POEMS WHICH INFLUENCED BURNS

The Life and Death of Habbie Simson, the Piper of Kilbarchan

Kilbarchan now may say alas!
For she hath lost her game and grace,
Both *Trixie* and *The Maiden Trace;*   [*tunes*]
But what remead?
For no man can supply his place:
Hab Simson's dead.

Now who shall play *The Day it Dawis,*
Or *Hunt's Up,* when the cock he craws?
Or who can for our kirk-town cause
Stand us in stead?
On bagpipes now nobody blaws
Sen Habbie's dead.   *since*

Or wha will cause our shearers sheer?
Wha will bend up the brags of weir,   *raise war*
Bring in the bells, or good play-meir   *hobby-horse*
In time of need?
Hab Simson could, what needs you speir?   *ask*
But now he's dead.

So kindly to his neighbours neist   *next*
At Beltan and St. Barchan's feast
He blew, and then held up his breast,
As he were weid: *mad*
But now we need not him arrest,
For Habbie's dead.

At fairs he play'd before the spear-men,
All gaily graithed in their gear men: *accoutered*
Steel bonnets, jacks, and swords so clear then
    Like any bead:
Now wha shall play before such weir-men   *warriors*
    Sen Habbie's dead?

At clark-plays when he wont to come,
His pipe played trimly to the drum;
Like bikes of bees he gart it bum,   *hives   made   hum*
    And tun'd his reed:
Now all our pipers may sing dumb,
    Sen Habbie's dead.

And at horse races many a day,
Before the black, the brown, the gray,
He gart his pipe, when he did play,
    Baith skirl and skreed: *scream   shriek*
Now all such pastime's quite away
    Sen Habbie's dead.

He counted was a waled wight-man,   *chosen   strong-*
And fiercely at football he ran:
At every game the gree he wan   *prize*
    For pith and speed.
The like of Habbie was na than,
    But now he's dead.

And then, besides his valiant acts,
At bridals he wan many placks;
He bobbit ay behind folk's backs
    And shook his head.
Now we want many merry cracks
    Sen Habbie's dead.

He was convoyer of the bride,
With Kittock hinging at his side;
About the kirk he thought a pride
    The ring to lead: *bridal procession*
But now we may gae but a guide,   *go without*
    For Habbie's dead.

So well's he keepèd his decorum,
And all the stots of *Whip-meg-morum;*   *bouncing turns*

He slew a man, and wae's me for him,
   And bure the feid!   *feud*
But yet the man wan hame before him,
   And was not dead.

Ay whan he play'd the lasses leugh
To see him teethless, auld, and teugh,
He wan his pipes besides Barcleugh,
   Withouten dread!
Which after wan him gear eneugh;   *wealth*
   But now he's dead.

Ay when he play'd the gaitlings gedder'd,   *children*
And when he spake the carl bleddered,   *old man* *babbled*
On Sabbath days his cap was fedder'd,
   A seemly weid;
In the kirk-yeard his mare stood tedder'd
   Where he lies dead.

Alas! for him my heart is sair,
For of his spring I gat a skair,   *a quick air* *share*
At every play, race, feast, and fair,
   But guile or greed;
We need not look for piping mair,
   Sen Habbie's dead.
                    Robert Sempill of Beltrees

The Last Dying Words of Bonnie Heck,
A Famous Grey-hound in the Shire of Fife

     Alas, alas, quo' bonnie Heck,
     On former days when I reflec';
     I was a dog much in respec'
         For doughty deed:
     But now I must hing by the neck
         Without remeid.

     O fy, sirs, for black burning shame,
     Ye'll bring a blunder on your name?
     Pray tell me wherein I'm to blame.
         Is't in effec'

Because I'm cripple, auld, and lame?
    Quo' bonnie Heck.

What great feats have I done mysel
Within clink of Kilrenny bell,
When I was souple, young, and fell,   *strong*
    But fear or dread;   *Without*
John Ness and Paterson can tell,
    Whose hearts may bleed.

They'll witness that I was the vier   *rival*
Of all the dogs within the shire;
I'd run all day and never tire;
    But now my neck,
It must be stretchèd for my hire,
    Quo' bonnie Heck.

How nimbly could I turn the hare,
Then serve myself; that was but fair;
For still it was my constant care
    The van to lead.
Now what could sery Heck do mair?
    Syne kill her dead.

At the King's-muir and Kelly-law,
Where good stout hares gang fast awa',   *went*
So cleverly I did it claw,
    With pith and speed;
I bure the bell before them a'
    As clear's a bead.

I ran alike on a' kind grunds;
Yea, in the midst of Ardry whins,   *furze*
I gripped the maukins by the buns,   *hares*
    Or by the neck;
When naething could slay them but guns,
    Save bonnie Heck.

I wily, witty, was, and gash,   *lively*
With my auld fellin pawky pash;   *very sly head*
Nae man might ance buy me for cash
    In some respec';
Are they not then confounded rash,
    That hangs poor Heck?

I was a hardy tyke, and bauld;   *dog   bold*
Tho' my beard's grey, I'm not so auld.
Can any man to me unfauld
       What is the feid,   *feud*
To stane me ere I be well cauld?
       A cruel deed!

Now honesty was ay my drift;
An innocent and harmless shift,
A kail-pot lid gently to lift,
       Or aumrie sneck,   *cupboard latch*
Shame fa' the chafts dare call that thift,   *jaws   theft*
       Quo' bonnie Heck.

So well's I cou'd play Hocus-Pocus,
And of the servants mak Jodocus,
And this I did in every Locus
       Throw their neglec':
And was not this a merry Jocus?
       Quo' bonnie Heck.

But now, good sirs, this day is lost
The best dog in the East-Neuk coast;
For never ane durst brag nor boast
       Me, for their neck,
But now I must yield up the ghost,
       Quo' bonnie Heck.

And put a period to my talking;
For I'm unto my exit making:
Sirs, ye may a' gae to the hawking,
       And there reflec'
Ye'll ne'er get sic a dog for maukin   *hare*
       As bonnie Heck.

But if my puppies ance were ready,
Which I gat on a bonnie lady,
They'll be baith clever, keen, and beddy,
       And ne'er neglec'
To clink it like their ancient daddy,
       The famous Heck.

William Hamilton of Gilbertfield

An Elegy on John Cowper*

I warn ye a' to greet and drone;   *weep*
John Cowper's dead — Ohon! Ohon!
To fill his post alake there's none
      That with sic speed
Could sa'r sculdudry out like John,   *smell whoring*
      But now he 's deid.

He was right nacky in this way,   *clever*
And eydent baith be night and day,   *diligent*
He wi' the lads his part could play,
      When right sair fleed,
He gart them good bill-siller pay;   *stud fees*
      But now he 's dead.

Of whore-hunting he gat his fill,
And made be 't mony a pint and gill;
Of his braw post he thought nae ill,
      Nor didna need;
Now they may mak a kirk and mill
      O 't, since he 's dead.

Altho' he was nae man of weir,   *war*
Yet mony a ane, wi' quaking fear,
Durst scarce afore his face appear,
      But hide their head;

* It is necessary, for the illustration of this clergy to strangers, to let them a little into the history of the kirk-treasurer and his man. The treasurer is chosen every year, a citizen respected for riches and honesty; he is vested with an absolute power to seize and imprison the girls that are too impatient to have their green gown before it is hemmed. Them he strictly examines, but no liberty is to be granted till a fair account be given of those persons they have obliged: it must be so; a list is frequently given, sometimes of a dozen or thereby, of married or unmarried unfair traders, whom they secretly assisted in running their goods: these his lordship makes pay to some purpose, according to their ability, for the use of the poor. If the lads be obstreperous, the kirk-sessions, and worst of all, the stool of repentance, are threatened, a punishment which few of any spirit can bear. The treasurer, being changed every year, never comes to be perfectly acquainted with the affair; but their general servant, continuing for a long time, is more expert at discovering such persons, and the places of their resort, which makes him capable to do himself and customers both a good and ill turn. John Cowper maintained this post with activity, and good success, for several years. *Ramsay's note.*

The wylie carle, he gather'd gear,   *fellow*
    And yet he 's dead.

Ay, now to some part far awa',
Alas he 's gane and left it a';
May be to some sad whilliwha   *deceitful fellow*
    Of fremit blood;   *not akin*
'Tis an ill wind that disna blaw
    Somebody good.

Fy upon Death! he was to blame,
To whirl poor John to his lang hame;
But tho' his arse be cauld, yet fame,
    Wi' tout of trumpet,
Shall tell how Cowper's awfu' name
    Could flie a strumpet.

Shame fa' ye'r chandler-chafts',* O Death!
For stapping of John Cowper's breath,
The loss of him is public skaith.   *loss*
    I dare well say,
To quat the grip he was right laith
    This mony a day.

POSTSCRIPT.

Of umquhile John to lie or bann,   *denounce*
Shaws but ill will, and looks right shan,   *pitiful*
But some tell odd tales of the man;
    For fifty head
Can gie their aith they've seen him gawn†
    Since he was dead.

Keek but up thro' the Stinking Stile,‡
On Sunday morning a wee while,
At the kirk door, out frae an aisle,
    It will appear:
But tak good tent ye dinna file   *foul*
    Ye'r breeks for fear.   *breeches*

* Lean or meagre cheeked; when the bones appear like the sides or corners of a candlestick, which in Scots we call a chandler. *Ramsay's note.*
† The common people, when they tell their tales of ghosts appearing, say, he has been seen "gawn," or stalking. *Ramsay's note.*
‡ Opposite to this place is the door of the church, which he attended, being a beadle. *Ramsay's note.*

For well we wat it is his ghaist:
Wow, wad some fouk that can do't best,*
Speak til't, and hear what it confest;
　　　'Tis a good deed
To send a wand'ring saul to rest
　　　Amang the deid.

He ken'd the bawds and louns fou well,
And where they used to rant and reel,
He pawkily on them could steal,
　　　And spoil their sport;
Aft did they wish the muckle deil
　　　Might take him for 't.

But ne'er a ane of them be spar'd,
E'en tho' there was a drunken laird
To draw his sword, and make a faird,　　　*bullying bustle*
　　　In their defence;
John quietly put them in the guard,
　　　To learn mair sense:

There maun they lie till sober grown,
The lad neist day his fault maun own;
And to keep a' things hush and lown
　　　He minds the poor; †
Syne after a' his ready's shown,
　　　He damns the whore.

And she, poor jade, withoutten din,
Is sent to Leith-wynd-fit‡ to spin,
With heavy heart, and cleathing thin,
　　　And hungry wame,
And ilka month a well-paid skin,　　　　*beating*
　　　To make her tame.

But now they may scour up and down,
And safely gang their wakes aroun,
Spreading their claps thro' a' the town,

---

* It is another vulgar notion that a ghost will not be laid to rest till some priest
speak to it, and get an account of what disturbs it. *Ramsay's note.*
† Pays hush-money to the treasurer. *Ramsay's note.*
‡ The house of correction at the foot of Leith-wynd. *Ramsay's note.*

But fear or dread;   *without*
For that great kow to bawd and lown,   *goblin rogue*
John Cowper's dead.

Allan Ramsay

Familiar Epistles

WHICH PASSED BETWEEN LIEUT. HAMILTON*

AND ALLAN RAMSAY

EPISTLE I.

Gilbertfield, June 20th, 1719.
O fam'd and celebrated Allan!
Renown'd Ramsay! canty callan!
There's nowther Highland-man nor Lawlan,
   In poetrie,
But may as soon ding down Tamtallan,   [*castle*]
   As match wi' thee.

For ten times ten, and that's a hunder,
I ha'e been made to gaze and wonder,
When frae Parnassus thou didst thunder,
   Wi' wit and skill;
Wherefore I'll soberly knock under,
   And quat my quill.

Of poetry the hail quintescence
Thou hast suck'd up, left nae excrescence
To petty poets, or sic messens,   *lap-dogs*
   Tho' round thy stool
They may pick crumbs, and lear some lessons
   At Ramsay's school.

Tho' Ben and Dryden of renown   *Ben Jonson*
Were yet alive in London town,
Like kings contending for a crown,
   'Twad be a pingle,   *hard task*
Whilk o' you three wad gar words sound
   And best to gingle.

* Hamilton was a retired officer on half pay.

Transform'd may I be to a rat,
Wer't in my power, but I'd create
Thee upo' sight the laureat
    Of this our age,
Since thou may'st fairly claim to that
    As thy just wage.

Let modern poets bear the blame,
Gin they respect not Ramsay's name,
Wha soon can gar them greet for shame,   *make   weep*
    To their great loss,
And send them a' right sneaking hame
    Be Weeping-cross.

Wha bourds wi' thee had need be wary,   *jests*
And lear wi' skill thy thrust to parry,
When thou consults thy dictionary
    Of ancient words,
Which come from thy poetic quarry
    As sharp as swords.

Now tho' I should baith reel and rottle,
And be as light as Aristotle,
At Ed'nburgh we sall ha'e a bottle
    Of reaming claret
Gin that my half-pay siller shottle   *drawer*
    Can safely spare it.

At crambo then we'll rack our brain,   *a rhyming game*
Drown ilk dull care and aching pain,   *each*
Whilk aften does our spirits drain   *which*
    Of true content;
Woy, woy! but we's be wonder fain,   *we'll   merry*
    When thus acquaint.

Wi' wine we'll gargarize our craig,   *throat*
Then enter in a lasting league,
Free of ill aspect or intrigue;
        And, gin you please it,   *if*
Like princes when met at the Hague,
    We'll solemnize it.

Accept of this, and look upon it
With favour, tho' poor I've done it:

Sae I conclude and end my sonnet,
    Who am most fully,
While I do wear a hat or bonnet,
    Yours,
        Wanton Willy.

POSTSCRIPT.

By this my postscript I incline
To let you ken my hail design   *know   whole*
Of sic a long imperfect line   *such*
    Lies in this sentence,
To cultivate my dull engine
    By your acquaintance.

Your answer therefore I expect;
And to your friend you may direct
At Gilbertfield; do not neglect,   *[near Glasgow]*
    When ye have leisure,
Which I'll embrace with great respect,
    And perfect pleasure.

ANSWER I.

                        Edinburgh, July 10th, 1719.
Sonse fa' me, witty, Wanton Willy,   *good fortune*
Gin blyth I was na as a filly;   *If*
Not a fou pint, nor short-hought gilly,
    Or wine that's better,
Could please sae meikle, my dear Billy,   *much*
    As thy kind letter.

Before a lord and eik a knight,
In gossy Don's be candle-light,
There first I saw't, and ca'd it right,
    And the maist feck   *part*
Wha's seen't sinsyne, they ca'd as tight   *since then*
    As that on Heck.

Ha, heh! thought I, I canna say
But I may cock my nose the day,
When Hamilton the bauld and gay
    Lends me a heezy,   *good lift*

In verse that slides sae smooth away,
Well tell'd and easy.

Sae roos'd by ane of well-kend mettle,
Nae sma' did my ambition pettle,
My canker'd critics it will nettle,
    And e'en sae be 't:
This month I'm sure I winna settle,
    Sae proud I 'm wi't.

When I begoud first to cun verse,   *began*
And could your Ardry whins rehearse,
Where Bonny Heck ran fast and fierce,
    It warm'd my breast;
Then emulation did me pierce,
    Whilk since ne'er ceast.

May I be licket wi' a bittle,   *fuller's club*
Gin of your numbers I think little;   *If*
Ye're never rugget, shan, nor kittle,   *silly   knotty*
    But blyth and gabby,
And hit the spirit to a tittle
    Of standard Habby.

Ye'll quat your quill! — that were ill, Willy,
Ye's sing some mair yet, nill ye will ye,
O'er meikle haining wad but spill ye,   *saving   spoil*
    And gar ye sour;   *make*
Then up and war them a' yet, Willy,   *excel*
    'Tis in your pow'r.

To knit up dollars in a clout,
And then to card them round about,
Syne to tell up, they downa lont   *Then   bow down*
    To lift the gear;   *money*
The malison lights on that rout,
    Is plain and clear.

The chiels of London, Cam, and Ox,
Ha'e rais'd up great poetic stocks
Of Rapes, of Buckets, Sarks, and Locks,
    While we neglect
To shaw their betters; this provokes
    Me to reflect

On the learn'd days of Gawn Dunkell;*
Our country then a tale could tell,
Europe had nane mair snack and snell   *clever sharp*
 At verse or prose:
Our kings† were poets too themsell,
 Bauld and jocose.

To Ed'nburgh, Sir, whene'er ye come,
I'll wait upon ye, there's my thumb,
Were't frae the gill-bells to the drum‡
 And tak' a bout,
And faith I hope we'll not sit dumb,
 Nor yet cast out.

Hallow-Fair

At *Hallowmas,* whan nights grow lang,
 And *starnies* shine fu' clear,   *little stars*
When *fock,* the nippin cald to bang,   *folk defeat*
 Their winter *hap-warms* wear,   *mantles*
Near Edinbrough a fair there hads,   *holds*
 I wat there 's nane whase name is,
For strappin dames and sturdy lads,
 And cap and stoup, mair famous *cup tankard more*
  Than it that day.

Upo' the tap o' ilka lum   *every chimney*
 The sun began to keek,   *peep*
And bad the trig made maidens come
 A sightly joe to seek   *lover*
At *Hallow-fair,* whare browsters rare *brewers*
 Keep gude ale on the gantries,   *stands*
And dinna scrimp ye o' a skair   *do not share*
 O' kebbucks frae their pantries,   *cheeses*
  Fu' saut that day.

* Gavin Douglas (1475?–1522), bishop of Dunkeld, and translator of the *Aeneid.*
† James the First and Fifth. *Ramsay's note.*
‡ From half an hour before twelve, at noon, when the music-bells begin to play, (frequently called the gill-bells, from people taking a whetting dram at that time,) to the drum at ten o'clock at night; when the drum goes round to warn sober folks to call for a bill. *Ramsay's note.*

Here country John in bonnet blue,
  An' eke his Sunday claise on,   *also*
Rins efter Meg wi' *rokelay* new,
  An' sappy kisses lays on;
She'll tauntin say, Ye silly coof!
  Be o' your gab mair spairin;
He'll tak the hint, and criesh her loof   *grease palm*
  Wi' what will buy her fairin,   *lunch*
    To chow that day.

Here chapman billies tak their stand,   *pedlar fellows*
  An' shaw their *bonny wallies;*   *wares*
Wow, but they lie fu' gleg aff hand   *readily*
  To trick the silly fallows:
Heh, Sirs! what cairds and tinklers come, *gypsies and tinkers*
  An' *ne'er-do-weel* horse-coupers,
An' spae-wives fenzying to be dumb,   *fortune-tellers*
  Wi' a' siclike landloupers,   *vagabonds*
    To thrive that day.

Here Sawny cries, frae Aberdeen;
  "Come ye to me fa need: *who*
The brawest *shanks* that e'er were seen *hose*
  I'll sell ye cheap an' guid.
I wyt they are as protty hose
  As come fae *weyr* or *leem*:   *wire loom*
Here tak a rug, and shaw's your pose: *bargain money*
  Forseeth, my ain's but teem   *own's empty*
    An' light this day."

Ye wives, as ye gang thro' the fair,   *go*
  O mak your bargains hooly!
O' a' thir wylie lowns beware,   *these rogues*
  Or fegs they will ye spulzie.   *figs spoil*
For fairn-year *Meg Thamson* got,   *last-year*
  Frae thir mischievous villains,   *these*
A scaw'd bit o' a penny note,   *worthless*
  That lost a score o' shillins
    To her that day.

The dinlin drums alarm our ears,
  The serjeant screechs fu' loud,
"A' gentlemen and volunteers

That wish your country gude,
Come here to me, and I shall gie
Twa guineas and a crown,
A bowl o' *punch*, that like the sea
Will soum a lang dragoon   *swim*
Wi' ease this day."

Without the cuissers prance and nicker,   *lancers*
An' our the ley-rig scud;   *grass-field drive*
In tents the carles bend the bicker,   *old men tankard*
An' rant an' roar like wud.   *mad*
Then there's sic yellowchin and din,   *yelling*
Wi' wives and wee-anes gablin,   *children*
That ane might true they were a-kin   *believe*
To a' the tongues at Babylon,
Confus'd that day.

Whan *Phoebus* ligs in *Thetis* lap,
Auld Reekie gies them shelter,   *Edinburgh*
Whare cadgily they kiss the cap,   *gaily cup*
An' ca't round helter-skelter.
Jock Bell gaed furth to play his freaks,   *pranks*
Great cause he had to rue it,
For frae a stark Lochaber aix   *strong*
He gat a *clamihewit*   *heavy blow*
Fu' sair that night.

"Ohon!" quo' he, "I'd rather be
By *sword* or *bagnet* stickit,   *bayonet*
Than hae my crown or body wi'
Sic deadly weapons nicket."
Wi' that he gat anither straik   *stroke*
Mair weighty than before,
That gar'd his feckless body aik,   *made useless ache*
An' spew the reikin gore,
Fu' red that night.

He peching on the cawsey lay, *breathing hard pavement*
O' kicks and cuffs weel sair'd;   *served*
A *Highland* aith the serjeant gae,   *oath gave*
"She maun pe see our guard."   *must be seeing*
Out spak the weirlike corporal,   *warlike*
"Pring in ta drunken sot."

They trail'd him ben, an' by my saul,   *in*
  He paid his drunken groat,
    For that neist day.   *next*

Good fock, as ye come frae the fair,   *folk*
  Bide yont frae this black squad;   *keep away from*
There's nae sic savages elsewhere
Allow'd to wear cockade.
Than the strong lion's hungry maw,
  Or tusk o' Russian bear,
Frae their wanruly fellin paw   *unruly*
Mair cause ye hae to fear
    Your death that day.

A wee soup drink dis unco weel   *very well*
  To had the heart aboon;   *hold above*
It's good as lang's a canny chiel
Can stand steeve in his shoon.   *upright*
But gin a birkie's owr weel sair'd,   *chap's*
  It gars him aften stammer   *makes*
To *pleys* that bring him to the guard,
An' eke the *Council-chawmir,*
    Wi' shame that day.

                                                       Robert Fergusson

The Farmer's Ingle

Whan gloming grey out o'er the welkin keeks,   *peeps*
  Whan Batie ca's his owsen to the byre,   *oxen*
Whan Thrasher John, sair dung, his barn-door steeks,   *beaten*
  And lusty lasses at the dighting tire: *winnowing*
What bangs fu' leal the e'enings coming cauld,   *defeats truly*
  And gars snaw-tapit winter freeze in vain;
Gars dowie mortals looks baith blyth and bauld,   *melancholy*
  Nor fley'd wi' a' the poortith o' the plain;   *frightened poverty*
Begin, my Muse, and chant in hamely strain.

Frae the big stack, weel winnow't on the hill,
  Wi' divets theekit frae the weet and drift,   *sods   thatched*
Sods, peats, and heath'ry trufs the chimley fill,   *turfs*
  And gar their thick'ning smeek salute the lift;   *make smoke   sky*

The gudeman, new come hame, is blyth to find,
  Whan he out o'er the halland flings his een,   *partition*
That ilka turn is handled to his mind,   *every*
  That a' his housie looks sae cosh and clean;   *snug*
For cleanly house looes he, tho' e'er sae mean.

Weel kens the gudewife that the pleughs require   *ploughmen*
  A heartsome meltith, and refreshing synd   *meal*   *wash down*
O' nappy liquor, o'er a bleezing fire: *heady*
  Sair wark and poortith douna weel be join'd.   *..poverty* *cannot*
Wi' buttered bannocks now the girdle reeks,   *griddle*
  I' the far nook the bowie briskly reams   *wooden milk-vessel* *foams*
The readied kail stand by the chimley cheeks,   *broth* *chimney side*
  And had the riggin het wi' welcome steams,   *holds*   *roof*
Whilk than the daintiest kitchen nicer seems.   *Which*

Frae this lat gentler gabs a lesson lear;   *mouths*   *learn*
  Wad they to labouring lend an eidant hand,   *diligent*
They'd rax fell strang upo' the simplest fare,   *grow*
  Nor find their stamacks ever at a stand.
Fu' hale and healthy wad they pass the day,
  At night in calmest slumbers dose fu' sound,
Nor doctor need their weary life to spae,   *foretell*
  Nor drogs their noddle and their sense confound,   *drugs*
Till death slip sleely on, and gi'e the hindmost wound.

On sicken food has mony a doughty deed   *such*
  By Caledonia's ancestors been done;
By this did mony wight fu' weirlike bleed   *warlike*
  In brulzies frae the dawn to set o' sun: *broils*
'Twas this that brac'd their gardies, stiff and strang,   *arms*
  That bent the deidly yew in antient days,
Laid Denmark's daring sons on yird alang,   *earth*
  Gar'd Scottish thristles bang the Roman bays;
For near our crest their heads they doughtna raise.

The couthy cracks begin whan supper's o'er,   *sociable gossip*
  The cheering bicker gars them glibly gash   *beaker* *makes* *talk*
O' simmer's showery blinks and winters sour,
  Whase floods did erst their mailins produce hash: *farms*
'Bout kirk and market eke their tales gae on,
  How Jock woo'd Jenny here to be his bride,

And there how Marion, for a bastard son,
    Upo' the cutty-stool was forc'd to ride,   *stool of repentence*
The waefu' scald o' our Mess John to bide.   *scolding   Clergyman*

The fient a chiep's amang the bairnies now;   *murmur's children*
    For a' their anger's wi' their hunger gane:
Ay maun the childer, wi' a fastin mou',   *children*
    Grumble and greet, and make an unco mane,   *cry moan*
In rangles round before the ingle's low: *clusters fire's glow*
    Frae gudame's mouth auld warld tale they hear,
O' Warlocks louping round the Wirrikow,   *Goblin*
    O' gaists that win in glen and kirk-yard drear,   *dwell*
Whilk touzles a' their tap, and gars them shak wi' fear.   *rumple top*
    makes

For weel she trows that fiends and fairies be
    Sent frae the de'il to fleetch us to our ill;   *flatter*
That ky hae tint their milk wi' evil eie,   *cows lost*
    And corn been scowder'd on the glowing kill.   *scorched kiln*
O mock na this, my friends ! but rather mourn,
    Ye in life's brawest spring wi' reason clear,
Wi' eild our idle fancies a' return,   *age*
    And dim our dolefu' days wi' bairnly fear;   *childish*
The mind's ay cradled whan the grave is near.

Yet thrift, industrious, bides her latest days,
    Tho' age her sair dow'd front wi' runcles wave,   *faded wrinkles*
Yet frae the russet lap the spindle plays,
    Her e'enin stent reels she as weel's the lave.   *stint rest*
On some feast-day, the wee-things buskit braw   *dressed finely*
    Shall heeze her heart up wi' a silent joy,   *lift up*
Fu' cadgie that her head was up and saw   *happy*
    Her ain spun cleething on a darling oy,   *own grandchild*
Careless tho' death shou'd make the feast her foy.   *farewell feast*

In its auld lerroch yet the deas remains,   *site dais*
    Whare the gudeman aft streeks him at his ease,   *stretches*
A warm and canny lean for weary banes
    O' lab'rers doil'd upo' the wintry leas: *sore-worn*
Round him will badrins and the colly come,   *puss*
    To wag their tail, and cast a thankfu' eie
To him who kindly flings them mony a crum
    O' kebbock whang'd, and dainty fadge to prie;   *cheese sliced thick cake*
This a' the boon they crave, and a' the fee.

Frae him the lads their morning counsel tak,
  What stacks he wants to thrash, what rigs to till;   *ridges*
How big a birn maun lie on bassie's back,   *burden   old horse's*
  For meal and multure to the thirling mill.   *toll of meal*
Niest the gudewife her hireling damsels bids
  Glowr thro' the byre, and see the hawkies bound,   *Look   cowshed   cows*
Take tent case Crummy tak her wonted tids,   *tantrums*
  And ca' the leglin's treasure on the ground,   *milking   pails*
Whilk spills a kebbuck nice, or yellow pound.   *cheese*

Then a' the house for sleep begin to grien,   *yearn*
  Their joints to slack frae industry a while;
The leaden God fa's heavy on their ein,
  And halflins steeks them frae their daily toil: *half-way   shuts*
The cruizy too can only blink and bleer,   *rush-light*
  The restit ingle's done the maist it dow;   *fire's   can*
Tacksman and cottar eke to bed maun steer,   *Tenant*
  Upo' the cod to clear their drumly pow,   *pillow   muddled head*
Till wauken'd by the dawning's ruddy glow.

Peace to the husbandman and a' his tribe,
  Whase care fells a' our wants frae year to year;
Lang may his sock and couter turn the gleyb,   *ploughshare   coulter*
  And bauks o' corn bend down wi' laded ear.   *strips   /glebe*
May Scotia's simmers ay look gay and green,
  Her yellow har'sts frae scowry blasts decreed;   *showery*
May a' her tenants sit fu' snug and bien,   *comfortable*
  Frae the hard grip of ails and poortith freed,   *poverty*
And a lang lasting train o' peaceful hours succeed.

                                   Robert Fergusson

Leith Races

In July month, ae bonny morn,
  Whan Nature's rokelay green   *mantle*
Was spread o'er ilka rigg o' corn   *every ridge*
  To charm our roving een;   *eyes*
Glouring about I saw a quean,   *Staring   lass*
  The fairest 'neath the lift;   *sky*
Her EEN ware o' the siller sheen,
  Her SKIN like snawy drift,
    Sae white that day.

Quod she, "I ferly unco sair,   *wonder*
    That ye sud musand gae,   *should   musing go*
Ye wha hae sung o' HALLOW-FAIR,
    Her winter's pranks and play:
Whan on LEITH-SANDS the racers rare,
    Wi' Jocky louns are met,   *rogues*
Their orro pennies there to ware,   *extra   waste*
    And drown themsel's in debt
        Fu' deep that day."

An' wha are ye, my winsome dear,
    That takes the gate sae early?   *yay*
Whare do ye win, gin ane may spier,   *dwell   if   ask*
    For I right meikle ferly,   *much   wonder*
That sic braw buskit laughing lass   *such   finely   dressed*
    Thir bonny blinks shou'd gi'e,   *These   glances   give*
An' loup like HEBE o'er the grass,   *leap*
    As wanton and as free
        Frae dule this day.   *From sorrow*

"I dwall amang the caller springs   *fresh*
    That weet the LAND o' CAKES,
And aften tune my canty strings   *merry*
    At BRIDALS and LATE-WAKES:
They ca' me MIRTH; I ne'er was kend   *known*
    To grumble or look sour,
But blyth wad be a lift to lend,
    Gif ye wad sey my pow'r   *try*
        An' pith this day."

A bargain be't, and, by my feggs,   *truly*
    Gif ye will be my mate,   *If*
Wi' you I'll screw the cheery pegs,
    Ye shanna find me blate;   *bashful*
We'll reel an' ramble thro' the sands,
    And jeer wi' a' we meet;
Nor hip the daft and gleesome bands   *miss*
    That fill EDINA's street
        Sae thrang this day.   *busy*

Ere servant maids had wont to rise
    To seeth the breakfast kettle,   *boil*
Ilk dame her brawest ribbons tries,   *Each   finest*

To put her on her mettle,
Wi' wiles some silly chiel to trap,   *fellow*
    (And troth he's fain to get her,)   *glad*
But she'll craw kniefly in his crap,   *crow briskly*
    Whan, wow! he canna flit her   *fly*
        Frae hame that day.

Now, mony a scaw'd and bare-ars'd lown
    Rise early to their wark,
Enough to fley a muckle town,   *frighten   large*
    Wi' dinsome squeel and bark.
"Here is the true an' faithfu' list
    O' Noblemen and Horses;
Their eild, their weight, their height, their grist,   *age   contents*
    That rin for PLATES or PURSES
        Fu' fleet this day."

To WHISKEY PLOOKS that brunt for wooks   *Pimples   burned   weeks*
    On town-guard soldiers faces,
Their barber bauld his whittle crooks,   *razor*
    An' scrapes them for the races:
Their STUMPS erst us'd to *filipegs*,   *kilts*
    Are dight in spaterdashes
Whase barkent hides scarce fend their legs   *encrusted   protect*
    Frae weet, and weary plashes
        O' dirt that day.

"Come, hafe a care (the captain cries),
    On guns your bagnets thraw;   *twist*
Now mind your manual exercise,
    An' marsh down raw by raw."
And as they march he'll glowr about,
    'Tent a' their cuts and scars: *Note*
'Mang them fell mony a gausy snout   *very big*
    Has gusht in birth-day wars,
        Wi' blude that day.

Her *Nanesel* maun be carefu' now,   *[The Captain himself]*
    Nor maun she pe misleard,   *must   unmannerly*
Sin baxter lads hae seal'd a vow   *baker*
    To skelp and clout the guard:
I'm sure AULD REIKIE kens o' nane   *Edinburgh knows   none*
    That wou'd be sorry at it,

Tho' they should dearly pay the kane,   *rent*
An' get their tails weel sautit
    And sair thir days.   *sore*

The tinkler billies i' the Bow   *tinker fellows*
Are now less eidant clinking,   *diligently*
As lang's their pith or siller dow,   *silver allows*
They're daffin', and they're drinking.
Bedown LEITH-WALK what burrochs reel
Of ilka trade and station,   *every*
That gar their wives an' childer feel   *make   children*
Toom weyms for their libation   *Empty stomachs*
    O' drink thir days.

The browster wives thegither harl   *brewer   drag*
A' trash that they can fa' on;
They rake the grounds o' ilka barrel,
To profit by the lawen: *reckoning*
For weel wat they a skin leal het   *know   truly hot*
For drinking needs nae hire;
At drumbly gear they take nae pet;   *muddy goods*
Foul WATER slockens FIRE
    And drouth thir days.

They say, ill ale has been the deid   *death*
O' mony a beirdly lown;   *stout fellow*
Then dinna gape like gleds wi' greed   *kites*
To sweel hail bickers down;   *swill whole tankards*
Gin Lord send mony ane the morn,   *If   many a one next day*
They'll ban fu' sair the time   *curse   sore*
That e'er they toutit aff the horn   *blew the horn (drank)*
Which wambles thro' their weym   *belly*
    Wi' pain that day.

The Buchan bodies thro' the beech
Their bunch of *Findrums* cry,   *fish*
An' skirl out baul', in Norland speech,   *scream   bold   Northland*
"Gueed speldings, fa will buy."   *good dried fish   who*
An' by my saul, they're nae wrang gear   *goods*
To gust a stirrah's mow;   *give taste to a man's mouth*
Weel staw'd wi' them, he'll never spear   *stowed   ask*
    The price o' being fu'
        Wi' drink that day.

Now wyly wights at ROWLY POWL,
    An' flingin' o' the DICE,
Here brake the banes o' mony a soul   *bones*
    Wi' fa's upo' the ice:
At first the gate seems fair an' straught,   *way*
    So they had fairly till her;   *hold   to*
But wow! in spite o' a' their maught,   *might*
    They're rookit o' their siller   *cheated   silver*
        An' goud that day.   *gold*

Around whare'er ye fling your een,
    The HAIKS like wind are scourin';   *Horses*
Some chaises honest folk contain,
    An' some hae mony a WHORE in;
Wi' rose and lilly, red and white,
    They gie themselves sic fit airs,
Like DIAN, they will seem perfite;   *perfect*
    But its nae goud that glitters   *gold*
        Wi' them thir days.

The LYON here, wi' open paw,
    May cleek in mony hunder,   *hook   hundreds*
Wha geck at SCOTLAND and her law,   *toss the head in disdain*
    His wyly talons under;   *cunning*
For ken, tho' JAMIE's laws are auld,
    (Thanks to the wise recorder),
His Lyon yet roars loud and bawld,   *bold*
    To had the Whigs in order   *keep   Hypocrites*
        Sae prime this day.   *prim*

To town-guard DRUM of clangor clear,
    Baith men and steeds are raingit;   *ranged*
Some liveries red or yellow wear,
    And some are tartan spraingit: *striped*
And now the red, the blue e'en-now
    Bids fairest for the market;
But, 'ere the sport be done, I trow
    Their skins are gayly yarkit
        And peel'd thir days.

Siclike in ROBINHOOD debates,   *Thus*
    Whan twa chiels hae a pingle;   *chaps   argument*
E'en-now some couli gets his aits,

An' dirt wi' words they mingle,
Till up loups he, wi' diction fu',
   There's lang and dreech contesting,   *dreary*
For now they're near the point in view;
   Now ten miles frae the question
      In hand that night.

The races o'er, they hale the dools,   *sorrows*
   Wi' drink o' a' kin-kind;
Great feck gae hirpling hame like fools,   *most* *limping*
   The cripple lead the blind.
May ne'er the canker o' the drink
   E'er make out spirits thrawart,   *bad tempered*
'Case we git wharewitha' to wink
   Wi' een as BLUE's a BLAWART   [*a plant*]
      Wi' *straiks* thir days!

Auld Reike, July 21. [1773]   *Edinburgh*

                    Robert Fergusson

APPENDIX B

MEDICAL OPINION AND DATA
UPON WHICH IT IS BASED

Dr. Stanley Bardwell has written especially for this biography the follow-ing clinical analysis of the health record of Robert Burns to be found below.

1. One of the outstanding characteristics of rheumatic fever is its clinical variability. Usual complaints include malaise,* prostration,* feverishness,* loss of appetite,* and migrating joint pain,* redness, and swelling. Once a person is victimized by rheumatic fever, recurrences are the rule. It is apt to wax and wane. Death due to rheumatic fever is a consequence of carditis, an infection of the lining, or the body, or the containing sac of the heart.

2. Rheumatic fever is caused by a preceding infection with a ubiquitous bac-teria called beta-hemolytic streptococcus.

3. Assured diagnosis of rheumatic fever and carditis may be established only with a careful history, physical examination, and electro-cardiagraphic, X-ray, and laboratory studies.

4. In the vast majority of instances, bacterial endocarditis occurs in a set-ting in which a heart valve has been previously damaged by rheumatic fever. Therefore, it can be distinguished from rheumatic fever only by the use of blood culture studies, although it is manifested as well by skin hemorrhages,† enlargement of a painful spleen,† blood in the urine,† and paralysis† due to breaking off of vegetations which occur on the affected heart valve.

5. Bacterial endocarditis has as its principal symptoms: weakness,‡ malaise,‡ feverishness,‡ sweating, weight loss,‡ skin hemorrhages,‡ large tender spleen, occasional joint pains‡ (1/3 of patients), and paralysis.

There is nothing in the record to suggest either venereal disease or the usual stigma of alcoholism. Almost certainly Burns had recurrent attacks of

* Burns mentions all of these symptoms. RTF.
† There is no mention of any of these symptoms in the record. RTF.
‡ Burns mentions these symptoms. RTF.

rheumatic fever. Bacterial endocarditis may have been present terminally, but not necessarily. If rheumatic heart disease is not granted, then endocarditis as a diagnosis is not justified.

Prompt recognition of symptoms, and assessment of the clinical situation would today lead to appropiate treatment with penicillin, or other suitable antibiotics, and possibly cortisone or one of its derivatives.

THE HEALTH RECORD OF ROBERT BURNS
Compiled from his correspondence and other sources

1. Burns in adolescence, as reported later by his brother Gilbert: "My brother, at the age of thirteen, assisted in threshing the crop of corn, and at fifteen was the principal labourer on the farm, for we had no hired servant, male or female. The anguish of mind we felt at our tender years, under these straits and difficulties, was very great. To think of our father growing old (for he was now above fifty) broken down with the long continued fatigues of his life, with a wife and five other children, and in a declining state of circumstances, these reflections produced in my brother's mind and mine sensations of the deepest distress. I doubt not but the hard labour and sorrow of this period of his life, was in a great measure the cause of that depression of spirits with which Robert was so often afflicted through his whole life afterwards. At this time he was almost constantly afflicted in the evenings with a dull headache, which, at a future period of his life, was exchanged for a palpitation of the heart, and a threatening of fainting and suffocation in his bed, in the night time." (Currie I, 70.)

2. Burns at 22, to his father, December 27, 1781: "My health is much about what it was when you were here only my sleep is rather sounder and on the whole I am rather better than otherwise tho it is but by very slow degrees. — The weakness of my nerves has so debilitated my mind that I dare not, either review past events, or look forward into futurity." He goes on to say that he is weary of life, sees nothing ahead for him, and would welcome death. (F I, #4, 40.)

3. "Previous to his leaving Ayrshire," 1786: "At that early period these nocturnal faintings and suffocations were so frequent he always kept a large tub filled with cold water in the place where he slept, and often during the night he rose and plunged himself among the cold water which gave instant relief." Reported by a "bedfellow," to James Grierson of Dalgoner. (*Robert Burns His Associates and Contemporaries*, Chapel Hill, 1953. 54.) See below, no. 45.

4. Burns to his former schoolmaster, John Murdoch, January 15, 1783: "Though indolent, yet so far as an extremely delicate constitution permits, I am not lazy." (F I, #13, 14.)

5. Burns in his Commonplace Book, "March — 84": "There was a certain period in my life that my spirit was broke by repeated losses & disasters, which threatened, & indeed effected the utter ruin of my fortune. My body too was attacked by that most dreadful distemper, a Hypochondria, or confirmed Melancholy." (*Robert Burns's Commonplace Book*, eds. J. C. Ewing and D. W. Cook, Glasgow, 1938. 8.)

6. Of the same period Burns writes to Dr. Moore: "The finishing evil that brought up the rear of this internal file was my hypochondriac complaint being irritated to such a degree, that for three months I was in a diseased state of body and mind, scarcely to be envied by the hopeless wretches who have just got their mittimus." (F I, #125, 112.)

7. Burns' headnote in his Commonplace Book, August, 1784, to a versified prayer probably written in 1781: "A prayer when fainting fits & other alarming symptoms of a Pleurisy or some other dangerous disorder, which indeed still threaten me, first put Nature on the alarm." (Ewing and Cook, 18.)

8. Burns to John Tennant, Jr., September 13, 1784: "My unlucky illness on friday last did not do me a greater disservice than in disappointing me of the pleasure I had promised myself in spending an hour with you." (F I, #18, 19.)

9. Burns to John Ballantine of Ayr, December 13, 1786, describing his arrival in Edinburgh after a convivial party en route: "I have suffered ever since I came to town [he had been there two weeks] with a miserable head-ach & stomach complaint; but am now a good deal better." (F I, #63, 56.)

10. Burns after his first winter in Edinburgh, 1786–1787; comment by Dugald Stewart: "I should have concluded in favour of his habits of sobriety, from all of him that ever fell under my own observation. He told me indeed himself, that the weakness of his stomach was such as to deprive him entirely of any merit in his temperance. I was however somewhat alarmed about the effect of his now comparatively sedentary and luxurious life, when he confessed to me, the first night he spent in my house after his winter's campaign in town, that he had been much disturbed when in bed, by a palpitation at his heart, which, he said, was a complaint to which he had of late become subject." (Currie I, 141.)

11. Burns in his Journal of his Border Tour, May 23–24, 1787: "I am taken

extremely ill with strong feverish symptoms, & take a servant of Mr Hood's
to watch me all night — embittering Remorse scares my fancy at the
gloomy forebodings of death — I am determined to live for the future in
such a manner as not to be scared at the approach of Death." By the 25th
he was about and active. (*Robert Burns His Associates and Contemporaries*,
Chapel Hill, 1953. 118.)

12. Burns to William Nicol, July 29, 1787: "A lingering indisposition has
hung about me for some time and has beaten me out of the use of pen and
ink." (F I, #123, 103.)

13. Burns to Mrs. Dunlop, July 31, 1787: "I have indeed been ailing."
(F I, # 124, 104.)

14. Burns to Dr. John Moore, August 2, 1787: "Of late I have been confined with some lingering complaints originating as I take it in the
stomach. — To divert my spirits a little in this miserable fog of Ennui,
I have taken a whim to give you a history of Myself." (F I, #125, 104.)

15. Burns in his Journal of his Highland Tour, September 15, 1787, at
Kinross: "A fit of the Colic." (*Journal of a Tour in the Highlands made in
the Year 1787*, ed. J. C. Ewing, London and Glasgow, 1927. 17.)

16. Burns to Patrick Miller, October 20, 1787: "I was still more unlucky
in catching a miserable cold for which the medical gentlemen have ordered
me into close confinement, 'under pain of Death!' the severest of penalties.
— In two or three days, if I get better, . . . I will take a ride to Dumfries directly." (F I, #144, 131.)

17. From a poem, *Address to the Toothache*, probably of this period: "Thou
hell of a' diseases." Burns continued to suffer from the toothache. See
below, no. 54, 56.

18. Burns to Robert Ainslie, November 23, 1787: "You will think it romantic when I tell you, that I find the idea of your friendship almost
necessary to my existence. You assume a proper length of face in my
bitter hours of blue devilism, and you laugh fully up to my highest wishes
at my good things." (F I, #153, 140.)

19. Burns to John Beugo, December 4?, 1787: "A certain sour-faced old
acquaintance called Glauber's salts hinders me from my lesson tonight."
Burns and Beugo were taking French lessons together. (F I, #156, 142.)

20. Burns to various correspondents, early December, 1787, to early
March, 1788, about an injury to his knee:
a. To Agnes M'Lehose (Clarinda), December 8, 1787: "Tonight I was to
have had the very great pleasure [of seeing you] — I was intoxicated with

the idea. — but an unlucky fall from a coach has so bruised one of my knees, that I can't stir my leg off the cushion." (F I, #159, 143.)

b. To Margaret Chalmers, December 12, 1787: "I am here under the care of a surgeon, with a bruised limb extended on a cushion; and the tints of my mind vying with the livid horror preceding a midnight thunderstorm. A drunken coachman was the cause of the first, and incomparably the lightest evil; misfortune, bodily constitution, hell and myself, have formed a 'Quadruple Alliance' to guarantee the other. I got my fall on Saturday, and am getting slowly better." (F I, #160, 144.)

c. To Clarinda, December 12, 1787: "I stretch a point indeed, my dearest Madam, when I answer your card on the rack of my present agony." (F I, #161, 145.)

d. To Margaret Chalmers, December 19, 1787: "The atmosphere of my soul is vastly clearer than when I wrote you last. For the first time, yesterday I crossed the room on crutches. It would do your heart good to see my bardship, not on my *poetic*, but on my *oaken* stilts; throwing my best leg with an air." (F I, #162, 145.)

e. To Clarinda, December 20, 1787: "My limb now allows me to sit in some peace; to walk I have yet no prospect of, as I can't mark it to the ground." (F I, #162, 147.)

f. To Clarinda, December 27(?), 1788: "My limb is vastly better; but I have not any use of it without my crutches. Monday, for the first time, I dine at a neighbour's, next door. As soon as I can go so far, *even in a coach*, my first visit shall be to you." The dating of this letter is discussed in *Studies in Scottish Literature*, VI, 4, April 1969, 260–262. (F I, # 169, 153.)

g. To Clarinda, January 4, 1788: "Tomorrow evening I intend taking a chair, and paying a visit at Park-Place to a much valued old friend." If Clarinda is to be at home, he will call on her. (F I, #170, 155.)

h. To John Ballantine, January, 1788: "Some weeks bypast indeed I have been a cripple in one of my legs, owing to a fall by the drunken stupidity of a coachman. — I am got a good deal better, but can walk little yet without my crutches." (F I, #173, 158.)

i. To Clarinda, January 14, 1788: "My limb has been so well today that I have gone up and down stairs often without my staff. Tomorrow, I hope to walk once again on my own legs to dinner. It is only next street." (F I, #178, 164.)

j. To Clarinda, January 20, 1788: "The impertinence of fools has joined with a return of an old indisposition to make me good for nothing today. . . . A little alarm last night and today that I am mortal, has made such a revolution in my spirits! . . . I can scarce hold up my head." Next day, he writes, "I am, my lovely friend, much better this morning, on the whole; but I have a horrid languor on my spirits." (F I, #182, 168.)

k. To Mrs. Dunlop, January 21, 1788: "After six weeks' confinement, I am beginning to walk across the room. They have been six horrible weeks; anguish and low spirits made me unfit to read, write, or think." (F I, #184, 171.)

l. To Margaret Chalmers, January 29, 1788: "Now for that wayward unfortunate thing, myself. . . . The sport, the miserable victim of rebellious pride, hypochondriac imagination, agonizing sensibility, and bedlam passions! . . . Seriously though, life presents me with but a melancholy path: but my limb will soon be sound, and I shall struggle on." (Date corrected by Professor G. Ross Roy, PBSA, 1967. 357.) (F I, #185, 177.)

m. To John Tennant, February 7, 1788: "I met with an ugly accident about ten weeks ago, by the drunkeness of a Coachman; I fell and dislocated the cap of my knee, which laid me up a cripple, that I have but just lately laid aside my crutches. — I shall not have the use of my limb as formerly, for some months, perhaps years to come." (F I, #197, 183.)

n. To John Richmond, February 7, 1788: "I have not got, nor will not for some time, get the better of my bruised knee; but I have laid aside my crutches." (F I, #196, 182.)

o. To the Rev. John Skinner, February 14, 1788: "I have been a cripple now near three months, though I am getting vastly better." (F I, #203, 188.)

p. To William Cruikshank, March 3, 1788: (Burns has left Edinburgh where the accident occurred, and where he lived with Cruikshank.) "My unlucky knee is rather worse, and I fear for some time will scarcely stand the fatigue of my Excise instructions." (F I, #214, 199.)

21. Burns to Richard Brown, March 20, 1788: "Watching, fatigue, and a load of Care almost too heavy for my shoulders, have in some degree actually fever'd me." (F I, #228, 212.)

22. Burns to Mrs. Dunlop, April 28, 1788: "I prepared with the sincerest pleasure to meet you at the Mount, and came to my brother's on Saturday night, to set out on Sunday, but for some nights preceding I had slept in an apartment where the force of the winds and rains was mitigated by being sifted through numberless apertures in the windows, walls, &c. In consequence I was on Sunday, Monday, and part of Tuesday, unable to stir out of bed, with all the miserable effects of a violent cold." (F I, #238, 220.)

23. Burns to John Ballantine, July, 1788: He would transcribe a poem for Ballantine except that he has a "bruised finger." A brief note only. (F I, 259, 240.)

24. Burns to Robert Graham of Fintry, September 23, 1788: "Though I am scarce able to hold up my head with this fashionable influenza, which

is just now the rage hereabouts, yet with half a spark of life, I would thank you for your most generous favor of the 14th." (Burns is now living in a far from weathertight hut on a newly rented farm while the farmstead is abuilding.) (F I, #273, 259.)

25. Burns to Dr. James Mundell(?), October, 1788: "As my symptoms are continuing milder, I have not waited on you; but my liquid drug has failed. — You will please send me by my servant the bearer, a recruit of the g —— d D —— n. — I am still using the unction, tho' thank Heaven, not extreme unction." (F I, #277, 265.)

26. Burns to William Cruikshank, December, 1788: "My knee, I believe, never will be entirely well; and an unlucky fall this winter has made it still worse." (F I, #292, 281.)

27. Burns to Mrs. Dunlop, June 21, and July 7, 1789: "Will you take the effusions, the miserable effusions, of low spirits, just as they flow from their bitter spring? I know not of any particular cause for this worst of all my foes besetting me; but for some time my soul has been beclouded with a thickening atmosphere of evil imaginations and gloomy presages." "As I mentioned to you in a letter you will by this time have received, I have since I was at Dunlop been rather hurried and out of spirits." (F I, #350, 341, 343.)

28. Burns to Mrs. Dunlop, November 8, 1789: (He is now riding thirty to forty miles a day in all weathers as an Exciseman.) "I have somehow got a most violent cold; and in the stupid, disagreable predicament of a stuffed, aching head and an unsound, sickly crassis [temperament, disposition], do I sit down to thank you for yours of the nineteenth." (F I, #371, 368.)

29. Burns to Mrs. Dunlop, December 13, 1789: "I am groaning under the miseries of a diseased nervous System; . . . For now near three weeks I have been so ill with a nervous head-ach, that I have been obliged to give up for a time my Excise-books, being scarce able to lift my head, much less to ride once a week over ten muir Parishes." He continues with comments on the rapid shifts between health and illness, and adds reflections on death and immortality. (F I, #374, 372.)

30. Burns to William Nicol, December 13, 1789: "I have been so ill, my ever dear Friend, that I have not been able to go over the threshold of my door since I saw you." (F I, #375, 375.)

31. Burns to Lady Winifred Maxwell Constable, December 16, 1789: He speaks of an "unlucky indisposition" which had prevented his keeping an engagement. (F I, #377, 376.)

32. Burns to Lady Elizabeth Cunningham, December 23, 1789: He thanks her for a letter which "came very seasonably to his aid amid the cheerless gloom and sinking despondency of December weather and diseased nerves." (F I, #379, 378.)

33. Burns to his brother Gilbert, January 11, 1790: "I have not in my present frame of mind much appetite for exertion in writing. — My nerves are in a damnable State. — I feel that horrid hypochondria pervading every atom of my body & soul. — This Farm has undone my enjoyment of myself. — It is a ruinous affair on all hands. — But let it go to hell! I'll fight it out and be off with it." (F II, #381, 1.)

34. Burns to William Dunbar, January 14, 1790: "I have had a tract of bad health most part of this winter, else you had heard from me ere now. — Thank Heaven, I am now got so much better as to be able to partake a little in the enjoyments of life." (F II, #382, 2.)

35. Letter to Mrs. Dunlop, January 25, 1790: "My health is greatly better, and I now begin once more to share in satisfaction and enjoyment with the rest of my fellow-creatures." (F II, #385, 4.)

36. Burns to Clarinda, February ?, 1790: "I have indeed been ill, Madam, the whole winter. An incessant head-ache, depression of spirits, and all the truly miserable consequences of a deranged nervous system, have made dreadful havoc of my health and peace. Add to all this, a line of life into which I have lately entered obliges me to ride, on the average, at least 200 miles each week. However, thank Heaven, I am now greatly better in my health." (F II, #388, 7–8.)

37. Burns to Alexander Dalziel, October 5, 1790: "A few days after I received yours I was seized with a slow, illformed fever from which I am just risen out of a weary bed of Sickness; & if this is not apology enough, I must inform you farther that I have likewise had a most malignant Squinancy [subacute phlegonous tonsillitis] which had me very near the precincts of the Grave. — I am now got greatly better, though by no means in a confirmed state of health. — Yesterday, for the first time, I rode as far as Dumfries [from Ellisland, about six miles]." (F II, #422, 43–44.) Dr. Douglas Guthrie of Edinburgh was kind enough to search out the definition of "squinancy."

38. Burns to Mrs. Dunlop, October 6, 1790: "I was just beginning to get the better of a malignant squinancy & slow fever which had tormented me for three weeks & had actually brought me to the brink of the grave." (F II, #423, 45.)

39. Burns to Mrs. Dunlop, February 7, 1791: "When I tell you, Madam,

that by a fall, not from my horse but with my horse, I have been a cripple some time, & that this is the first day my arm & hand have been able to serve me in writing, you will allow that it is too good an apology for my seemingly ungrateful silence." (F II, #435, 55.)

40. Burns to Peter Hill, March, 1791: "I have been this week plagued with an indigestion." (F II, #440, 62.)

41. Burns to Mrs. Dunlop, April 11, 1791: "This is the greatest effort my broken arm has yet made." (F II, #443, 69.) Burns refers here, apparently, to a later accident than the one mentioned in no. 38 above.

42. Burns to A. F. Tytler, April, 1791: He speaks of "the unfortunate accident I have met with," and adds later, "A day or two after I received your letter my horse came down with me and broke my right arm." (F II, #445, 70.)

43. Burns to Lady Winifred Maxwell Constable, April 25, 1791: He speaks of "the unlucky accident of having lately broken my right arm." (F II, #448, 72.)

44. Burns to Peter Hill, October, 1791: "A poor devil nailed to an elbow chair, writhing in anguish with a bruised leg, laid on a stool before him, is in a fine situation truly for saying bright things." (F II, #475, 95.) This accident is Burns' fourth since moving to Ellisland farm in June, 1788, and his third in 1791.

45. Mrs. Dunlop to Burns, December 30, 1792 and March 16, 1793: "[Dec. 30] I was so ill that morning you left us I could not leave my bed till towards dinner time. It was no cordial for my disappointment in not seeing you when I heard from Keith how much you were complaining yourself, and when Adair on his arrival confirmed the continuance of your still doing the same as long as he and you were together." [Burns and Adair had made a visit to Harvieston, in the Devon Valley, in the autumn of 1787.] "[March 16] How does the cold bath suit this weather? We are in snow here." (*Robert Burns and Mrs. Dunlop*, London, 1898. 371 and 380.) These references seem to say that Burns had continued his cold baths at Harvieston in 1787, and at Dunlop in 1792. See above, no. 3.

46. Burns to Mrs. Dunlop, January 2, 1793: "I am better, though not quite free of my complaint." (F II, #529, 190.)

47. Burns to Robert Graham of Fintry, January 5, 1793: (Graham was on the Excise Board and Burns is trying to get a better post.) He urges his "hardy constitution." Burns obviously considers himself a vigorous and

active man who has suffered from bouts of illness. And he leads, as he always has done, a vigorous and active life. (F II, #530, 145.)

48. Burns to Maria Riddell, November, 1793: "Here I sit, altogether Novemberish, a damn'd melange of Fretfulness & melancholy; not enough of the one to rouse me to passion, nor of the other to repose me in torpor; my soul flouncing & fluttering round her tenement, like a wild Finch caught amid the horrors of winter & newly thrust into a cage. (F II, #596, 217.)

49. Burns to James Johnson, February, 1794: "I have, all this winter, been plagued with low spirits & blue devils, so that I have almost hung my harp upon the willow trees." (F II, #616, 233.)

50. Burns to Alexander Cunningham, February 25, 1794: "For these two months I have not been able to lift a pen. My constitution and frame were, ab origine, blasted with a deep incurable taint of hypochondria, which poisons my existence." (F II, #619, 234-35.)

51. Burns to Mrs. Dunlop, June 25, 1794: After an apology for neglect of his correspondence, he writes, "To tell you that I have been in poor health, will not be excuse enough, though it is true. I am afraid that I am about to suffer for the follies of my youth. My medical friends threaten me with a flying gout; but I trust they are mistaken." (F II, #628, 246.) Burns is now 35. The following definition of "flying gout" received through the courtesy of Dr. Douglas Guthrie of Edinburgh: "a term applied to gouty or rheumatic cases in which there is no swelling of the joints, but pain in their interior, which frequently changes its seat."

52. Burns to Mrs. Dunlop, September, 1794: "I am so poorly today as to be scarce able to hold my pen." (F II, #638, 258.)

53. Burns to Maria Riddell, Spring, 1795: "I am so ill as to be scarce able to hold this miserable pen to this miserable paper." (F II, #668, 299.)

54. Burns to William Creech, May 30, 1795: "At present the delightful sensations of an omnipotent Tooth-ach so engross all my inner man, as to put it out of my power even to write Nonsense." (F II, #671, 302.)

55. Burns to Maria Riddell, June or July, 1795: "The health you wished me in your Morning's Card is I think, flown from me forever. — I have not been able to leave my bed today, till about an hour ago." (F II, #674, 304.)

56. Burns to George Thomson, July 3, 1795: "I am at present quite occupied with the charming sensations of the Tooth-Ach." (F II, #673, 303.)

57. Burns to Mrs. Dunlop, January 31, 1796: "The Autumn robbed me of my only daughter & darling child, & that at a distance too & so rapidly as to put it out of my power to pay the last duties to her. — I had scarcely begun to recover from that shock, when I became myself the victim of a most severe Rheumatic fever, & long the die spun doubtful; until after many weeks of sick-bed, it seems to have turned up more life, & I am beginning to crawl across my room, & once indeed have been before my own door in the street." (F II, #688, 316.)

58. Burns to George Thomson, April, 1796: "Alas! my dear Thomson, I fear it will be some time ere I tune my lyre again! . . . Almost ever since I wrote you last [in February], I have only known Existence by the pressure of the heavy hand of Sickness; & have counted time by the repercussions of Pain! Rheumatism, Cold, & Fever have formed, to me, a terrible Trinity in Unity, which makes me close my eyes in misery, & open them without hope." (F II, 693, 319.)

59. Burns to George Thomson, May, 1796: "I cannot boast of returning health. I have now reason to believe that my complaint is a flying gout: — a damnable business!" (F II, #694, 321.)

60. Letter to James Johnson, about June 1, 1796: "How are you, my dear Friend? & how comes on yr fifth volume? — You may probably think that for some time past I have neglected you & your work; but, Alas, the hand of pain, & sorrow, & care has these many months lain heavy on me! — Personal & domestic affliction have almost entirely banished that alacrity & life with which I used to woo the rural Muse of Scotia. — In the meantime let us finish what we have so well begun. —. . . Many a merry meeting this Publication has given us, & possibly it may give us more, though, alas! I fear it — This protracting, slow, consuming illness which hangs over me, will, I doubt much, my ever dear friend, arrest my sun before he has well reached his middle carreer, & will turn over the Poet to far other and more important concerns than studying the brilliancy of Wit or the pathos of Sentiment. — However, Hope is the cordial of the human heart, & I endeavour to cherish it as well as I can." (F II, #696, 322.)

61. Burns to Maria Riddell, June 1, 1796: "I am in such miserable health as to be utterly incapable of shewing my loyalty in any way. — . . . Would you have me in such circumstances copy you out a Love-song? No! if I must write, let it be Sedition, or Blasphemy, or something else that begins with B [Bawdy?], so that I may grin with the grin of iniquity, & rejoice with the rejoicing of an apostate Angel." (F II, #697, 323.)

62. Burns to James Clarke, June 26, 1796: (Burns had helped Clarke with

a loan, which Clarke was repaying in installments.) "Still, still the victim of affliction; were you to see the emaciated figure who now holds the pen to you, you would not know your old friend. — Whether I shall ever get about again, is only known to Him, the Great Unknown, whose creature I am. — Alas, Clarke, I begin to fear the Worst! As to my individual Self, I am tranquil; — I would despise myself if I were not: but Burns's poor widow! & half a dozen of his dear little ones, helpless orphans, there I am weak as a woman's tear." (F II, #698, 323–24.)

63. Burns to George Thomson, July 4, 1796: "I recd. your songs: but my health being so precarious nay dangerously situated, that as a last effort I am here at a sea-bathing quarters. — Besides inveterate rheumatism, my appetite is quite gone, & I am so emaciated as to be scarce able to support myself on my own legs. — Alas! is this a time for me to woo the Muses? However, I am still anxiously willing to serve your work; & if possible I shall try." (F II, #699, 324.)

64. Burns to Alexander Cunningham, from Brow, July 7, 1796: "Alas! my friend, I fear the voice of the Bard will soon be heard among you no more! For these eight or ten months I have been ailing, sometimes bedfast & sometimes not; but these last three months I have been tortured with an excruciating rheumatism, which has reduced me to nearly the last stage. — You actually would not know me if you saw me. — Pale, emaciated, & so feeble as occasionally to need help from my chair — my spirits fled! fled! — but I can no more on the subject — only the Medical folks tell me that my last & only chance is bathing & country quarters & riding." He continues, asking how he can afford it, with his pay reduced and his family to support. (F II, #700, 325.)

65. Burns to James Armour, his father-in-law, July 10, 1796: "I have now been a week at salt water, & though I think I have got some good by it, yet I have some secret fears that this business will be dangerous if not fatal." (F II, #701, 326.)

66. Burns to his brother Gilbert, July 10, 1796: "It will be no very pleasing news to you to be told that I am dangerously ill, & not likely to get better. — An inveterate rheumatism has reduced me to such a state of debility, & my appetite is tottaly gone, so that I can scarcely stand on my legs. — I have been a week at sea-bathing, & I will continue there or in a friend's house in the country all summer." (F II, #703, 326–27.)

67. Burns to his cousin, James Burness, of Montrose, July 12, 1796: (He is being dunned by a tailor, partly for the expense of his volunteer's uniform, and asks his cousin for ten pounds.) "The worst of it is, my health was coming about finely; you know & my Physician assures me that

melancholy & low spirits are half my disease, guess then my horrors since this business began." (F II, #705, 328.)

68. Burns to James Gracie, July 13, 1796: "It would be doing high injustice to this place not to acknowledge that my rheumatisms have derived great benefit from it already; but, alas, my loss of appetite still continues." (F II, #707, 329.)

69. Burns to his wife, July 14, 1796: "I have delayed writing until I could tell you what effect sea-bathing was likely to produce. It would be injustice to deny that it has eased my pains, and I think has strengthened me; but my appetite is still extremely bad. No flesh nor fish can I swallow: porridge and milk are the only things I can taste." (F II, #708, 329.)

70. Maria Riddell, describing her last meeting with Burns, during the time he was at Brow: "I was struck with his appearance on entering the room. The stamp of death was imprinted on his features. He seemed already touching the brink of eternity. His first salutation was, 'Well, Madam, have you any commands for the other world?' I replied that it seemed a doubtful case which of us should be there soonest, and that I hoped he would yet live to write my epitaph. (I was then in a bad state of health.) He looked in my face with an air of great kindness, and expressed his concern at seeing me look so ill, with his accustomed sensibility. At table he ate little or nothing, and he complained of having entirely lost the tone of his stomach. We had a long and serious conversation. . . . I had seldom seen his mind greater or more collected. There was frequently a considerable vivacity in his sallies, and they would probably have had a greater share, had not concern and dejection I could not disguise, damped the spirit of pleasantry he seemed not unwilling to indulge." (Currie I, 221, 223.)

71. John Syme to Alexander Cunningham, July 17, 1796: "I have your favour covering letter to the Bard which I delivered personally. He poor fellow is in a very bad state of health — I am extremely alarmed, not only by the cadaverous aspect and shaken frame of Burns, but from the accounts which I have heard from the first Faculty here — But I entertain strong hopes that the vigor of his former stamina will conquer his present illness, and that by care & the attention & advice he receives from Dr Maxwell he will recover — I do not mean to alarm you but really poor Burns is very ill — " (From author's transcript. See P. S. for p. 365.)

72. John Syme to Alexander Cunningham, July 19, 1796: "The illness is — the whole system debilitated & gone." (Author's transcript.)

73. Notes taken down from Mrs. Burns by John M'Diarmid: "Burns

thought himself dying before he went to the Brow. He seemed afraid however of dwelling on the subject, considering Mrs. B's situation [momentarily expecting a baby]. On one occasion he said distinctly, 'Dont be afraid: I'll be more respected a hundred years after I'm dead than I am at present.' He was not above a week at the Brow when he returned. [It was 15 days.] Mrs. Burns was so struck with the change in his appearance, that she became almost speechless. From this period he was closely confined to bed, and was scarcely 'himself' for half an hour together. By this, it is meant that his mind wandered, and that his nervous system was completely unhinged. He was aware of the infirmity himself, and told his wife that she was to touch him, and remind him that he was going wrong. The day before he died, he called very quickly and with a hale voice, 'Gilbert! Gilbert!' Three days before he died, he got out of bed, and his wife found him sitting in a corner of the room with the bed clothes around him. Mrs. B got assistance, and he suffered himself to be gently led back to bed. But for the fit, his strength would have been unequal to such an exertion." (Life and Works of Robert Burns, ed. P. Hately Waddell, Glasgow, 1867. II, xxiv.)

74. John Syme to Alexander Cunningham, July 21, 1796: "Burns departed this morning at 5 oClock." (Author's transcript. See P. S. for p. 365.)

75. "According to popular tradition, 'early in the month of January [1796], when his health was in the course of improvement, Burns tarried too late at a jovial party in the Globe Tavern. Before returning home, he unluckily remained for some time in the open air and, overpowered by the effects of the liquor he had drunk, fell asleep. In these circumstances and in the peculiar condition to which a severe medicine had reduced his constitution, a fatal chill penetrated to his bones; he reached home with the seeds of a rheumatic fever already in possession of his weakened frame.'" (The Life and Works of Robert Burns, ed. Robert Chambers, rev. William Wallace, Edinburgh and London, 1896. IV, 254.)

76. "From October 1795, to the January following, an accidental complaint confined him to the house. A few days after he began to go abroad, he dined at a tavern, and returned home about three o'clock in a very cold morning, benumbed and intoxicated. This was followed by an attack of rheumatism, which confined him about a week." (Currie I, 219.) But Josiah Walker, who visited Burns in November, 1795, "observed no unfavorable change in his looks," and found him active, and happy to go on walks. However, Burns wrote to Robert Cleghorn, January, 1796: "Since I saw you, I have been much the child of disaster. — Scarcely began to recover the loss of an only daughter & darling child,* I became

* Elizabeth Riddell Burns died in September, 1795.

myself a victim of a rheumatic fever, which brought me to the borders of the grave. — After many weeks of a sick-bed, I am just beginning to crawl about." (F II, #687, 315.) The record above reveals that Burns had fallen victim to a rheumatic fever long before the exposure mentioned by Currie and Chambers, if indeed, it did occur. There is no substantiated source for the story.

77. Hately Waddell quotes both a Gilbert Baird and a Mrs. Marion Hunter, who claimed to have known Burns, as saying he was pockmarked. (II, xxvii and xxxix.) This is the only suggestion that he may have had smallpox. There was an epidemic of it in Irvine the winter Burns was there. (Strawhorn, *Ayrshire at the Time of Burns*, 1959, 20.)

APPENDIX C

BURNS' AUTOBIOGRAPHICAL
LETTER TO DR. JOHN MOORE

S<small>IR</small>

For some months past I have been rambling over the country, partly on account of some little business I have to settle in various places; but of late I have been confined with some lingering complaints originating as I take it in the stomach. — To divert my spirits a little in this miserable fog of Ennui, I have taken a whim to give you a history of MYSELF. — My name has made a small noise in the country; you have done me the honor to interest yourself very warmly in my behalf; and I think a faithful account of, what character of a man I am, and how I came by that character, may perhaps amuse you in an idle moment. — I will give you an honest narrative, though I know it will be at the expence of frequently being laughed at; for I assure you, Sir, I have, like Solomon whose character, excepting the trifling affair of WISDOM, I sometimes think I resemble, I have, I say, like him "Turned my eyes to behold Madness and Folly;" and like him too, frequently shaken hands with their intoxicating friendship. — In the very polite letter Miss Williams did me the honor to write me, she tells me you have got a complaint in your eyes. — I pray God that it may be removed; for considering that lady and you are my common friends, you will probably employ her to read this letter; and then goodnight to that esteem with which she was pleased to honor the Scotch Bard. — After you have perused these pages, should you think them trifling and impertinent, I only beg leave to tell you that the poor Author wrote them under some very twitching qualms of conscience, that, perhaps he was doing what he ought not to do: a predicament he has more than once been in before. —

I have not the most distant pretensions to what the pye-coated guardians of escutcheons call, A Gentleman. — When at Edinr last winter, I got acquainted in the Herald's Office, and looking through that granary of Honors I there found almost every name in the kingdom; but for me,

" — My ancient, but ignoble blood
Has crept thro' Scoundrels ever since the flood" —

Gules, Purpure, Argent, &c. quite disowned me. — My Fathers rented land
of the noble Kieths of Marshal, and had the honor to share their fate. — I
do not use the word, Honor, with any reference to Political principles;
loyal and disloyal I take to be merely relative terms in that ancient and
formidable court known in this Country by the name of CLUB-LAW. —
Those who dare welcome Ruin and shake hands with Infamy for what they
sincerely believe to be the cause of their God or their King — "Brutus and
Cassius are honorable men." — I mention this circumstance because it
threw my father on the world at large; where after many years' wanderings
and sojournings he pickt up a pretty large quantity of Observation and
Experience, to which I am indebted for most of my little pretensions to
wisdom. — I have met with few who understood "Men, their manners and
their ways" equal to him; but stubborn, ungainly Integrity, and headlong,
ungovernable Irascibillity are disqualifying circumstances: consequently I
was born a very poor man's son. — For the first six or seven years of my
life, my father was gardiner to a worthy gentleman of small estate in the
neighbourhood of Ayr. — Had my father continued in that situation, I must
have marched off to be one of the little underlings about a farm-house;
but it was his dearest wish and prayer to have it in his power to keep his
children under his own eye till they could discern between good and evil;
so with the assistance of his generous Master my father ventured on a
small farm in his estate. — At these years I was by no means a favorite
with any body. — I was a good deal noted for a retentive memory, a
stubborn, sturdy something in my disposition, and an enthusiastic, idiot
piety. — I say idiot piety, because I was then but a child. — Though I
cost the schoolmaster some thrashings, I made an excellent English scholar;
and against the years of ten or eleven, I was absolutely a Critic in sub-
stantives, verbs and particles. — In my infant and boyish days too, I
owed much to an old Maid of my Mother's, remarkable for her ignorance,
credulity and superstition. — She had, I suppose, the largest collection in
the county of tales and songs concerning devils, ghosts, fairies, brownies,
witches, warlocks, spunkies, kelpies, elf-candles, dead-lights, wraiths, ap-
paritions, cantraips, giants, inchanted towers, dragons and other trumpery.
— This cultivated the latent seeds of Poesy; but had so strong an effect on
my imagination that to this hour, in my nocturnal rambles, I sometimes keep
a sharp look-out in suspicious places; and though nobody can be more
sceptical in these matters than I, yet it often takes an effort of Philosophy
to shake off these idle terrors. — The earliest thing of Composition that I
recollect taking pleasure in was, The vision of Mirza and a hymn of

Addison's beginning — "How are Thy servants blest, O Lord!" I particularly remember one half-stanza which was music to my boyish ear —

"For though in dreadful whirls we hung,
"High on the broken wave" —

I met with these pieces in Mas[s]on's English Collection, one of my school-books. — The two first books I ever read in private, and which gave me more pleasure than any two books I ever read again, were, the life of Hannibal and the history of Sir William Wallace. — Hannibal gave my young ideas such a turn that I used to strut in raptures up and down after the recruiting drum and bagpipe, and wish myself tall enough to be a soldier; while the story of Wallace poured a Scotish prejudice in my veins which will boil along there till the flood-gates of life shut in eternal rest. — Polemical divinity about this time was putting the country half-mad; and I, ambitious of shining in conversation parties on Sundays between sermons, funerals, &c. used in a few years more to puzzle Calvinism with so much heat and indiscretion that I raised a hue and cry of heresy against me which has not ceased to this hour. —

My vicinity to Ayr was of great advantage to me. — My social disposition, when not checked by some modification of spited pride, like our catechism definition of Infinitude, was "without bounds or limits." — I formed many connections with other Youngkers who possessed superiour advantages; the youngling Actors who were busy with the rehearsal of PARTS in which they were shortly to appear on that STAGE where, Alas! I was destined to drudge behind the SCENES. — It is not commonly at these green years that the young Noblesse and Gentry have a just sense of the immense distance between them and their ragged Playfellows. — It takes a few dashes into the world to give the young Great man that proper, decent, unnoticing disregard for the poor, insignificant, stupid devils, the mechanics and peasantry around him; who perhaps were born in the same village. — My young Superiours never insulted the clouterly appearance of my ploughboy carcase, the two extremes of which were often exposed to all the inclemencies of all the seasons. — They would give me stray volumes of books; among them, even then, I could pick up some observations; and ONE, whose heart I am sure not even the MUNNY BEGUM's scenes have tainted, helped me to a little French. — Parting with these, my young friends and benefactors, as they dropped off for the east or west Indies, was often to me a sore affliction; but I was soon called to more serious evils. — My father's generous Master died; the farm proved a ruinous bargain; and, to clench the curse, we fell into the hands of a Factor who sat for the picture I have drawn of one in my Tale of two dogs. — My father was advanced in life when he married; I was the eldest of seven children; and he, worn out by early hardship, was unfit for labour. — My father's spirit was soon irritated, but not easily broken. — There was a freedom in his lease in two years more, and to weather these two years we retrenched expences. — We lived very poorly; I was a dextrous Ploughman for my years; and the next eldest to me was a brother, who could drive the plough very well and help me to thrash. — A Novel-Writer might perhaps have viewed these scenes with some satisfaction, but so did not I: my indignation yet boils at the recollection of the scoundrel tyrant's insolent, threatening epistles, which used to set us all in tears. —

This kind of life, the chearless gloom of a hermit with the unceasing moil of a galley-slave, brought me to my sixteenth year; a little before which period I first committed the sin of RHYME. — You know our country custom of coupling a man and woman together as Partners in the labors of Harvest. — In my fifteenth autumn, my Partner was a bewitching creature who just counted an autumn less. — My scarcity of English denies me the power of doing her justice in that language; but you know the Scotch idiom, She was a bonie, sweet, sonsie lass. — In short, she altogether unwittingly to herself, initiated me in a certain delicious Passion, which in spite of acid Disappointment, gin-horse Prudence and bookworm Philosophy, I hold to be the first of human joys, our dearest pleasure here below. — How she caught the contagion I can't say; you medical folks talk much of infection by breathing the same air, the touch, &c. but I never expressly told her that I loved her. — Indeed I did not well know myself, why I liked so much to loiter behind with her, when returning in the evening from our labors; why the tones of her voice made my heartstrings thrill like an Eolian harp; and particularly, why my pulse beat such a furious ratann when I looked and fingered over her hand, to pick out the nettle-stings and thistles. — Among her other love-inspiring qualifications, she sung sweetly; and 'twas her favorite reel to which I attempted giving an embodied vehicle in rhyme. — I was not so presumtive as to imagine that I could make verses like printed ones, composed by men who had Greek and Latin; but my girl sung a song which was said to be composed by a small country laird's son, on one of his father's maids, with whom he was in love; and I saw no reason why I might not rhyme as well as he, for excepting smearing sheep and casting peats, his father living in the moors, he had no more Scholar-craft than I had. —

Thus with me began Love and Poesy; which at times have been my only, and till within this last twelvemonth have been my highest enjoyment. — My father struggled on till he reached the freedom in his lease, when he entered on a larger farm about ten miles farther in the country. — The nature of the bargain was such as to throw a little ready money in his hand at the commencement, otherwise the affair would have been impractible. — For four years we lived comfortably here; but a lawsuit between him and his Landlord commencing, after three years tossing and whirling in the vortex of Litigation, my father was just saved from absorption in a jail by phthisical consumption, which after two years promises, kindly stept in and snatch'd him away — "To where the wicked cease from troubling, and where the weary be at rest."

It is during this climacterick that my little story is most eventful. — I was, at the beginning of this period, perhaps the most ungainly, aukward being in the parish. — No Solitaire was less acquainted with the ways of the world. — My knowledge of ancient story was gathered from Salmon's and Guthrie's geographical grammars; my knowledge of modern manners, and of literature and criticism, I got from the Spectator. — These, with Pope's works, some plays of Shakespear, Tull and Dickson on Agriculture, The Pantheon, Locke's Essay on the human understanding, Stackhouse's history of the bible, Justice's British Gardiner's directory, Boyle's lectures, Allan Ramsay's works, Taylor's scripture doctrine of original sin, a select Collection of English songs, and Hervey's meditations had been the extent of my reading. — The Collection of Songs was my vade mecum. — I pored over them, driving my cart or walking to labor, song by song, verse by verse; carefully noting the true tender or sublime from affectation and fustian. — I am convinced I owe much to this for my critic-craft such as it is. —

In my seventeenth year, to give my manners a brush, I went to a country dancing school. — My father had an unaccountable antipathy [to (deleted)] against these meetings; and my going was, what to this hour I repent, in absolute defiance of his commands. — My father, as I said before, was the sport of strong passions: from that instance of rebellion he took a kind of dislike to me, which, I believe was one cause of that dissipation which marked my future years. — I only say, Dissipation, comparative with the strictness and sobriety of Presbyterean country life; for though the will-o'-wisp meteors of thoughtless Whim were almost the sole lights of my path, yet early ingrained Piety and Virtue never failed to point me out the line of Innocence. — The great misfortune of my life was, never to have AN AIM. — I had felt early some stirrings of Ambition, but they were the blind gropins of Homer's Cyclops round the walls of his cave: I saw my father's situation entailed on me perpetual labor. — The only two doors by which I could enter the fields of fortune were, the most niggardly economy, or the little chicaning art of bargain-making: the first is so contracted an aperture, I never could squeeze myself into it; the last, I always hated the contamination of the threshold. — Thus, abandoned of [every (deleted)] aim or view in life; with a strong appetite for sociability, as well from native hilarity as from a pride of observation and remark; a constitutional hypochondriac taint which made me fly solitude; add to all these incentives to social life, my reputation for bookish knowledge, a certain wild, logical talent, and a strength of thought something like the rudiments of good sense, made me generally a welcome guest; so 'tis no great wonder that always "where two or three were met together, there was I in the midst of them." — But far beyond all the other impulses of my heart was, un penchant á l'adorable moitiée du genre humain. — My heart was compleatly tinder, and was eternally lighted up by some Goddess or other: and like every warfare in this world, I was sometimes crowned with success, and sometimes mortified with defeat. — At the plough, scythe or reap-hook I feared no competitor, and set Want at defiance; and as I never cared farther for my labors than while I was in actual exercise, I spent the evening in the way after my own heart. — A country lad rarely carries on an amour without an assisting confident. — I possessed a curiosity, zeal and intrepid dexterity in these matters which recommended me a proper Second in duels of that kind; and I dare say, I felt as much pleasure at being in the secret of half the amours in the parish, as ever did Premier at knowing the intrigues of half the courts of Europe. —

The very goosefeather in my hand seems instinctively to know the well-worn path of my imagination, the favorite theme of my song, and is with difficulty restrained from giving you a couple of paragraphs on the amours of my Compeers, the humble Inmates of the farm-house and cottage; but the grave sons of Science, Ambition or Avarice baptize these things by the name of Follies. — To the sons and daughters of labor and poverty they are matters of the most serious nature: to them, the ardent hope, the stolen interview, the tender farewell, are the greatest and most delicious part of their enjoyments. —

Another circumstance in my life which made very considerable alterations in my mind and manners was, I spent my seventeeth summer on a smuggling [coast] a good distance from home at a noted school, to learn Mensuration, Surveying, Dialling, &c. in which I made a pretty good progress. — But I made greater progress in the knowledge of mankind. — The contraband trade was at that time very successful; scenes of swaggering riot and roaring dissipation were as yet new to me; and I was no enemy to social life. — Here, though I learned to look unconcernedly on a large tavern-bill, and mix without fear in a drunken squabble, yet I went on with a high hand in my Geometry; till the sun entered Virgo, a month which is always a carnival in my bosom, a charming Fillette who lived next door to the school overset my Trigonomertry, and set me off in a tangent from the sphere of my studies. — I struggled on with my Sines and Co-sines for a few days more; but stepping out to the garden one charming noon, to take the sun's altitude, I met with my Angel,

——"Like Proserpine gathering flowers,
"Herself a fairer flower" —

It was vain to think of doing any more good at school. — The remaining week I staid, I did nothing but craze the faculties of my soul about her, or steal out to meet with her; and the two last nights of my stay in the country, had sleep been a mortal sin, I was innocent. —

I returned home very considerably improved. — My reading was enlarged with the very important addition of Thomson's and Shenstone's works; I had seen mankind in a new phasis; and I engaged several of my schoolfellows to keep up a literary correspondence with me. — This last helped me much on in composition. — I had met with a collection of letters by the Wits of Queen Ann's reign, and I pored over them most devoutly. — I kept copies of any of my own letters that pleased me, and a comparison between them and the composition of most of my correspondents flattered my vanity. — I carried this whim so far that though I had not three farthings worth of business in the world, yet every post brought me as many letters as if I had been a broad, plodding son of Day-book & Ledger. —

My life flowed on much in the same tenor till my twenty third year. — Vive l'amour et vive la bagatelle, were my sole principles of action. — The addition of two more Authors to my library gave me great pleasure; Sterne and Mckenzie. — Tristram Shandy and the Man of Feeling were my bosom favorites. — Poesy was still a darling walk for my mind, but 'twas only the humour of the hour. — I had usually half a dozen or more pieces on hand; I took up one or other as it suited the momentary tone of the mind, and dismissed it as it bordered on fatigue. — My Passions when once they were lighted up, raged like so many devils, till they got vent in rhyme; and then conning over my verses, like a spell, soothed all into quiet. — None of the rhymes of those days are in print except, Winter, a dirge, the eldest of my printed pieces; The Death of Poor Mailie, John Barleycorn, And songs first, second and third: song second was the ebullition of that passion which ended the forementioned school-business. —

My twenty third year was to me an important era. — Partly thro' whim, and partly that I wished to set about doing something in life, I joined with a flax-dresser in a neighbouring town, to learn his trade and carry on the business of manufacturing and retailing flax. — This turned out a sadly unlucky affair. — My Partner was a scoundrel of the first water who made money by the mystery of thieving; and to finish the whole, while we were giving a welcoming carousal to the New year, our shop, by the drunken carelessness of my Partner's wife, took fire and was burnt to ashes; and left me like a true Poet, not worth sixpence. — I was obliged to give up business; the clouds of misfortune were gathering thick round my father's head, the darkest of which was, he was visibly far gone in a consumption; and to crown all, a belle-fille whom I adored and who had pledged her soul to meet me in the field of matrimony, jilted me with peculiar circumstances of mortification. — The finishing evil that brought up the rear of this infernal file with my hypochondriac complaint being irritated to such a degree, that for three months I was in [a] diseased state of body and mind, scarcely to be envied by the hopeless wretches who have just got their mittimus, "Depart from me, ye Cursed." —

From this adventure I learned something of a town-life. — But the principal thing which gave my mind a turn was, I formed a bosom-friendship with a young fellow, the first created being I had ever seen, but a hapless son of misfortune. — He was the son of a plain mechanic; but a great Man in the neighbourhood taking him under his patronage gave him a genteel education with a view to bettering his situation in life. — The Patron dieing just as he was ready to launch forth into the world, the poor fellow in despair went to sea; where after a variety of good and bad fortune, a little before I was acquainted with him, he had been set ashore by an American Privateer on the wild coast of Connaught, stript of every thing. — I cannot quit this poor fellow's story without adding that he is at this moment Captain of a large westindiaman belonging to the Thames. —

This gentleman's mind was fraught with courage, independance, Magnanimity, and every noble, manly virtue. — I loved him, I admired him, to a degree of enthusiasm; and I strove to imitate him. — In some measure I succeeded: I had the pride before, but he taught it to flow in proper channels. — His knowledge of the world was vastly superiour to mine, and I was all attention to learn. — He was the only man I ever saw who was a greater fool than myself when WOMAN was the presiding star; but he spoke of a certain fashionable failing with levity, which hitherto I had regarded with horror. — Here his friendship did me a mischief; and the consequence was, that soon after I resumed the plough, I wrote the WELCOME inclosed. — My reading was only encreased by two stray volumes of Pamela, and one of Ferdinand Count Fathom, which gave me some idea of Novels. — Rhyme, except some religious pieces which are in print, I had given up; but meeting with Fergusson's Scotch Poems, I strung anew my wildly-sounding, rustic lyre with emulating vigour. — When my father died, his all went among the rapacious hell-hounds that growl in the kennel of justice; but we made a shift to scrape a little money in the family amongst us, with which, to keep us together, my brother and I took a neighbouring farm. — My brother wanted my harebrained imagination as well as my social and amorous madness, but in good sense and every sober qualification he was far my superiour. —

I entered on this farm with a full resolution, "Come, go to, I will be wise!" — I read farming books; I calculated crops; I attended markets; and in short, in spite of "The devil, the world and the flesh," I believe I would have been a wise man; but the first year from unfortunately buying in bad seed, the second from a late harvest, we lost half of both our crops: this overset all my wisdom, and I returned "Like the dog to his vomit, and the sow that was washed to her wallowing in the mire. — "

I now began to be known in the neighbourhood as a maker of rhymes. — The first of my poetic offspring that saw the light was a burlesque lamentation on a quarrel between two revd Calvinists, both of them dramatis person in my Holy Fair. — I had an idea myself that the piece had some merit; but to prevent the worst, I gave a copy of it to a friend who was very fond of these things, and told him I could not guess who was the Author of it, but that I thought it pretty clever. — With a certain side of both clergy and laity it met with a roar of applause. — Holy Willie's Prayer next made its appearance, and alarmed the kirk-Session so much that they held three several meetings to look over their holy artillery, if any of it was pointed against profane Rhymers. Unluckily for me, my idle wanderings led me, on another side, point-blank within the reach of their heaviest metal. — This is the unfortunate story alluded to in my printed poem, The Lament. — 'Twas a shocking affair, which I cannot yet bear to recollect; and had very nearly given [me] one or two of the principal qualifications for a place among those who have lost the chart and mistake the reckoning of Rationality. — I gave up my part of the farm to my brother, as in truth it was only nominally mine; and made what little preparation was in my power for Jamaica. — Before leaving my native country for ever, I resolved to publish my Poems. — I weighed my productions as impartially as in my power; I thought they had merit; and 'twas a delicious idea that I would be called a clever fellow, even though it should never reach my ears a poor Negro-driver, or perhaps a victim to that inhospitable clime gone to the world of Spirits. — I can truly say that pauvre Inconnu as I then was, I had pretty nearly as high an idea of myself and my works as I have at this moment. — It [is] ever my opinion that the great, unhappy mistakes and blunders, both in a rational and religious point of view, of which we see thousands daily guilty, are owing to their ignorance, or mistaken notions of themselves. — To know myself had been all along my constant study. — I weighed myself alone; I balanced myself with others; I watched every means of information how much ground I occupied both as a Man and as a Poet: I studied assiduously Nature's DESIGN where she seem'd to have intended the various LIGHTS and SHADES in my character. — I was pretty sure my Poems would meet with some applause; but at the worst, the roar of the Atlantic would deafen the voice of Censure, and the novelty of west-Indian scenes make me forget Neglect. —

I threw off six hundred copies, of which I had got subscriptions for about three hundred and fifty. — My vanity was highly gratified by the reception I met with from the Publick; besides pocketing, all expences deducted, near twenty pounds. — This last came very seasonable, as I was about to indent myself for want of money to pay my freight. — So soon as I was master of nine guineas, the price of wafting me to the torrid zone, I bespoke a passage in the very first ship that was to sail, for

Hungry ruin had me in the wind —

I had for some time been sculking from covert to covert under all the terrors of a Jail; as some ill-advised, ungrateful people had uncoupled the merciless legal Pack at my heels. — I had taken the last farewel of my few friends; my chest was on the road to Greenock; I had composed my last song I should ever measure in Caledonia, "The gloomy night is gathering fast," when a letter from Dr Blacklock to a friend of mine overthrew all my schemes by rousing my poetic ambition. — The Doctor belonged to a set of Critics for whose applause I had not even dared to hope. — His idea that I would meet with every encouragement for a second edition fired me so much that away I posted to Edinburgh without a single acquaintance in town, or a single letter of introduction in my pocket. — The baneful Star that had so long shed its blasting influence in my Zenith, for once made a revolution to the Nadir; and the providential care of a good God placed me under the patronage of one of his noblest creatures, the Earl of Glencairn: "Oublie moi, Grand Dieu, si jamais je l'oublie!" —

I need relate no farther. — At Edinr I was in a new world: I mingled among many classes of men, but all of them new to me; and I was all attention "to catch the manners living as they rise." —

You can now, Sir, form a pretty near guess what sort of a Wight he is whom for some time you have honored with your correspondence. — That Fancy & Whim, keen Sensibility and riotous Passions may still make him zig-zag in his future path of life, is far from being improbable; but come what will, I shall answer for him the most determinate integrity and honor; and though his evil star should again blaze in his meridian with tenfold more direful influence, he may reluctantly tax Friendship with Pity but no more. —

My most respectful Compliments to Miss Williams. — Her very elegant and friendly letter I cannot answer at present, as my presence is requisite in Edinburgh, and I set off tomorrow. —

If you will oblidge me so highly and do me so much honor as now and then to drop me a letter, Please direct to me at Mauchline, Ayrshire. —

I have the honor to be, Sir,
your ever grateful humble servt

Mauchline 2d August ⎱
1787 ⎰

ROBT BURNS

APPENDIX D

THE CHILD IN HIGHLAND
MARY'S GRAVE

A letter from Mr. W. Hillhouse Carmichael, J.P., in reply to an inquiry, and a memorandum by Mr. Carmichael and Mr. Archibald MacPhail, quoted below, provide additional details of the exhumation of Mary Campbell's remains.

76 Finnart St
Greenock
Scotland
30th Octr. 1933

Robert T. Fitzhugh Esq.
College Park
Maryland U.S.A.

DEAR MR. FITZHUGH,

I duly received your letter of Septr 5th. I regret not having been able to see you when in Greenock. My friend Mr. Archibald McPhail and myself have collaborated in drawing up a report of what happened at the removal of *all* the contents of the three lairs, in one of which Burns' Highland Mary was interred, in the Old West Burying Ground. When permission had been given by Parliament to include the ground where a Church and Burying Ground existed, into the site of a shipbuilding yard, it was agreed, in certain ways, as to the disposal of the old tombstones and what was below them. The owners of the shipbuilding yard had to transfer *all* the contents of the three lairs, in one of which Highland Mary was buried, to suitable ground in the New Cemetery, along with the Memorial Stone. This was done as stated in the report enclosed herewith. At the date (Novr. 8th 1920) of the removal of the contents of the three lairs, I was convener or chairman of the Cemetery and Parks Committee of the Greenock Corporation and was present in that capacity. Mr. McPhail, who is a student of Burns, was present at my invitation. It is within our knowledge, that in 1827, an infant aged 6 weeks, was buried in one of the lairs, as per enclosed document.* You are quite at liberty to print anything sent you herewith. With regards,

I am,

Yours faithfully,

W. HILLHOUSE CARMICHAEL

Mr. Carmichael also supplied the following supplementary details:

Removal of the contents of the three lairs in Old West Church Burying Ground, Greenock, Scotland (Novr. 8th 1920) in one of which Burns' Highland Mary was buried. All the contents of the three lairs (earth bones and wood) were taken up to the New Cemetery, where a suitable excavation had been made, to receive the contents of the three lairs. The Memorial Stone† was re-erected in New Cemetery. Suitable receptacles to contain, separately, bones, wood and earth having been provided, the excavation was proceeded with. There were three lairs, lying approximately North & South. The lairs were four feet deep, when what was taken for the old shore consisting of clay and gravel was reached. There were some springs of water visible at this level draining into the river Clyde, which flows not far from the Old Burying Ground. The excavation was carried out decently and in order. When a certain depth had been reached, bones, wood of the old coffins (the wood rotten and in small pieces) and what were evidently small pieces of human remains, black flecked with small white spots, "chemicalized" by mother earth. Three skulls were found and one jaw bone with teeth in a good state of preservation. *All* the bones and skulls were those of grown people. In the north lair and in the northwest corner, lying on the old shore, was found (lying in spring water) the bottom board of an infant's coffin, perfect in shape in good condition but sodden with water. No infant's bones, so far as we saw, were exposed. When the earth, wood, bones &c. were thrown up each was placed separately in different receptacles for transferrence to New Cemetery. All the bones found were placed in a coffin and were reverently interred in New Cemetery.

(signed)   W. HILLHOUSE CARMICHAEL J. P.

ARCHIBALD MACPHAIL

Past-Presidents
of Greenock (the mother) Burns Club.

After correspondence, on July 23, 1934, Mr. Carmichael added the following details: "There is no doubt that the place of Highland Mary's burial was known. She was buried in McPherson's ground (McP. was a ship's carpenter) for the same reason that the Hendry child was i.e. either

---

* The Duncan M. Hendry memorandum of October 23, 1933.
† Permission to mark the grave had been asked by the Greenock Burns Club, February 23, 1803.

poverty precluding buying ground or else a neighbourly obligation. This sort of thing is done in Scotland among folk not very well off."

The late James D. Sloan of Ayr generously supplied a transcript from the *Campbeltown Courier*, October 25, 1930 containing information about the Hendry burial from Miss J. Hendry, 2 Margaret Street, Greenock:

The suggestion that the baby found in Highland Mary's grave was Mary Campbell's child is utter rubbish. The baby was Agnes Hendry my father's sister. Of that there is not the slightest doubt. The baby's father, my grandfather, was Captn. Duncan Hendry, a Campbeltown man, who came to reside in Greenock, where the child was born.

My grandfather had no burial ground in Greenock. The family burial ground was in Campbeltown, and, being a friend and neighbour of the McPherson's he was allowed to bury the child in the same grave as Highland Mary. That was the custom in those days.

Had it been a grown-up person, of course, a new lair would have been taken, but not in the case of a baby. I have often heard my father talk about it.

Shortly after Highland Mary's remains were re-interred in Greenock Cemetery, ten years ago, it was recorded in the local paper, the "Greenock Telegraph" that the coffin found in Highland Mary's grave was that which had contained the baby Hendry. The first suggestion that the child was Highland Mary's was made in an American newspaper. I paid no attention to that at the time, but now that it has cropped up again in Mrs. Carswell's book I feel bound to state the true facts of the case.

Another point which proves that Mrs. Carswell's book is wrong, is that if the child had been Mary Campbell's, it would have been laid in the same coffin with her.

All our family have been keenly interested in the controversy, and only the other day I had a letter from my cousin in Tarbrax, in which she said, — "I see that woman slandering our Highland Mary. Oh! that mistake of burying our wee auntie in her grave."

LIST OF
MAJOR SOURCES

POST SCRIPTS

INDEX

LIST OF
MAJOR SOURCES

Currie   *The Works of Robert Burns, with an account of his life,* by James Currie, 4 volumes, was first published in Liverpool in 1800, and reissued many times, with revisions. I have used the London, 1806 edition, which includes the revisions.

Museum   *The Scots Musical Museum.* James Johnson. Edinburgh 1787–1803. 6 volumes. I have used the facsimile reprint of William Stenhouse's 1853 annotated edition in 4 volumes, issued by Folklore Associates, Hatboro, Pennsylvania, 1962.

M'Lehose   *The Correspondence between Burns and Clarinda,* ed. W. C. M'Lehose. Edinburgh and Dublin, 1843. Also New York, 1843. I have used the New York edition.

Scott Douglas   *The Works of Robert Burns,* ed. William Scott Douglas. Edinburgh, 1877–79. 6 volumes.

Chronicle   *The Annual Burns Chronicle and Club Directory,* Kilmarnock, 1892, and annually thereafter under several variations of title.

Chambers– Wallace or Ch–W   *The Life and Works of Robert Burns,* ed. Robert Chambers, rev. William Wallace. Edinburgh and London, 1896. 4 volumes.

H & H   *The Poetry of Burns,* ed. William Ernest Henley and Thomas F. Henderson. Edinburgh, 1896. 4 volumes. In the interest of providing an agreeable text for general readers, quotations from Burns' poems and songs in this volume have been taken largely from H & H. Those readers who prefer a text edited on more recent and more rigorous principles, and without a marginal gloss, are urged to consult Professor Kinsley's excellent edition. See "Kinsley" below.

RB & Mrs. D   *Robert Burns and Mrs Dunlop.* Correspondence, ed. William Wallace. London, 1898.

Dick   *The Songs of Robert Burns,* ed. James C. Dick. London, Edinburgh, Glasgow, New York, 1903.

Dick I M   *Notes on Scottish Song by Robert Burns,* ed. J. C. Dick. London, Edinburgh, Glasgow, New York, and Toronto, 1908. (The Interleaved *Museum*)

Carswell   *The Life of Robert Burns,* by Catherine Carswell. London, 1930; New York, 1931. I have used the New York edition.

F   *The Letters of Robert Burns,* ed. J. DeLancey Ferguson. Oxford, 1931. 2 volumes. References to this edition are so arranged that they may be used with the revised edition now in preparation by Professor G. Ross Roy.

Snyder   *The Life of Robert Burns,* by Franklyn Bliss Snyder. New York, 1932.

P & P   *Pride and Passion, Robert Burns,* by DeLancey Ferguson. New York, 1939.

Fitzhugh   *Robert Burns His Associates and Contemporaries,* ed. Robert T. Fitzhugh, and *The Journal of the Border Tour,* ed. DeLancey Ferguson. Chapel Hill, 1943.

Daiches   *Robert Burns,* by David Daiches. New York, 1950.

Skinner   *Burns: Authentic Likenesses,* by Basil Skinner. Edinburgh and London, 1963.

Crawford   *Burns, A Study of the Poems and Songs,* by T. Crawford. Edinburgh and London, 1960. Second edition, 1965. I have used the second edition.

Egerer   *A Bibliography of Robert Burns,* by J. W. Egerer. Edinburgh and London, 1964. Corrected and reprinted 1965. I have used the 1965 edition.

Kinsley   *The Poems and Songs of Robert Burns,* ed. James Kinsley. Oxford, 1968. 3 volumes.

Supplementary List
of Books on Burns

Readers of Burns may find interest in the following books not mentioned
elsewhere in this volume.

Barke, James, *Immortal Memory*, a novelized life of Burns in five volumes,
1946–1954:
    The Wind That Shakes the Barley, early years.
    The Song in the Green Thorn Tree, creative period.
    The Wonder of All the Gay World, Edinburgh sojourn.
    The Crest of the Broken Wave, post Edinburgh period.
    The Well of the Silent Harp, final years and death.
Craig, David, *Scottish Literature and the Scottish People 1680–1830*.
    London, 1961.
Gibbon, Lewis Grassic, (pseud. for J. Leslie Mitchell), *Sunset Song*. 1932.
    A novel of country people in the Mearns, the district from which
    William Burnes came.
Hecht, Hans, *Robert Burns: The Man and His Work*. London, Edinburgh,
    Glasgow, 1936. Translated by Jane Lymburn.
Kinsley, James, ed., *Scottish Poetry: A Critical Study*. London, 1955.
Reid, J. B., *A Complete Word and Phrase Concordance to the Poems and
    Songs of Robert Burns*. Glasgow, 1889. Reissued, New York, 1968.
Speirs, John, *The Scots Literary Tradition*. London, 1940; rev. 1962.
Wilson, Sir James, *The Dialect of Robert Burns*. Oxford, 1923.
Wilson, Sir James, *The Scottish Poems of Robert Burns in his Native Dialect*.
    Oxford, 1924.
Wittig, Kurt, *The Scottish Tradition in Literature*. London and Edinburgh,
    1958.

POST SCRIPTS

Preface

Epigraph. From *Thoughts suggested . . . near the Poet's residence.*

I. Profile

Page 1

Epigraph. L. A. Marchand, *Byron*, New York, 1957. I, 426.
"not his *forte*." Maria Riddell, Currie I, 253.
Nicol. From author's transcript of original in library of Edinburgh University. See author's unpublished dissertation, 1935, Cornell University Library, 240–43. See also, R. D. Thornton, *James Currie, The Entire Stranger, and Robert Burns*, Edinburgh and London, 1963. 332.

Page 2

sophisticated audience. cp. J. W. Egerer, "Burns and 'Guid Black Prent,'" *The Age of Johnson*, New Haven, 1949. 269–79.
no wish to repeat. F I, #379, 379; also #319, 312; #333, 326.
burden. F I, #373, 370; II, #473, 93; #610, 228. Also, McDiarmid Notes, P. Hately Waddell, *The Life and Works of Robert Burns*, 2 vols., Glasgow, 1867. II, xxi–xxv. See dissertation, 525–47.

Page 3

Syme. Author's transcript of original in Nat. Lib. of Scotland (Watson Collection, 1190). See dissertation, 339.
Commonplace Book. *Robert Burns's Commonplace Book*, eds. J. C. Ewing and D. Cook, Glasgow, 1938. 7–8.
Maria Riddell. Currie I, 253ff. See also, J. C. Weston, "The Text of Maria Riddell's Sketch of Burns," *Studies in Scottish Literature*, V, 3 (January, 1968). 194–97.

Page 4

"so discerning." H & H II, 421.

Page 5

"continual struggle." Crawford, 40, 41.

Page 6

"earliest friend." F II, #440, 63.
"extremely deferential." J. G. Lockhart, *The Life of Robert Burns*, ed. W. Scott Douglas, London, 1882. 113.
"blood-royal." F II, #556A, 165.
lovemaking. Gilbert Burns, Currie I, 71.

Page 7

"a very Poet." F II, #646, 271–72.
locked in a room. Fitzhugh, 44.
To Ainslie. F I, #215, 199–200; also *The Merry Muses of Caledonia*, published for the Burns Federation, 1911. 137–38.

Page 8

formula. F I, #272, 257.
eggs. F II, #393, 13–14.

Page 9

"twa wives." Ch-W III, 365n.
Syme. Author's transcript of original, then the property of the late J. C. Ewing. See dissertation, 335.
Maria Riddell to Currie. *Chronicle* 1921, 108.
Telford letter. R. T. Fitzhugh, "The Paradox of Burns' Character," *Studies in Philology*, XXXII, 1 (January, 1935). 113–14.

Page 10

Sharpe. *Chronicle* 1903, 100.
Carswell. Copy in author's library of *Outlook* I, 5 (Aug., 1936). 60.
"defecates." Ch-W IV, 428n.
"occasional hard drinking." F II, #529, 140.
Syme. Author's transcript. See dissertation, 331.
Findlater. J. Currie, *The Life and Works of Robert Burns*, ed. Alexander Peterkin, Edinburgh, 1815. I, xcv.

Page 11

Scott. *The Letters of Sir Walter Scott*, ed. H. J. C. Grierson, London, 1936. X, 401.

Page 12

"more respected." Waddell II, xxiv; also Fitzhugh, 41.
Nature's Fire. See F, index, under "Scots Poetry."
"absolutely crazed." F I, #147, 134.
Kinsley. J. Kinsley, "The Music of the Heart," *Renaissance and Modern Studies*, V, iii (1964). 33.

Page 13

To Thomson. F II, #586, 200.
To Thomson. F II, #644, 265.

Page 14

Bawdy. F II, #592, 213.

Page 15

Syme. Author's transcript. See dissertation, 336; also P.S. for p. 9.
religion. Waddell II, xxiii–iv; F I, #261, 242; II, #395, 16; I, #353, 348; #89, 79; #252, 231; II, #392, 13. Also F I, # 350, 343; #221, 207; #374, 373; II, #506, 120; #649, 281. See also F, index, under "Religion."

Page 16

Currie. *Chronicle* 1919, 14.

II. Growth

Although often sparse, the details of Burns' early life are well established, except for a few relating to his stay in Irvine; but one does wish that original texts of material printed by Dr. Currie were available. The story of Burns' development as a poet, however, remains obscure, and must be reconstructed from hints in his letters and his Commonplace Book. It is greatly to be regretted that we cannot follow this growth as we can that of John Keats, for example, in similarly unpromising circumstances.

Page 18

"auld clay biggin." A building with two rooms, outer, "but," and inner, "ben," hence a but and ben. See P & P. 11; and *Ayrshire at the Time of Burns*, ed. John Strawhorn, 1959. 34–94; also index for Dr. Alexander Campbell and William Fergusson (Doonholm).

Page 19

"lived very sparingly." Currie I, 69–70; 62–63.

Page 22

"retentive memory." F I, #125, 106.
midwife. J. M. Murdoch, *Familiar Links with Robert Burns*, Ayr, 1933. 58.
chest. Fitzhugh, 59.
gable blown in. Currie I, 378.

Page 23

Murdoch. Currie I, 87–89.
Titus Andronicus. Currie I, 61–62.

Page 24

Dr. Dalrymple. Ch-W I, 34n.
further schooling. Currie I, 65, 66.
Kirkoswald. F I, #125, 111.

Page 25

"reader when he could get a book." Currie I, 60; also 64.

Page 26

"fluency and precision." Dugald Stewart, Currie I, 137.
harvest partner. F I, #125, 108.

Page 28

young love. *Commonplace Book*, Ewing and Cook, 3.
"a darling walk." F I, #125, 112.

Page 29

dancing school. F I, #125, 109; Snyder, 93, n. 9.
"tinder." F I, #125, 110.
"An Aim." F I, #125, 109.
"vive l'amour." F I, #125, 111.
"to see and observe." F I, #13, 13–14.
"Though when young." Currie I, 71.

Page 30

Robert. F I, #125, 110.
Bachelor's Club Rules. Currie I, 104–6.

Page 31

"views of matrimony." F I, #18, 20.
new members. Currie I, 107.

Page 32

Rules. Currie I, appendix, 363–67.
July 4, 1781. *Chronicle* 1929, 139.
subsequent separation. *Chronicle* 1929, 141.

Page 33

"Caledonia's Bard." F I, #77, 67. *Chronicle* 1937, 94–102; 1947, 37–43.
"two doors." F I, #125, 109–10.
"Egotisms." *Reliques of Robert Burns,* ed. R. H. Cromek, London, 1808.
339. See also J. D. Ferguson, "In Defense of R. H. Cromek," *Philological Quarterly,* IX. 239–48; and D. Cook, *Chronicle* 1922, 1–21.

Page 34

"jilted." F I, #125, 112.
five drafts. F I, #5, 6, 7, 8, 9, 5–11.

Page 35

ownership of shop. *Chronicle* 1905, 33–42.
Robert Fergusson. F I, #125, 113; *Chronicle* 1956, 1–2.
To Dr. Moore. F I, #125, 113.

Page 38

religious ferment. *Commonplace Book,* Ewing and Cook, 8, 18; Crawford, 12–16.

Page 39

Adam Smith. *Commonplace Book,* 5.
heart-wrung comment. F I, #162, 146.

Page 40

early letters. Currie I, 64.
To William Burns. F I, #4, 4–5.

Page 41

"dangerous disorder." *Commonplace Book,* 18. (Heading to prayer)

Page 42

To James Burness. F I, #17, 18–19.

Page 44

"man seeking work." Currie III, Appendix, 382.
Lochlea troubles. McVie, *Chronicle* 1935, 69–87. See also Snyder, 77–83; Strawhorn, *Ayrshire,* 133.

Page 45

Murdoch.   Currie I, 94, 95.

Page 46

Currie.   Currie I, 82.
M'Kenzie.   *Poems of Robert Burns*, Edinburgh, 1811. (Morison's Burns)
II, 261–62.

Page 47

early poetry.   F I, #125, 112.
To Peter Hill.   F I, #276, 263.

Page 48

collection of songs.   *Chronicle* 1935, 12; F I, #125, 109.

Page 49

"ill-spawned monsters."   F I, #319, 311–12; see also F I, #333, 326.
Burns' diction.   Crawford, ix–xv, and discussions of individual poems,
   passim; Raymond Bentman, "Robert Burns's Use of Scottish Diction,"
   From Sensibility to Romanticism, New York, 1965; and R. Crombie
   Saunders, "Burns in Two Tongues," *Saltire Review* I, 3 (1954). 41–45;
   also a review of Crawford: McD. Emslie, "Burns and the Alien Diction,"
   Essays in Criticism X, 4 (Oct., 1960). 451–61.

III. Poet

By his early twenties, the record of Robert Burns has become fairly full,
but little poetry of these years has survived. Apparently he destroyed it when
he thought he was going to Jamaica in 1786. A representative selection of
poetry which influenced Burns is offered in Appendix A — poems not easily
available for the general reader. They will illustrate Burns' freely acknowledged debt, and the irony of his being at once a highly imitative and a highly
original poet.

Knowledge of the quality and tone of peasant life in Ayrshire is important
for an understanding of his poems. It also reveals that Burns was a fairly
normal product of his environment. Section III seeks to provide some lively
evidence on this point.

Mary Campbell (the "Highland Mary" of much romantic confusion) had
minor importance for Burns before her death (see P & P. 144–50). The
extended section on Mary is presented to give full and circumstantial information about her from reliable sources, which readers may interpret for

themselves. At very least it establishes the girl as a flesh and blood person —
tall, fair-haired, blue-eyed, a native of Cowal, and victim of a fever. It
should be noted that the Lord Eglinton mentioned by Train did, indeed,
have a brother, despite claims to the contrary (McVie, *Chronicle* 1956.
107). Also that the Hendry response to Mrs. Carswell's story of the coffin
found in Mary's grave (Appendix D) was prompt, and not suspiciously
delayed as has been charged.

Page 51

Epigraphs. Aileen Ward, *John Keats*, New York, 1963. 275. F I, #299, 292.

Page 52

Gilbert's recollection. Currie III, 378–79.
To Sillar. F I, #355, 350.
Wen Yuang-Ning, *Chronicle* 1945, 6.

Page 55

models and themes for epistles. See J. C. Weston, "Robert Burns' Use of the
Scots Verse-Epistle Form," *Philological Quarterly*, April, 1970.

Page 59

six-line stanza. H & H I, 336–42.

Page 62

"Polemical divinity." F I, #125, 107.
Sillar's comment. Morison's Burns II, Appendix I, 259–60.

Page 63

To Dr. Moore. F I, #125, 113–14.

Page 64

Kirk dissension. Crawford, 25–48; for auld lichts and new lichts, see Kinsley
III, 1045; also R. W. Chambers, *The Life and Works of Robert Burns*,
4 vols., Edinburgh and London, 1880. I, 122–23.
Fisher. H & H II, 321; *The Glenriddell Manuscripts of Robert Burns*,
printed not published, John Gribbel, Philadelphia, 1914. Facsimile, 2 vols.
(1 verse, 1 letters).

Page 65

Hamilton. Synder, 110–11, and 146, n.18; see also Kinsley III, 1047–53.

Page 68

Elizabeth Burns.   Ch-W I, 119–20.

Betty Paton's settlement.   *Scribners Magazine,* Dec. 1933. 383–84.

Page 72

The blacksmith.   Synder. 175–76, 185, n.35.

Page 73

Aiton.   Strawhorn, *Ayrshire,* "Holding the Fair." 73–75.

Page 84

Henley.   H & H IV, 274.

"Natural ideas."   Ch-W II, 129.

Page 85

"study men."   F I, #13, 14.

"rural imagery."   F II, #557, 168.

vernacular.   cp. F II, #507, 122; #511, 126.

Ramsay.   Quoted by D. Daiches, "Eighteenth Century Vernacular Poetry,"
Scottish Poetry, a Critical Study, ed. J. Kinsley, London, 1955. 159. Burns
mentions "Theocrites" in his Kilmarnock preface.

Page 92

news "not the most agreable."   F I, #21, 22.

legal marriage.   James Smith may have been a witness. In F I, #251, 230.
Burns asks Smith to write a letter which can be shown, saying that "such
things are" about his marriage.

To Arnot.   F I, #29, 26–30; see also Strawhorn, 137.

Page 94

To Brice.   F I, #31, 30–31.

Jean writes to Kirk Session.   Ch-W I, 344n.

To Richmond.   F I, #33, 32.

Page 95

To Brice.   F I, #34, 33.

Page 96

To Richmond.   F I, #36, 35.

To Smith.   F I, #37, 36.

dates.   F I, #40, 37, 38; #43, 40; #49, 44.

new edition.   F I, #53, 46–47.

Page 97

To Richmond, Sept. 1. F I, #43, 40.
To Richmond, Sept. 3. From transcript supplied the author by the late
DeLancey Ferguson. See also, Kinsley #124, I. 294.

Page 98

assignment. F I, #35, 33–34.
Dundonald Mary Campbell. Ch-W I, Appendix VIII. 470–75.

Page 99

Cromek. *Reliques,* 237.

Page 100

To George Thomson. F II, #511, 127. October 26, 1792.

Page 101

To Mrs. Dunlop. F I, #374, 373.

Page 102

Train MS. Fitzhugh, 54–55.

Page 103

another note. Fitzhugh, 57–58.

Page 104

Anthony Dunlop. RB & Mrs. D, xxv–xxvi; also xxvi n.
Grierson notes. Fitzhugh, 34–36; p. 36, Grierson adds, "Highland Mary
from Dunoon Parish Cowal." See map of Northern Scotland.

Page 105

"texts connected with the name." Those who wish to pursue the matter of
Mary Campbell further are referred to Snyder, 129–46.

Page 106

Aiken. F I, #53, 47.

Page 107

Returns from Kilmarnock edition. Ch-W I, 468–70.

Page 108

Review notices. Egerer, 4.

Page 114

"Burns's verse." H & H I, v.
Raleigh. Walter Raleigh, *Some Authors, A Collection of Literary Essays,
1896–1916,* Oxford, 1923. 221–22.

Page 119

"sober science." F I, #31, 31.
"last foolish action." F I, #31, 31.

Page 120

Blacklock. F I, #80, 71.
dozen copies. Thornton, *Currie*, 26on. Also, *Chronicle* 1939, 50, #276 (2).

Page 121

candor. RB & Mrs. D, 48; 108–11; 175; 286–87; 296–97.
sympathy. RB & Mrs. D, 179; 264; 271–72; 275; 365.

Page 122

"idle project." F I, #330, 325; #351, 344.
commission. F I, #90, 82.
Dunlop quarrel. F II, #649, 281; also 349.
Last letter to Mrs. Dunlop. F II, #702, 326.

IV. *Lion*

Much of the information in Section IV is standard, but Burns' own feelings about his Edinburgh patrons, and about his publisher, William Creech, have been emphasized. His friendship with William Nicol has been clarified, also. Details of the gentry's carousing provide a background against which Burns' own exploits seem modest. Indeed, as Professor Ferguson has remarked, Burns was not so much a conspicuous sinner as one who sinned conspicuously. The upper social class of many Crochallan Fencibles should be noted. (McVie, *Chronicle* 1964, 10.)

The Clarinda affair is given full coverage, but perhaps the best comment on it is Jean's, to John M'Diarmid. Allan Cunningham identified the heroine of "Had we never lov'd sae kindly" as a "frail dame of Dumfriesshire," but M'Diarmid adds (Waddell II, xxiv), "Mrs. Burns thinks it was no one but Clarinda."

Details about Learned Pigs are a novelty in Burns scholarship.

Page 124

Epigraph. To Muir. F I, #64, 57.
Scott. J. D. Lockhart, *The Life of Robert Burns*, ed. W. Scott Douglas, London, 1882. 113.
"hare-brained ramble." F I, #309, 300.
"Greenland bay." Fitzhugh, 111.

Page 125

Duchess. Ch-W II, 60.

Page 126

advertisement. Ch-W II, 22.

Page 127

appearance. Lockhart, Scott Douglas edition. 112; Currie I, 230–31; *Chronicle* 1906, 75–76.
"like coals." Ch-W IV, 218. John Syme to H. Constable, Nov. 1829; quoted in Syme's obituary, *Dumfries Weekly Journal*, Dec. 16, 1831.
pock-marked. Waddell II, xxvii, xxxix.

Page 128

"his deportment." Morison's Burns I, lxv–vi.
learned pig. Fitzhugh, 32.
rusticity. Ch-W II, 137.
whip. R. Kerr, *Memoirs of the Life, Writings, and Correspondence* of *William Smellie*, Edinburgh, 1811. II, 350–51.
swelled head. Author's transcript of original (National Library of Scotland, Ms. number 22.4.17). See also F, index, under "David Ramsay."
Lockhart. Scott Douglas edition, 126ff.

Page 129

Mackenzie. *The Anecdotes and Egotisms of Henry Mackenzie,* ed. H. W. Thompson, London, 1927. 151–52.

Page 130

Anderson. *Chronicle* 1925, 14ff.

Page 132

poor verses. *Chronicle* 1925, 12.

Page 133

eccentric clergyman. Ch-W II, 76–77.
To Hamilton. F I, #62, 55.
To Ballantine. F I, #63, 57.

Page 134

To Aiken. F I, #65, 58.
Mrs. Carfrae. F I, #77, 67–68.

Page 135

To Dr. Moore.   F I, #97, 85.
To Mrs. Dunlop. F I, #98, 86.
"Great people."   F I, #189, 175.
To Nicol.   F I, #216, 201.
To Dunbar.   F I, #236, 217.
To Cleghorn.   F I, #230, 214.
To Mrs. Dunlop.   F I, #98, 86.
To Smith.   F I, #113, 95.

Page 136

To Clarinda.   F I, #171, 156.
Blair.   *The Works of Robert Burns,* ed. W. Scott Douglas, 6 vols., Edinburgh, 1877–79. VI, 391.
gaffe.   Ch-W II, 76.

Page 138

"ludicrous."   Ch-W II, 23.
Smellie.   F II, #440, 63.

Page 139

Crochallans.   McVie, *Chronicle* 1964, 10.
Dr. Stuart.   Kerr, *Smellie,* I, 502–3.

Page 140

Williamson.   Robert Chambers, *Traditions of Edinburgh,* rev., Edinburgh and London, 1868. 182–83.

Page 141

Edinburgh edition.   Edwin Wolf, 2nd, " 'Skinking' or 'Stinking'?", *Library Chronicle of . . . University of Penna.* xiv (April, 1947). 3–14.

Page 142

agreement.   Reproduced, Snyder, 224.
To Creech.   Text printed by Professor G. Ross Roy, *Papers of the Bibliographical Society of America,* 1965. 358. He writes that Currie probably had the letter but did not print it for fear of offending Burns' "superiors." See also S. Parks, PBSA, 1966. 453–64.
final settlement   F I, #315, 308.
To Mrs. Dunlop.   F I, #324, 317.

Page 145

To a Haggis. Fitzhugh, 37–38.
pirated editions. J. W. Egerer, "Burns and 'Guild Black Prent,'" *The Age of Johnson,* New Haven, 1949. 269–79.

Page 146

"inundation of nonsense." F I, #333, 326; see also F I, #319, 312.
To Lady Elizabeth Cunningham. F I, #379, 379.
To Dr. Moore. F I, #291, 284.
Drama. J. D. Ferguson, "Burns and the Drama," *Scots Magazine* XXI (1934). 278–86.
"Mr. Miller." F I, #77, 67.

Page 147

To Smith. F I, #113, 95–96.
To Nicol. F I, #114, 96.
Milton's Satan. F I, #113, 95.
To Mrs. Dunlop. F I, #254, 234.
To Ainslie. F I, #122, 102.

Page 148

Border Tour. Fitzhugh, Journal text edited by DeLancey Ferguson. 108–22.
People Burns met. Journal: Minister at Dunse, Dr. Bowmaker, 107, 117; Brydone, 109; Rutherford, 110–11.

Page 149

Somerville. Ch-W II, 105.
Miss Lindsay. Journal, 111ff.
Esther Easton. Journal, 113.

Page 152

plough horses. Journal, 115.
Ladies. Betsy Grieve, 116; Miss Clarke, 117; Rachel Ainslie, 118; also Ch-W II, 116n.

Page 153

illness. Journal, 118.
roup. Journal, 119.
Meg Cameron. Ch-W II, 121. For "Meg," not "May," see DeLancey Ferguson, "Some New Burns Letters," PMLA LI, 4 (Dec., 1936). 979.
To Ainslie. F I, #246, 226. Here dated "about 1 June, 1788," which is a year too late.

Page 154

To Ainslie. F I, #116, 98.
To Ainslie, July 29, 1787. See "Meg Cameron" above.
"Highland wench." F II, #586, 203.

Page 156

Dumbarton. *Chronicle* 1927, 82–84.
To Smith. F I, #117, 98–100.
Sterne. *Tristram Shandy* II, 9.

Page 158

Creech. Ch-W II, 141; 145–46; F I, #294, 285.
Meg Cameron. Ch-W II, 145–46.
Cockburn. *Memorials of His Time*, Edinburgh, 1856. 4.

Page 159

Nicol. Fitzhugh, 65–67; 97–98.

Page 161

To Ainslie. F I, #130, 119–20.
three weeks. F I, #131, 120.
Journal. *Journal of a Tour in the Highlands . . . by Robert Burns*, ed.
J. C. Ewing, London and Glasgow, 1927. Transcript pp. 11–17.

Page 163

Burns at Blair Athole. Ch-W II, 162; Currie I, 178–82; cp. *post* xxx–xx
and F II, #441, 64–65.

Page 164

"debts." F I, #135, 123.
"obstinate son of Latin Prose." F I, #145, 131.

Page 165

later letter. F I, #149, 136.
messenger and guide. Ch-W II, 172.
Bishop Skinner. *Chronicle* 1944, 35.

Page 167

To Gilbert. F I, #137, 125.

Page 168

Edinburgh patrons. F I, #324, 317.
To Mrs. Dunlop. F II, #510, 125.
To Mr. Miller. F I, #139, 126–27.
Adair. Currie I, 168–72.
proposal. F II, 334.

Page 169

Murdoch sisters. Ch-W II, 153.
To Hamilton. F I, #132, 121–22.
Burns' itinerary. F I, #140, 128; #141 and #142, 128–29.

Page 170

Marriage of Adair and Charlotte Hamilton. Ch-W II, 188 n.

Page 171

Ramsay. Currie I, 188–89.

Page 172

To Mr. Miller. F I, #144, 130, 131.
return from Dumfries. F I, #155, 141.

Page 173

To Margaret Chalmers. F I, #207, 192.
Clarinda. *Burns and Clarinda,* ed. W. C. M'Lehose, New York, 1843.
  (Originally published in Edinburgh the same year); see also R. L. Brown,
  Clarinda, Dewsbury, England, 1968.

Page 174

Mrs. M'Lehose and her husband. M'Lehose, 17, 28.

Page 175

method of censorship. M'Lehose, 186.
caress. M'Lehose, 176.

Page 176

Mr. Kemp. M'Lehose, 174.
theological position. F I, #174, 159.

Page 177

To Mrs. Dunlop. F I, #374, 374.
mid-February. F I, #204, 189.
diary. M'Lehose, 53.

Page 178

mulatto child. Brown, *Clarinda,* 64–65.
1791 letters. F II, #484, 101; #485, 101; #486, 102.
Feb. 1788 letters. F I, #197, 183; #207 and #208, 192.
trip to Mauchline. F I, #209, 194; #211, 195; #214, 198.

Page 179

"disgusted." Fitzhugh, 43; F I, #210, 194.
To Ainslie. F I, #215, 199–200.
To Brown. F I, #220, 206.
Mr. Pattison. F I, #209, 193–94.

Page 180

"Compliment to Mr. Miller." F I, #210, 195.

Page 181

To Margaret Chalmers. F I, #207, 192.
To Hill. F II, #475, 95.
lease. F I, #223, 208; lease reprinted by Snyder, 503–7.
To Clarinda. F I, #225, 210.
Creech. F I, #228, 212.
"dearest angel." F I, #225, 210.
loves her. F I, #224, 209.
To Brown. F I, #228, 212.

Page 182

To Clarinda. F I, #320, 312.

Page 183

acidulous exchange. F II, #388 and #389, 7 and 8.
Ainslie to Clarinda. R. Fitzhugh, "Burns at Ellisland," *Modern Language Notes,* LII (Nov. 1938). 525–26.

Page 185

To Clarinda, 1794. F II, #629, 247–48.
Sweet Sensibility. F II, #462, 82.

Page 186

Jenny Clow's appeal. M'Lehose, 262–63.
Burns' reply. F II, #483, 100.

Page 187

To Clarinda. F II, #544, 155; #629, 247.
Cunningham to Syme. Author's transcript of original; see P.S. for p. 365.
For details of Cunningham, see *Chronicle* 1933, 94ff.

Page 188

Maria Riddell. *Chronicle* 1923, 76.
Mrs. M'Lehose. Fitzhugh, 40; M'Lehose, 52.

details of Burns' marriage.   Fitzhugh, 58; F I, #251, 230; Snyder, 303.
To Ainslie.   F I, #249, 229.

Page 189

To Beugo.   F I, #268, 252.
To Mrs. Dunlop.   F I, #247, 227.
To Dunbar.   F I, #236, 217.

Page 190

From Nicol.   Author's transcript. See P.S. for p. 1.
Gray.   J. Currie, *The Works of Robert Burns*, with additions by Gilbert
Burns, London, 1820. I, 439.

V. Married Man

The anticlimax of Burns' later years is rendered more poignant by his unrecognized infection. From a biographer's point of view, there is almost too
much information about Burns during these years when his life was less interesting than before, and his poetic output generally less striking. It should
be noted that Burns himself eagerly sought employment in the Excise, which
offered a desirable and steady income, and good prospects for promotion.
He was a faithful officer, and a brave one, as the *Rosamond* incident reveals.

The full truth of Burns' life in Dumfries is probably not known, but from
comments such as those by Syme, Cunningham, Thomas Telford, James
Gray, and C. K. Sharpe, the outline is clear enough. Some relatively fresh
details appear here about Burns' friend Robert Riddell, but the puzzle of the
Riddell quarrel cannot be solved on the basis of presently available information. It is hoped the note on Jenny Little will be of interest. And one of the
rich adornments of the book, certainly, is Mrs. Walter Riddell's portrait.

Page 191

To Mrs. Dunlop.   F I, #184, 171.

Page 192

"defy the teeth of time." F I, #288, 275.

Page 193

To Thomson.   F II, #511, 126; #507, 123.
George Thomson.   J. Cuthbert Hadden, *George Thomson, The Friend of
Burns*, London, 1898; J. D. Ferguson, "Cancelled Passages in the Letters
of Robert Burns to George Thomson," PMLA XLIII (1928). 1110–20;
see also *passim*, Dick (Historical Notes), Kinsley (Notes and Commentary), and R. D. Thornton, unpublished Harvard dissertation.
docket.   F II, #706, 328–29.

Page 194

Thomson's contribution. J. G. Lockhart, *The Life of Robert Burns,* ed. W. Scott Douglas, London, 1882. 277.

Page 195

"Rhinoceros." F I, #268, 251.
Did Thomson meet Burns? Hadden, 134–38.
"ill at ease." F II, #627, 245.
"thumb-phial." F I, #290, 277.
To Deborah Davies. F II, #556A, 165.
To Mrs. Dunlop. F I, #244, 224.

Page 196

To Hill. F II, #430, 51–52.

Page 197

To Cunningham. F II, #441, 64–65.

Page 198

To Dr. Moore. F I, #322, 315.

Page 199

Glenriddell Collection. *The Glenriddell Manuscripts of Robert Burns,* printed not published, John Gribbel, Philadelphia, 1914. Facsimile, 2vols. (1 verse, 1 letters).

Page 200

"Jacobitism." Dick I M, 27.
To Mrs. Dunlop. F II, #397, 18.
"beef-witted." Dick I M, 5.
Edinburgh Evening Courant. F I, #283, 269–71.

Page 203

To Mrs. Dunlop, 1. F II, #403, 26.
To Mrs. Graham. F II, #402, 25.
To Mrs. Dunlop, 2. F II, #510, 125.
To Dunbar. F II, #382, 2.

Page 205

To Hill. F I, #255, 235.
Ellisland. F I, #247, 226; #272, 257.
"elbow of existence." F I, 381.

Page 206

To Graham. F I, #269, 253.

Excise. John Sinton, *Burns, Excise Officer and Poet*, Glasgow and Edinburgh, 4th edition, 1897; R. W. Macfadzean, "Burns's Excise Duties and Emoluments," *Chronicle* 1898, 53ff.; J. Macfadzean, "Robert Burns and the Scotch Excise Board," *Chronicle* 1903, 26ff.; B. R. Leftwich, "Burns and the Excise," *Chronicle* 1936, 65ff.

Page 207

To Graham. F I, #273, 259.

To Mrs. Dunlop, 1. F I, #363, 360.

Twelve cows. M'Diarmid Notes, Waddell II, xxii.

To Mrs. Dunlop, 2. F I, #324, 317–18.

To Jean. F I, #278, 265.

Page 208

uncle Robert. F I, #314, 307–8.

Agnes. M'Diarmid Notes, Waddell II, xxii.

Page 209

To Mrs. Dunlop. F I, #330, 324.

"business." F I, #378, 377.

To Graham. F I, #341, 335; #353, 347.

To Mrs. Dunlop. F I, #359, 356.

September 7. *Chronicle* 1936, 68.

October 27. Snyder, 317.

October 10. Ch-W III, 96; Snyder, 316.

"expectant." F I, #367, 364.

"most violent cold." F I, #371, 368.

"diseased nervous system." F I, #374, 372.

Page 210

"hypochondria." F II, #381, 1.

"slow, illformed Fever." F II, #422, 44.

"with my horse." F II, #435, 55.

broken arm. F II, #445, 70.

Janet Little. RB & Mrs. D, see index; Hilton Brown, *Chronicle* 1950, 15–20; *The Poetical Works of Janet Little, the Scotch Milkmaid*, Air, 1792. This volume carries a subscription list of nearly 700 names, among them, Dr. Adair, Edinburgh; Mr. Robert Ainsley, writer, Edinburgh; Mr. Robert Burns, Dumfries; and James Boswell, Esq., of Auchinleck. Hilton

Brown, who cites no authority, reports that "Jenny is said to have made fifty pounds" from her volume. She wrote in English, and preferred quatrains and couplets.

Mrs. Dunlop's letters to Burns contain many references to Janet, or Jenny, Little, and her poetry, with quotations. While Mrs. Dunlop did not rate Jenny's work highly, she offered the woman encouragement in her benevolent-officious way, and tried to engage Burns' interest and assistance. Jenny herself sought Burns' patronage by addressing an epistle to him in his favorite stanza, her only use of that form. A few stanzas will suffice:

> To hear thy song, all ranks desire;
> Sae well thou strik'st the dormant lyre.
> Apollo, wi' poetic fire,
>   Thy breast did warm,
> An' critics silently admire
>   Thy art to charm.
>
> . . . .
> When slighted love becomes thy theme,
> An' woman's faithless vows you blame,
> With so much pathos you exclaim,
>   In your Lament,
> But glanc'd by the most frigid dame,
>   She wad relent.
>
> . . . .
> Did Addison or Pope but hear,
> Or Sam, that critic most severe,
> A plough-boy sing, wi' throat sae clear,
>   They, in a rage,
> Their works wad a' in pieces tear
>   An' curse your page.

This salutation prompted Burns to write Mrs. Dunlop (F I, #362, 359), calling it "a very ingenious but modest composition." Nothing daunted by Burns' silence, Jenny presented herself at Ellisland on the day of his accident, which she celebrated with another modest composition. It begins by reciting her disappointment at not having been able to see him earlier, and bursts out as he comes into view:

> Hark! now he comes, a dire alarm
>   Re-echoes through his hall!
> Pegasus kneel'd, his rider's arm
>   Was broken by a fall.
>
> The doleful tidings to my ears
>   Were in harsh notes convey'd;
> His lovely wife stood drown'd in tears,
>   While thus I pond'ring said:

"No cheering draught, with ills unmix'd,
Can mortals taste below;
All human fate by heav'n is fix'd,
Alternate joy and wo."

With beating breast I view'd the bard;
All trembling did him greet:
With sighs bewail'd his fate so hard,
Whose notes were ever sweet.

A year later, however, (F II, #491, 106) Burns gallantly assures Mrs. Dunlop, "I am glad to hear so good an account of Jenny Little's affairs. I have done next to nothing for her yet, but I shall now set about & fill up my Subscription bill."

"elbow chair." F II, #475, 95.
despondency. M'Diarmid Notes, Waddell II, xxii.
To Brown. F I, #369, 365–66.
To Lady Elizabeth Cunningham. F I, #379, 379.
To Ainslie. F I, #367, 364.

Page 211

To Cleghorn. F II, #473, 93.
Exciseman's duties. *Chronicle* 1898, 53ff.

Page 212

To Graham. F II, #419, 40–41.
To Mitchell. F II, #417, 38.
To Cleghorn. F II, #473, 94.

Page 213

Syme to Cunningham. Author's transcript. See P.S. for p. 365.
Nicol to Ainslie. Ch-W III, 200.
Mrs. Dunlop. RB & Mrs. D, 155; 241, 245, 249.
To Mrs. Dunlop. F II, #396, 17.

Page 215

Ellisland lease. Snyder, 503–7; Ch-W III, 296.
To Cleghorn. F II, #473, 93.
sale of crops. F II, #466, 87.
sale of "farming things." F II, #481, 98.
To Mrs. Dunlop. F II, #491, 105.
Nov. 11, 1791. P & P, xviii.

Page 216

To Hill.   F II, #495, 109.
Excise records.   Sinton, 59.
Maria Riddell.   F II, #497, 110.
Burns' Excise record.   F, index; *Chronicle* 1936, 66–69; Sinton, *passim*.
promotion.   Sinton, 60.

Page 217

Findlater. *Glasgow Courier*, March, 1834.
To Heron.   F II, #660, 292.
Rosamond.   *Scotsman,* and *Glasgow Herald,* Nov. 11, 1932; *Chronicle* 1934,
   43–52.

Page 220

Gazetteer.   P & P, xviii.
To Mrs. Dunlop.   F II, #524, 137.

Page 223

To Mrs. Dunlop.   F I, #376, 321.
To Graham.   F I, #528, 139–40.

Page 224

To Mrs. Dunlop.   F II, #529, 140.
To Graham.   F II, #530, 143–45.

Page 226

"tippling Ballad."   *When Princes and Prelates.*
Syme to Peterkin.   Author's transcript. See dissertation, 334; also P.S. for
   p. 9.
Findlater.   Author's Cornell Univ. dissertation, 234–37.
To Erskine of Mar.   F II, #558, 169–70.

Page 228

Nicol.   Gribbel facsimile, Glenriddell letter book. See P.S. for p. 64.

Page 230

To Nicol.   F II, #537, 150–51.
To Cunningham.   F II, #536, 149–50.

Page 231

To Mrs. Dunlop.   F II, #649, 281.
To Mrs. Dunlop.   F I, #254, 234.
"suitable to his feelings."   F I, #207, 192.

Page 232

"talent and humour." Author's transcript. See dissertation, 332; also P.S. for p. 9.

Page 233

Ellisland. F I, #270, 254; #271, 255–56; and M'Diarmid Notes, Waddell II, xxi–xxii.
list of correspondents. *Chronicle* 1933; 1939.
Helen Maria Williams. F I, #358, 352–55.

Page 234

To Bruce Campbell. F I, #284, 271–72.
To Ainslie. F I, #252, 231.
To Stewart. F I, #253, 232–33.
To Mrs. Dunlop. F I, #264, 245.

Page 235

To Jean. F I, #270, 254–55.

Page 236

To Mrs. Dunlop. F I, #285, 272–75.
To Dr. Blacklock. F I, #287, 274.
To Mrs. Dunlop. F I, #290, 277.

Page 237

To Mrs. Dunlop. F I, #293, 282–83.
To Ainslie. F I, #295, 286–87.
To James Burness. F I, #314, 307–8.

Page 239

To Mrs. Dunlop. F I, #330, 324.
To Rev. Patrick Carfrae. F I, #333, 327.

Page 240

To William Burns. F I, #337, 332.
To James Johnson. F I, #348, 340; see *The Scots Musical Museum*, originally published by James Johnson, with illustrations by William Stenhouse, reissued by Folklore Associates, Hatboro, Penna. 1962.

Page 241

To Mrs. Dunlop. F I, #350, 342.
To Mrs. Dunlop. F I, #352, 346.

Page 242

To Hill.　F II, #387, 6–7.

Page 243

Creech.　Ch-W III, 164n.

Page 244

To Nicol.　F II, #390, 8–10.

Page 246

To William Burns.　F II, #391, 10–11.

Page 247

To Mrs. Dunlop.　F II, #403, 27–28.

Page 248

To John Wilson.　F II, #420, 42–43.

Page 249

To Rev. George Husband Baird.　F II, #438, 60–61.
Blair and Moore.　Ch-W III, 240.
To Dr. Moore.　F II, #437, 58.

Page 250

To Findlater.　F II, #460, 81–82.

Page 251

To Newall.　F II, #398, 20.
"chequered."　F II, #443, 68.
To Sillar.　F II, #461, 82.
To Boyd.　F II, #458, 80.

Page 252

Gilbert's wedding.　F II, #457, 79; P & P, xviii.
Archers.　F II, #441, 64–65.
Lord Buchan.　F II, #465, 85.

Page 253

Creech.　F II, #475, 95.
Robert Riddell.　See account of Riddell in DNB; Dick. xliii; Kerr, *Smellie*,
　　II. 364, 365; R. D. Thornton, *Chronicle* 1953, 44–67; Stenhouse, *Museum*,
　　I, lxxvi.
Friars' Carse.　For punctuation see Gribbel, Glenriddell letter book, p. 6.

Page 254

degree. Under date of January 23, 1794, the minutes of "Edin. Coll." record, "A report was made to the Meeting that Robert Riddell Esqr. of Glenriddell F. S. A. of London & of Edinburgh had been judged by the Law Faculty a proper candidate for receiving the Degree of Doctor of Laws; and he was recommended as a Gentleman of uncommon knowledge as an Antiquarian.

"The Senatus Academicus having considered the Said Report & recommendation, unanimously consented to confer the Said Degree upon Mr. Riddell, and ordered his Diploma to be issued in the usual form." From a Xerox copy of the Minutes, courtesy C. P. Finlayson, Esq., Keeper of MSS, The University Library, Edinburgh.

Stenhouse, *Museum*, I, lxxvi.

Scott.   P & P, 121.

Young.   Fitzhugh, 77.

Page 255

borrow a laborer.   F I, #271, 255.

Page 256

1792 quarto.   Not listed in H & H, Egerer, or Kinsley.
interleaved set.   Dick I M; F II, #513, 129.

Page 257

Glenriddell Collection.   See P.S. for p. 64.
wedding anniversary song.   Cromek, *Reliques*, 269.

Page 258

To Riddell.   F I, #271, 255.
Cromek.   Dick I M, 73; Cook, *Chronicle* 1922, 1–22; J. D. Ferguson, "In Defense of R. H. Cromek," *Philological Quarterly*, IX (1930). 239–48.
librarian.   M'Diarmid Notes, Waddell II, xxiv.
Statistical Account.   F II, #469, 89–90.

Page 260

drinking.   F II, #529, 140.
Whistle contest.   Ch-W III, 102–9; M'Diarmid Notes, Waddell II, xxiii.

Page 261

To Grose.   F II, #401, 22–24.

Page 264

Douglas Graham.   H & H I, 437.

Pages 264–65

composition of *Tam o' Shanter*. H & H I, 438; Morison's Burns II, 340; F II, #443, 68; Egerer, 160n. 4 and 5; F I, #298, 289; #294, 284; #299, 272.

Page 265

Anne Park. Ch-W III, 364–65; Snyder, 307; Maria Riddell to Currie, *Chronicle* 1921, 108.

"Yestreen I had . . ." *The Merry Muses of Caledonia*, ed. G. Legman, New Hyde Park, N.Y., 1965. 9–10.

Tam o' Shanter. See H & H I, 433–41; Kinsley III, 1347–64.

Page 273

Walter Riddell and Woodley Park. F II, #626, 244.

To Smellie. F II, #492, 106–7.

Smellie to Maria Riddell. Kerr, *Smellie* II, 361–63; 366–67.

Page 274

Maria Riddell's *Voyages*. Ch-W III, 313n; F II, #517, 132.

strained relations. F II, #509, 124.

To Maria Riddell. F II, #675, 306; #555, 163.

Thornton. R. D. Thornton, *Currie*, 293–94 & 304; see also Kerr, *Smellie* II, 390.

Page 275

Maria Riddell. See Sharpe, *Chronicle* 1903, 100; *Chronicle* 1920, 1921, 1923, 1924; Kerr, *Smellie, passim*.

"Dearest Friend." F II, #497, 110.

"vive l'amour." F II, #509, 124.

"enviable creature." F II, #520, 133–34; see also *Chronicle* 1935, 4.

request. F II, #516, 131.

Page 276

"trifling present." F II, #556, 163.

French gloves. D. Ferguson, "Some New Burns Letters," PMLA LI, 4 (Dec. 1936). 982.

"The music of thy voice." *Farewell, thou stream;* H & H III, 235.

Walter Riddell to West Indies. Thornton, *Currie*, 294; Kerr, *Smellie* II, 371–73.

epigram. F II, #590, 211.

four letters. F II, #594, 215; #595, 216; #596, 216–17; #597, 217.

Page 278

letter from Hell. F II, #608, 226–27.
Walter Riddell away. Thornton, *Currie*, 294.
"Mrs. R*****" Currie II, 449.

Page 279

To Maria Riddell. F II, #609, 227–28.

Page 280

returning Common Place Book. F II, #611, 229–30.
"rag." Carswell, 367–68; see also Ainslie, *ante*, 205–7.

Page 281

Sharpe. *Chronicle* 1903, 100.
Rachel Kennedy. Thornton, *Currie*, 296–97.
Robert Riddell. F II, #621, 239; #623, 241; #626, 244; #630, 249.
Walter Riddell. F II, #689, 317.

Page 282

To Margaret Chalmers. F I, #185, 172.
To Maria Riddell. F II, #611, 230.
To Mrs. Dunlop. F II, #634, 254.
To Clarinda. F II, #629, 248.
Epigram to Patrick Miller, Jr. F II, #622, 240.

Page 284

To Maria Riddell. F II, #650, 282; #658, 289–90; #668, 299; #674, 304; #675, 305–6; #679, 309; #681, 310; #683, 314; #697, 323.

Page 285

politics and alcohol. F II, #501, 113; #600, 220 (*Chronicle* 1968, 30); #617, 333–34; #618, 234; #631, 249–50.

VI. Song

This section attempts to give a comprehensive account of Burns' work in Scots song. If it seems detailed, that in turn has seemed the only way to make clear what Burns achieved, and also the limits of his accomplishment. The section owes much, of course, to Burns' correspondence with George Thomson, and to the Stenhouse edition of Johnson's *Museum* (Folklore Associates reissue, 1962), but without the work of Henley and Henderson, J. C. Dick, and James Kinsley, it could not have been written.

Page 288

Epigraph.   Prologue to the *Canterbury Tales,* l. 95.
early interest in song.   F I, #125, 106, 112; II, #511, 127; Dick I M,
28, 29.
"vade mecum."   F I, #125, 109.
To Candlish.   F I, #193, 179.

Page 289

comment on song.   J. Kinsley, "Music of the Heart," *Renaissance and Mod-
ern Studies* VIII (1964). 5–52, particularly 27, 28, & 36.
"Scotch Songs."   *Commonplace Book,* Ewing and Cook, 37–38, 39. See
P.S. for p. 3.

Page 290

Later he comments.   Ewing and Cook, 39–40.
Finally.   Ewing and Cook, 41.

Page 291

Love and Liberty.   H & H II, 291–313; Kinsley III, 1148–62; Crawford,
130–46; *The Jolly Beggars,* ed. J. C. Weston, Northampton, Mass., 1963;
J. C. Weston, "The Text of Burns' 'The Jolly Beggars,'" *Studies in Biography* 13 (1960). 239–47; D. Daiches, *Robert Burns,* New York, 1950.
215–32. (Also later revisions.)
"dissuaded."   J. D. Ferguson, "Burns and Hugh Blair," *Modern Language
Notes* XLV (Nov., 1930). 440–46.
To Thomson.   F II, #586, 202.

Page 302

"I set about composing."   Ewing and Cook, 42.
"all the music."   F II, #452, 75.

Page 303

musicians.   Janet Cruikshank, Morison's Burns I, lxxxi. Kirsty Flint, Dick
I M, xlvii. "an able fiddler," F I, #258, 239. Nathaniel Gow, F II, #591,
212. "a musical Highlander," F II, #576, 189. Fraser, F II, #567, 179.
"Singing Master," F II, #684, 313.

Page 304

fading interest in vernacular poetry.   F I, #379, 379; #333, 326; #319,
311–12.
songs.   Dick I M; Dick (Historical Notes); Kinsley (Notes and Commentary); and H & H (Notes); all *passim.*

tunes and music. Dick I M, xlviii, liii.

notes on song. Dick I M; Cook, *Chronicle* 1922; Ferguson, "Cromek," *Philological Quarterly* IX. 239–48.

"paid more attention." Dick I M, 5.

Page 305

letters. Dick (Historical Notes) makes full use of the Johnson material.

Thomson. Dick I M (xxxix n.), acknowledges a debt to Hadden's *George Thomson, the Friend of Burns*, but asks, "Why the friend of Burns?" See also R. D. Thornton's unpublished Harvard dissertation; and F II, #522, 134; #575, 188; and for *Scots Wha Hae*, F II, #584, 197.

Page 306

"Let me in this ae night." F II, #637, 257.

Simplicity. F II, #511, 126; #554, 161; #507, 122; #535, 148; #554, 162; #588, 210; Dick I M, 15.

Page 307

To Thomson. F II, #647, 276.

Page 308

Thomson's niggling. F II, #644, 268; #647, 277.

tampering. F II, #554, 161.

elegant modification of music. F II, #559, 172.

formal knowledge of music. *Commonplace Book*, Ewing and Cook, 42; F II, #637, 256; #582, 194.

need for a tune. F II, #637, 256; #514, 129; #694, 321.

Page 309

To Rev. John Skinner. F I, #147, 133–34.

Page 310

apologies Dick I M, 24, 26.

originality. F II, #651, 283.

Pages 311–12

To Thomson on music. F II, #515, 130; #586, 202; #569, 182; #644, 268; #646, 271. For Johnson, see Dick (Historical Notes), 368, #48.

Page 313

methods of composing. F II, #577, 190; #637, 256; #636, 255; #506, 200–201; #644, 265.

Page 314

Dick.   Dick I M, xlviii & xliii–iv; also Dick, Preface, xiii.
"whole cycle." Dick I M, l; Dick (Historical Notes), #152, 403–4; see also Kinsley, commentary on songs, III.

Page 315

Scott.   Review of Cromek's *Reliques, Quarterly Review,* Feb. 1, 1809.

Page 316

To Jean McMurdo.   F II, #572, 185.

Page 324

"extra syllables."   Crawford, 290–91.

Page 328

Auld Lang Syne.   Kinsley, #240, III, 1289–91; Dick (Historical Notes), #234, 438–40.
To Thomson.   F II, #646, 274.

Page 329

"a Covenanting Clergyman."   *Chronicle* 1922, 6–7.
Jean Glover.   Dick I M, 57.
Bush.   Dick I M, 20.
Dumbarton's Drums.   Dick I M, 31.

Page 330

Cunningham the player.   Dick I M, 13.

Page 331

polite versions.   Legman, *Merry Muses,* xli–xlii.
Gavin Grieg.   *Chronicle* 1950, 28.

Page 332

"indecorous traditionary verse." Quoted by S. G. Smith in "Robert Burns and the Merry Muses of Caledonia," *Hudson Review* VII, 3 (Autumn, 1954). 334.
"truly remarkable."   G. Legman, *The Horn Book,* New Hyde Park, N.Y., 1964 (2nd printing 1966). 163.
Cunningham.   Author's transcript. See P.S. for p. 365.
origins in . . . bawdy songs.   See notes in H & H, Dick, Kinsley, and Legman's *Merry Muses.* Also *The Merry Muses of Caledonia,* ed. James Barke and Sydney Goodsir Smith, with preface by J. DeLancey Ferguson, Edinburgh, 1959. Also, New York, 1964.

Page 333

Mr. Gracie. Legman, *Horn Book*, 132–34.

Page 334

Merry Muses. See Egerer, #311, 154–56; also Legman, *Merry Muses*, 260–97.

Page 341

To Cleghorn. F II, #592, 212.

Page 346

"A droll Scots song." F II, #637, 257.

VII. Last Years

Burns' friendship with John Syme began before he had moved to Dumfries from Ellisland in 1791, and continued until his death. Although remarks by Syme have appeared from time to time throughout the earlier parts of this book, it has seemed best to continue here the general principle of presenting relationships as a whole. And since this one began late in Burns' life and really continued beyond his death, the appropriate place for the main part of this vivid record is near the end of the book, even though certain events in it, chronologically, fall earlier than some already presented. See the Chronological Table, pp. xv–xviii.

Page 350

convivial parties. Syme to Cunningham, author's transcript. See P.S. for p. 365.
assistance. Peterkin's Currie I, lxxxix–xc.
"cold and frugal." Author's transcript. See dissertation, 390.

Page 351

jar of brandy. F II, #493, 107–8.
To Cunningham. F II, #506, 120.

Page 352

To Provost Staig. F II, #534, 147–48.

Page 353

Maria Riddell and seal. *Chronicle* 1921, 100. See representation of Burns' seal on title page.
To Cunningham. F II, #620, 237–38.
"a bit of a Herald." see McVie, *Chronicle* 1952, 56–63.

Page 354

To Thomson.   F II, 625, 243.
To Thomson.   F II, #642, 278.

Page 355

Burns' position in Dumfries.   *Chronicle* 1937, 102; Ch-W IV, 54–55; F II, #542, 154; Snyder, 372.

Page 356

James Gray.   Snyder, 378; 438 (n. 40); F II, 364. Peterkin's Currie I, lxxxv–vi; Gilbert Burns' Currie I, 433–34.

Page 358

Sharpe.   *Chronicle* 1903, 99–100.
Archibald Lawrie.   F II, 357; Ch-W IV, 14.

Page 359

Josiah Walker.   Morison's Burns I, cxii–v.

Page 361

David McCulloch.   F II, #627, 245.
king's birthday, May 24.   This date kindly supplied by Mrs. Isobel Dewar of the Nat. Lib. of Scotland; see Lockhart, Scott Douglas edition, 224; and Ch-W IV, 121–22.

Page 362

Grace Aiken.   Ch-W IV, 262.

Page 363

Jesse Lewars.   Ch-W IV, 119.

Page 364

John Syme.   Ch-W IV, 217–18; *Chronicle* 1920, 115–16. I am deeply indebted to Mr. Desmond Donaldson, County Librarian, Dumfriesshire, for sending me a copy of Syme's obituary in the *Dumfries Weekly Journal* of December 6, 1833. Syme had died November 24, after an illness of two days.
Syme to Cunningham.   Author's transcript. See P.S. for p. 365.
Maria Riddell and Currie.   *Chronicle* 1924, 86.

Page 365

Syme-Cunningham correspondence.   The originals of this correspondence, then in the Burns Cottage Museum, Alloway, were kindly made available to the author in 1933 by the late Lieut. Col. T. C. Dunlop, head of the

Trustees. For selections, see *Chronicle* 1934, 1935, 1936, 1938, 1939, 1940. The author's transcript is in his doctoral dissertation, in the Library of Cornell University.

Syme to Cunningham. Author's transcript. See above.

Page 369

To Thomson. F II, #582, 194–96.

Page 371

Mr. Carson. Ch-W IV, 20–21.

Page 372

Syme to Cunningham. Author's transcript. See above.

Page 373

two passages. Author's transcript. See above.

Page 374

Syme to Cunningham. Author's transcript. See above.

Page 375

Stobbie. Currie I, 229.

financial details. Ch-W IV, 264n; Peterkin's Currie I, xc.

estate. Money owed him by his brother Gilbert (*Chronicle* 1900, 77–90), and personal property, including his library which was appraised after his death at £90 (Alloway Cottage document 184).

Cunningham to Syme. Author's transcript. See above p. 365.

Page 376

Peterkin proof sheets. Author's transcript. See above p. 365.

Page 378

Brow. Sir James Crichton-Browne, *Burns from a New Point of View*, London, 1926. 1–3. Courtesy of the publishers, Hodder and Stoughton, Ltd.

Page 379

Maria Riddell. Currie I, 221–23.

Page 381

To Thomson. F II, #699, 324.

To Cunningham. F II, #700, 325.

Page 382

To James Armour. F II, #701, 326.

Page 383

To Gilbert Burns.   F II, #703, 326–27.
To James Burness.   F II, #705, 327–28.

Page 384

To Jean.   F II, #708, 329.
To John Clark.   F II, #709, 330.
To James Armour.   F II, #710, 330.

Page 385

Syme to Cunningham.   Author's transcript. See above, p. 365.

Page 386

funeral.   Currie I, 224–25; D. Ferguson, "The Earliest Obituary of Burns,"
   Modern Philology, XXXII (Nov. 1934). 179–84. Also dissertation, 237–
   40.

Page 387

subscription.   Chambers (1880) IV, 306–9; and Syme-Cunningham correspondence.
returns from Currie edition.   T. Besterman, *The Publishing Firm of Cadell
   and Davies*, 1938. xxi.

Page 388

Betty Paton.   Some details of Betty Paton's descendants may be found in
   Chronicle 1922, 114.

Addendum to Page 209
   Dr. James Currie kept a notebook in which he made entries to assist him
in writing his Life of Burns. The following entry is further evidence that
Robert Burns had discussed giving up Ellisland with his brother Gilbert even
before he went on active Excise duty:

Gilbert Burns to Rob[t]
6 Aug 89
—Not that I would have you give up your farm which I am afraid may be
your idea, as I knew that you are a little disgusted with the cares of farming, & your poetic sensibility & love of ease makes you think that you cannot
too much avoid that which gives you uneasiness" he goes on to argue very
sensibly ag[t]. giving it up.

R. D. Thornton, "Burns Letters and
the Currie Notebook," *Studies in
Scottish Literature*, VII, 1 & 2 (1970).

INDEX

A

Abercrombie, Col. and Mrs.: R.B. meets at Gordon Castle, 164
Aberdeen, 18; R.B. visits on Highland tour, 162, 165
Aberdeen, Lord, 165
Abridgement of all the Statutes now in Force Relative to the Revenues of the Excise in Great Britain, 211
Academy, The, Dumfries, 356
Accidents: R.B. injures his knee, 173, 178; R.B. falls from his horse, 210
Achitophel (Burns Ainslie), 161
Act Sederunt of the Session, 341–42 (quoted)
Acting Supervisor of Excise, Dumfries, R.B. serves as, 231
Adam Armour's Prayer, 111
Adam, Dr. Alexander, Rector, Edinburgh High School, 160, 161, 182n
Adair, Anne McKittrick (Mrs. Archibald Lawrie), sister of Dr. J. M. Adair, 358
Adair, Dr. James McKittrick, Edinburgh, 161n; tours with R.B., 168–71; marriage to Charlotte Hamilton, 170n, 467
Adair, Mrs. J. M. (Charlotte Hamilton), 168–70, 170n, 358
Addison, Joseph, *How Are Thy Servants Blest, O Lord,* 288
Address of Beelzebub, 109–10 (quoted from)
Address to a Haggis, 111, 145; "stinking" or "skinking," 141n
Address to Edinburgh, 125, 143
Address to the Deil, 67, 70; 81–83 (quoted from)
Address to the Shade of Thomson, 252
Address to the Unco Guid, 145
Agriculture, Professorship of, proposed for R.B., 122
Aiken, "A Great Critic on Songs," 311. *See also* Currie, I, 147
Aiken, Andrew Hunter, son of Robert Aiken, 111
Aiken, Grace, daughter of Robert Aiken, 262–63
Aiken, Robert, lawyer, Ayr, 65, 67–68, 92, 105–6, 111, 134, 362
Ainslie family: R.B. describes, 148
Ainslie, Rachel, sister of Robert Ainslie: R.B.'s epigram on, 87 (quoted); 148, 152–53
Ainslie, Robert, 7–8, 87, 179; tour with R.B., 147–55; and Meg Cameron, 153, 154, 156; birth of bastard son to, 154–56, 161; and Agnes M'Lehose, 176, 182, 182n, 183–85, 187; 187n; 188–89, 210–11, 213, 234, 237, 467
Airds Hill, 366, 371
Airs: R.B. must like, before he can compose words for, 309; Scots', difficult to fit words to, 309; always better with words, 310
Aiton, William, *A General View of Agriculture in the County of Ayr,* 73–75
Alcohol and politics, and R.B., 285–87
Alison, Rev. Archibald, *Essays on the Nature and Principles of Taste,* 9
Allan, David, artist, 354–55
"All good to me is lost" (*Paradise Lost*), 284 (quoted)
Alloway kirk, 261–63, 266n

Alloway, near Ayr: R.B. born at, 18; 22; the Burnes' home life at, 45; R.B.'s schooling at, 22, 303
"Altho' my bed were in your muir," 1st line of a song by R.B. to illustrate the desirability of "irregularity" in rhyme, 290 (quoted)
"A man's a man for a' that," Jacobin cry, 202
Ambiguities in R.B.'s life, 231
American Congress of 1776, 202
American Revolution, 14, 201–2
Anchor Close, Edinburgh, location of Dawney Douglas' tavern, 139, 140
Anderson, ———, mason, Paisley, son of James Anderson, Ardrossan, 104
Anderson, Dr. Harry B., Toronto, 204n
Anderson, James, mason, Ardrossan, brother-in-law of Mary Campbell, 104
Anderson, Mrs. James, Ardrossan (Anne Campbell), sister of Mary Campbell, 104
Anderson, Robert, carpenter, Greenock, son of James Anderson, Adrossan, 104
Anderson, Dr. Robert, Edinburgh, editor and biographer, 130–33
Andrew and His Cutty Gun, 345–46, (quoted)
Angusshire Fencibles, at R.B.'s funeral, 386
Annan and the Rosamond seizure, 218
Annandale, 159; political "warriors" from, 247; 358
Anne, Queen, 229
Annuities for Agnes M'Lehose, 175
Antigua, 272, 275
Antiquities of England and Wales, by Francis Grose, 241
Antiquities of Scotland, by Francis Grose, 241–42, 260, 266n
Appearance of R.B. in Edinburgh, 127, 130, 130n
Appearance of R.B. in Tarbolton, 63
Arbigland, home of the Craik family, 277n–78n
Arbroath, 167
Archers, Royal Company of, admit R.B. to membership, 252
Ardrossan, 104
Ardwell, Kirkcudbrightshire, 361

Argyle, Duke of, 104
Arianism, 177
Arminianism, 177
"Armorial bearings," for R.B., 353, 353n. See also this book's title page
Armour, James, Mauchline, father of Jean Armour: and warrant for R.B.'s arrest, 6, 96, 98, 107; 238, 381, 382, 384–85
Armour, Mr. and Mrs. James, Mauchline, parents of Jean Armour, 92, 99; set trap for R.B., 147
Armour, Mrs. James, Mauchline, mother of Jean Armour, 92, 95, 96, 180, 382, 384–85
Armour, Jean (Mrs. Robert Burns): her love affair with R.B., 6–9, 63, 91–98, 101, 107, 147, 154, 154n, 158, 178–79, 179n; her marriage to R.B., 7, 92–93, 177, 179, 180, 182, 188, 188n, 189, 192, 238 (See also Marriage of R.B.); her life with R.B., 8n, 231, 350n, 363, 380, 381, 384–85, 386; her later years and death, 216, 227n, 387. Also, 12, 52, 53, 106, 111, 117, 121, 176, 189, 204–5, 207–8, 215, 229, 235–36, 245, 249, 260, 264, 303, and under M'Lehose, Agnes Craig
Arnold, Matthew, 291
Arnot, John, of Dalquhatswood, Ayrshire, 92–94, 96, 106
Arrochar, Loch Long; R.B.'s epigram on, 156 (quoted)
Arthur's Seat, 133
As I Cam o'er the Cairney Mount, 347 (quoted)
Athole, children of Duke and Duchess of: the Marquis; Lords James, Edward, and Robert; Ladies Charlotte, Amelia, and Elizabeth, 163
Athole, Duchess of, 163
Athole, Duke of, 163
Auchmithie, 167
"Auld clay biggin," R.B.'s birthplace, 18
Auld Farmer's New-Year Morning Salutation to his Auld Mare, Maggie, The: use of the "Doric" in, 85; quotations from, 90, 113
Auld Lang Syne, 327–28 (quoted)
"Auld Licht" Calvinism in Ayrshire, R.B. challenges, 5

"Auld Lichts" (Conservatives) vs. "New Lichts" (Liberals) in Ayrshire, 63–64
Auld, Rev. William, Mauchline, 95
Auld Rob Morris, 307
Autobiographical letter of R.B. to Dr. John Moore, quoted in full, 430–37
Ayr, 18, 22, 24, 245, 262, 263, 362
Ayr, Bailies and Provost of, Trustees for funds subscribed for Jean Burns and her children, 387
Ayrshire, 17, 18, 53; R.B. wished to celebrate, 57–58; the Kirk's power and position in, and dissensions, 63–64; peasant life in, 72–75, 454 (R.B. a normal product of); 106, 156, 198, 208, 215, 242
Ay Waukin, O, 315–16 (quoted)

B

Bab the Bowster, a dance, 156, 156n
Bachelor's Club, The, Tarbolton: history of, 30–31; rules of, 32, 52n
Bailie, Lady Grizel, *Werena My Heart Licht I Wad Die*; R.B. quotes from, 362
Bailies and Provost of Ayr, Trustees for funds subscribed for Jean Burns and her children, 387
Baird, Rev. George Husband, R.B. offers him *Tam o' Shanter*, 249
Baker, an English squire, 221n–22n
Balaak, 284
Balaam, 284
Ballad: R.B. uses the term for song, which he thinks of as a little story, a dramatic lyric; R.B. knows the ballad form well but is little interested in ballads, 316–17
Ballantine, John, banker, Ayr, 111, 125, 133, 134
Banff, Banffshire, 165
Bank Street (formerly the Wee, or Stinking, or Carwart's Vennel), Dumfries: R.B. moves to, from Ellisland, 369, 370
Bannockburn, battlefield, 162, 369, 370
Barclay, Mr., friend of R.B. and James Johnson, 241
Bard's Epitaph, A, 386–87 (quoted from)
Bardwell, Dr. Stanley, 204, 204n, 415–16

Barnard, Lady Anne, 330
Bawdry, R.B.'s taste for, 14
Bawdry, Scots: traditional and contemporary, 332–33; anthology of, 335–49
BBC, 53
Beattie, James, poet, 48, 138
Begbie, Alison or Ellison, 34–35
Begg, Mrs. John (Isabella Burns), sister of R.B., 34
Belfast 1787 edition of R.B.'s poems, 51
Bell, Dr. George, Manchester, at school with Alexander Young, 254
Belles of Mauchline, The, mentions Bettsy Miller, 98n
Ben Lomond, 157
Benson, Anna Dorothea (Mrs. Basil Montagu), 277n–78n
Beppo, by Lord Byron, 86
Berrywell, the Ainslie home, Dunse, 152
Berwick, 148n
Beuge, John, engraver, 127, 188–89
Bible: copy of, given Mary Campbell by R.B., 103, 104–5, 104n; 166, 189, 205
Biggar, Lanarkshire, 107
Biographical Dictionary of Eminent Scotsmen, ed. Robert Chambers, 143
Birth of R.B., 18, 20
Blackguards, R.B. courts acquaintance of, 2
Black joke (Jock), The, tune to a bawdy song, 155
Blacklock, Dr. Thomas, Edinburgh, 119–20, 163, 169, 191, 236
Blair Athole, 163–64, 197
Blair, Rev. Hugh, Edinburgh, 136, 138, 247, 291
Blair, Robert, poet, 48
Boat o' Rhone, Kenmore, Kirkcudbrightshire, 371
Bonie brucket lassie, The, 312
Bonnie Heck, 393–95
Bordeaux wine cellar, destination of a witch company, 263–64
Border tour of R.B. and Robert Ainslie, 147–55, 156, 162
Borelan, Maggy, character in *The Court of Equity*, 344
Borough reform and R.B., 225, 226, 228, 242, 285, 286
Boswell, James, the biographer, 11, 234, 369, 467

Botany Bay, Thomas Muir transported to, 203
Bower of Bliss, The, 234
Bowie, Euphan, 99n
Bowmaker, Rev. Robert, Dunse, 148
Boyd, Thomas, builder, Dumfries, 9, 189, 251–52
Braes of Ballenden, The, 300
Braes of Ballochmyle, The, 240
Brandy, smuggled: R.B. sends to Mrs. Dunlop, 351
Bray, The Vicar of, 229
Breadalbane, Earl of, 108, 359
Breckenridge, Jean (Mrs. Gilbert Burns), marriage of, 252
Bremner, Robert, editor of songs, 289, 289n
Breughel, Pieter, 75
Brice, David, Mauchline, 94–95, 98, 119
Brigs of Ayr, The, 111, 145
British Constitution, The, by John De Lolme, 224n
British Museum, 305
Brodie, James, of Brodie, naturalist, 164, 165
Broun, Agnes (Mrs. William Burnes), mother of R.B., 6, 7, 18, 45, 68
Broun, Samuel, Kirkoswald, brother of Agnes Broun, 24
Brow, Dumfriesshire, 378–79, 381, 384, 385
Brown, Alexander, Tarbolton, member of the Bachelor's Club, 31
Brown, Hilton, journalist, 467–68
Brown, John, character in The Court of Equity, 344
Brown, Richard, 35, 36, 178, 179, 181–82, 210, 233
Bruce, Andrew, merchant, Edinburgh, 175
Bruce, Edmund, W. S., a Crochallan, 139
Bruce, Michael, poet, 249
Bruce, Mrs. Catherine, Clackmannan, 170–71
Bruce, Robert, 171, 369, 370
Brydone, Patrick, a celebrated traveler, 148
Buccleugh, Duke of, 247
Buchan, David Stewart Erskine, Earl of, 125, 252
Buchan, Mrs. Elspat, leader of an orgiastic cult, Irvine, 42, 43

Buchanites, The, Irvine, 42, 43
Bunyan, John, 133
Burgess, R.B. made a: at Jedburgh, 148n; Dumfries, 148n; Dumbarton, 156; and Sanquhar (See F II, 375.)
Burke, Mrs., aunt of Dr. J. M. Adair, 170n
Burn, Robert, erected a stone for R.B. over Robert Fergusson's grave, 216
"Burnes," pronunciation of, 17n
Burnes, Elspet (Mrs. John Caird), sister of William Burnes, 167
Burnes, Isbal (Mrs. William Brand), sister of William Burnes, 167
Burnes, Jean, sister of William Burnes, 167
Burnes, Robert, brother of William Burnes, 6, 121, 208, 238
Burnes, William, father of R.B., 4–5, 17–25, 26, 38, 40–41, 43; Lochlea troubles of, 44–45; 45–47, 50, 261
Burness, James, lawyer, Montrose, R.B.'s cousin, 42, 167, 233, 237–39, 375, 381, 383
Burnett, Elizabeth, daughter of Lord Monboddo, 126
Burnett, James, Lord Monboddo, Judge of the Court of Session, 126
Burns, Agnes, sister of R.B., 18, 204, 208
Burns, Alexander Cunningham, name promised by R.B. for unborn child if a son; in ignorance of the promise, his mother named him Maxwell, 382
Burns, Annabella, sister of R.B., 18
Burns Chronicle, The, 372; editor of, 375
Burns, Elizabeth Hyslop (Park), daughter of R.B. and Anne Park, 9, 265n, 388
Burns, Elizabeth (Paton), daughter of R.B. and Elizabeth Paton, 6, 68, 107, 399
Burns, Elizabeth Riddell, daughter of R.B. and Jean Armour Burns, 284, 350n
Burns, Fanny, daughter of William Burnes' brother Robert, 121, 208, 238
Burns Federation, publisher of an edition of Merry Muses, 334
Burns, Francis Wallace, son of R.B. and Jean Armour Burns, 215, 245, 246, 265, 387

Burns from a New Point of View, by Sir James Crichton-Browne, 204n, 378–79 (quoted from)

Burns, Gilbert, brother of R.B.: details from, of R.B. until Mossgiel, 18n, 19, 23–24, 29, 31, 36n, 45, 47, 50, 52, 204; his later relations with R.B., 68, 98, 107; R.B.'s aid to, 142–43, 206, 207, 213, 482; his marriage, 252; in a storm at sea, 364. *Also*, 121, 167, 209, 210, 233, 235, 356–57, 381, 383

Burns, Mrs. Gilbert (Jean Breckenridge), 252

Burns, Isabella (Mrs. John Begg), sister of R.B., 34

Burns, James Glencairn, son of R.B. and Jean Armour Burns, xviii, 222n, 350n, 382, 387

Burns, Jean, daughter of R.B. and Jean Armour, twin to Robert Burns, Jr., died an infant, 7, 98, 154, 154n

Burns, John, brother of R.B., xv, xvi

Burns, John, son of William Burnes' brother Robert, 238

"Burns," Mademoiselle (Margaret Matthews), Edinburgh whore, 242–43; R.B.'s epigram on, 243n (quoted)

Burns, Maxwell, son of R.B. and Jean Armour Burns, 386, 387

Burns, Robert, *passim*. Specific references to R.B. are to be found in association with other persons, topics, or places

Burns, Robert, Jr., "The Laird," son of R.B. and Jean Armour, twin to Jean, 7, 98, 208, 215, 245, 387

Burns, Mrs. Robert. *See* Jean Armour

Burns, Sarah, daughter of James Glencairn Burns, 387

Burns Street (formerly Mill Vennel), Dumfries, 216

Burns, William, brother of R.B., xvii, 24, 208, 233, 240, 246

Burns, William Nicol, son of R.B. and Jean Armour, 215, 229, 265, 387

Burns, William, son of William Burnes' brother Robert, 208, 238

Bush Aboon Traquair, The, 329

"By all on high adoring mortals know!" 1st line of verses sent by R.B. to Maria Riddell, 277

Byron, Lord, 1, 50, 86

C

Cadell, London, publisher of Maria Riddell's *Voyages*, 274

Caesar, aristocrat of *The Twa Dogs*, 11

"Ça ira," revolutionary slogan, heard in Dumfries theatre, 220, 222, 225, 229

Caird, John, Sr., Stonehaven, husband of Elspeth Burnes, 167

Caird, John, Jr., Stonehaven, son of John, Sr., 42

Caledonian Hunt, The, 125, 143–44, 221n–222n, 278n

Caledonian Hunt, The, a song, 240

Caledonian Mercury, Edinburgh, 145

Caller Water, by Robert Fergusson, 111

Calvinism: Agnes M'Lehose a convert and orthodox, 174, 176; Maria Riddell no Calvinist, 275

Calvinism and R.B.: influence on him of William Burnes' views, 5, 25; his challenge to the "Auld Lichts," 5; his belief in the "reverse" of original sin, 15–16; 25; his inner conflict at Irvine, 38–39, 40–41; 62; he satirizes, 65–68, 75–80, 110, 336–37

Calvinism in Ayrshire, "Auld Licht," vs. "New Licht," 63–64

Cameron, Meg, 153, 154, 158

Campbell, ———, Ayr, R.B.'s first teacher, 22

Campbell, Agnes, Dunoon, mother of Mary Campbell, 104

Campbell, Alexander, Greenock, uncle of Mary Campbell, 104

Campbell, Anne (Mrs. James Anderson), Ardrossan, sister of Mary Campbell, 104

Campbell, Archibald, father of Mary Campbell, 104

Campbell, Bruce, Milrig, 234

Campbell, Sir Islay, Lord Advocate, Edinburgh, R.B.'s epigram on, 87–88 (quoted)

Campbell, Mary ("Highland Mary"), 91, 98–107, 156, 440–42, 454–55

Campbell, Thomas, poet, 168

Campbeltown, Argyllshire, 442

Campbeltown Courier, interview in, with Agnes Hendry, 442

Candlish, James, 6, 288

Canongate Kilwinning Lodge of Masons, Edinburgh, 125

Canterbury Tales, The, 86
Carfrae, Mrs., R.B.'s and John Richmond's landlady, Edinburgh, 134
Carfrae, Rev. Patrick, Morham, 145–46, 239–40
Carlisle, 148n, 208
Carlyle, Jane Welsh (Mrs. Thomas Carlyle), 277n
Carlyle, Thomas, 91
Carmichael, Rebekah, Edinburgh, 133, 133n
Carmichael, W. Hillhouse, J.P., Greenock, 440, 441
Carnegie, Mr., friend of William Nicol, 167
Carrick, southern Ayrshire, 242, 262, 263
Carronades from the *Rosamond*, 217, 220
Carson, Mr., Kenmore, 371–72
Carswell, Catherine (Mrs. Donald), biographer of R.B., 10, 280, 442, 454
Carwart's (or the Wee, or Stinking) Vennel, now Bank Street, Dumfries, 216
Case of Conscience, The, bawdy parody of Calvinism, 336–37 (quoted)
Castle of Kenmore, 366
Cathcart, Miss, R.B. meets, at Blair Athole, 163
Cato, pseudonym of Robert Riddell, 226
Cauld Kail in Aberdeen, 381
Cawdor, 162
"Cease, ye prudes, your envious railing!" 1st line of R.B.'s epigram on "Mademoiselle Burns," 243 (quoted)
Certificate as a bachelor: R.B. promised, 95; qualifies for, 98
Chalmers, Cochran (Lady Mackenzie), sister of Margaret Chalmers, 169
Chalmers, Mrs. Euphemia (née Murdoch), mother of Margaret Chalmers, 169
Chalmers, Margaret, 39, 146, 168–69, 173, 174, 181, 194, 282
Chambers, Robert, author, editor, publisher, 9, 140, 143, 332, 334, 364, 365, 371
Champman, Dr., schoolmaster, Dumfries, 254
Charles, Prince, The Young Pretender, 162, 378
Chaucer, 86, 288

Cherry and the Slae, The, 55, 90
Chevy Chase, 245
China, 53, 54
Choruses to songs, R.B. not fond of, 316–17, 317n
Christabel, 17
Christinson, Mr. and Mrs. Alexander, 133
Christis Kirk on the Green, 80
Cinque Ports Cavalry, at R.B.'s funeral, 386
Clackmannanshire, 170
Clark, John, of Locherwoods, 384
Clark, Miss, Dunbar, 152
Clarke, James, schoolmaster, Moffat, and later Forfar, 199, 259–60
Clarke, Samuel, Jr., lawyer, Dumfries, 285, 286
Clarke, Stephen, organist, Edinburgh, 240, 303
Clarinda. *See* Agnes Craig M'Lehose (Mrs. James)
Class consciousness and feeling in R.B., 15, 135, 194–99, 282
Cleghorn, Robert, farmer, Edinburgh, a Crochallan, 1, 14, 135, 139, 141, 211, 340
Clow, Jenny, 186, 216
Club life in Edinburgh, 138–41
Clyde, river, 96, 314, 441
Cockburn, Henry, Edinburgh, *Memorials of His Time*, 158–59
Coldstream, 148n
Collection of Scotch, Galwegian, and Border Tunes, A, ed. Robert Riddell, 254, 254n
Collection of songs, unidentified, R.B.'s *vade mecum* in youth, 217
Comin' Thro' the Rye, 305, 325–26 (quoted)
Common Place Book, Maria Riddell's, 280, 282
Commonplace Book of Robert Burns, 1783–1785, 3, 27, 28, 29, 33, 155n, 288–90, 332
Commonplace Book of Robert Burns, 1787, 125, 133, 136
Composition of songs, R.B.'s methods of, 13–14, 313–314
Conjugal love inferior to Nature's Law as a topic for songs, 312–13
Constitution, British, and R.B., 223, 225, 228
Copland, Mrs., Dumfries, 362–63

Copyright to Edinburgh 1787 edition of R.B.'s poems, 142
Corbet, Mrs. William, friend of Mrs. Dunlop, 122
Corbet, William, General Supervisor of Excise, 213, 213n–14n, 226, 228, 286–87
Corn Rigs, 36–38 (quoted), 84
Correspondence of R.B. at Ellisland, 1788–1791, 233–51 (quotations from)
Cotter's Saturday Night, The, 46, 48, 113–14, 120
Court of Equity, The, or Libel Summons, or The Fornicators Court, 59n, 70, 70n, 108, 111, 341–45 (quoted)
Court of Session, The, William Burnes' Appeal to, 45
Covenanters, The, 16
Covington Mains farm, near Biggar, Lanarkshire, 107
Cowgate, Highland wench in the (Meg Cameron?), 154
Cowper, John, Elegy on, by Allan Ramsay, 396n, 396–99 (quoted)
Craig, Andrew, surgeon, Glasgow, father of Agnes Craig (M'Lehose), 174, 175
Craig, William, later Lord Craig, Judge of the Court of Session, cousin of Agnes Craig (M'Lehose), a Crochallan, 139, 175
Craigie, Mrs. Dunlop's ancestral estate, 120
Craigie: R.B. mentions to James Burness, 167
Crawford, Robert, poet, 329
Crawford, Thomas, critic, 324
Crawford, Riding Master Walter, Excise officer, 217–19
Creech, bookseller and publisher, Edinburgh: and the 1787 edition of R.B.'s poems, 7, 125, 126, 138; R.B.'s difficulties with, 126–27, 126n, 142, 143, 147, 158, 168, 180, 181; and the 1793 edition, 253, 351n; and "Mademoiselle Burns," 243. Also, 134, 155, 183n, 458
Crichton-Browne, Sir James, Burns from a New Point of View, 204n, 378–79
Crieff, Perthshire, 162
Criffell, Kirkcudbrightshire, 379
Cro Chalein ("Colin's Cattle"), Dawney Douglas' favorite song, 139

Crochallan (Cro Chalein) Fencibles, convivial Edinburgh club, 138–41, 233, 303, 333, 458
Crombie, Alexander, Dumfries, 252
Cromek, Robert Hartley, ed. Reliques of Robert Burns, 33, 99–100, 257–58
Cromlongan Castle, 379
Cruickshank, Janet, daughter of William Cruickshank, 303
Cruickshank, William, schoolmaster, Edinburgh, 182n, 303
Cullen, Banffshire, 164
Cullie, Mr. and Mrs. David, R.B.'s predecessors at Ellisland, 205
Culloden battlefield, 162
Cumberland and Westmoreland mountains, 379
Cunningham, Alexander, lawyer and jeweler, Edinburgh, a Crochallan, 139, 141, 174n, 187, 197–98, 210, 213, 221n–22n, 227n, 230–31, 252, 332, 351–52, 353, 365–75, 380–82, 385, 465
Cunningham, Mrs. Alexander, 369
Cunningham, Allan, biographer of R.B., 254, 277n–78n, 333
Cunningham, Lady Elizabeth, sister of Lord Glencairn, 146
Cunningham, James, Earl of Glencairn, 125, 162, 210, 251
Cunningham, John, actor, 330
Cunningham, northern Ayrshire, 242
Currie, Dr. James, Liverpool, biographer of R.B.: on R.B.'s candor as a proof of genius, 16; on William Burnes, 46; at school with Alexander Young, 254; embroiders John Syme's account of the 1793 tour with R.B., 372, 372n; raises £70 for Jean in Liverpool, and £1400 with his Life and Works of R.B., 387. Also, 9, 22, 130, 158, 168, 169, 188, 275, 278, 282, 305, 359, 364, 365, 375, 376
Customs, R.B. writes Maria Riddell about a position in, for a protégé of hers, 284

D

Daer, Basil, Lord, son of the 4th Earl of Selkirk, 89, 111, 368n
Dalgoner, n. w. Dumfriesshire, 104
Dallas, William, W. S., Edinburgh, a Crochallan, 139

Dalrymple, James, of Orangefield, nephew of Rev. William Dalrymple, 24, 125

Dalrymple, Rev. William: baptized R.B., 24, 125

Dalrymple village, Ayrshire, 24

Dalswinton, Nithsdale, Dumfriesshire, estate of Patrick Miller, 11, 126, 148n, 168, 172, 247

Dalzell, Andrew, Professor of Greek, Edinburgh University, 133

Dalzell, J., Dumfries, and Scots Wha Hae, 369

Dalzell, L., Kirkcudbright, friend of John Syme, 368

Dancing schools, R.B.'s attendance at, 27–28

Davidson, Betty, "an old Maid" of R.B.'s mother's, 264, 431

Davies, Miss Deborah Duff, 195

Day Returns, The, R.B.'s song for Robert and Elizabeth Riddell, 256

Death and Dr. Hornbook, 89, 145

Death and Dying Words of Poor Mailie, The, 36, 48, 57, 289

Death of Mary Campbell, 104, 105, 107

Death of Robert Burns, 385

Dedication to the Edinburgh 1787 edition of the poems of R.B., 143–44 (quoted), 222n

Dedication to Gavin Hamilton, of Kilmarnock edition, 110 (quoted from)

Dee, river, Kirkcudbrightshire, 366, 371

Deism, R.B. contemns, 15–16

De Lolme, John, The British Constitution, 224n

Deserted Village, The, by Oliver Goldsmith, 48

Despondency, an Ode, 108

Devon valley, Clackmannanshire, 168, 170, 194

Dick, James C., on R.B. and Scots song: R.B. "embodied the whole cycle of Scottish song"; collected and edited airs, 314

Discouragement and loneliness of R.B., 4, 190, 194–95, 210, 361, 362, 362n

Dods, Captain, Dumfries, 286

Don, Lady Henrietta, sister of Lord Glencairn, 264

Doon, river, 262

Doonholm, estate of Dr. William Fergusson, provost of Ayr, employer of

William Burnes at Alloway, and the Mt. Oliphant landlord, 18

Doric, 85

Douglas, Donald (Dawney), tavern keeper, Anchor Close, Edinburgh, host of the Crochallan Fencibles, 139

Douglas, Gavin, poet, 266, 403, 403n

Dow, John, keeper of the Whitefoord Arms inn, Mauchline, character in The Court of Equity, 345

Dow, Sandy, character in The Court of Equity, 343, 344, 345

Drama, the, and R.B., 146. See also Theatre, the, and R.B.; and P.S. for p. 146

Dramatic lyrics, R.B. thinks of his songs as, 316–17

Drinking and R.B., 4, 10–11, 106, 132, 138–41, 159, 165–66, 178, 180, 184–85, 260, 274, 277n–78n, 278–80, 285–87

Drumlanrig, Duke of Queensberry's estate, Dumfriesshire, 260

Dryburgh, Roxburghshire, 148, 148n

Dublin 1787 edition of R.B.'s poems, 51

Duff House, seat of Earl of Fife, 165

Dulsie, Invernessshire, 164

Dumbarton, 156, 157, 158

Dumbarton's Drums Beat Bonny, O, 329–30

Dumfries, 2, 42; R.B. made a burgess of, 148n, 153; 172, 183, 194 208; R.B. and the Excise and loyality inquiry there, 215–31; Caledonian Hunt meeting there, 221n–22n; 238, 247, 254, 255, 272, 273, 277n, 303, 328, 335–53; R.B.'s position and life there, 350–63; 368, 369, 378, 379, 380, 381, 384, 385; R.B.'s funeral in, 386; 387

Dumfries Academy, The, 356

Dumfries Royal Volunteers, 15, 356, 373–74, 386

Dumfriesshire, few there to understand R.B., 358

Dumfries Town Hall, site of R.B.'s funeral, 386

Dunbar, town, 148n, 152

Dunbar, William, poet, 86

Dunbar, William, W.S., Edinburgh, a Crochallan, 135, 138, 189–90, 203–4

Duncan Davidson, 333

Duncan Gray, 318–19 (quoted), 333

Duncan, king, 162
Dundas family attitude to R.B., 197–98. *See also* Archers, 252
Dundas, Henry, later Lord Melville, 10, 163, 197
Dundas, John, W.S., Edinburgh, a Crochallan
Dundas, Robert, Lord Arniston, President, The Court of Session, 197–98, 198n
Dundas, Robert, Jr., Solicitor General, 197–98, 198n
Dundee, 162, 238
Dundonald parish, which includes Irvine, 98
Dunfermline Abbey, 171
Dunlop, Major Andrew, of Dunlop, son of Mrs. Frances Dunlop, 121, 242
Dunlop, Anthony, son of Mrs. Frances Dunlop, friend of James Grierson of Dalgoner, 104, 247
Dunlop House, 178, 241, 358
Dunlop, John, of Dunlop, husband of Frances Anna Wallace, 120, 121
Dunlop, John, of Moreham Mains farm, Haddington, son of Mrs. Frances Dunlop, 121
Dunlop, Mrs. John (Frances Anna Wallace), of Dunlop: her Portuguese friend, 53; details of, 119–23; sends Kilmarnock edition to Dr. Moore, 158; comments unfavorably on William Nicol, 158n; dislikes R.B.'s "outspokenness" in his poems, 175; helps R.B., 213, 214; breaks with R.B., 122, 231; and *Tam o' Shanter*, 264–65, 266n. *Also*, 10, 101, 104, 135, 142–43, 147, 168, 189, 191–92, 199, 203, 206, 207, 209, 210, 215, 223, 224, 232, 233, 234–35, 236–37, 239–40, 241–42, 247, 260, 274, 282, 283, 350n, 357, 358, 381
Dunlop, Miss Keith, daughter of Mrs. Frances Dunlop, 236
Dunlop, Miss Rachel, daughter of Mrs. Frances Dunlop, 236
Dunlop, Susan (Mrs. James Henri), Loudon Castle, daughter of Mrs. Frances Dunlop, 121
Dunlop village and estate, Ayrshire, 119
Dunnotar, Kincardineshire, home of William Burnes, 18

Dunoon, birthplace of Mary Campbell, 104
Dunse, Berwickshire, site of Ainslie family home, 148
Durham, 222n
"Dweller in you dungeon dark," opening line of quotation from R.B.'s *Ode to the Memory of Mrs. Oswald*, 199

E

Earlston, Berwickshire, 148n
East India Company, 356, 387
Easton, Esther, R.B. meets on his Border Tour, 149, 152
Ecclefechan, Annandale, Dumfriesshire, 159, 218
Echo, Mrs. John Gordon's lap dog; epitaph on, by R.B., 366 (quoted)
Edinburgh, 7, 10, 18, 107, 108, 119; R.B.'s "hare-brained ramble" in, 124–41; R.B.'s manner in, 127–33; R.B.'s impressions of, 133–36; a general description of, 136–37; club life, 138–41; 141, 147, 162, 163, 167, 171; Clarinda episode in, 172–88; R.B. injures knee in, 173, 178; 191, 206, 218, 231, 248, 249; the interest in song in, 303; 303n, 358, 365, 387
Edinburgh Castle, 137
Edinburgh Evening Courant, ed. David Ramsay, 128, 200
Edinburgh Herald, 266n
Edinburgh High School, 159, 170
Edinburgh Magazine, 125, 266n
Edinburgh Magazine and Review, ed. Gilbert Stuart, 139
Edinburgh 1787 edition of R.B.'s poems, 2, 6, 51, 96, 107, 126; details of, 141–45; 222n, 238
Edinburgh 1793 edition of R.B.'s poems, 253, 351, 351n
Edinburgh 1794 edition of R.B.'s poems, he superintended, 351
Edinburgh Society and R.B., 124, 135, 141, 147n, 303, 375
Edinburgh University, 137, 254
Education of R.B., 5, 22–26
Eglinton, Earl and Countess of, present R.B. with 10 gns., 125
Eglinton, Hugh Montgomerie, Earl of, 102, 102n, 455
Elbow, The, Mauchline public house, 102, 103n

Elegy XVIII He Repeats the Song of Colin, a Discerning Shepherd, Lamenting the State of the Woolen Manufactory, by William Shenstone, 48

Elegy on John Cowper, An, by Allan Ramsay (model for *Poor Mailie's Elegy* and *Tam Samson's Elegy, III*), 396–99 (quoted)

Elegy Written in a Country Churchyard, 48, 133

Eliot, Jane, poet, 330

Elizabeth I, Queen, 14, 250

Elliott, the Herriotter, 161

Ellisland farm, 8n, 16, 143; Kirn night at, 183–85; lease of, 181, 189, 189n; the "elbow of existence," 204–6; farmhouse at, still unfinished, 208; 209, 210; a "ruinous bargain," 214; R.B. leaves with little loss, 215; 216, 231–33; R.B.'s correspondence there, 206, 233–51; 232, 253, 260, 303; letter from Gilbert Burns about, 482

Ellisland Hallowe'en, and the Riddell quarrel, 280

Eloïsa to Abelard, by Alexander Pope, 283

England, 148n, 240

English Convention of 1688, 202

English usage of R.B., 26

Epigrams of R.B., 87–88, 367

Epistle to Davie, 52, 53–55 (quotations from), 57, 90

Epistle to Dr. Blacklock, 191 (quotation from)

Epistle to Hugh Parker, 205 (quoted from)

Epistle to James Smith, 59–62 (quoted), 90

Epistle to J. Lapraik, 55–57 (quotation from)

Epistle to a Young Friend (Andrew Aiken, son of Robert Aiken), 111

Epistles in verse of R.B., 53–62

Equality, 83, 202

Erskine, Andrew, 333

Erskine, David Stewart, Earl of Buchan, brother of Henry Erskine, 125, 252

Erskine, Hon. Henry, Dean of the Faculty of Advocates, Edinburgh, a Crochallan, 51; R.B.'s epigram on, 87–88 (quoted); 125, 139, 264

Erskine, Lady Isabella, sister of Henry

Erskine and wife to the Hon. and Rev. John Cunninghame, younger brother of Lord Glencairn, 125

Erskine, John Francis, of Mar, 227–28, 227n

Estate of R.B., 375

Euclid, 152

Evergreen, The, ed. Allan Ramsay, 55

Ewie wi' the Crooked Horn, The, by Rev. John Skinner, 166

"Excellent wretch!/Perdition catch my soul but I do love thee!" quoted by R.B. about Jean, 179

Excise, The, 2, 8n; R.B.'s early thoughts of, 96, 105; 122, 124, 163, 167–68; R.B.'s appointment to, and instruction in, 173, 181, 189; 192; R.B.'s seeking active duty, 206–7; R.B.'s feelings about, 209, 210–11; the *Abridgement* of its regulations, 211; R.B.'s duties and difficulties in, 211–13; R.B.'s life in, at Ellisland, 183–84, 207, 209–17; and in Dumfries, 215–31; R.B.'s hopes of promotion in, 213–14, 217; report of R.B.'s Supervisor in, 213–14; R.B. made Acting Supervisor in, at Dumfries, 216, 231; R.B. and, in the *Rosamond* seizure, 217–20; inquires into R.B.'s loyalty, 223–31; 233, 246, 248, 250–51, 286–87; R.B.'s suggestion for improvement in, Dumfries, 352–53; 375, 381, 465

Expositor, The, by William Frederick Pinchbeck, 128n

Extempore Pinned to a Lady's Coach (Maria Riddell's), 283 (quoted)

Eyemouth, 148n, 152

F

Fairest Maid on Devon's Banks, 194 (quoted)

"Fair maid you need not take the hint," 1st line of R.B.'s epigram on Rachel Ainslie, 87 (quoted)

Fair, Mrs., sister of Miss Lookup, 149

Falstaff, 341, 365

Family loyalty of R.B., 6, 142–43, 206, 231–32, 383. *See also* Burnes and Burness

Farewell of R.B. and Mary Campbell, 100

Farmer's Ingle, The, by Robert Fergusson, 406–9 (quoted)

"Fencibles" explained, 139

Ferdinand, Count Fathom, by Tobias Smollett, 36

Ferguson, Professor Adam, Edinburgh University, 126

Ferguson, De Lancey, editor and biographer of R.B., 8, 121, 193, 206, 216, 338, 352, 369

Fergusson, Alexander, of Craigdarroch, J.P., "Whistle" contest winner, 260

Fergusson, Robert, poet, 1, 35, 36, 47, 49; author, *Caller Water,* 111; 134–35; his poems used by R.B. for models, 80–81; author, *Hallow-Fair,* 409–14 (quoted); author, *The Farmer's Ingle,* 406–9 (quoted); author, *Leith Races,* 409–14 (quoted)

Fergusson, Dr. William, Doonholm, Provost of Ayr, William Burnes' employer at Alloway and landlord at Mt. Oliphant, 19, 43

Fife, Earl of, 165

Findlater, Alexander, Supervisor of Excise, Dumfries, 8n, 10-11, 213n–14n, 216, 217, 226, 250, 352, 353

Findlay, James, Exciseman, Tarbolton, instructor of R.B., 185

Fintry, near Dundee, 238

Fisher, William ("Holy Willie"), 64, 65

Five Carlins, The, election ballad 1790, 248

Flax, R.B. raises, at Lochlea, 35

Flax dressing, R.B. goes to Irvine to learn, 35

Flint, Kirsty, sang for R.B., 303

Fochabers, Elginshire, seat of Gordon Castle, 164

Fontenelle, Miss Louisa, actress, Dumfries, 220, 221, 226

Fornicator, The, 70–71 (quoted), 108, 111

Fornicators Court, The, or *The Court of Equity,* or *Libel Summons,* 59n, 70n, 108, 111, 341–45 (quoted)

Fort George, Invernesshire, 164

Fox, Charles James, 132

Fraser, Luke, Latin master at Edinburgh High School, 160

Fraser, Thomas, musician ("hautboy"), 303, 359, 369

Fraternity, 202

Freedom, 44, 83

French gloves, smuggled, for Maria Riddell, 276

French Revolution, and R.B., 14, 122–23, 202–3; carronades for, 220; 222–31, 286

Friars' Carse, estate of Robert Riddell, 253, 255, 256, 257, 258, 260, 273, 281

From Esopus to Maria, 283–84 (quotation from)

Frost, Robert, poet, 84

Funeral of Robert Burns, 386

G

Galloway, Lord, R.B.'s epigram on, 87 (quoted), 367

Galloway hills, 379

Galloway tour 1793 of R.B. with John Syme, 365–72

Galloway tour 1794 of R.B. with John Syme, 361, 365n

Gardner, Jean, a Buchanite lass, 43

Garry, river, 163

Gatehouse-of-Fleet, Kirkcudbrightshire, 361, 367

Gazetteer, The, Edinburgh, ed. William Johnston, 220, 225, 226, 253

Geddes, Jenny, R.B.'s mare, 157, 210n

Gedes, Jenny, vegetable seller, 157n

General Assembly of the Church of Scotland, 137

General View of Agriculture in the County of Ayr, A, by William Aiton, 73–75

Gentle Shepherd, The, by Allan Ramsay, 172, 354

George I, II, and III, R.B.'s "beefwitted" Hanoverian kings of England, 14

Gethsemane, of R.B., 379

Giblet Pie, The, 334n

Gibson, Poosie Nancie, 291, 292

Gillespie, Rev. John, Kells, 271–72

Gillies, Lord, Judge of the Court of Session, a Crochallan, 139

Glasgow, 42, 175, 178, 181, 291

Glasgow Courier, 226

Glencairn, Dowager Countess of, 139

Glencairn, James Cunningham, Earl of, 125, 162, 210, 251

Glendonwynnes of Parton, R.B. and John Syme dine at, 366

Glenkens, John Gordon's barge, 371

Glenkens, Kirkcudbrightshire, 372
Glenriddell MSS., 92, 187n, 199, 227, 228, 257
Glens, Kirkcudbrightshire, 361
Glorious Revolution, the, 200, 201, 202
Glover, Jean, O'er the Moor amang the Heather, 329
God Save the King, 220, 229
Goldilea (Woodley Park), Walter Riddell purchases, 273
Goldsmith, Oliver, author, 48
Gordon, Mrs., R.B. meets, at Gordon Castle, 164
Gordon, Hon. Alexander, advocate, a Crochallan, 139
Gordon, Lady Charlotte, 164
Gordon, Duke and Duchess of, 164–65
Gordon, Jane, Duchess of, 125
Gordon, John, of Kenmore, later Viscount Kenmure, 366, 371, 372
Gordon, Mr. and Mrs. John, Kenmore, Kirkcudbrightshire, 366
Gordon, Lady Madelina, 164
Gordon, Miss Patricia, Halleaths, Dumfriesshire, 222n
Gordon Castle, Fochabers, Elginshire, 164, 166
Gow, Nathaniel, fiddler, son of Neil Gow, 303
Gow, Neil, fiddler, 162
Gracie, I., Dumfries, son of James Gracie, 333
Gracie, James, banker, Dumfries, 333
Gracie MS, of bawdy songs, 333
Graham, Douglas, of Shanter Farm, 264
Graham, Robert, of Fintry, Commissioner of Excise, 122, 163, 173; R.B. suggests active duty to, 206–7, 236; 209, 212, 213; and the loyalty inquiry, 223–28; 238, 375
Graham, Mrs. Robert, 203
Grant, Mrs., R.B. meets, at Kilravock, 164
Grant, Sir James, of Grant, 164
Granton, Rt. Hon Charles Hope, Lord, 160–61, 168
Grassmarket, Edinburgh, 128, 186
Grave, The, by Robert Blair, 48–49
Gray, James, schoolmaster, Dumfries, 190, 194, 356, 465
Gray, Thomas, poet, 48, 133
Greenfield, Rev. William, Edinburgh, 136

Green Grow the Rashes, O, bawdy version, 97–98 (quoted); 324–25 (quoted); 333
Greenock, 100, 104, 214, 440, 441, 442
Greenock Burns Club, 441, 441n
Greig, Gavin, 331
Gretna, 148n
Grey Goose and the Gled, The, 346–47 (quoted)
Grierson, James, of Dalgoner, Dumfriesshire, 102–5, 126n, 178–79, 188, 188n
Grieve, Miss Betsy, Eyemouth, 152
Grim Grizel, 339–41 (quoted)
Grose, Capt. Francis, 241–42; Antiquities of England and Wales, 241; Antiquities of Scotland, 241–42; 256; and Tam o' Shanter, 260–64, 266n
Guthrie, Rev. William, Trial of a Saving Interest, 229

H

Habbie Simpson, 59, 391–93
"Had we never loved sae kindly," 1st line of four quoted, from song by R.B. to Agnes M'Lehose
Halleaths, 272n, 275
Halliday, James, laborer, 251
Hallowe'en, 85, 89 (quoted from), 108
Hallow-Fair, by Robert Fergusson, 81, 403–6 (quoted)
Hamilton, Mrs. Barbara (née Murdoch), mother of Charlotte Hamilton, Gavin Hamilton's stepmother, 168
Hamilton, Charlotte (Mrs. J. M. Adair), Gavin Hamilton's half-sister, 168–70, 170n, 358
Hamilton, Gavin, lawyer, Mauchline, R.B.'s landlord at Mossgiel, 45, 65, 65n, 102, 110, 133, 168, 169, 188
Hamilton, Mr. and Mrs. Gavin, 99
Hamilton, Grace, Charlotte Hamilton's sister, 169
Hamilton, Capt. John, of Allershaw, R.B.'s Dumfries landlord, 216
Hamilton, Lieut. William, of Gilbertfield, poet, 52, 55; Bonnie Heck, 393–95 (quoted); his verse epistles, 399–401 (quoted from)
Handsome Nell, 27, 28, 37
Hannibal, life of, R.B. delighted in, as a boy, 25n

Hanover, the house of, R.B.'s caustic comments on, 162, 200

Harvieston, estate of John Tait, 168–70, 171, 194

Hay, Charles, later Lord Newton as Judge of the Court of Session, a Crochallan, 139, 198n

Hay, John, and the Mauchline Kirk Session, 99, 99n

Hay, Lewis, banker, Edinburgh, husband of Margaret Chalmers, 168

Hazlitt, William, critic, 48, 265

Health Record of R.B., 38, 41, 41n, 173, 203, 204, 207, 209–10, 233, 282, 362–63, 381–82, 415–29, 465

"Heaventaught Ploughman," the role R.B. played in Edinburgh, 145

Helvellyn, 379

Henderson, Capt. Matthew, a Crochallan, 139

Henderson, T. F., editor, 114. See also Henley and Henderson

Hendry, Agnes, the infant buried in Mary Campbell's grave, 106, 441, 442

Hendry, Daniel S., brother of Agnes Hendry, 106

Hendry, Duncan M., memorandum from, 106, 441n

Hendry, Miss J., Greenock, niece of Agnes Hendry, 442

Hendry response prompt to story that baby's coffin was found in Mary Campbell's grave, 445

Henley, W. E., and T. F. Henderson, editors, The Poetry of Burns (Centenary Edition), their comment on R.B.'s poetry, 114

Henley, W. E., editor, 84, 114

Henri, James, Loudon Castle, husband of Susan Dunlop, 121

Henri, Mrs. James (Susan Dunlop), 121

Henryson, Robert, poet, 86

Herald's office, R.B. visits, 353n

Herd, David, song collector, 314

"Here cursing, swearing Burton lies," 1st line of R.B.'s epigram, 87 (quoted)

Here's His Health in Water, 332

"Here Stewarts once in glory reign'd," 1st line of R.B.'s indiscreet lines at Stirling, 162 (quoted)

Hermitage, The, at Friars' Carse, 255–56

Heron, Rev. James, Kirkungeon, 245

Heron, Patrick, of Heron, M.P., 217

Heron's, 182

Highland Airs, ed. Malcolm McDonald, 312

Highland Mary, 100–101 (quotation from), 308

"Highland Mary." See Mary Campbell

Highland Society, the Right Honorable, 109

Highland tour of R.B. with William Nicol, 157n, 158, 161–67

"Highland wench in the Cowgate" (Meg Cameron?), 154

High School, Edinburgh, 159, 170

Hildebrode, John, epitaph on, 159

Hill, Peter, bookseller, Edinburgh, 47, 181, 196–97, 205, 216, 241–43, 58, 274

"His very foot has music in't," 1st line of passage quoted from There's Nae Luck about the House, 307

Hog, James, Edinburgh, 153

Hog, Mrs. James, Buchannan's Land, Canongate, Edinburgh, 153

Hogg, James, poet, 331

Holy Fair, or "sacramental occasion," 72

Holy Fair, The, 63, 64, 70, 72–80 (quoted), 80–81, 175

Holyrood Palace, 137

Holy Willie's Prayer, 63–68 (quoted), 70, 84

Homer, Pope's translation, 152

Hood, Mr., R.B.'s host on the Border tour, 153

Hope, Rt. Hon. Charles, later Lord Granton, 160–61

Hope, John, later Lord Hopetoun, 161

Hopetoun, James, Earl of, 161, 199, 247

"How are thy servants blest, O Lord," hymn by Joseph Addison, 288

Hoy, James, librarian at Gordon Castle, 164

Humble Petition of Bruar Water, The, 164

Hume, David, philosopher, 137

Hunter, William, character in The Court of Equity, 343, 345

Hyslop, Mr. and Mrs. William, Globe Inn, Dumfries, 265n

I

"If you rattle along like your mistress's tongue," 1st line of R.B.'s epigram on Maria Riddell, 285 (quoted)
"Ilka lassie hae her laddie," 1st line of stanza of *Comin' Thro' the Rye*, not by R.B., 326
I'm o'er Young to Marry Yet, 321–22 (quoted)
Independence, 369
India, 356
Inquiry into R.B.'s loyalty, 223–31
Interleaved *Scots Musical Museum*, 328, 329, 330
"In this strange land, this uncouth clime," 1st line of *Epistle to Hugh Parker*, 205 (quoted from)
"Inundation of Nonsense," provoked by R.B.'s success, 146
Inventory, The, 111
Inverleithing, 148n
Inverness, 162, 164
Ironies in R.B.'s life, 231–32, 386
Irvine, David, 376
Irvine, Dundonald Parish, Ayrshire, 35–36, 38–39, 40–41, 42, 50, 98, 135, 178, 204
Irvine Hogmanay, and the Riddell quarrel, 280
Iscariot, Judas, 250
Isle, The, Kirkcudbright, seat of Lord Selkirk, 367–68
Isle, The, Nithsdale, country house of David Newal offered R.B., 208
Is There for Honest Poverty, 311

J

Jacobinism and R.B., 199–203, 280, 378
Jacobitism and R.B., 14, 199–203, 378
Jamaica, 6, 59n, 92, 95, 96, 106, 175, 178
James I and V, kings of Scotland, 403
James Currie the Entire Stranger and Robert Burns, by Robert D. Thornton, 187n
Jedburgh, Roxburghshire, 148, 148n, 149, 152
John Anderson, my jo, 333; bawdy version, 348–49 (quoted)
John Highlandman, 292
Johnie Faa, 330

Johnson, James, engraver, Edinburgh, publisher of *The Scots Musical Museum*, 13, 108, 139, 141, 148, 161, 192, 194, 235, 236, 240–41, 254, 254n, 302–3, 304, 305, 311, 312, 314, 315, 332
Johnson, Dr. Samuel, 120, 369
Johnston, Capt. William, editor of *The Gazetteer*, Edinburgh, 225, 247, 248, 253
Jolly Beggars, The, or *Love and Liberty*, 84, 111, 131n, 291–92, 293–302 (quoted), 332

K

Kate of Aberdeen, by John Cunningham, actor, 330
Keats, John, 51, 82
Kelso, Roxburghshire, 148n
Kemp, Rev. John, Edinburgh, Agnes M'Lehose's spiritual adviser, 176
Ken, Loch, Kirkcudbrightshire, 371
Ken, river, Kirkcudbrightshire, 366
Kenmore, Castle of, 366
Kenmore, or Kenmure, Kirkcudbrightshire, 366, 367, 371
Kenmure, John Gordon, Viscount, 366n
Kennedy, Elizabeth (Mrs. Robert Riddell), 253, 255, 257, 258, 260
Kennedy, Rachel, sister of Elizabeth Kennedy, 281
Kerr, Robert, *Memoir of the Life, Writings, and Correspondence of William Smellie*, 140
Killiecrankie, 87
Killiecrankie battlefield, 162
Kilmarnock, 119, 178, 231, 252, 329
Kilmarnock and Edinburgh 1787 editions of R.B.'s poems, inspirers of "inundations of nonsense," 145–46
Kilmarnock edition of the poems of R.B., 1, 2, 6, 51, 52, 68; publication of, 95, 96, 98, 106; 107–8, 119, 134, 158, 175, 191, 291, 386
Kincaid, Alexander, his assignees, publisher of Bible given Mary Campbell by R.B., 104
King, Mrs., R.B. meets, at Blair Athole, 163
King's birthday, 1794, Dumfries, 316
Kinross, 167
Kinsley, James, editor of *The Poems and*

Songs of Robert Burns, 12, 289, 326, 328, 337, 338, 339, 347

Kirkcudbright, 367–69, 373

Kirk in Ayrshire, The, its position and inner stresses, 63–64

Kirkoswald, Ayrshire, 28, 264

Kirkpatrick, Rev. Joseph, Dunscore, Dumfriesshire, R.B.'s Ellisland parish, 241, 245

Kirkpatrick, Nelly, heroine of *Handsome Nell,* 26, 27

Kirk Session, The, and R.B., 6; Tarbolton (?), 68; Mauchline, 63, 65, 70, 92, 95, 98, 188

Kirk tyranny, R.B.'s challenge to, 83

Kirk Wad Let Me Be, The, 329

Kiroughtree, Dumfriesshire, 361

Knee, R.B.'s, injured, 173, 178

Kyle, central district of Ayrshire, 205, 242

L

Laing collection, Edinburgh University Library, R.B.'s notes on song in, 304, 328

Lament, 108

Lament for James Earl of Glencairn, 251

Langwell, David Balfour Graham, *The Lawrie Family,* 170n

Lapraik, John, addressee of R.B.'s *Epistle,* 55, 55n, 56, 289

Large, Mr., from Ireland, 372–73

Largieside, home farm of Elizabeth Paton, 68

Last Dying Words of Bonnie Heck, The, by William Hamilton of Gilbertfield, 52, 59, 393–95 (quoted)

Last May a Braw Wooer, 317–18 (quoted)

Lawrence, Rev. Archibald, Kirkmahoe, 245

Lawrie, Archibald, son of Rev. George Lawrie, 120, 168, 358–59

Lawrie, Mrs. Archibald (Anne McKittrick Adair), 358

Lawrie, Christina, sister of Archibald Lawrie, 120

Lawrie Family, The, by David Balfour Graham Langwell, 170n

Lawrie, Rev. George, Newmilns, Loudon, Ayrshire, 119, 120

Lawrie, Sir Walter, M.P., "Whistle" competitor, 260

Learned Pig, The, 128, 128n, 458

Lease for Ellisland, 181, 189, 189n

Leeward Isles, 272

Legman, G., 332

Leith Races, by Robert Fergusson, 81, 409–14 (quoted)

Let Me In This Aye Night, 306

Letter from a Blacksmith, 71–73

"Letter from Hell," 278–80, 281

Letters on Religion Essential to Man, by Dr. John Taylor, 62–63

Lewars, Jesse, sister of John Lewars, 363

Lewars, John, Exciseman, Dumfries, 218, 219–220, 359, 363

Libel Summons, or *The Court of Equity,* or *The Fornicators Court,* 59n, 70, 70n, 108, 111, 341–45 (quoted)

Liberty, R.B.'s warm response to cries for, 44, 109, 202, 226, 369

Library, public, Dumfries, R.B. made a member of, 355

Library of Robert Riddell, R.B.'s access to, 258

Life and Death of Habbie Simpson, by Robert Sempill, of Beltrees, 59, 391–93 (quoted)

Lindsay, Miss Isabella, 149, 152

Lines on Meeting with Lord Daer, 89 (quotation from), 111

Linlithgow, 157, 157n, 458

Little, Janet or Jenny, poetess, 210, 465, 467–68 (quotation from)

Livelihood, R.B.'s difficulty in choosing a means of, 33, 105–6, 107, 119, 126, 146–47, 157, 168, 172, 173, 180–81, 189, 206–7, 209–17, 231–33, 482

Liverpool, 362, 364, 387

Lochaber, 304

Loch Erroch Side, 156

"Lo, Children are God's heritage," 1st line of versified psalm, quoted by R.B. on the birth of Robert Ainslie's bastard son, 154

Loch Ken, Kirkcudbrightshire, 371

Lochlea farm, Tarbolton parish, Ayrshire, 18, 25, 29–30, 35, 40; William Burnes' troubles with landlord of, 43–45; 45, 232, 233

Loch Lomond, 156–57

Loch Long, 156
Lochmaben, Dumfriesshire, 336
Lockhart, John, biographer of R.B., 11, 102, 128–29, 362, 362n
Logan, John, of Laight, 208
London, 24; R.B.'s poems reviewed in, 108; 208, 272, 387
London 1787 edition of R.B.'s poems, 51
Loneliness and discouragement of R.B., 4, 190, 194–95, 210, 361, 362, 362n
Lonsdale, Lord, 283
Lookup, Miss, sister of Mrs. Fair, 149
Lord Gregory, R.B. recites his version, 368
Loretto, 106
Lorimer, Jean, daughter of William Lorimer, 250
Lorimer, William, Kemmis-hall, near Ellisland, 250
Loudon Castle, Ayrshire, home of Mr. and Mrs. James Henri, 121
Loudon parish, Ayrshire, the charge of Rev. George Lawrie, 119, 358
Lounger, The, Edinburgh, review of Kilmarnock edition in, 124, 145
Love and Liberty, or The Jolly Beggars, 14, 84, 131n, 291–92, 293–302 (quoted), 332
Low, or Lowe, Rev. John, Mary Weep No More for Me, or Mary's Dream, 366, 371
Loyal Native Club, Dumfries, 373
Loyalty of R.B., inquiry into, by the Excise Board, 223–31
Luath, ploughman's collie in The Twa Dogs, 111–13
Lyle, Lord (Sir William Montgomerie), Stewarton Lasses, 230

M

Macbeth, location of witch scene in, 162
Manly, Quartermaster, commander of party at the seizure of the Rosamond, 219
Man of Feeling, The, by Henry Mackenzie, 25, 41
Manual of Religious Belief, A, by William Burnes and John Murdoch, 25
Man Was Made to Mourn, 44, 108–9 (quoted from)
Marriage of R.B., 8–9, 63, 92, 93, 146, 182, 188, 188n, 189, 231, 456 (P.S. to p. 92). See also Armour, Jean

Marriage, R.B.'s views on, 31, 53, 188–89, 236, 352
Maryport, Cumberlandshire, 364
Mary Queen of Scots, 14, 162, 200
Mary Weep No More for Me, or Mary's Dream, by Rev. Robert Low, or Lowe, 366, 371
Masonry and R.B., 15, 29, 32–33, 45, 50, 103, 125, 355, 361n
Masterton, Allan, teacher of writing and music, Edinburgh High School, 139, 141
Mauchline, 1, 2, 6, 7, 47, 51, 72, 96, 98, 99n, 102, 147, 148n, 156, 157n, 158, 169, 178, 204, 205, 206, 208, 291, 333, 343n, 345
Maule, Hon. William Ramsay, of Panmure, 221n–22n
Maxwell, Dr. James, Dumfries, R.B.'s physician, 374, 377–78, 385
Maxwell, Kirkonnel, father of James Maxwell, 377–78
Maxwell, Robert, Provost of Lochmaben, 336
Medical opinion on health record of R.B., by Dr. Stanley Bardwell, 415–16
Medical Sketches, by Dr. John Moore, London, 158
Melrose, Roxburghshire, 148, 148n
Merry Muses, The, 322–49; bibliographical details of, 333–34; anthology of bawdry associated with R.B., 335–49
Miers, John, artist, 107
Miller, Miss Bettsy, Mauchline, 91, 98n
Miller, Patrick, of Dalswinton, Nithsdale, Dumfriesshire, R.B.'s Ellisland landlord, 11, 126, 141, 146–47, 168, 172, 180; R.B.'s lease with, 181, 189, 189n; no Maecenas, 146–47, 207; lease with, given up by R.B., 215; 234–35, 247, 260, 280
Miller, Mrs. Patrick, 234–35
Miller, Capt. Patrick, Jr., Patrick Miller's son, 11, 247, 283
Mill, Mill, O, The, 289
Mill Vennel (Now Burns Street), Dumfries; R.B.'s last residence in, 216
Milton, John, 39, 81, 84, 129n, 135, 147
Miniature of R.B., by Alexander Reid, 284

Minstrel, The, or The Progress of Genius, by James Beattie, 48

Mitchell, Jeany, character in The Court of Equity, 344

Mitchell, John, Collector of Excise, Dumfries, 209, 213–14, 223, 352, 353

Mitchell, Walter, member of the Tarbolton Bachelor's Club, 31

Mitchelson, Samuel, lawyer, Edinburgh, Robert Ainslie's employer, 155, 155n

Moffat, Dumfriesshire, 199

Monboddo, James Burnett, Lord, as Judge of the Court of Session, 126

Monkland Friendly Society, The, a book club established by Robert Riddell and R.B., and managed by R.B., 258–59, 259n

Monody on a Lady Famed for Her Caprice (Maria Riddell), 282–83 (quoted from)

Montagu, Mrs. Basil (Anna Dorothea Benson), 277n–78n

Montgomerie, Alexander, The Cherry and the Slae, 55

Montgomerie, Col. Hugh, later Earl of Eglinton, 102n

Montgomerie, Capt. James, brother of Col. Hugh Montgomerie, and Master of St. James Lodge of Masons, Tarbolton, 102, 102n, 103

Montrose, Forfarshire, home of James Burness, 161, 162, 167

Moore, Capt. Graham, R.N., son of Dr. John Moore, and friend of Dr. James Currie, 158

Moore, Dr. John, London, 25n, 26, 33–34, 36, 37n, 62, 63, 121, 135, 146, 158, 176, 198, 210n, 233, 249–50, 257, 264, 266n, 430–39

Moore, Sir John, son of Dr. John Moore and hero of the battle of Coruña, 158

Morin, John, of Laggan, 215, 215n, 367, 367n; R.B.'s epigram on, 368 (quoted)

Morning Chronicle, London, 283

Moray Firth, 162

Morgan Library, New York, 305

Mossgiel farm, Mauchline parish, Ayrshire, 6, 16, 45, 50, 63, 65, 98, 232, 233

Mt. Oliphant farm, near Ayr, 18–19, 25, 43, 45, 62, 203

Muir, Robert, wine merchant, Kilmarnock, 101, 124

Muir, Thomas, politician, transported to Botany Bay, 203

Murdoch, Barbara (Mrs. Hamilton, Mauchline), mother of Charlotte Hamilton, 169

Murdoch, Charlotte (Mrs. John Tait, Harvieston), 169

Murdoch, Euphemia (Mrs. Chalmers), mother of Margaret Chalmers, 169

Murdoch, John, schoolmaster, R.B.'s teacher at Alloway, 22–26, 45–46, 234, 246, 303, 303n

Murray, Captain, R.B. meets, at Blair Athole, 163

Murray, Miss, painter, R.B. meets, at Blair Athole, 163

Murray, Sir William, of Auchtertyre, near Crieff, 163, 171

Music, and R.B.: his knowledge of, 131, 131n, 301–3, 308–9, 311–12; his concern with, in The Scots Musical Museum, 304; his taste in, 308–9; his feeling about, in airs for songs, 309, 310; the musicians who assisted him, 303

"Music of thy voice I heard, The," 1st line of song to Maria Riddell, 276 (quoted)

My Father Was a Farmer, 39

My Girl, She's Airy, 155 (quoted), 155n, 332

"My kimmer & I lay down to sleep," 1st line of passage quoted by R.B. to illustrate "simplicity," 307

Mylne, James, farmer-poet, 239–40

My Lovely Nancy, 183

McClure, David, the Lochlea landlord, 44–45

McCulloch, David, Ardwell, 195, 361, 361n, 365n

McCulloch, Elizabeth (Mrs. Thomas Scott), sister of David McCulloch, 362n

MacDiarmid, Hugh (pseud. for C. M. Grieve), poet, 332

MacDonald, Mr., of Glengary, 109

MacDonald, Malcolm, editor of Highland Airs, 312

McDowell, a notorious smuggler, 218

M'Gavin, William, member of the Tarbolton Bachelor's Club, 31

Mackay, Mr., proprietor of the White
Hart Inn, Edinburgh, 186
McKay, Miss Georgina, friend of Keith
and Rachel Dunlop, 236
M'Kenzie, of Applecross, 109
Mackenzie, Henry, lawyer and author,
25, 41, 125, 129–30, 129n, 138, 142,
145, 164
M'Kenzie, Dr. John, Mauchline, 46–47,
169, 180
McLaggan, Mr., R.B. meets, at Blair
Athole, 163
M'Cletchie, Agnes, 99n
M'Lehose, Agnes Craig (Mrs. James),
"Clarinda," 7, 136, 146; her affair
with R.B., 172–88; her marriage and
separation, 174–75; her Calvinism,
174, 176; her fervent meetings with
R.B., 175–77, 181; her later relations
with R.B., 177–83, 185–87, 216; her
connection with the Adam-Nicol
quarrel, 182n; her letter from Robert
Ainslie from Ellisland, 183–85; and
Jenny Clow, 185, 186; 187, 188,
188n; and Maria Riddell, 187–88,
275–77, 282–83; Jean's comment on,
458
M'Lehose, James, husband of Agnes
Craig, 174, 175
M'Lehose, W. C., grandson of Agnes
M'Lehose, 174, 188
M'Math, Rev. John, Tarbolton, 65, 108
McMurdo, John, Chamberlain to the
Duke of Queensberry, Drumlanrig,
260, 285, 358
McMurdo, Jean, daughter of John Mc-
Murdo, 316–17
McNaught, Duncan ("Vindex"), edi-
tor of The Merry Muses for the Burns
Federation, 334
MacPhail, Archibald, Greenock, 440–41
McPherson, ship's carpenter, 441, 442
McPherson, widow, Greenock, 104

N

Nairne, Carolina Oliphant, Baroness,
poet, 330, 331
Nasmyth, Alexander, painter, 127
National Library of Scotland: Rosamond documents in, 219; Watson collection, 375
Nature's Law, 111

Nelson, Rev. Mr., Kirkbean, 245
Newal, David, The Isle and Dumfries,
208, 251
Newcastle-on-Tyne, 208, 240
New Cumnock, Ayrshire, 198
"New Licht" (Liberal) vs. "Auld Licht"
(Conservative) in Ayrshire, 63–64
New Modes of poetry for R.B., after
the Edinburgh 1787 edition of his
poems, 146
New York 1788 edition of the poems of
R.B., 57
Nicol, Ned, son of William Nicol, 246
Nicol, William, Latin master, Edin-
burgh High School, a Crochallan, 1,
25n, 135, 139, 141, 147; Cockburn,
Young, and Hope account of, 158–61;
Adair account of, 170; his Highland
tour with R.B., 161–67; 168, 182n,
190, 213, 228–29, 229–30, 232, 244–
46, 458
Nicol, Mrs. William, 229, 245
Nicolson, Peg, a mad washerwoman
who attempted to assassinate George
III; the name given William Nicol's
mare, 244
Night Thoughts on Life, Death, and
Immortality, by Edward Young, 48
Nimmo, Miss Erskine, Edinburgh,
friend of Agnes M'Lehose and Mar-
garet Chalmers, 174
Nine Inch Will Please a Lady, 338–39
(quoted)
Ninetieth Psalm Versified, The, 39
Nith, river, Dumfriesshire, 215, 238,
359
Nithsdale, Dumfriesshire, 205, 208, 246
Notes on Scots song by R.B., 328–30

O

Ochtertyre, near Crieff, seat of Sir Wil-
liam Murray, 171
Ochtertyre, near Stirling, seat of John
Ramsay, 171
Ode Sacred to the Memory of Mrs. Os-
wald of Auchencruive, 198–99
(quoted from)
Ode to Spring, 310 (quoted)
O'er the Moor Amang the Heather, by
Jean Glover, 329
Old Tar, The, Mauchline public house
keeper, 103n

"O May, thy morn was ne'er sae sweet," 1st line of song for Agnes M'Lehose, 178 (quoted)

On Lord Galloway, 87, 367

On seeing a fellow wound a hare with a shot, 239

On Some Commemorations of Thomson, 226, 252–53 (quoted)

On the Late Captain Grose's Peregrinations Thro' Scotland, 90, 260–61 (quoted from)

Ordination, The, 108, 145

O Saw Ye Bonie Lesley, 311

Ossian's grave, near Crieff, 162

O, Steer Her up an' Haud Her Gaun, 323 (quoted)

Oswald, Mrs. Mary Ramsay, of Auchencruive, 198–99, 282

Othello, 179

O Thou Dread Power, 120

P

Paisley, Dumbartonshire, 92, 94, 104, 158, 178, 179–80

Pamela, 36

Paradise Lost, 39, 81, 129n, 135, 147, 184

Paraphrase of the First Psalm, 38

Parenthood troubles R.B., 192, 203–4, 284, 351, 383

Park, Anne, niece of Mrs. Walter Hyslop, Globe Inn, Dumfries, and mother of Elizabeth Hyslop Burns by R.B., 5, 6, 68, 98, 99, 107, 108, 388

Patriarch, The, 111, 337–38 (quoted)

Patricians, in Edinburgh, R.B.'s opinions of, 124, 135, 147; lukewarm to the subscription for Jean, 141, 387; 303

Patriotism (Scots) of R.B., 199–202

Pattison, Alexander, merchant, Paisley, 179–80

Patty, Alexander, Master of the *Rosamond*, 219

Peacock, R.B.'s partner in Irvine, 35

Peacock, Mary (later Mrs. James Gray), friend of Agnes M'Lehose, 356

Peasant life in Ayrshire, 72–75

Pebble for R.B.'s seal, 353

Pegasus, R.B.'s horse, 198, 210n

Pegasus at Wanlockhead, 210n

"Peg Nicolson was a good bay mare," 1st line of R.B.'s ballad on William Nicol's mare, 245 (quoted)

Perth, 162, 167

Peterhead, Aberdeenshire, 162, 166

Peterkin, Alexander, solicitor and editor, 226, 356, 365, 376–77

Philadelphia 1788 edition of R.B.'s poems, 51

Philosophy of Natural History, by William Smellie, 273

Pinchbeck, William Frederick, 128n

Piper of Kilbarcham, The (Habbie Simpson), 59

Pitt, William, 10, 11, 132, 164

Plenipotentiary, The, 234

Pleyel, Joseph, George Thomson's musical editor, 308

Pockmarked, was R.B.?, 127, 429

Poems Chiefly in the Scottish Dialect, Kilmarnock, 1786. See Kilmarnock edition of the poems of R.B.

Poems Chiefly in the Scottish Dialect, 1787, 1788, 1793, 1794. See under Belfast, Dublin, Edinburgh, London, New York, Philadelphia edition of the poems of R.B.

Poetry of R.B.: 2, 12, 16, 26, 27; its relation to the 18th century English tradition, 47–49 (see also T. Crawford, *Burns, passim*); in the vernacular, 49–53; *Epistles*, 53–62; rime couée, 59; 63; satires, 64–68, 75–83; Bard, and paradoxes in, 84–91; 108; Henley on, 114; "inspiration," pose of, in, 132; new modes in, 145–46, 454

Poet's Welcome to His Bastart Wean, The, 36, 69–70 (quoted), 108

Poet's Welcome to His Love-Begotten Daughter, The, 36, 69–70 (quoted), 108

Politics and R.B., 14–15; influence of landlords on, 43–45; his support of Pitt and the king, 130n, 132; Jacobinism and Jacobitism, 199–203; reform, 122, 220–31, 285–86; 247

Poor Mailie's Elegy, 111; *An Elegy on John Cowper*, 396–99 (quoted)

Poor Thresher, The, 240

Pope, Alexander, 29; greatly admired and much quoted by R.B., 48; 41, 50, 86, 283

Port Division of Excise, Dumfries, R.B. promoted to, 216
Port Glasgow, a lucrative Excise post, 214
Port officer, R.B. desires to be one, 214
Portraits of R.B., Edinburgh, 127
Portuguese friend of Mrs. Dunlop, 53
Poverty, R.B. discusses, 196–97, 203–4
Prayer in the Prospect of Death, A, 38
"Pray who are these Natives, the rabble so ven'rate?" 1st line of R.B.'s epigram, 373 (quoted)
Presbytry of Ayr, 65
Presbytry Relief, a religious sect, 42
Princes Street, Edinburgh, 137
Proceeds from Edinburgh 1787 edition of R.B.'s poems, 142–43
Proceeds from Ellisland sales, 216
Professorship of Agriculture proposed for R.B., 122
Promotion in the Excise, R.B.'s hopes for, 213–14, 213n–14n, 216–17
Pronunciation of English by R.B., 40, 126
Proverbial quality in R.B.'s poetry, 86

Q

Queensberry, Duke of, 247, 248, 250, 260
Queensferry, 162, 167

R

R * * * * *, Mrs., 278, 279, 281
Raleigh, Professor Sir Walter, 114–15
Ramsay, Allan, poet: R.B.'s familiarity with, 47, 48, 52n, 55, 80, 288; The Gentle Shepherd, 354; Elegy on John Cowper, 396–99 (quoted); verse epistles exchanged with William Hamilton, 399–403 (quotations from)
Ramsay, John, of Ochtertyre, near Stirling, 171–72
Ramsay, David, editor Edinburgh Evening Courant, 128, 133
Rankine, John, Adamhill farm, near Lochlea, 350
Rannoch, Loch, 163
Rantin Dog, The, 332
Rape of the Lock, The, 118n
Raving Winds around Her Blowing, 235
Reading, the, of R.B., before his 26th year, 22, 23, 24, 25, 25n, 26, 36n, 47, 48–49

Rebellious young manhood of R.B., 5–6
Reform, political, and R.B., 14–15, 43–44, 132, 199, 203; his sympathy for the French Revolution, 122, 220–31, 286; 247; Borough reform, 224–26, 228, 242, 285, 286
Reid, Alexander, miniaturist, 284
Reid, Hugh, member of the Tarbolton Bachelor's Club, 31
Religion and R.B., 5, 15–16, 25; ferment at Irvine, 38–39, 40–41; the Buchanites, 43; 62, 153; statements to Mrs. M'Lehose and Mrs. Dunlop, 176–77, 241; statement to Alexander Cunningham, 351–52
Remorse, 39
Resentment by R.B. of wealth and dullness, 195–99
Reviews in Edinburgh of Kilmarnock edition, The Lounger and the Edinburgh Magazine, 125
Revision of another's poetry, R.B.'s opposition to, 308
"Rhinoceros," 195
Richmond, John, lawyer's clerk, Mauchline and Edinburgh: character in The Court of Equity, 59n, 343, 343n, 345; R.B.'s letters to, about the Armour affair, 95–98, 98n; his details of Mary Campbell, 102–3; R.B. his bedfellow in Edinburgh, 124; and The Jolly Beggars, 291
Riddell, Elizabeth Kennedy (Mrs. Robert), 255, 279, 281–82
Riddell, Maria Banks Woodley (Mrs. Walter): her account of R.B., 3–4; 9; her relations with Agnes M'Lehose, 187–88, 275–77, 282–83; 190, 194, 216; her relations with R.B., 272–85; her Voyages, 273–74; her correspondence with James Currie and William Smellie, 273, 274, 275, 364–65; her early relations with R.B., 274–276; intense relations with, 276–77; quarrel with, 278–84; Rachel Kennedy's letter about, 281; the reconciliation with R.B. and the Reid miniature, 284–85; R.B.'s last visit to, 285, 379–80; and R.B.'s seal, 353, 353n; 465
Riddell quarrel, the, 278–84, 285, 464
Riddell, Capt. Robert, of Glenriddell (see Glenriddell MSS): his interleaved

Museum and R.B., 199–200, 304; his library open to R.B., 202, 258; as "Cato," 226; 227; host to Francis Grose, 242, 260; accounts of, by C. K. Sharpe, 254, 256, 358; by Sir Walter Scott, 254, 256; by Alexander Young, 254–55; interest in song and antiquities and R.B., 253–55; helps James Clarke, 259–60; and the "Whistle" contest, 260; 274; quarrel with R.B., 277–81; death, 282; 285, 465

Riddell, Mrs. Robert (Elizabeth Kennedy), 255, 279, 281–82

Riddell, Walter, brother of Robert Riddell, 222n, 272, 273, 274–75, 279, 281

"Rights of Man," and R.B., 15, 44, 202

Rights of Woman, The, 220–21 (quoted), 226

Ritson, Joseph, scholar-antiquarian editor, 307, 314

Robene and Makyne, by Robert Henryson, 86

Robertson, Major William, of Lude, 285–86

Rosamond seizure, the, 217–20; R.B. commands party in, 219

Roscoe, William, attorney and author, Liverpool, 160

Rose, Miss, Kilravock, sings for R.B., 164

Rose, Mrs. Elizabeth, Kilravock, Invernesshire, 164

Rosinante, 157

Rothemurche's Rant, 309

Rothiemurche, 194

Roxburgh, 148, 148n

Royal Company of Archers, 252

Royal Dumfries Volunteers, 15, 356, 373–74, 386

Rutherford, Captain, R.B. meets, on Border tour, 119

Rutherford, Miss, daughter of Captain Rutherford, 149

S

St. Abbs, Berwickshire, 148n

St. Andrew's Lodge of Masons, Dumfries, 361n

St. Andrew's Lodge of Masons, Edinburgh, 32

St. Bees Head, 364, 379

St. David's Lodge of Masons, Tarbolton, 32

St. James' Lodge of Masons, Tarbolton, 32, 125

St. Kitts, Leeward Isles, 272

Sacramental Occasions ("Holy Fairs") in Ayrshire, 72

Saddleback, 379

Salisbury Craigs, Edinburgh, 133

Salt officer, a post suggested for R.B., 122

Sanquhar, Dumfriesshire, 198, 247

Sarcasm of R.B., 127–28, 129, 129n, 358

Satan, as in Paradise Lost, R.B.'s admiration for, 39, 129n, 135, 147; R.B. parodies, 81

Saul, dead march from, played at R.B.'s funeral procession, 386

Schooling of R.B., 22–26

Scone, 162

Scorpion in a thumb phial, 195

Scotch Drink, 110

Scots Magazine, 145

Scots Musical Museum, The (See also James Johnson): R.B.'s early interest in, 141, 148; his correspondence with James Johnson, 240, 288–312 passim, 305, 425; Robert Riddell's interleaved set of, 199–200, 256, 257–58, 304, 328, 329, 330; R.B.'s concern for music in, 304; as a standard anthology, 331; 332–33, 347. Also, 164, 235, 254, 256, 303, 312, 351

Scots patriotism of R.B., 199–202

Scots song, R.B.'s notes on, 328–30

Scots usage of R.B., 26

Scots Wha Hae: and George Thomson, 192, 305; 202; composition of, and thrust of, 369–71 (quoted)

Scott, Sophia (Mrs. John Lockhart), Sir Walter Scott's daughter, 362n

Scott, Thomas, Sir Walter Scott's brother, 362n

Scott, Sir Walter, 11, 84n, 124, 125, 128, 137; his interest in the Rosamond seizure, 320; his comments on Robert Riddell, 254, 256; his praise of R.B. as a song writer, 315; 331, 362n; and the sword story, 377

Seal for R.B., 353–55; see representation of, on title page.

Seasons, The, by James Thomson, 48, 252

Second Epistle to J. Lapraik, 57 (quoted from)

Sedition trials of 1793, Edinburgh, 203, 220

Select Collection of Original Scotish Airs, A, 332. See also Thomson, George

Selkirk, 148n

Selkirk, Lord, 367, 368

Sempill, Robert, of Beltrees, poet, *The Life and Death of Habbie Simpson,* 59, 391–93 (quoted)

Settlement of R.B. with Elizabeth Paton, 68, 98

Shakespeare, 50, 86, 162

Sharpe, Charles, of Hoddam, father of C. K. Sharpe, 358

Sharpe, Charles Kirkpatrick: reports R.B.'s intemperance "venial," 10; his comments on Robert Riddell, 254, 256; 277n; his report on Maria Riddell, 280–81; his comments on R.B. in Dumfries, 357; 465

Shenstone, William, poet, 48

Sillar, David ("Davie"), Tarbolton, 52n; R.B.'s *Epistle* to, 53–55 (quotations from); 55n; his comment on R.B. in Tarbolton, 62–63; 233, 251

Sillar, Janet, 99n

Simplicity in songs, R.B.'s taste for, 306–8

Simpson, William, schoolmaster, Ochiltree, Ayrshire, 57n, 117; R.B.'s *Epistle* to, 134–35 (quotation from)

"Sing, up wi't Aily, Aily," 1st line of a stanza quoted by R.B., 155

Sinton, John, *Burns Excise Officer and Poet,* 148n

Skiddaw, 379

"Skinking" or "stinking," Edinburgh 1787 editions, 141, 141n

Skinner, Rev. John, Langside, song writer, 165, 309–10, 330

Skinner, Rt. Rev. John, Jr., Episcopal Bishop of Aberdeen, later Primate of Scotland, son of Rev. John Skinner, 165

Sloan, James D., Ayr, 442

Sloan, Thomas, 215

Slop, Dr., character in *Tristram Shandy;*

Francis Grose compared to, by R.B., 242

Smellie, William, printer and author, Edinburgh, a Crochallan: account of, 138–40; man of R.B.'s caliber, 232; 233n; 253; and Maria Riddell, 273–75

Smith, Captain of the *Nancy,* 96

Smith, Adam, *Theory of Moral Sentiments,* 39, 122, 126

Smith, James, Mauchline merchant, 59; a character in *The Court of Equity,* 59n, 343; his death in St. Lucia, 59n; 96, 98n, 135, 147; R.B.'s account to, of his ride down Loch Lomonside, 156–57; 157n, 158; and *The Jolly Beggars,* 291; his probable witnessing of the marriage of R.B., 456 (P.S. for p. 92)

Smith, Leonard, Exciseman, 206–7, 209

Smith, Dr. S. Watson, 204n

Smith, Sydney Goodsir, 332

Socinianism, 177

"Solemn League and Covenant, The," 1st line of R.B.'s epigram on, 16 (quoted)

Solway Firth, scene of the *Rosamond* seizure, 217, 218, 219, 238, 378–79

Somerville, Rev. Thomas, Jedburgh, 149

Songs: R.B.'s early interest in, 12–14, 288–91; a collection of his *vade mecum* in youth, 48, 288; 108; Edinburgh interest in Scots song delights R.B., 145, 303; R.B.'s excited activity in providing songs for Johnson's collection: Border, 148; Highlands, 161, 165–66, 167; interest in, of Robert Riddell and R.B., 256–57; 279; breadth of R.B.'s interest in and knowledge of (airs, lyrics, scenes associated with), and his desire to "embody" all Scots song, 304–5; R.B.'s notes on, 304, 328–30

R.B.'s critical principles relating to primacy of melody, desirability of "irregularity," and "escape from jingle," and the need for "Scotch syllables" (Commonplace Book, 1783–1785), 288–91; the desirability of "simplicity" in, 306–8; R.B.'s dislike of choruses in, and his thinking of, as dramatic lyrics, 316–17, 317n; 310–11, 312–13

R.B.'s songs always written for

tunes, and to be *sung*, 111, 291, 315, 323, 324; R.B.'s feeling that tunes are always improved by having words for them, often a difficulty for Scots tunes, 309–10; R.B.'s concern for musical settings, 302–3, 308–9, 311–12
Musicians who assisted R.B., 164, 303, 368. R.B. had a harsh voice and *spoke* his songs when he was called on for them, 131, 170, 368
R.B.'s method of composing songs, 13–14, 313–14, 290; 308; R.B. a folk artist who "localized" traditional material, 314–15; *The Merry Muses*, 322–349; R.B.'s achievement in song, 14, 331
See also Music and R.B.
Spenser, Edmund, poet, 84
Staig, David, Provost, Dumfries, 352–53
Stair, Ayrshire, 98, 99
Stamp office, Dumfries, R.B.'s rooms above, 215
Stanzas Written in the Prospect of Death, 38
Star, The, London, 199
Statistical Account of Scotland, The, ed. Sir John Sinclair, R.B.'s account in, of the Monkland Friendly Society, 258–59
Stenhouse, William, editor of Johnson's *The Scots Musical Museum*, 254, 256
Sterne, Laurence, 25, 26n, 93, 156
Stewart, Mr. and Mrs., R.B. meets, at Blair Athole, 163
Stewart, Professor Dugald, Edinburgh University, 125, 129–30, 129n, 138, 368n
Stewart, William, factor on the Closeburn Estates, Dumfriesshire, 234
Stewarton Lasses, by Sir William Montgomerie, 330
"Stinking" or "skinking" Edinburgh 1787 editions, 141, 141n
Stinking (or the Wee, or Carwart's) Vennel, Dumfries, now Bank Street, to which R.B. moved from Ellisland, 216
Stirling, R.B.'s indiscreet lines at, 162 (quoted), 168, 169–70; 200, 214
Stobbie, Adam, Excise expectant who assumed R.B.'s duties without pay during R.B.'s illness, 375

Stock and horn, R.B.'s concern with, on his seal, 353–55
Stonehaven, home of R.B.'s relatives, 161, 162, 166
Struan-Robertson estate, near Blair Athole, 163
Stuart, Dr. Gilbert, editor, a Crochallan, 139
Stuart, Peter, proprietor of *The Star*, London, 199
Stuart kings, R.B.'s sympathy for, 200–202
Subscription for Jean Armour after R.B.'s death, 375
Supervisor of Excise, Galloway, the illness of, and R.B.'s interest in the post, 226
Surgeoner, Jenny, later Mrs. John Richmond, 97
Surgeons of Glasgow grant an annuity to Agnes M'Lehose, 175
Sutherland, George Stephens, manager of the theater, Dumfries, 245
Sweet Afton, 326–27 (quoted)
Sweet Sensibility How Charming, 185
Sweet Tibbie Dunbar, 315 (quoted)
"Sylvander," Agnes M'Lehose's Arcadian name for R.B. *See* Agnes M'Lehose
Syme, John, of Ryedale (a Cabin), Troqueer, near Dumfries, Distributor of Stamps, Dumfries: his friendship with R.B., 364–77, 385; an account of, 364, 365, 374; particulars of R.B. from, 3, 9, 10, 15, 350; to Alexander Peterkin, 226, 275–77; describes conviviality in Dumfries, 221n–22n, 372–73; describes his 1793 tour of Galloway with R.B., 365–72; visits R.B. in his last illness, 374–75, 385; arranges R.B.'s funeral, 386; makes efforts to collect a subscription for Jean in Dumfries with limited success, 387. *Also*, 187–88, 213, 227n, 277n, 279, 283, 361, 377, 380–81, 479, 485

T

Tait, John, of Harvieston, 169
Tait, Mrs. John (Charlotte Murdoch), 169
Tam Glen, 320–21 (quoted)
Tam o' Shanter: background, composition, and chronology of, 261–65.

Tam o' Shanter (*cont'd*)
266n; 266–72 (quoted). *Also*, 2, 84, 107, 146, 192, 232, 249, 264, 266, 293, 351

Tam o' Shanter, who could see witches and warlocks, 278n

Tam Samson's Elegy, 111, 145. *Cp. An Elegy on John Cowper*, 396–99 (quoted)

Tannahill, Robert, poet, 331

Tarbolton, Ayrshire, 18, 33, 47, 51, 62–63, 189, 298

Tarbolton Bachelor's Club, 29, 30–32

Tarbolton penny bridal, a, and the Riddell quarrel, 280

Tarbrax, Lanarkshire, 442

Taste in music, R.B.'s simple, 308–9

Taylor, Dr. John, *Letters on Religion Essential to Man*, 62–63

Taylor, Peter, painter of R.B.'s portrait, Edinburgh, 127

Tea-Table Miscellany, The, ed. Allan Ramsay, 288

Telford, Thomas, engineer, 9, 465

Tenant farming and R.B., 124, 141, 168, 180–81

Tennant, John, of Glenconner, a Crochallan, 139, 180–81

Tennant, John, Jr., 31

Theatre, and R.B., 220, 221, 222, 225, 226, 244–45. *See also* Drama and R.B.

"The light that led astray/Was light from heaven," 53

"Then hey, for a merry good fellow," 1st line of final stanza of *I'll Tell You a Tale of a Wife* (*The Case of Conscience*, quoted (336–37), 155 (quoted), 155n

"Theocrites," 446 (P.S. for p. 85)

Theocritus, 85

Theory of Moral Sentiments, by Adam Smith, 39

There's Nae Luck about the House, 307 (quoted from)

There'll Never Be Peace Till Jamie Comes Hame, 312

Tho' Fickle Fortune, 39, 135

Thomas a' Kempis, 133

Thomas-a-Rhymer, 157

Thomson, George, Edinburgh, editor of *A Select Collection of Original Scotish Airs*, 6–7; R.B.'s relations with, 192–95, 305, 375, 381; and R.B.'s

seal, 354–55; R.B.'s comments to, on songs: his methods of composing, 13–14, 313–14; his early songs the "breathings of ardent Passion," 100, *The Jolly Beggars* forgotten, 291, the difficulty of ascertaining the truth about songs, 328; and *Scots Wha Hae*, 192, 305, 369–70; 311–12. *Also*, 108, 276, 304, 305, 306–8, 313–14, 317, 332

Thomson, James, poet, *The Seasons*, 48; 138, 225, 252

Thomson, Peggy, Kirkoswald, 25

Thornton, Robert D., *James Currie The Entire Stranger and Robert Burns*, 187, 274

Thou Lingering Star, 100

Tho' Women's Minds, 333

Tilt, river, 163

Tinwald Downs, 222n

Tinwald House, residence of Walter and Maria Riddell after Woodley Park, 275

Titus Andronicus, 23

Todlin' Hame, 307

To a Louse, 114–16 (quoted)

To a Mountain Daisy, 114

To a Mouse, 88, 90 (quotations from), 114

Toasting, 18th Century style, 272–73

To the Hon. Wm. R. Maule, of Panmure, R.B.'s epigram on, 222n (quoted)

To the Rev. John M'Math, 58–59 (quoted from)

To Ruin, 108

Tours of Galloway of R.B. and John Syme: 1793, 365–72; 1794, 361, 365n

Tours of Scotland by R.B.: The Borders, with Robert Ainslie, 147–55; The West Highlands, 156–58; The Highlands, with William Nicol, 158–67; Stirlingshire, Clackmannanshire, Perthshire, and Fifeshire, with Dr. J. M. Adair, 168–72. *See also* Tours of Galloway of R.B. and John Syme

To William Simpson of Ochiltree, 57–58, 117 (quotations from)

Traditions of Edinburgh, by Robert Chambers, 140

Train, Joseph, Collector of Excise, Castle Douglas, 102–4, 102n, 220

Traquair, Earl of, 329

Trial of a Saving Interest, by Rev. William Guthrie, 229
Tristram Shandy, 21, 110
Troqueer, near Dumfries, John Syme's cabin at, 365
Tudor, the house of, 201
Tullochgorum, by Rev. John Skinner, 156, 165–66
Tummel, loch and river, 163
Turn Again, Thou Fair Eliza, 312
Twa Dogs, The, 91 (quoted from), 111–13 (quoted from)
Twa Herds, The, 63, 64
Twins to R.B. and Jean Armour: first set, 107, 111; second set, 179n
Tytler, Alexander Fraser, 351

U

Urbani, Pietro, musician, 368, 370, 371
Usage of English and Scots by R.B., 26

V

Vernacular poetry of R.B., 52–53, 57
Vernacular tradition in Scots, R.B.'s debt to, 49. See also Village rhymers
Verses in Friars' Carse Hermitage, 255–56 (quoted)
Vicar of Bray, The, 229
View of Society and Manners in France, Switzerland, and Germany (1779); *in Italy* (1781), by Dr. John Moore, 158
Village rhymers, in Scotland, 63n
"Vindex" (Duncan McNaught), editor of a *Merry Muses* for The Burns Federation, 334
Virgin Mary, the, 166
Vision, The, 53, 90–91, 117–19 (quotations from); 118n, 120
Volunteers, Dumfries Royal, 15, 356, 373–74, 386
Voyages to the Madeira and Leeward Islands, by Maria Riddell, 273, 274

W

Walker, Josiah, biographer of R.B., 162, 308, 359–61
Walker and Gordon, agents for Charles Sharpe of Hoddam, 358
Wallace, Sir William, 25n, 120
Wanlock-head miners as political support troops, 247
Warrant for R.B.'s arrest, 96, 97, 98, 107

Watson Collection, National Library of Scotland, 375
Wealth and dullness, R.B.'s resentment of, 195–99
Wee, The (or Stinking, or Carwart's) Vennel, now Bank Street, Dumfries, to which R.B. moved from Ellisland, 216
Welcome to a Bastart Wean, A (*See* also *A Poet's Welcome* . . .), 36, 69–70 (quoted), 108
Welsh, Harry, hedgehogged, 222n
Wen Yuan-ning, Dr., on R.B.'s appeal to Chinese, 53
Werena My Heart Licht I Wad Die, by Lady Grizel Bailie; R.B. quotes from, 362
West Highlands, 100; R.B.'s tour to, 156–58
West Indies, 274
Westminster Divines, 93
Westmoreland and Cumberland mountains, 379
Weston, Professor John C., University of Massachusetts, 118n
Wha Is That at My Bower Door, 320 (quoted), 332
Wha'll Mow Me Now, 70n (quotation from), 335 (quoted)
What Can a Young Lassie, 322–23 (quoted)
When Maukin Bucks, 310–11 (quoted)
When Princes and Prelates, 226
"Where Love is Liberty and Nature Law," a better basis for songs than conjugal love according to R.B., 312–13
Whigham, Edward, Bailie of Sanquhar, 198
Whistle, The, 260, 286
"Whistle o'er the lave o't," a phrase of bawdy ambiguity, 292
Whitefoord, Sir John, Edinburgh, formerly of Ballochmyle, Ayrshire, 125
Whitefoord Arms, a Mauchline inn, 345
White Hart Inn, Grassmarket, Edinburgh, 186
Whitehaven, Cumberlandshire, 364
"Whoe'er he be that sojourns here," 1st line of R.B.'s epigram at Arrochar, 156 (quoted)
Whyte, Rev. Hugh, Irvine, a convert to Buchanism, 42

Wigton, 367
Williams, Helen Maria, London, pro-
    tégé of Dr. John Moore, and author
    of a poem, *The Slave Trade*, 233–34
Williamson of Cardrona, a Crochallan,
    139
Willie Wastle, 319 (quoted)
Wills, Dr. William Charles, London, at
    school with Alexander Young, 254
Will Ye Go to the Indes, My Mary?, 100
Wilson, John, printer of the Kilmarnock
    edition, 96, 106
Wilson, John, Tarbolton, 248–49
Wilson, Mrs. John, 249
Wilson, Laird, character in *The Court
    of Equity*, 344
Wilt Thou Be My Dearie?, 286
Winter, a Dirge, 36, 38
Wood, Alexander, surgeon, Edinburgh,
    173, 197
Woodley, William, father of Maria
    Banks Woodley (Mrs. Walter Rid-
    dell), 272
Woodley Park, near Dumfries, estate of
    Walter Riddell, 273, 274, 279, 280,
    281

Woods, William, actor, Dumfries, 330
Wordsworth, William, 84, 86
Wright, Alexander, a Crochallan, 139
Wright, Thomas, member of the Tar-
    bolton Bachelor's Club, 31
Writers of Glasgow arrange an annuity
    for Agnes M'Lehose, 175
Written in Friars' Carse Hermitage,
    255–56 (quoted)

Y

Ye Banks and Braes, 324 (quoted)
Ye Flowery Banks o' Bonie Doon, 324
"Yestreen I Had a Pint o' Wine," line
    from R.B.'s song to Anne Park,
    265n (quoted from)
York, the house of, 201
Young, Alexander, of Harburn, W.S.,
    159–60, 168, 254–55
Young, Edward, poet, 48

Z

Zeluco, a novel, by Dr. John Moore,
    London, 158
Zimri (Burns Ainslie), 161

87852

PR
4331   Fitzhugh
F57   Robert Burns: the
        man and the poet
             10.00

Date Due
